The Multilingual Origins of Standard English

Topics in English Linguistics

Volume 107

The Multilingual Origins of Standard English

Edited by
Laura Wright

ISBN 978-3-11-099510-7
e-ISBN (PDF) 978-3-11-068754-5
e-ISBN (EPUB) 978-3-11-068757-6

Library of Congress Control Number: 2020941972

Bibliographic information published by the Deutsche Nationalbibliothek
The Deutsche Nationalbibliothek lists this publication in the Deutsche Nationalbibliografie; detailed bibliographic data are available on the Internet at http://dnb.dnb.de.

This volume is text- and page-identical with the hardback published in 2020.
Typesetting: Integra Software Services Pvt. Ltd.
Printing and binding: CPI books GmbH, Leck

www.degruyter.com

For Ruth Kennedy

Acknowledgements

This volume is produced under the British Arts and Humanities Research Council's Open World Research Initiative umbrella *Multilingualism: Empowering Individuals, Transforming Societies*, grant no. RG78116AA, strand 'Standard languages, norms and variation: comparative perspectives in multilingual contexts'. It is a companion to Wendy Ayres-Bennett and John Bellamy (eds.) *The Cambridge Handbook of Language Standardisation*, Cambridge University Press.

I thank Prof Wendy Ayres-Bennett, Principal Investigator, for the care with which she has overseen every stage of this endeavour and enabled it to come to fruition. I thank Prof Susan Fitzmaurice, editor of the Topics in English Linguistics series at Mouton, not only for her incisive criticism but also for her generosity of vision, as the chapters here cover ground from linguistics to medieval studies and several languages. I also thank the forty reviewers whose criticisms have immeasurably improved the chapters.

https://doi.org/10.1515/9783110687545-202

Contents

Acknowledgements —— VII

Part 1: **The orthodox version**

Laura Wright
Introduction —— 3

Laura Wright
1 A critical look at previous accounts of the standardisation of English —— 17

Merja Stenroos
2 The 'vernacularisation' and 'standardisation' of local administrative writing in late and post-medieval England —— 39

María José Carrillo-Linares and Keith Williamson
3 The linguistic character of manuscripts attributed to the Beryn Scribe: A comparative study —— 87

David Moreno Olalla
4 Spelling practices in late middle English medical prose: A quantitative analysis —— 141

Jacob Thaisen
5 Standardisation, exemplars, and the Auchinleck manuscript —— 165

Moragh Gordon
6 Bristol <th>, <þ> and <y>: The North-South divide revisited, 1400–1700 —— 191

Juan M. Hernández-Campoy
7 <th> *versus* <þ>: Latin-based influences and social awareness in the Paston letters —— 215

Terttu Nevalainen
8 Early mass communication as a standardizing influence? The case of the Book of Common Prayer — 239

Part 2: **The revised version**

Alpo Honkapohja and Aino Liira
9 Abbreviations and standardisation in the *Polychronicon*: Latin to English and manuscript to print — 269

Herbert Schendl
10 William Worcester's *Itineraria*: mixed-language notes of a medieval traveller — 317

Philip Durkin
11 The relationship of borrowing from French and Latin in the Middle English period with the development of the lexicon of Standard English: Some observations and a lot of questions — 343

Louise Sylvester
12 The role of multilingualism in the emergence of a technical register in the Middle English period — 365

Megan Tiddeman
13 More sugar and spice: Revisiting medieval Italian influence on the mercantile lexis of England — 381

Richard Ashdowne
14 *-mannus* makyth *man(n)*? Latin as an indirect source for English lexical history — 411

J. Camilo Conde-Silvestre
15 Communities of practice, proto-standardisation and spelling focusing in the Stonor letters — 443

Jesús Romero-Barranco
16 A comparison of some French and English nominal suffixes in early English correspondence (1420–1681) — 467

Joanna Kopaczyk
17 Textual standardisation of legal Scots *vis a vis* Latin — 487

Laura Wright
18 Rising living standards, the demise of Anglo-Norman and mixed-language writing, and Standard English — 515

Index — 533

Part 1: **The orthodox version**

Laura Wright

Introduction

This collaboration by nineteen historical linguists shows why the current textbook explanations of the origins of Standard English are incorrect (Part One, the Orthodox Version), and suggests an alternative explanation (Part Two, the Revised Version). Textbook authors have been aware of the issues we discuss for quite some time, but, despite many scholars' misgivings over the years, these origin myths have continued to be repeated, especially in textbooks aimed at undergraduates.

But before we consider previous accounts, what do we mean by the origins of Standard English? For mid nineteenth-century scholars it meant vocabulary. For early twentieth-century scholars it meant phonology, as indicated by spellings for vowels in stressed syllables. For mid-twentieth-century scholars it meant orthography (majority spellings, ignoring minority ones). For late twentieth-century scholars it meant morphology – the rise of auxiliary *do*, third-person present-tense *-s*, *you/thou*, the *wh-* pronouns. We work with Trudgill's (1999) definition that Standard English is a dialect, largely distinguishable from other English dialects by means of its grammar and preeminently used in writing. In these pages we are concerned with the initial phase, which was propelled by reduction of variants and in particular, loss of geographically-restricted variants. Middle English was characterised by great variety, and it was not until variant reduction began that all the other things that go along with standardisation such as selection, diffusion, elaboration, codification, prescription and implementation could follow. In searching for variant reduction we examine syntax, morphology, wordstock (open-class as well as closed-class), spelling, letter-graphs, and also the the pan-European medieval abbreviation and suspension system, in texts from Edinburgh to Bristol. The mere fact of consistency, even though the feature under consideration may not have been (indeed, was usually not) the one that ended up in modern Standard English, constituted the beginning of the long process of standardisation – which did not appreciably slow down until the nineteenth century.

In the first chapter (Wright: A critical look at previous accounts of the standardisation of English), I track the development of the orthodox origin explanations. These inform readers that the precursor of Standard English was an East Midlands variety (or Central Midlands, depending on the book) that became adopted in London and disseminated therefrom; that manuscripts of the fifteenth century can be divided into four Types, and that the fourth Type,

https://doi.org/10.1515/9783110687545-001

dating after 1435 and labelled 'Chancery Standard', provided the mechanism by which this 'Standard' spread. Type 4 was given this label because it was the supposedly relatively cohesive dialect in which letters from the King's Office of Chancery emanated. Working backwards from scholar to scholar, I identify the nineteenth-century origin of these explanations, which although reasonable according to evidence available in the early 1870s, are in need of updating a century and a half later.

Next, whereabouts should we be looking for the origin of Standard English? The 'when' is over the fourteenth and fifteenth centuries because specific changes in writing practices are identifiable in those centuries, but the 'where' is less apparent, although textbooks assert that it emanated from an original source somewhere in the Midlands, and spread via London. Yet Standard English is characterised by its lack of affiliation to a single region, and defining what constituted fourteenth and fifteenth London English dialect is hard to pin down, partly because variation was still common at this time (meaning that regional features were also present in London writing), and partly because most writing that can be ascribed to London with any certainty during the period was mostly not written in monolingual English and has yet to be analysed. Pre-Standard regional focussing over the fifteenth century (and well into the sixteenth) led to supralocal clusters of morphemes, closed-class words and spelling-sequences fanning out from various provincial centres, as shown, for example, in the lower frequency of regionally-marked spellings in wills from urban York versus those from rural Swaledale (Fernández Cuesta 2014), the urban-hopping of less regionally-marked features in Cheshire and Staffordshire (Thengs 2013), or the more London-like, less Midlands/East Anglia-like, writing of Cambridge (Bergstrøm 2017).[1] Supralocalisation processes are one type of variant reduction, and the fifteenth century was effectively the century of the supralocal spread – which by definition, cannot be geographically pinpointed. As people in cities and towns did business with each other (using the term 'business' in its widest application: administration, bureaucracy, estate-management, trade, commerce, industry, law, medicine, accountancy, and any other activity that caused people to write to those whom they did not know in a family or very local capacity), such morphemes, words and spelling-sequences were transferred around the country by means of speaker-contact and writer-contact from places of greater density to those of lower. London as a high-density administrative, bureaucratic and trading centre was highly influential, but it was two-way traffic: the provinces contributed too (present singular *-s*, plural *are*,

1 See Milroy (1993) for an overview, and Nevalainen (2000) for a discussion of supralocalisation and standardisation.

auxiliary *do*; spellings in <g> in *again, guildhall*), and I show (Wright, Chapter 18: Rising living standards, the demise of Anglo-Norman and mixed-language writing, and Standard English) that in particular, the more uniform conventions of written Anglo-Norman provided a model for reduction of variants.

Then, at what should we be looking? The history of English has traditionally been based on studies of monolingual English literary and religious writing, that is, poetry and prose. But language change happens in a dialogue situation, when people communicate back and forth, and the purpose of dialogue – the pragmatics of the situation – is crucial: who spoke or wrote to whom, for what purpose, when, where, and with what result. Most of the writing extant in archives around the British Isles dating from the late fourteenth and fifteenth century was not written in monolingual English but in varying proportions of Medieval Latin, Anglo-Norman and Middle English. Communities of practice such as accountants auditing income and outgoings, merchants keeping track of payments and wares, or lawyers writing letters on behalf of clients, led to the development of specific writing conventions for specific spheres of activity.[2] More recent scholarship has included the internally dated and located non-literary documents of various administrative, bureaucratic and legal sorts such as those analysed by Stenroos and her colleagues and Cuesta and her colleagues, in which it is less easy to ignore the multilingual component.[3] Stenroos and her colleagues' surveys for the *Corpus of Middle English Local Documents* found that during the fifteenth century local administrative writing throughout England was predominantly written in Latin. She reports (Chapter 2: The vernacularisation and standardisation of local administrative writing in late and post-medieval England) that there was no sudden change from Latin to English but decades of switching back and forth, with English emerging in the fifteenth century in functional slots previously held by Anglo-Norman. She distinguishes between formulaic content for internal pragmatic use by other professionals which was usually written in Latin, and the more unpredictable components that needed to be understood by non-professionals which were written in Anglo-Norman until the early fifteenth century and in English thereafter. The switch from French to English in the more oral components was relatively swift, but the Latin components predominated well into the sixteenth century, lasting into the eighteenth. Administrative documents were therefore not the harbinger of Standard

2 See Kopaczyk and Jucker (eds.) (2013) for the introduction of communities of practice to historical linguistics as an explanatory framework.

3 Cuesta et al: *Seville Corpus of Northern English*, http://www.helsinki.fi/varieng/CoRD/corpora/SCONE/; Stenroos et al: *A Corpus of Middle English Local Documents*, http://www.uis.no/meld.

English, as letters written in English sent from the King's Office of Chancery were proportionately few in terms of ratios of English to Latin; because letters in English were written by petitioners *to* the Office of Chancery not from it; and also because there was no obvious variant reduction in the English components – a pool of variants still persisted at the turn of the sixteenth century.[4] The meme of 'Chancery Standard' as the fount of Standard English does not bear scrutiny.

With regard to Samuels' other Types, Peikola (2003: 32), examining Type 1 spelling ratios in the orthography of 68 hands who wrote manuscripts of the Later Version of the Wycliffite Bible, concluded: "it is difficult to sustain a 'grand unifying theory' about C(entral) M(idland) S(tandard)"; and "the alleged status of L(ater) V(ersion) as the prototypical 'invariable' Type 1 text has to be questioned when variation is measured at a graphemic level" (Peikola 2003: 32, 40). On analysis of the orthography of texts forming Type 2, Thaisen (Chapter 5: Standardisation, exemplars, and the Auchinleck manuscript) also found no consistent similarities between different scribes' spelling choices and no obvious overlap of selection signalling incipient standardisation. Horobin (2003: 18) examined spelling in texts labelled Type 3 and reported "such variation warns us against viewing these types of London English as discrete ... we must view Samuels' typology as a linguistic continuum rather than as a series of discrete linguistic varieties". Another part of the origin orthodoxy turns out to hold no explanatory power.

Gordon (Chapter 6: Bristol <th>, <þ> and <y>: the North-South divide revisited, 1400–1700) investigates Benskin's (1982) claim that there was a regional North-South distribution with regard to thorn and yogh spellings in the fifteenth century, with <y> graphs supposedly not used to indicate voiced and voiceless dental fricatives in the South. She surveys various text-types amounting to *c.*100,000 words emanating from the south-western city of Bristol 1404–1711, and finds that on the contrary, <y> graphs representing word-initial dental fricatives in function words occur in substantial amounts in the letters of affluent Bristol merchants and their families. As well as reopening the topic of regional distribution, Gordon shows that standardisation was far from complete by 1711, that variation still prevailed amongst educated writers although at lower frequencies, and that text-type and register greatly influenced scribal choices. Hernández-Campoy (Chapter 7: <th> versus <þ>: Latin-based influences and social awareness in the

4 Auer, Gordon and Oudesluijs's *Emerging Standards: Urbanisation and the Development of Standard English, c.1400–1700* survey of published calendared editions of civic, administrative and legal texts produced in York, Coventry and Bristol also found that the predominant language of written record over the period continued to be Latin.

Paston letters) also considers <þ>/<th> distribution and also finds that the purpose of the text influenced choice. First introduced from Latin in the Old English period and then reinforced by Anglo-Norman usage, the <th> digraph gradually came to replace the monograph <þ> over the Early Modern period. In his study of the Paston family's letters 1425–1503, Hernández-Campoy tracks fluctuation between the two, adducing evidence that during this period <th> was a sociolinguistic variable with indexical meaning: the higher the social rank, the higher the frequencies of the prestige variant <th>. However he also shows how individuals could tweak ratios to give the impression of being more or less humble, according to the purpose of their text. He suggests that Sir John Paston II (1442–1479) used only 33% <th> when writing to the king (even though his father had used 100% <th> when writing to royalty) in order to position himself as an ordinary, put-upon citizen seeking redress. The individual speaker/writer is the crucial ingredient in the diffusion of linguistic practices and innovations.

Turning now to wordstock: Medieval Latin and, to a lesser extent, Anglo-Norman French were the usual languages of written record (with Anglo-Norman occuring in more oral text-types) until the late fourteenth century, when a century of intense written multilingualism ensued – meaning that writings using all three languages are apparent in archives, added to which was the system of mixed-language writing used for accounts and inventories (although as Schendl (Chapter 10: William Worcester's *Itineraria*: mixed-language notes of a medieval traveller) shows, it was also used in personal journals).[5] We agree with the nineteenth-century scholars identified in Chapter 1 that vocabulary is relevant to the development of Standard English, and we foreground multilingual writing – in particular, mixed-language writing – as the mechanism by which so much late fourteenth-century French and Latin-derived vocabulary became regarded as part of English. Durkin reports (Chapter 11: The relationship of borrowing from French and Latin in the Middle English period with the development of the lexicon of Standard English: some observations and a lot of questions) that

5 For a discussion of mixed-language business writing see Wright (2018) and references therein. A note on labels: the term 'Anglo-Norman' is sometimes objected to on the grounds that the language wasn't half-English, half-Norman but fully French, that the original inputting dialects were more varied, and that lexical and grammatical developments took place over centuries in Britain, with the result that over time, it became unlike the French of the Angevin areas of France. In particular, lexemes belonging to the realm of law were coined in Britain so that 'Law French' was a British phenomenon (see Löfstedt 2014). As the historical dictionary of the wordstock is known as the *Anglo-Norman Dictionary*, we retain the traditional title in order to preserve continuity with previous scholarship (for a more reasoned justification, see Trotter 2013: 141–2). I do not discuss here Old Norse and Middle Dutch/Low German, but they added to the lexicon too.

present-day high-frequency Standard English vocabulary shows a higher proportion of late Middle English borrowing from French and Latin than the rest of the lexicon, with a "huge spike" in the late fourteenth century. Given that by the late fourteenth century Anglo-Norman was no longer a mother-tongue in Britain, this huge spike would be inexplicable were it not for the equally huge amount of mixed-language accounts and inventories extant from this period, mostly unpublished.[6] Sylvester (Chapter 13: The role of multilingualism in the emergence of a technical register in the Middle English period) makes the point that within the realm of vocabulary, the process of elimination of variants to the vanishing-point of one single standard form did not apply. Rather, a multiplicity of near-synonyms deriving from several languages enabled nuances of semantics, pragmatics and register to develop. Sylvester demonstrates this by examining the semantic fields of dress/armour and sheepfarming, taken from the *Lexis of Cloth and Clothing in Britain c. 700–1450* and the *Bilingual Thesaurus of Everyday Life in Medieval England*, which include vocabulary from Middle English, Anglo-Norman, Medieval Latin and Older Scots. She deliberately surveys vocabulary to do with sheepfarming in order to demonstrate that Anglo-Norman vocabulary was far from being limited to the higher registers, as is often reported. On the contrary, it was prevalent in land-administration, land-ownership being the backbone of legal day-to-day writing in any century.

Ashdowne (Chapter 14: *-mannus makyth man(n)*? Latin as an indirect source for English lexical history) considers Latin lexical items in *-mannus* as evidence of English – there are 64 such *-mannus* lexemes recorded in the *Dictionary of Medieval Latin from British Sources*, and more than 300 ending in *-man(n* attested before 1500 in dictionaries of English. Ashdowne makes the point that a study of this highly-productive set that depended on monolingual English evidence alone would miss a significant amount of data. Both monolingual Latin and mixed-language writing provides evidence of English words either not attested in monolingual English, or attested with different meanings, or earlier. "Evidence for English lexical history is available in sources written in a variety of languages by users from a variety of linguistic heritages", and Latin is key because Anglo-Norman administrators initiated Latin as the main language of written record, admixed with both French and English. Ashdowne's chapter also makes the point that it was not a one-way street, as English vocabulary crossed over into what

6 Mixed-language consisted of Medieval Latin (and to a lesser extent, Anglo-Norman) as a grammatical matrix, with nouns, verb-stems, modifiers and *-ing* forms appearing variably in Middle English. Alcolado Carnicero (2013) has demonstrated that the London Mercers' Company Wardens' Accounts, for example, entered into five generations of mixed-language writing after 1380, before committing to monolingual English in the mid fifteenth century.

could fairly be considered monolingual Latin. Both Medieval Latin as written in Britain and Anglo-Norman as written in Britain contained considerable influence from English. Tiddeman (Chapter 13: More sugar and spice: revisiting medieval Italian influence on the mercantile lexis of England) countermands the usual textbook assertion that Italian words predominantly entered English via the works of Dante, Petrarch and Boccaccio, influencing the poetical vocabulary of Chaucer, Gower and Lydgate, and again during the Renaissance in cultural fields such as music and architecture. She augments the work of previous lexicographers and historians by adding to the list of late medieval trade borrowings from Italian, which greatly outnumbered the later, erudite ones. In many cases these are the names of goods which passed through Italian rather than originated in Italian, and which were then written down in Anglo-Norman and mixed-language in British customs accounts and port books as commodities from the Near, Middle and Far East were ferried over to Britain (notably to Southampton) by Italian merchants. In particular, Tiddeman identifies Anglo-Norman as the buffer language through which Tuscan, Genoese and Venetian trade-terminology was transmitted into Middle English, a role hidden from sight by dictionaries which blanket this route with 'Old French', or simply 'French'.

These discussions of the late medieval wordstock have all depended on evidence taken from mixed-language documents, even though mixed-language is invisible in textbook histories of English. Schendl (Chapter 10: William Worcester's *Itineraria*: mixed-language notes of a medieval traveller) analyses the mixed-language usage of a single scribe, William Worcester, who was secretary to Sir John Fastolf. In the late fifteenth century Worcester made various journeys around Britain noting down what he saw. His *Itineraries* are a hotchpotch of miscellaneous facts and descriptions of all sorts, some written at a slant on the hoof as he travelled. The importance of his diaries cannot be overstated: he used mixed-language not for professional accountancy, mercantile or notarial reasons but for his own personal jottings and note-keeping. Very little other fifteenth-century ephemera has survived, so this is a surprise glimpse as to how mixed-language also pervaded the personal sphere.

Moving now to monolingual English, assumptions have been made about the pre-eminence of London English, with certain scribes assumed to have worked there in the fifteenth century. One such is the Beryn scribe. Carrillo-Linares and Williamson (Chapter 3: The linguistic character of manuscripts attributed to the Beryn Scribe: a comparative study) analyse his spellings using the comparative method of the *Linguistic Atlas of Late Medieval English*. Williamson was instrumental in the creation of the *Linguistic Atlas of Late Medieval English*, so if the Beryn scribe were locatable in London by this method, Carrillo-Linares and Williamson would be able to show us how. However, they conclude that on the contrary, by means of spelling-comparison the Beryn scribe cannot be localised and could have come from anywhere over a large swathe of the midland and southern half of the country, and that he copied exemplars from various regions. He didn't impose his own dialect in a uniform manner but retained certain features from his exemplars whilst using certain features from his idiolect and others that he'd picked up along the way, as a result of long copying experience. Carrillo-Linares and Williamson come to the view that most fifteenth-century professional scribes would, over the length of a copying career, have written in mixed dialectal styles like this. The culmination of features amassed from the scribe's idiolect, from the supralocal norm, from the exemplar at hand, and those ported over from copying previous texts, would have constituted normal professional fifteenth-century scribal behaviour. As the Beryn scribe was writing within the the period of the supralocal spread, geographical pinpointing is not possible (and in Wright (2012) I make the same point about the non-localisability of the Hammond scribe, who flourished in the late fifteenth century). Carrillo-Linares and Williamson also report that a handful of the scribe's spellings are completely invariant, although none became Standard. The mere fact of consistency signals the onset of the long standardisation process. In Chapter 18 (Rising Living Standards, the Demise of Anglo-Norman and Mixed-Language Writing, and Standard English) I identify another copying phenomenon, that of given versus new information. In any early fifteenth-century mixed-language weekly-payments account from the London Bridge archive, the first half of each week's entry shows invariant spellings and the second half shows variation. The first part (details of the permanent staff) was copied over verbatim from the previous week, then what followed (the individual weekly incomings and outgoings) was new and more varied. I call this the payroll phenomenon: high-intensity copying led towards a more uniform look on the page.

Honkapohja and Liira (Chapter 9: Abbreviations and standardisation in the *Polychronicon*: Latin to English and manuscript to print) also noticed certain consistent spellings across all English manuscripts of their much-copied text, the *Polychronicon*. In different versions of the *Polychronicon* they find that reduction in spelling variation was preceded by reduction in abbreviations, that the rate of abbreviation loss in Latin portions differed from the rate of loss in English portions, and that different abbreviation types disappeared at different rates. Individual scribes varied considerably in their use of abbreviations, but abbreviation densities of scribes were found to be similar across manuscripts. That is to say, individuals had their own preferred patterning of abbreviation usage – the fifteenth-century abbreviation variant pool remained, but individuals selected fairly consistently from that pool. The relative amount of spelling variation also held steady between the various witnesses, with no decrease from the early manuscripts to the mid-fifteenth century.

To take stock so far: the fifteenth century was a century of of multilingual writing, which can be seen in present-day high-frequency vocabulary, and of supralocal spread, rather than standardisation *per se*. Latin continued in use. Incipient standardisation cannot be detected by influence from London, nor by a reduced fifteenth-century feature pool as such, but what can be detected is the behaviour of individual scribes selecting consistently from that pool. Individuals narrowed down their selection but not in a universally-shared manner, so that the feature pool itself continued on. Moreno-Olalla (Chapter 4: Spelling practices in Late Middle English medical prose: a quantitative analysis) considers four herbals written in Middle English during the 1460s–1490s. He finds that, like the Beryn scribe, each scribe had a collection of certain invariant preferences, certain near-invariant preferences, and that each scribe's preferred spellings were not universally shared by the others. Moreno-Olalla finds a discrepancy between the final part of a word (he focusses on distribution of word-final *-e* spellings) and stems: spelling of stems remained varied, whereas the scribes were progressing towards an 'imperfect agreement' about what the end of a word should look like.

Conde-Silvestre (Chapter 15: Communities of practice, proto-standardisation and spelling focusing in the Stonor letters) constructs a community of practice, that of the cofeoffees of Thomas Stonor II (1424–1474). From this network he analyses 21 letters written in English, and compares them to a control group. He finds a prevalence among the cofeoffees of spelling-focussing in words of Romance origin, which reflects the pragmatics of law and administration – which were usually written in Anglo-Norman, Medieval Latin and mixed-language. This is a direct indication that the conventions of Anglo-Norman and Medieval Latin business writing had an effect on written English. In Chapter 16, Romero-Barranco (A comparison of some French and English nominal suffixes in Early English correspondence (1420–1681)) surveys the usage of nine French and English nominal suffixes over a 260–year period, as exemplified by the *Parsed Corpus of Early English Correspondence*. He finds that the gentry and the professionals were the main users of French suffixes, leading their diffusion at the beginning of the Early Modern English period, in contradistinction to the nobility and the lower commoners. It is notable that the professionals were instrumental here as it is in keeping with the underlying theme of multilingual dissemination by mercantile, legal and other business communities of practice. Nevalainen (Chapter 8: Early mass communication as a standardizing influence? The case of the Book of Common Prayer) assesses whether liturgical language had any influence on Standard English. She compares three versions of the Book of Common Prayer: of 1549, 1552, and revised in 1661. She finds that the versions of 1549 and 1552 were both written in "middle of the road" southern dialect, neither particularly conservative nor particularly modern, but that the 1661 version was somewhat more varied, modernising some features but retaining others. She concludes that the *Book of Common Prayer* did not exert an identifiable formative standardizing influence on Early Modern English grammar. Like the advent of print, it has often been asserted that the language of the Bible and Liturgy was formative, but it is not easy to marshall evidence supporting either claim.

Kopaczyk (Chapter 17: Textual standardisation of legal Scots *vis a vis* Latin) considers the influence of Latin on Scots, as evidenced by medieval burgh laws. Kopaczyk extracts invariant Latin chunks from selected Scottish burgh laws from seven Latin manuscripts, and compares them with seven extant Scots manuscripts of 1455–1602 in order to see how these standardised Latin chunks were rendered into Scots. The second aim is to establish whether there were any traces of standardisation on the level of text which were not prompted by Latin. She finds the Scots versions show more variation than their Latin counterparts, but within limits. That textual stability seems to have been largely independent of Latin and may be interpreted as incipient standardisation. Scots is an interesting case in that the process of standardisation was set in train but did not go to completion: during the medieval and Early Modern period standardising scenarios were developing in parallel on both sides of the border, with separate standardisation trajectories. As yet we do not know if patterns spread from urban to rural settings, or even where the hubs of standardisation in Scotland were located.[7] Standard English did eventually arrive in Scotland of course, but only after a series of seventeenth and eighteenth century political and cultural events.

Summary of the revised version

Where: Supralocal centres all over England, not specifically East or Central Midlands, not specifically London. Spreading out from centres of population density to rural areas, driven by language contact (both written and spoken) in a business context resulting in loss of regional features.

When: Second half of the fourteenth century onwards, not completing until the 1800s.

Who: All writers: scribes, clerks, accounts-keepers, copyists of all kinds.

7 Kopaczyk, Joanna. 2013. *The legal language of Scottish burghs. Standardisation and lexical bundles (1380–1560)*, Oxford University Press, pp. 43, 258–260. Previous research suggests that Edinburgh was a strong draw.

Which text types: No one single text-type. There is no obvious text-type that should be excluded. Even ephemera provide evidence.

What kind of pragmatics: Stenroos (chapter 2) found that language choice was conditioned by who needed to understand the text (if professional, then Latin, if non-professional, then Anglo-Norman until the mid fifteenth century and English thereafter). Carrillo-Linares and Williamson (chapter 3) found that scribes accrued 'souvenirs' along the way; invariant items from individual copying projects that stayed with them and became part of their invariant repertoire. I (chapter 18) found that the pragmatics of high-intensity copying influenced variant reduction, the payroll effect. Latin and French had long been conventionalised on the page and their range of variation was limited, whereas Middle English was not conventionalised and reflected the variation inherent in the 'linguistics of speech'. When Middle English took over the pragmatic roles of written Anglo-Norman, it took over its tendency towards visual uniformity too.

Which features: All linguistic features are relevant to standardisation, including wordstock, and the under-studied abbreviation and suspension system. The early stage of standardisation can be identified by reduction of grammatical and orthographical variants and loss of geographically-marked variants (however, Sylvester (chapter 12) points out that words did not get eliminated, rather, they increased as foreign words were absorbed into English, allowing technolects with nuanced meanings to develop). The fifteenth century was still the century of the large variant pool but towards the end of the century individuals began to select fewer choices from that pool. Thus consistency began with individuals curtailing their range, although individuals differed from each other so the feature pool itself still remained large (Moreno-Olalla, chapter 4). This alone speaks against any kind of imposition of a model, whether governmental or bureaucratic, or a single dialect – Midland, London, or anywhere else.

How: Communities of practice; both strong-tie and weak-tie social networks; the repeat back-and-forth encounters inherent in trading activity.

Why: Politics and economics (Wright, chapter 18). In the later fourteenth century living standards rose, exerting a demand for goods, which themselves began to standardise. Trade patterns altered: continental merchants made repeat visits to London, and London became a nexus of trade countrywide, resulting in weak-tie networks both throughout Britain and extending to the continent. As their circumstances improved, the people who belonged to trade and craft guilds began to express themselves on the page in their mother-tongue. Trade and craft guilds correlate with early adoption of monolingual supralocal English.

Why wordstock should be included: The Anglo-Norman administration brought Medieval Latin as a written language and Anglo-Norman as a spoken language to Britain. Over time, British Medieval Latin became more and more informed by Anglo-Norman, which developed lexically and grammatically in ways unlike that of France. Mixed-language, so prevalent in the late fourteenth and first half of the fifteenth centuries, is really written Latin which had absorbed its spoken French reflex (and because Anglo-Norman was used in England, it absorbed vocabulary from English too). When the social circumstances of the trading classes changed and they became more powerful, ratios inverted: instead of a Latin matrix swollen with Anglo-Norman vocabulary, the language of written record became an English matrix swollen with Anglo-Norman vocabulary.[8]

Why multilingual: all of the chapters in this volume answer this question but I single out here Sylvester (chapter 12), who focusses on the development of a technolect (itself a property of standardised languages) via synonyms of English, Latin and French derivation taking on domain-specific nuances of meaning, and Conde-Silvestre (chapter 15), who pinpoints reduction of variation beginning first in Romance-derived vocabulary in the subset of Stonor letters he studies. Schendl (chapter 10) shows how mixed-language writing was used not just for professional, outward-looking purposes such as institutional accounts or wills and testaments (aimed at specific audiences of accountants, auditors, lawyers and legatees) but also inward-looking purposes such as the personal travel journal he discusses. Everything in this volume points towards the conventions of written Anglo-Norman as the key factor catalysing the development of Standard English.

In sum: the 'Chancery Standard' meme was successful not only because it is a catchy label, but also because top-down imposition by the Crown fits with modern perceptions of medieval feudalism. Therefore, our revised account needs a nutshell version in order to compete. It is this:

> Over the fourteenth century, living standards rose, enabling a new class of people to find their voice. Monolingual English, shaped by its Anglo-Norman antecedent, was the written record of the trading classes.

8 I use 'trading classes' instead of working or labouring classes because those terms have modern social implications. By 'trade' I mean any commercial or professional exchange.

References

Alcolado Carnicero, José Miguel. 2013. *Social Networks and Mixed-Language Business Writing: Latin/French/English in the Wardens' Accounts of the Mercers' Company of London, 1390–1464*. University of Castilla-La Mancha: PhD thesis.

Auer, Anita, Moragh Gordon, Mike Olson. 2016. English Urban Vernaculars, 1400–1700: Digitizing Text from Manuscript. In María José López-Couso, Belén Méndez-Naya, Paloma Núñez-Pertejo and Ignacio Palacios-Martínez (eds.). *Corpus linguistics on the move: Exploring and understanding English through corpora*, Language and Computers Series 79 Amsterdam: Brill/Rodopi, 21–40.

Bergstrøm, Geir. 2017. *Yeuen at Cavmbrigg': A Study of the Late Medieval English Documents of Cambridge*. University of Stavanger: PhD thesis.

Bex, Tony and Richard J. Watts (eds.). 1999. "Standard English: what it isn't". *Standard English: the Widening Debate*. London: Routledge, 117–128.

Cuesta, Julia Fernández. 2014. "The Voice of the Dead: Analyzing Sociolinguistic Variation in Early Modern English Wills and Testaments". *Journal of English Linguistics* 42/4, 330–358.

Horobin, Simon. 2003. *The Language of the Chaucer Tradition*. Chaucer Studies 32. Woodbridge: D. S. Brewer.

Kopaczyk, Joanna and Andreas H. Jucker (eds.). 2013. *Communities of Practice in the History of English*. Amsterdam: John Benjamins.

Löfstedt, Leena. 2014. 'Notes on the Beginnings of Law French'. *Romance Philology* 68, 285–337.

Milroy, James. 1993. "The notion of "standard language" and its applicability to the study of Early Modern English pronunciation". In Dieter Stein and Ingrid Tieken-Boon van Ostade (eds.). *Towards a Standard English: 1600–1800*. Berlin: Mouton de Gruyter. 19–29.

Nevalainen, Terttu. 2000. "Processes of supralocalisation and the rise of Standard English in the Early Modern Period". In Ricardo Bermúdez-Otero, David Denison, Richard M. Hogg and Chris McCully (eds.). *Generative Theory and Corpus Studies*. Berlin: Mouton de Gruyter. 329–371.

Peikola, Matti. "The Wycliffite Bible and 'Central Midland Standard': Assessing the Manuscript Evidence". 2003. *Nordic Journal of English Studies* 2, 1. 29–51.

Schipor, Delia. 2018. *A Study of Multilingualism in the Late Medieval Material of the Hampshire Record Office*. University of Stavanger: PhD thesis.

Thengs, Kjetil V. 2013. *English medieval documents of the Northwest Midlands: A study in the language of a real-space text corpus*. University of Stavanger: PhD thesis.

Trotter, David. 2013. "Deinz certains boundes: where does Anglo-Norman begin and end?" *Romance Philology* 67/1, 139–177.

Wright, Laura. 2012. "The Hammond scribe: his dialect, his paper, and folios 133–155 of Trinity College Cambridge MS O.3.11". In Claudia Lange, Beatrix Weber and Göran Wolf, (eds.). *Communicative Spaces: Variation, Contact, and Change*. Frankfurt am Main: Peter Lang. 227–258.

Wright, Laura. 2018. "A Multilingual Approach to the History of Standard English". In Pahta, Paivi, Janne Skaffari and Laura Wright (eds.). *Multilingual Practices in Language History: English and Beyond*. Language Contact and Bilingualism 15. Berlin: Mouton de Gruyter. 339–358.

Laura Wright

1 A critical look at previous accounts of the standardisation of English

Twenty years ago, handbooks discussing the origins of Standard English gave the impression that its beginnings were well understood. Readers were informed that there had been a written variety called Late West Saxon Standard in the Old English period, replaced by a written variety called Chancery Standard in the late fourteenth/early fifteenth century. Readers were told that Chancery Standard was based on Central Midlands writing (or East Midlands, if they were reading an older textbook), and it was explained that the Midlands dialect was more easily understood than other dialects because it was spoken in the middle of the country. How Chancery Standard came to derive from the Midlands dialects was said to be due to migration of Northerners into London (although some authors claimed a migration from the East Midlands, and yet others from the Central Midlands). Handbooks which went into more detail classified Chancery Standard's evolution as stemming from Type 4 of four prototypical Types into which London Middle English writing had been divided, which was writing from the King's Office of Chancery. And there was sometimes a nod to the language of the court, to the varieties of English used by scholars in Oxford and Cambridge, and to the invention of print. The actual mechanism of how Standard English supposedly focussed and diffused both geographically out from the Midlands (whether East or Central) and through different text-types was not detailed. That all that had been originally explicitly stipulated under the label 'Chancery Standard' were spellings for twenty-one common words, the third-person plural pronoun forms *they/their*, and the *-inde/-ende/-ande* morpheme, was not specified. Syntax, morphology, sentence structure, social context and discourse norms, pragmatics, word-choice, register, text-types, reduction of variation, reduction of abbreviations and suspensions, the abandonment of letter-graphs *thorn* and *yogh*, and the multilingual backdrop – the convention of keeping accounts in mixed-language Anglo-Norman/Medieval Latin/Middle English, the continuing custom of alternating passages of monolingual Anglo-Norman and Medieval Latin, and the rise of Neo-Latin as a politico-scholarly medium of international communication – these were barely mentioned.

In various publications (Wright (1994, 1996, 2001a, 2005, 2013, 2017) and Wright, ed. (2000)) I traced how this narrative came to be accepted orthodoxy

https://doi.org/10.1515/9783110687545-002

when its empirical underpinnings are, as this volume shows, unverifiable. I sorted the competing handbook versions into five groups:[1]

1. Standard English evolved from the speech and writing of Middle English speakers from the East Midlands because:
   a. merchants spoke the East Midland dialect (Leith)
   b. there was an influx of immigrants from the East Midlands (Strang, Freeborn)
   c. the East Midlands was culturally, economically and administratively important (Barber)
   d. the East Midlands was the largest of the major dialect areas (Baugh and Cable)
   e. the University of Cambridge was influential (Leith, Barber, Baugh and Cable)
2. Standard English evolved from the speech and writing of Middle English speakers from the Central Midlands because:
   a. the East Midlands dialect was too "peripheral and remote" whereas the Central Midlands dialect had a "more systematic patterning"; therefore the Central Midlands dialect became adopted as a standard instead, despite there being no fresh wave of migration from the Central Midlands (Strang)
   b. there was later, massive, immigration from the Central Midlands (Crystal)
3. Oxford, Cambridge and London naturally influenced the developing standard because:
   a. that is where the educated speakers were (Leith, Barber, Crystal)
   b. but the University of Oxford had no influence (Baugh and Cable)
4. The Midlands dialect was the obvious dialect to standardise because it was more easily understood than the Northern or Southern dialects (Baugh and Cable)
5. Standard English evolved from the usage of the clerks of the office of Chancery (Strang, Crystal)

These five versions are contradictory. The authors did not provide evidence for their assertions about migration, nor why one dialect should have been more

1 Summarised from Wright (1996: 103): Leith (1983 [1987]: 38–9), Blake (1992: 11), Pyles and Algeo (1964 [1993]: 141), Barber (1964: 160), Baugh and Cable (1951 [1993]: 187–190), Strang (1970 [1986]: 162–3), Freeborn (1992: 95), Burnley (1989: 23), Crystal (1995: 41, 55). Stenroos (this volume) provides equivalent accounts from more recent handbooks. Our lists are not exhaustive: Chancery Standard has been a successful meme over the last fifty years, bearing much repetition.

comprehensible than another. More recent accounts no longer repeat these 'facts' verbatim but elements are still occasionally repeated: in particular, the supposed influence of speakers from either the East or Central Midlands, the supposed migration of Northerners to London, and a conflation of London English with Standard English.[2] One more recent handbook account which does confront these difficulties is Schaefer (2012), who reports that the fifteenth century was when a set of written discourse traditions were taken over from French and Latin models into English, and when written variation started to reduce for supralocal use. However she still devotes subsections to "Types I–III" and "Chancery English", reporting on them in detail because "Regarding "Chancery English" as the direct ancestor of "modern written English" . . . has very much become the received wisdom", even though she then goes on to discredit these notions, emphasising instead "that putting "Chancery English" into place means situating it in the multilingual discourse community" (Schaefer 2012: 525).[3]

Herein lies the paradox: scholars who work on the origins of Standard English no longer accept that "Chancery Standard" was a cohesive entity, and believe that the multilingual context of late Medieval Britain (both written and spoken) had an important influence, but authors of chapters in handbooks aimed at undergraduates still feel compelled to give "Chancery Standard" room due to its pervasive repetition, with the result that students new to the subject learn that a) there was a written variety known as "Chancery Standard" but b) it never actually existed. Let us now see where these versions came from, and why belief in them has been so long-held.

1 East Midlands, Central Midlands

These contradictory versions stem from work by earlier scholars. Eilert Ekwall (1877–1964), a Swedish scholar, summarised changes observed by earlier German linguists Lorenz Morsbach (1850–1945) and Wilhelm Heuser (fl.1886–1930) in English writing of the fourteenth century produced in London. Of Morsbach (1888), Ekwall reported (1956: xiv–xv):

2 For a discussion of what different scholars have meant by 'standard' and 'standardisation' with resultant contradictions, and the classification of Late West Saxon Standard as a set of orthographic norms rather than a standardised dialect, see Kornexl (2012).

3 Schaefer is not the only recent scholar taking this approach of detailing Chancery Standard before pointing out its deficiencies, see also, for example, Beal (2016).

> ... he examined a number of texts from the 14th and 15th centuries which he supposed to have been written in London proper, such as the Appeal of Thomas Usk (1384–5), some among *the Fifty Earliest English Wills* (1387 ff.) and a number of Gilds (1389). Other groups of texts Morsbach calls Staatsurkunden and Parlamentsurkunden (royal writs, Parliamentary papers and the like). Morsbach found that the language in these texts is on the whole uniform and agrees with the later Standard language. He concludes that the Standard language developed in London and spread from there to the remainder of the country. The language in the late ME London texts is East Midland.
>
> But London is situated in Old Saxon territory, was in fact the capital of the kingdom of Essex. Its language should therefore have been East Saxon. The London language must thus have undergone a change from East Saxon to East Midland. ... The change, in his opinion, is due to the vicinity of the Anglian area (the Midland and the North), which is more than double that of the Saxon-Kentish area. He does not work out his theory in any detail, and the statement that the Anglian area immediately adjoins London is not correct. ... The general results of Morsbach's investigations can on the whole still be accepted. The language found in the texts used by him ... does agree in the main with the later Standard language. But the whole problem is more complicated than it appears in Morsbach's presentment of it, and a convincing explanation of the change from a Saxon to an East Midland dialect is missing.

There are statements here that surprise present-day readers, such as "the language in these texts is on the whole uniform", that it "agrees with the later Standard language",[4] and that despite Ekwall's reservations, "the general results of Morsbach's investigations can on the whole still be accepted". Ekwall also summarised Heuser's work (1956: xvi):

> In 1914 appeared Wilhelm Heuser's important study *Alt-London*, in which the early London language was shown to have been definitely East Saxon. ... The chief criteria of the early London dialect are:
> 1. *a* from OE *ae:*, as *strate* from OE *strae:t*.
> 2. *a* from OE *ae* (*e*) from *i*-mutated *a* before a nasal, as *fan* (in *Fancherche* 'Fenchurch') from OE *fen* 'fen'.
> 3. *e* from OE *y*, *y:*, as *bregge*, *hethe* from OE *brycg* 'bridge', *hy:th* 'landing-place'.
> 4. *e* from *eo* in *melk* 'milk', *selver* 'silver', as in *Melk-*, *Selver-strate* 'Milk Street', 'Silver Street'.

Ekwall reported that Heuser's work on early ("East Saxon") London texts contradicted Morsbach's, yet although "Morsbach's starting-point is thus doubtful", nevertheless "This need not affect his general results" (Ekwall 1956: xvii). Ekwall accepted wholesale both the change from 'East Saxon' to 'East Midland' dialect and that late fourteenth-century London texts "agree in the main with

4 For a discussion of variation in the 1389 guild certificates see Wright (1995). For a discussion of multilingual language in the *Fifty Earliest English Wills* see Wright (2015).

the later Standard language". He explained what he meant by "in the main": distinguishing what he called "genuine London forms" *strate* 'street', *fan* 'fen', *gert* 'girt', *hethe* 'hythe' from forms that occurred "by the side" *strete, fen, -igurt, hithe*. Ekwall's own specification of "obvious Midland features" were three: present plural *-e(n*, present participle *-ing* replacing what he called "Essex *-ande*", and *they* replacing *hi* (1956: xviii).

In order to provide an explanation for what he thought was a dialect change from East Saxon to East Midland, Ekwall collected together evidence of people who came to London between the Norman Conquest of 1066 and 1360 from somewhere more northerly (a "relatively small" amount), or who had a surname derived from a more northerly place ("extremely numerous", 1956: xxxi). He was well aware of and discussed many of the difficulties with this local-surname approach as a means of proving immigration, and his survey effectively revealed considerable variation not easily reducible to generalisation. He did not pretend otherwise: "The early material points to a good deal of dialectal variation in the early London language".

However from a Neogrammarian perspective such variation was in need of explanation and so Ekwall invoked homophonic clash (*hull* instead of 'expected' *hell* 'hill'), analogy (*whelk* influenced by *melk* 'milk'), "internal sound-substitution" (*bury*), and "Midland" influence (*calf, cold* instead of word-initial affricates) (1956: xviii–xxxi). His results were N = 2,890, made up of 1,970 from East Midland counties (Suffolk, Norfolk, Cambridgeshire, Bedfordshire, Huntingdonshire, Northamptonshire, Rutland, Lincolnshire, Leicestershire, Nottinghamshire), 380 from West Midlands counties (Warwickshire, Herefordshire, Staffordshire, Derbyshire, Cheshire, Lancashire), 405 from the North and Scotland, and 135 of Midland or Northern origin not included in the above. Note that the East Anglian counties were included under the label "East Midlands" and Lancashire and Derbyshire under the label "West Midlands": classifications that affect the results. He repeated the exercise for the Home Counties (Essex, Middlesex, Hertfordshire, Kent, Surrey, Buckinghamshire) and found 3,000 immigrants, or the same as the North and the Midlands (in his definition of it!) taken together (1956: lx). For the south (Sussex, Hampshire, Berkshire, Oxfordshire, Wiltshire, Dorset, Somerset, Devon, Cornwall, Gloucestershire, Worcestershire – again, note the unusual categorisation) he estimated somewhat over 1,000 persons. In other words, his survey did not support the immigration theory (regardless of the labels, by his surname method, most immigrants were from London's hinterland), and he was well aware of it: "The question may then be raised whether it is probable that linguistic influence due to immigration from the Midlands and the North can have been sufficiently strong to affect the City dialect". Nevertheless he adduced an argument that it could, as he claimed that Midland immigrants included "upper-class merchants" who affected the speech of the "upper classes" in the City: "the London language as we find it towards the end of the fourteenth century was a class dialect, the language spoken by the upper stratum of the London population". For reasons he did not give, he discounted trade: "London as a centre of commerce attracted traders from all parts. Some scholars have seen in this fact the chief reason or one of the chief reasons for the dialectal change in the London language, for instance H. C. Wyld, who in *Colloquial English*, p. 8, even suggests that the strong East Midland influence came from the great business centre of Norwich. This cannot of course be accepted".[5] However Ekwall also found counterarguments: "I have sometimes wondered whether, and even suggested many years ago in lectures, that the marked East Midland element in the London language may to some extent be bound up with the fact that this part of England was the old Danelaw, where an extensive infusion of Scandinavian blood took place, and where Scandinavian customs left strong traces".

Was there really a change from "East Saxon" to "East Midland" dialect in London in the fourteenth century? The only features mentioned by Ekwall (1956) were four: certain <a> graphs and <e> graphs in stressed syllables, present plural *-e(n*, present participle *-ing*, and pronoun *they* – and no mention of ratios of major to minor variants. Indeed variation posed a problem: "The curious case of the Subsidy of 1307 with its 13 *Meneter* and 13 *Min(e)ter* is an illustration of the variation between old London and Midland forms ... The material as a whole gives us a glimpse of the flux in the language of early London" (Ekwall 1956: xxx). Ekwall, born a generation after the Neogrammarians, was expecting uniformity. For him, categorical shift from *men-* to *min-* would have indicated categorical shift from Saxon to Anglian. The fact that there were 26 tokens showing both spellings equally was explicable only as change from one to the other. Yet despite his theoretical underpinning causing him to maintain the concept of discrete dialects, his observations of the data were, repeatedly, that there was variation. His data and Neogrammarian theory were at odds, and he had a hard time reconciling the two.

Let us take stock: Morsbach reported that Standard English developed in London and derived from the East Midland dialect. For Ekwall, the label "East Midland" included East Anglia (Suffolk, Norfolk, Cambridgeshire) and Bedfordshire (also not usually regarded as a Midland county, neighbouring

5 Ekwall (1956: lxii). My only suggestion for his outright rejection is that 'trade' was thought to be vulgar in the first half of the twentieth century and perhaps Ekwall suffered from this prejudice, coming from an illustrious and prominent family himself. Certainly he assumed that fourteenth-century London Aldermen and Sherriffs were members of the upper class, and that the documents he was analysing – tax lists – reflected upper-class language use.

Hertfordshire, Buckinghamshire and Cambridgeshire and covering part of the Chilterns). Even working with this expanded understanding of the label, Ekwall found that Londoners with locative surnames came predominantly from the surrounding hinterland. Nevertheless he sought to rescue the "East Midland" theory by suggesting that a preponderance of immigrants from this region came from the upper class, assuming that language change was mediated by the upper classes (again, this is not the present-day expectation). However he was not dogmatic about it, also suggesting that features typical of dialects North of London may have entered London speech via "industrial" "freer peasants" from Danelaw areas. A scrupulous scholar, Ekwall discussed motivation, the plusses and the defects of his survey, its preliminary nature, and proffered more than one interpretation.

More recent scholarship is less concerned with macrodialect labels and pays more attention to text-type, as the pragmatics of a text determine the language used. Two recent surveys from the Middle English Local Documents project at the University of Stavanger have shown that parish guild documents were more conservative than other administrative documents from the same date and place (Thengs 2013, Bergstrom 2017; see also Wright 2001b), and one of the findings of the project is that administrative texts show supralocalisation earlier than literary texts. Supralocalisation (meaning the spreading out of variants from centres around the country over time, usually discussed with reference to variants which became near-categorical over a specific region but which were not then adopted in Standard English) is found before standardisation, and it is why Ekwall's report that "Morsbach found that the language in these texts is on the whole uniform and agrees with the later Standard language" is so startling. A late fourteenth century text can look modern with regard to variant reduction yet look old-fashioned with regard to feature-selection. This is not a paradox: when English became a language of written record, firstly, variants began to be reduced (on the Latin and Anglo-Norman model), and secondly, certain features became selected as majority variants. Which spellings/morphemes were selected as majority variants differed from region to region and text-type to text-type, with some becoming supralocal but not national, and others eventually becoming more widely accepted. This movement from supralocal to national equates to standardisation (although there is more to standardisation than spellings and morphemes). An illustration comes from Bergstrom's work on administrative texts post 1399 from Cambridge. Cambridge is shown to have been rather advanced when compared with administrative documents from the surrounding areas of East Anglia and further into the Midlands. As well as showing fewer variants, Cambridge texts were considerably more southern in dialect. This is not due to standardization *per se* – word-final verbal <-th> is present in late medieval Cambridge administrative documents in high ratios, yet it did not last in Standard English.

To return to my discussion of influential scholars: the next was Michael Samuels in *English Studies*, a paper published seven years after Ekwall (1956). Samuels was one of the editors of the *Linguistic Atlas of Late Medieval English* which was to be finished more than two decades later and on which he was working at the time. In this short paper (Samuels 1963 covers thirteen pages but just seven of those pages consist of printed text, the rest being full-size dot maps, diagrams and tables), Samuels classified late medieval London (and other) texts into Types I–IV, introduced the term "Central Midlands dialect", and the label "Chancery Standard". He too was not dogmatic, stating, like Ekwall, that his work was preliminary, but he was metaphorical, and it seems that his water metaphor had appeal for generations of literary medievalists: "consultation of any of the large classes of documents at the Public Record Office will show clearly that, until 1430–35, English is the exception rather than the rule in the written business of administration; after that, there is a sudden change, and the proportions are reversed, from a mere trickle of English documents among thousands in Latin and French, to a spate of English documents" (Samuels 1963 [1989]: 70). Inundation aside, this classification of manuscripts into four types has subsequently proved problematical, partly because Samuels did not specify exactly which manuscripts fall into which class, and partly because others do not see the internal cohesiveness he proclaimed. For Type I, he specified "the majority of Wycliffite manuscripts (though by no means limited to them) . . . it becomes apparent that this is a standard literary language based on the dialects of the Central Midland counties". For Type II he specified just eight manuscripts: Auchinleck MS hands 1 and 3, the Early English Prose Psalter in BL Add. 17376, MS BL Harley 5085, three manuscripts by one scribe: Magdalene College Cambridge Pepys 2498, Bodley Laud Misc. 622 and BL Harley 874, St John's College Cambridge MS 256, and Glasgow Hunterian MS 250. For Type III he specified a number (but not exactly which) of the documents in Chambers and Daunt (1931) and Furnivall (1882), some Chaucer manuscripts (but not exactly which) "as vouched for by a concensus of the best MSS", *Piers Plowman* in Trinity College Cambridge B.15.17, and the works of Hoccleve. Type IV "(which I shall call 'Chancery Standard')" was specified as "that flood of government documents that starts in the years following 1430. Its differences from the language of Chaucer are well known, and it is this type, not its predecessors in London English, that is the basis of modern written English" (Samuels 1963 [1989]: 67–71). This sounds authoritative, but so far as I can gather from the data presented, it is based on spellings for wordforms *again, -ande/-ende/-inde, any, but, each, gave, given, much, neither, not, old, saw, self, should, stead, such, their, these, they, though, through, while, will, world.* Just as Morsbach, Heuser and Ekwall used the term "language" to mean essentially phonology (spellings for vowels in stressed syllables, and consonants, with a considerably smaller amount of space devoted to part-of-speech morphology); so Samuels used it to mean mainly orthography. And methodologically, there are problems: "if we exclude those documents and wills that, on the evidence of their dialectal forms, must have been written by immigrants into London, Type III may still be taken as representative of London English of 1400; but any form of written standard is conspicuous by its absence". I agree that a written standard is absent from texts written in 1400 but I would like to know Samuels' principles of exclusion, in order for the result not to be a self-fulfilling prophecy. His wording is extreme: "it was only at the stage represented by Type IV (a stage of London English changed beyond all recognition from that of a century previous) that it was finally adopted by the government offices for regular written use; from then on, it was backed by the full weight of the administrative machine" (Samuels 1963 [1989]: 70–1). The phrases "beyond all recognition" and "the full weight of the administrative machine" are rhetorical overstatements.[6]

Samuels disagreed with Morsbach and Ekwall's East Midland theory, because his analysis of East Anglian documents for *LALME* showed spellings that differed from those of Types I-IV. Plotting dot maps of major variants (minor variants were ignored) for *they, though, give, gave, their, them*, "notably the so-called northern forms", he wrote "the nearest point from which they could have spread was in the North Central Midlands". He then (partially) reported Ekwall (1956): "Professor Ekwall has shown, firstly, that in the late thirteenth and early fourteenth centuries, immigration into London was highest from Norfolk, with Essex and Hertfordshire next, and then the remaining Home Counties. ... But Ekwall has also shown that in the fourteenth century a significant change took place: immigration from Northamptonshire and Bedfordshire increased, that from the Home Counties decreased, while that from Norfolk continued .... This immigration from the Central Midlands in the fourteenth century amply explains the great difference btween our Types II and III ... as it will explain the further changes from Type III to Type IV ('Chancery Standard')." (Samuels 1963 [1989]: 73–4). Again, this sounds authoritative, but Samuels omitted Ekwall's discussions of the limitations of his survey,

6 See Stenroos, this volume, for a refutation of Chancery's "spate" and "flood" of documents in English.

such as the fact that data was not distributed evenly over the decades between the Norman Conquest and 1360, rendering the deduction that immigration from the Home Counties decreased in the fourteenth century unsafe. Samuels stated that the Central Midlands dialect was "easily understood all over the country", whereas East Anglian English was "peripheral, and … unsuitable as a means of communication with either native Londoners or strangers and immigrants" (Samuels 1963 [1989]: 74). No new evidence was provided for these assertions.

A dense paper packed with ideas, Samuels (1963) was both looking back – disagreeing with Ekwall – and looking forward to *LALME* to come. It is disjointed, and the first footnote explains that it was printed substantially the same as an oral presentation given to a meeting of University Professors in 1962 (explaining oral features such as "flood of documents" and "beyond all recognition"). He gave the caveat that it was interim ("a first attempt"), the project being then ten years into its thirty-four year duration at that point, and I assume the grouping of Types was Samuels' method of trying to find anchor texts for *LALME*. Anchor texts are those which are irrefutably anchored in time and place to which other texts can be compared, and because the editors discounted the obvious (the explicitly dated and located documents included in the Middle English Local Documents project of 2017, which are usually multilingual), they had to survey all kinds of religious, literary, and other texts and date and locate them on internal and linguistic grounds. There is of course a danger of circularity in this, and Samuels' assignation of Types and "best" Chaucer texts shows his process of sifting and sorting.

I return to Samuels' assertion that *they, though, give, gave, their, them* spread from the North Central Midlands. Positing migration as the mechanism by which language change spreads entails identification of a wave of migrants. It is not *prima facie* parsimonious, but there have been points in history when large-scale migrations have occurred. Kerswill (2018) tackles the question of how linguists might identify the point at which a dialect becomes influenced by incomers (that is, when the founder dialect is *swamped*), but rather than conceptualising dialects as discrete entities, he envisages a *dialect landscape*:

> a 'dialect landscape' consisting of a series of geographically distributed but interlinked communities across which a continuum of language varieties is spoken. … Communities are in flux, composed as they are of individuals with overlapping and changing social networks, and boundaries are diffuse. For our limited purposes, namely the actuation and spread of linguistic change, it is useful to see the community as reflecting concentrations of people who are potentially in contact with each other. (Kerswill 2018: 12)

For a dialect to be thus changed, Kerswill states that there needs to be, at a given point in time, a minimum proportion of incomers who have not acquired the local dialect. He cites studies supporting 50% as this minimum, with additional requirements of a high proportion of children and adolescents, which conditions must persist for at least a dozen years. Trudgill (2011) also cites cases of around 50% of incomers effecting change in natives' speech, with data from Bergen, Norway; Hackney, London; urban Swedish, and native-speaker English in the United States (Trudgill 2011: 57–8, references therein). If we take London's population in 1377 to be about 30,000, then Ekwall's total of 2,890 named immigrants would have been nowhere near enough to make dialect shift plausible.[7] The conclusion must be that London speech continued, shifting over the years as all language does, and that written Standard English developed as a separate entity.

Back to Morsbach (1888) and Samuels (1963). I have reason to believe that both scholars had the same text open on their desks as they composed their works, despite the 85 year gap between them. This is a text that resonates behind all of the claims discussed so far, and it was published in a source which is no longer a first port of call for linguists. In 1878, the Ninth Edition of the *Encyclopaedia Britannica* printed a long, comprehensive article entitled "English Language", written by J. A. H. M. I have been unable to consult the Ninth Edition, but by the Eleventh Edition (1910–11), which I have been able to consult, the initials H. M. R. M. had also become appended to this article. These initials belong to no less a figure than James Augustus Henry Murray, together with his daughter Hilda Mary Ruthven Murray.[8] Morsbach quoted directly from Murray's article of 1878, and Samuels, although not citing it, adheres to its content, for instance passing comment on "the Welshman Pecock".

7 Unwin (1918: 43): "In 1377 there appear to have been 23,314 lay persons over 14 in London, which suggests a total lay population of about 30,000". There are 23,314 persons listed in the poll tax of 1377, of which 2,890 equals about 12%. Presumably there were more people in London than appeared on the poll tax list, and more immigrants than those noted by Ekwall, most of whom were located in London between 1250–1350, although weighted towards the later end. 'The London lay subsidy of 1332: II, Size, wealth and occupations of population', in *Finance and Trade Under Edward III the London Lay Subsidy of 1332*, ed. George Unwin (Manchester, 1918), pp. 43–50. *British History Online* http://www.british-history.ac.uk/manchester-uni/london-lay-subsidy/1332/pp43-50 [accessed 8 February 2018].

8 Later to become Sir James, Editor in Chief of the *Oxford English Dictionary*. Hilda Murray was styled "Lecturer on English Language, Royal Holloway College" in the encyclopaedia but "Lecturer in Germanic Philology" at the college (1899–1915). She was later to become Vice-Mistress of Girton College, University of Cambridge (Thomas 1992: 174). Sir James wrote his 1878 version whilst living at "Sunnyside", Hammer's Lane, Mill Hill; by 1910 when he and his daughter Hilda revised it, they were living at "Sunnyside", Banbury Road, Oxford. When Hilda Murray retired from Girton College she and her mother and younger sister moved to "Sunnyside", Kingsley Green, Haslemere, Surrey.

In *Encyclopaedia Britannica*'s "English Language" the Murrays give the text of the Proclamation of Henry III "or rather of Simon de Montfort in his name, which ... has sometimes been spoken of as the first specimen of English". They wrote:

> The dialect of this document is more southern than anything else, with a slight midland admixture. It is much more archaic inflectionally than the *Genesis and Exodus* or *Ormulum*; but it closely resembles the old Kentish sermons and *Proverbs of Alfred* in the southern dialect of 1250. It represents no doubt the London speech of the day. London being in a Saxon county, and contiguous to Kent and Surrey, had certainly at first a southern dialect; but its position as the capital, as well as its proximity to the midland district, made its dialect more and more midland. Contemporary London documents show that Chaucer's language, which is distinctly more southern than standard English eventually became, is behind the London dialect of the day in this respect, and is at once more archaic and consequently more southern.... During the next hundred years English gained ground steadily. ... Every reason conspired that this "English" should be the midland dialect. It was the intermediate dialect, intelligible, as Trevisa has told us, to both extremes, even when these failed to be intelligible to each other; in its south-eastern form, it was the language of London, where the supreme law courts were, the centre of political and commercial life; it was the language in which the Wycliffite versions had given the Holy Scriptures to the people; the language in which Chaucer had raised English poetry to a height of excellence admired an dimitated by contemporaries and followers. And accordingly after the end of the 14th century, all Englishmen who thought they had anything to say to their countrymen generally said it in the midland speech.

They quoted a passage from the writing of Pecock against the Wycliffites (taken from Skeat): who "has still the southern pronouns *her* and *hem* for the northern *their, them*" and "verbal inflections in *-en* in a state of obsolescence". They considered standardisation to be more or less complete by Caxton:

> In the productions of Caxton's press ... the earlier of these have still an occasional verbal plural in *-n*, especially in the word *they ben*; the southern *her* and *hem* of Middle English vary with the northern and Modern English *their, them*. ... By its exclusive patronage of the midland speech, it raised it still higher above the sister dialects, and secured its abiding victory. ... Modern English thus dates from Caxton."

The Murrays presented a full-page diagram of the history of English, which by means of its layout suggests that Northern English equates to Anglian, Midland English to Saxon, and Southern English to Kentish. Wycliffe, Chaucer and Gower are placed in the "Midland English, Saxon" column with sideways heading "Early Southern and S.W. English", whereas the Proclamation of Henry III of 1258 is in the "Southern English, Kentish" column, with sideways heading "Middle Kentish". The Murrays then surveyed recent work by Prince Louis Lucien Bonaparte and A. J. Ellis:

> The researches of Prince L. L. Bonaparte and Dr Ellis were directed specially to the classification and mapping of the existing dialects, and the relation of these to the dialects of Old and Middle English. They recognized a *Northern* dialect lying north of a line drawn from Morecambe Bay to the Humber, which, with the kindred Scottish dialects (already investigated and classed [by Murray – *LCW*]), is the direct descendant of early northern English, and a *South-western* dialect occupying Somerset, Wilts, Dorset, Gloucester and western Hampshire, which, with the *Devonian* dialect beyond it, are the descendants of early southern English and the still older West-Saxon of Alfred. This dialect must in the 14th century have been spoken everywhere south of Thames; but the influence of London caused its extinction in Surrey, Sussex and Kent, so that already in Puttenham it had become "far western". An *East Midland* dialect, extending from south Lincolnshire to London, occupies the cradle-land of the standard English speech, and still shows the least variation from it."

In this article, Murray laid down all the main concepts: the change from Saxon to Midland, the quoting of the comment from Trevisa's translation of Higden that midland English was the most comprehensible, the equating of London English with Standard English, adducing as main (only) evidence for the dialect shift personal pronouns in *th-* and verbal plurals in *-n*, and the label "East Midland", covering ground from south Lincolnshire to London. The Murrays' article makes for exuberant reading, encompassing the whole of the English language as known at that date. Essentially, it is their adumbration of the standardisation of English that has been repeated so often over the last century.

2 The multilingual background

When the Murrays, Morsbach and Heuser were undertaking their studies a comparative approach was the norm. What is missing from previous discussions of standardisation is the fourteenth and fifteenth-century multilingual background against which English began to be written. Acolado Carnicero (2015) observed that scholars' datings of "first" writings in English in any given archive vary wildly and can even be contradictory. This is because fourteenth and fifteenth century scribes switched back and forth between languages, so a run of English for several years would then be followed by further decades of Anglo-Norman and Medieval Latin, and oaths and ordinances (for example) would be translated in all three languages. The timespan between first use of English and the switch to monolingual English in a given archive could be more than a hundred years, but in reporting passages of English, systematic notice is rarely taken of surrounding proportions of Medieval Latin and Anglo-Norman. As a rough rule of thumb, from the thirteenth century to the last quarter of the fourteenth, most writing was in Medieval Latin, Anglo-Norman French and mixed-language (by which I mean the system of codeswitched Medieval Latin/Anglo-Norman/Middle English as used in accounts, inventories, day-books and testimonies). From 1375 to 1440 most writing switched between Medieval Latin, Anglo-Norman, Middle English, and mixed-language. From 1440 to 1500 most writing switched between Medieval Latin, Middle English and mixed-language (that is, Anglo-Norman was used less); and from 1500 onwards most writing was in Neo-Latin and Early Modern English (with a shift away from both the mixed-language system and Medieval Latin and towards monolingualism). From the late fourteenth century to the late fifteenth century, London archives show that use of all four systems was the norm: Medieval Latin, Anglo-Norman, Middle English, and mixed-language. Monolingualism was the exception during this century, with switching occuring within the word, the phrase, the clause, the paragraph; from paragraph to paragraph; from text to text; between text-body, margin, heading, gloss and annotation; and with different text-types following different conventions. The switchover can be characterised as a movement from Medieval Latin, Anglo-Norman and mixed-language, to a transition period of intense switching back and forth, to an eventual outcome of monolingual English and monolingual Neo-Latin. It is not until the sixteenth century that monolingual English settled down as a written norm for numerous purposes, and supralocal varities still persisted at that date.

The century of intense language switching 1375–1475 co-occurred with a rise in London's involvement in national and international trade, as observed by H. C. Wyld. Wright (2013: 66–71) discusses the locations of debtors owing debts to Londoners in 1329 and 1424.[9] In 1329, Londoners' debtors lived mainly in the Home Counties, with just a few reaching into Norfolk and Dorset. A hundred years later, Londoners' debtors lived all over England, from Cornwall to the borders. This expansion in trade was due to shifting demand: the Black Death of 1348-9 caused depopulation in England, with a shrunken population exerting less pressure on basic resources and an increased demand for manufactured goods. These goods were supplied by the expanding markets of Antwerp, Ghent and Bruges, with a shift in transport systems causing Antwerp to take over from Bruges as a financial hub. London also became a hub for merchants, national and foreign, buying manufactured woollen cloth. Doing business with people from afar acted as a means of linguistic diffusion, of levelling, of introduction of regional features from elsewhere (present plural *-s*, auxiliary *do*, *-ing*, *are*, were all present in London English but at different stages of their trajectories), and, for foreign

9 As identified by the "Metropolitan Market Networks *c.* 1300–1600" project undertaken at the Centre of Metropolitan History, University of London. Plotted by Keene, Galloway and Murphy, taken from Keene (2000).

merchants, as a catalyst for a learners' target. The rise of Neo-Latin is important because it became a relatively fixed written system at the same time that written Standard English also came to be relatively fixed, as did all the European standards.[10] Trade explains the when, the where, and also why London English is not the same as Standard English. Standardisation does not come about if speakers stay still in one place and remain homogenous, unless it is consciously imposed for political reasons. Trudgill (1986: 107–8) defines a *koiné* as "a historically mixed but synchronically stable dialect which contains elements from the different dialects that went into the mixture, as well as interdialect forms that were present in none". Standard English can be used as an illustration, with levelling (such as the reduction of adverbial *-liche* to *-ly*, and the loss of regionally-marked *-th*, *-n* and *-s* as plural indicative present-tense markers and the subsequent adoption of zero); elements from different dialects (such as *are*, the *th-* pronouns, third person singular *-s* and auxiliary *do*); and interdialect (such as *-ing* replacing regionally-marked *-and(e, -end(e, -ind(e)*. Koinéisation happens when multidialectal or multilingual speakers need to find common ground, and koinéisation is the underpinning of the standardisation of English – a change from a relatively homogenous usership to a considerably more heterogenous one.

3 Babies and bathwater

I have been critical of the work of my predecessors yet much from their endeavours is valid. I now pay tribute to their contributions:

James and Hilda Murray: in context, it becomes apparent that their concept of the "East Midlands" was the land stretching from south Lincolnshire in the north to London in the south. Thus they had not envisaged a dramatic dialect shift in London from local south-eastern to the dialect of Northampton or Leicester. Rather, they wrote of a shift in influence from the counties south of London to the counties north of London. There is no need, therefore, to posit migration as an explanation.

Lorenz Morsbach: Morsbach gathered together the London English material later published by Chambers and Daunt: the *Appeal of Thomas Usk*, the *Petition of the Folk of Mercery*, the London guild certificates of 1388-9

10 Although see Demo (2014) and references therein for diversity within Neo-Latin. Medieval Latin and Anglo-Norman were far less variable than English: by the fifteenth century they were no longer languages learnt naturally in infancy via maternal speech, but had become languages learnt consciously by tuition.

that were written in English. He also included the wills written in English in Furnivall's Early English Text Society selection, and the rest of his material was made up of English passages from *Rotuli Parliamentorum*. These were his "Londoner Urkunden": he read through Medieval Latin archives and pulled out the English as it appeared here and there (remember that this is the century of switching between languages, a simplified schema of the progression being from monolingual Latin, to a tip period of switching, to monolingual English). Morsbach also included what he called state witness (*Staatsurkunden*, mostly taken from the Close Rolls and *Rotuli Parliamentorum*) and parliament witness (*Parlamentsurkunden*, also taken from the *Rotuli Parliamentorum*), showing less variation than the *Londoner Urkunden* – as is to be expected if fewer scribes contributed to the rolls of parliament, a single entity, than to the various wills, petitions and guild certificates. Under *Staatsurkunden* he grouped some extracts as stemming from the *Hof* or *Staatskanzlei*, the head or state chancery. The introduction of chancery to the history of Standard English thus enters from German, but Morsbach made no special claim for it. His technique was to group examples of spellings illustrating vowels in stressed syllables, consonants, nouns, adjectives, numerals, pronouns, and verb morphology, meaning that he presented type variation but not tokens thereof. For example, on page 51 of his *Londoner Urkunden* he presents the spellings "chirche-ȝerd W 21/23; chirch-ȝerd W 84/6. 85/4; cherche-ȝerd W 67/5; chircheyerd W 132/14; chirche-yerd W 104/8; chircheyerde W 98/6. 99/9; Pouleschirche-yerd W 96/5; aber churchȝard W 83/13", where W stands for a will in Furnivall (1882), so that the reader can see the variation but not the ratios. Morsbach informed the reader that Medieval Latin and Anglo-Norman were the norm and English the exception (with Latin continuing as an official language until 1733), and he also noted the relevance of London as the "Centrum des englischen Handels und Verkehrs", the centre of commerce and traffic (Morsbach 1888: 5 fn 2, 7). He also presented Higden's opinion (in Trevisa's translation) that "men of myddel Engelond" were understood better than the "syde longages".

Heuser: Heuser's contribution was to add to Morsbach's local London evidence the house, street and placenames found in Sharpe's (1889) edition of the Hustings Rolls, providing earlier London evidence and revealing further variation. He arranged his material in the same way as Morsbach, so that the reader can see type variation but not token numbers. It is interesting to see that Heuser draws attention to variants *-hethe, -huthe, -hithe*; *bregge, brigge, brugge, hull, hill, hell, -bury, -bery, -biry, Crepelgate, Crupelgate, Cripelgate*, so that Ekwall's reduction of his findings to <a> and <e> graphs was in fact highly selective.

Ekwall: Ekwall's compiled a list of immigrants' locative bynames, showing that by this method immigration to London from elsewhere in the country was around 12%, far too low for dialect swamping (contrary to his own interpretation), and also contributing further evidence of late medieval variation. The Murrays' article is not in Ekwall's bibliography, and it is clear that he did not realise what they had meant by the label "East Midland".

Samuels: Samuels, in seeking to show the many exciting purposes to which the then-forthcoming *Linguistic Atlas of Late Medieval English* could in future be put, unsettled the "East Midlands" orthodoxy.

4 Centre of the universe: Rutland

James Murray, writing for the 1878 recension of the *Encyclopaedia Britannica*, had a book open on his desk as he worked, which deduction I make from the fact that he cited it in his bibliography. It was written by Thomas Laurence Kington-Oliphant (1831–1902), and it was called *The Sources of Standard English.*[11] Kington-Oliphant's primary application of the term 'Standard English' was not with regard to phonology, like Morsbach, Heuser and Ekwall, nor orthography, like Samuels, but the word-stock. Thus, for Kington-Oliphant, how many obsolete words a medieval author contained determined how Standard it was (he was for "Teutonic" and agin French and Latin: "Alfred's Teutonic has been replaced by the French and Latin that Tyndale was driven to use, owing to the heedlessness of the Thirteenth Century".[12] His book was published in 1873, and was

---

11 Born at "Charlton House", Wraxall, Somerset of an English father and a Scottish mother, T. L. Kington-Oliphant M.A. (Oxon), barrister, Fellow of the Society of Antiquaries, Justice of the Peace, Deputy Lieutenant, wrote his *The Sources of Standard English* at "Charlton House", Wimbledon. It may be relevant that his wife's family was from Lincolnshire. (http://www.thepeerage.com/p12505.htm#i125048). The Kington family fortune was derived from slaving (https://www.ucl.ac.uk/lbs/person/view/44502).

12 This is footnote 57 of his Chapter 5; some of his more enjoyable footnotes include: "I remember in Somerset a yoke of oxen called *Good Luck* and *Fortune*"; "I wish that the Parker Society had published Tyndale's works in his own spelling."; "*The Art of Rhetorique*, written by Wilson, about 1550. Can he have had a prophetic glimpse of the *Daily Telegraph* of 1873? [a complaint about inkhorn terms, and one of two footnotes in Chapter 5 about the *Daily Telegraph* – *LCW*]"; "Of course, I use *nicely* neither in the sense of 1303, nor in that of 1873." [he means 'precisely' – *LCW*]; "*Tendimus in Latium* is a bad watchword for England, whether in religion, in architecture, or in philology."; "I grieve to say that he is guilty of 'on the *tapis*;' a vulgarism more suited to a schoolgirl than to a scholar."; "The Secretary of the Society [E.E.T.S. – *LCW*] is G. Joachim, Esq., St. Andrew House, Change Alley, London. I wish they would print more works written before 1400, and fewer works written after that year." For more on the influence of Kington-Oliphant and Murray, see Matthews (1999: xxx–xxxiii). I do not know whether Kington-Oliphant knew Furnivall, but they were much the same age, both lived in London at the same time and shared a lively written style.

based mainly on the literary and religious medieval texts that had been collected in print at that date. The familiar points rehearsed above – East Midlands, Bishop Pecock, Trevisa, Caxton – are all found within (I quote at length as his delightful style is not easy to reduce):

> It may often be remarked that one form of a great speech drives another form before it. Thus, in our own day, the High German is always encroaching on its Northern neighbour the Low German; and the Low German, in its turn, is always encroaching upon its Northern neighbour the Scandinavian. Something of the like kind might have been seen in England six hundred years ago; but with us the Dano-Anglian speech of the Midland was working down Southwards towards London and Oxford all through the Thirteenth Century. Its influence may be seen so early as the Essex Homilies of 1180; many years later we find a still clearer token of the change. In some hundred Plural substantives that had been used by Layamon soon after 1200, the Southern ending in *en* was replaced by the Midland ending in *es*, when Layamon's work came to be written out afresh after 1250. East Midland works became popular in the South, as may be seen by the transcript of the Havelok and the Harrowing of Hell. In the Horn, a Southern work, we find the Present Plural *en* of the Midland verb replacing the older Plural in *eth*. In the Alexander (perhaps a Warwickshire work) the Midland *I, she, they*, and *beon* encroach upon the true Southern *ich, heo, hi*, and *beoth*. Even in Kent we find marks of change: in the sermons of 1290 the contracted forms *lord* and *made* are seen instead of *louerd* and *maked*. Already *mid* (cum) was making way for the Northern *with*. This was the state of things when the Handlyng Synne was given to England soon after 1303; it was believed, though wrongly, to be the translation of a work of Bishop Robert's, and it seems to have become the great pattern; from it many a friar and parson all over England must have borrowed the weapons wherewith the Seven Deadly Sins (these play a great part in English song) might be assailed. Another work of Robert Manning's is entitled Medytacyuns of the Soper of our Lorde, a translation from Buonaventura, the well-known oracle of Franciscans abroad. The popularity of these works of the Lincolnshire bard must have spread the influence of the East Midland further and further. We know not when it made a thorough conquest of Oxford, the great stronghold of the Franciscans; but its triumph over the London speech was most slow, and was not wholly achieved until a hundred and sixty years after Manning's first work was begun. That poet, as may be seen by the Table at the end of the foregoing chapter, heralded the changes in English, alike by his large proportion of French words and by his small proportion of those Teutonic words that were sooner or later to drop. . . . It may seem strange that England's new Standard speech should have sprung up, not in Edward the First's Court, but in cloisters on the Nen and the Welland. We must bear in mind that the English Muse, as in the tale of the Norfolk bondman, always leaned towards the common folk; it was the French Muse that was the aristocratic lady. (256–8)

> Throughout the Fourteenth Century the speech of the shires near Rutland was spreading in all directions; it at length took possession of Oxford and London, and more or less influenced such men as Wickliffe and Chaucer. Gower, when a youth, had written in Latin and French; when old, he wrote in English little differing from that of Manning. This dialect moreover made its way into the North: let any one compare the York Mysteries of 1350 with the version of them made forty years later, and he will see the influence of the Midland tongue. (259)

> The Southern dialect, the most unlucky of all our varieties, gave way before her Mercian sister: Dane conquered Saxon. (260)

> Mandeville's language is far more influenced by the Midland forms than that of Davie had been fifty years earlier; in the new writer we find *sche*, *I*, *thei*, *theirs*, *have*, *are*, and *ben*, forms strange to the Thames, at least in 1300; the Southern ending of the Third Person Plural of the Present tense is almost wholly dropped, being replaced by the Midland ending in *en*; even this is sometimes clipped, as also is the *en* of the Infinitive, and the Prefix of the Past Participle. A hundred years would have to pass before these hoary old relics could be wholly swept away from Standard English. (264)

Murray, synthesising for the *Encyclopaedia Britannica*, omitted mention of Rutland, the Nene and the Welland, but kept the gist; Rutland, the Nene and the Welland being the centre of localities that Kington-Oliphant associated with *Havelok the Dane*, the *Harrowing of Hell* and *Handlyng Synne* – especially the latter.[13] Here is Kington-Oliphant's own synthesis (320–1):

Twelfth Century	Break-up of the Old English grammar; a variety of dialects prevail for two centuries, with no fixed standard.
Thirteenth Century	Loss of thousands of Old English words, which are slowly replaced by French words.
Fourteenth Century	The New English, or Dano-Anglian, which had long been forming, gains possession of London and Oxford, and is spoken at Court.
Fifteenth Century	The Printing-press fixes the language, which had lost nearly all its inflections.
Sixteenth Century	The Reformation brings Standard English home to all men, and imports many Latin words.

Chapter 5, footnote 46 reads "Mr. Earle tells us (*Philology of the English Tongue*, p. 97) that 'a French family settled in England and edited the English language;' he means the Plantagenets. I suspect that the Queen's English owes more to a Lincolnshire monk, on whom I have bestowed some pains, than to all our Kings put together who have reigned since the year 901." The book he refers to here was written by John Earle (1824–1903),[14] and section 67 of Earle (1871 [1879]) under the subhead 'The King's English', reads:

---

13 Trudgill (1999), describing the present-day dialects of England, shows that the area with fewest distinguishing dialect features equates to central and eastern Northamptonshire bordering on Rutland, northern Bedfordshire, and central and western Cambridgeshire, which could be described as the lands of the Welland and the Nene.

14 Priest and Professor of Old English at the University of Oxford (1849–1851 (the chair was tenable only for five years at that time), and then again 1876–1903, his death) https://doi.org/10.1093/ref:odnb/32954. Earle lived at no. 84, Banbury Road, Oxford; Sir James Murray lived at no. 78.

> We have a phenomenon to account for. In the midst of this Babel of dialects there suddenly appeared a standard English language. It appeared at once in full vigour … Piers Plowman is in a dialect; even Wiclif's Bible Version may be said to be in a dialect; but Chaucer and Gower write in a speech which is thenceforward recognised as THE ENGLISH LANGUAGE, and which before their time is hardly found. This seems to admit of but one explanation. It must have been simply the language that had formed itself in the court about the person of the monarch. … If we want to describe the transition from the Saxon State-language of the eleventh century to the Court-English of the fourteenth, and to reduce the description to its simplest terms, it comes in fact to just this: That a French family settled in England, and edited the English language.

So the idea of a change from Saxon to something else had already been introduced in 1871, but this change was simply the addition of Anglo-Norman French lexemes due to the Norman Conquest, not a wholesale shift in dialect. For Earle, the sublimity of Chaucer's English was largely due to its admission of so much French vocabulary, which fact he explained by Chaucer's being a courtier (he called the Proclamation of Henry III of 1258 "overcharged rudeness and broadness", "crude and laboured", and "an artificial conglomerate of confused provincialisms"; he regarded regional dialects to be relatively free from French). Kington-Oliphant offered up Rutland as an alternative, and it is the Rutland hypothesis – passed down to posterity as East Midland – that has reigned ever since.

References

Alcolado Carnicero, José Miguel. 2015. "Dating the shift to English in the financial accounts of some London livery companies: A reappraisal". *Multilingua* 34/3. 373–404.

Barber, Charles. 1964. *The Story of English*. London: Pan.

Baugh, Albert C. and Cable, Thomas. 1951, 1993 reprint. *A History of the English Language*. London: Routledge.

Beal, Joan C. 2016. "Standardization". In Merja Kytö and Päivi Pahta (eds.). The Cambridge Handbook of English Historical Linguistics. Cambridge: Cambridge University Press. 301–317.

Bergstrøm, Geir. 2017. *Yeuen at Cavmbrigg' A Study of the Late Medieval English Documents of Cambridge*. University of Stavanger: PhD thesis.

Blake, Norman (ed.). 1992. *The Cambridge History of the English Language*. Volume 2, 1066–1476. Cambridge: Cambridge University Press.

Burnley, J. David. 1989. "Sources of Standardisation in Later Middle English". In Joseph B. Trahern, (ed.). *Standardizing English: Essays in the History of Language Change in Honour of John Hurt Fisher*. Knoxville: University of Tennessee Press.

Chambers, R. W. and Marjorie Daunt (eds.). 1931. *A Book of London English 1384–1425*. Oxford: Clarendon Press. 22–31.

Crystal, David. 1995. *The Cambridge Encyclopedia of the English Language*. Cambridge: Cambridge University Press.
Demo, Šime. 2014. " Diversity in Neo-Latin: Example of Administrative Ecclesiastical Texts". *Rasprave* 40/1. 111–125.
Earle, John. 1871, 3rd ed. 1879. *The Philology of the English Tongue* Oxford: Clarendon Press.
Ekwall, Bror Eilert, 1956. *Studies on the Population of Medieval London*. Stockholm: Almqvist and Wiksell.
Freeborn, Dennis. 1992. *From Old English to Standard English*. Basingstoke: Macmillan.
Furnivall, Frederick J. (ed.). 1882. *Fifty Earliest English Wills in the Court of Probate, London : A. D. 1387–1439*. Early English Text Society, Old Series, 78. London: Oxford University Press.
Keene, Derek. 2000a. "Project Reports. 1. Metropolitan Market Networks *c*. 1300–1600". In *Centre for Metropolitan History Annual Report 1999–2000*, 5–9. London: University of London School of Advanced Study Institute of Historical Research.
Kerswill, Paul. 2018. "Dialect formation and dialect change in the Industrial Revolution: British vernacular English in the nineteenth century". In Laura Wright (ed.). *Southern English Varieties Then and Now*. Berlin: Mouton de Gruyter. 8–38.
Kington-Oliphant, Thomas Laurence. 1873. *The Sources of Standard English*. London: Macmillan & Co.
Kornexl, Lucia. 2012. "Old English: Standardization". *English Historical Linguistics* Volume 1. Handbooks of Linguistics and Communication Science 34/1. Berlin: De Gruyter Mouton. 373–385.
Heuser, Wilhelm. 1914. *Alt-London mit besonderer Berücksichtigung des Dialekts*. Strassburg: Karl J. Trübner.
Leith, Dick. 1983, 1987 reprint. *A Social History of English*. London: Routledge and Kegan Paul.
Matthews, David. 1999. *The Making of Middle English, 1765–1910*. Minneapolis: University of Minnesota Press.
McIntosh, Angus, Michael Louis Samuels and Michael Benskin (eds.). 1986. *A Linguistic Atlas of Late Medieval English*. Aberdeen: Aberdeen University Press.
Moessner, Lilo. 2012. "Early Modern Standardization". In Alexander Bergs and Laurel J. Brinton (eds.). *English Historical Linguistics* Volume 1. Handbooks of Linguistics and Communication Science 34/1. Berlin: De Gruyter Mouton. 698–714.
Morsbach, Lorenz. 1888. *Über den Ursprung der neuenglischen Schriftsprache*. Heilbronn: Henninger.
Murray, J. A. H. and H. M. R. 1910–11. "English Language". *Encyclopaedia Britannica*. Eleventh Edition. 587–600.
Pyles, Thomas and Algeo, John. 1964, 1993 reprint. *The Origins and Development of the English Language*. Fourth edition. San Diego: Harcourt Brace Jovanovich.
Samuels, Michael Louis. 1963. "Some Applications of Middle English Dialectology". *English Studies* 44. 81–94. Reprinted in Angus McIntosh, Michael Louis Samuels & Margaret Laing (eds.). 1989. *Middle English Dialectology: essays on some principles and problems*. Aberdeen: Aberdeen University Press. 64–80.
Schaefer, Ursula. 2012. "Middle English: Standardization". In Alexander Bergs and Laurel J. Brinton (eds.). *English Historical Linguistics* Volume 1. Handbooks of Linguistics and Communication Science 34/1. Berlin: De Gruyter Mouton. 519–533.
Sharpe, Reginald Robinson. 1889. *Calendar of Wills Proved and Enrolled in the Court of Husting, London, A.D. 1258-A.D. 1688*. London: Her Majesty's Stationery Office.

Strang, Barbara M. H. 1970, 1986 reprint. *A History of English*. London: Methuen.
Thengs, Kjetil V. 2013. *English Medieval Documents of the Northwest Midlands. A Study in the Language of a Real-Space Text Corpus*. University of Stavanger: PhD thesis.
Thomas, Gillian. 1992. *A Position to Command Respect: Women and the Eleventh Britannica*. Metuchen, N. J.: Scarecrow Press.
Trudgill, Peter. 1986. *Dialects in Contact*. Oxford: Basil Blackwell.
Trudgill, Peter. 1999. *The Dialects of England*. Oxford: Basil Blackwell.
Trudgill, Peter. 2011. *Sociolinguistic Typology: Social Determinants of Linguistic Complexity*. Oxford: Oxford University Press.
Wright, Laura. 1994. "On the Writing of the History of Standard English". In Francisco Fernández, Miguel Fuster, Juan José Calvo (eds.). *English Historical Linguistics 1992*. Current Issues in Linguistic Theory 113. Amsterdam: Benjamins. 105–115.
Wright, Laura. 1995. "The London Middle English Guild Certificates of 1388/89: The Texts". *Nottingham Medieval Studies* 39. 119–145.
Wright, Laura. 1996. "About the Evolution of Standard English". In Elizabeth M.Tyler and M. Jane Toswell (eds.). *Studies in English Language and Literature: 'Doubt Wisely' Papers in honour of E. G. Stanley*. London: Routledge. 99–115.
Wright, Laura. 2001a. "The role of international and national trade in the standardisation of English". In Isabel Moskowich-Spiegel Fandiño, Begona Crespo-García, Emma Lezcano González, and Begona Simal González (eds.). *Re-interpretations of English. Essays on Language, Linguistics and Philology* (I). A Coruña: Universidade da Coruña, 189–207.
Wright, Laura. 2001b. "Some Morphological Features of the Norfolk Guild Certificates of 1388/9: an exercise in variation". Peter Trudgill and Jacek Fisiak (eds.). *East Anglian English*. Woodbridge: D. S. Brewer. 79–162.
Wright, Laura. 2005. "Medieval Mixed-Language Business Texts and the Rise of Standard English". *Opening Windows on Texts and Discourses of the Past*. In Janne Skaffari, Matti Peikola, Ruth Carroll, Risto Hiltunen and Brita Wårvik (eds.). Pragmatics and Beyond New Series 134. Amsterdam: John Benjamins. 381–399.
Wright, Laura. 2013. "The Contact Origins of Standard English". In Daniel Schreier and Marianne Hundt (eds.). *English as a Contact Language*. Studies in English Language. Cambridge: Cambridge University Press, 58–74.
Wright, Laura. 2015. "On medieval wills and the rise of written monolingual English". In Javier Calle Martín and Juan Camilo Conde Silvestre (eds.). *Approaches to Middle English. Contact, Variation and Change*. Frankfurt am Main: Peter Lang. 35–54.
Wright, Laura. 2017. "A Multilingual Approach to the History of Standard English". In Päivi, Pahta, Janne Skaffari and Laura Wright (eds.). *Multilingual Practices in Language History: English and Beyond*. Language Contact and Bilingualism 15. Berlin: Mouton de Gruyter.
Wright, Laura. 2000. (ed.). *The Development of Standard English, 1300–1800: Theories, Descriptions, Conflicts*. Cambridge: Cambridge University Press.

Merja Stenroos

2 The 'vernacularisation' and 'standardisation' of local administrative writing in late and post-medieval England

1 Introduction

1.1 Aims of the chapter

This chapter addresses linguistic usage in local administrative writing in fifteenth- and early sixteenth-century England, with reference to the processes of 'vernacularisation' and 'standardisation' often assumed to take place in this period. Most textbooks of the history of English suggest that the fifteenth century saw both the standardisation of written English and its adoption as the language of administration and government; however, recent scholarly work has shown that the evidence of government documents does not, on the whole, agree with these accounts (see e.g. Benskin 2004; Dodd 2011a, 2011b, 2012).

The present study is based on documentary evidence from local administration, that is, from sources outside the central government offices: the records of cities, churches, manors, local courts and private transactions, as sampled in *A Corpus of Middle English Local Documents* (MELD). It is sometimes assumed that the 'standardisation' of English proceeded through this type of texts, a point made most explicitly by Benskin (1992: 75). This chapter considers the question to what extent the MELD materials show developments that might corroborate the ideas of a major fifteenth-century process of anglicisation and standardisation.

The overall finding concerning the first question – that local administrative writing continued to be predominantly Latin – comes as no surprise to those who work on documentary texts. The patterns of use of English and Latin in this period are, it is held here, crucial for understanding what goes on in the development of written English. No attempt is made to trace the usage of individual texts or groups (even though such studies are important): instead, the focus is on the general variability. The study considers

Merja Stenroos, University of Stavanger

https://doi.org/10.1515/9783110687545-003

both formulaic phrases and spelling, tracing in detail the spelling variation in five highly frequent lexical items.

Given the scope of the material and the complexity of the questions involved, this study can only present preliminary findings, and much more work is needed. It should also be pointed out that the concepts discussed – vernacularisation and standardisation – are relative and variously defined, and there can thus be no absolute answers: rather, the aim is to discuss some of the claims made in light of the patterns found in the material. The discussion is restricted to administrative materials throughout: no attempt is made to deal with these processes in other kinds of materials, such as literary or scientific texts.

1.2 The textbook ideas of 'vernacularisation' and 'standardisation'

In most introductory textbooks and histories of English, the late Middle English period is marked by two more or less cataclysmic events: the rise of English as a major written language (sometimes referred to as the 'triumph' or 'restoration' of English, or the 'vernacularisation' of text production) and the standardisation of written English. For example, Millward and Hayes (1990: 148) note that, at the end of the Middle English period, '[t]he revival of English as the national language of England was assured, and a national standard English based on London speech was being disseminated throughout the country'. The classic history by Strang gives more detail:

> Official documents continue to be only exceptionally written in English until 1430, when English becomes the norm and documentation is abundant. It is written in a kind of Standard, Type IV or Chancery Standard, which thereafter reigns supreme.
>
> (Strang 1970 [2015: 63])

In a more recent textbook of the History of English, van Gelderen (2014: 17) states that '(a)t the end of the Middle English period (in 1420 to be precise), scribes working at the Chancery began writing in English rather than in Latin' and notes that 'Chancery English may be the beginning of a written standard' (van Gelderen 2014: 18).

These accounts all go back to a single source, the 1963 article by Samuels titled 'Some applications of Middle English dialectology'. This article, which arguably presents the single most influential narrative of the standardisation of written English, expressly connects this process with the appearance of English in official writing:

> Type IV (which I shall call 'Chancery Standard') consists of that flood of government documents that starts in the years following 1430. Its differences from the language of Chaucer are well known, and it is this type, not its predecessors in London English, that is the predecessor of modern written English... it was... adopted by the government offices for regular written use; from then on, it was backed by the full weight of the administrative machine. (Samuels 1963 [1989: 71])

While Samuels does not claim that English immediately replaced all other languages in government documents, his formulation ('adopted by the government offices for regular written use') does suggest a major, irreversible change. Samuels further claims that the English adopted by the government offices represented a specific, definable variety, the predecessor of 'modern written English'.

Samuels' ideas have had an enormous influence on scholarly views of the standardisation of English, and they are repeated in virtually all later textbooks (see Wright 1996 and Chapter 1.). A highly influential account based on Samuels' theory was developed by Fisher (1977, 1979, 1992, 1996), who added the idea that the 'Chancery Standard' was enforced through deliberate control, as part of government policy. Through Fisher's work, a whole generation of scholars were taught that the 'Chancery Standard' was imposed by Chancery as a national standard of English writing. As adopted in textbooks, this idea sometimes seems to owe more to modern assumptions of standardisation than to actual historical evidence:

> [T]he emergence of a new standard language began to re-institute a linguistic norm for written supraregional English. This development was a natural consequence of the acceptance of English in public domains, and was speeded up by the change-over to English as the Chancery language in 1430. It is important to realise that this process almost automatically devalued the use in writing of all forms that were locally or otherwise deviant... Obviously, cases of deliberate neglect of the pressure towards conforming were rare. (Görlach 1999: 459–60)

It may be noted that Görlach's narrative has travelled far from Samuels' original, far more guarded, account: the adoption of English from the late 1430s has become a change-over in 1430, and the beginning standardisation has become a 'linguistic norm'.

Later work has adjusted many of Samuels' premises. It is now clear that the adoption of English in government documents was neither general nor sustained (Dodd 2011a, 2011b, 2012), and that the English produced by the government departments, including Chancery, shows highly variable usages (Benskin 2004: 31–33). Accordingly, the idea of a regulated and enforced 'Chancery Standard' is no longer generally accepted, and most scholars see the process of standardisation as a considerably more complex and gradual one.

While Samuels saw standardisation as a direct consequence of the adoption of English in goverment documents, he did not elaborate on the spread of the standard forms. Benskin, in another a classic paper, points out that we cannot talk about standardisation until such a usage has spread to different parts of the country:

> It is... in its adoption as a second-learned competence that the language of the capital qualifies as a national standard at all: the displacement of local conventions is not an epiphenomenon, but standardisation itself. Without attention to provincial usage, 'the rise of standard English' simply cannot be understood, and it is above all in administrative and legal writings that the early standard appears. (Benskin 1992: 75)

Benskin sees the usage of the local administrative documents throughout the country as the decisive *locus* of standardisation. Other scholars have called in question the entire idea of a single origin of Standard English, whether as government usage or another specific model variety (e.g. Wright 2000a: 6; Hope 2000: *passim*; see also 4.1 below). However, the idea that English administrative documents functioned as a major medium of standardisation has not been seriously called into question.

A Corpus of Middle English Local Documents (MELD) has now made available a large sample of local administrative texts from the period 1399–1525. This material makes it possible to start addressing the questions of 'vernacularization' and 'standardisation' beyond the scope of a single archive or text type: to what extent, and when, did English supplant French and Latin as the language of administration outside central government, and how far does the evidence support a fifteenth-century process of standardisation in the written English of local administration?

2 The material: Middle English local documents

The texts concerned here are the kind of texts that were referred to as 'documentary texts' in the *Linguistic Atlas of Late Mediaeval English* (McIntosh, Samuels and Benskin 1986; henceforth LALME), often in contrast with 'literary texts'. Documentary texts were described in LALME (I: 40) as 'legal instruments, administrative writings, and personal letters: the type of material that is calendared by historians, likely to be of known date and local origins'. Because of their connection to specific localities, this type of texts were used as 'anchor texts' in LALME, providing the initial framework for localisation. More recently, historical sociolinguists in particular have developed an interest in these practically oriented texts as linguistic evidence in themselves, precisely because they represent the linguistic output of language users in a specific historical context.

A Corpus of Middle English Local Documents (MELD) defines documentary texts as follows:[1]

a) they relate to a specific situation at a specific point of time, involving specific people, whether or not all of these are explicitly stated (for example, we may not know the precise year when a letter was written, but we know that it relates to that precise moment of time and no other)
b) they have a pragmatic function – transferring values, recording a decision, communicating information or whatever – not an aesthetic or scholarly or didactic function.

This definition includes a wide range of administrative and private texts, including wills, sales, accounts, inventories, receipts, letters and all kinds of memoranda. It excludes such practically oriented texts as recipes or law texts, which are meant to have a general applicability: however, local ordinances, such as guild rules, are included in MELD as long as they are dated and refer to a specific, geographically and institutionally defined group. Most documentary texts are connected to a specific geographical location or area. Such connections can be of three main kinds: an explicit localizing clause ('given at x'), the people or places referred to, or the physical context of a text, such as a town cartulary. As used here, the term 'local document' refers to texts that show any of these kinds of local affiliation. This excludes documents produced by the central government offices, but includes the local documents that were produced in London: conveyances and letters by Londoners, church accounts, municipal declarations and memoranda.

By far most documentary texts from this period may be defined as administrative: personal letters are the main exception, but even they are most often written for a specific, practical purpose, such as requesting an action or conveying information. The texts represent a range of domains and institutions, including manorial, monastic, ecclesiastical, commercial, academic, legal and municipal administration as well as private papers. Most of this type of texts are held in county record offices and municipal archives; others are found in university and cathedral libraries and some remain in private collections.

For the compilation of MELD, the team visited 82 archives and identified more than five thousand documentary texts from the period 1399–1525, written in or containing English. The so far compiled corpus covers the whole of England, with a few texts from bordering areas of Wales; altogether it includes 2,017 texts from 766

1 For a fuller description of the corpus and of local documentary texts in general, see the MELD Introduction (http://www.uis.no/meld).

different locations. While the corpus is not in itself designed to be a multilingual one, the process of identifying texts involved going through archive collections systematically, either identifying English texts from catalogue entries or, far more commonly, physically sifting through thousands of Latin documents in order to find texts or passages in English, making notes of the language of all medieval documents viewed.[2]

Detailed surveys of code selection have, in addition, been carried out in specific archives. In her MA thesis, Delia Schipor carried out a study of the Beverley Town Cartulary (Schipor 2013), and her recent PhD thesis (Schipor 2018) provides a detailed study of code selection and multilingual practices in three collections at the Hampshire Record Office in Winchester. In addition, the present author has collected systematic data on code selection in several smaller collections at different archives.[3]

The local documents form a highly complex universe of texts, relating to different but overlapping communities of practice. Different institutions had their own conventions for record keeping, and employed their own scribes. At the same time, the same administrators may turn up in several contexts: in the towns in particular, several institutions (town administration, craft guilds and parish churches) would draw on the same pool of writers. From the point of view of the English texts, however, the most striking feature of the material is its spread, both with regard to the number of scribes and the number of locations involved. While there are clusters of texts belonging to the same community or produced by the same scribe, the overall picture is one of widely dispersed text production.

3 The 'rise of English' as the language of administration

3.1 The languages of administration: Overview

England in the late medieval and early modern periods was a highly multilingual country. The languages spoken and written included Celtic languages as well as the languages of various immigrant groups. In this chapter, the concern

2 By far most archive catalogues do not state the language of the individual documents.

3 These collections include the Buxton and Coke of Weasenham papers in the Cambridge University Library, as well as several family collections at the Herefordshire and North Yorkshire Archives.

is with what Ad Putter (2016: 126) has called the Big Three: Latin, French and English. These three languages were used on the national scale, and all were major administrative languages. However, their distribution varies greatly over time and between communities and text types.

Of the three languages, English is the only one that may be said to have been used by all parts of the population, while a sizeable minority were using French and/or Latin as well. All three languages were restricted in function. English was used in speech, and increasingly in reading and writing; however, its use had not yet spread to all areas of writing. Latin was mainly (although not exclusively) used for writing or ritual use, and was not the native language of anyone. French, whether Anglo-Norman or continental, had also become a language that had to be learnt, even by the previously francophone upper classes. From a widely used administrative and literary language its functions were eventually restricted, even though it survived for a long time in legal usage; indeed, remnants of legal French survive to the present day in parliamentary records and ritual.

In official functions, the uses of English had been highly restricted since the Norman Conquest. As is well known, the fourteenth century marks the beginnings of a change, as English appears as the official spoken language in legal and parliamentary contexts, in virtually all cases taking over from French. For the written language, a date that is often quoted as decisive is 1417, the year when Henry V's official letters first appeared in English, rather than French. Subsequent historians of English have made much use of Samuels' reference to a 'flood' of English documents from the government offices from the 1430s onwards. While this has often been interpreted as a wholesale shift from Latin to English in the government offices, and Chancery in particular, this does not agree with the archival evidence, as shown in the important work by Benskin (2004) and Dodd (2011a, 2011b, 2012).

First of all, Benskin (2004) has pointed out that Latin continued to be the regular language of Chancery writing until the eighteenth century, making the term 'Chancery English' a considerable misnomer:

> The great bulk of Chancery's routine administration was effected by writs, and Chancery writs were composed almost exclusively in Latin. Much has been made of Chancery's hundred-and-twenty disciplined scribes, and their supposed conversion of the English in documents initiated outside Chancery into the official Chancery forms... They did, but that standard was Latin... Chancery Standard was Latin, and save for nine years during the Commonwealth, it remained so until 1731, when for official purposes it was abolished altogether by Act of Parliament (Benskin 2004: 38)

The language of incoming formal petitions from the king's subjects did, however, change from French to English. As Dodd (2011a: 122) shows, these petitions to the Crown show a shift in the second quarter of the fifteenth century: 'in c. 1425 almost all were written in Anglo-Norman French; by c. 1450, if not earlier, almost all were written in English.' Dodd notes the late 1430s as the turning point, when English supplications began to outnumber French ones.

Such documents form a considerable proportion of the texts printed in the *Anthology of Chancery English* (Fisher *et al.*, 1984). The petitions were not, however, in any formal sense commissioned by the Chancery, but were simply presented to the department. As Dodd (2011a: 119) points out, the question of whose language they represent is problematic: they 'fit comfortably neither into the category of records produced by the Crown nor into the designation of "local" documents written independently of influence from the royal secretariat'. While there is 'scholarly agreement that most petitioners engaged the services of a professional scrivener, clerk, or lawyer' (Dodd 2011a: 119, see also Myers 1937: 387–89), the identities and backgrounds of these clerks are generally not known.

While Latin remained the main language of Chancery documents, English was adopted, at least temporarily, in the other, smaller, government departments, replacing French. After the first English royal letter of 1417, English gradually took over from French in royal correspondence, and signet letters came to be regularly written in English under Henry VI (after a temporary reversion to French). English also appeared in privy seal records during this period, taking over both from French and mixed-language writing; however, as Dodd (2012: 262 and *passim*) has shown, the dominance of English was short-lived and, by the second half of the fifteenth century, Latin takes over as the majority language.

Accordingly, while English appeared in government documents during the second quarter of the fifteenth century, and became the regular language of signet letters, there was no sustained takeover: the main change was the reduction in the use of French, and the long-term development was towards more Latin, not less. On the whole, the output of government documents in English continued to be small compared to Latin.

Government usage has generally been taken as the driving force of changes in administrative language. However, the overwhelming majority of administrators in late- and post-medieval England were not working for the government offices, but were producing texts locally at hundreds of locations throughout England, on behalf of institutions, local government and individuals. Most studies of code selection in local documents have involved urban texts, especially London ones. Wright (2000b, 2005, 2011, 2012, 2013, 2015) has carried out important studies of multilingualism in a range of types of administrative and business documents, and there have also been studies of the language shift from Latin and French to English in London guild records and ordinances, as well as in the records of other urban centres (see e.g. Alcolado Carnicero 2013, Britnell 2013).

As with government documents, English most commonly takes over from French. French was used fairly commonly in local documents in the fourteenth century; Britnell (2013) finds it used extensively as the language of lawyers, especially in York and London, up to the early fifteenth century. French is also retained in the record keeping of London craft guilds, some of which retained it as their language of record until the mid-fifteenth century (Britnell 2013: 87). In general, however, French was falling out of use by the early fifteenth century, and was often, but by no means always, replaced by English; Latin, on the other hand, was not falling out of use, and its role in relation to English is much more complex. The following sections address the roles and contexts of these languages in the material surveyed in connection with MELD.

3.2 The local documentary material: The proportions of English, French and Latin

The archive collections surveyed for the MELD project vary greatly with regard to the proportions of English, French and Latin. However, the general pattern is clear: texts in Latin dominate throughout the period, while texts in French are exceptional and mostly confined to the first two decades of the fifteenth century. In addition, a considerable number of texts, mainly inventories and lists, contain the kind of mixed language that has been described most fully by Wright (e.g. 2000b, 2011, 2012, 2013), and that seems to belong mainly to the period of transition from monolingual Latin or French to monolingual English (Thengs 2016; Wright 2015: 47). A few such texts are included in MELD, but are problematic in the context of a corpus of English texts: extracting the 'English' elements out of their context makes little sense, and determining the language of a specific word or phrase is often impossible, as in this example from a 1502 churchwarden's account from Oxford:

> Jtm' Solut' e' pur le studdis ~ iij d
> Jtm' Solutu' est pur le Sute of vestm*entes* of blewe velvet. . .
> (D2314, Oxfordshire History Centre: PAR213/4/F1/1/10 (fol. 19))

It is arguable that such texts should not be considered in terms of their French, English or Latin elements at all, but rather seen to represent a code of their own, used for specific functions (cf Wright 2000b: 151).

Even when texts can be sensibly defined as English, Latin or French, a considerable proportion of them contain multilingual events. Latin texts commonly include personal and place names, titles and occupational terms in English (sometimes French); conversely, Latin appears in dating clauses, formulaic phrases and the like in texts mainly written in English or French. In the following discussion, texts referred to as 'English', 'French' or 'Latin' include such multilingual texts, as long as their main language is indisputable.

Few French texts are found in the local archives from dates later than *ca* 1420. In Schipor's study of the Hampshire Record Office materials in the period 1399–1425, only 20 out of a total of 7,049 texts (less than 0.3%) are in French (Schipor 2018: 102); of these, all except one are dated to the first quarter of the fifteenth century (Schipor 2018: 143). Most collections show similar patterns; it may also be noted that the only French elements to be found in MELD consist of an address clause in a letter and a set of subheadings in a London inquest, from 1418 and 1421 respectively. From then on, with the exception of mixed-language texts, local documents were written either in Latin or in English, with very few exceptions.

In most parts of the country, English texts are few in the first part of the period but become gradually more common. This is perhaps less clearly the case in northern archives: certainly early texts in English are much more readily found here. The distribution of texts per quarter century in MELD shows a steady rise in numbers of non-northern texts, while the number of northern texts peaks in the second quarter of the fifteenth century (see Figure 2.1). The subsequent declining pattern may simply reflect a skewing in the collection of texts for the

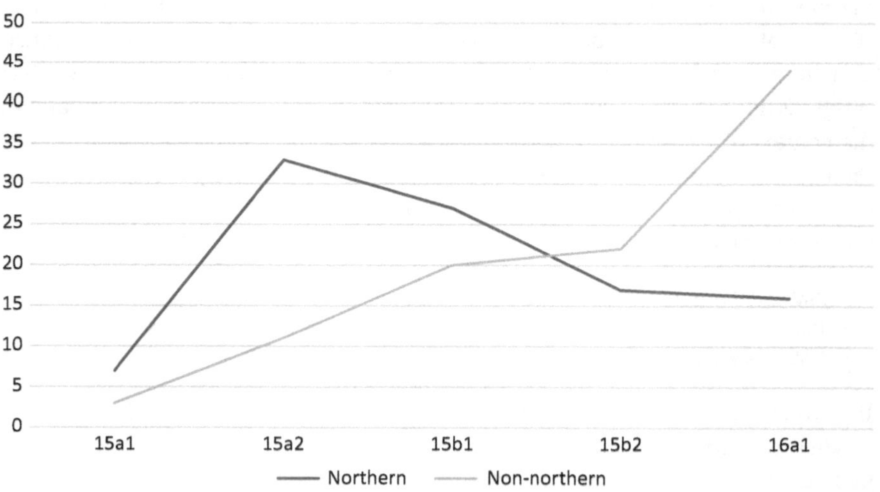

Figure 2.1: The distribution of texts in MELD over quarter-centuries: northern and non-northern texts (proportional). The northern counties are defined as: Cumberland, Durham, Lancashire, Northumberland, Westmorland and Yorkshire.

corpus, caused by the abundance of earlier texts listed in the LALME Index and suggested by archivists; however, early texts in English are certainly found in much larger numbers in northern archives than in non-northern ones.

Where systematic counts have been carried out of specific collections, considerable differences are found between kinds of collection, as well as between individual collections of the same type. Generally, bishop's registers contain the most solidly Latin materials, while the records of parish churches are to a large extent in English or in mixed code. Manorial collections, which often form the bulk of the material at local archives, are highly variable, and generally show clear patterns in terms of text type and chronology. Schipor's study of code selection in the Jervoise family papers, housed at the Hampshire Record Office and comprising 458 texts in all, shows a gradual and steady increase in English texts over time, French being present only in the first quarter of the fifteenth century; at the same time, Latin still remains the majority language a century later (Figure 2.2; Schipor 2018: 124).

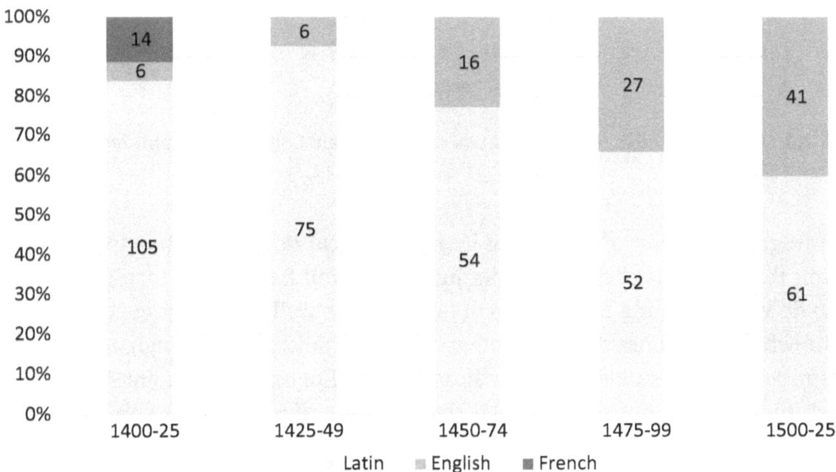

Figure 2.2: Latin, English and French texts in the Jervoise family collection, Hampshire Record Office (from Schipor 2018: 124).

Schipor's study of the Jervoise papers also shows that, during the period surveyed, some text types, such as leases and receipts, show a proportional shift from Latin to English; other text types, however, show no such changes, and in most text types, indeed, Latin remains dominant (see Schipor 2018: 125–127). The increase in English texts does not simply reflect English taking over functions from the other languages: in some cases it also reflects changes in the types of surviving documents. This may be illustrated by the collection of papers relating to the Coke family of Weasenham, held at the Cambridge University Library (see Figure 2.3). At first sight, the use of English seems to increase dramatically around 1500. However, a closer look at the material shows that the English texts from 1500–25 all belong to text types that are not represented in the earlier periods in any language: rentals, terriers, receipts and memoranda.

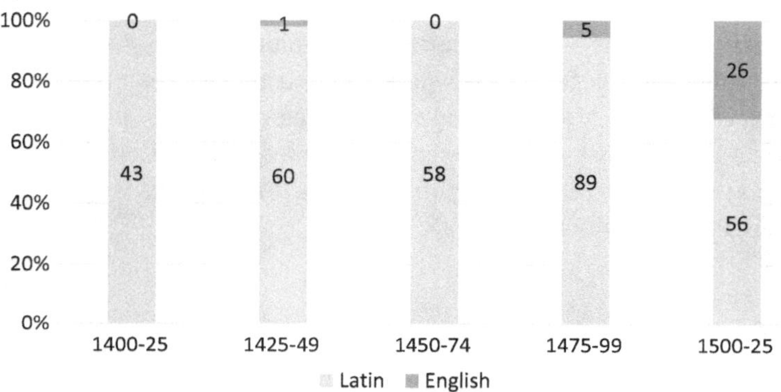

Figure 2.3: Latin and English texts in the Coke of Weasenham Collection (Cambridge University Library).

Accordingly, the study of the use of English in local documents has to take into account the functions of the texts, not just the overall figures: the 'rise of English' has to do with changing frequencies of text types as well as with linguistic choice. On the whole, the figures suggest no sudden dramatic change: English local administration did not suddenly switch from Latin to English at any point during this period. Indeed, it is not unusual that the accounts of a manor or church switch from Latin to English, and then, twenty years later with a change of accountant, change back from English to Latin. The long-term tendency was for English to gain frequency; however, this was not a unidirectional process.

3.3 The functions of the languages

Machan (2003: 35) has commented on the introduction of written French in the official documents of the early thirteenth century: 'at a time when the semantic content of documents was beginning to rival their symbolic import, intelligibility demanded, in some cases, translation into French.' In other words, French came to be used, instead of Latin, when it was important that the people using the documents were able to understand them. In the fourteenth century, French seems to appear in largely the same functions in which English appears in the fifteenth: correspondence, ordinances, oaths, conditions of obligation and occasional leases and sales. These general findings from the MELD project agree with the findings of Britnell (2013: 87), who finds that French in urban administration was used mainly in speech-related genres such as proclamations, ordinances and oaths, as well as in correspondences, especially letters and petitions to authorities. Britnell relates the use of French in the fourteenth and early fifteenth centuries to two main functions: 'oral language' and the display of status. However, he finds it difficult to account for some of the typical uses of French:

> Ordinances were characteristically directed at ordinary workers and tradesmen, and needed to be understood by them if they were to take effect, and oaths had to mean something to the people who swore them if they were not to be an invitation to perjury.
> (Britnell 2013: 87)

The suggestion here is that such problems were, indeed, central in the shift from French to English. Since the early thirteenth-century situation described by Machan, French had largely lost its usefulness for reaching the literate lay population: literacy was no longer confined to the aristocracy, and the latter no longer had French as their first language. French was no longer a language intelligible to document users on the whole – rather, its use had become conventional, carried on in record-keeping by professional groups such as lawyers (Rothwell 2001: 541), and, presumably, also used for status-marking (Britnell 2013: 87).

A general overview of the kind of texts that appear in English in the fifteenth and early sixteenth centuries, based on the MELD materials, suggests that English was adopted precisely in those texts where intelligibility (from the point of view of the users) was important. English is generally found in the following text types (the list is far from exhaustive but includes the most common types found in the archives):

a) *As a rule:* letters, including petitions and complaints (except formal letters from ecclesiastical/monastic authorities)
b) *Commonly:* arbitrations, churchwarden's accounts, commissions, conditions of obligation, marriage agreements, memoranda, statements (such as affidavits, attestations and testimonies)
c) *As a substantial minority:* agreements, bailiff's accounts, guild ordinances and records, leases, municipal records, receipts, rentals, sales, surveys and inventories, wills
d) *Rarely:* enfeoffments, exchanges, gifts, grants

English virtually never occurs in bonds, final concords, inquests post mortem, letters of attorney, manorial court rolls, probates of wills and quitclaims. This means that Latin dominates the most common types of documents: in virtually any archive, the most common medieval documents are bonds, gifts, grants and quitclaims, as well as manorial court rolls, all documents that are for the most part written in Latin.

One might wonder why Latin lingered on in so many types of documents, even though English had already in the late fourteenth century taken over in most spoken official functions, and had, after all, become a perfectly acceptable written language in many types of texts, including such inherently prestigeous ones as royal letters. It should, of course, be borne in mind that Latin was still the default written language of professionals, and continued to be the norm in documents produced within a professional or institutional context and meant for internal use. Thus, court proceedings and episcopal records were produced in Latin as a matter of course, with the exception of the records of spoken statements, such as witness statements, vows and abjurations. As Britnell points out, these had to be understood to make sense, and in the fifteenth century they generally appear in English.

However, Latin also remained the norm in several document types that would have been kept and used by lay people without competence in Latin. One of the most common of such document types, which virtually always appears in Latin, is the bond, or obligation. This is generally a short and completely formulaic document, the wording of which is practically invariable; the only elements that vary are the names, sums and dates. In the following example, the parts that are formulaic have been highlighted in bold:

> **Nou*er*int vniu*er*si *per* presentes me** Thomam Synnagh de Briggewater' in Com' Som*er*s' March*a*unt **teneri & firmit' obligari** Thome houper' & Ric'o Osgod in viginti libris **legal' monete anglie soluend' eisdm'** Thome & Ric'o **aut suis cert' attorn' sen executor' suis ad que' quidm' soluco*n*em bene & fidelit' faciend obligo me heredes & executores meos *per* presentes Jn cui*us* rei testiom' p*re*sentibz sigillu' meum appos' Dat'** octauo die augusti anno regni Regis henrici octaui quinto.
>
> (D0629; Taunton, Somerset Archives: D\B\bw/390)

Reading the sums and dates in Latin would not require particular Latin skills, as these formed closed systems that were highly conventional; in addition, sums would often be written in Roman numerals rather than, as here, written out as *viginti libris* 'twenty pounds'.

Bonds are commonly accompanied by a condition, often (if not always) written in English. Unlike the bond, the condition describes detail that is specific to that particular document: the tasks or further payments that the bound person has to carry out in order to make the bond void. Accordingly, a large part of the text would not be predictable, only the opening and concluding phrases being formulaic, as seen in the condition accompanying the bond cited above:

> **The condicion of this obligacon is suche that if the seid** Thom*a*s Synnagh do make New howsse well and sufficiently billyd longyng to the roode Ile of Briggewater yn Dampyate in the South *par*tie of the Tenement of the Master of the hospitall of Seynt Jonnes of Briggewater A this sid the Feeste of seynt Mighell tharchangell that shal be in the yere of o*ur* lord Ml v hundred and xiiij **that then this p*re*sent obligacon to be voyd And of none effecte or els to stond in his full strengh and vertue**.
>
> (D0629; Taunton, Somerset Archives: D\B\bw/390)

One may assume that understanding the content of a condition of obligation would be important for all parties involved, and – unlike that of the bond itself – it would be impossible to access without a full command of the language. The use of English in conditions would therefore be a purely pragmatic choice, addressing a need for intelligibility not present in the completely formulaic bond. From the same point of view, it makes sense that the first documentary texts which routinely appear in English are letters, both official and private. No matter how formulaic medieval letters may appear, with their set greetings and closing phrases, they almost by definition contain information that is not predictable, whether it be news, instructions or arguments to back up a petition. Similarly, the function of a memorandum, also a document typically written in English, is to record something that needs to be remembered, and that cannot be inferred from the context.

By the fifteenth century, there was a large range of document types that were used to transfer rights (property or otherwise) to others, referred to as *conveyances* in MELD. Of these, leases and sales are fairly commonly written in English, while this is extremely rare for feoffments, gifts, grants and quitclaims. The four latter document types are all highly formulaic, usually short and completely predictable in form: a quitclaim, for example, simply states that the named person gives up all claims for a property. In contrast, leases and sales tend to be more informative. Sales (properly 'bargains and sales') begin to appear in the fifteenth century as an alternative to gifts or enfeoffments: a court 'enrolment' or registration here replaces the traditional oral ritual of livery of seisin. Sales typically provide more detail than gifts or enfeoffments: the financial transaction is usually stated in full and the landholdings may be described in more detail. Similarly, leases frequently contain details about the payment of rent and other conditions, and sometimes describe the landholdings involved, as in this Berkshire lease of 1522:

> **This indenture made** the First Day of Septembre Jn the Reygne of kyng Harry the Sevynthe the viiith yere **betwene** John Jsbury esquyer Lord of grauntsunȝ **on̓ that on̓ part / And** Wyllyam Mundy Smythe of Alborn̓ **on̓ that other part Witnessythe that the**

> **seyde** john **hathe graunted and to Ferme lete to the seide** william **his eyres and Assignes** a plotte of voyde grounde counteynyng xxiiij fote in lengthe by fore the kynges hye-wey in Chepyng Lamborn afore seynt Antony crosse **To haue and to hold** that forseide voyde ground to bylde and make there a newe Mancion w[t] a smythys forge set þeron̛ Well and sufficiently at hys owne proper costes.
>
> (D0461, Reading, Berkshire Record Office: D/Q1/T3)

While leases typically contain much unpredictable content, they are, like most administrative documents, based on specific formulae that make them recognizable as a text type. Unlike the equivalent Latin formulae, however, the English ones show little standardisation, not just with regard to spelling but also with regard to vocabulary and syntax. Most English leases begin with a formula corresponding to the Latin *Hec indentura testatur quod ... ad firmam dimisit* 'this indenture witnesses that X has let to farm'. The following seven examples are all taken from Essex and Suffolk texts, to minimise geographical variation:

a) Thise indenture... beres witnes that... hath*e* dimised and latten' to ferme (Essex D2682, 1459)
b) This endenture... witnesseth that... han' letyn to ferme (Essex D2708, 1473)
c) This bille Indentid... Beryth wytnese that... hath latyn to ferme (Essex D3017, 1433)
d) This indentur̛ ... Witnessith that... hath Demysed graunted and to ferme lete (Suffolk D0518, 1498)
e) Thys indentur̛ wytnessyt that .... have let to ferme (Suffolk D3018, 1492)
f) This Indentur ... witnesseth that... hath g*ra*unted dymysed and to Ferme leten̛ and by thes p*re*sent*es* g*ra*unteth dymyseth and to Ferme leteth (Suffolk D3026, 1511)
g) Thes Jndenters̛... beryth wytnes y[t] ... hathe g*ra*untyd and letyn̛ to Ferm̛ (Suffolk D3027, 1502)

The examples show a considerable range of lexical and syntactic choices. The subject appears variously as *bille indentid, indenture* or the plural *Jndenters*. The verb phrase shows two basic alternative constructions, 'bears witness' and 'witnesses' (see Thengs 2015 for a discussion) and the Latin phrase *ad firmam dimisit* is rendered as five different constructions:

hath latyn to ferme
hath*e* dimised and latten' to ferme
hath Demysed graunted and to ferme lete
hath g*ra*unted dymysed and to Ferme leten̛
hathe g*ra*untyd and letyn̛ to Ferm̛

This kind of semi-formulaicness – repeating the same basic content but varying considerably in form – is typical of late medieval English local documents in general (cf also Thengs 2015, Solberg-Harestad 2018). Developing consistent English formulae that could be simply reproduced, just like the Latin ones were, would presumably have been useful from the point of view of both the scribes and the users. Eventually such stable formulae would develop; however, in the fifteenth and early sixteenth centuries, the documents still show much variation in detail.

In the case of highly formulaic documents, with largely predictable content, continuing to use the standard Latin formulae would therefore plainly be the easiest option for the reasonably competent scribe. The use of formulaic Latin might also have been seen as the best guarantee of legality for the layman, as long as the content was predictable and did not require specific language skills. Some of the commonest types of documents, such as quitclaims and bonds, continued to be routinely written in Latin until 1731, when an Act of Parliament decreed that English was to be used to record all official information in the law courts.

In sum, when English appeared in local administrative writing, it appeared above all in the functional slots that had been occupied by French: the text types which required an understanding of the contents by lay people, and that were not predictable. In other words, rather than being a process of 'vernacularisation', the early fifteenth-century shift basically entailed the introduction of a new written vernacular replacing an earlier one. This change from French to English was completed over a short timespan. The actual process of vernacularisation, the shift from Latin to English, was a far more gradual process, and even though English gained in frequency, Latin remained the majority language of administration throughout the period here considered.

4 Local documents and standardisation

4.1 What do we mean by 'standardisation'?

It is suggested in LALME that Southern English local documents are standardised from the mid-fifteenth century, or even earlier (LALME I: 35). Benskin (1992: 71) writes that '[t]he development of what became standard written English is essentially a fifteenth-century phenomenon'. The opening clauses of fifteenth- and early sixteenth-century Essex and Suffolk leases quoted above would seem difficult to reconcile with most people's expectations of a standardised language; as noted above, a similar degree of variation has been found in other studies of late medieval English formulae.

The term 'standard' is problematic when used to discuss early historical developments. It carries much political baggage, including powerful ideas of nationality and civilization (cf Milroy 2000). Standard languages have been identified at unlikely times and places: the 'AB-language' found in two thirteenth-century manuscripts has been called an early 'literary standard'

(Hulbert 1946; cf Black 1999: *passim* for a discussion), and scholars refer to a 'Wycliffite' or 'Central Midland' Standard, again based on Samuels (1963: 67–70), despite evidence that Wycliffite texts, like Middle English writing in general, show highly variable language (see e.g. Peikola 2003: *passim*).

The classic description of standardisation is that by Haugen (1966): a sequence of processes defined as selection, acceptance, elaboration of function and codification. This well-known model has not, however, been very popular in the study of early historical materials, presumably because few identified 'standards' may be said to have gone through all the processes. Internal consistency (embedded in Haugen's concept of codification as 'minimal variation in form') is involved in most discussions of standardisation; as this is a highly relative concept, some scholars have dated the beginning of standardisation to the fourteenth century (e.g. Schaefer 2006), while others date it to the eighteenth (e.g. Beal 2010: 21). Benskin's statement about the development of standard English as a fifteenth-century phenomenon is linked to his suggestion that 'local forms of language' disappear in this period: standardisation thus becomes the absence of geographical variation (Benskin 1992: 72).

The loss of geographical distinctions and a reduction of variation overall may presumably both be considered necessary parts of the development of a national 'standard', and both will be considered in the study presented here. Another criterion sometimes applied in studies of standardisation, the extent to which the attested forms agree with those current in present-day Standard English, is more problematic: such comparisons may give a misleading picture, assuming a unidirectional development towards a predetermined model.

The assumption that a specific model variety of written English existed in the fifteenth and early sixteenth centuries does not seem to be backed up by concrete evidence. It was noted in section 1.1 that the idea of an officially enforced 'Chancery' language has been shown to be untenable. Chancery as a department could not have had a major effect on English writing, as its routine production of texts was in Latin. In addition, Benskin (2004: 30–32) shows that the English produced by the writers of Chancery documents, when available, shows no particular signs of standardisation, but rather represents various clearly regional usages. Instead, Benskin suggests that '[t]he development of a written standard, even in the offices of government, was more complex and less determined than it has sometimes been made to appear, and government English is not the whole story' (Benskin 2004: 36). He notes that London's sheer size and commercial importance could have played a role independently of government texts, and also that '"colourless regional standards" arise independently of London or government English, but interact with them as well'.

The idea of a single source for standard English has been called in doubt even more forcefully by other scholars. The complexity of the process was a major theme of an important collection of papers published in 2000; Wright (2000a: 6) formulates this point in the Introduction:

> Standard English is to some extent a consensus dialect... meaning that no single late Middle English or early Early Modern authority will show all the features that end up in Standard English... it did not progress as a bundle of features, but in piecemeal fashion.'
>
> (Wright 2000a: 6)

Instead of trying to isolate entire varieties that may be labelled actual or incipient 'standards', later research has therefore tended to focus on the spread of individual forms and their adoption by writers (e.g. Nevalainen and Raumolin-Brunberg 2003, Bergs 2005). This development is in line with a general shift from *varieties* to *variation* as the focus of study: considering the distribution of forms in the material rather than attempting to classify a variable reality into unified 'dialects' (cf Upton 2006: 311). The remainder of this paper will take up this line of enquiry in order to address the remaining question: to what extent does the written language of fifteenth- and early sixteenth-century local documents show a standardising development (here defined as a reduction in variation and a loss of geographical patterns) at the level of individual items? This study will deal with spellings, which were also the focus of much of the earlier work cited, and which show by far the greatest variation.

4.2 Spelling variation: A study of five lexical items

No attempt is made here to measure the variability of texts as a whole. While degrees of internal variability may be measured, they are difficult to compare because of the numerous factors that make a difference: length and number of texts, topic, and range of vocabulary. Instead, the aim here is to focus on the variant forms of specific items and study their distribution in the material. As virtually any lexical item of any length will present a large number of variants, and their distribution should be studied both in relation to geography and time, the scope of the present study allows for only a limited number of items.

To provide geographical comparison, the study is based on four subcorpora of MELD, representing two regions and two municipalities, and making up a total of 954 texts (443,185 words):

- The Northern counties (Cumberland, Durham, Lancashire, Northumberland, Westmorland, Yorkshire) – 370 texts (156,115 words)

- The Western counties (Cheshire, Derbyshire, Shropshire, Staffordshire, Warwickshire, Worcestershire) – 356 texts (169,820 words)
- Cambridge (with immediate surroundings) – 143 texts (90,075 words)
- London – 85 texts (27,175 words)

While the two regional subcorpora are of a similar size, the Cambridge and London corpora are smaller, the London one considerably so. The sizes of these corpora reflect the compilation history of MELD: the Cambridge materials were the subject of a doctoral dissertation (Bergstrøm 2017), while London was not. As the Cambridge data were shown to be relatively homogeneous, and also different from the surrounding counties, it seemed reasonable to include them in the study. The London data are too scanty to be strictly comparable in terms of the amount of variation; however, it was felt that they had to be included to give some idea of the variants present in the capital.[4] Each subcorpus has been further divided into three chronological sections, corresponding to the regnal periods of the three ruling dynasties during the period covered by the corpus: Lancaster (1399–1461), York (1461–85) and Tudor (1485–1525).[5]

The following five items were surveyed: 'abovesaid', 'lawful', 'other', 'seals' and 'these'. These items were chosen as they occur commonly in many types of documentary texts and may be expected to appear in reasonable numbers; also, it was felt to be important to include items other than those traditionally included in studies of the 'Chancery Standard', here represented by 'other' and 'these'. Altogether, the survey found 222 variant forms (or types) of the five items, realized as 4,296 tokens. An overview of the number of tokens and variants collected for the three periods is given in Table 2.1; it should be noted that the figures are somewhat smaller, as not all texts can be precisely dated to a single regnal period. While the figures for the different periods are not directly comparable (most importantly, variants will be proportionally fewer the higher the number of tokens and texts), it is clear that all periods show a considerable degree of variation.

Many texts show internal variation for some of the items, and some variants appear only as minority forms. In order to compare the frequencies of

4 The London corpus is currently being expanded and studied in a PhD project by Kenneth Solberg-Harestad, University of Stavanger.

5 The Tudor reign does not, of course, end in 1525: the date reflects the scope of the corpus. The three regnal periods have turned out to provide a useful chronological division for MELD (see e.g. Thengs 2013: 63–64); it is here preferred to quarter centuries in order to keep the sample sizes reasonably large.

Table 2.1: An overview of the material collected in MELD for 'abovesaid', 'lawful', 'other', 'seals' and 'these' in the periods surveyed.

Period	Number of tokens	Number of variants	Number of texts
Lancaster (1399–1461)	1,398	135	279
York (1461–1485)	707	103	148
Tudor (1485–1525)	1,918	112	250
TOTAL	4,023	212	677

the individual forms, figures are calculated on the basis of each variant's proportional frequency within a text. The sole form of a text is calculated as 1.0, while variant forms are calculated at their approximate proportions (up to two decimals): if a text contains three occurrences of *other* and one of *oder*, the figures will be 0.75 and 0.25 respectively. The figures are then added to obtain a total for each variant form within the sample considered.

Only four abbreviation symbols appear in the material collected. Following the MELD conventions, they are indicated with unique identifiers in italics (or underlining, when the entire form is cited in italics), based on the classification in Hector (1966: 30–35): thus *er* indicates Hector 3, *ur* indicates Hector 4, *n* indicates a macron (Hector 2) and *es* indicates Hector 9. The abbreviation identifiers should not be read as equivalent to the letter values but as spellings in their own right (*oder* is, in other words, not the same as *oder*). Substantial final flourishes (cf Parkes 1979: xxix) are transcribed as an apostrophe: *odir'*.

Abovesaid

The word 'abovesaid' is a frequently occurring item in documents concerned with the dealings of people, such as conveyances, arbitrations and many types of memoranda, used to refer to persons (and sometimes places) already named in the document, e.g. 'the abovesaid John'. It is the most variable of the items included in this study, with 68 variant forms distributed in altogether 332 occurrences:

> aboesayde, abofesaid, abofesayd, abofesayde, aboffesayd, aboffesayde, abofsaid, abon'said, abon'sayde, abouen'said, abouen*n*said, abouensaid, abouensaide, abouensayd, abouenseid, abouenseid*es*, abouersaid, abouesade, abouesaid, abouesaide, abouesaid*es*, abouesaidez, abouesaidz, abouesayd, abouesayde, aboueseid, aboueseide, aboueseid*es*, aboueseyd, aboueseyde, aboun'said, aboun'seid, abounesaid, abounesaide, abouneseyde, aboun*n*said, abou*n*nsayd, abou*n*said, abou*n*saide, abounsayd, abounsayde, abounseid, abousaid, abovesaid, abovesaide, abovesayd, abovesayde, abovesayed, aboveseid, aboveseide, aboveseyd,

aboveseyde, abovn'seyd, abovyn'seyd, abowen'said, abowesaid, abowesayd, abowesayde, abowfesayd, abown'sayd, abownseyde, abowynseyd, aboyfsayd, abufeseid, abuffeseid, abuffsaide, abufsaid, abufseid

In the entire material, the most commonly used variants of 'abovesaid' are *abouesaid* (40.85), *aboueseid* (23.24), *abovesaid* (8.5), *abouesaide* (7.5), *abouesayd* (6.5), *aboueseyd* (5.06) and *aboveseyd* (5). As the other forms have frequencies of less than 5.0, they might at first sight be dismissed as minor; however, as Tables 2.2–2.4 in the Appendix show, many cluster in specific periods and areas, appearing as major forms in particular samples.

In the northern subcorpus, *abouensaide* is the most common form in the Lancastrian period, and forms with *-n (abounsayde, abounesaid, abouensayd, abouen'said, abouennsaid, abouensaid, abownseyde, abovnseyd, abouneseyde*) far outnumber *-n*-less forms at this point (see Appendix, Table 2.2). These forms gradually decrease in frequency but are still well evidenced in the Tudor period (4.0 out of a total of 19.0). Even though *abouesaid* is the most frequent form in the York and Tudor periods, it is closely matched by *abofesayde* (York) and *abouesade* (Tudor).

In the western subcorpus, on the other hand, *abouesaid* is closely matched by *aboueseid* throughout the survey period (see Appendix, Table 2.3). Only Cambridge (Table 2.4) shows *abouesaid* as the clearly dominant form: in the Tudor period, which is the only one for which materials are reasonably plentiful, *abouesaid* accounts for 12.0 out of a frequency total of 22.

London (Table 2.5) is the one area that stands out, in that the form *abouesaid* is in a clear minority, occurring only in one Tudor text and accounting for only 1.0 out of 11.0. in all; however, it should be noted that the London material is too scanty to be strictly comparable.

The variation in the first element of 'abovesaid' shows clear patterns in relation to geography and chronology. The variants may be grouped into types as follows (with some overlap):

- the <f> type: *abofesaid, abofesayd, abofesayde, aboffesayd, aboffesayde, abofsaid, abowfesayd, aboyfsayd, abufeseid, abuffeseid, abuffsaide, abufsaid, abufseid*
- the <n> type: *abon'said, abon'sayde, abouen'said, abouennsaid, abouensaid, abouensaide, abouensayd, abouenseid, abouenseides, aboun'said, aboun'seid, abounesaid, abounesaide, abouneseyde, abounnsaid, abounnsayd, abounsaid, abounsaide, abounsayd, abounsayde, abounseid, abovn'seyd, abovyn'seyd, abowen'said, abown'sayd, abownseyde, abowynseyd*
- the <u> type: *abouersaid, abouesade, abouesaid, abouesaide, abouesaides, abouesaidez, abouesaidz, abouesayd, abouesayde, aboueseid, aboueseide, aboueseides, aboueseyd, aboueseyde, abousaid*

- the <v> type: *abovesaid, abovesaide, abovesayd, abovesayde, abovesayed, aboveseid, aboveseide, aboveseyd, aboveseyde, abovn'seyd, abovyn'seyd*
- the <w> type: *abowesaid, abowesayd, abowesayde, abowen'said, abowfesayd, abown'sayd, abownseyde, abowynseyd*

Of these, the <u> type is the most frequent and appears in all samples: all the others are restricted in geography and time. The only other type to occur evenly throughout the period is the <v> type, which appears in 36 texts, by far most of which belong to the Western subcorpus.

The <f> type is restricted to the northern subcorpus as well as three Cheshire texts, appearing altogether in fourteen texts, all from the fifteenth century. The <n> type, which is the most common type in the northern area in the earliest period, appears in 24 texts and is also limited to northern subcorpus, with the exception of two Warwickshire texts. Finally, the <w> type appears in 10 texts, all except one of which belong to the northern or western subcorpora; the only sixteenth-century text, from 1515, was produced in London. Both <n> and <w> types appear mainly in the fifteenth-century material.

The data for 'abovesaid' would seem to show a pattern that is largely in agreement with the development of regional standards described by Benskin (1992: 82–84): the most strongly regional forms (in particular the <f> and <n> types) have become rare or disappeared in the sixteenth century, but the material still remains highly variable. The overall majority form, *abouesaid,* is the most frequent form overall by a large margin; however, with the exception of Cambridge, it is not an unchallenged majority form in any of the samples. Similarly, while a few forms, including *abouesaid,* appear in all or most samples, the Northern and Western sets of forms are otherwise quite different throughout the period, both with regard to the attested forms and their relative frequencies.

Lawful

The word *lawful* usually appears in the phrase 'of lawful English money' in reference to sums of money owed. In the material here surveyed, there are 437 occurrences with 32 different spellings:

> laffull, laful, lafull, laghefull, laghfull, lauffull, laufull, laufull', laufulle, laweful, lawefule, lawefull, lawffull, lawful, lawfull, leaffull, leafull, leefull, lefalle, leffull, lefoll, lefolle, leful, lefull, lefulle, lefwll, leueful, leuefull, levefull, lewfull, loufull, lowfull

By far the most common form overall is *lawfull* (87.38), followed by *laufull* (49.65) and *lefull* (41.5). *Lawfull* is also the most common form in all samples for which material is plentiful, although sometimes with a very small margin (see Appendix, Table 2.7). As with *abouesaid, lawfull* is for the most part not a clear majority form, but has close contenders. Here, however, the other two most frequent forms also appear in all geographical areas, and seem to undergo the same development in all of them, the form *lefull* being overtaken by *laufull* in the Tudor period. The forms with <e> appear in all subcorpora and periods, with no noticeable pattern; the form *laufull,* on the other hand, increases considerably in frequency during the period, with more than half the occurrences being from the sixteenth century. Forms with single <l>, such as the present-day standard form *lawful,* are generally in minority everywhere, except for the scanty early Cambridge and London texts (Appendix, Tables 2.8 and 2.9); however, they disappear almost completely in the Tudor period.

The most obviously 'regional' forms in the material are those with <gh>: *laghefull* and *laghfull.* As might be expected, these forms are mainly restricted to northern texts (Appendix, Table 2.6), but also appear in a Derbyshire text from the Tudor period; they all belong to the latter half of the fifteenth century.

Unlike 'abovesaid', the forms of 'lawful' show several developments that seem to take place simultaneously throughout the country, regional differences being less notable, with the exception of the northern <gh> forms. At the same time, the variation remains considerable even in the Tudor period, with a very wide range of different forms.

Other

The item 'other' occurs most frequently of all items surveyed, with 2,000 tokens; these are realized as 36 variant forms:

> od*er*, oder', odere, odir, odir', odr', odre, od*ur*, odur', odurȝ, odyr, odyr', oth^{e}r, otheire, other, other', othere, other*er*, othir, othir', othire, othor, othr, othr', othre, oth*ur*, othur', othyr, othyr', othyre, oþ*er*, oyer', oþ*er*e, oþir, oþ*ur*, oþyr

The present-day form *other* is a clear majority form overall, only the early Cambridge materials showing *othr'* as the principal form. Despite of this, and the fact that the overall number of variants is among the lowest in this study, every sample (except the scantily represented York period in London) shows a high number of minor variants (see Appendix, Tables 2.10–2.13).

The most interesting variation concerns the medial consonant, in particular the variation between medial <d> and spellings indicating a fricative, most commonly <th> but also <þ> and, in the north, <y>. Of the spellings suggesting fricatives, <th> is completely dominant, even though <þ> appears in most samples, most notably in the early London materials, where it is more common than <th>.

The appearance of <d> spellings in ‘other’ and similar words (‘either’, ‘leather’) in the fifteenth century has been noted by Thengs (2013: 219–225) and Bergstrøm (2017: 147–149) in their studies of the Western and Cambridge materials respectively; it seems to coincide with or precede the appearance of spellings suggesting a fricative for the ‘father’ set which had historical [d]. Whether the *oder* type forms simply represent back spellings, reinterpreting <d> as a spelling for the dental fricative, or whether they reflect an actual sound change is not completely clear: however, Thengs (2013: 223–225) has suggested that the geographical pattern of their spread might indicate a sound change.

The <d> forms are thus a recent innovation, but one that does not end up in Standard English. Except for the North where they peak in the York period at 32%, they increase throughout the period. In the West, <d> forms leap from 11% in the Lancaster and York periods to 21% in the Tudor period. Except for a single appearance as a very minor form in an early Cambridge texts, <d> forms only appear in Cambridge and London in the Tudor period, when they make up 13% and 10% of the total respectively.

The final vocalic element in ‘other’, finally, shows a clear geographical pattern. Forms ending in *-ur* (*othur, odur*) appear only in the Western subcorpus and in one Lancashire text, and seem to remain fairly constant in the Western area, with 8% in the Lancaster period and 7% in the Tudor period. The *a*-shaped abbreviation used for Latin *-ur* and conventionally expanded as *ur* (Hector 4; see Hector 1966: 31) shows largely the same pattern: with the exception of one London text, it appears only in the Western subcorpus, as well as in two texts from the bordering area to the North, from Lancashire and the West Riding of Yorkshire respectively. It is also retained fairly constantly throughout the period.

Accordingly, ‘other’ shows a complex picture: on the one hand, the modern standard form is clearly the majority form in all areas; on the other hand, the minor variants show no sign of disappearing, and they show both a solid retention of traditional dialect features (*-ur*) and an overall increase in innovative forms that do not end up in the later standard (the *oder* type).

Seals

The item ‘seals’ occurs commonly at the end of indentures, usually in the phrase ‘X and Y have set to their seals’; there are 384 occurrences in the material. As this is a short word with fairly invariable consonants, one might not expect much variation; however, it turns out to be realized in 39 different spelling variants:

seales, sealex, sealez, sealis, sealles, seallez, seallis, sealls, seallus, seallys, seallz, seals, sealse, sealus, sealx, sealys, seeles, seelez, seellus, seels, seiles, seilles, seillys, seles, selez, selis, selles, sellez, sellis, sellus, sellys, selys, seyles, seylles, seyllys, seyls, seylus, seylys, sielles

The most common form is *seales* (93.83), followed by *seals* (46.5), *sealles* (27) and *sealles* (25); however, there is much variation between the different samples, and only in the western subcorpus does *seales* appear as the most common form throughout (see Appendix, Tables 2.14–2.17). By far the most variable element is the plural ending; however, there is also variation in the vowel and between single and double <l>. As regards the vowels, the <ea> forms are by far the most common; it may be noted that the <ei> and <ey> spellings are restricted to the north in the fifteenth century, but appear in four western texts in the late fifteenth and early sixteenth centuries.

As with 'other', the material for 'seals' shows a solid presence of <u> in the inflectional ending in the western subcorpus: forms with *-us* (*seallus, sealus, seellus, sellus, seylus*) appear in all periods, and do not show up anywhere else. Two other plural endings that show a regional or local patterning are in fact increasing in frequency. The form *-ez (sealez, seallez, seelez, selez, sellez)* is by far most common in the North, but also appears in the Lancaster and York periods in Cambridge: in the north, it shows a considerable increase in frequency from 8% to 28%.

Perhaps the most interesting feature here, however, is the <x> ending. The overwhelming majority of attestations are found in Cheshire, where, as Thengs (2013: 308) has shown, they are particularly typical of documents from Nantwich; they also appear in two texts from nearby counties, Staffordshire and the West Riding of Yorkshire respectively, and in two London texts. As Thengs notes, this feature, which also appears in words such as *espouselx, catelx* and *spirituelx*, seems to derive from French and is a late innovation in English: it only occurs in words of a French origin with final <l>, which would have had a plural formed with <x> in Anglo-Norman as well. There are occasional early occurrences in the material, of which the earliest is found in London (1419); however, by far the majority of the occurrences appear in the late fifteenth and early sixteenth centuries.

The <x> spellings would seem to be largely restricted to documentary texts in the fifteenth century; the Middle English Grammar Corpus (MEG-C), which contains a range of genres, shows no occurrences in the non-documentary texts. Bearing in mind that, as English comes to be used in documentary texts, it for the most part takes over the functions of French, it is not surprising that specifically French writing conventions would be taken over in discourse communities engaging in this area of writing; what is interesting is its seemingly late spread in the material. In all, it seems that 'seals' shows the opposite development from that of 'abovesaid' and 'lawful': rather than showing the loss of older, local forms, it shows the appearance and increase of innovating forms with clear geographical distributions.

These

The item 'these' was one of the eight forms Samuels used to illustrate the difference between the 'Chancery Standard' and 'Type 3', or the language of Chaucer (as 'vouched for by the best MSS'): Chancery Standard had *these* compared to Chaucerian *thise* (Samuels 1963[1989: 70–71, 80]). The present material contains 1,143 occurrences of 'these', realized in altogether 49 different forms:

> thease, theer', thees, theez, theis, theise, theiz, ther, there, thes, thes', these, theses, thesse, theus, theys, þ^{eys}, theyse, thez, þ^{ez}, þ^{e}z, thies, þies, thiez, thir, þir', thir', this, thise, thyes, thyez, thyr, thys, thyse, þ^{z}, yees, y^{e}es, yeis, yes, y^{e}s, y^{es}, yese, yez, yiez, yir, yis, y^{is}, yise, y^{s}

The most common forms are *thes* (103.15) and *these* (98.21). While the other forms are considerably less frequent overall (e.g *thies* 36.76, *theis* 22.6), there is considerable variation between the samples, and it is notable that the later standard form, *these,* in fact decreases in relative frequency over time in all four subcorpora (see Appendix, Tables 2.18–2.21).

In the northern subcorpus, forms with initial <y> appear throughout but become markedly less common towards the end of the period. In the Lancaster and York periods they account for 30% and 33% respectively of the overall tokens, with *y^{es}* appearing as the most frequent form overall in the York period; however, in the Tudor period they only appear in four texts and account for 6% of all tokens. Even more dramatically, the traditionally northern *thir* type with final <r> (*theer', ther, there, thir, þir', thir', thyr, yir*) disappears completely, going from 21% in the Lancaster period (with *yir* the fourth most common form) to 4% in the York period and no occurrences at all in the Tudor period. The material still shows variation in the Tudor period; however, the typically northern forms are by now very rare.

The western subcorpus shows no similar changes: here, the *these* and *thes* forms remain in majority, with a number of medium-frequency forms (*theis, thees, theys, thies, thys)* also retaining their position. In the Cambridge corpus, however, there is a dramatic change from *thes/these* to *thise* and *thies,* which suddenly appear around 1500 (there is only one occurrence in the fifteenth century, in 1491) and become completely dominant. There is no similar change in the other subcorpora, most of which show *thies* as a stable medium-frequency form throughout. It might be noted that Benskin's (2004: 36) study of government documents suggests a surge in the popularity of *thies* and *thise* in Signet letters during the Yorkist period (see 6 below).

Again, the material for 'these' shows a complex picture: the loss of traditional regional forms in the north, stable variation in the west, and a sudden dramatic change in Cambridge, bringing in a dominant variant that did not eventually end up in the standard.

Discussion

This limited survey shows that spelling in the early sixteenth century is still highly variable. At the same time, all five items surveyed have developed overall top-scoring forms that appear in all or most areas: *abouesaid, lawfull, other, seales/seals* and *thes/these*. As Table 2.22 shows, these forms generally account for approximately 20–50% of the total frequency count for each period. However, these forms are seldom completely dominant in the samples: their prominence in the total frequency counts simply reflects the fact that the other forms are more geographically restricted in use.

Table 2.22: The overall leading forms: proportion of the total frequency count for each item per period. The overall number of variants in each period is given in brackets.

Form	Lancaster period 1399–1461	York period 1461–1485	Tudor period 1485–1525
abouesaid	20% (26 variants)	18% (24 variants)	31% (26 variants)
lawfull	34% (18 variants)	35% (14 variants)	39% (17 variants)
other	49% (26 variants)	35% (21 variants)	52% (27 variants)
seales	21% (31 variants)	40% (22 variants)	24% (20 variants)
thes/these	48% (30 variants)	50% (20 variants)	50% (22 variants)

The material shows the gradual loss of certain strongly regional forms, such as *abounsaid* and *thir*. On the other hand, other similarly traditional regional forms are retained (*othur*, the plural ending *-us*) and there is an actual increase in innovative forms with clear geographical distributions, such as the <d> forms of 'other', the <x> plurals of 'seals' and *thies, thise* 'these'. Regional variation, in other words, does not disappear, but the variants change over time.

Perhaps the most important point is, however, that the overall patterns of variation show relatively little change over time. The leading forms themselves are without exception there from the beginning. As Table 2.22 shows, their proportion of the overall forms increases slightly over time, but the changes are for the most part neither consistent nor major, and the number of variants remains fairly constant for most items (bearing in mind that the York material is considerably smaller compared to the other periods in terms of the number of texts and tokens, cf Table 2.1). The overall amount of variation does not seem to be reduced substantially: it is the actual pool of forms taking part in the variation that changes over time, as one would expect of a variable, dynamic system.

5 Concluding comments

This chapter has dealt with two ideas that are traditionally connected in the history of English: the rise of English as a written language in administrative writing and the standardisation of written English. Both these developments – or their decisive phases – have been dated to the fifteenth century, and related to the assumed adoption of English as the regular language of government documents. While many of the basic assumptions behind such accounts have been adjusted by more recent work, the central role of administrative writing in the standardisation of English has not generally been called into question; the present study suggests that this role is far from self-evident.

Archive searches for the MELD project showed clearly that English remained a minority language in local administration throughout the fifteenth and early sixteenth centuries. The distribution of English and Latin in the material suggests that English was generally adopted in text types with a fairly low degree of formulaicness – that is, largely unpredictable content – that were intended for the use of non-professionals. Highly formulaic texts, and texts intended for internal use by administrators, continued to be largely written in Latin. As such texts would have formed the majority of the texts encountered by most administrators, it should not be surprising that writing conventions for the English documents were slow to develop.[6]

The survey of spelling variation in the MELD corpus, based on five frequently occurring items, showed that the spelling of local documents remained highly variable in the fifteenth and sixteenth centuries. While all items have 'leading' forms that account for 20–50% of the overall usage, their relative frequency increases only slightly during the period. The appearance of such forms

6 It is unknown to what extent clerks might have made use of model exemplars when producing English documents. Formal education focussed on the mastery of Latin, even though English would be used in the earlier stages: before printing, however, the English of school texts was extremely variable (cf Stenroos 2016: 120–22).

could in itself be seen as an indication of 'standardisation'; however, this would be missing an important point about the material. There seems to be no substantial change towards greater homogeneity: in the early sixteenth century, the usage remains extremely variable, and as older, regionally marked forms disappear, new forms take their place in the pool of variants.

Of the 'innovative' forms (*laufull, oder, sealx, thies, thise*) that appear or become more frequent towards the end of the period, none survive into Standard English. In studies of Early Modern English variation, 'innovative' is sometimes equated with 'standard', suggesting an inexorable progress towards a set model. However, innovations continued to take place in the written language, and not nearly all of them were in the direction of the future standard. Benskin (2004: 36) makes this point very clearly, with reference to signet documents from the Yorkist period, well after the period covered by *An anthology of Chancery English* (Fisher *et al.* 1984):

> [N]o-one then could know that *nat* and *thise* and *thies* would not survive into the later standard, and some of the clerks to Henry VIII did not know it either. Only in the long view can such forms be recognised as deviations from some true path, and it is a question how far any writers during the fifteenth century thought in terms of a written standard as fixed for even the foreseeable future. A standard need be no more than a fashion widely accepted, and changes in fashion proceeded often enough from the royal court.

The idea of a standard as 'no more than a fashion widely accepted' is clearly rather different from the 'predecessor of modern written English ... backed by the full weight of the administrative machine' (Samuels 1963 [1989: 71]). In their work on late middle and early modern English variation, Nevalainen and Raumolin-Brunberg (2003: 13, 157) have dispensed with the term 'standardisation' altogether, preferring to refer to the 'supralocalization' of individual forms. Referring to standardisation in the context of the present material certainly makes little sense: rather, dispensing with the term – and the compulsion to keep tracing a standardisation process – allows us to study the linguistic variation in late medieval and early modern documents on its own terms, without treating it as a puzzle from which Present-Day Standard English is meant to emerge.

Much of this linguistic variation is still unexplored, perhaps not surprisingly given the idea that, as stated in LALME (I: 3), 'in the course of the fifteenth century ... regional diversity gives way increasingly to Chancery Standard'. The present data show that, even in the early sixteenth century, diversity – including regional diversity – is very much present, even though some of the older dialect markers have fallen out of use. Certainly, there are no particular indications that local documents would be 'leading' a process of standardisation.

Appendix: Tables 2.2–2.21

Table 2.2: The Northern subcorpus: 'abovesaid'.

Lancaster		York		Tudor	
abouensaide	3	abouesaid	3.25	abouesaid	4
abouesaide	2.3	abofesayde	3	abouesade	3
abovesaid	2	abofesayd	1	abon'said	2
abounesaide	2	abofsaid	1	abouesaid*es*	2
abouesaid	2	aboueseid	1	abon'sayde	1
abovesaide	1.5	abowen'said	1	abouesayd	1
abouesayde	1.2	abou*n*said	1	abouenseid*es*	1
abouen'said	1	abou*n*saide	1	abouersaid	1
abouensayd	1	abown'sayd	1	aboueseid	1
abouesayd	1	abowynseyd	1	aboueseid*es*	1
abounesaid	1	aboffesayd	0.75	abovesayed	1
abounsayde	1	abouesaide	0.75	abowesayd	1
abousaid	1	aboffesayde	0.25		
abowfesayd	1				
aboyfsayd	1				
abufsaid	1				
abouensaid	0.5				
abouen'said	0.5				
abouneseyde	0.33				
abovn'seyd	0.33				
abownseyde	0.33				
abufeseid	0.33				
abuffeseid	0.33				
abufseid	0.33				
Number of texts	26		16		19

Table 2.3: The Western subcorpus: 'abovesaid'.

Lancaster		York		Tudor	
abouesaid	3.6	abouesaid	4	abouesaid	7.5
abovesaid	3	aboueseid	3.67	aboueseid	7.4
aboueseid	2.67	abovesaid	2.5	aboveseyd	3
abovesaide	2	abovesayd	1.5	aboueseyd	2.6
abovesayde	2	aboueseyd	1.13	abouesaidez	2.5
abouesaide	1.2	aboffesayd	1	abouesaidz	2.5
abouensaid	1	aboueseyde	1	aboveseid	2
aboveseid	1	aboveseid	1	abofesaid	1
abuffsaide	1	aboveseyde	1	abovesayd	1
abouesayde	0.7	abowesaid	1	aboveseide	1
aboesayde	0.5	abowesayd	1	aboveseyde	1
aboueseyd	0.33	abouenseid	0.5	abowesayd	1
		abovyn'seyd	0.5	abouesaid*es*	0.5
		abouesayd	0.2		
Number of texts	19		20		33

Table 2.4: The Cambridge subcorpus: 'abovesaid'.

Lancaster		York		Tudor	
abouesaid	3	aboueseid	1.5	abouesaid	12
		abouesayd	1	abouesayd	3.3
		abouesaid	0.5	aboueseid	3
				abouesaide	1
				aboueseide	1
				abovesaid	1
				abouesayde	0.7
Number of texts	3		3		22

Table 2.5: The London subcorpus: 'abovesaid'.

Lancaster		York		Tudor	
abouesaide	1	abouesaide	2	abouesaid	1
aboueseid	1	aboueseid	1	aboueseid	1
aboueseyd	1			aboveseyd	1
aboveseyd	1			abowesayde	1
Number of texts	4		3		4

Table 2.6: The Northern subcorpus: 'lawful'.

Lancaster		York		Tudor	
lawfull	11.3	lawfull	7.9	lawfull	8.7
lefull	9.33	lefull	4.9	laufull	8.3
leffull	3.17	lawful	2	lefull	3.1
leful	2.5	laufull	1.2	lawful	1
lawefull	2	laghefull	1	lefalle	0.3
lawful	2	laghfull	1	lefolle	0.3
lafull	1.2	leffull	1	lefoll	0.3
laghfull	1	leuefull	1		
laufulle	1				
lawefule	1				
laufull	0.5				
Number of texts	35		20		22

Table 2.7: The Western subcorpus: 'lawful'.

Lancaster		York		Tudor	
lawfull	11	lawfull	7	laufull	20.35
laufull	3	lefull	6.5	lawfull	20.47
lefull	2.8	laufull	4	lefull	6.55
lawefull	2.2	lafull	1	lafull	7
leful	2	lauffull	1	leafull	2
laful	1	lawful	1	leefull	1.27
lafull	1	leafull	1	laffull	1
leefull	1	lowfull	1	laghfull	1
leueful	1	loufull	0.5	leaffull	1
levefull	1			lawffull	0.33
lewfull	1			lawful	0.03
laweful	0.5				
leffull	0.5				
Number of texts	28		23		61

Table 2.8: The Cambridge subcorpus: 'lawful'.

Lancaster		York		Tudor	
lawful	2	lawfull	4	lawfull	15.02
lawfull	1	lefull	3.34	laufull	10
leefull	1	lawful	2	lefull	2.98
		lawffull	0.33	leffull	1
		leffull	0.33		
Number of texts	4		10		29

Table 2.9: The London subcorpus: ‘lawful’.

Lancaster		York		Tudor	
lawful	1	lefull	1.5	laufull	1.8
leful	1	laufull	0.5	lawfull	1
				lawefull	1
				lefull	0.5
				lefwll	0.5
				leefull	0.2
Number of texts	2		2		5

Table 2.10: The northern subcorpus: ‘other’.

Lancaster		York		Tudor	
other	51.01	other’	8.3	other	14.58
other’	18.27	od*er*	7.2	other’	5.58
othir	9.6	othir	5	oþ*er*	5.33
othir’	5.7	other	4.55	od*er*	3.5
odyr	3.71	othre	4	othir	2.33
othere	3.67	oder	3.5	oder	1.17
othyr	3.05	othir’	2.9	odir	1
oþ*er*	2.33	odyr	2.8	odr’	1
oder	2.31	othyr	2	odre	1
od*er*	2	oþ*er*	1	odyr	1
oy*er*e	1.7	othere	0.4	oth*er*	1
odir’	1.5	otheire	0.2	othre	1
odyr’	1.33	oþ*er*e	0.2	oth*ur*	1
odir	1			othyr	1
othyr’	1			oder’	0.5
oy*er*	1				

Table 2.10 (continued)

Lancaster		York		Tudor	
oyer'	1				
oþ*ere*	1				
oyir	1				
othur	0.7				
oþer	0.55				
oder'	0.5				
oþer'	0.05				
od*ur*	0.01				
Number of texts	114		42		41

Table 2.11: The western subcorpus: 'other'.

Lancaster		York		Tudor	
other	47.15	other	28.6	other	47.36
othir	9.3	oþ*er*	6.86	other'	11.7
other'	4.9	other'	6.82	od*er*	5.2
oþ*er*	3.98	od*ur*	4.75	oþ*er*	4.2
othur'	2.94	othir	2.95	othir	3.9
od*ur*	2.5	othr'	2	oder	3.83
oth*ur*	2.5	othir'	1.4	odur	3.3
odyr	1.75	odur	1.25	othre	3
oder	1.25	oder	1	od*ur*	2.05
odir'	0.67	oder'	1	oder'	2
	0.67	odur'	1	othyr'	1.55
oþur	0.5	oþ*ur*	1.14	odere	1.5
oþer	0.5	othr	0.75	othur'	1.5
odur'	0.33	oþ*ere*	0.33	odur'	1.45

Table 2.11 (continued)

Lancaster		York		Tudor	
othir'	0.33	othyr	0.17	oth*er*	1.3
othir'	0.33			othir'	1.05
o*þur*	2			oth*ur*	1
odyr'	0.2			othur	1
				odyr	0.6
				othor	0.3
				odyr'	0.2
Number of texts	80		60		98

Table 2.12: The Cambridge subcorpus: 'other'.

Lancaster		York		Tudor	
other	2.37	other	4.5	other	38.1
othr'	2.29	othir	1.33	other'	7.82
o*þer*	1.14	othyr	0.8	odir	3.03
othir	0.72	o*þer*	0.67	oder	1.92
other'	0.67	other'	0.5	oder'	0.6
othere	0.33	othyre	0.2	odyr	1
oder	0.2			othr'	0.67
odyr	0.14			othr	0.33
othyr	0.14			odir'	0.25
				od*er*	0.15
				othir	0.13
Number of texts	8		8		54

Table 2.13: The London subcorpus: 'other'.

Lancaster		York		Tudor	
other	5.67	other	3.5	other	7.61
oþ*er*	3.33	other'	1.5	oþ*er*	1.78
oþer	2.17	odir	1	oder	1.5
oþyr	1.33	othir	1	other'	1.1
othir	1			othir'	1
oþir	0.5			oth*ur*	1
				othyr	0.56
				othir	0.22
				othyr'	0.22
Number of texts	14		7		15

Table 2.14: The northern subcorpus: 'seals'.

Lancaster		York		Tudor	
seals	14	seales	10	seallez	5
seales	10.5	selys	6	seall*es*	5
seles	10.5	sellys	4	seales	5
selys	6	sealles	3	seals	3
sealez	3.3	seallys	3	sealez	3
selis	3	sealez	2	sealys	2
sellys	3	seyllys	2	seal*es*	2
sealles	2	sealis	1	sellis	1
seal*es*	1.3	seals	1	selles	1
seallez	1	sealx	1	sell*es*	1
seallis	1	seels	1	sealles	1
sealls	1	selles	1		
seels	1	seyl*es*	1		

Table 2.14 (continued)

Lancaster		York		Tudor	
seiles	1	seyll*es*	1		
seill*es*	1				
seillys	1				
selles	1				
sellez	1				
seyles	1				
seyllys	1				
seyls	1				
selez	0.3				
Number of texts	66		37		29

Table 2.15: The western subcorpus: 'seals'.

Lancaster		York		Tudor	
seales	18	seales	23	seales	14
seals	15	sealles	4	seals	8.5
seles	14	seals	4	sealx	7.5
sealles	6	seall*es*	2	seall*es*	6
sealx	2	sealx	2	sealles	5
sealez	1	seel*es*	2	seallez	4
seallz	1	selys	2	sealls	2
sealse	1	sealls	1	seallus	2
sealus	1	seallus	1	sealys	2
seeles	1	sealys	1	seiles	2
seellus	1	seeles	1	selles	2
sellus	1	seles	1	seal*es*	1
sielles	1	seylus	1	sealez	1

Table 2.15 (continued)

Lancaster		York		Tudor	
				seallis	1
				seallys	1
				selys	1
				seyll*es*	1
Number of texts	63		45		61

Table 2.16: The Cambridge subcorpus: 'seals'.

Lancaster		York		Tudor	
seelez	1	seales	2	seall*es*	13
seallez	1	sealez	2	seales	6.33
sealles	1	sealles	2	seal*es*	3
		seeles	1	sealis	2
				sealles	1
				seallys	1
				sealys	1
				sealez	0.67
Number of texts	3		7		28

Table 2.17: The London subcorpus: 'seals'.

Lancaster		York		Tudor	
sealx	1	seall*es*	1	seales	5
				seals	1
				sealx	1
				sealys	2
Number of texts	1		1		9

Table 2.18: The northern subcorpus: ‘these’.

Lancaster		York		Tudor	
thes	14.5	y^{es}	3.5	thes	13.5
these	10.9	thies	3	thies	4.3
yes	5.35	these	2.5	theis	3.5
this	4.65	thes	2	thiez	3.3
thir	4	this	2	thez	1.55
yise	3.7	yes	2	these	1.5
yir	3.5	yese	2	thees	1
thees	3.3	thees	1.5	theiz	1
yis	3.05	theis	1.5	yis	1
yir’	3	theys	1.5	y^{es}	0.75
thies	2.25	thiez	1	this	0.7
thir’	2	thyr	1	thes’	0.5
thyr	1.8	þiez	1	y^{is}	0.3
yees	1.7	thyes	0.5		
yeis	1.5	thyez	0.5		
thys	1.2	$y^{e}s$	0.5		
$þ^{es}$	1.2	y^{is}	0.5		
theys	1	yez	0.5		
thez	1				
y^{es}	1				
yese	1				
þies	1				
thyes	1				
þir’	1				
þis	1				
yies	0.5				

Table 2.18 (continued)

Lancaster		York		Tudor	
ther	0.5				
thiez	0.3				
þise	0.3				
theer'	0.25				
theis	0.25				
theses	0.2				
Number of texts	78		27		33

Table 2.19: The western subcorpus: 'these'.

Lancaster		York		Tudor	
these	18.52	these	14.5	thes	29.73
thes	17.13	thes	13.34	these	25.71
theis	3.83	thys	5.83	theis	5.86
thees	2.7	thies	4	thies	5.51
theys	2	thise	1.5	thys	3.29
thys	2	theus	1	theez	2.25
this	1.6	thesse	0.5	theys	1.83
yese	1.56	þes	0.5	thees	1.75
yes	1.54	yes	0.5	thise	1.67
þis	1.14	thees	0.33	y^{is}	1.17
þes	1.03			thesse	1.1
thies	1			thez	1
theise	0.67			yes	0.11
yis	0.67				
y^{e}es	0.4				
thesse	0.33				

Table 2.19 (continued)

Lancaster		York		Tudor	
þ^{e}s	0.33				
yees	0.33				
y^{s}	0.2				
Number of texts	57		42		81

Table 2.20: The Cambridge subcorpus: 'these'.

Lancaster		York		Tudor	
these	5	thes	4	thise	18.45
thees	0.67	these	3.67	thies	14.5
thes	0.33	theis	1.14	theis	6.5
		theys	0.57	these	5.73
		theyse	0.29	thes	3.9
		þese	0.33	theise	2
				theys	0.5
				theyse	0.07
				thyse	0.1
				þ^{e}z	0.1
				þ^{es}	0.05
				þ^{ez}	0.05
				þ^{z}	0.05
Number of texts	6		10		52

Table 2.21: The London subcorpus: 'these'.

Lancaster		York		Tudor	
these	4.5	these	2.15	thes	4.25
þes	2	thise	1.85	these	3.5
thies	1			thise	2
thes	0.5			thies	1.2
				thease	1
				thiez	0.8
				thys	0.25
Number of texts	8		4		13

References

Alcolado Carnicero, José Miguel. 2013. *Social Networks and Mixed-Language Business Writing: Latin/French/English in the Wardens' Accounts of the Mercers' Company of London, 1390–1464*. Universidad de Castilla-La Mancha. PhD thesis.

Beal, Joan C. 2010. Prescriptivism and the suppression of variation. In R. Hickey (ed.), *Eighteenth-century English: Ideology and Change*, 21–37. Cambridge: Cambridge University Press.

Benskin, Michael. 1992. Some new perspectives on the origins of standard written English. In J.A. van Leuvensteijn and J.B. Berns (eds.), *Dialect and Standard Language in the English, Dutch, German and Norwegian Language Areas*, 71–105. Amsterdam: Koninklijke Nederlandse Akademie van Wetenschappen.

Benskin, Michael. 2004. Chancery Standard. In C. Kay, C. Hough and I. Wotherspoon (eds.), *New Perspectives on English Historical Linguistics: Selected Papers from 12 ICEHL*, 1–40. Amsterdam: John Benjamins.

Bergs, Alexander. 2005. *Social Networks and Historical Sociolinguistics: Studies in Morphosyntactic Variation in the Paston Letters (1421–1503)*. Berlin: Mouton de Gruyter.

Bergstrøm, Geir. 2017. *'Yeuen at Cavmbrigg': A study of the late medieval English documents of Cambridge*. University of Stavanger: PhD thesis.

Black, Merja. 1999. AB or simply A? Reconsidering the case for a standard. *Neuphilologische Mitteilungen* 100: 155–174.

Britnell, Richard. 2013. French language in medieval English towns. In J. Wogan-Browne (ed.), *Language and Culture in Medieval Britain: The French of England, c.1100–c.1500*, 81–89. Cambridge: Boydell and Brewer.

Dodd, Gwilym. 2011a. The rise of English, the decline of French: supplications to the English Crown, c. 1420–1450. *Speculum* 86: 117–146.

Dodd, Gwilym. 2011b. The spread of English in the records of central government, 1400–1430. In E. Salter and H. Wicker (eds.), *Vernacularity in England and Wales, c. 1300–1550*, 225–66. Turnhout: Brepols.
Dodd, Gwilym. 2012. Trilingualism in the Medieval English Bureaucracy: The Use – and Disuse – of Languages in the Fifteenth-Century Privy Seal Office. *Journal of British Studies* 51 (2): 253–283.
Fisher, John H. 1977. Chancery and the emergence of standard written English in the fifteenth century. *Speculum* 52 (4): 870–899.
Fisher, John H. 1979. Chancery Standard and modern written English. *Journal of the Society of Archivists* 6: 136–144.
Fisher, John H. 1992. A language policy for Lancastrian England. *Publications of the Modern Language Society of America* 107: 1168–1180.
Fisher, John H. 1996. *The Emergence of Standard English*. Lexington: University Press of Kentucky.
Fisher, John H, Malcolm Richardson & Jane L. Fisher (eds.), 1984. *An Anthology of Chancery English*. Knoxville: University of Tennessee Press.
Görlach, Manfred. 1999. Regional and social variation. In Roger Lass (ed.), *The Cambridge History of the English Language. Volume III: 1476–1776*. Cambridge: Cambridge University Press.
Haugen, Einar. 1966. Dialect, language, nation. *American Anthropologist* 68 (6): 922–935.
Hector, Leonard C. 1966. *The handwriting of English documents*. 2nd edn. London: Edward Arnold.
Hope, Jonathan. 2000. Rats, bats, sparrows and dogs: linguistics and the nature of Standard English. In Laura Wright (ed.), *The Development of Standard English 1300–1800: Theories, Descriptions, Conflicts*, 49–56. Cambridge: Cambridge University Press.
Hulbert, J.R. 1946. A thirteenth-century English literary standard. *Journal of English and Germanic Philology* 45: 411–414.
Machan, Tim William. 2003. *English in the Middle Ages*. Oxford: Oxford University Press.
McIntosh, Angus, Michael L. Samuels & Michael Benskin. 1986. *A Linguistic Atlas of Late Mediaeval English*. 4 vols. Aberdeen: Aberdeen University Press.
MEG-C = The *Middle English Grammar Corpus*. Version 2011.1. Compiled by Merja Stenroos, Martti Mäkinen, Simon Horobin and Jeremy J. Smith. University of Stavanger. www.uis.no/meg-c
MELD = *A Corpus of Middle English Local Documents*. Version 2017.1. Compiled by Merja Stenroos, Kjetil V.Thengs and Geir Bergstrøm. University of Stavanger. www.uis.no/meld
Millward, Celia M. and Mary Hayes, 1990. *A Biography of the English Language*. 3rd edn. Boston: Wadsworth.
Milroy, James. 2000. Historical description and the ideology of the standard language. In Laura Wright (ed.), *The Development of Standard English 1300–1800: Theories, Descriptions, Conflicts*, 11–28. Cambridge: Cambridge University Press.
Myers, A. R. 1937. Parliamentary petitions in the fifteenth century. *English Historical Review* 52: 385–404, 590–613.
Nevalainen, Terttu and Helena Raumolin-Brunberg. 2003. *Historical Sociolinguistics: Language Change in Tudor and Stuart England*. London: Longman.
Parkes, Malcolm. 1979. *English cursive book hands, 1250–1500*. London: Scolar Press.
Peikola, Matti. 2003. The Wycliffite Bible and 'Central Midland Standard': Assessing the manuscript evidence. *Nordic Journal of English Studies* 2: 29–51.

Putter, Ad. 2016. The linguistic repertoire of medieval England, 1100–1500. In Tim Machan (ed.), *Imagining Medieval English: Language Structures and Theories, 500–1500.* 126–144. Cambridge: Cambridge University Press.

Rothwell, William. 2001. English and French in England after 1362. *English Studies* 6: 539–559.

Samuels, Michael L. 1963. Some applications of Middle English dialectology. *English Studies* 44: 81–94. Reprinted in: Margaret Laing (ed.), 1989. *Middle English Dialectology: Essays on some Principles and Problems*, 64–80. Aberdeen: Aberdeen University Press.

Schaefer, Ursula (ed.), 2006. *The Beginnings of Standardization*. Frankfurt am Main: Peter Lang.

Schipor, Delia. 2013. Multilingual practices in late medieval English official writing: an edition of documents from the Beverley Town Cartulary. University of Stavanger: MA thesis.

Schipor, Delia. 2018. *A Study of Multilingualism in the late medieval material of the Hampshire Record Office*. University of Stavanger: PhD thesis.

Solberg-Harestad, Kenneth. 2018. Genre, text type and the nature of formulaicness in Late Medieval and Early Modern English abjuration texts. University of Stavanger: MA thesis.

Stenroos, Merja. 2016. Regional language and culture: the geography of Middle English linguistic variation. In Tim Machan (ed.), *Imagining Medieval English*, 100–125. Cambridge: Cambridge University Press.

Strang, Barbara. 2015. *A History of English*. [first published 1970] Abingdon: Routledge.

Thengs, Kjetil V. 2013. *Studies in the dialect materials of medieval Staffordshire*. University of Stavanger: PhD thesis.

Thengs, Kjetil V. 2015. Compactness of expression in Middle English legal documents. *Filologia Germanica – Germanic Philology* 7: 163–181.

Thengs, Kjetil V. 2016. St Michael at the North Gate and St Peter in the East: English churchwardens' accounts of late medieval Oxford. Paper presented at ICEHL 19, 22–26 August 2016, University of Duisburg-Essen.

Upton, Clive. 2006. Modern regional English in the British Isles. In Linda Mugglestone (ed.), *The Oxford History of English*, 305–333. Oxford: Oxford University Press.

van Gelderen, Elly. 2014. *A History of the English Language*. Revised edition. Amsterdam: John Benjamins.

Wright, Laura. 1996. About the evolution of Standard English. In Elizabeth M.Tyler and M. Jane Toswell (eds.), *Studies in English Language and Literature: 'Doubt Wisely' Papers in honour of E. G. Stanley*, 99–115. London: Routledge.

Wright, Laura. 2000a. Introduction. In Laura Wright (ed.), *The Development of Standard English 1300–1800: Theories, Descriptions, Conflicts*, 1–8. Cambridge: Cambridge University Press.

Wright, Laura. 2000b. Bills, accounts, inventories: everyday trilingual activities in the business world of later medieval England. In D.A. Trotter (ed.), *Multilingualism in Later Medieval Britain*, 149–156. Cambridge: D.S. Brewer.

Wright, Laura. 2005. Medieval mixed-language business discourse and the rise of Standard English. In Janne Skaffari, Matti Peikola, Ruth Carroll, Risto Hiltunen and Brita Wårvik (eds.), *Opening Windows on Texts and Discourses of the Past*, 381–399. Amsterdam: John Benjamins.

Wright, Laura. 2011. On variation in medieval mixed-language business writing. In Herbert Schendl and Laura Wright (eds.), *Code-switching in Early English*, 191–218. Berlin: De Gruyter Mouton.

Wright, Laura. 2012. On variation and change in London medieval mixed-language business documents. In Merja Stenroos, Martti Mäkinen and Inge Særheim (eds.), *Language Contact and Development around the North Sea*, 95–115. Amsterdam: John Benjamins.
Wright, Laura. 2013. Mixed-language accounts as sources for linguistic analysis. In J.A. Jefferson and Ad Putter (eds.), *Multilingualism in Medieval Britain (c.1066–1529) Sources and Analysis*, 123–136. Turnhout: Brepols.
Wright, Laura. 2015. On medieval wills and the rise of written monolingual English. In Javier Calle-Martin and Juan Camilo Conde-Silvestre (eds.), *Approaches to Middle English: Variation, Contact and Change*, 35–54. Oxford: Peter Lang.

María José Carrillo-Linares and Keith Williamson

3 The linguistic character of manuscripts attributed to the Beryn Scribe: A comparative study

1 Introduction

This chapter examines the copying behaviour of a 15th-century Middle English scribe – the so-called Beryn Scribe[1] – from the viewpoint of his written language. The language of one of the Beryn Scribe's manuscripts was analysed for *A Linguistic Atlas of Late Mediaeval English, 1380–1450*. A Linguistic Profile (number 6040) was made of the language of Alnwick Castle MS 455 and localised to South Essex, near Basildon. This led some researchers on the work of the Beryn Scribe to suppose that the language of this manuscript therefore represents that of its copyist and so to localise the other manuscripts copied by him to this same place. Other scholars have concluded that the Beryn Scribe must have trained in South Essex, but then he migrated to London to work, probably in a 'scriptorium', since the likelihood of such a place for copying books in the Basildon area seemed unlikely to them. They propose further that features of the Beryn Scribe's language can be connected to the emergence of the written 'standard' language of 15th-century London.

Our own linguistic investigation of the language of the Beryn Scribe has caused us to question these ideas, and our aim in this chapter is to provide a

1 Called so because he was the copying scribe of the unique copy of the pseudo-Chaucer 'Tale of Beryn' in the collection of the 'Canterbury Tales' in Alnwick Castle MS 455.

Note: We are grateful to the staff of the Centre for Research Collections, University of Edinburgh Main Library, for their support during the research for this project. We are also grateful to the British Library for providing digital copies of the manuscripts held there and to the Bodleian Library for letting us take additional photos from their manuscripts in the Mackerras Reading Room; to Cambridge University Library for allowing us to transcribe from manuscript Kk.I.3 and to make images from it; to Christopher Hunwick, archivist at Alnwick Castle Library, and to the staff in Special Collections at Princeton University Library for facilitating our access to on-line digital copies of their manuscripts. Special thanks to Dr. Petra Hofmann, Librarian at Oxford, St. John's College for her help during our visit to the College Library. Likewise, we thank Merja Stenroos and Jacob Thaisen for letting us have a draft of their chapters in this volume.

https://doi.org/10.1515/9783110687545-004

more detailed linguistic account than hitherto of his production and copying practice by analysing the forms of English found in the different texts attributed to him. We compare the linguistic evidence of his productions having regard to: the degree of consistency in the language of the manuscript texts, elements common to all or most that might be attributable to the scribe's own linguistic repertoire, variants distinctive to any of them, and connection of his usage with the supposed language of London and associated notions of written 'Standard English'. We have considered possible provenances of assemblages of forms found in the scribal language of his different productions and we are driven to conclude that the linguistic connections of the Beryn Scribe with London and South Essex are not supported by the linguistic evidence. The notions of what have been held up as 'London language' and 'standard language' as the linguistic milieu for the Beryn Scribe's written usage are, we suggest, questionable.

2 Review of the literature on the Beryn Scribe

2.1 The Beryn Scribe's manuscripts

In *A Descriptive Guide to the Manuscripts of the 'Prick of Conscience'* (Lewis and McIntosh 1982) provided a description for the copy of the Main Version of the poem found in Oxford, St. John's College 57 (SJC 57). The authors date this manuscript in the 15th century, sometime after 1432.[2] The *Prick of Conscience* occupies folios 1 to 137. It is written in an Anglicana script, in single columns with between 29 and 35 lines per page (Lewis and McIntosh 1982: 117). In the unpublished materials used for the creation of *A Linguistic Atlas of Late Mediaeval English, 1350–1450* (henceforth 'the *Atlas*'), palaeographical and linguistic links between this manuscript and Northumberland, Alnwick Castle 455 (AC 455) were made (see further below, § 4.1).

Horobin (2000) identifies another manuscript as being copied in the same hand as that of AC 455: the so-called 'Helmingham' manuscript of *Canterbury*

2 The date is based on that of the last entry for the *Chronicle of London*, also copied by the Beryn Scribe, preserved in ff. 138–223 of SJC 57. However, Hanna (2003) notes: "the book is on two paper stocks; although the scribal hand is continuous throughout, I think there is no likelihood that Stock A (fols 1–137) predates 1441, and stock B (fols 138–240, including the *Chronicle*) most resembles papers of later 1450s." On palaeographical grounds Mooney and Matheson (2003: 354) place it closer to mid-century, in the 1440s or 1450s.

Tales, now Princeton Firestone Library 100.[3] Through palaeographical and linguistic analysis Horobin concluded that the paper section of this volume (fols. 1–165, 203–215) could be ascribed to the same person who copied AC 455. Manly and Rickert (1940: 390) assigned a similar origin for the language of these two manuscripts of the *Canterbury Tales* (AC 455 and Helmingham): they designate the Alnwick Castle manuscript's language as 'East Midlands showing some Northern influence', although the language of Helmingham they consider to be even more markedly East Anglian (Manly and Rickert 1940: 258).[4]

Mooney and Matheson (2003) – at the time unaware of Horobin's work – identified six other manuscripts copied by the same scribe, namely,

- two manuscripts containing complete copies of the prose *Brut Chronicle*
  London, British Library Harley 1337 (Hrl 1337)
  London, British Library Harley 6251 (Hrl 6251);
- lengthy portions of the *Brut Chronicle* in three other manuscripts
  Ann Arbor, University of Michigan, Hatcher Library, MS 225 (Mi 225)
  Oxford, Bodleian Library, Hatton 50 (Hatton 50)
  Oxford, Bodleian Library, Tanner 11 (Tanner 11);
- a version of John Lydgate's *Life of Our Lady* in
  Cambridge, University Library, Kk.I.3, part 10* (CUL Kk.I.3)

And to these they added the volume containing the four texts in the same hand in SJC 57. They also dubbed the copyist 'the Beryn Scribe'.

Mosser (2010) assessed the watermarks and paper stock of the manuscripts attributed to the Beryn Scribe, with the aim of establishing their dates and a relative chronology. His analysis concluded that the scribe must have been copying these manuscripts between ca 1430 and 1455. From the analysis of the paper stocks, and comparison of them with the closest analogues discovered so far, Mosser provided a possible chronology for the Beryn Scribe's production in paper.[5] He considered that the paper portion of Helmingham is the earliest surviving example of the scribe's production. SJC 57, Tanner 11, and Mi 225 are,

3 As it is more familiarly known by the 'Helmingham' designation, we use that name to refer to this manuscript below.

4 "Nl [i.e. AC 455] may be assigned to the same region as He[lmingham] (q.v.) The fact that the dialect in the ReT [Reeve's Tale] is for the most part lost may mean that the scribe or his exemplar came from further South; but some Northern forms appear throughout the manuscript. The peculiar forms found in He occur, but less regularly – e.g. the v for w, while almost always in vomman, vommen in other words is less frequent than in He" (Manly and Rickert 1940: 390).

5 His chronology does not include the manuscripts or portions of manuscripts copied in parchment, that is, Helmingham, Hatton 50, Hrl 1337 and Hrl 6251.

according to him, likely to be from the early to mid-1440s. Mosser also included another manuscript of the *Brut Chronicle*, Oxford, Bodleian Library Rawlinson C. 901 (Raw C. 901), and placed this manuscript at the end of the scribe's production. Placing CUL Kk.I.3 was problematic for him because one of the watermarks has not been identified. He provided a tentative location of the production of these copies in London.

Mosser and Mooney (2014) go further on the Beryn Scribe. There they argued that, contrary to what Horobin (2000) had stated, this scribe copied both the paper (fols. 1–165, 203–215) and the parchment (fols. 166–202) sections of Helmingham. They also argued that this same scribe copied the Oxford fragments (Rosenbach 1084/2 and Manchester, John Rylands Library English 63) of *Canterbury Tales*.[6] Further, they identified another *Brut Chronicle* manuscript (Raw C. 901)[7] as one copied by the Beryn Scribe and suggested that the *Regiment of Princes* copy that follows *Life of our Lady* in CUL Kk.I.3 is the work of one of the Beryn Scribe's 'cohort' (Mosser and Mooney 2014: 74).

We do not challenge the palaeographical identification of the manuscripts cited above as being in the same hand. We assume in what follows that the Beryn Scribe was indeed the copyist of these manuscripts.

2.2 The Beryn Scribe's language

The scribal language of the Beryn Scribe is discussed in Matheson (2008) as part of a wider study of the language of 'prolific' East Anglian scribes apparently working in London in the mid fifteenth century. Matheson's study is concerned with the relation of these scribes' spellings systems with the genesis, development, adoption and dissemination of standard English. He accepts the evidence of the *Atlas* Linguistic Profile 6040 as representing the Beryn Scribe's language and its localisation in South Essex. Further, Matheson (2008: 49) concluded from recurrent forms observable from across his productions that the scribe was "a consistent

6 Horobin (2009) ascribed these fragments to another prolific scribe who was heavily associated with Lydgate's work, designated the 'Edmund–Fremund scribe'. However, Mosser and Mooney (2014: 61) observe that the spelling peculiarities which are so common in other texts copied by the Beryn Scribe and which are shared by the scribe of these fragments, do not occur in any other texts supposedly copied by the Edmund–Fremund scribe. We have not included in our analysis here the data from these fragments: they are very short and a Linguistic Profile of them contains too many gaps to allow a firm conclusion. Nevertheless, such evidence as our examination of their linguistic features provides is not inconsistent with the result of our analysis of the Beryn Scribe's manuscripts discussed here.

7 This manuscript had already been mentioned earlier in Mosser (2010).

translator into his own language". He also noted a cluster of linguistic forms that are partly included in Type III and partly in Type IV in M.L. Samuel's classification of types of London 'standard' language (Samuels 1963 [1989]: 66; Samuels (1983 [1988]), although Matheson observed that the Beryn Scribe also retained a set of distinctive features that he considers were "the result of his local Essex background and original training"; however "such blend of language was perfectly acceptable in London" (Matheson 2008: 50). We examine these claims below.

3 Data and methodology

The sources of our data are the manuscripts ascribed to the Beryn Scribe and our methodology draws on that which underpins the *Atlas*, which we have used as a resource and particularly the on-line 'electronic version'.[8]

8 *A Linguistic Atlas of Late Mediaeval English, 1350–1450* was compiled as a dialect atlas for *written* forms of late Middle English. A 'Questionnaire' to record a set of items, e.g. the manuscript forms for words corresponding to such Present-day English words as THEY, SHE, EACH, MUCH, AGAINST, WORLD, CHURCH as well as the manuscript forms for verb endings such as the 3rd Present Indicative Singular and Plural, Weak and Strong Past endings. The Questionnaire for the electronic version of the *Atlas* can be viewed within the web-site <http://www.lel.ed.ac.uk/ihd/elalme/elalme.html>. Using documentary texts with non-linguistic associations as a base, a set of maps was made for each Questionnaire item by plotting on them the forms recorded in the texts analysed. These maps established a series of distributions for each form. The maps taken together form a dialect matrix. A new text, whose provenance is otherwise unknown, could then be 'fitted' into this matrix by eliminating those areas on each map where the corresponding forms in the text to be localised do *not* fit. In principle, as each form is compared, the area for a possible localisation of the combinations of forms becomes smaller and smaller. Eventually the aim is to find an area into which the set of forms in the text to be localised 'fit' as a combination or *assemblage*, i.e. each form may have a different area of distribution, but taken together they can be found on the map only in some smaller, well-defined area. This method of adding information to the dialect map is known as the 'fit'-technique. (See *A Linguistic Atlas of Late Mediaeval English*, Introduction § 3.2; for a worked example of a fit using the *Atlas*, see Benskin 1991. On the sources and base texts of the *Atlas*, see Benskin (1977); for introductions to methodology in historical dialectology and on the dialectology of Middle English, see Williamson (2012a, 2012b); for more detailed accounts of principles, methods and applications see the collections in Laing (1989) and Smith (1988)). The *Atlas* is the principal frame of reference for the present study. In response to any who would still question the validity of this work and therefore our dependence on it here, let us state that we accept that it is neither 'perfect' nor 'definitive' (both states impossibilities in reality). Revisions are desirable, localisations can be questioned (cf Hanna 2005). Indeed, here and in Carrillo-Linares and Williamson (2019) we do just that. In the preparation for the on-line version (2013) the compilers of the *Atlas* themselves took the opportunity to re-examine a number of manuscript texts, especially for the Southern area of survey, and this resulted in re-localisation of some texts. (See the Introduction to

We transcribed to disk samples from all the manuscripts listed above from the texts attributed to the Beryn Scribe. Transcription was from either the original manuscripts or digital photographic reproductions. In some cases the latter were available on-line. Our samples amount to some 130,000 words. From the transcribed texts we created Linguistic Profiles using an extended version of the Questionnaire in the *Atlas* to include some further items that seemed to us relevant for the copying practice of the Beryn Scribe. This was done by adding identifying reference numbers to the appropriate forms. The Linguistic Profiles were then generated by a specially written computer program. The output also gives frequency counts of each form rather than a notional presentation of the levels of occurrence. This system has allowed us to select material for analysis more precisely. Items may be added to the Questionnaire and the Linguistic Profiles are easily revised. In the case of SJC 57, we had already made a full annotation by 'lexico–grammatical tagging', which offers the possibility of investigating wider linguistic questions.[9]

In the case of long works, samples were made from different parts of the text to cover beginnings and ends of different sections as well as parts from the middle. The length of the original manuscripts varies so our selections are likewise uneven in length. For the *Canterbury Tales* manuscripts parallel texts were selected. The language displayed in the various Linguistic Profiles for every section of every work has been compared. We use a smaller selection of items for the analysis presented in this chapter.[10]

the on-line version (*eLALME*): 'Scope of Revision'.) The overall picture of Middle English linguistic geography that the *Atlas* presents is sound (and *falsus in uno* does not entail *falsus in omnibus*), while the underlying principles and methodology stand on both rational and empirical grounds.

9 This analysis was made for a different piece of research on the *Prick of Conscience* text in this manuscript (Carrillo-Linares and Williamson, 2019). Lexico-grammatical tagging involves adding a label comprising a lexical element and / or a grammatical element to each text word in the manuscript text. The analysis is exhaustive and not selective as with the use of a questionnaire. On the questionnaire and lexico-grammatical tagging methods of analysis, see Williamson (2012b). For the application of lexico-grammatical tagging to Early Middle English texts, see Laing and Lass (2013: Ch. 4).

10 Tables including 75 items and features have been produced for the analysis presented here. These items are: AGAIN, AGAINST, ANY, ARE, BEFORE, BROTHER, CHURCH, DAUGHTER, EACH, EITHER, FELL, FIRE, GAVE, HUNDRED, IF, IT, LAND, MANY, LENGTH, MOTHER, MUCH, NEITHER … NOR, NOT, ONE, PEOPLE, SAW, SHALL, SHOULD, SISTER, STRENGTH, SUCH, THAN, THE-ONE, THE-OTHER, THEIR, THEM, THEN, THEY, THROUGH, TWO, UPON, WAS, WEEK, WERE, WHEN, WHERE, WHICH, WHILE, WIGHT, WILL, WITEN, WORK, WORLD, YE, YEAR, YOU, YOUR, Substantive Plural, 3rd Person Singular Present Indicative, Plural Present Indicative, Weak Past, Weak Past Participle, Present Participle, Past Participle Prefix, Infinitive Ending, Negation with NE, -ABLE, -LY, -ASE (for -ACE), <atte> (for AT THE), <butte> (for BUT THE), <scl-> (for 'sl'-), <v> for etymological 'w', and <v> or <u> for non-initial /v/.

In our discussions of the dialectal character of the various texts, references are made to the *Atlas*'s Dot Maps and to the 'User-defined Maps' function in the online version.[11] The latter was used to access diatopic details discussed. The User-defined Maps supplement the Dot Maps, which often deal with more general orthographic types and the distributions of specific details are not recoverable from them. We localised the language of our Linguistic Profiles two ways: first by applying the McIntosh 'fit'-technique 'by hand' (see footnote 9), i.e. using pencil and tracing paper over the *Atlas* Dot Maps and on User-defined Maps made with the electronic *Atlas*, secondly by means of a computer program, CompFT3.[12]

4 Challengeable assumptions about the Beryn Scribe

In the literature cited above regarding the Beryn Scribe, several assumptions or conjectures have been made about his origins, the character of his repertoire, localisation of his scribal language, consistency in his language, as well as the relation of his language with London English and 'standard' English. Furthermore, most of the hypotheses about the scribe's provenance – based on his linguistic features – and about his working environment and location follow from these assumptions. Our own examination of the linguistic evidence drawn from all his

11 The Dot Maps appear in both the printed and electronic versions of the *Atlas* and show the distribution of a form or a set of forms having some feature in common (constituting a 'type'). A black dot (hence the name) on the map indicates the places to which the manuscript texts containing the relevant forms have been localised. User-Defined Maps are a feature of the electronic version and allow the user interactively to make their own Dot Maps in effect. One or more Questionnaire item may be selected and within each one a single form or any set of forms may be chosen for mapping. The dots in the resulting maps may be clicked to view in a window all the forms for the Questionnaire item attested in each Linguistic Profile associated with the dot's location. From this window the full Linguistic Profile may be accessed.

12 This program generates an enriched overall dialect map, effectively filling in the adjacent *terra incognita* around the *Atlas* survey points, with data projected into it from the localised Linguistic Profiles. The enriched map allows many more potential sites of fit, which now contain supplementary Linguistic Profiles. These contain a presumption of occurrence of the features in the original Linguistic Profiles on the principle of a dialect continuum, viz. that language varies in an orderly way across geographical space. The idea for the algorithm that CompFT3 uses was proposed first in Benskin (1981). Its further development as a computer program with theoretical background is outlined in Williamson (2000). For a detailed application of an earlier version, see Laing and Williamson (2004).

known productions suggests to us that all or some part of these assumptions are challengeable.

4.1 Provenance

In their *Descriptive Guide to the Manuscripts of the* Prick of Conscience (1982), Lewis and McIntosh did not claim to have made a close analysis of the dialects of all the manuscripts discussed. They used three categories to describe their provenances: (a) texts that can confidently be placed in a particular county; (b) those that cannot be localised firmly enough to place them in one particular county; and (c) those for which only a tentative localisation could be provided (Lewis and McIntosh 1982: 29–30). SJC 57 falls into the first of these categories and this version of the *Prick of Conscience* is assigned to Essex, although there is no comment as to why.

As noted in the introduction above, the *Atlas* localised the language of AC 455 to South Essex, near Basildon. It appears from information in the Middle English Dialect Project Archive,[13] that Angus McIntosh analysed Books I and II of the *Prick of Conscience* in SJC 57. Similarities are noted between the language of SJC 57 and the analysis of AC 455, discounting its "Northern traits". The evidence of the analyses indicated that the language of the *Prick of Conscience* in the SJC 57 is mixed. It seems likely, then, that identification of at least a partial similarity between the language of the two manuscripts led Lewis and McIntosh (1982) to adopt Essex also as the provenance for the Oxford, St John's College version of the *Prick of Conscience* in their *Guide*. This information in Lewis and McIntosh (1982: 117–118) does not appear in the original printed *Atlas*, but it has since been added to the Index of Sources in the revised electronic version of the *Atlas* (2013), where Lewis and McIntosh (1982) is cited as the source. The Alnwick Castle manuscript does have a Linguistic Profile 6040 in both the printed edition, vol. 3 (1986: 115–116) and the revised on-line edition, and it is localised to Essex, near Basildon. This South Essex localisation of AC 455 seems to have formed the basis for the subsequent localisation of the language of the other manuscript texts copied in the same hand.[14]

---

13 We are grateful to Dr Rhona Alcorn, then Deputy Director of the Angus McIntosh Centre for Historical Dialectology, for aiding us with access to the Middle English Dialect Project Archive.
14 SJC 57 contains: *Prick of Conscience* (ff. 1r-135r + supplement ff. 135v-137r), *Chronicle of London* (ff. 138r-223r), Chaucer's *Parliament of Fowls* (ff. 224r-236r), and *Statues and Ordinances for the Army by Henry V* (ff. 337r-240v).

Other scholars, whose work we have described above, had meanwhile fixed Essex as the place of origin of all the texts written by this scribe. In addition, Hanna (2003: unpaginated) states that SJC 57 "has long been seen as representative of Essex English" and that "connecting the hand with the Northumberland *Canterbury Tales* would place it in a precisely analysed context". Mooney and Matheson (2003) conclude that the Beryn Scribe must have trained in South Essex and then migrated to London to work in a 'scriptorium' and they connect some features of his language to the emergence of the putative written 'standard language' of 15th-century London.

One cannot assume that the scribal language of an individual text is that of the person who copied that text. McIntosh (1974 [1989]: 47) observes that there are texts whose language "seems to derive, not from the person who copied them, but directly from the language of the exemplar used. In such cases we shall not be able in any meaningful way to characterise the 'scribe' by means of a Spoken Linguistic Profile, because what he has written reflects some other kind of spoken language than his own; another text copied by him may well display quite different S-features". Any claim that the language of the *Prick of Conscience* in SJC 57 is the same as that of AC 455 has to take into consideration McIntosh's observation.

So far as we know, no detailed comparative analysis of these two manuscript texts was otherwise undertaken.[15] To decide if the Beryn Scribe was at all times, or on different occasions, a translator or a partial translator or a *literatim* copyist[16] requires very close analysis and comparison of all the features of all his productions. With respect to SJC 57 and AC 455 there are indeed shared features between the texts in the two manuscripts, but those features only can be attributable *prima facie* to the presumed common scribe.

In this chapter, we argue that the Beryn Scribe was not, in fact, a consistent translator but rather a partial one. In each production, he generated a greater or lesser degree of mixed language. Thus, when considering the provenance of the language of his copies in SJC 57 and AC 455, their non-Beryn Scribe features have to be considered separately as a diatopic set. Our argument is based on a comparison of the languages of both manuscripts and our attempts to 'fit' them.

---

15 Mooney and Matheson (2003: 361) state that "full dialectal analyses of the language of the Beryn Scribe, the scribes with whom he worked, and other associated manuscripts and scribes, together with the implications for scribal collaboration and manuscript production, will be the topics of a future study, which will add further variant spellings and forms to the Beryn Scribe's repertoire".

16 These are the three manners of scribal copying practice proposed in McIntosh (1973 [1989]: 92).

So far as we are aware no detailed attempt to localise of any of the other works copied by the Beryn Scribe has been published. Due to the limitations in space for the present chapter, we cannot include full detail of our localisations. Our manual fittings of the languages of each of them (summarised in Table 3.1)

Table 3.1: Preliminary attempt to 'fit' the language of the Beryn Scribe's copied texts.

Manuscript	**Text**	**Counties and areas in which the language of each manuscript text 'fits'**
Oxford, St John's College 57	Prick of Conscience	North-West Norfolk, Isle of Ely, Soke of Peterborough, Rutland, South Lincolnshire, North Northamptonshire
	Chronicle of London	(1) South Suffolk, Essex (2) Surrey
	Parliament of Fowls	(1) Essex, Hertfordshire, East Surrey (2) Gloucestershire, Herefordshire
Cambridge University Library Kk.I.3, part 10	Life of Our Lady	Essex, South Suffolk, London, Surrey
London, British Library, Hatton 50	Brut Chronicle	(1) Essex, London, North Surrey (2) Worcestershire
London, British Library, Harley 1337		Essex, Surrey
London, British Library, Harley 6251		(1) East Essex, London (2) Northamptonshire
Oxford, Bodleian Library, Tanner 11		East Hertfordshire, Essex, Surrey
Ann Arbor, University of Michigan, Hatcher Library, 225		(1) South Suffolk, Essex (2) South Oxfordshire, South Berkshire, South Buckinghamshire, North Hampshire (3) Somerset
Oxford, Bodleian Library, Rawlinson C 901		(1) South Suffolk, Essex, London, Surrey (2) Northamptonshire
Northumberland, Alnwick Castle 455	Canterbury Tales	(1) Essex, London, Surrey Hertfordshire (2) Oxfordshire (3) Warwickshire (4) South part of Northamptonshire
Princeton Firestone Library 100	Canterbury Tales	London, Essex and South West Suffolk.

show that, although Essex cannot be excluded, many other areas are also possible.[17] London, Surrey and Northamptonshire recur as possible areas of fit. The only text which does not fit in Essex is *Prick of Conscience* in SJC 57. Our conclusion from the fitting by hand is that the language of the Beryn Scribe is not so easy to pin down to a specific area and that the language of his different manuscripts varies although clearly Southern and generally Eastern in character.

4.1.1 The language of Alnwick Castle MS 455

The main source of information for the language of AC 455 has been Linguistic Profile 6040 in the *Atlas,* where a description is given in the Index of Sources:

> **Alnwick** Castle: Duke of Northumberland's MSS, 455 (*olim* 55). *ca.* 1460, MED. Hand of (a) Chaucer, *Canterbury Tales*; and of (b) *Tale of Beryn.* (a) analysed from Chaucer Soc. 81, *Specimens* i (1890); (b) from F.J. Furnivall and W.G. Stone, ed., *The Tale of Beryn*, EETS ES 105 (1909, repr. 1973). Grid 567 185. Essex.

There is no explicit statement that the full texts in these editions were analysed to make the Linguistic Profile or, if not, what specific pages (and corresponding manuscript folios) were used. Linguistic Profile 6040 was made as part of the southern area of survey, so the northern items of the *Atlas* Questionnaire were not included. The Linguistic Profile was not among those revised for the electronic version of the *Atlas.*

Our analysis of the language of this manuscript is based on our own Linguistic Profile, made from the *Physician's Tale*, the *Second Nun's Tale* and the *Squire's Tale*, the *Tale of Melibee* and also from the anonymous pseudo-Chaucer *Tale of Beryn* with its *Prologue.*[18] As our objective is not only localisation of the language but also to have a wider repertoire of the forms from the Beryn Scribe,

17 Although we refer to forms as belonging (or not) to Essex, features of Middle English orthography had distributions of different extents and densities and were not confined by political or administrative boundaries. Nor do the authors of the paper suppose this. The county boundaries in the *Atlas* are used as a convenient method for dividing up the geographical space and discussion about Essex as a provenance is likewise intended as a convenient way of referring to the purported provenance of the Beryn Scribe, without being too precise about it. In fact, he is made to be of South Essex, according to the *Atlas*. We are concerned simply to consider the features identified in his manuscript productions, jointly and severally, as being typical of the area in which his Beryn manuscript was localised.

18 The source of our transcription for AC 455 has been a digitised version of the manuscript online at https://www.senshu-u.ac.jp/socio/ms_anglo/anglo/shahon/ss/ct/ct58/kmview.html. We are grateful to Dr Christopher Hunwick, Archivist at Alnwick Castle, for directing us to this web-site.

we collected data for all the items of the *Atlas* Questionnaire plus other forms that seemed to us of interest, viz. his spellings for: the suffixes -ABLE and -ABLY, the singular and plural preterites of (BE)FALL and WIGHT.[19] We produced individual Linguistic Profiles for each of the *Canterbury Tales* texts, to reveal any variation within a Tale or across the Tales. This has provided us with a far more exhaustive linguistic analysis than afforded by Linguistic Profile 6040.

Close examination of the items and features displayed in each of our Linguistic Profiles shows that the language is fairly consistent across all of them. Only a few forms stand out, mainly – and perhaps not surprisingly – in the *Tale of Beryn* section. Morphological features, such as the endings of 3rd Person Singular Present Indicative or Plural Present Indicative (see Tables 3.2 and 3.3) account for some of the differences.[20] The ending for the singular is almost exclusively a '-th' type ending in the texts we analysed (99%). In our samples, 70% of the endings were <-ith>. Only in the *Tale of Beryn* is there 's' type, with three cases of <-is> (1%), two of these on words in rhyme position. In the plural the forms overall are '-th' type (41%) and '-n' type (36%), with a small number of zero endings (10%). However, both the *Tale of Melibee* and the *Tale of Beryn* show a preference for 'th' type endings. In our sample of the *Tale of Beryn* there is only one recorded 'n'-type and that is in rhyme. There are also forms in rhyming position in the *Tale of Beryn* that do not always agree with the patterns in the other texts, which suggests a possible alternative provenance for the original *Tale of Beryn*.[21] In the end, we resolved these data into a single Linguistic Profile for further comparisons.

The comparison of the forms in our Linguistic Profile for the Alnwick Castle manuscript with their distributions displayed in the *Atlas* maps, shows that many of the forms in our combined Linguistic Profile have widespread occurrence across the whole country. Others are very common in the South and Midlands, but not in the North. The following *Atlas* items and forms are selected to fit 'by hand': THEIR <hir[-]>; EACH<ech[e]>; MANY <many>; ANY <eny>; MUCH <muche>; ARE <been>; WILL <woll>; NOT <nat>; BEFORE <to[-]fore[e]>; GAVE <gaff>; UPON <oppon>. Their occurrence is consistent in all the manuscript text samples analysed.

---

19 We have also recorded forms and features that are common to most texts attributed to this scribe.

20 In the tables, the numbers after each form indicate the total frequency of occurrence of the form in all the samples. Where a superscript number in () is attached to the frequency, this gives the number of cases where the form is found in rhyme, so $4^{(2)}$ signifies four tokens of the form with two of them occurring in rhyme position; $3^{(3)}$ would signify three tokens with all of them in rhyme position. Where a number has no superscript annotation, it means that the form was not found in rhyme position.

21 Keith Williamson is preparing a paper on the rhymes of the *Tale of Beryn*.

Table 3.2: 3rd person present singular indicative in Alnwick Castle 455.

	C+	V+	
Physician	-ith 8 -eth 1	-ith 5 -th 1	15
Second Nun	-ith 13 -yth 5	-ith 1	19
Squire	-ith 17 -yth 1	-ith 5 -yth 1	24
Melibee	-ith 48 -yth 7 -eth 6 -ithe 1 -th 1	-th 38 -ith 13	114
Beryn Prol	-ith 22 -es 1[(1)] -eth 1 -yth 1	-ith 2	27
Beryn	-ith 34[(1)] -yth 9 -eth 4 -is 3[(2)]	-ith 12[(2)] -th 3	65
	all: 183 = 69.3%	*all*: 81 = 30.7%	264
	-ith 142 = 54%, -yth 23 = 9%, -eth 11 = 4%, -is 3 = 1%, -es 1 = <1%, -ithe 1 = <1%, -th 1 = <1%	-ith 42 = 16%, -th 38 = 14%, -yth 1 = <1%	

Table 3.3: Present plural indicative in Alnwick Castle 455.

	C-	V-	
Physician	-ith 2	-n 1[(1)]	3
Second Nun	-en 5 -yth 1	-en 3 -ith 1[(1)] -n 1	11
Squire	-yn 4 -en 4 -ith 2 -yne 1[(1)]	-n 1 -en 1	13
Melibee	-ith 8 ∅ 3 -en 1	∅ 3 -th 3 -n 1	19
Beryn Prol	-en 3 -yn 2 -in 1 -eth 1 -ith 1 -yth 1	-en 1 -ith 1	11
Beryn	-ith 8 -yth 1	-ith 4 -th 1 ∅ 1 -n 1[(1)]	16
	all: 49 = 67% **'th'** type: 25 = 27% **'n'** type: 16 = 22%	*all*: 24 = 33% **'th'** type: 10 = 14% **'n'** type: 10 = 14%	73
	-ith 21 = 29%, -en 13 = 18%, -yn 6 = 8%, **-yth** 3 = 4%, ∅ 3 = 4%, -eth 1 = 1%, **-in** 1 = 1%, -yne 1 = 1%	**-ith** 6 = 8%, -n 5 = 6%, **-en** 5 = 7%, -th 4 = 6%, ∅ 4 = 6%	

The features used for the final fitting of CompFT3 were: THESE <these>, <þese>; SHE <she>; HER <hir>, <hire>, <hir*e*>; THEY <they>, <þey>; THEM <hem>, <he*m*>; SUCH <such>, <suche>; WHICH <wich>; EACH <ech>, <eche>, <echon[-]>; MANY <many>, <ma*n*y>; MAN <man>, <ma*n*>; ANY <eny>, <e*n*y>; MUCH much; ARE <been>, <bee*n*>; SHALL *1/3sg* <shal[l]>; SHALL *pl* shul[l]; SHOULD 1/3sg <shuld>; WILL *1/3sg* <wol>, <woll>; WILL *pl* <wol>, <woll>; WOULD *1/3sg* <wold>; FROM <fro>; FROM <from>; FROM <from>; AFTER aftir; THEN <then>, <the*n*>, <þen>, <þe*n*>; THOUGH <thouȝ[e]>, <þouȝ[e]>; IF yf[-]; AGAIN <a-geyn>, <a-geyn>, <ageyn>, <ageyn>; ERE <or(-)>; YET <ȝit>; NOT <nat>; NOR <ne>; WORK *sb* <work[-]>; WORK *vb* <worch[-])>; MIGHT *vb* <myȝt>, <myȝte>; Present Indicative 3sg <-ith>; ASK <ax(-)>; BEFORE *adv / prep* <to-fore>, <to-fore>, <tofore>, <tofore>; CALLED *ppl* <[-]clep(-)>; CHURCH <chirch[e]>; EYES <eyen>; HIGH <hiȝe>; LITTLE <litil>, <litill>, <littil>, <littill>; SAY *pres* <sey(-)>; SAW *pret-sg* saw(e); TWO <to>, <too>; UNTIL <till(-)>, <tyll(-)>; WHETHER <whether>, <whether>, <whether>, <whethir>, <wheþer>, <wheþer>, <wheþir>.

The result of a manual fitting (Map 3.1) is not conclusive since the text seems to contain different layers of language: the language(s) of the original texts and that of the scribe. The possible area where the language of this manuscript can be fitted is very wide. The areas where the forms analysed seem to have coexisted as seen on Map 3.1 are: Essex, London, Surrey, Hertford, Oxfordshire, Warwickshire and the South part of Northamptonshire.

CompFT3 (run using a projection of 20km)[22] similarly produced an inconclusive result, with no single locus. Map 3.2 shows a number of widely distributed large sites of fit along with some smaller ones, geographically scattered. The sites of fit cover: (1) a small part of East Berkshire; (2) North-East Surrey and much of Middlesex; (3) a large area covering central and East Essex, extending into North-East Hertfordshire and South-East Cambridgeshire; (3) a patchwork of areas in the central and West central Midlands, the main area of these in South Northamptonshire and West Warwickshire; (4) a small area of North-East Somerset. The scribal language of AC 455, reckoned as a single entity, seems not to be localisable. Such a result is what one might expect in the case of a text with a degree of mixed language (or *Mischsprache*), including many forms which have a wide geographical currency. The kind of *Mischprache* that seems to be characteristic of the Beryn Scribe's productions is examined

22 The data for the Alnwick Castle MS's Linguistic Profile (6040) were, of course, excluded from consideration by the program.

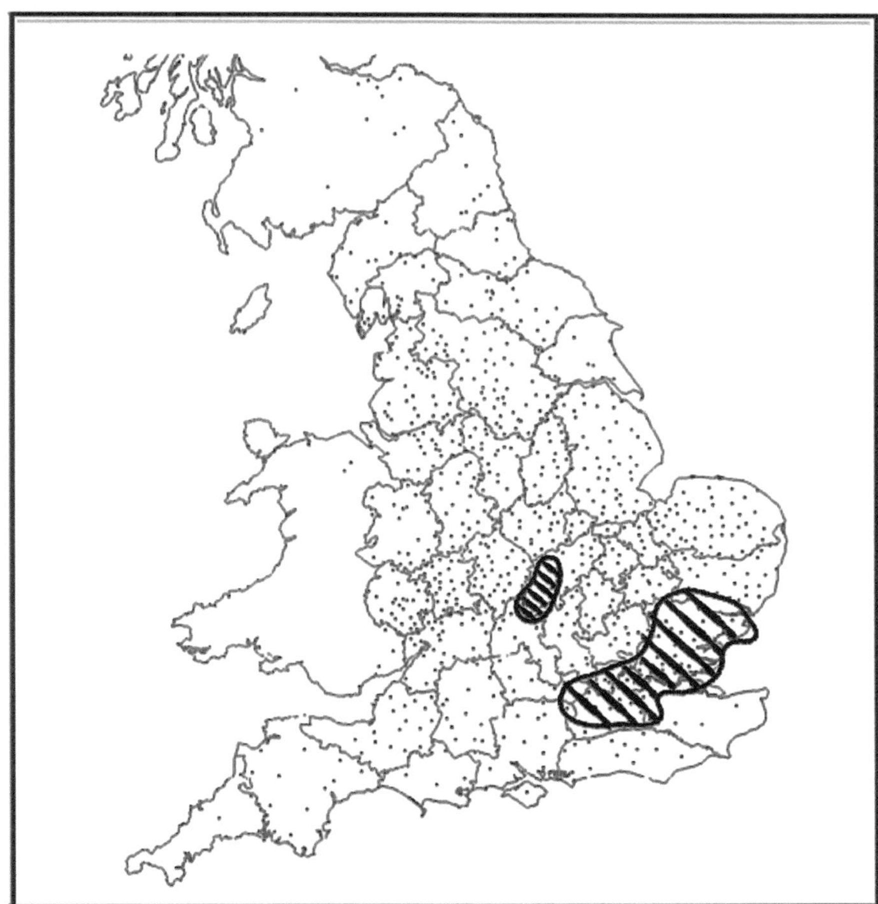

Map 3.1: Result of fit 'by hand' of Alnwick Castle MS 455.

below. (On the notion of *Mischsprache* and its possible types, see *A Linguistic Atlas of Late Mediaeval English*, General Introduction, Ch. 3, <http://www.lel.ed.ac.uk/ihd/elalme/intros/atlas_gen_intro.html>.)

4.1.2 The language of *Prick of Conscience* in Oxford, St John's College MS 57

We had originally lexico-grammatically tagged our samples of text from SJC 57 *Prick of Conscience*. These samples consist of 2,700 lines out of 8,618, being

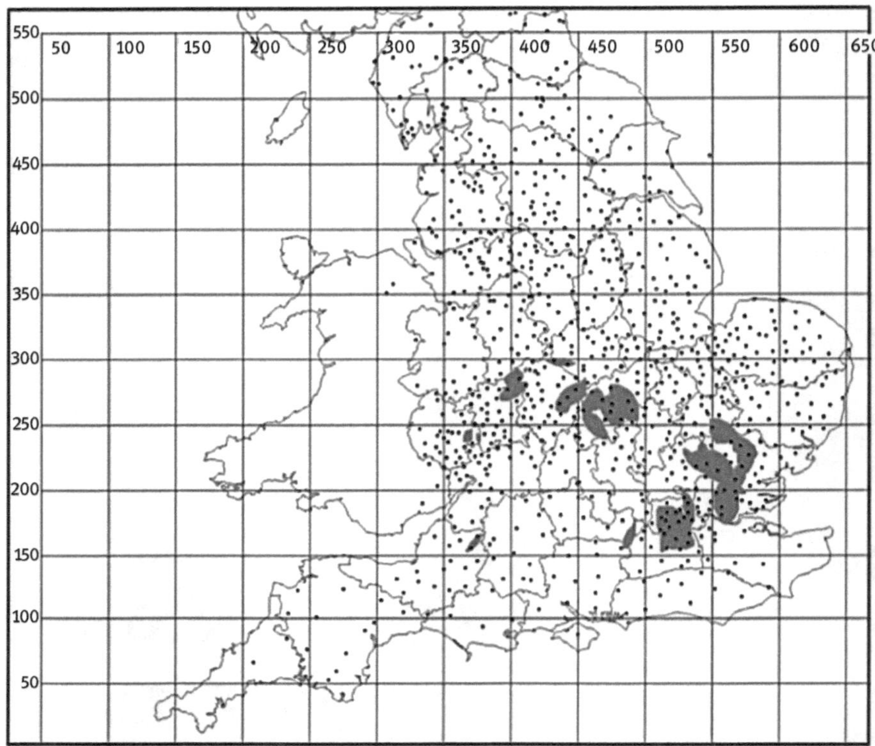

Map 3.2: CompFT3 'fit' of Alnwick Castle 455.

around 20,000 words or 31.3% of the whole text.[23] Comparison with the electronic version of the *Atlas* data reveals both orthographic and morphological features that do not accord with an Essex provenance. A set of salient items and features relating to the orthography are shown in Table 3.4 in bold.

Where frequencies of occurrence are low we consider them as minority forms. However, in the case of some items (e.g. forms for EACH, MUCH, FIRE and HUNDRED) all the majority forms are alien to Essex; the scribe used no alternative forms for these in the text, even if, taking into account his other productions,

23 The tagged portions were selected from the introduction and from the beginning and the end of each of the seven 'books' of the text. SJC 57 is the subject of a separate paper by the authors (Carrillo-Linares and Williamson, 2019), and includes a detailed analysis of its language. It was for this paper that we made the original lexico–grammatical tagging, but we have mined the tagged version for the present chapter.

Table 3.4: Evidence from the *Prick of Conscience* in Oxford, St John's College 57.

SUCH	suche 17 **swilk** 1	18
WHICH	wiche 21 → 42%; the-wich 12 → 24%; **the-wilk** 8 → 16%; wilk 6 → 12%; þe-wiche 2 → 4%; **wilke** 1 → 2%	50
EACH	ilk-a 30 → 35%; ilk 21 → 25%; **ilkon** 16$^{(2)}$ → 19$^{(1)}$%; Jlkon 5 → 6%; Jlk-a 5 → 6%; **ilkone** 4$^{(2)}$ → 5%; **Jlk** 2 → 2%; ilk-oon 1 → 1%; ***ilkone*** 1 → 1%	85$^{(2)}$
MUCH	**mykill** 16$^{(2)}$ **mykil** 9 **muche** 5 **mikill** 3 **mikil** 1	34$^{(2)}$
THERE	*there* 75$^{(2)}$ → 54$^{(1)}$%; there 16$^{(3)}$ → 11$^{(2)}$%; *þere* 16 → 11%; **thore** 12$^{(11)}$ → 9$^{(8)}$%; ther 6 → 4%; þer*e* 5 → 4%; þere 3 → 2%; thare 2$^{(2)}$ → 1%; þare 2$^{(2)}$ → 1$^{(1)}$; **þore** 2$^{(2)}$ → 1$^{(1)}$; ȝer 1 → <1%	140$^{(22)}$
WORLDLY	**wordely** 2	2
FIRE	fei*re* 25$^{(2)}$ **feir** 10 fi*re* 1$^{(1)}$	36$^{(3)}$
HUNDRED	**hundrit** 7	7
AMONG	amonge 8$^{(5)}$ among 8$^{(1)}$ a-monge 2$^{(1)}$ **amang** 1	19$^{(7)}$
KNOW	knowe 17$^{(3)}$ → 41$^{(7)}$%; knowis 5$^{(3)}$ → 12$^{(7)}$%; knowen 4$^{(2)}$ → 10$^{(5)}$%; knowing 4$^{(2)}$ → 10$^{(5)}$%; knowying 2$^{(1)}$ → 5$^{(2)}$%; **knawe** 2$^{(2)}$ → 5$^{(5)}$%; knowithe 2 → 5%; know 2 → 5%; knowith 1 → 2%; **knawen** 1$^{(1)}$ → 2%; **knaw** 1 → 2%; knowinge 1$^{(1)}$ → 2$^{(2)}$%	42$^{(15)}$
ONE	oon 15 a 10 **an** 5 **ane** 2	32

we might have expected the scribe to substitute them with more southern forms. <feir[e]> (FIRE) is mainly attested in Norfolk and North Suffolk. The forms for EACH, MUCH and WHICH that show no palatalisation of /k/ occur very frequently in the text, but are not recorded in Essex. <hundrit> (HUNDRED) is a rare form, recorded (the Alnwick Castle Linguistic Profile aside) only in three Linguistic Profiles in West Norfolk, North Devon and Surrey.

Among the morphological peculiarities of this text are the endings for the 3rd Person Singular, as shown in Table 3.5. The most frequent representation of the 3rd Person Singular indicative ending is <-is>. This is a salient feature of Northern (including Lincolnshire) and North Midlands texts.[24] There are only occasional occurrences in the South. Moreover, for the 3rd Person Plural, as shown in Table 3.6,

24 See *Atlas*: Dot Map, 3sg pres ind: '-is' and '-ys'.

Table 3.5: 3rd person singular present indicative in Oxford, St John's College 57, *Prick of Conscience.*

C+	-is 79$^{(14)}$ → 52$^{(9)}$%; -es 38$^{(9)}$ → 25$^{(6)}$; ∅ 13$^{(10)}$ → 9$^{(7)}$%; -ys 8$^{(2)}$ → 5$^{(1)}$%; -ithe 7 → 5%; -ethe 2 → 1%; -yth 2 → 1%; -s 2$^{(2)}$ → 1$^{(1)}$%; -ith 1 → <1%	152
V+	-s 63(16) → 66(17)%; -is 14(10) → 15(11)%; -the 8 → 8%; -es 6(3) → 6(3)%; -ithe 4 → 4%	95
All	-is 93$^{(24)}$ → 38$^{(10)}$%; -s 65$^{(18)}$ → 26$^{(7)}$%; -es 44$^{(12)}$ → 18$^{(5)}$%; ∅ 13(10) → 5$^{(4)}$%; -ithe 11 → 5%; -the 8→ 3%; -ys 8$^{(2)}$ → 3$^{(<1)}$%; -ethe 2 → <1%; -yth 2 → <1%; -ith 1 → <1%	247

Table 3.6: Present plural indicative in Oxford, St John's College 57, *Prick of Conscience.*

C-	∅ 72$^{(23)}$ → 39$^{(12)}$%; -is 48$^{(23)}$ → 26$^{(12)}$%; -es 23$^{(7)}$ → 12$^{(4)}$%; -en 19$^{(1)}$ → 10$^{(<1)}$%; -ithe 11$^{(1)}$ → 6$^{(<1)}$%; -ys 5$^{(2)}$ → 3$^{(<1)}$%; -ith 4$^{(1)}$ → 2$^{(<1)}$%; -yn 2 → <1%; -ythe 1 → <1%	185
V-	∅ 21$^{(5)}$ → 40(9)%; -n 8 → 15%; -s 8$^{(4)}$ → 15(8)%; -ithe 6 → 11%; -is 5(3) → 9(6)%; -se 3$^{(3)}$ → 6(6)%; -the 1 → 2%; -ith 1 → 2%	53
All	∅ 93$^{(28}$) → 39$^{(12)}$%; -is 53$^{(26)}$ → 22$^{(11)}$%; -es 23$^{(7)}$ → 10$^{(3)}$%; -en 19$^{(1)}$ → 8$^{(<1)}$%; -ithe 17$^{(1)}$ → 7$^{(<1)}$%; -n 8 → 3%; -s 8$^{(4)}$ → 3$^{(2)}$%; -ith 5$^{(1)}$ → 2$^{(<1)}$%; -ys 5$^{(2)}$ → 2$^{(<1)}$%; -se 3$^{(3)}$ →; -yn 2 → <1%; -ythe 1 → <1%; -the 1 → <1%	238

there are 93 (39%) instances of no inflexion (out a total of 238 tokens). Zero endings were not recorded systematically in the *Atlas*. Grammars of Middle English treat the absence of inflection in present plural verb forms as a Northern and North Midlands phenomenon. Of verbs with an inflectional plural ending, <-is> is the preferred form with 53 (22%) of tokens. Other 's' types are: <-es> and <-ys>, which occurs only post-consonant; <-s>, which only occurs after a vowel; and <-se>, also only post-vowel. '-s' type is typically northern and extends in the East through Lincolnshire as far south as The Wash.[25] Although the *Atlas* data for Plural Present Indicative were only collected for the Northern area of survey, the distribution of 's' type endings ceases before the southern edge of the distribution of Northern survey points. The implication is that it is not to be expected in the southern area.

Since, on this linguistic evidence, Essex did not seem to us to be a convincing localisation for this text, we attempted ourselves to localise it by using different assemblages of the manuscript forms, first 'by hand' using electronic *Atlas* Dot

25 See *Atlas*: Dot Map, Pres ind pl: '-s' type, incl abbr. *-es* and *-us*.

Map 3.3: Result of fit 'by hand' of Oxford,St John's College 57, *Prick of Conscience*.

Maps and User-defined Maps, secondly by using CompFT3. The assemblage for fitting 'by hand' (Maps 3.3) was: THEIR <þeir>, <hir>; EACH <ilk>; ANY <eny>; MUCH <mykill>, <mikill>; ARE <are>, <been>; WILL <woll>; NOT <nat>, <nouȝt[e]>; BEFORE <to[-]fore[e]>; 3rd sg present indicative '-s', '-th'. The features used for CompFT3 fitting of Oxford, St John's College 57, *Prick of Conscience* (Maps 3.4) were: THESE these þese; THEY <they>, <þey>; THEM <hem>, <hem(-)>, <he*m*>; THEIR <þeir>, <their>; SUCH <suche>; WHICH <[-]wich[-]>, <wich[-]>; WHICH <the-wilk>, <the-wilke>, <wilk>, <wilke>, <þe-wilk>, <þe-wilke>; EACH <ilk[-]>; MAN <man>; ANY <eny>, <eny>; MUCH <mikil[l]>, <mykil[l]>; ARE <are>; WERE <were>;

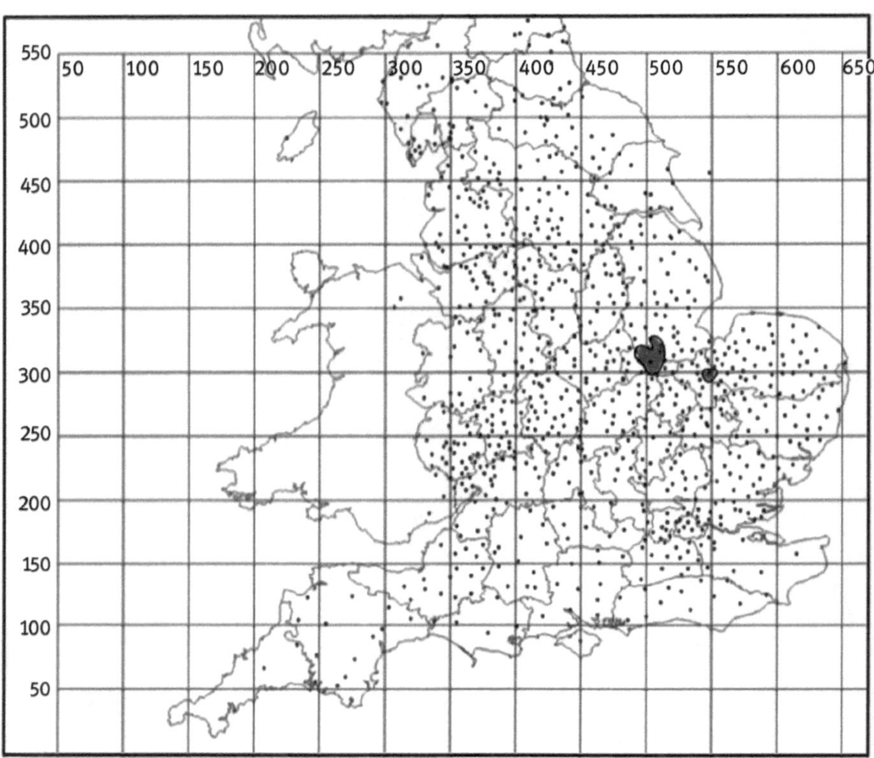

Map 3.4: CompFT3 'fit' of Oxford,St John's College 57, *Prick of Conscience*.

SHALL *1/3 sg* <shal>, <shall>; SHALL *pl* <shul>, <shull>; WILL <woll>; WOULD <wold>; THEN <þen>, <þe*n*>, <then>, <the*n*>; THAN <than>, <þan>; THAN <then>, <þen>; THOUGH <thouȝ(e)>, <þouȝ(e)>; IF <yf>, <yff>; SINCE *conj* <sithen[-]>, <sithe*n*[-]>; YET <ȝit>; NOT <nat>; NOT <nauȝt[e]>, <nouȝt[e]>; THERE <ther[e]>, <þer[e]>; THROUGH <thurgh>, <þurgh>; Sb-pl <-is>, <-ys>; Present Indicative 3sg: <-is>; CALLED <callid>; CHURCH <chirch(e)>; CHURCH <kirk[e]>; LITTLE <litil>, <litill>; TOGETHER <to[-]gidir[-]>. When alternative forms for the same item have a considerable number of occurrences, we have used both for the assemblage for fitting. The possible areas of localisation for both fittings are shown in Maps 3.3 and 3.4.

Our conclusion about the provenance of the *Prick of Conscience* in SJC 57 is that the scribe deploys a kind of language that is not inconsistent with those of texts from the North-East or Central Midlands. The language of this manuscript version fits within the area covered by North-West Norfolk, Isle of Ely, Soke of Peterborough, North Northamptonshire, Rutland and South Lincolnshire.

Thus, given the above re-evaluation of provenance, the proposition

(1) the *language* of Alnwick Castle 455 is of Essex
(2) the *scribe* of Oxford, St John's College 57 = the *scribe* of Alnwick Castle 455
(3) ∴ the *language* of Oxford, St John's College 57 is of Essex

collapses on closer examination of the linguistic evidence – if it was not already dubious in principle (see §4.1 Provenance above).

4.2 Language consistency

Another related belief about the Beryn Scribe is that the language of the manuscripts copied by him is consistent throughout. It has been accepted that in all the texts he copied the spelling forms were the same as those recorded in Linguistic Profile 6040 as representing the language for AC 455, with "only a few extra variant spellings." (Matheson 2008: 49). The linguistic evidence provided for any of the *Brut Chronicle* manuscripts and the *Life of Our Lady* cited in Mosser and Mooney (2014: 70–71) is insufficient to take such a claim for granted.[26] The authors compare sixteen items,[27] twelve of which comprise a limited set of features which seem to be a set of 'idiosyncratic' forms which the scribe reproduces in all his copies. The other four are frequently occurring and widespread forms. They do not serve for attempting to establish the provenance of the scribe's language: they are either not geographically distinctive, being used almost everywhere in the country and by numerous other writers and copyists or they are sporadic or occur rarely.[28] Regarding the manuscripts containing *Canterbury Tales*, most of their studies also analyse linguistic aspects which they consider to be 'idiosyncratic'. They compare those features in AC 455 with both the paper and the parchment sections of Helmingham. However, no comparison is made with the other manuscripts produced by the Beryn Scribe, and none of the studies makes any reference to or reveals any details about the works copied in SJC 57.

26 But see footnote 15, where we quote the authors' intentions to make a more detailed linguistic analysis of the Beryn Scribe's manuscripts.

27 They compare evidence for sixteen items in seven manuscripts. The items they use are the following; 'w for v', 'which', 'upon', 'you', 'your', 'if', 'much', 'scl- for sl', 'any', '-ed', 'ij', '-ve', 'strength', 'high', 'such', 'while', 'through'.

28 These forms are those found in the manuscripts they analysed for the items IF, MUCH, ANY and SUCH.

We agree that the scribe has certain orthographic shibboleths that recur across the manuscripts attributed to him and these support the argument in favour of a single person copying them. Apart from the above-mentioned features we have collected others which also show consistency across the Beryn Scribe's productions. Of these features some are not uncommon and were shared by other scribes. Among them, we find consistency in the spelling for the suffix '-able', which apart form two single exceptions (2% of the occurrences) is always spelt '-abil[l]'. There is also a common tendency to spell words of the FACE class with <-ase> rather than <-ace>, and although both spellings occur in all the texts, the occurrences of <-ace> are approximately 28% of the type. Another written feature is the use of <v> instead of <u> for non-initial /v/. In the texts found in SJC 57 only 4.7% of the occurrences are spelt with medial <u>. In CUL Kk.I.3 the percentage of usage of medial <u> is 6.5%. Among the manuscripts containing the *Brut Chronicle*, Tanner 11 shows <u> in 6.4% of the cases in the sample, Hatton 50 in 1.5%, Hrl 6251 in 6.5%. In Mi 255 <u> occurs in 7.1% of the total in 13 occurrences, seven of which are in abbreviations. The exception is Raw C. 901 in which <u> is used in 50.6% in the samples, but 38.27% correspond to cases where there is an abbreviation of the sequence <er> after the /v/ and only 12.34% occur in non-abbreviated environments. The scribal practice in this manuscript seems to be different from the rest in some other aspects too. <u> for non-initial /v/ occurs in 7.6% of potential environments in the samples from AC 455 and in 2.9% in those from Helmingham (both parts).

A different group of written features is found in contracted forms such as <atte> for AT THE, and <butte> for BUT THE. The form <atte> occurs systematically in all the texts, whereas <butte> turns up in three different works only (*Canterbury Tales*, *Prick of Conscience* and *Chronicle of London*). However, in the four manuscripts containing *Brut Chronicle*, in SJC 57 *Parliament of Fowls* and in *Canterbury Tales* in Helmingham paper and parchment there are no attestations of BUT THE in our samples. Only two copies of *Brut Chronicle* (Raw C. 901 and Hatton 50) and that of *Life of Our Lady* show an uncontracted form. Likewise, the forms for THE ONE and THE OTHER are consistent throughout all the texts and occur respectively as: <the- / þe-toon> and <the- / þe-todir> or <the / þe-tothir>. These items were collected only for the northern area of the survey in the *Atlas*, and although the forms found for the Beryn Scribe are not extremely common, the *Atlas* shows them to be scattered in different areas.

Additionally, the spelling <scl-> for etymological 'sl-' is found as a majority form in eleven out of the thirteen texts analysed. This possibly reflects a spoken feature, rather than a purely written one. It is only absent in our samples from Helmingham (paper and parchment). In the electronic version of the *Atlas* it was recorded for the southern area of survey and appears, when mapped, in a very scattered distribution across the South West and South and East. Likewise, the scribe seems to have a strong preference for 'v' instead of 'w' in certain words, such as WOMAN spelt <voman> or WORM spelt <vorm>, and this feature is repeated throughout all his productions. VENUS, however, is spelt with 'w', <wenus>.

The endings for the weak past and the weak past participle are shown in Tables 3.7 and 3.8 and show variation in all the manuscripts analysed. At first sight it looks as if the scribe had no consistency of form in this feature, but closer examination reveals patterning in the endings. The most frequent ending is <-id>, followed by <-ed> and <-yd>. The ending <-it> also turns up in all the Beryn Scribe's copies. In the *Atlas*, the weak past participle only was collected for the southern area of survey, and then only forms other than <-ed>. The electronic *Atlas* data show instances in a scatter of southern Linguistic Profiles,

Table 3.7: Weak past in all MSS.

SJC 57 (PoC)	-id $18^{(1)}$ → $37^{(2)\%}$; -d 16 → $33^{\%}$; -ed 10 → $20^{\%}$; -it 2 → $4^{\%}$; -yd 1 → $2^{\%}$; -de 1 → $2^{\%}$; -t 1 → $2^{\%}$	49
SJC 57 (PoF)	-id 8 → $35^{\%}$; -ed $7^{(1)}$ → $30^{\%}$; -d $6^{(1)}$ → $26^{\%}$; -ithe 1 → $4^{\%}$; -de $1^{(1)}$ → $4^{(4)\%}$	23
SJC 57 (CL)	-id 74 → $59^{\%}$; -ed 33 → $26^{\%}$; -it 17 → $14^{\%}$; -yd 1 → $<1^{\%}$; -d 1 → $<1^{\%}$	126
AC 455	-id $179^{(10)}$ → $69^{(4)\%}$; -d 37 → $14^{\%}$; -ed $29^{(1)}$ → $11^{(<1)\%}$; -yd $23^{(2)}$ → $9^{(<1)\%}$; it $18^{(1)}$ → $7^{(<1)\%}$; -t $2^{(1)}$ → $<1^{(<1)\%}$; -de 2 → $<1^{\%}$; -yt 1 $<1^{\%}$	261
Helmingham (Paper)	-id 41 → $55^{\%}$; -d $17^{(1)}$ → $23(1)^{\%}$; -yd $9^{(1)}$ → $12^{(1)\%}$; -ed $5^{(1)}$ → $7^{(1)\%}$; -t 1 → $1^{\%}$; -dyn 1 → $1^{\%}$	74
Helmingham (Parchment)	-d 3 -yd 2 -ed 1	6
CUL Kk.I.3	-id 20 -ed 7 -de 3 -yd 3 -it 2 -d 1	36
Tanner 11	-id 75 → $48^{\%}$; -ed 34 → $22^{\%}$; -d 24 → $15^{\%}$; -de 15 → $10^{\%}$; -it 7 → $4^{\%}$; -ede 1 → $1^{\%}$; -yd 1 → $<1^{\%}$	157
Mi 225	-id 116 → $45^{\%}$ -ed 69 → $27^{\%}$ -d 56 → $22^{\%}$ -yd 6 → $2^{\%}$ -it 6 → $2^{\%}$ -de 1 → $< 1^{\%}$ -den 1 → $<1^{\%}$ -it 1 → $< 1^{\%}$ -t 1 $< 1^{\%}$	257
Hrl 1337	-id 42 → $74^{\%}$; -d 14 → $25^{\%}$; -ed 7 → $12^{\%}$; -it 3 → $5^{\%}$; -yd 1 → $2^{\%}$	57
Hrl 6251	-id 97 → $46^{\%}$; -ed 80 → $37^{\%}$; -d 28 → $13^{\%}$; -it 12 → $6^{\%}$; -yd 1 → $<1^{\%}$	218
Hatton 50	-id 38 → $59^{\%}$; -ed 4 → $6^{\%}$; -it 3 → $5^{\%}$; -d 1 → $2^{\%}$	64
Raw C. 901	-ed 91 → 56%; -id 34 → 21%; -d 19 → 12%; -yd 13 → 8%; -it 3 → 2%; -ud 1 → <1%; -ede 1 → <1%; -itt 1 → <1%;	163

Table 3.8: Weak past participle in all MSS.

SJC 57 (PoC)	-id $76^{(9)}$ → $48^{(6)}$%; -ed $46^{(6)}$ → $29^{(4)}$%; -yd $10^{(2)}$ → $6^{(1)}$%; -d $9^{(3)}$ → $6^{(4)}$%; -it 8 → 5%; -t 5 → 3%; -de $2^{(2)}$ → $1^{(1)}$%; -ede $2^{(2)}$ → $1^{(1)}$%; -yte 1 → <1%	$159^{(24)}$
SJC 57 (PoF)	-id $20^{(3)}$; -ed $8^{(1)}$; -it 4; -yd 2; -d 1; -de $1^{(1)}$	36
SJC 57 (CL)	-id 90 → 46%; -it 49 → 25%; -ed 44 → 23%; -d 5 → 3%; -yd 4 → 2%; -t 2 → 1%; -de 1 → <1%	195
AC 455	-id $211^{(53)}$ → $62^{(16)}$%; -yd $48^{(8)}$ → $14^{(2)}$%; -it $44^{(3)}$ → $13^{(<1)}$%; -ed $24^{(3)}$ → $7^{(<1)}$%; -de $7^{(5)}$ → $2^{(2)}$%; -d $6^{(1)}$ → $2^{(<1)}$%; -yde $1^{(1)}$ → <$1^{(<1)}$%; -t $1^{(1)}$ → <1($^{<1}$)%	342(75)
Helmingham (Paper)	-id $70^{(7)}$ → 67(7)%; -yd $25^{(4)}$ → $24^{(4)}$%; -ed 4 → 4%; -it 3 → 3%; -d 2 → 2%	104
Helmingham (Parchment)	-id 32 → 70%; -d 6 → 13%; -yd 5 → 11%; -it 2 → 4%; -t 1 → 2%	46
CUL Kk.I.3	-id 70 → 64%; -ed 19 → 17%; -it 8 → 7%; -yd 8 → 7%; -et 2 → 3%; -d 2 → 2%; ∅ 1 → <1%	110
Tanner 11	-id 560 → $62^{\%}$; -ed 18 → $19^{\%}$; -d 8 → $8^{\%}$; -it 5 → $5^{\%}$; -yd 4 → $4^{\%}$; -t 1 → $1^{\%}$	96
Mi 225	-id 87 → $80^{\%}$; -ed 12 → $11^{\%}$; -it 4 → $4^{\%}$; -yd 2 → $2^{\%}$; -de 2 → $2^{\%}$; -d 2 → $2^{\%}$	109
Hrl 1337	-id 70 → 71%; ed 16 → 16%; -it 5 → 5%; -yd 4 → 4%; -d 3 → 3%	98
Hrl 6251	-id 71 → 71%; -ed 19 → 19%; -it 5 → 5%; -yd 2 → 2%; -d 2 → 2%	99
Hatton 50	-id 28 -ed 5 yd 4 -it 1	38
Raw C. 901	-id 31 → 59%; -ed 15 → 28%; -it 3 → 6%; -yd 2 → 4%; -d 2 → 4%	53

including two in Essex in addition to AC 455.[29] Mooney and Matheson (2003) and Mosser and Mooney (2014) consider this ending for both the past and past participle to be one of the scribe's idiosyncrasies. This ending occurs with low frequency in most of his copies: its proportions of occurrence are usually from 3% to 7% in most texts. There are higher proportions in SJC 57 *Parliament of Fowls* (11%) and in the AC 455 texts (13%). Most marked with respect to this

29 The ending is also found in the North for both weak past and weak past participle, where it is attested mainly in the North West Midlands. Data for the weak past in the South is lacking in the electronic *Atlas*.

form is SJC 57 *Chronicle of London* where it occurs in 25% of the instances marking weak past participle and in 14% marking weak preterite forms. The form of the verbal ending depends on the final consonant in the stem: <-it> is used when the final consonants in the verbal forms are 'd','g' or the sequences 'ng', 'bl' or 'dr'; <-ed> is used after a nasal and occasionally after 't', 's' and 'x'; <-id> and the alternative <-yd> are used after any other consonant and only rarely after a vowel; <-d> is used after a vowel, 'i' / 'y' or 'u' / 'w'.

Five other uncommon forms deserve attention, since they occur throughout the Beryn Scribe's productions with consistency and high frequency. Among the uncommon spellings is <ʒew[e]> (YOU), which occur in every manuscript copied by him except for Raw C. 901, where there are no attestations of YOU in our sample. Very occasionally alternative forms turn up in the other texts, but they constitute only a tiny proportion of the forms for the item. The item YOU was not collected systematically for the southern area of survey in the *Atlas*, but occurrences of the spellings <ʒew> and <yew> were noted. However, including the northern area of survey these spellings are recorded in only six linguistic profiles, in addition to that for AC 455. One is localised in Norfolk, one in Lincolnshire, two in Worcestershire and one in Somerset, so that the form has no clear provenance.

The form consistently used by the scribe for UPON is <oppon>. The spelling with <o> and <pp> is not very common according to the *Atlas* data, although the item was collected only for the Northern area. HUNDRED is spelt with final <it>, i.e. <hundrit>. This word does not turn up in all the texts and occurrences are restricted to three manuscripts, but this is the Beryn Scribe's unvarying form. 'pepill' (PEOPLE) is likewise rare in the *Atlas* data, but the scribe is again consistent in this spelling, as with the form he uses for the simple past of the verb FALL, which is always <fill>, and likewise he has <befill> for BEFALL. Such adherence solely to an unvarying form is unusual, especially in long texts. More usual in Middle English texts of this period is the favouring of one or maybe two forms most of the time against a set of occasional minor variants.

In spite of this apparent consistency, there is a high degree of variation to be observed in forms for items that might be used either to identify the dialectal provenance of a manuscript copy or, in the case of those features common to all the scribe's copies, to identify his area of origin. Our analysis is based on application of an extended version of the *Questionnaire* used in the electronic *Atlas*.[30] We invoked the items and sub-items without regard to their geographical

30 This version contains 504 main items with 331 sub-items.

restriction, the actual number varying, of course, according to the attestations of each manuscript and work. A selection of items where consistency along the scribe's production is not found is offered below, although the list is far from being exhaustive. We group the features in three categories:

a) words with spellings which imply phonological differences, for example those in which the spelling suggests absence or present of palatalisation, e.g. EACH, WHICH, MUCH, and CHURCH;
b) verbal morphological features, e.g. 3rd Singular Present, Plural Present, Present Participle, and Present Plural form of BE;
c) certain common lexical items, e.g. AGAIN, AGAINST, NOT, MANY, THEIR.

The different forms for WHICH and EACH are shown in Tables 3.9 and 3.10. The spellings for the forms for EACH (Table 3.9) in most manuscripts imply a palatal post-tonic consonant, /tʃ/. The 'lk' type occurs in only two of our manuscript samples: once in AC 455 *Second Nun's Tale* as <ilk-oon> in rhyme position,[31] but exclusively in SJC 57 *Prick of Conscience*. The occurrence in the AC 455 manuscript might hint that this 'lk' form had slipped through from the scribe's own repertoire. In principle, if the 'lk' type found in the *Prick of Conscience* were in the exemplar they could have been altered if the scribe had so wished to do so. Change to palatalised types are to be observed in copies of the *Prick of Conscience* localised in the Midlands and South. That the scribe perpetrated them consistently in his copy suggests familiarity and acceptance of them, if they originated in his exemplar. Otherwise we would have to suppose that he imposed these forms himself.

The data for WHICH (Table 3.10) are slightly different. Only SJC 57 *Prick of Conscience* has forms with 'lk', but only in a minority of cases, 15x being 30% of forms. Otherwise, the form is <wiche> 21x (42%) and with preceding determiner, <the-wiche> 12x (24%), <þe-wiche> 2x (4%). The northern origins of *Prick of Conscience* would explain the presence of the 'lk' forms. They may have been in the exemplar from which the scribe copied and he brought them over into his copy. If the exemplar contained the northern forms, the scribe took the trouble to change only some leaving almost one-third of the forms where the reflex implies a non-palatalised consonant. The proportion is high enough to allow us to consider that <wilk[e]> was not alien to him, although clearly not his preferred form. <wiche> is the preferred form in the other texts within SJC 57, but <wich> occurs 3x out of 23 (13%) occurrences for the item in the *Parliament of Fowls*, and

31 The rhyme falls on the second syllable and is with <aloon> in the next line, ll. 339–40 (corresponding to ll. 377–78 in the *Riverside Chaucer* edition, p. 267).

Table 3.9: EACH in all MSS.

SJC 57 (PoC)	ilk-a 30 → 35%; ilk 21 → 25%; ilkon 16[(2)] → 19%; Jlkon 5 → 6%; Jlk-a 5 → 6%; ilkone 4[(2)] → 5%; Jlk 2 → 2%; ilk-oon 1 → 1%; ilkon*e* 1 → 1%	85
SJC 57 (PoF)	eche 7	7
SJC 57 (CL)	eche 1 euery-chone 1	2
AC 455	ech 17 → 38%; eche 13 → 29%; echone 4[(3)] → 9[(7)]%; echon 3[(3)] → 7[(7)]%; everich 2 → 4%; everichone 1 → 2%; eu*er*ychoon 1[(1)] → 2[(2)]%; ilk 1 → 2%; echon*e* 1[(1)] → 2%; echeon 1 → 2%; ilk-oon 1 → 2%	45[(8)]
Helmingham (Paper)	everych 1 ech 1 echon 1[(1)]	3[(1)]
Helmingham (Parchment)	–	
CUL Kk.I.3	eche 6 ech 3 echoon 1 echon 1 echeone 1 echone 1 eu*er*erych 1 eu*er*ychon 1	15
Tanner 11	eche 2 echon 1	3
Mi 225	eche 5 echoon 2 echon 1	8
Hrl 1337	eche 3 echon 2 eu*er*ychone 1	6
Hrl 6251	eche 5 eche oon 1 echon 1 everychon 1 eu*er*ychone 1	9
Hatton 50	eche 5 echon 1	6
Raw C. 901	echon 1 ech 1 eche-oon 1	3

17x out of 118 (14%) in the *Chronicle of London*. However, his other manuscript productions, in Tanner 11, Hrl 1337, and Hrl 6251 (all *Brut*s) attest <wiche> as dominant. Otherwise, <wich> tends to be predominant in his manuscript copies and <wiche> is rare or absent.

The occurrences for the items MUCH and CHURCH are shown in Table 3.11. The Beryn Scribe's preferred forms for MUCH – as evidenced in his other productions – are <much> or <muche>. However, in SJC 57 *Prick of Conscience* 'much[e]' is the minority type, occurring only in 15% of the sampled text, while the non-palatalised disyllabic type constitutes 85% of the total. Substitution of the disyllabic /k/-forms with monosyllabic /tʃ/-forms such as these, would in principle alter the metric of the line. That said, in other copies of the *Prick of Conscience* localised in to the Midlands and southern counties, MUCH is often realised with disyllabic

Table 3.10: WHICH in all MSS.

SJC 57 (PoC)	wiche 21 → 42%; the-wiche 12 → 24%; the-wilk 8 → 16%; wilk 6 → 12%; þe-wiche 2 → 4%; wilke 1 → 2%	50
SJC 57 (PoF)	wiche 16; wich 2; the-wiche 2; wiche-that 2; wich-that 1	23
SJC 57 (CL)	wiche 38 → 66%; wich 17 → 29%; þe-wiche 2 → 3%; the-wiche 1 → 2%	58
AC 455	wich 31 → 63%; the-wich 9 → 18%; wich-that 6 → 12%; wich-þat 1 → 2%; þe-wich 1 → 2%; wiche 1 → 2%	49
Helmingham (Paper)	wich 35 → 67%; wich-that 11 → 21%; the-wich 4 → 8%; wich-þat 2 → 4%	52
Helmingham (Parchment)	wich 6; the-wich 3; þe-wich 2; wich-that 1	12
CUL Kk.I.3	wich 35 → 75%; the-wich 11 → 23%; wiche 1 → 2%	47
Tanner 11	wiche 4 the-wiche 2 þe-wich 2 þe-wiche 2 +te-wiche 1 wich 1	12
Mi 225	wich 4 wiche 3 the wiche 2 þe wiche 2 þe wich 1 wich that 1	13
Hrl 1337	wiche 4 þe-wiche 4 the-wiche 3 wiche-þat 2	13
Hrl 6251	wiche 8 wich 1 the-wiche 2 the-wich 1 þe-wiche 1 þe-wich 1	14
Hatton 50	wich 11 wiche 1	12
Raw C. 901	wich 2 the-wich 1 þe-wich 1 the-wiche 1	5

'mVchVl' type (with 'ch' instead of 'k') or the monosyllabic 'mVch[e]' type. In the Beryn Scribe's production, only in Helmingham *Squire's Tale* is there another occurrence of the non-palatalised type.[32]

CHURCH is not attested in all the manuscripts. There are instances of it only in six works in five manuscripts. <chirch> is the preferred form in four of the manuscripts, lacking in the two SJC 57 texts which attest the item: *Prick of Conscience* and *Chronicle of London*, the former having <chirche> and <kirk>, the latter <chirche>, but with plural <chirchis> 1x. Raw C. 901 alone has <church> (1x). The instances of <kirk> in SJC 57 *Prick of Conscience* occur in both in non-rhyming and rhyming positions. In the *Prick of Conscience*, the tendency seems to have

32 '… / There ["where"] he is hurt that is as mykil to seyn / ȝee mot with the plat swerd ageyn / Stroke hym in the wound and it wol close', ll. 157–59 (corresponding to ll. 163–65 in the *Riverside Chaucer* edition).

Table 3.11: MUCH and CHURCH in all MSS.

SJC 57 (PoC)	mykill $16^{(2)}$ mykil 9 muche 5 mikill 3 mikil 1	$34^{(2)}$	chirche 5 kirk $4^{(3)}$ chirchis *gen* 3 chirche *gen* 1	$13^{(3)}$
SJC 57 (PoF)	–	–	–	–
SJC 57 (CL)	muche 19 much 3	22	chirche 8 chirchis *pl* 1	9
AC 455	much $28^{(1)}$ muche 1 mych 1	$30^{(1)}$	chirch $14^{(2)}$ church 2 chirchward $2^{(2)}$	$18^{(4)}$
Helmingham (Paper)	much 5 mykil 1	6	chirch $2^{(1)}$	$2^{(1)}$
Helmingham (Parchment)	much 2	2	–	–
CUL Kk.I.3	much 3 muche 1	4	chirch 3	3
Tanner 11	muche 21 much 5	26	–	–
Mi 225	much 25 muche 13	38	–	–
Hrl 1337	muche 23 much 10 much*e* 1	34	–	–
Hrl 6251	muche 27 much 6	33	–	–
Hatton 50	much 37	37	–	–
Raw C. 901	much 4 muche 3	7	church 1	1

been to retain <kirk> in rhyming position, although instances of <chirch> and <chirche> also occur in rhyme.[33]

Verbal morphological features that show variation are: 3rd Singular Present, Plural Present, Weak Past, Weak Past Participle, Present Participle, and Present Plural form of BE. Regarding the endings for the 3rd person singular present indicative, as shown in Table 3.12, SJC 57 *Prick of Conscience* shows a significant majority of '-s' type endings, constituting 85% of the total occurrences. These occurrences fall in both rhyming and non-rhyming positions. 10% of the endings are '-th' type. 5% are verbs with no ending for the 3rd person singular, the majority of these occurring in rhyming position. The picture found in *Prick of Conscience* is not repeated in any of the other works in SJC 57,

33 Global numbers for the occurrences of 'kirk' and 'chVrch[e]' types in the *Prick of Conscience* collected for the whole manuscript are: in rhyming position, 'kirk' 7x and 'chirch[e]' 3x. In non-rhyming position, 'chirch[e]' 25x and 'kirk' (5x).

Table 3.12: 3rd person present singular indicative in all MSS.

SJC 57 (PoC)	-is $93^{(24)}$ → $38^{(10)}$%; -s $65^{(18)}$ → $26^{(7)}$%; -es $44^{(12)}$ → $18^{(5)}$%; ∅ 13(10) → $5^{(4)}$%; -ithe 11 → 5%; -the 8→ 3%; -ys $8^{(2)}$ → $3^{(<1)}$%; -ethe 2 → <1%; -yth 2 → <1%; -ith 1 → <1%	247
SJC 57 (PoF)	-ithe $24^{(3)}$ → $49^{(6)}$%; -ith $13^{(2)}$ → $27^{(4)}$%; -ethe 3 → 6%; -yth $3^{(1)}$ → $6^{(2)}$%; -eth 2 → 4%; -the 2 → 4%; -is 1 → 2%;-ythe 1 → 2%	49
SJC 57 (CL)	-ithe 3	3
AC 455	**-ith $179^{(3)}$** → $68^{(1)}$%; **-th 43** → 16%; **-yth 24** → 9%; -eth 12 → 5%; -is $3^{(2)}$ → $1^{(<1)}$%; -ithe 1 → <1%;-es $1^{(1)}$ → <1%	$263^{(3)}$
Helmingham (Paper)	**-ith 73** → 71%; **-ith 12** → 12%; -yth 12 → 12%; -eth 5 → 5%; -ythe 1 → 1%	103
Helmingham (Parchment)	**-ith 23** → 42%;**-th 15** → 34%;-yth 6 → 14%	44
CUL Kk.I.3	-ith 70 → 81%; yth 9 → 11%; -th 4 → 5%; -∅ 3 → 4%; -jth 2 → 2%; -eth 1 → 1%; -ist 1 → 1%	90
Tanner 11	-ithe 6 -ith 5	11
Mi 225	-ith 13 -ithe 12	25
Hrl 1337	-ith 2 -ithe 2 -[t]h 1 -ethe 1 -ythe 1	7
Hrl 6251	-ithe 1 -yth 1 -ith 2	4
Hatton 50	-ith 6 -yth 3	9
Raw C. 901	-ith 16 -ithe 2 -th 2	20

or in any other manuscripts copied by the scribe. <-ith(e)>, <-yth(e)> and, in a minority of cases, <-eth[e]> are found in the rest of the works, although AC 455 shows three instances of '-s' type endings as well, but with only one in non-rhyming position. Retention of the '-s' type verbal endings of his *Prick of Conscience* exemplar suggests that they were acceptable for him and part of a repertoire of forms with which he was familiar. Changing these would not have disrupted the metric structure of the poem. The number of instances of these endings in SJC 57 *Prick of Conscience* is too large to be considered any sort of accidental retention.

Regarding the Present Indicative Plural endings (see Table 3.13), the degree of variation in forms ending in '-s', '-n' or '-th' and ∅ is high. In the manuscripts containing Chaucer's works the tendency to have '-n' type endings is higher than

Table 3.13: Present plural indicative in all MSS.

SJC 57 (PoC)	∅ $93^{(28)}$ → $39^{(12)}$%; -is $53^{(26)}$ → $22^{(11)}$%; -es $23^{(7)}$ → $10^{(3)}$%; -en $19^{(1)}$ → $8^{(<1)}$%; -ithe $17^{(1)}$ → $7^{(<1)}$%; -n 8 → 3%; -s $8^{(4)}$ → $3^{(2)}$%; -ith $5^{(1)}$ → $2^{(<1)}$%; -ys $5^{(2)}$ → $2^{(<1)}$%; -se $3^{(3)}$ → $1^{(1)}$%; -yn 2 → <1%; -ythe 1 → <1%; -the 1 → <1%	238
SJC 57 (PoF)	-en 6 -∅ $5^{(3)}$ -n 2 -ithe $2^{(1)}$ -ith 1 -ythe 1 -yn 1	$18^{(4)}$
SJC 57 (CL)	-yth 1 -ithe 1	2
AC 455	-ith $33^{(1)}$ → $41^{(1)}$%; -en 18 → 23%; -∅ 7 → 9%; -yn 6 → 8%; -n 5 → 6%; -yth 4 → 5%; -th 4 → 5%; -in 1 → 1%; -eth 1 → 1%; -yne $1^{(1)}$ → $1^{(1)}$%	$81^{(2)}$
Helmingham (Paper)	-yn $22^{(1)}$ → 43%; -ith 11 → 22%; -en 5 → 10%; -∅ $4^{(1)}$ → 8%; -n $4^{(1)}$ → $8^{(2)}$%; -yth 3 → 6%; -in 1 → 2%; -th 1 → 2%	$51^{(3)}$
Helmingham (Parchment)	-n 2 -en 1	3
CUL Kk.I.3	-∅ 14 -en 5 -ith 4 -n 3	26
Tanner 11	-en 2 -ith 1 -yn 1	4
Mi 225	-ith 2 -ithe 1 -yth 1 -en 1 +n 1 ∅ 1	7
Hrl 1337	-en 4 -ithe 2 -∅ 1	7
Hrl 6251	-ithe 3 -ith 1	4
Hatton 50	-ith 2	2
Raw C. 901	-n 1	1

any other endings, although '-th' type occur as well. Conversely, in most of the *Brut Chronicle* manuscripts and in SJC 57 *Chronicle of London* we only find a '-th' type ending. In CUL Kk.I.3 *Life of Our Lady* the most frequent ending is ∅, followed by '-n' type and then '-th' type. In SJC 57 *Prick of Conscience* ∅ and 's' type occur in almost equal proportions (39% and 38% respectively), followed by, in almost equal proportions, 'n' and 'th' types (12% and 11% respectively).

We compared the output for this feature in SJC 57 *Prick of Conscience* with the other *Prick of Conscience* manuscripts genealogically most closely related in a sub-group of Group II (in the classification of Lewis and Macintosh 1982). Although all the texts of the sub-group overlap in their inflectional types for this ending, each copyist imposed a distinctive combination of the different types with varying frequencies of use. In the present plural, all these related *Prick of Conscience* texts are '-s'-type dominant for this ending. However, ∅ is also a shared feature of texts in the sub-group and also the '-n' type, while the '-th' type is shared only with the copy of the *Prick of Conscience* found in Cambridge Magdalene College F.4.18.[34]

The present participle forms show diversity only in SJC 57 *Prick of Conscience* (see Table 3.14), where the following endings are found: <-and> (34x), <-ande> (12x), <-yng> (7x), <-ynge> (1x), <-inge> (1x), <-ing> (1x), <-ond> (1x). In the other manuscripts only forms ending in <-ng[e]> are present with the exception of 1x of <-and> occurring in rhyme in AC 455. In the case of the *Prick of Conscience*, the northern origin of the poem would explain the presence of the northern '-nd[e]' type endings for the present participle and the scribe decided to leave them unaltered. We cannot tell if the Beryn Scribe's exemplar also contained '-ng[e]' type

Table 3.14: Present participle in all MSS.

SJC 57 (PoC)	-and $34^{(17)}$ → 60%; -ande $12^{(12)}$ → $21^{(21)}$%; -yng $7^{(1)}$ → 12%; -ynge $1^{(1)}$ → $2^{(2)}$%; -inge $1^{(1)}$ → $2^{(2)}$%; -ing $1^{(1)}$ → $2^{(2)}$%; ˙ond $1^{(1)}$ → $2^{(2)}$	$57^{(34)}$
SJC 57 (PoF)	-yng 7 -ing $6^{(1)}$	13
SJC 57 (CL)	-ing 14 -yng 10	24
AC 455	-ing $55^{(5)}$ → 62%; -yng $33^{(2)}$ → 37%; -and $1^{(1)}$ → $1^{(1)}$%	89
Helmingham (Paper)	-yng $11^{(2)}$ -ing$7^{(3)}$	18
Helmingham (Parchment)	-yng 2 -ing 1	3
CUL Kk.I.3	-ing 10 -yng 7	17
Tanner 11	-yng 5 -ing 2 -ynge 1	8
Mi 225	-ing 8 -yng 6 -ynge 1	15
Hrl 1337	-ing 7	7
Hrl 6251	-ing 1 -yng 1	2
Hatton 50	-ing 6 -yng 2	8
Raw C. 901	-ing 2 -yng 1 -eng 1	4

34 A more detailed account of the relation of the *Prick of Conscience* in SJC 57 and the other genealogically-related texts in the group is covered in Carrillo-Linares and Williamson (2019).

endings, which he took over as well or if he was solely responsible for introducing them.

The variant forms for the plural present of BE are shown in Table 3.15. The commonest form in all *Brut* manuscripts and in the *Life of Our Lady* is 'been', while 'be' occurs as a minority form. <been> is also the commonest form found in AC 455 where it occurs in 67% of the occurrences, with <be> as a variant (19% of cases). <beth> (8x) is also a minor variant, along with <beith> (1x) and also <is> (4x). Both the Helmingham paper and parchment show a majority form 'ben' which is not found in any other of the Beryn Scribe's productions. Finally, SJC 57 *Prick of Conscience* deviates completely from the Southern and Midlands forms found in the manuscripts, and shows a majority form <are> in two-thirds of cases (105 → 64%), although there are also some instances of

Table 3.15: Present plural of BE in all MSS.

SJC 57 (PoC)	are $105^{(3)}$ → $64^{(2)}$%; been 22 → 14%; is 17 → 10%; be 13 → 8%; ar 2 → 1%; bee 1 → <1%; er 1(1) → $<1^{(<1)}$%; ere $1^{(1)}$ → $<1^{(<1)}$%; ys $1^{(1)}$ → $<1^{(<1)}$%	163
SJC 57 (PoF)	been 5 be 2 bene 1 are 1	9
SJC 57 (CL)	been 1 be 1 are 1	3
AC 455	been $66^{(1)}$ → $67^{(1)}$%; be $19^{(2)}$ → $19^{(2)}$%; beth 8 → 8%; is 4 → 4%; beith 1 → 1%	$98^{(3)}$
Helmingham (Paper)	ben 26 → 62%; be 9 → 21%; is 3 → 7%; been 2 → 5%; beth 1 → 2%; bene $1^{(1)}$ → $2^{(2)}$%	42
Helmingham (Parchment)	ben 5 be 3	8
CUL Kk.I.3	been 4 be 1	5
Tanner 11	been 2	2
Mi 225	be 1	1
Hrl 1337	been 5 be 1	6
Hrl 6251	been 4 be 2	6
Hatton 50	been 4 be 1	5
Raw C. 901	been 1 be 1	2

<bene> (14%) and <be> (8%) as in the rest of the manuscripts. 'is' also occurs as a minor variant (10%).[35]

For the item AGAIN (see Table 3.16) the Beryn Scribe uses 'ageyn[e]' type in most of his copies. <ageyn> has a dense, coherent distribution in Isle of Ely, North Cambridgeshire, Norfolk, Central Suffolk. The distribution extends from this sporadically across the North Midlands and also southwards through Essex to London. The variant with final 'e' occurs very sporadically and widely scattered within this same area of distribution, with a few further attestations in the central South.[36] However, Raw C. 901 has as the dominant form <a[-]ʒeen>. 'a[-]ʒeen'

Table 3.16: AGAIN in all MSS.

SJC 57 (PoC)	ageyn $14^{(9)}$ gayn 1	$15^{(9)}$
SJC 57 (PoF)	ageyn 2	2
SJC 57 (CL)	ageyn 7 agey*ne* 4 a-geyn 3	14
AC 455	a-geyn $11^{(2)}$ ageyn $5^{(2)}$ agey*ne* $2^{(1)}$ a-ʒe $2^{(2)}$ a-ye $2^{(1)}$ ageyns 1	$23^{(8)}$
Helmingham (Paper)	aʒen 2 a-ʒen 2 ageyn~ $2^{(2)}$ a-gayn 1	$7^{(2)}$
Helmingham (Parchment)	a-geyn 1	1
CUL Kk.I.3	ageyn 6 a-geyn 1	8
Tanner 11	ageyn 5 a-geyn 4 agayn 1	10
Mi 225	ayeyn 12 a-geyn 2	14
Hrl 1337	ageyn 7 agey*ne* 2 a-gey*ne*2	11
Hrl 6251	ageyn 10 a-geyn 3	13
Hatton 50	ageyn 7	8
Raw C. 901	a-ʒeen 9 a-geyn 2	11

35 The occurrence and use of <is> for ARE in SJC 57 *Prick of Conscience* seems to reflect a partial operation of the Northern Present Tense Rule, for which there is evidence from other verbal forms in his copy. Given the linguistic origins of the *Prick of Conscience*, the Beryn Scribe may well have encountered this in his exemplar. This matter is discussed further in Carrillo-Linares and Williamson (2019).

36 See electronic *Atlas:* User Defined Map AGAIN: *ageyn*; User Defined Map: *ageyne*; and *Atlas*: Dot Map, AGAIN: 'medial *-ei-* or *-ey-* (*agein, a-yeyn, oʒeine*, etc)'; Dot Map, AGAIN, 'forms with *-g-* (*a-gayne, ageyn*, etc)'.

forms are otherwise attested in only six *Atlas* Linguistic Profiles, two localised in Norfolk, two in Essex and one each in Northamptonshire and Suffolk. In the paper section of Helmingham the Beryn Scribe also uses forms with medial 'ʒ': <a[-]ʒen> and <aʒen>. The latter variant is attested widely across southern England from Norfolk to the South-West, including the South-West Midlands.[37] These forms co-occur in several places with the <ageyn>, notably in Norfolk, Suffolk, Isle of Ely, Cambridgeshire, North Essex and Hertfordshire.[38] AC 455 has <a[-]ʒe> 2x and <a[-]ye> 3x, but except for one instance of <a[-]ye> these are in rhyme and all occur in the *Tale of Beryn*. This suggests they are imports from the *Beryn* exemplar. <a[-]ʒe> is attested in only two southwestern Linguistic Profiles; a third has <aye>.

For the item AGAINST (see Table 3.17) the spellings are varied, but a high degree of diversity for this item is not unusual. The scribe uses forms with pretonic <g> in *Prick of Conscience* and *Parliament of Fowls* in SJC 57, but his forms have <ʒ> in all the *Brut* manuscripts and in the *Life of Our Lady*. In the

Table 3.17: AGAINST in all MSS.

SJC 57 (PoC)	ageyn 8 agaynes 1 ageynst 1 -ageyn 1 -ageyn*e* 1	12
SJC 57 (PoF)	ageynst 1 ageyn 1	2
SJC 57 (CL)	a-ʒenst 3 ageyn 2 ageyn*e* 1 ageynst 1	7
AC 455	a-geyn 3 a-ʒenst 2 geyn 2 ageyns 1 a-geyn*e* 1 a-gayns 1 a-geyns 1 ageyn 1 a-ʒenste 1 a-ʒe 1[(1)]	14[(1)]
Helmingham (Paper)	aʒenst 3 ageynst 1	4
Helmingham (Parchment)	a-ʒenst 1	1
CUL Kk.I.3	aʒenst 1	1
Tanner 11	a-ʒenst 3	3
Mi 225	a-ʒenst 3	3
Hrl 1337	a-ʒenst 1 aʒenst 1	2
Hrl 6251	–	–
Hatton 50	aʒenst 2	2
Raw C. 901	aʒenst 2 aʒane 1	3

37 See electronic *Atlas*: User Defined Map, AGAIN: *aʒen*.
38 See electronic *Atlas*: User Defined Map, AGAIN: *ageyn*.

Canterbury Tales and *Chronicle of London* manuscripts, he uses both. In AC 455 forms with <ȝ> are in the minority, 4 out of 13 attestations of the item.[39] <g>-forms can occur almost everywhere in the country, but they are attested more frequently in the North.[40] <ȝ>-forms are preferred in the South and Midlands. In East Anglia, and areas in the West, forms with both 'g' and 'ȝ' types seem to have co-existed more frequently than in more northern or southern areas.[41]

The scribe's personal preferences with regard to the item MANY (Table 3.18) are not clear. In some of his productions <many> is the majority form; <meny> occurs as a minority form in SJC 57 *Parliament of Fowls*, but it is the predominant form in *Prick of Conscience* and *Chronicle of London* in that manuscript. In AC 455 it occurs once against dominant <many> (97%). Out of three instances of MANY in each of, CUL Kk.I.3 and, Tanner 11, <meny> occurs 2x in both cases against 1x for <many>. <meny> 2x and <many> 2x occur also in Mi 225. Some instances of 'mony' have also been recorded. The form 'many' is widespread and should not be alien to

Table 3.18: MANY in all MSS.

SJC 57 (PoC)	meny 29 many 9^(1) mony 1	39^(1)
SJC 57 (PoF)	many 5 meny 1	6
SJC 57 (CL)	meny 21 many 3	24
AC 455	many 71 → 97%; meny 1 → 1%; mony 1 → 1%	73
Helmingham (Paper)	many 21 mony 4	25
Helmingham (Parchment)	many 4 mony 2 meny 1	7
CUL Kk.I.3	meny 2 many 1	3
Tanner 11	meny 2 many 1	3
Mi 225	many 3 meny 2	5
Hrl 1337	many 7	7
Hrl 6251	many 5 meny 1	6
Hatton 50	many 4 meny 1	5
Raw C. 901	many 2	2

39 One of these is a single instance of <a[-]ȝe> in rhyme position.

40 See *Atlas*: Dot Map, AGAINST: 'forms with *-g-* (*agaynst*, *a-geyn*, etc)'.

41 See *Atlas*: Dot Map, AGAINST: 'forms with *-ȝ-* (*a-ȝayn*, *a-ȝenste*, etc)'.

any late Middle English scribe, while the form 'meny' is much more restricted in provenance, with a more western and southern distribution. The *Prick of Conscience* is not the only work where <meny> is found, and the likelihood of this form being carried over from his exemplar in this case is not high, given its distribution – it is unlikely to have come from a source with such a strongly northern pedigree. If the exemplar for SJC 57's *Prick of Conscience* did not provoke <meny> as a passive repertoire form, then we might wonder if he produced it spontaneously on occasions from his own usage. It seems unlikely that the exemplar had 'many' type, for he would have had no problem taking that type over, as he does so in other manuscripts. It is possible that he found rather 'mony' forms, and he preferred to change these to <meny> as a form from his spontaneous usage. One of the other four *Prick of Conscience* manuscripts with which SJC 57 forms a sub-group (Douai Abbey, Woolhampton, Berkshire 7, localised to East Lancashire) also has <mony> for MANY, so that there is at least indirect evidence for the occurrence of this type in a close relative.[42] <meny> for MANY also is congruent with the other features which we have used to suggest tentatively a possible location for the scribe's own language (see § 4.3 and Map 3.5).

THEIR (Table 3.19) is represented in the Beryn Scribe's productions by a variety of forms: 'h-' type – <hir>, <hire>, <hir*e*>, <her>, <here>, <her*e*>, <heer>; 'th-' type – <ther>, <ther*e*>, <their>, <their*e*>, <þere>, <þeir>, <þeire>, <þeir*e*>. 'th-' type forms are commoner in the North and Midlands, although in the 15th century this type was spreading rapidly into southern areas. 'h-' type forms are found in the South and also across the Midlands in the 15th century. In the only text with a northern origin the 'th-' type forms outnumber the 'h-' type forms. The occurrence of a minority of the occasional 'th-' type in some of his other manuscripts suggests scribal familiarity with it, e.g. in the *echt*-Chaucer of AC 455, Tanner 11, Hrl 1337, Hrl 6251 and Raw C. 901. Among the 'h-' type his preferred forms are <hir> and <hire>, but in Helmingham paper and parchment only <her>, <here> or <heere> occur (with <heere> 1x). This 'her[e]' type also crops up in SJC 57 *Prick of Conscience* and *Chronicle of London* (<hire> and <here>*1x* in each case), Hrl 1337 and Raw C. 901 (where it is dominant). It seems likely that preference for 'hir[e]' or 'her[e]' types was provoked by whichever type the scribe encountered in his exemplar.

42 SJC 57 retains traces of 'thore' and 'whore' type forms for THERE and WHERE. We have inferred elsewhere (Carrillo-Linares and Williamson 2019) that the exemplar for SJC 57 contained this 'o' type and a small cluster of *Atlas* Linguistic Profiles records these forms together with 'mony' for MANY in the West Riding of Yorkshire (Linguistic Profiles 30, 100, 115, 494). Their locations are not very distant from that of the Douai Abbey manuscript.

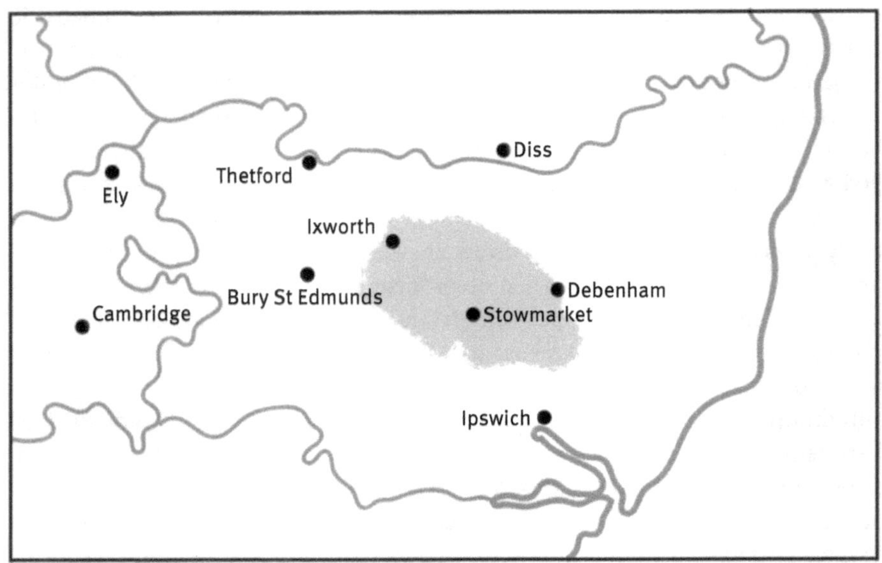

Map 3.5: CompFT3-generated provenance for a set of the Beryn Scribe's consistently deployed forms.

The dominant form of NOT (Table 3.20) is 'nat', which occurs in all the Beryn Scribe manuscripts more frequently than any other form for the negative adverb, except in SJC 57 *Prick of Conscience*, where it is almost equalled in number by forms with <-ȝt->, notably <nouȝt[e]>. We might suppose that this choice was influenced by the exemplar, but <nouȝt> is not a northern form; it has a widespread distribution across the South into the North Midlands, including Lincolnshire, Isle of Ely and Norfolk. These <-ȝt-> forms are also occasionally found in the *Canterbury Tales* manuscripts. When copying *Prick of Conscience*, the Beryn Scribe still used his preferred form <nat>. A second variant that he uses albeit with low frequency is <ne>. This occurs in all his copies except SJC 57 *Prick of Conscience*. Especially in the copies of *Canterbury Tales*, though it also turns up as a minor variant in the *Brut* copies. 'ne . . . nat' is found in the Chaucer texts and, in this case he seems to have adhered to the syntactic structure of the original works, rather than imposing his own preference. All these different strategies for dealing with what he found in his sources provide us with evidence for a better understanding of his copying practice.

Table 3.19: THEIR in all MSS.

SJC 57 (PoC)	þeir 39 → 39%; hir 18 → 18%; their 12 → 12%; theire 10 → 10%; þair 5 → 5%; þere 4 → 4%; hire 4 → 4%; there 3 → 3%; þeire 2 → 2%; þeire 1 → 1%; hire 1 → 1%; here 1 → 1%	100
SJC 57 (PoF)	hir 20 hire 2	22
SJC 57 (CL)	hir 24 hire 1 here 1	26
AC 455	hir 55 → 49%; hire 53 → 47%; there 3 → 3%; þere 1 → <1%; here 1 → <1%	113
Helmingham (Paper)	her 16 here 11 heere 1	28
Helmingham (Parchment)	here 4 her 1	6
CUL Kk.I.3	hir 29 hire 7 hire 1	37
Tanner 11	hire 36 → 88%; þeir 3 → 8%; þere 1 → 2% their 1 → 2%	41
Mi 225	hire 14 hir 9 hire 1 there 1 þere 1	26
Hrl 1337	hire 16 hire 5 hir 3 here 1 there 1 þeir 1	27
Hrl 6251	hire 35 hir 2 theire 1	38
Hatton 50	hir 35 → 85%; hire 5 → 12%; hire 1 → 2%	41
Raw C. 901	here 9 her 2 hire 1 their 1	13

4.3 Scribe's personal repertoire

It has been widely accepted that all the texts copied by the Beryn Scribe share linguistic features that must constitute his personal repertoire. This assumption is also used to bolster the idea that he was a consistent translator into his own variety of English. Yet the evidence presented in the previous sections shows that this was not the case. The extant manuscripts attributed to this scribe in most cases consist of significant Middle English works preserved in many other manuscripts, for which he produced single or multiple copies.[43] These are only the Beryn Scribe's copies that have

43 *Brut Chronicle* (6 copies), *Canterbury Tales* (2 copies, plus fragments); single copies of pieces which are all also preserved in a large number of manuscripts, such as Chaucer's *Parliament of Fowls*, Lydgate's *Life of our Lady*, *Prick of Conscience* and a 15th-century *Chronicle of London*.

Table 3.20: NOT in all MSS.

SJC 57 (PoC)	nat $46^{(1)}$ → 47%; nouȝt $19^{(1)}$ → 19%; nouȝte $18^{(14)}$ → 18; nauȝt $6^{(1)}$ → $6^{(1)}$%; ne 7 → 7%; not 1 → 1%; noȝte $1^{(1)}$ → $1^{(1)}$%	$98^{(18)}$
SJC 57 (PoF)	nat 35 → 78%; ne 5 → 11%; nouȝt 3 → 7%; nouȝte $2^{(1)}$ → $4^{(2)}$%	$45^{(1)}$
SJC 57 (CL)	nat 22 not 1	23
AC 455	nat 190 → 82%; ne 20 → 9%; ne-nat 9 → 4%; no $5^{(3)}$ → $2^{(1)}$%; nauȝt $5^{(3)}$ → $2^{(1)}$%; nouȝt $2^{(2)}$ → $<1^{(<1)}$%; not 1 → <1%	$232^{(8)}$
Helmingham (Paper)	nat 67 → 74%; ne 19 → 21%; noght $2^{(2)}$ → $2^{(2)}$%; not 2 → 2%; ne-nat 1 → 1%	$91^{(2)}$
Helmingham (Parchment)	nat 17 ne-nat 3 ne 2	22
CUL Kk.I.3	ne 24 ne 7	31
Tanner 11	nat 8 ne 1	9
Mi 225	nat 13 nouȝte 1 ne 1	15
Hrl 1337	nat 11 ne 1	12
Hrl 6251	nat 14 ne 1	15
Hatton 50	nat 14 ne 2	16
Raw C. 901	nat 13 ne 1	14

survived (or that we know of so far), but the Beryn Scribe could have made more copies of these works as well as of others. However, most of these works have an origin in the Midlands or in the London area, and many of the other preserved copies of the works he undertook show 15th-century Midlands characteristics (either West or East Midlands).[44] Of all his extant works the only exception to this is SJC 57 *Prick of Conscience*, originally written in Northern Middle English, and other manuscripts closely related to the

44 The electronic *Atlas* localises some of the *Brut Chronicle* manuscripts to Essex (6), Surrey (3), Herefordshire (3), Northamptonshire (1) and Wiltshire (1). Most of Chaucer manuscripts were copied in the Midlands with the exception of a manuscript in which the language is possibly of Lincolnshire, or more southerly but with Northern overlay. None of the multiple copies for *Life of Our Lady* are included in the electronic *Atlas* Index of Sources, but other localised Lydgate's works were produced in the Midlands as well.

SJC 57 version are localised to Lancashire and Ireland.[45] As previous research on the Beryn Scribe has not included any linguistic evidence for the text of *Prick of Conscience*, the picture is incomplete and what has been believed to be the Beryn Scribe's repertoire may just represent common variants for the Midlands dialects carried over into the scribe's output. These features were probably not inconsistent with his own features in many respects, but there might have been others as well which were not shown in the texts originating in the Midlands. Thus, as SJC 57 *Prick of Conscience* deviates a great deal from the evidence found in the rest of the texts originally composed in the Midlands, the need to include evidence from this manuscript is imperative to try to establish what may have comprised the scribe's own repertoire.

The proposed assemblage of features for this includes some of his persistent idiosyncrasies – which are essentially the consistent features in section 4.2 above – and other items that appear to be common in all his productions.[46] A fitting 'by hand' of all these features suggests as possible locus for the assemblage in North and Central Suffolk. For a fitting using CompFT3 other features have been used,[47] but the result is the same (see Map 3.5). The area of fit lies in the centre of Suffolk, north of Ipswich and East of Bury St Edmonds, covering roughly a triangle whose points are Stowmarket, Ixworth and Debenham.

One interpretation of the consistent use of these features is that they form part of the Beryn Scribe's active repertoire and he imposes them instinctively on his copies. Such behaviour is explicable if these features were

---

45 We tried to 'fit' a set of the features common to all the manuscripts of the *Prick of Conscience* subgroup to which SJC 57 *Prick of Conscience* belongs. The aim was to try to establish a possible area of origin of the exemplar from which all the manuscripts in the subgroup derive. The set was consonant with two potential provenances, one in North-West Yorkshire on the border with North-East Lancashire, South Yorkshire and the other in the area around the meeting of the boundaries of Yorkshire, North-West Lincolnshire and North Nottinghamshire and also a small area of West Central Nottinghamshire.

46 Additional features considered here are: 'feir', 'feyr' (FIRE), atte (for AT THE), and butte (for BUT THE) 'the / þe toon' and 'the / þe todir' or 'the / þe tothir'. '-it' for Past Participle, and Weak Past.

47 The features used for the compFT3 fitting were: THEIR hir hire hir*e*; WHICH (-)wich wich(-); MANY meny; MUCH much; ARE been bee*n*; AFTER afft*er* afftir afftyr; IF yff yff-; AGAIN a-geyn a-geyne ageyn ageyne; Present 3rd singular -ith -yth; FIRE feir feyr feyr<e>; TOGETHER to-gidir togidir; <w> + glide-vowel *attestation*; <scl> for 'sl' *attestation*; <v> for 'w' *attestation*. As well as Suffolk, a small area in Northamptonshire shows up as a potential 'site of fit', with two non-attestations registered, but no rejections. However, the non-attestations here are for <w> + glide vowel and <v> for 'w'. Since these items require simple occurrence, in effect they may be taken as negative evidence for these features there.

adopted during his acquisition of written English. We thus suggest an alternative potential locus for the scribe's training than that proposed in Mooney and Matheson (2008). They claim '. . . the Beryn scribe probably learned his spelling in south central Essex, somewhere in the general area bounded by Basildon, Brentwood, Havering and the north bank of the Thames' (Mooney and Matheson 2008: 49). Such an origin does not of course preclude the Beryn Scribe having migrated to London, or round about, or in fact to anywhere else. He may well have carried out his profession in the metropolis for all or part of his career, but it is worth remembering that people copied and made manuscripts in places such as Bury St Edmonds, Ipswich and Cambridge.

4.4 Standardisation

With respect to the English of the Beryn Scribe's copies, claims have been made about South Essex provenance (Matheson 2008) and conformance in some respects at least to 'London standard' (Horobin 2000). In this section we examine these claims by comparing the scribe's linguistic forms and his copying behaviour in relation to 'London standard English' as defined by M.L. Samuels, although we question if the notion 'standard' can be said to have any evidential content in the first half of the fifteenth century.

The codicological and palaeographical investigations of the Beryn Scribe's manuscript productions suggests that his *floruit* as a copyist was between *ca* 1430 to *ca* 1455. His early linguistic formation must be presumed to predate this period of copying activity. We do not know his age when he made the earliest extant copies attributed to his hand nor the place(s) where he acquired literacy in English. If the extant copies he produced belong to the early part of his career, then his own variety of English, acquired in speech and learned for writing, must have been drawn from the varieties of English to which he was exposed from at least the 1420s, if not earlier. If his copies belong to later in his career, then his linguistic formation would have to be antedated accordingly. It seems reasonable to date the period of his linguistic formation in both speech and writing to the first quarter to third of the 15th century.

'London English' we define here by a set of linguistic features recorded in the *Atlas* Linguistic Profiles localised therein to 'London' and an immediately surrounding area, encompassing parts of the neighbouring counties of Middlesex, Surrey and Essex. This set of Linguistic Profiles overlaps in the main with the evidence drawn from the texts used by M.L. Samuels to define his 'Types' 'standard' in the 14th century and the early part of the 15th century (Samuels 1963 [1989], Samuels 1983 [1988]) and localised in the *Atlas* in and around London. If the period of the Beryn Scribe's linguistic formation is taken as the first quarter to third of the 15th century, then contemporaneous with this would be Samuels's Type III, with Type IV forms to consider as potential options during the Beryn Scribe's later copying career. Type II forms might be relevant for texts he copied whose authorship goes back to the second half of the 14th century.

We may compare forms recorded in our Linguistic Profiles from the Beryn Scribe's manuscripts samples with the set of items and forms displayed in Samuels (1983 [1988]: 28–29) as representing characteristics of 'London Standard' Types between the mid 14th century and the mid 15th century. These Types are, to say the least, problematic. They represent sets of linguistic characteristics salient in a small corpus of London-associated texts from different periods.[48] A number of these defining characteristic carry over from one period / Type to another and mix with other forms with a wider provenance. Nevertheless, since they have formed part of the discourse concerning the Beryn Scribe's provenance and working milieu, we consider the degree to which his productions agree or diverge from the Types. In Table 3.21 those forms in the Beryn Scribe's manuscripts which agree with those given in Samuels (1983 [1988]: 28–29) are flagged with the Type numerals (annotated): II = Type II (early–mid 14th century), $\mathrm{II_b}$ = Type II (late 14th century), $\mathrm{III_{14}}$ = Type III (late 14th century), $\mathrm{III_{15}}$ = Type III (early 15th century), IV = Type IV ('Chancery Standard', *ca* 1430 and later).[49] The Beryn Scribe's forms in bold correspond to those in one or more of the standard Types. (When we refer to 'standard' it is in

48 Samuels's characterisation of these 'Standard' types as representative of London language has become embedded in much of the discussion about the standardisation of English, either assumed or re-assessed (See Hanna, 2005 and Benskin, 2004).

49 Type II is defined by Edinburgh, National Library of Scotland, Advocates' 19.2.1 (*olim* Auchinleck) (electronic *Atlas* Linguistic Profile 6510), Cambridge, St John's College 256 (Linguistic Profile 6430), London, British Library, Add. 17376 (Linguistic Profile 6280); Type $\mathrm{II^b}$ by (1) Cambridge, Magalene College Pepys 2498, (2) London, BL, Harley 874, (3) Oxford, Bodleian Library, Laud Misc. 622 (Linguistic Profile 6260); $\mathrm{III^{14}}$ (1) London documents – 'East London' (Chambers and Daunt 1931: 47–57), 'Petition of the Folk of Mercerye' (Chambers and Daunt 1931: 33–37), (2) *Equatorie of the Planetis* = Cambridge, Peterhouse College 75.I; Type $\mathrm{III^{15}}$ by Aberystwyth, National Library of Wales, Peniarth 392 D (*olim* Hengwrt 154) (Linguistic Profile 6400), Cambridge, Corpus Christi College 61 (*Troilus and Criseyde*), Cambridge, Trinity College B.15.17 (*Piers Plowman*), Huntington Library, San Marino (California), HM 111 and 744 'and other autograph MSS of Hoccleve'; IV by 'typical forms in documents written by Chancery-trained scribes, in PRO, Early Chancery Proceedings and Exchequer TR Council and Privy Seal'. See Samuels (1983 [1988]: 23–24). The annotations on the 'Type' numerals are ours.

relation to these Types – for the sake of the argument – not from a belief that there existed such a thing at the time the Beryn Scribe was operating.)

The Beryn Scribe uses a number of forms that belong to one or more of the Types. From Table 3.21 it is clear that the sets of forms that define (in some measure) the Types are not exclusive to any one Type: some forms show continuity through the time-periods of the Types. Some of the Beryn Scribe's forms belong to earlier Types, though most to the later ones, closer to, if not contemporaneous with, the putative period of his copying activity. IF <ȝyff>, BEFORE <aforn>, <to[-]fore>, <to-forne> are associated with the early Types II and $\mathrm{II_b}$, of the 14th century. <ȝyff> is a minority form in the SJC 57 *Prick of Conscience* (8x). Rather than having significance as a kind of standard feature, the form is to be found in a coherent cluster in South Norfolk, with other sporadic attestations in

Table 3.21: Comparision of forms found in the BS manuscript samples with forms representative of M.L. Samuels' Standard 'Types' (after Samuels 1988 [1983]: 28–29).

Item	Form	Manuscript	II	$\mathrm{II_b}$	$\mathrm{III_{14}}$	$\mathrm{III_{15}}$	IV
SUCH	**such**	SJCf* AC HEr HEt CU MI* HT	–	–	X	(X)	X
	suche	SJCpfc TR* MI H1* H6	–	–	X	((X))	–
	swilk	SJp*	–	–	–	–	–
MUCH	much	SJc AC HEr HEt CU TR MI H1 H6 HT RA	–	–	–	–	–
	muche	SJpc CU* TR MI H1 H6 RA	((X))	–	–	X	X
	muche	AC* H1*	–	–	–	–	–
	mykil(l)	SJp	–	–	–	–	–
	mikil(l)	SJp					
SHALL *pl*	shal	SJpf HEr* HEt HT* H1 H6*	–	–	–	–	–
	shall	SJpf* SJc AC*r CU TR MI HT* H1 H6* RA*	–	–	–	–	–
	shul	SJp AC HEr HEt HT*	X	–	–	X	X
	shull	SJp AC* CU TR H1 H6	–	–	–	–	X
IF	**if**	SJpf* AC HEr HEt	((X))	–	X	X	X
	if-that	AC					
	Iff	SJp HEr*	–	–	–	–	–
	yf	SJpfc AC HEr HEt CU TR MI HT* H1 H6 RA	–	–	–	–	–
	yf-	AC HErt	–	–	–	–	–
	that/þat/þ[t]	SJpf AC MI* HT	–	–	–	–	–
	yff	HEr*	–	–	–	–	–
	hyf	SJp	X	–	–	–	–
	ȝyff	AC					
	and	SJc* AC					
	&						

Table 3.21 (continued)

Item	Form	Manuscript	II	II$_b$	III$_{14}$	III$_{15}$	IV
AGAINST	**a[-]geyn**	SJpc AC HEr	–	–	–	X	X
	a-geyn*e*	SJc* AC*	–	–	–	–	X
	ageynst	SJp*f*c* HEr*	–	–	–	–	–
	a-geyns	AC	–	–	–	X	–
	a-gayn	HEr*	–	–	X	X	–
	a-gayns	AC	–	–	X	X	–
	agaynes	AC	–	–	–	–	–
	ogeyn	SJp*	–	–	–	–	–
	a[-]ȝenst	AC* HEr HEt* CU* MI H1 HT RA	–	–	–	–	–
	a-ȝenste	AC*	–	–	–	–	–
	a-ȝe	AC**r*	–	–	–	–	–
AGAIN	**a[-]geyn**	TR*	–	–	–	–	–
	a[-]geyn*e*	SJpfc AC HEr HEt CU TR MI H1 H6 HT RA	–	–	–	X	X
	a-ye	SJp* SJc AC H1	–	–	–	–	X
	a-ȝe *rh*	AC	–	–	–	–	–
	ayeyne	ACr	–	–	–	–	–
	a-ȝeen	MI*	–	–	–	–	–
		RA	–	–	–	–	–
NOT	**nat**	SJpfc AC HEr HEt CU TR MI H1 H6 HT RA	–	–	X	X	–
	not	SJp*f*c* AC* HEr	–	–	–	(X)	X
	ne	SJf AC HEr HEt CU TR* MI* H1* H6* HT RA*	–	–	–	–	–
	no	AC	X	(X)	–	–	–
	nauȝt	SJp AC	X	–	(X)	X	–
	nauȝte	SJp ACr		–			–
	noȝt	SJp	(X)	–	–	X	–
	nouȝt	SJp AC	X	–	(X)	X	–
	nouȝte	SJp AC**r* HErr MI*		–			–
	noght	HErt	–	–	–	X	–
	nenat	AC	–	–	–	–	–
WORK *vb*	**work(-)**	SJp*f* AC* HEr HEt* CU	–	–	(X)	(X)	X
pres. stem	**werk-**	HEr* CUL	X	–	–	X	X
	worch(-)	AC	–	–	–	–	–
BEFORE	**a[-]fore**	SJc* AC* HEr* H1 H6* RA	–	–	(X)	(X)	X
adv. / prep.	**aforn**	CU*	(X)	–	–	–	–
	fore	AC* H1* HT*	–	–	–	–	–
	be-for	HEr*	–	–			–
	be[-]fore	SJp AC HEr	–	–	X	X	X
	before	SJc*	–	–			
	be[-]forn	SJf* HEr HEt	–	–	X	X	–
	to[-]fore	SJpc AC CU TR MI H1 H6 HT RA	X	X	–	–	–
	to-forn	AC**r* CU	X		–	X	–
	to-forne	AC**r*	X	X	–		–

Table 3.21 (continued)

Item	Form	Manuscript	II	II_b	III_{14}	III_{15}	IV
SAW *1/3sg*	**saw**	AC HT	–	–	–	X	–
	sawe	SJf AC HEr* HEt CU TR MI H1* H6 HT* RA	–	–	–	X	X
	say	AC*r HEr*r	–	–	X	X	–
	sy	HEr	–	–	–	X	–

MS and work abbreviations:
SJ Oxford, St John's College 57 – SJp = Prick of Conscience, SJf = Parliament of Fowls;
SJc = Chronicle of London
AC = Alnwick Castle MS 455
HE = 'Helmingham MS' – HEr = paper part, HEt = parchment part
CU = Cambridge University Library Kk.I.3, part 10
TR = Oxford, Bodleian Library Tanner 11
MI = Michigan University Library MS 255
H1 = London, British Library, Harley 1337
H6 = London, British Library, Harley 6251
HT = Oxford, Bodleian Library, Hatton 50
RA = Oxford, Bodleian Library, Rawlinson C.901
Annotations on the abbreviations:
* form occurs only once in the manuscript sample
X in one of the columns for the Types indicates that the form corresponds to that Type, – that it does not. Parentheses around the X, e.g. (X), ((X)) represent the level of occurrence of the form(s) within the Type as given in Samuels (1988 [1983]: 28–29) and follows *LALME* practice.

Lincolnshire and across the West Midlands, and so its significance may rather be dialectal. Other forms, AGAIN(ST) <a[-]geyn>, <a[-]geyn*e*>, NOT <not>, SAW 1/3sg <saw>, <sawe>, <sy> correspond only to Types III_{15} and IV, that is, the later standard types.

<a[-]geyn> (AGAINST) occurs in only four manuscript samples. In SJC 57 (*Prick of Conscience, Chronicle of London*) and AC 455 it is the majority form; in Helmingham paper it is a lesser form. <a[-]geyn> (AGAIN) has a much wider spread across the manuscripts, occurring in all except Raw C. 901 as a majority form, where it is a lesser form. <a[-]geyn*e*> (AGAINST) occurs only in SJC 57 *Chronicle of London* and AC 455, once in each case. <a[-]geyn*e*> (AGAIN) is a minority form in SJC 57 *Prick of Conscience, Chronicle of London* and AC 455 and a lesser form in Hrl 1337.

<sawe> for SAW 1/3 sg has the widest spread of occurrence across the manuscript samples (ten), although it occurs only once in Helmingham

paper, Hrl 1337 and Hrl 6251. It is otherwise the majority form. <saw>, by contrast, is restricted to AC 455 and Hatton 50. <sy> occurs only in Helmingham paper.

Of these later standard forms, only <a[-]geyn> (AGAIN) and <sawe> (SAW 1/3sg) have much currency in the Beryn Scribe's usage, and one might argue for them being part of his general repertoire.

The predominantly Type IV <not>, nevertheless occurs mainly as a one-time occurrence, in SJC 57 (*Prick of Conscience*, *Parliament of Fowls*, *Chronicle of London* and AC 455); in Helmingham paper it occurs only 2x.

The form <to[-]fore> is counted standard in Types II, II_b, but not in later Types. It is nevertheless, the preferred form for BEFORE adv / prep in ten manuscript samples. In SJC 57 *Prick of Conscience* it is a lesser form. Otherwise, it is the majority form in the samples. It is also geographically widespread. As preposition the form is generally not to be found in the North-East Midland counties.

Of the Beryn Scribe's favoured *non-standard* forms, we note the following. His form of MUCH with the widest spread across the manuscript samples (eleven) is <much>. In three of these – SJC 57 *Chronicle of London*, Tanner 11 and Hrl 6251 – it is a minority form. The geographical distribution of <much> is rather sporadic. There are three main clusters: (1) in the West Midlands; (2) SW England, in Somerset and Gloucestershire; (3) mainly in a band from Hampshire, Surrey, Middlesex and Essex. We can contrast this with the standard <muche>, which occurs as majority form in only four of the Beryn Scribe's manuscripts – SJC 57 *Chronicle of London*, Tanner 11, Hrl 1337 and Hrl 6251. It is a lesser form in Raw C. 901 and Mi 225, a minority form in SJC 57 *Prick of Conscience*. In CUL Kk.I.3 it occurs only once. <muche> has a widespread and dense geographical distribution across the southern half of England. It is densely attested in the West Midlands, in a band across the South of England, extending northeastwards through the London area into Essex and Suffolk.

For AGAINST, the Beryn Scribe's most favoured form is the non-standard <a[-]ȝenst>. It occurs in eight manuscript samples, but in three – AC 455, Helmingham paper and CUL Kk.I.3 – it occurs only once in each case. Otherwise, it is the majority form.

<yf> is the Beryn Scribe's preferred form for IF. It is found across all the manuscript samples. Geographically, it is widespread, but with a less dense pattern of coverage compared with the standard <if>, which occurs as a minority form in five only of the samples.

After, <nat> for NOT, the most favoured form is <ne>, in eleven samples. In Hrl 1337, Hrl 6251, Mi 225, Tanner 11 and Raw C. 901 it occurs once. It is a lesser form in Tanner 11 and elsewhere a minority form. <ne> is widely scattered across the southern counties, with a cluster centred on North-West Gloucestershire.

While some of the forms corresponding to the standard Types may be found across the samples from the Beryn Scribe's manuscripts, their occurrences are not consistent. They are found in a few of the manuscripts, often as minority or lesser forms or as single occurrences. The forms with the widest spreads across the manuscript samples are in fact non-standard ones. We may add this fact to: (1) the character of the Types, where forms may belong to more than one Type according to period; (2) the fact that we cannot tell on what grounds the Beryn Scribe was selecting the forms that happen to conform to one or other of the Types; (3) the fact that the Beryn Scribe was copying manuscripts with texts written originally in an earlier period and so he may have introduced forms into his copies from these earlier-written texts. Finally, his view of the written language of his time as he encountered it in manuscripts and our view and interpretations of the language are inevitably quite different. Given all this, at the very least it would be unsafe to claim that the Beryn Scribe's language was conforming to or tending towards any kind of standard, certainly as defined by the Samuels Types. Many of the forms that the Beryn Scribe deploys – 'standard' and 'non-standard' – had wide, but not equivalent, geographical distributions with varying densities of attestation, across Southern England. But they are only part of his repertoire. He also consistently used forms with very widely sporadic, even rare, occurrences. It is clear also, that he was influenced to greater or lesser degrees by his exemplars, the most striking case being SJC 57 *Prick of Conscience*, where he tolerated a substantial intake of northernisms.

We made an extended assemblage of features from the 15th-century London Linguistic Profiles, making use of a wider set of items, and attempted to fit this using compFT3. We found that the assemblage could fit widely across the West and Central Midlands and in the South-East, from the counties West of and around London, across Essex into Suffolk and Cambridgeshire. The foci of the areas of fit seem to be centred on towns with significant manuscript production. It would not be surprising if, in the 15th century, certain forms were 'city-hopping' as manuscripts moved around to be copied in different centres of production, some from London, others to London, as well as to and from other centres as part of a growing culture of book production. Wright (2000: 6) comments:

> Standard English is to some extent a consensus dialect, a consensus of features from authoritative texts, meaning that no single late Middle English or early Early Modern authority will show all the features that end up in Standard English. Sixteenth-century witnesses who show standardisation of a given feature do not necessarily show standardisation in any other feature: it did not progress as a bundle of features, but in piecemeal fashion.

In the 15th century, as texts circulated and copyists gained more familiarity with different varieties of English with the expansion of book culture, gradually regional and wider assemblages of consensus or supralocalised forms appeared.[50] Eventually, aspects of these consensus varieties coalesced into a broad core of usage that we perceive as an early manifestation of the linguistic construct we call 'Standard English'. It is in this gelling yet still very fluid context that the activity of the Beryn Scribe should be interpreted.

5 Concluding remarks

Our analysis of the language of AC 455, the manuscript in which the Beryn Scribe's South Essex provenance was established, reveals that the precision of this Essex localisation is far from accurate and there is not enough linguistic evidence to point exclusively to this area. While many of the linguistic features deployed in AC 455 as an assemblage could have been used in Essex, they could also co-occur in London, Surrey, Hertfordshire, Oxfordshire, Warwickshire and the South Northamptonshire. Moreover, the language of SJC 57 *Prick of Conscience* is very different to that of AC 455 in many respects. Our attempts to localise it point to a provenance in the area of North-West Norfolk, Isle of Ely, Soke of Peterborough, North Northamptonshire, Rutland and South Lincolnshire. The wider comparative analysis of the other texts attributed to the Beryn Scribe clearly demonstrates that the language portrayed in each of them is not consistent throughout, and, although there are a number of features common to all of them, there is clear internal variation within each manuscript, and there is clear variation between the works copied. Different copies of the same work show some degree of similarity, which might imply that they were sourced from the same, or from very closely related, exemplars. Not all the linguistic features common to the Beryn Scribe's texts are necessarily his original personal repertoire acquired in his place of origin or training. There are certain forms he uses consistently that are probably a personal stylistic preference.[51] Some of these features are widespread

50 Supralocalisation refers to the spread of a linguistic feature from its region of origin to neighbouring areas (Nevelainen, 2000). Such supralocalised varieties would correspond to M.L. Samuels' 'colourless regional standards', but without the fixedness implied by the terms 'regional' and 'standard', i.e. the provenance of features is extensive but shifting and there is variability.

51 Other 15th century scribes, such as the so-called Hammond scribe, may have also their idiosyncratic spellings which "may be no more than personal preference, with no implications for regional dialect at all" (Wright, 2012: 230–31).

forms likely to have been accepted and carried over from the exemplars he used, and some could eventually become part of his written repertoire. Additionally, there is no evidence in his texts that may support the thesis of his language moving towards a single written standard.

In summary, we propose four strands which may occur with varying emphasis in his productions:

(1) a set of recurring idiosyncratic features. Dialectally – on the evidence of the electronic *Atlas* – these are sporadic geographically and / or of rare occurrence;
(2) a set of features that are distinctive to each manuscript and distinct from the Beryn Scribe's other strands and which are likely to be carry-overs from his exemplars;
(3) a set that seems to cohere with consensus usage across the Midlands, from West to East and the South-East;
(4) a set drawn from and internalised as a result of Beryn Scribe's experience as a copyist.

With respect to sets (2), (3) and (4) we can expect some degree of intersection between them. Such a combination of strands would not make the Beryn Scribe special with respect to his profession. In his case, we have the good fortune to be able to observe the results of his scribal behaviour in a number of productions, to allow us to compare them one with another and to make some inferences from his consistencies and his variability in usage.

Our understanding of the Beryn Scribe's behaviour is that, having different models for each of his productions, he was led in each of them to produce a language with different layers of different depths. The Beryn Scribe can be considered a 'partial translator': he deploys a number of his own preferred forms, that do not necessarily have to be forms in his original dialect. He readily carries over features, to a greater or lesser extent, from his exemplars. Taken as a whole, the linguistic evidence of the Beryn Scribe's productions cannot tell us that they were made in London and used by a London community or that the scribe was originally from Essex. If the Beryn Scribe was of South-East Essex / London – as the 'several scholars' assert – why did he produce such a limited dialectal conversion of the *Prick of Conscience*, retaining a great deal of the text's northern linguistic character? Did he feel a more thorough-going translation was beyond him? Were the constraints more linguistic than structural? The Chaucer and Lydate texts may have been closer to his own spontaneous language, but again he retains characteristics of their language. Copying a poetic text probably resulted in a more constrained approach for a late Middle English scribe, especially where the exemplar was in a dialect substantially different from that into which it was being converted. We do not, of course, know the provenance of the Beryn Scribe's own dialect. We have made only a tentative suggestion above, based on some of the features consistent across his productions. SJC 57 provides us with evidence of how the Beryn Scribe dealt with a text in a language much more distinct from those of the other texts he copied and which have survived. However, the copying approach seems to us to be the same: a tendency to respect a great deal of what he found in his exemplars. The language features displayed in his texts were highly dependent on individual textual histories and his experience as a professional copyist, and they cannot be exclusively associated with Essex, London nor with any type of putative emerging standard. The work of the Beryn Scribe remains, of course, open to further investigation and interpretation given a wider range of sources for London English in the fifteenth century that extends beyond that currently offered in the *Atlas* and better understanding of the processes of supraregionalisation in the period.

To determine how typical the copying practices of the Beryn Scribe were among his contemporaries as professional copyists would, of course, require investigation of other cases of manuscripts in the same hand and comparison of their language. Nevertheless, we would be prepared to hazard that he was probably not untypical, that he was part of the cadre of productive professionals exposed through their exemplars to a range of variant orthographic systems. From these, consciously and subconsciously, they drew and retained characteristics to add to their repertoires, reproducing them to greater or lesser degree in response to what they encountered in manuscripts subsequently to be copied. During the course of a copying career, the scribes must have developed an awareness of and sensitivity to what was becoming more widely used within English manuscript culture. Thus, certain variants gained wider currency and acceptance. Such a scenario, we can propose, was the genesis of standardisation of English.

References

Benskin, Michael. 1977. Local Archives and Middle English Dialects, *Journal of the Society of Archivists* 5(8): 500–514.

Benskin, Michael. 1981. Dialect Maps for the Past. Unpublished Working Paper. Edinburgh University: Middle English Dialect Project.

Benskin, Michael. 1991. The "Fit"-technique Explained. In Felicity Riddy (ed.), *Regionalism in Late Medieval Manuscripts and Texts*, 9–26. Cambridge: D.S. Brewer.

Benskin, Michael, Margaret Laing, Vasilis Karaiskos and Keith Williamson. 2013 *e-LALME An Electronic version of A Linguistic Atlas of Late Mediaeval English*. <http://www.lel.ed.ac.

uk/ihd/elalme/elalme.html>. Edinburgh, The University of Edinburgh. (Accessed from September 2013 to December 2018).

Benskin, Michael, 2004. Chancery standard. In Christian Kay, Carole Hough & Irené Wotherspoon (eds.), *New perspectives on English historical linguistics, vol. 2, Lexis and transmission*, 1–40. Amsterdam: John Benjamins.

Carrillo-Linares, María José and Keith Williamson. (2019). A Reconsideration of the Dialectal Provenance of the *Prick of Conscience* in Oxford, St John's College, 57. *Anglia* 137/2: 303–350.

Chambers, R.W. and Margaret Daunt (eds.), 1931. *A Book of London English, 1384–1425*. Oxford: Oxford University Press.

Hanna, Ralph. 2003. Review of Mary-Rose McLaren, The London Chronicles of the Fifteenth Century: A Revolution in English Writing. *History in Focus*. <www.history.ac.uk/reviews/review/340> (accessed from June 2017 to September 2018).

Hanna, Ralph. 2005. *London Literature 1300–1380*. Cambridge: Cambridge University Press.

Horobin, Simon. 2000. The Scribe of the Helmingham and Northumberland Manuscripts of the Canterbury Tales. *Neophilologus* 84: 457–465.

Horobin, Simon. 2009. The Edmund-Fremund Scribe Copying Chaucer, *Journal of the Early Book Society* 12: 193–203.

Laing, Margaret (ed.), 1989. *Middle English Dialectology: Essays on some Principles and Problems*. Aberdeen: Aberdeen University Press.

Laing, Margaret and Keith Williamson. 2004. The Archaeology of Medieval Texts. In Christian. J. Kay and Jeremy J. Smith (eds.), *Categorization in the History of English*, 85–145. Amsterdam / Philadelphia: John Benjamins.

Laing, Margaret and Roger Lass. 2013. *A Linguistic Atlas of Early Middle English*. Introduction, Ch. 4 <http://www.lel.ed.ac.uk/ihd/laeme2/laeme_intro_ch4.html>. Edinburgh: The University of Edinburgh.

Lewis, Robert and Angus McIntosh. 1982. *A Descriptive Guide to the Manuscripts of the 'Prick of Conscience'*, Medium Aevum Monographs NS 12. Oxford: The Society for the Study of Mediæval Languages and Literature.

Manly, John and Edith Rickert. 1940. *The Text of the Canterbury Tales: Studied on the Basis of All Known Manuscripts*, 8 vols. Chicago: University of Chicago Press.

McIntosh, Angus. 1973. Word Geography in the Lexicography of Mediaeval English, *Annals of the New York Academy of* Sciences 211: 55–56. Reprinted in 1989 in Margaret Laing (ed.), *Middle English Dialectology: Essays on Some Principles and Problems*, 86–97. Aberdeen: Aberdeen University Press.

McIntosh, Angus. 1974. Towards an Inventory of Middle English Scribes, *Neuphilologische Mitteilungen* 75: 602–624. Reprinted in 1989 in Margaret Laing (ed.), *Middle English Dialectology: Essays on Some Principles and Problems*, 46–63. Aberdeen: Aberdeen University Press.

McIntosh, Angus, Michael L. Samuels and Michael Benskin [with the assistance of Margaret Laing and Keith Williamson]. 1986. *LALME: A Linguistic Atlas of Late Medieval English*. Aberdeen: Aberdeen University Press.

Matheson, Lister. 2008. Essex/Suffolk Scribes and Their Language in Fifteenth-century London. In Marina Dossena, Richard Dury and Maurizio Gotti (eds.), *English Historical Linguistics 2006. Volume III: Geo-Historical Variation in English*, 45–65. Amsterdam: John Benjamins.

Mooney, Linne R. and Lister Matheson. 2003. The Beryn Scribe and his Texts: Evidence for Multiple-Copy Production of Manuscripts in Fifteenth-Century England. *The Library*. 4(4): 347–370.
Mosser, Daniel. 2010. The paper Stocks of the Beryn Scribe. *Journal of the Early Book Society for the study of Manuscripts and Printing History*. 13: 63–93.
Mosser, Daniel and Linne R. Mooney. 2014. More Manuscripts by the Beryn Scribe and his Cohort. *The Chaucer Review*. 49(1): 39–76.
Nevelainen, Terttu. 2000. Processes of Supralocalisation and the Rise of Standard English in the Early Modern Period. In Ricardo Bermúdez-Otero, David Denison, Richard M. Hogg and Chris McCully (eds.), *Generative Theory and Corpus Studies*. Berlin: Mouton de Gruyter, 329–371.
Samuels, Michael L. 1963. Some Applications of Middle English dialectology. *English Studies* 44. 81–94. Reprinted in: Margaret Laing (ed.), 1989. *Middle English Dialectology: Essays on some Principles and Problems*, 64–80. Aberdeen: Aberdeen University Press.
Samuels, Michael, L. 1983. Chaucer's Spelling. In Douglas Gray and Eric G. Stanley (eds.), *Middle English Studies Presented to Norman Davis*, 17–37. Oxford: Oxford University Press. Reprinted in 1988 in Jeremy Smith (ed.), *The English of Chaucer and his Contemporaries*. Aberdeen: Aberdeen University Press.
Smith, Jeremy J. (ed.), 1988. *The English of Chaucer and his Contemporaries*. Aberdeen: Aberdeen University Press.
Williamson, Keith. 2000. Changing Spaces: Linguistic Relationships and the Dialect Continuum. In Irma Taavitsainen, Terttu Nevalainen, Päivi Pahta and Matti Rissanen (eds.), *Placing Middle English in Context*, 141–179. Berlin / New York: Mouton de Gruyter.
Williamson, Keith. 2012a. Middle English: Dialects. In Alexander Bergs and Laurel J. Brinton (eds.), *English Historical Linguistics: an International Handbook*, vol. 1 (Handbooks of Linguistics and Communication Science 34.1, 480–505. Berlin / New York: Mouton de Gruyter. Reprinted in 2017 in Laurel Brinton and Alexander Bergs (eds.), *The History of English, vol. 3: Middle English*, 134–164. Berlin, Boston: De Gruyter.
Williamson, Keith. 2012b. Historical Dialectology. In Alexander Bergs and Laurel J. Brinton (eds.), *English Historical Linguistics: an International Handbook*, vol. 2 (Handbooks of Linguistics and Communication Science, 34.2), 1421–1438. Berlin: / New York: Mouton de Gruyter.
Wright, Laura. 2000. *The Development of Standard English, 1300–1800: Theories, Descriptions, Conflicts*. Cambridge: Cambridge University Press.
Wright, Laura. 2012. The Hammond Scribe: His Dialect, His Paper, and Folios 133–155 of Trinity College Cambridge MS 0.3.11. In Claudia Lange, Beatrix Weber and Göran Wolf (eds.), *Communicative Spaces: Variation, Contact, and Change*, 227–258. Frankfurt am Main: Peter Lang.

David Moreno Olalla

4 Spelling practices in late Middle English medical prose: A quantitative analysis

1 Introduction

Medical *Fachprosa* is a text-type that remains *terra incognita* as far as the standardization processes of English go. The scholarly neglect of medieval scientific prose (be it editorial or linguistic) is well-known,[1] but the lack of interest in the actual written forms used by the copyists of herbals, phlebotomies or surgeries is surprising, all the more so after Taavitsainen (2000) undercut the notion of the so-called 'Central Midland Standard' by showing that the copyists of an assortment of scientific texts used a bundle of features similar to those of many Wycliffite tracts, baptized 'Type I' in an extremely influential article (Samuels 1989: 67). Taavitsainen suggests that the influence may have been in fact the other way around: that scientific discourse (and some of the more common words and morphemes used therein) influenced Wycliffite tracts, since sectarian literature circulated secretly, whereas scientific treatises could not only be read in the open but frequently enjoyed official sanction as well (Taavitsainen 2000: 146). Just like any other medieval text-type, Middle English medical prose did not constitute a homogeneous block when it comes to normative writing, linguistic registers or indeed anything else, but there is good reason to believe that, just like the scriveners of personal or business letters, the authors and copyists of medical prose were freer in their linguistic choices than the average literary or legal scribe. Judging from the comparatively small number of copies (single versions of a given treatise are not uncommon), many of these translations are likely to have been privately commissioned, presumably enjoying limited circulation and with intended readerships not larger than those of a manor, a monastic infirmary or the lower echelons of the medical profession such as barber-surgeons.[2] As a consequence, one might assume that the need

1 Some of the causes for such editorial invisibility were listed in Moreno Olalla (2013a: 388–390), which supplements Pahta and Taavitsainen (2004: 4). Some remarks on the current academic status of early medieval Medicine studies made in Horden (2011: 5–6) also apply, although the situation is less dire for the late Middle Ages than it is for the Carolingian period.
2 Take for instance the collection of gynaecological treatises called *Trotula*, which was independently translated at least five times, but spawned a proper textual family just once (Translation A, consisting of five members; Green 1992: 64–68).

https://doi.org/10.1515/9783110687545-005

for a standardized version of the language would not have been particularly pressing.

The following pages discuss a collection of graphic variants used in four manuscripts containing herbals and in particular, scribal decisions concerning *-e*. The manuscripts I have selected for the task are Oxford, Bodleian Library, Additional MS A.106, ff. 244r–259r and the following three volumes from the Sloane collection: London, British Library, Sloane MS 5, ff. 13r–57r, Sloane MS 404, ff. 3v–243r, 294r–319v and Sloane MS 770, ff. 1r–48v (i.e. the whole manuscript).[3] Since a substantial part of the wordstock is shared by all four manuscripts, my method is to compare the most frequent words in each of the four witnesses in order to see whether there were preferred spellings. The findings indicate that all four scribes chose from a reduced pool of spellings when writing any particular word; that is, a single form is the rule for a substantial number of words, and many more occur with just a single alternative form (as a rule, due to variation in the usage of *-e*). The feature-pool of variant spellings remained wide during the second half of the fifteenth century, but individual scribes had narrowed their choices from that pool.

2 The manuscripts

A brief description of the four manuscripts that compose the corpus is provided below. I record the contents, likely composition dates, dialect and, whenever this is known and has a bearing on the dialect, a short history of the book.

2.1 Additional A.106

This herbal (siglum *A*106) is a prose translation of one of the most widely-read medical texts of the Middle Ages, Macer Floridus's *De Viribus Herbarum*, a poem on the healing powers of 77 plants that was composed in hexameters.[4]

3 An edition of Sloane 5, the so-called *Lelamour Herbal*, has been completed (Moreno Olalla 2018a) and Sloane 770 has been the object of a recent Ph.D. dissertation (Carmona Cejudo 2019); the other two have been transcribed and are currently being edited.

4 See Moreno Olalla (2013b, 2017) for further details on this textual family, which I call *Northern Macer*. This version of the Latin text is incomplete (retaining only 68 out of the 77 canonical entries found in the original) and fully independent from another, more popular English rendering that seems to have circulated around the Midlands (Frisk 1949: 51–54 tentatively suggests Oxford as the origin).

Identification of this text as a translation of *De Viribus Herbarum* passed unnoticed until recently since the expected order of the entries was scrambled during the transmission of the Latin text.[5] The Bodley translation is in a Northern dialect, located in South Humberside, most likely somewhere not far from Grimsby and perhaps in some religious establishment (Moreno Olalla 2013b: 934–936). The hand can be dated in the 1470s.

2.2 Sloane 5

This herbal (siglum *S*5) was taken until recently to be a translation of *De Viribus Herbarum* made in 1373 by an otherwise unknown schoolmaster from Hereford called John Lelamour. However, it is now known that the treatise is actually a conflation of several sources, mainly the very popular herbal called *Agnus Castus*, and a selection of entries from the same Northern translation of Macer Floridus's poem that served also as the subarchetype of *A*106, together with a second, independent translation of the same Latin poem, plus an uncertain number of minor sources, most of them still unidentified. The hand and the watermark on its paper pages indicate that the book was written sometime in the 1460s. The dialect, while displaying a number of layers due to the several sources employed by the compiler and the complicated transmission of the text, has been located near the London-Essex border (Moreno Olalla 2018a: 47–48).[6] The Essex location for this herbal is reinforced by the fact that it seems likely that not just the *Lelamour Herbal* but also the bulk of *S*5 (ff. 13–193)[7] was copied by a professional scribe called John Vynt, who lived in Barking in SW Essex. Vynt, about whom we know very little, was a ward of the first known owner of the volume, a barber-surgeon called Richard Dod, who was London-based but had family connections in SW Essex. Dod also owned a copy of Henry Daniel's *Liber*

5 See Moreno Olalla (2018b) on the possible exemplar for this textual tradition.

6 A Hereford location was suggested in *LALME* (McIntosh et al. 1986: I.199) and repeated in Black (1997: 81–85), where a more definite place of composition was proposed "in the southern part of Herefordshire, corresponding on the geographical map to the plain between Hereford and the upland regions of Archenfield" (1997: 82). In this account, a second scribe is posited who wrote all texts copied after the *Lelamour Herbal*. This is surely wrong: from f. 13r to the end of the book, the same bastard Anglicana hand, written with a quill cut and held in the same angle and dipped in the same greyish black ink (and the same red one in titles and capital letters), is found on the same type of paper pages bearing the same griffin watermark. Even the elongated shafts of some letters and the flourishes used as decoration are clearly the same.

7 The first twelve folios contain a 14th-century *synonyma* and were bound at an unknown date to what in all likelihood must have been an already complete manuscript.

Uricrisiarum.[8] This manuscript was copied in the same hand as *S5*. It is possible, therefore, that John Vynt the scribe was commissioned to copy both texts by his guardian Dod.

2.3 Sloane 404

Sloane 404 (siglum *S404*) is the longest and most recent of the four manuscripts, having been copied by a single scribe sometime in the mid-1480s or 1490s, judging from its hand. It is also the least well-known. I have been unable to find any mention of *S404* in Keiser (1998) and, while it is referenced in the Voigts-Kurtz database with the eVK number 719.00, the information provided there is far from accurate.[9] It is described as an incomplete version of Platearius's *Circa Instans*, but this is demonstrably not so. *S404* is a complete anonymous translation, into what seems to be a very much watered-down Midlands dialect with some Western features, of a Latin incunabulum variously called *Herbarius Moguntinus*, *Herbarius Latinus*, *Herbarius Patavinus*, *Tractatus virtutibus herbarum* and *Aggregator practicus de simplicibus*.[10] The *Aggregator* is an alphabetical book of *simples* (i.e. a collection of mineral, vegetable and animal substances thought at the time to have some medicinal value and therefore used as ingredients in ointments, pills, potions, etc.) that was first printed in 1484 by Peter Schöffer.[11] The book became a best-seller and at least twelve editions appeared during the next seventy years. Initially attributed to Arnaldus de Villanova due to a misleading reference on the front page of its 1491 Vicenza edition, the author of this compilation remains unknown but is sometimes assumed to have been Johannes de Cuba (Johann von Wonnecke Caub, 1430–1503), the same person who composed the *Gart der Gesundheit*, the first printed German book on natural history, which Schöffer published the year after the *Aggregator*. Since there is no positive proof for this attribution, Anderson (1977: 88) prudently suggests that the treatise may be "an original compilation constructed in Schoeffer's printing establishment" from materials which were ultimately drawn from Vincent of Beauvais's *Speculum naturale*.

8 Now San Marino, Huntington Library MS HM 505, described in Hanna (1994: 190–192) and Keiser (2008: 297); see Moreno Olalla (2018a: 60–64) for a more detailed account of the lives of Dod and Vynt.

9 Voigts and Kurtz (2000), available at cctr1.umkc.edu/search, and consulted 25/03/2019.

10 For a fuller list of titles see Anderson (1977: 83–84).

11 This work is no. 91 in the list of known books and broadsides printed by this disciple of Gutenberg (Lehmann-Haupt 1950: 111–123).

2.4 Sloane 770

This manuscript (siglum *S770*) once contained a large number of medical treatises, only four of which now remain. Three herbals, written by the same scribe using a variety of Anglicana hands that can be dated palaeographically to the late 1460s or 1470s, make up most of the volume. The longest of these herbals (ff. 6v–43v) was ascribed to Gilbert Kymer in a near-contemporary inscription on the top margin of its opening page, but this is best taken either as a mistake or as a case of wilful misattribution.[12] Carmona Cejudo (2019) has demonstrated that the main herbal was created through the compilation of several sources, mostly *Circa Instans* and *Agnus Castus*, with the addition of a substantial number of Latin quotations taken from the *Regimen Sanitatis Salernitanum* and *De Viribus Herbarum* (Carmona Cejudo 2019: 97–99). The other two herbals (ff. 44r–45r and 45v–48v) are partial translations of *Circa Instans*. The fourth text of the manuscript (ff. 1v) is a brief astrological treatise on the phases of the Moon based on the Dominical letters, while 2r–5v contain a detailed index of the original contents of the book. Linguistically, all three herbals seem to be homogeneous and contain features regularly associated with dialects from the North, the South and the West, less so to those from the East. The editor tentatively suggests that they might have been copied in some relatively central location in the Midlands but not too far from the Western counties (Carmona Cejudo 2019: 156). Locating the text via the 'fit-technique' of the electronic version of the *Linguistic Atlas of late Mediaeval English* seems to push the location some miles north into NW Leicester, near Derbyshire (Carmona Cejudo 2019: 369–377).

3 The corpus

The four manuscripts that compose the corpus were transcribed and morphologically lemmatized according to the system employed in the *Annotated Corpus of Middle English Scientific Prose*.[13] The total number of items in the corpus is

12 Gilbert Kymer *ca.* 1411–1463, physician to Humphrey, Duke of Gloucester, and then to his nephew, Henry VI (Talbot and Hammond 1965: 60–63).

13 Described in Moreno Olalla and Miranda García (2009: 128–134) and Calle Martín and Moreno Olalla (2012: 18–19). A new field MEDNumber was added cross-referencing tokens to the electronic *Middle English Dictionary*. Entries in the *MED* are recorded as separate files in the same server directory, ranging from MED1, referring to the first entry in the dictionary (ā, *n.*[1] "the letter A of the alphabet") to MED54083, the last word of the dictionary (zucarīne, *adj.*, without a proper definition in the dictionary but meaning 'sugary'). The grammatical

131,423, but this figure is reduced to just 124,092 tokens once the names of medical *auctoritates* and Latin and other foreign-language quotations/borrowings are removed. Roman and Arabic numbers and apothecary symbols are also ignored, as are about a score of words that remain as yet unidentified.

Much of the omitted material consists of section headings, text-organisers such as such as *item* "also", *ut supra* "as above" and Latin synonyms for plant-names.

*S*404 contains c.150 Middle High German words, most of which the translator was unable to interpret, presumably because he did not read German and the words had been printed with a Fraktur type in his exemplar, and were misspelt in the English version as a consequence.[14]

Breaking down the corpus into grammatical categories yields the following figures: nouns 23.94% (29,702 tokens), verbs 17.53% (21,752 tokens), prepositions (including the preposition-cum-article ‹atte›) 13.53% (16,791 tokens), determiners (including articles) 12.33% (15,299 tokens), conjunctions 12.2% (15,142 tokens), pronouns 8.51% (10,562 tokens), adjectives 7.03% (8,724 tokens), adverbs 4.93% (6,120 tokens) (Table 4.1). With the exception of the TOTAL row, where they indicate the weight of each manuscript within the corpus, percentages in Table 4.1 refer to the relative number of tokens by category in each of the four manuscripts.

Table 4.2 indicates the number of word types per manuscript and calculates their lexical richness. Several mathematical formulas, designed to tackle the issue of skewness when texts of different length are compared, have been developed to find an accurate way to represent this.[15] Text length in the four herbals is very variable, as seen from the TOTAL row of Table 4.1, so *a priori* a method such as Mean Segmental Type-Token Ratio or Measure of Textual Lexical Diversity, which require the division of the texts into equal chunks,

categories used in the electronic *Middle English Dictionary* were retained but modified: for example, *tǭ*, which *MED* tags as a particle if appearing immediately before an infinitive (MED46049), is taken together with the preposition (MED46047). Similarly, the different cases of personal pronouns, which are segregated in *MED* (eg *thǒu* MED45409, *thę̄* MED45072, *thīn* MED45296), were lumped together into a single type under the nominative form, although singular and plural forms were kept apart. The tags *ger.* and *ppl.*, which *MED* employs to indicate present and past participles when functioning as adjectives or nouns, were dropped and the tags *Adje* or *Noun*, according to context, used instead.

14 Eg ‹ybiszmorczel› *S*404.11r/6 instead of ‹ybißwortzel› and ‹Misz niszworcz› *S*404.96r/8 instead of ‹wiß nißwortz›, respectively glossing ‹Altea› and ‹Ellebor*us* alb*us*› and corresponding to Present-Day German *Eibischwurzel*, "marshmallow, *Althaea officinalis* L." and *weiße Nieswurz*, "white hellebore, *Veratrum album* L.".

15 See Tweedie and Baayen (1998). Torruella and Capsada (2013: 448–449) present recent developments, although with errors and incorrect references.

Table 4.1: Number of ME tokens according to MS and category.

	A106	*S5*	*S404*	*S770*
Nouns	2,296 (24.15 %)	6,592 (24.07%)	15,643 (23.6%)	5,171 (24.73%)
Verbs	1,849 (19.44%)	5,165 (18.86%)	10,886 (16.42%)	3,852 (18.42%)
Prepositions	1,068 (11.23%)	3,103 (11.33%)	10,020 (15.11%)	2,600 (12.43%)
Determiners	1,095 (11.52 %)	3,215 (11.74%)	8,669 (13.08%)	2,320 (11.1%)
Conjunctions	1,476 (15.52%)	2,926 (10.69%)	8,274 (12.47%)	2,466 (11.79%)
Pronouns	843 (8.87%)	2,734 (9.98%)	5,405 (8.15%)	1,580 (7.56%)
Adjectives	534 (5.62%)	2,025 (7.4%)	4,496 (6.78%)	1,669 (7.98%)
Adverbs	348 (3.66%)	1,622 (5.92%)	2,899 (4.37%)	1,251 (5.98%)
TOTAL	9,509 (7.66%)	27,382 (22.07%)	66,292 (53.42%)	20,909 (16.85%)

would be the obvious approach. However Torruella and Capsada show that type-token ratio formulas based on logarithmic functions, and Maas's *a*-index in particular (expressed through the formula $a^2 = (\log N - \log V)/\log N^2$),[16] are able to render very similar results and require neither text splitting nor any other sort of normalization procedure.

Table 4.2: Lexical richness of the four manuscripts in the corpus.

	A106	*S5*	*S404*	*S770*
N	9,509	27,382	66,292	20,909
V	784	1,693	2,214	1,583
a^2	0.0303	0.0267	0.0276	0.0261

4 Analysis

Since my purpose was to detect spelling trends on a per-wordtype basis, wordtypes recorded just once or twice in each manuscript of the corpus were of no discriminatory interest and dropped. Depending on the length of the actual text, even a wordtype appearing three or four times may prove to be not

16 N refers to the total number of tokens and V to the number of wordtypes; lexical richness is therefore inversely proportional to its index value; see Maas (1972) for details.

particularly relevant to the general argument, so I have settled for an analysis of wordtypes fulfilling the condition $f = N{\cdot}100/V \geq 0.05$, which means studying the top 230–265 most frequent wordtypes in each text, appearing on average at least 11 times in the corpus. These figures represent 85.58% of the total number of tokens recorded more than twice in the corpus, as seen in Table 4.3. Therefore, the selected tokens of the corpus form, unsurprisingly, the lion's share of a regular Zipf-Pareto distribution.[17]

Table 4.3: Accepted and discarded corpus data.

	A106	*S5*	*S404*	*S770*
Accepted wordtypes	230	233	250	265
Accepted tokens	8,598 (≥ 5×)	23,511 (≥ 13×)	56,546 (≥ 30×)	17,662 (≥ 10×)
% Accepted tokens	90.42%	85.86%	85.3%	84.47%
Discarded tokens	399 [116]	2,634 [479]	8,342 [884]	2,136 [465]
% Discarded tokens	4.16%	9.62%	12.58%	10.21%

Since the corpus is lemmatized, deviation based on the number of hits of a given word will be completely annulled, and the similar lexical richness between all witnesses, as shown in Table 4.2, ensures that skewness due to the different number of wordtypes will be minimal. A simple classification of the accepted wordtypes in each manuscript according to their number of variants, using the same tokens in the chart above, generated Chart 4.1 below.

The distribution of variants per wordtype shows that for most wordtypes a comparatively reduced number of spellings was used. Although there are a few outliers, most obviously, the sixteen different spellings in *S404* for *mug-wort*, meaning either the common mugwort (*Artemisia vulgaris* L.) or the akin species wormwood (*Artemisia absinthium* L.),[18] as a rule scribes employed no more than five separate spellings per wordtype. The copyists of *A106* and *S770* seem to have worked with an even more constrained number of choices, since for

17 Note that 'discarded tokens' in the table refers to items appearing more than twice in the text but below the 0.05 threshold; the figures between square brackets in that row refer to the number of discarded wordtypes. The figures of accepted tokens are followed by the minimal number of hits per manuscript that allowed inclusion in the group of valid data.

18 The list of spellings for this word are: ‹mogeworte›, ‹mogewortte›, ‹moughworte›, ‹moughwortte›, ‹mough wortte›, ‹mougwort›, ‹mougworte›, ‹moug worth›, ‹mougwortte›, ‹moug wortte›, ‹mugewort›, ‹muge worte›, ‹mugewortte›, ‹mugwort›, ‹mugworte› and ‹mugwortte›.

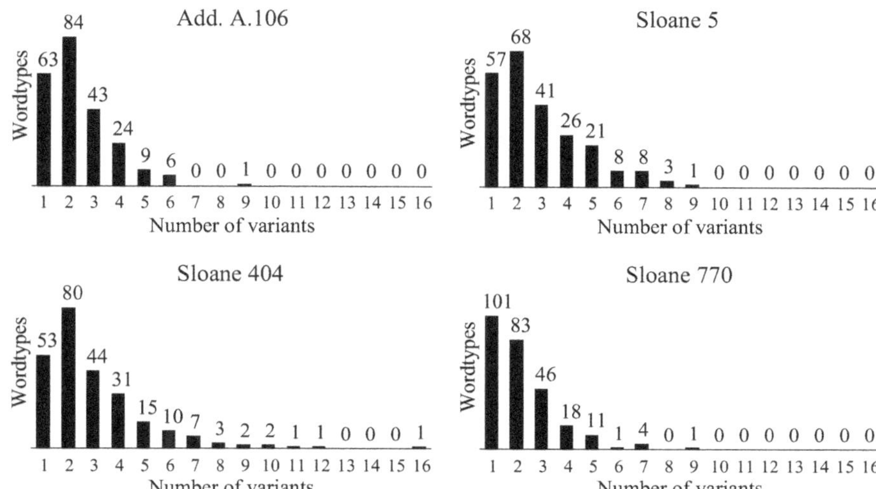

Chart 4.1: Wordtypes according to their number of variants (raw data).

over 93% of the wordtypes (93.04% and 93.58%, respectively) the limit is four spellings or fewer. Perhaps the most interesting finding is that about a third of the most frequent wordtypes in each manuscript take just two spellings: 36.52% in *A*106, 29.18% in *S*5, 32% in *S*404 and 31.32% in *S*770.

Chart 4.2, which distributes the wordtypes into quartiles, supports the preceding analysis of all four manuscripts in the corpus as being orthographically homogeneous, despite initial appearances to the contrary: μ = 2.17 [*S*770], 2.37 [*A*106], 2.84 [*S*5], 3.02 [*S*404]. The dispersion of variants in the witnesses seems negligible (σ = 1.31 [*A*106], 1.34 [*S*770], 1.75 [*S*5], 2.14 [*S*404]), yet the comparatively high coefficient of variation (i.e. the ratio between the standard variation and the mean) proves that this is in fact not so: 62% for all MSS except for *S*404, where it is even larger (c_v = 71%).

The raw data presented in Chart 4.1 and Chart 4.2 above were then refined by bundling together certain orthographical features, as Middle English scribes could represent the same sound with two or more graphic symbols (see Chart 4.3). To put it in medieval parlance, the different *litterae* (graphs) having the same *potestas* (perceived phonological value) were ignored.[19]

19 On the useful tripartite distinction between *litterae*, *figurae* and *potestates*, which dates back at least from Priscian, see Irvine (1994: 97); Horobin (2013: 21–23) and especially Pérez Rodríguez (2002). These equivalences are built in the understanding that, to the best of our current knowledge, scribes would have regarded some sets of forms as being fully interchangeable, substitution

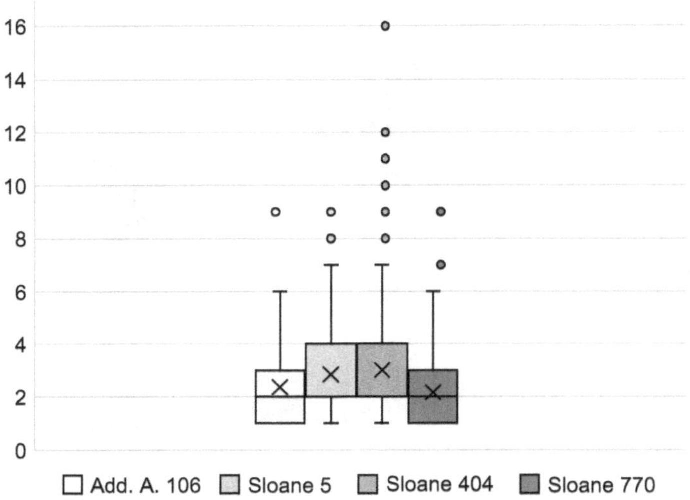

Chart 4.2: Spelling variants (quartiles).

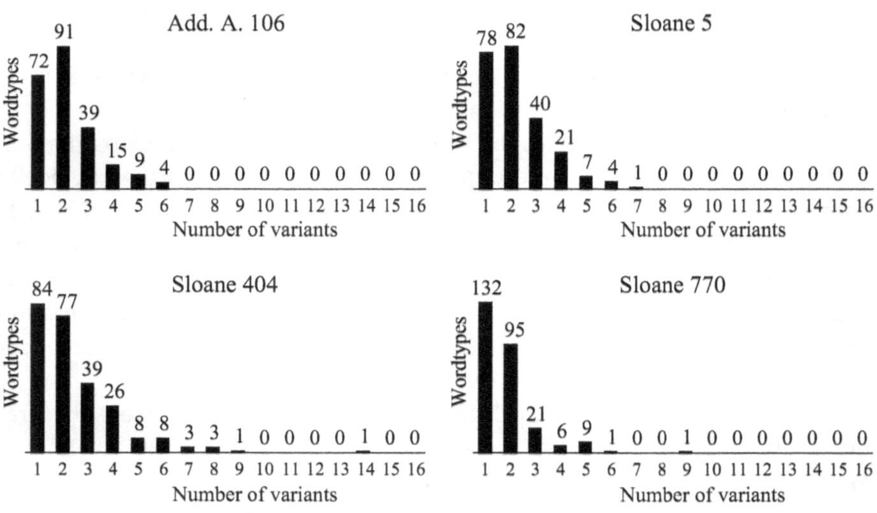

Chart 4.3: Wordtypes according to their number of variants (refined data).

of one form by the other(s) having no actual linguistic implications, be they phonological, morphological, syntactic or dialectal. The interchangeable sets were not fixed in time but shifted according to the time, the space and the social class to which the scribe belonged.

The list includes ‹ȝ› and ‹gh› to represent /x/, ‹þ› and ‹th› to represent /θ/, ‹y›, ‹i› and ‹j› to represent /i(:)/ and ‹u› and ‹v› to represent both /v/ and /u(:)/.

These substitutions are not just a convenient theoretical consideration but can be demonstrated practically by analysing copy blunders. Take for example the copyist of a popular ophthalmological treatise by Benvenutus Grassus, variously called *Practica oculorum* or *De probatissima arte oculorum* and which is now Glasgow, Glasgow University Library, Hunter MS 503 (V.8.6), a manuscript from the last quarter of the 15th century (Eldredge 1996: 25). He inadvertently duplicated on page 13 the same fragment that he had copied on page 11, thus giving us the opportunity of having exactly the same words, drawn from the same exemplar, arranged in the same order and written by the same person, reproduced twice.[20] The two versions are similar in almost every detail, suggesting that the person who copied Hunter 503 must have been basically an A-type or *literatim* scribe (Laing 2004: 52) – and yet the two versions of the fragment are not *exactly* the same. Ignoring some differences in the punctuation, a copy mistake (‹whytishe› 11/5, misspelt as ‹whytylhe› 13/5), a small scribal addition (‹as the› 11/7 : ‹as of the› 13/7–8) and a couple of divergences on the choice between the ampersand and the full form of the copulative conjunction, at least 28 out of the 111 words which compose the otherwise identical text offer some sort of spelling modification. That means that over a quarter of the words of the text were spelt in different ways. Changes include alternations between ‹th› and ‹þ›, ‹i› and ‹y›, the endings ‹-or› and ‹-o*ur*›, single and double letters (either to spell long vowels or to indicate preceding short ones), and the presence or absence of -*e*.[21]

20 See Eldredge (1996: 30–37) on the transmission of this textual family. The parallel passage can be found in Miranda García (2011: 164–166), but note that abbreviated words have been silently expanded and there are several minor transcription mistakes.

21 It is important to stress that the scribe's spelling freedom was not mirrored by a similar level of dialectal variation. Very few of the alternative spellings used by the scribe would raise the eyebrow of your regular dialectologist – and then even so slightly. Of course, ‹mech› 13/11 instead of ‹much› 11/11 would draw some attention, and it is just possible that the pairs ‹comu*n*ly› 11/6 vs. ‹comonly› 13/6–7, ‹causid› 11/8 vs. ‹caused› 13/8–9 and ‹yndegest› 11/15 vs. ‹indigest› 13/15 could merit some passing remark. This reinforces the hypothesis that the scribe of Hunter 503 must have been quite conservative in his writing habits. Though I must concede that there is something of a circular argument here, the very opposition between the dialectal discretion exhibited by the scribe of Hunter 503 while doing his copying job and the number of spelling changes he made while replicating page 11 of the manuscript gives support to the assumption that for him the differences between ‹th› and ‹þ›, ‹i› and ‹y›, and even the presence or absence of certain letters, were factually immaterial and hence these alternations would better be regarded as being in fact the same.

On the other hand, some graph-combinations that had similar phonetic values were kept separate. This is the case of the group formed by ‹sch›, ‹sh›, ‹ssh› (and, depending on the precise word and manuscript, ‹s›, ‹ss› and ‹x› as well). Although these letters were used interchangeably to represent the postalveolar voiceless fricative /ʃ/, one could argue that, at least for some scribes, the choice here was not free but constrained by considerations having to do with syllable structure (theoretically at least, ‹sh› would be used after long vowel, while ‹ssh› represents its doubled form and hence would be found after a short one).[22] Moreover, some authors consider ‹sch› a Northern feature (Jordan 1974: §181), so there were possible dialectal considerations advising against that move as well.

Phonotactic variants across word boundaries were also interpreted as a single spelling but only if it is the sole distinguishing feature: hence, ‹a› and ‹an› were grouped together as the alternation follows the usual rule in all MSS;[23] on the other hand, ‹ane› is considered separately. (This is actually the sole example: possessive adjectives/pronouns, which would also qualify for this type of external sandhi, did not fulfil the frequency condition and hence are not included as valid wordtypes.) Split words such as ‹a bout› or ‹de gre› were joined together to form single words, while about a hundred clear scribal oversights and obvious copy mistakes were corrected, trying to be as non-invasive as possible. Emendations consisted for the most part of adding a missing letter or brevigraph mark.[24]

The results of the changes to the wordtypes corpus are presented as Chart 4.3. Although interventions were minor, it resulted in considerable changes in the distribution of spellings, and strongly suggests that the four scribes were working with what was basically a collection of binary spellings for most wordtypes: 64.4% of the corpus in *S*404, 68.38% in *S*5, 70.87% in *A*106 and 85.66% in *S*770.

---

22 The reverse trend seems to be true in the case of *S*404. While the rule was only very loosely applied and counterexamples abound, ‹ssh› was used after a long vowel, ‹sh› after a short one: cf. ‹flessh› or ‹fressh› (OE *flǣsc*, OF *freis*, *fresche*) vs. ‹fishes› or ‹radysh(e)› (OE *fisc*, OF *radis*/Pr. *raditz*). Such behaviour is not confined to this digraph: using a single consonant after a short vowel, a double one after a long one – broadly speaking, the opposite of the system employed in the *Orrmulum* – is a peculiar feature of this manuscript, at least with some consonants (mainly voiceless ones), cf. ‹dyppe› "deep" (OE dēop), ‹mette› "food, meat" (OE *mete*), ‹rosse› "rose" (OE *rōse*), ‹rotte› "root" (late OE *rōt*/ON *rót*).

23 As expected, this includes choosing the *n*-variant not only before vowels but also /h-/, as in ‹an hondfull› *S*5.146, ‹an hoolle yere› *S*404.8r/8 or ‹an hote botche› *S*770.7v/14–15.

24 Eg ‹myke› *A*106.249r/12 for *MYLKE, or ‹chyapite› *S*404.116v/11 instead of *CHYAPITRE. Less certain cases, such as ‹an› instead of ‹and› appearing four times in *S*5 and once in *S*404, or a collection of peculiar spellings for the definite article in the translation of the *Aggregator* (including ‹to›, ‹de› and ‹te›) were treated separately.

(For comparison, it should be borne into account that the percentage of binary choices in the case of raw, non-edited data was just 32% as an average.) The parallel figures for tokens after the intervention are also revealing: 76.27% (6,554) of *A*106, 75.79% (17,819) of *S*5, 57.52% (32,528) of *S*404 and 91.74% (16,230) of *S*770 present binary choices.[25]

The figures suggest that standardization processes, while far from complete, were well on their way by the second half of the fifteenth century, at least in this sort of text-type, but perhaps we could dig yet a bit deeper. I have demonstrated in Moreno Olalla (2011: 56–58) that the perceived instances of singular nouns displaying an opposition between spellings ending with a final consonant and with *-e* in *S*5 (i.e., cases like ‹maner› : ‹manere›, ‹wyn› : ‹wyne›) were to a very large extent more apparent than real. For most nouns in that herbal there was a clear preference for one version or the other so, in actual practice, its scribe used a single form, which he spelt differently just a very small number of times.[26] Only 16.45% of the nouns in that manuscript did *not* have a clearly-preferred orthography.

Does this observation apply to the *Lelamour Herbal* alone or is it valid for the other manuscripts of the corpus too? After checking that *-e* did not serve a morphological function in any of the four herbals (see Minkova 1991 for a discussion of the loss of schwa), valid wordtypes were grouped according to the presence or absence of the final vowel in their tokens, without any editorial tampering. Chart 4.4 presents the initial results, suggesting that, for many wordtypes, ± *-e* was clearly very much alive.[27]

25 The noticeably lower figure in the case of the *Aggregator* is due to the fact that the definite article, the verb *bẹ̄n* and the prepositions *in* and *with* were spelt using three or more variants in that particular manuscript.

26 The numbers are very revealing in the case of the words quoted above: ‹maner› 70× : ‹manere› 1× (98.28% : 1.72%) and ‹wyne› 189× : ‹wyn› 12× (94.03% : 5.97%). Such cases are not exceptional but regular in *S*5, as seen by the (incomplete) collection of wordtypes quoted in Moreno Olalla (2011: 58).

27 Wordtypes with a vocalic consonant in their final syllables were included in the reckoning because they represent the same syllable structure whenever the final consonant is a sonorant, so spelling variations between -‹el› and -‹le›, -‹en› and -‹ne›, and -‹er› and -‹re› were considered separately. (There are no instances of -‹em›/-‹me› in the part of corpus under scrutiny.) Tokens spelt with -‹ul›, -‹il›, -‹ur›, -‹ir›, etc. were included in the same block as -‹el›, -‹er› and the like, unless the same wordtype is also spelt with two or more different vowels before the consonant in the manuscript. Monosyllables ending in *-e* were omitted (the list includes the personal pronouns *hẹ̄, shẹ̄* and *wẹ̄*, the conjunction and adverb *ne*, the definite article and the like; and the bisyllabic *dēgrẹ̄* belongs here as well since *-e* was stressed, cf. OFr *degré* < MLat *dēgradus*). Verbs appearing only as inflected forms and nouns recorded in the corpus only in either the plural or the genitive singular case were also omitted. (This is the reason why the numbers of

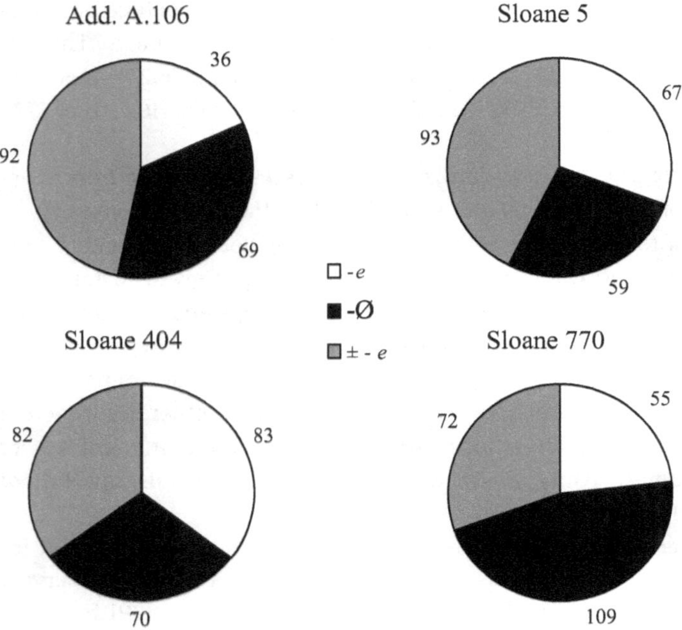

Chart 4.4: Distribution of final *-e* (raw data).

Chart 4.5 is a refined version of Chart 4.4, where the cases of ± *-e* have been classified according to their most frequent variant. The number of variants with an unstable *-e* were reckoned, the hits of each of the two main variants compared and the wordtype added to either the *-e* or the *-Ø* group only when the following condition is met: one of the two spelling variants must be found at least twice as much as the other. Re-distributing the wordtypes through the application of this simple rule changed dramatically the figures for ± *-e*: *A*106 passed from 46.7% of such wordtypes to just 11.17%, *S*770 from 29.66% to 5.51%, *S*5 from 42.47% to 5.02% and *S*404 from 33.62% to 2.55%. Ignoring cases where the ratios are 1 : 1, 2 : 1, etc. and thus of lesser statistical consequence, the following are the only wordtypes which each scribe *really* varied:

valid wordtypes per manuscript here do not tally those in previous charts, and why it is possible to find very small ratios of opposing variants in this section, even though wordtypes must be recorded ≥ 11× as an average to qualify into the corpus: nouns like *eie* or *ēre* and verbs like *cŏmen* or *sęthen*, which are included in the corpus because they do fulfil the above condition, are in fact seldom found without an ending.)

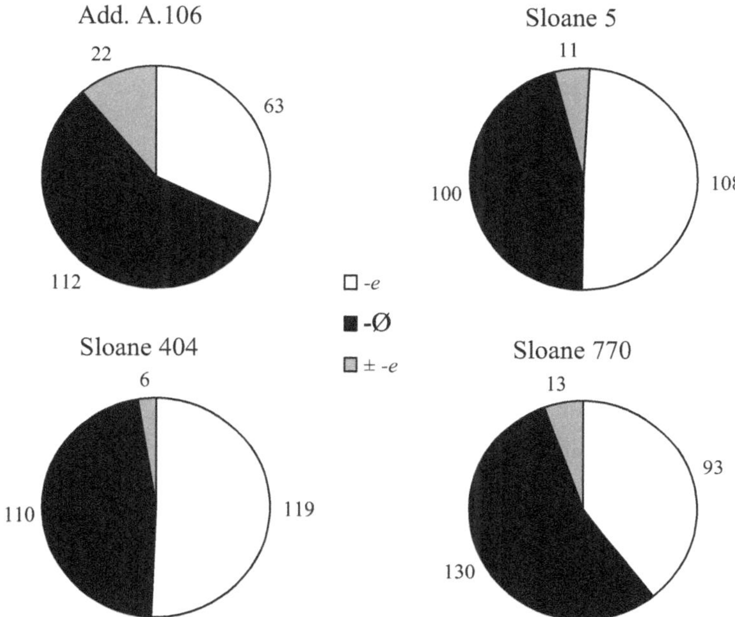

Chart 4.5: Distribution of final *-e* (refined data).

> *A*106: ‹body› 5 : ‹bodye› 4; ‹both› 4 : ‹bothe› 5; ‹chyld› 6 : ‹chylde› 4; ‹dry› 29 : ‹drye› 16; ‹hard› 5 : ‹harde› 4; ‹hed, heyd› 14 : ‹hed(d)e› 16; ‹hot(t)› 24 : ‹hotte, hatte› 22; ‹man› 15 : ‹mane› 10; ‹mych› 5 : ‹myche› 4; ‹ros› 4 : ‹ro(y)se› 5; ‹seth› 5 : ‹sethe› 7; ‹veton› 5 : ‹vetone› 5.

> *S*5: ‹betony› 8 : ‹betonye› 6; ‹brennyng› 8 : ‹brennynge› 10; ‹brest› 14 : ‹breste› 12; ‹com› 7 : ‹come› 7; ‹distroy› 19 : ‹distroye› 14; ‹drop(e)sy› 12 : ‹drop(e)sye› 12; ‹fallyng› 8 : ‹fallynge› 6; ‹mylt› 7 : ‹mylte› 7[28]; ‹stoppyng› 7 : ‹stop(p)ynge› 10; ‹swellyng› 18 : ‹swellynge› 30.

> *S*404: ‹comf(f)ort(t)› 51 : ‹comf(f)ort(t)e› 66; ‹grow› 9 : ‹growe› 13; ‹flo(u)r› 77 : ‹flo(u)re› 44, ‹fruit› 13 : ‹fruit(t)e› 23; ‹warmo(a)d› 32 : ‹warmode› 20; ‹whit› 66 : ‹whyt(t)e› 37.

> *S*770: ‹acces› 7 : ‹accesse› 6; ‹al› 41 : ‹al(l)e› 32; ‹bla(c)k› 9 : ‹blak(k)e› 5; ‹colour› 9 : ‹col-oure› 5; ‹dry› 22 : ‹drye› 36; ‹jamciem› 5 : ‹jaundyce› 6; ‹medecyn(a)bul(l) 9 : ‹medicyn-able› 8; ‹streyn› 4 : ‹streyne› 7; ‹ther› 24 : ‹there› 19; ‹thees› 14 : ‹thise› 17; ‹tyl› 8 : ‹tylle› 6; ‹vertu› 39 : ‹vertue› 35.

Although the self-imposed "+50%" rule means that, from a strict point of view, there is significant scribal variation in these cases too, it would be possible to

28 Note that the variants for this wordtype were mistyped as "7:6" in Moreno Olalla 2011: 58.

argue that, in the case of *S5*, there was a scribal preference for ‹swellynge› over ‹swellyng›, while in *S404* the +-*e* variant seems to be the preferred one in the cases of *cŏmforten* and *fruit*, the opposite being true for *flŏur*, *wermōd(e* and *whīt*. As for *S770*, its scribe seems to have favoured the consonantal variant in the cases of *al*, *blāk*, *cŏlŏur* and (perhaps) *thĕ̄r*, but the final-vowel spelling in the case of *drīe* and, although this is less clear, *streinen* as well. That would in turn mean that in the case of *S404* only the preferred spelling for *grouen* would be dubious, and the number of cases of ± -*e* in *S770* would be literally halved, leaving *A106* as the sole manuscript presenting a substantial number of wordtypes displaying actual variation on the usage of -*e* (22 wordtypes).

There is surprisingly little one can say with any degree of confidence about a possible common distribution of -*e* in the same wordtypes. 82 lemmas in the corpus are common to the four manuscripts of the corpus *and* can be found more than twice in the core case (in the case of nouns) or in the infinitive/imperative (in the case of verbs, but with the exceptions of the wordtypes *bę̄n*, *mouen* and *shulen*, which stand here for their corresponding 3rd sg. present indicative forms, i.e. the attested spelling variants for ‹is› and ‹beth›, ‹may›, and ‹shall›, respectively). Of these 82 shared items, just the following 15 wordtypes were spelt the same way by the four scribes: *fleume* and *wŏrm* are always spelt with -*e*, and *hŏnī* plus a collection of function words (*alsō, and, anī, as, is, beth, hit, ŏ̄r, sō, that, thei, tǭ̆*, and *whanne*) are unexceptionally written without it. The rest of the shared items are distributed according to Table 4.4. The plus and minus signs in the table indicate that the presence or absence of final -*e* are the only variants for a particular wordtype in a particular manuscript, while ± indicates that the wordtype displays an -*e* that may appear in about 50% of the recorded instances. Those wordtypes with a plus or a minus sign followed by a ratio in square brackets are cases of unstable -*e* as well, but ones where there seems to have been a clear scribal preference for one spelling over the other if the "+50%" condition is applied.

Table 4.4 does not suggest many common patterns with regard to the presence/absence of -*e*. Only three wordtypes from the list, *grę̄ne*, *māken* and *washen*, are consistently spelt with -*e* by all the scribes (although even here the rare consonantal variants can be found), and there is no single wordtype in the list that the four copyists spell without -*e*. There seems to have been a shared preference for -*e* to appear whenever the coda of the stressed syllable was formed by a consonantal cluster, regardless of the quantity of the preceding vowel: long as in *chīld* or *cōld* or short as in *drinken or stampen.*[29] *Enointe(n* is the sole counterexample in the

29 The quantity of *brę̄st*, which should be included here, is not totally clear (Jordan 1974: §§23, 84, 281; divergent dialectal developments have been suggested, see Wright 1905: §196).

Table 4.4: Distribution of ±-*e* in shared wordtypes.

Wordtypes	*A*106	*S*5	*S*404	*S*770
a	– [72 : 2]	–	–	–
al	– [52 : 1]	–	+ [116 : 8]	±
awei	– [44 : 1]	– [97 : 10]	–	–
blāk	– [23 : 1]	– [33 : 3]	+	±
blọ̄d	– [8 : 3]	+	– [51 : 19]	+
bẹ̄n	–	– [25 : 12]	–	–
bŏ̄dī	±	–	–	–
brẹ̄st	–	±	+ [57 : 8]	–
but	–	– [67 : 1]	–	–
callen	±	–	+	+ [27 : 1]
chīld	±	+ [34 : 1]	+ [25 : 1]	+ [8 : 1]
cōld	–	+ [43 : 4]	+ [182 : 1]	+ [30 : 3]
drīe	±	+ [78 : 35]	+	±
drinken	+ [39 : 1]	+ [191 : 9]	+	+ [55 : 27]
enointen	– [21 : 2]	+	+ [34 : 1]	– [22 : 1]
ēre	±	+	+	+
fēver	– [14 : 1]	–	– [59 : 11]	–
flŏ̄ur	–	– [44 : 18]	±	+ [29 : 5]
flux	+	–	+ [124 : 33]	– [12 : 3]
for	– [88 : 6]	–	– [673 : 7]	–
from	±	–	+ [21 : 10]	–
gọ̄d	+ [35 : 17]	+	– [864 : 14]	+ [190 : 2]
grẹ̄ne	+ [9 : 2]	+	+	+
hēd	±	+	+ [84 : 24]	+
hŏ̄t	±	+	+ [231 : 4]	+ [67 : 2]
if	– [47 : 4]	–	–	–
in	–	–	– [1725 : 4]	– [662 : 1]
jaunĭ̄s	–	– [20 : 1]	– [41 : 1]	±
jūs	– [78 : 2]	– [275 : 10]	+	+ [102 : 11]
lĭ̄tel	–	–	– [193 : 4]	–
māken	+ [16 : 1]	+	+	+
man	±	– [74 : 2]	–	–
manēr(e	–	– [57 : 1]	–	– [20 : 1]
medicīn(e	±	+	–	–
mĕ̄te	±	+	– [8 : 4]	+
mouen	–	– [24 : 2]	–	–
mŏ̄uth	+ [19 : 2]	+ [40 : 1]	– [62 : 4]	+ [15 : 3]
much(e	±	+	+	+
nō	– [7 : 2]	–	–	–
of	– [330 : 8]	–	–	–
oil(e	– [22 : 1]	+ [57 : 1]	+	+

Table 4.4 (continued)

Wordtypes	*A106*	*S5*	*S404*	*S770*
on	–	–	– [47 : 1]	+ [51 : 3]
ŏut(e	–	+	+ [44 : 8]	–
plăstre	–	– [60 : 3]	– [63 : 3]	–
pŏudre	– [22 : 1]	–	–	– [80 : 10]
rēd	–	+	+ [41 : 13]	+
rōse	±	+	+	+
rǫte	– [30 : 1]	+	+ [94 : 1]	+
sẹd	– [24 : 8]	+ [96 : 1]	+	+ [63 : 1]
shulen	–	–	– [60 : 1]	– [75 : 3]
stampen	+ [25 : 3]	+ [128 : 1]	+	+ [33 : 10]
stomak	+	+ [62 : 8]	– [127 : 15]	+ [20 : 10]
stōn	+	+ [28 : 2]	+ [43 : 1]	– [12 : 1]
thanne	+ [7 : 1]	–	–	–
this	–	–	–	– [344 : 4]
tǫth	±	+	–	+ [17 : 2]
vertū	–	– [87 : 14]	– [171 : 35]	±
vinegre	– [5 : 1]	– [20 : 8]	+ [152 : 1]	+ [17 : 2]
washen	+ [12 : 3]	+	+	+ [25 : 2]
wăter	–	–	– [273 : 1]	–
wel	–	–	–	+ [84 : 1]
whīt	+	+	±	+
wīn(e	+ [86 : 4]	+ [189 : 12]	– [346 : 8]	+
with	– [99 : 6]	– [413 : 2]	–	– [207 : 3]
wŏmman	– [13 : 4]	– [41 : 3]	–	–
wŏund	– [5 : 2]	+ [13 : 2]	+	+ [20 : 1]
yēven	+	–	+	–

list, since *A106* and *S770* as a rule do not display a final vowel for this particular wordtype. If the coda is not a proper cluster but a doubled consonant, the tendency is unclear. John Vynt spells ‹al, all› and ‹wel, well› unexceptionally, and so does the Bodley scribe (but note ‹alle› just the once),[30] while the spelling behaviour of *S404* is not predictable for *al* and, in the case of the *S770* scribe, for neither *al* nor *wel*. The fact that a system for doubling affricates had not yet gained currency at the time may lie behind the spelling differences of *much(e*, which the Bodley scribe wrote without the final vowel ‹myche› 5× (including a misspelt

30 Notice also the regular spellings ‹oill, oyll› in Bodley, next to the forms ‹oile, oyle› that are used as a rule by the three Sloane scribes and where -*e* might be partially etymological. Vynt did write ‹oyll› and ‹oylle› three times in his work, but these spellings appear in entries derived from *Agnus Castus* and therefore they seem unrelated to the Bodley orthographies.

‹mythe› *A*106.257r/1, vs. ‹mych› 4×, but which the other three copyists spelt with a final vowel. It is possible that they regarded the digraph ‹ch› as yet another cluster. Another letter which must have posed gemination problems was ‹x›, and this probably explains the different spellings for *flux*: it always ends with a consonant in the case of *S*5, and the same form is also dominant in *S*770, while the copyist of *A*106 always added the final vowel. The scribe of *S*440 ended this word with a vowel too, but his majority spelling for this word is ‹fluxse› (119×, plus 2× in the plural ‹fluxses›).

Variants without -*e* are the rule in the case of wordtypes ending with a syllabic consonant and, to a lesser degree, when they end in a vowel other than ‹e› (as in *awei* or *vertū*). The four scribes preferred -Ø spellings in the only wordtype with a syllabic /l/ (*lĭ̄tel*), and the same is true in the case of syllabic /r/ (*fēver, manēr(e, plắstre, pŏ̄udre, vinegre, wā̆ter*) except for *vinegre*: the writers of *S*404 and *S*770 added a final vowel for this particular word.[31] There are no examples of [n̩] in the corpus but one may perhaps argue that *wŏ̄mman*, which must have had /-ən/ and which all scribes wrote almost unexceptionally without a final vowel, should be added here as well.

5 Conclusion

The main conclusion to be drawn from the foregoing analysis is, unsurprisingly, that some sort of standardization process of the English language must have been in motion by the late fifteenth century. The sample used as a corpus (four herbals written in Middle English during the 1460s–1490s) was small, but the image drawn here certainly fits that of other treatises I have tagged and lemmatized while contributing to the *Annotated Corpus of Middle English Scientific Prose*. Although counterexamples could be quoted, all four scribes chose from a reduced pool of spellings when writing any given word.

31 It is possible that the longer number of syllables in *vinegre* and the different stress placement in trisyllables depending on the weight of the last syllable (see Ritt 2012: 402–403) played a part. Although the following might turn out to be due to chance, I find it curious that the same scribes who preferred ‹vynegre›-type variants over ‹vyneger› ones chose *not* to write final -*e* in *medicīn(e* while the copyists of *A*106 and Sloane 5 did the exact opposite, and that only the latter two scribes used spellings such as ‹medcyne› or ‹medsyne›, while such syncopated forms for this word are never found in *S*404 or *S*770: their scribes always spelt a full penult here (as either ‹mede-› or ‹medi-›).

Once the graphic differences between several Middle English single letters and digraphs to represent the same phonetic value are ignored, it can be stated that collectively, scribes used no more than five different spellings per wordtype, a single form is the rule for a substantial number of words, and many more employed just a single alternative form (mostly a variation in the usage of *-e*). The figures for *S*770 are particularly revealing in this respect: 85.66% of the analysed wordtypes present either one or two spelling variants, and, on the matter of *-e*, only 5.51% of the wordtypes do *not* have a preferred writing form.

The study of these four medical works reinforces the finding that the top-to-bottom approach, such as the supposed existence of a Chancery Standard that either trickled down or was imposed upon every scribe in the country, cannot be accurate. The analysis shows that the four scribes did not follow a standard collection of orthographic norms (emanating from Chancery, Westminster or anywhere else) but rather they had their own orthographic norms, which were similar but not identical.[32] While the four scribes differed to a minor degree as to the spelling the final part of a word, they diverged dramatically when it came to spelling stems. The variation between single and double letters as length diacritics, for instance, is striking, and so is the fact that, other than function words, there are comparatively few wordtypes which all scribes spelt in the exact same way.[33] Another point in connection with the usage of final *-e* is that not a single one of the 'uncertain' wordtypes of Chart 4.5 are common to all four scribes. This may be construed

32 It would be a moot question to decide whether ME dialects played a part here. While the Northern scribe of *A*106 is freer in his choices and offers the highest number of orthographic variations, southern scribes seem to have had a comparatively more defined usage of *-e*. Among non-northern texts, the scribe of *S*404 – which may have been composed at or not far from Oxford – is strikingly homogeneous in his choices (just one wordtype, *grouen*, would present real spelling variance), while the one of *S*770, living in some neighbouring county if not in Oxfordshire too, would rank second in the list (seven wordtypes). The probable copyist of *S*5, John Vynt from Essex, would then stand in a middle ground here (ten wordtypes). A larger corpus, including many more manuscripts from other regions of the country (East Anglia, for instance), would be required to build a more definite case on the earlier acceptance of a more standardized form of English in the South than in the North, but it is surely worth mentioning that the figures and general impression here are concomitant with other findings on the topic. The Guild-book of the Barber-Surgeons of York, which is a very late work (1486), still maintains, as a whole, many dialectal traits, while texts copied in more Southern areas around the same years, for instance *The Commonplace Book of Robert Reyne of Acle*, composed in Norfolk, seem to deploy more standard spellings and choices (Taavitsainen 2000: 138).

33 See for instance the different spellings used for *ōld(e*: ‹ald›, less frequently ‹old› in *A*106, ‹olde› (once ‹woll› *S*5.2117, possibly a copying mistake for expected *WOLD, see Jordan 1974: §283) in *S*5 and 770, and ‹holde› (once ‹hold› *S*404.102v/14) in *S*404.

as another proof that standardization forces at this point of time did not yet work countrywide, but rather developed in an individual manner, scribe by scribe.

References

Anderson, Frank J. 1977. *An illustrated history of the herbals.* New York: Columbia University Press.

Barber, Charles Laurence. 1997. *Early modern English.* 2nd ed. Edinburgh: Edinburgh University Press.

Baugh, Albert Croll and Thomas Cable. 2002. *A history of the English language.* 5th ed. London: Routledge.

Benskin, Michael. 1982–1985. "The letters ⟨þ⟩ and ⟨y⟩ in Later Middle English, and some related matters". *Journal of the Society of Archivists* 7: 13–30.

Black, Merja Riita. 1997. "Studies in the dialect materials of medieval Herefordshire". University of Glasgow: PhD thesis.

Calle Martín, Javier and David Moreno Olalla. 2012. "*Body of evidence*: of Middle English annotated corpora and dialect atlases." In: Dance, Richard and Laura Wright (eds.). *The use and development of Middle English.* Frankfurt: Peter Lang. 17–33.

Carmona Cejudo, Jessica. 2019. "London, British Library, Sloane MS 770: A semi-diplomatic edition". Universidad de Málaga: PhD thesis.

Eldredge, Laurence M. (ed.). 1996. *Benvenutus Grassus. The wonderful art of the eye. A critical edition of the Middle English translation of his De probatissima arte oculorum.* Vol. 19. East Lansing: Michigan State University Press.

Freeborn, Dennis. 1998. *From Old English to standard English: a course book in language variation across time.* Studies in English language. 2nd ed. Basingstoke: Palgrave.

Frisk, Gösta (ed.) 1949. *A Middle English translation of Macer Floridus De Viribus Herbarum.* Uppsala: Almqvist & Wiksells Boktryckeri AB.

Green, Monica Helen. 1992. "Obstetrical and gynecological texts in Middle English". *Studies in the Age of Chaucer* 14: 53–88.

Hanna, Ralph. 1994. "Henry Daniel's Liber Uricrisiarum (Excerpt)." In: Matheson, Lister M. (ed.). *Popular and practical science of Medieval England.* East Lansing: Michigan State University Press. 185–218.

Horden, Peregrine. 2011. "What's wrong with early medieval Medicine?". *Social History of Medicine* 24: 5–25.

Horobin, Simon. 2013. *Does spelling matter?* Oxford: Oxford University Press.

Irvine, Martin. 1994. *The making of textual culture: 'grammatica' and literary theory, 350–1100.* Cambridge studies in medieval literature 19. Cambridge: Cambridge University Press.

Jordan, Richard. 1974. *Handbook of Middle English grammar: Phonology.* Trans. Crook, Eugene Joseph. Janua linguarum. Series practica 218. The Hague–Paris: Mouton.

Keiser, George R. 1998. *Works of science and information.* A manual of the writings in Middle English 1050–1500 10. New Haven: The Connecticut Academy of Arts and Sciences.

Keiser, George R. 2008. "Vernacular herbals: a growth industry in late medieval England." In: Connolly, Margaret and Linne R. Mooney (eds.). *Design and distribution of late medieval manuscripts in England.* Cambridge: Boydell & Brewer. 292–307.

Laing, Margaret. 2004. "Multidimensionality: time, space and stratigraphy in historical dialectology." In: Dossena, Marina and Roger Lass (eds.). *Methods and data in English Historical Dialectology*. Bern-Berlin-Bruxelles-Frankfurt am Main-New York-Oxford-Wien: Peter Lang. 49–96.

Lehmann-Haupt, Hellmut. 1950. *Peter Schoeffer of Gernsheim and Mainz. With a list of his surviving books and broadsides*. Printers' Valhalla [4]. Rochester (N. Y.): Printing House of Leo Hart.

Maas, Heinz-Dieter. 1972. "Über den Zusammenhang zwischen Wortschatzumfang und Länge des Textes". *Zeitschrift für Literatur und Linguistik* 2: 73–96.

McIntosh, Angus, Michael L. Samuels and Michael Benskin. 1986. *A linguistic atlas of late mediaeval English*. 4 vols. Aberdeen: Aberdeen University Press.

Minkova, Donka. 1991. *The history of final vowels in English: the sound of muting*. Topics in English linguistics 4. Mouton de Gruyter: Berlin.

Miranda García, Antonio. 2011. "Setting MSS Hunter 503 and 513 apart: A quantitative analysis." In: Miranda García, Antonio and Santiago González Fernández-Corugedo (eds.). *Benvenutus Grassus' On the well-proven art of the eye. Practica oculorum & De probatissima arte oculorum. synoptic edition and philological studies*. Bern: Peter Lang. 143–166.

Moreno Olalla, David. 2011. "Nominal morphemes in *Lelamour's Herbal*." In: Thaisen, Jacob and Hanna Rutkowska (eds.). *Scribes, printers and the accidentals of their texts*. Frankfurt: Peter Lang. 53–71.

Moreno Olalla, David. 2013a. "A plea for ME botanical synonyma." In: Gillespie, Vincent and Anne Hudson (eds.). *Probable truth. Editing medieval texts from Britain in the twenty-first century*. Brussels: Brepols. 387–404.

Moreno Olalla, David. 2013b. "The textual transmission of the *Northern Macer* tradition". *English Studies* 94: 931–957.

Moreno Olalla, David. 2017. "Reconstructing 'John Lelamour's' herbal: the linguistic evidence". *Anglia* 135: 669–699.

Moreno Olalla, David. 2018a. *Lelamour Herbal (MS Sloane 5, ff. 13r–57r). An annotated critical edition*. Late Middle English Texts 6. Frankfurt: Peter Lang.

Moreno Olalla, David. 2018b. "Notes on the Latin original of the Middle English *Northern Macer* herbal". *Manuscripta* 62: 33–56.

Moreno Olalla, David and Antonio Miranda García. 2009. "*An Annotated Corpus of Middle English Scientific Prose*: aims & features." In: Díaz Vera, Javier Enrique and Rosario Caballero Rodríguez (eds.). *Textual healing: Studies in medieval English medical, scientific and technical texts*. Bern: Peter Lang. 123–140.

Pahta, Päivi and Irma Taavitsainen. 2004. "Vernacularisation of scientific and medical writing." In: Taavitsainen, Irma and Päivi Pahta (eds.). *Medical and scientific writing in late medieval English*. Cambridge: Cambridge University Press. 1–22.

Pérez Rodríguez, Estrella. 2002. "La doctrina de Prisciano sobre la letra según sus comentaristas del s. XII." In: Pérez González, Maurilio (ed.). *Actas del III Congreso hispánico de Latín medieval*. Vol. 2. León: Universidad de León. 661–670.

Pyles, Thomas and John Algeo. 1993. *The origins and development of the English language*. 4 ed. Fort Worth: Harcourt Brace Jovanovich College Publishers.

Ritt, Nikolaus. 2012. "Middle English: Phonology." In: Bergs, Alexander and Laurel J. Brinton (eds.). *English historical linguistics: an international handbook*. Vol. I. Berlin: De Gruyter Mouton. 399–414.

Samuels, Michael Louis. 1989. "Some applications of Middle English dialectology." In: Laing, Margaret (ed.). *Middle English dialectology. Essays on some principles and problems*. Aberdeen: Aberdeen University Press. 64–80.
Taavitsainen, Irma. 2000. "Scientific language and spelling standadisation 1375–1550." In: Wright, Laura (ed.). *The development of standard English, 1300–1800. Theories, descriptions, conflicts*. Cambridge: Cambridge University Press. 131–154.
Talbot, Charles H. and E. A. Hammond. 1965. *The medical practitioners in medieval England. A biographical register*. London: Wellcome Historical Medical Library.
Torruella, Joan and Ramón Capsada. 2013. "Lexical statistics and tipological [*sic*] structures: a measure of lexical richness". *Procedia–Social and Behavioral Sciences* 95: 447–454.
Tweedie, Fiona J. and R. Harald Baayen. 1998. "How variable may a constant be? Measures of lexical richness in perspective". *Computers and the Humanities* 32: 323–352.
Voigts, Linda Erhsam and Patricia Deery Kurtz. 2000. *Scientific and medical writings in Old and Middle English: An electronic reference*. Vers. 1.0. Computer software. Ann Arbor: University of Michigan Press.
Wright, Joseph. 1905. *The English dialect grammar, comprising the dialects of England, of the Shetland and Orkney Islands, and of those parts of Scotland, Ireland and Wales where English is habitually spoken*. Oxford – London – Edinburgh – Glasgow – New York and Toronto: Henry Frowde.
Wright, Laura. 2012. "On variation and change in London medieval mixed-language business documents." In: Stenroos, Merja, Martti Mäkinen and Inge Særheim (eds.). *Language contact and development around the North Sea*. Amsterdam: John Benjamins. 95–115.

Jacob Thaisen

5 Standardisation, exemplars, and the Auchinleck manuscript

1 Introduction

Samuels' 1963-article "Some applications of Middle English dialectology" situated the first steps in the formation of present-day Standard English in fourteenth- and fifteenth-century London, the home of three of his four incipient standards. The orthographic forms respectively selected by Scribes 1 and 3 of the Auchinleck manuscript, National Library of Scotland, Edinburgh, MS Advocates' 19.2.1, dated *c.* 1330–40, exemplify the earliest of the London-based types, Type II. This type dies out suddenly *c.* 1380 and is replaced by Type III, which in turn is equally suddenly replaced by Type IV half a century or so later. Samuels' four types have been influential; for example, Kane and Donaldson (1975) explicitly selected Cambridge University Library, MS B.15.17 as the base text for their edition of the B version of *Piers Plowman* on the grounds that it is written in Type III. The types have come under fire in recent years but they continue to prove resilient despite the complete absence of contributions countering the criticisms. For example, the types are unconditionally accepted in a textbook on manuscript studies focusing on the late Middle English period (Kerby-Fulton et al 2012: 67), go entirely unquestioned in a widely used undergraduate linguistics textbook (Horobin and Smith 2002), and are reproduced in as many as three of the fifteen chapters in a recent handbook on Middle English (Brinton and Bergs 2017), including in the chapter specifically devoted to standardisation. It is time to lay the types to rest.

To fulfill this goal, this paper adds to the criticisms by questioning the basis for Type II. What follows details my methodology for orthographic analysis, which is able to discriminate the six scribes of the Auchinleck manuscript and the hands who produced the immediate exemplars. Relating how the exemplar hands are distributed to the manuscript's codicology strongly suggests the exemplars were obtained from local sources which also produced them. A later section discusses orthographic standardisation because there is evidence that the orthographic forms selected by Scribes 1 and 3 are no more similar than the forms selected by the manuscript's other scribes, contrary to what would be expected of a standard even at a very early stage in its formation. The final section summarises.

Note: Thanks are due to Laura Wright, Lawrence Warner, and two anonymous reviewers.

https://doi.org/10.1515/9783110687545-006

2 Perplexity distribution in the Auchinleck manuscript

How orthographically similar are two texts and why? A standard means of answering this question is to collect from both texts the orthographic forms they use for various pre-selected lexical, morphological, or phonological items. The items are ones that are very likely to occur in any text, such as function words and common lexical words, and analysis of their forms will typically concentrate on a specific part of them that is known to distinguish texts from each other. An example of such a part is how the third-person singular present indicative verbal suffix is represented, since its representation is known to differ between southern and northern texts. The number of forms considered is sometimes rather low, and the forms may have been collected from extracts. Any observed differences between the two texts in their inventory of forms and/or the forms' relative frequencies are explained as the result of variables having selected those forms. A variable often and correctly invoked is dialect, which, however, must be carefully distinguished from localisation. The latter represents a conflation of the total set of variables into a single one and cannot be assumed primarily to reflect the former. Williamson (2000) explains the distinction as the placing of a real-world locality on a map ('geographical localisation') versus the fitting of a text's orthographic profile into a typology ('linguistic localisation').[1] It is none the less standard to express linguistic localisation by reference to geographical space, a practice followed in this paper.

My methodology does not rely on pre-selected items and does not focus on any specific part of an orthographic form at the expense of other parts. Instead it takes into account every single orthographic form comprising the texts. I ask how well a probabilistic language model trained on all the forms found in one text is able to account for all the forms found in another text. Language models, including probabilistic ones, are a stable in natural language processing and are at the core of many applications involving pattern recognition, such as for example machine translation and optical character recognition. An extended example will clarify. A traditional linguistic profile of text A for a single item gives all the orthographic forms for that item found in text A. It may also give the orthographic forms' respective frequencies in absolute or relative terms. For example:

SUCH: <such> 28x, <suche> 23x, <swilk> 4x, <suylk> 1x

1 Whether a text's geographical localisation reflects the place where its scribe's received his training or the place where he copied the text is another matter.

A profile of text B contains the forms <such>, <suche>, and <swylk> for that same item. Disregarding frequency, it is reasonable to infer a high level of similarity between texts A and B from a comparison, since two forms are identical and the texts additionally share the features <swV> and <lk>, where V represents <i> or <y>; it is common for medieval scribes to use these two letters interchangeably. The level of similarity established, it is up to the researcher to put forward the variables that best explain how the similarity has come to be. Texts A and B might share exemplars if both are copies of the same literary work, or the form <lk> might suggest that they share a connection to a county like Lincolnshire where /l/ had not vocalised and /k/ had not palatalised.

A language model is an exhaustive version of the traditional linguistic profile, and "to train a model on text A" is just another way of saying "to compile a profile of text A". The unit that a model records could in principle be anything from the single letter to the whole word. Single letters record too little information to be useful for comparison of orthography. Units of two or three letters capture orthography well, whereas larger units capture less orthography and more lexicon. If the unit is three letters, a 3-gram, the recorded orthographic forms for SUCH in text A are:

#su, #sw, suc, swi, suy, uch, che, wil, ilk, uyl, ylk, ch#, he#, lk# (where # means beginning/end of word)

The linguistic profile for the item SUCH in text A corresponds to a 3-gram language model:

<#su> 51x, <#sw> 4x, <suc> 51x, <swi> 4x, <suy> 1x, <uch> 51x, <che> 23x, <wil> 4x, <ilk> 4x, <uyl> 1x, <ylk> 1x, <ch#> 28x, <he#> 23x, <lk#> 1x

To estimate the level of similarity between texts A and B is to calculate the probability of encountering the text B orthographic forms in text A. I do not give the equations here. Suffice it to say that they involve multiplying by the frequencies of the 3-grams that make up the forms, which has a consequence that text B's <swylk> will be assigned zero probability since <swy> and <wyl> are both unattested in text A. However, it can be inferred from the presence of both <swilk> and <suylk> that <swylk> *is* a possible form in text A, as was argued above, although it ought to receive a lower probability than <such> and <suche>.

To make the transition from a language model, which in essence is indistinguishable from a traditional linguistic profile, to a probabilistic language model is to incorporate two measures to simulate that inferential process. The one measure is to substitute the frequencies of the 3-grams <swy> and <wyl> with the frequencies of the constituent 2-grams <sw>, <wy>, and <yl>, and if this still leads to multiplication by zero, that is, if they too are unattested, then with the frequencies of the constituent 1-grams <s>, <w>, <y>, and <l>. This measure is termed "interpolation" or "backoff". The other measure is to add infinitesimal probability to every gram in the model, say by adding .01 to every frequency so that <#su>'s frequency is raised from 51 to 51.01, <#sw>'s from 4 to 4.01, and so forth. An unattested *gram* will thus be assigned the frequency .01, but notice that since every form is composed of several grams, two unattested *forms* will not receive the same probability. This measure is termed "smoothing", and while the example of adding a constant illustrates the principle, what is added to the frequencies in professional applications is not a constant but a variable, and there is some debate in the literature about what variable leads to the closest simulation of human inference. Scaling up by adding up all the probabilities of all the individual forms gives the level of similarity between texts A and B. If that probability is 1:69, the perplexity is just the denominator, which is always a positive integer. The lower the perplexity, the more similar are the two texts.

Note the asymmetry of these similarity metrics. The perplexity of a probabilistic language model trained on text A when tested on text B will not equal the perplexity of a probabilistic language model trained on text B when tested on text A.[2] Note also that the volume of training data affects a model's accuracy, for the greater this volume is, the less interpolation and smoothing will be required to handle unattested forms.

Quantification does not in and of itself explain why two texts are similar at a given level. Above, I pointed to shared exemplars and shared geographical localisation as possible explanatory variables. In what follows I elucidate methodology in a more technical and detailed manner, before establishing how perplexity is distributed in the Auchinleck manuscript and discussing a number of possible explanatory variables one by one. An important finding is that similar segments tend to be similar because they share a scribe.[3] "Scribe" must be the strongest

2 Most textbooks on Natural Language Processing that have a chapter on statistical language models will explain more exhaustively. Thaisen (2012) gives a fuller example of how perplexity is calculated for N-gram models of Middle English orthographic data.

3 In Thaisen (2009) I built separate probabilistic language models of all 50+ manuscript copies of two of the tales from Chaucer's *Canterbury Tales* and established the perplexity of every model on every tale. I found a strong tendency for the two tales by the same scribe always to have lowest perplexity relative to other combinations of tales and scribes/manuscripts. This tendency, then, meant that a shared scribe was the strongest predictor variable in that dataset.

explanatory variable, for the perplexity distribution closely matches the scribal stints that palaeographers have established.

I took the following steps to build probabilistic models of the Auchinleck manuscript. All punctuation was removed from a transcript of the manuscript downloaded from the Oxford Text Archive (Burnley and Wiggins 2003), and all emphatic letter shapes were made nonemphatic (lowercased). Tags were introduced to mark word- and line-boundaries. The transcript was then segmented at every 200th line, and the *SRI Language Modelling Toolkit* (Stolcke 2002) built a separate model for the gram length 3 for each segment. The toolkit assigned probability to every such gram based on its frequency in the segment.

3-grams spanning the space between consecutive words were excluded in order to reduce unwanted lexical effects, that is to say, in order to minimise the capture of a segment's lexicon in the process of modelling its orthography. If every line comprises thirty 3-grams and there are an average six words to a line, discarding the five 3-grams spanning the space between consecutive words within the line amounted to discarding around one-sixth of the data (30 less 5 is 25). Roughly speaking, the basis for the models, then, were 58,000 lines x 25 3-grams/line = 1,450,000 3-grams.

The models were smoothed according to the method devised by Witten and Bell, which weights the frequency-derived probability assigned to a gram according to the number of unique contexts in which it is attested so as further to reduce the undesirable lexical effects. The models were also linearly interpolated, that is to say models were built also for gram lengths 1 and 2. Any final segment shorter than 200 lines was ignored.

The toolkit next tested every segment on every model, returning a separate perplexity for each model on each segment. The resulting perplexity distribution had no noteworthy skew so no further action was taken to normalise it. The mean perplexity on all the segments and its standard deviation were established for every model and visualised by means of a scatterplot. The scatterplot revealed the perplexity distribution in the Auchinleck manuscript to comprise several groups of consecutive segments with similar means and standard deviations and such groups to be interrupted by abrupt shifts. The scatterplot is given in Figure 5.1 below.

The process of first segmenting the transcript, then modelling every segment separately, testing every model on every segment, and eventually identifying groups of models with similar perplexity was repeated with 2-gram models, with several other segment sizes, and with odd and even lines modelled and tested separately to ensure that the groups were no artefact of the method or property of the segments' lexicon. Their existence verified, the proposed groups were further isolated through exclusion of every 200-line segment

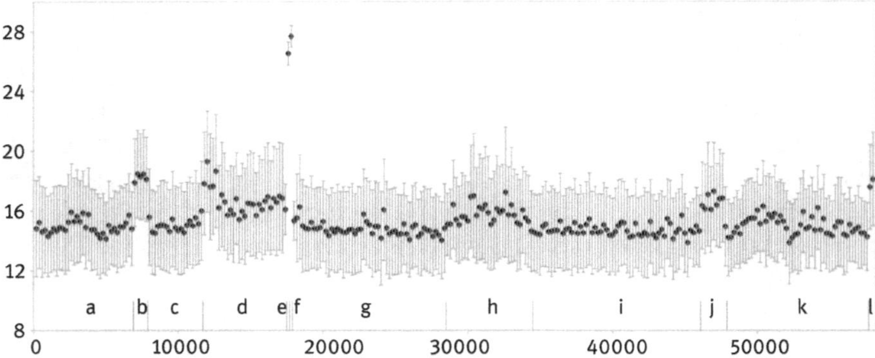

Figure 5.1: Perplexity distribution in the Auchinleck manuscript, based on 200-line segments.

falling at a transition between two groups. The *R* software environment for statistical computing subjected the groups to a one-way ANOVA test in conjunction with Tukey's Range Test, the latter with Kramer correction to compensate for the unequal number of segments in each group, to test the independence of the groups. Groups found not to be independent of each other were collapsed as sets, and the tests for independence repeated on the sets. Table 5.1 gives the final analysis. The groups are labelled alphabetically from "a" to "l" reflecting their order in the Auchinleck manuscript.[4]

Table 5.1 shows a division into six sets.[5] Groups a, c, g, i, and k form a single, non-consecutive set, as does groups b, e, and l. It can be seen from the p-values given in the table that the sets are clearly discriminated. The table identifies the scribe responsible for all text in a set, for the sets strongly correlate with the scribal stints established by palaeographers. These statistics, then, robustly show "scribe" to be a salient predictor variable in explaining the perplexity distribution. There is

4 What is visualised in Figure 5.1 is the mean perplexity on all the segments and its standard deviation for every model. These data were the input to the grouping procedure so that when a group of models was tested for independence from other groups, it was so on the mean of the mean perplexity of the models in the group. As a result, each group does not subsume an equal number of models – in particular groups b, e, f, and l subsume fewer models than the other groups – which could potentially render them incomparable, as one of the anonymous reviewers has rightly pointed out. However, Kramer correction, which was applied, is the variant of Tukey's Range Test designed for an unequal number of segments. An alternative strategy would have been to segment the transcript afresh along the boundaries of the proposed scribal stints, train models on the resulting segments, and repeat the analysis. I acknowledge that this strategy would have been a viable one.

5 Thaisen (2013), Table 1 gives the p-values for the groups prior to their merger into sets.

Table 5.1: Pairwise comparison of mean perplexities for sets of 200-line segments from the Auchinleck manuscripts, in p-values.

Set	scribe	a c g i k	b e l	d	f	h	j
a c g i k	1	–					
b e l	2	<.0000001	–				
d	3	<.0000001	<.0000001	–			
f	4	<.0000001	<.0000001	<.0000001	–		
h	5	<.0000001	<.0000001	<.0000001	<.0000001	–	
j	6	<.0000001	<.0000001	.1793072	<.0000001	<.0000001	–

one exception: The statistics do not show the respective sets corresponding to the stints executed by Scribes 3 and 6 to be statistically significantly different from each other.

The trouble with similarity metrics such as these is that all one can demonstrate is that the groups and sets exist. As was hinted at in the opening section, one can show that two texts have similar orthography but one cannot immediately tell why they are similar; this is so with traditional linguistic profiles too, of course. One cannot attribute the similarity to predictor variables other than by pointing to correlations, and one cannot gauge the strength of a variable by varying it while keeping all the other variables constant. While Table 5.1 provides a strong case for "scribe" as being a predictor variable that explains much of the variation in the perplexity distribution, it should be considered what other variables may explain or confound the metrics. Some can be ruled out. The sets do not correlate with any division of the Auchinleck manuscript by booklet, quire, ink, paraph, textual item, or theme-based grouping of textual items. There is no change of scribe within any textual item, and the genre-based *koiné* evidenced by rhyming usage does not show in these metrics either, but rhyming usage was not modelled separately from the rest of the line. I am unaware of obvious codicological or palaeographical traces of temporal constraints having operated on any of the six scribes, and there are no marked shifts in formality between different parts of the manuscript. Either variable could plausibly have influenced a scribe's selection of orthographic form at a given location of text.

By contrast, a variable for which a case can be made is spatiality. A need to cram the text into a preset space may, perhaps unsurprisingly, lead a scribe to select shorter orthographic forms among the alternatives available to him, while a perceived need to fill a generous such space may have the opposite effect (Peikola 2011; Thaisen 2011, 2013). This variable could explain the perplexity distribution in the three textual items copied by Scribe 2 of the Auchinleck manuscript (*Speculum Guy of Warwick; The Sayings of the Four Philosophers;*

The Simonie). Since one of them, *The Sayings,* is a mere 98 lines long and occupies a position between *Floris and Blancheflour* by Scribe 3 and *The Battle Abbey Roll* by Scribe 4, it constitutes a transitional segment in relation to the data summarised in Table 5.1 and so is omitted from them; but when segmentation is by textual item, the perplexity of the model trained on *The Sayings* does differ statistically significantly from the respective ones trained on Scribe 2's other two items. If this is not simply due to the sparsity of the data *The Sayings* provide, it could be because Scribe 2 writes *The Sayings* on folios ruled by Scribe 1 and compresses his script to fit the ruling, whereas no such compression characterises his other two items. In fact, Scribe 2 writes the *Speculum Guy* on pages ruled for fewer lines than the standard 44 lines and enlarges his script to fill them, and he writes *The Simonie* on folios laid out in single columns that provide ample space for accommodating its long lines; it would have required considerable squashing to fit the text within the double column format that is standard elsewhere in the manuscript.

Spatiality could also explain why the greatest variation between segments copied by a single scribe is found within Scribe 3's stint. The respective models trained on his first five 200-line segments all have higher perplexity than any of those trained on other segments copied by him. This difference is clearly visible in the illustrative scatterplot based on the 200-line segments (Figure 5.1) but it is not statistically significant. It stays non-significant when the methodology is repeated separately for each scribe's contribution so as to keep the predictor variable "scribe" constant. The five segments relate to *The Assumption of the Blessed Virgin,* which is laid out with generous spacing in the horizontal dimension as compared with the other three items. The result is that the scribe has filled up the lines by selecting longer orthographic forms from among the alternatives available to him.

Another variable for which a case can be made is language. The language of the Auchinleck manuscript is almost exclusively English but it does contain text in other languages. The probabilistic models are sufficiently robust for a Latin word or two to matter little to the similarity metrics but Scribe 2's *Sayings* contain as many as ten lines written in French. This amount of text may not be insignificant in a 200-line segment, let alone a 98-line poem. Similarly, Scribe 4's sole item, the *Battle Abbey Roll,* is an enumeration of 551 Norman surnames and as such does not follow English graphotactic rules.

It is well-known that scribes may spell non-identically in verse and prose. This variable is, however, often not perpendicular on spatiality, as verse and prose may be laid out differently. The distinction is not salient as a predictor variable in relation to the Auchinleck manuscript. There never was any potential for it to be so, for the simple reason that the manuscript does not contain any prose, save for the *Battle Abbey Roll* whose contents are not discursive. End-rhymed verse dominates the manuscript among the verse forms, but alliteration is found, in whole or in part, in *The Thrush and the Nightingale*, *Sir Tristrem*, *The Four Foes of Mankind*, and *The Simonie*. Three of these four textual items are excluded from the similarity metrics summarised in Table 5.1 on account of their falling at transitions between groups in the perplexity distribution for the models of the 200-line segments. The fourth item, *Sir Tristrem*, does none the less not constitute an independent group within the output of Scribe 1 according to the one-way ANOVA test. Nor do lines 1–474 form an independent group within *Sir Beves of Hampton*, despite the verse form changing from tail-rhyme to couplets at line 475, which is not a significant juncture in the narrative. A change in poetic form is present in the corresponding location in the Anglo-French version on which the English text is loosely based.

If the agreement between orthography and palaeography indicates that "scribe" is the strongest predictor variable, repetition of the methodology on text exclusively written in a single scribal hand will reveal the scribes behind the exemplars. Accordingly, I divided all text in the hand of Scribe 1 into 200-line segments, modelled each segment separately, computed each model's perplexity on each segment by means of the *Toolkit*, established each model's mean perplexity on all the segments and the standard deviation, visualised the perplexity distribution by means of a scatterplot, identified groups and transitional segments, eliminated transitional segments, and tested the independence of the groups and ultimately sets of groups by means of a one-way ANOVA and Tukey's Range Test.

I repeated these steps separately for each of the remaining scribes, resulting in Table 5.2 as the final analysis. It can be seen from the p-values given in the table that the sets are clearly discriminated. Each set is described as comprising one or more textual items just like Table 5.1 lists its sets by scribe. This is because I have not found a statistically significant change in perplexity within any of the textual items. Note that thirteen textual items do not appear in the table, for example both *The Sayings of the Four Philosophers* and *The Simonie* by Scribe 2. Their omission from consideration is due to them either occupying a transitional segment or constituting a stint less than 200 lines long that is sandwiched between stints by other scribes in the manner of *The Sayings*.

With these reductions in the amount of text considered, Table 5.2 strongly suggests that Scribe 1 worked from exemplars in four hands, Scribe 3 from ones in three hands, and Scribe 5 from ones in two hands, while no more than a single hand was behind the respective exemplars separately for each of Scribes 2, 4, and 6. The separation of scribes for the purpose of Table 5.2 does not permit one to determine any possible identity between an Auchinleck scribe and an exemplar hand, nor any possible instance of two of the scribes drawing on the

Table 5.2: Pairwise comparison of mean perplexities for sets of 200-line segments from the Auchinleck manuscript, in p-values.

Scribe 1					
Item		1 2 22 28 30 31	3 4 33 37 38 40	7 11 12 13 41 42	5 6 23 26 43
	1 2 22 28 30 31	–			
	3 4 33 37 38 40	<.0000001	–		
	7 11 12 13 41 42	<.0000001	<.0000001	–	
	5 6 23 26 43	.0008816	<.0000001	<.0000001	–
Scribe 2					
Item					10
	10				–
Scribe 3					
Item			16	17 18	19
	16		–		
	17 18		<.0000001	–	
	19		<.0000001	.0015620	–
Scribe 4					
Item					21
	21				–
Scribe 5					
Item				24	25
	24			–	
	25			.0000494	–
Scribe 6					
Item					32
	32				–

Key: 1. *The Legend of Pope Gregory;* 2. *The King of Tars;* 3. *The Life of Adam and Eve;* 4. *Seynt Mergrete;* 5. *Seynt Katerine;* 6. *St Patrick's Purgatory;* 7. *The Despute between the Body and the Soule;* 8. *The Harrowing of Hell;* 9. *The Clerk Who Would See the Virgin;* 10. *Speculum Guy of Warwick;* 11. *Amis and Amiloun;* 12. *Life of St Mary Magdalene;* 13. *Anna Our Lady's Mother;* 14. *On the Seven Deadly Sins;* 15. *The Pater Noster vndo on English;* 16. *The Assumption of the Blessed Virgin;* 17. *Sir Degarè;* 18. *The Seven Sages of Rome;* 19. *Floris and Blauncheflour;* 20. *The Sayings of the Four Philosophers;* 21. *The Battle Abbey Roll;* 22. *Guy of Warwick* (couplets); 23. *Guy of Warwick* (stanzas); 24. *Reinbrun;* 25. *Sir Beves of Hampton;* 26. *Of Arthur and of Merlin;* 27. *The Wenche that Loved a King;* 28. *A Penniworth of Witte;* 29. *How Our Lady Saute Was First Found;* 30. *Lay Le Freine;* 31. *Roland and Vernagu;* 32. *Otuel a Knight;* 33. *King Alisaunder;* 34. *The Thrush and the Nightingale;* 35. *The Sayings of St Bernard (=The Three Foes of Mankind);* 36. *David the King;* 37. *Sir Tristrem;* 38. *Sir Orfeo;* 39. *The Four Foes of Mankind;* 40. *Liber Regum Anglie (=The Anonymous Short English Metrical Chronicle);* 41. *Horn Childe and Maiden Rimnild;* 42. *Alphabetical Praise of Women;* 43. *King Richard;* 44. *The Simonie.*

Note: The following items are omitted (scribe indicated in square brackets): 8 [1], 9 [1], 14 [3], 15 [3], 20 [2], 21 [4], 27 [1], 29 [1], 34 [1], 35 [1], 36 [1], 39 [1], and 44 [2].

same exemplar hand (but see below). Every one of the hands who supplied Scribe 1 with exemplars did so for at least five textual items. Such recurrence of hands would be very unlikely if independently circulating individual textual items were collected and appropriated as exemplars. In addition, the absence of any statistically significant change in perplexity within a textual item shows that there was no change of hand within the exemplars for any individual textual item. This, in turn, implies that each scribe received the exemplars for each separate textual item as an integral whole.

The similarity metrics further show that Scribe 1 drew on exemplars prepared by the same hand on more than one occasion. This must be so in light of where the exemplar hands occur relative to the quiring, for their distribution preclude the possibility that Scribe 1 exhausted the exemplars written in one hand before turning to those written in other hands. For example, it is impossible to reconstruct a consecutive progress of copying for the first exemplar hand which reconciles its appearance in *The Legend of Pope Gregory* and *The King of Tars* as the first booklet's first two items with its appearance in *A Penniworth of Witte*. This is because the latter is situated in the middle of the fifth booklet following a stint by Scribe 5 *(Sir Beves of Hampton)*, a stint by Scribe 1 that is not based on the first exemplar hand (*Of Arthur and of Merlin)*, and another stint by Scribe 1 that is a based on an undetermined exemplar hand (*The Wenche that Loved a King)*. The same argument holds for the second exemplar hand, since it appears in the middle of the first booklet *(Seynt Mergrete)* but also opens the eighth and ninth booklets *(King Alisaunder* and *Sir Tristrem*, respectively). It can be appreciated from Table 5.2 that only Scribe 1 among the six scribes alternated between exemplar hands.

It is conspicuous that there is support for different exemplar hands for *Seynt Mergrete* and *Seynt Katerine* since scholars disagree on their possibly shared authorship (Bliss 1956, Görlach 1981); that *Lay Le Freine* and *Sir Orfeo* do not share their exemplar hand since they may share their author (Pearsall and Cunningham 1977: xi); and that *Of Arthur and of Merlin* and *King Richard* do not share their exemplar hand with *King Alisaunder* since Smithers (1957: 41) suggested there is linguistic evidence for a shared London authorship for them; and that *The Anonymous Short English Metrical Chronicle* groups with other textual items (second exemplar hand), since it has been proposed that Scribe 1 actively revised its text (M. Fisher 2012: 146–87). Scribe 1 appears on at least one other occasion to have largely resisted this revising impulse, for he transmitted *The Four Foes of Mankind* (unknown exemplar hand) "in a form which leaves no doubt as to its northern origin. Indeed the amount of change which it underwent at his hands is so minor that in its final form it must still have had as alien a linguistic flavour to a reader or listener in the London of the time as did the speech of the northern clerks in Chaucer's *Reeve's Tale* later in the century" (McIntosh 1978: 138).

3 The immediate exemplars for the Auchinleck manuscript

Codicologists agree that Scribe 1 played a key role in the production of the Auchinleck manuscript. He may have acted as *stacionarius* coordinating the work of all the scribes and interacting with the customer, as the manuscript was definitely compiled to order. The evidence not only is that he copied almost three-fourths of the total text (72 percent) but also that his hand appears outside the stints copied by himself; specifically, he is responsible for supplying paraphs and quire signatures throughout most of the manuscript, as well as for ruling the folios in the case of Scribe 2's *The Sayings*, as previously mentioned. He also furnished the textual items with item numbers and titles after the manuscript was illuminated. Add to this evidence that the manuscript is characterised by a general uniformity of layout with double columns and a fixed number of lines to the page. Such uniformity bespeaks some measure of advance planning, a supervisory presence (in the shape of Scribe 1), and ready access to exemplars for the textual items.

Disagreement has pivoted around the exact nature of the scribes' cooperation and continues to do so, for there are several interruptions to the general scheme. "[M]aybe the organisation was not very sophisticated", Pearsall and Cunningham comment (1977: ix). The order of copying is not settled; the four paraphers may have received the text of the manuscript piecemeal, in scribal stints or booklets (Shonk 2016); and someone other than Scribe 1 appears to have introduced corrections throughout the manuscript, including in Scribe 1's stints (Vaughan 2016).

One view, now abandoned in its strongest form, considers the Auchinleck manuscript as an example of booklet production. This mode of production would have entailed the various scribes producing booklets practically independently of each other at the behest of Scribe 1. One would, consequently, expect of a new scribe for him to have started a new textual item on the first recto of a new booklet and for this booklet to have a separate ruling pattern or be free-standing in other ways, such as by ending in a blank. The scribes would probably have worked on them each in their own workshop, before returning them to Scribe 1 for him to assemble the manuscript. He would have copied shorter items into the blanks at the ends of booklets at the time of assembly so as to fill the booklets up and create smooth transitions between them.

Booklet production of any manuscript gives the assembler flexibility in deciding the order of already copied materials and the possibility to include new material as it becomes available. It is theoretically possible in this production model for one or more booklets to have been copied prospectively, for several scribes each to have worked simultaneously on a booklet, and for exemplars to have been received piecemeal, resulting in a protracted copying process – in fact, there is good reason to think it was regular practice among scribes also to produce and stock exemplars as booklets (Hanna 1986, 1996; cf. Robinson 1980, Gillespie 2011).

The reason that this view is no longer considered entirely valid is that the Auchinleck manuscript does not fully meet the criteria, especially in relation to the roles of the six scribes. Heavy loss of folios hampers complete analysis but it can be confidently stated that scribal stints, textual boundaries, and quire/booklet boundaries do not always coincide. Codicologists recognise twelve booklets of between one and nine quires each with a regular quire size of eight folios. The second booklet spans quires 7–10. Scribe 2 opens this booklet and the *stacionarius* Scribe 1 concludes it, as expected in the booklet production model; but Scribe 2's stint, the *Speculum Guy*, ends already in quire 8 and what follows it, *Amis and Amiloun*, is not a short item helping to fill up a quire. The third booklet is started by Scribe 3 in the expected manner and does end in short items, only those items, *The Sayings* and the *Battle Abbey Roll*, are not supplied by Scribe 1 as one would expect but rather by respectively Scribes 2 and 4, who appear successively on fol. 105. A third example relates to the first of Scribe 5's two textual items, which are consecutive but straddle a booklet boundary. This item finishes a booklet started by Scribe 1, the fourth booklet, as if it was Scribe 5 who was the *stacionarius*.

Scribe 3, then, may have worked independently. So may Scribe 6, for the entire text of *Otuel*, his sole stint, occupies the seventh booklet, which is made up of the ten-folio quire 38, which is the manuscript's sole irregular quire. While Scribe 2 appears elsewhere in the manuscript as described in the preceding, it is possible that he prepared the twelfth booklet independently as it is a single-quire booklet with no other contents than *The Simonie* and does not have the alternating red and blue paraphs found elsewhere; however, this textual item ends imperfectly through loss of quires and it cannot be determined how the booklet ended.

Another abandoned view, this one fully abandoned, argues for readily available exemplars and closer contact between the scribes than the booklet theory allows. This view, associated with Hibbard Loomis (1942) and accepted by both Pearsall and Cunningham (1977) and Taylor (2003), holds that all the various artisans worked under one roof, including not only the scribes and illuminators but also the translators and versifiers who produced the exemplars and the binders who fixed the order of the booklets by binding the final manuscript. Professional lay scribes, in other words, organised themselves and their working methods along the lines of monastic scriptoria. A shared location would explain the codicological support for some form of collaboration among the six scribes, and the evidence that there are frequent thematic and other links between the textual items at the level of contents, such as verbal echoes. Very many of the items are translations from French and appear uniquely or in their earliest attested form in the Auchinleck manuscript. A good many of them are romances, including recently composed ones. It is unlikely that versions of all of them were simultaneously available anywhere else in England than London, be it in Parisian French, Norman French, or English.

It is widely, if not universally, accepted today that there were no organised scriptoria in London in the early fifteenth century, some two or three generations later. The basis for this view is a codicological examination of Trinity College, Cambridge, MS R.3.2 of John Gower's *Confessio Amantis* conducted by Doyle and Parkes (1978). The five scribes who each contributed booklets to that manuscript variously entered into joint ventures with other scribes and book artisans for the production of other manuscripts, suggesting the norm was *ad hoc* collaboration among them. The model is known as distribution copying. Each artisan plied his trade out of his joint living and working quarters, which were situated in close proximity to those of his peers but were none the less separate from them, except an apprentice could work in the same workshop as his master. Muniments relating to Paternoster Row and adjoining streets confirm such living and working arrangements for some book artisans and suggest the quarters' not-very-generous physical dimensions (Christianson 1989, 1990). This neighbourhood abutted the northern wall of St Paul's Cathedral but was not the sole locus of scribal activity in late medieval London. It tallies well with the distribution copying model that the Auchinleck manuscript's Scribe 3 appears to have worked more independently of its Scribe 1 than, for example, its Scribe 2.[6] And it tallies well with the model that the manuscript's Scribe 6 may in fact be its Scribe 1 copying a separate booklet at a moment in time before the manuscript was even conceived.

The absence of organised lay scriptoria two or three generations after the Auchinleck manuscript was produced starkly contrasts with the view of it as emanating from one and is why this view of its making is no longer current. However,

6 The six scribes of the Auchinleck manuscript do not reappear in other manuscripts, except that Scribe 2 possibly furnished British Library, London, MS Egerton 1993 with paraphs (Marshall 2010). There are more certain links to other London manuscripts in the decoration. The four surviving miniatures are in the same style found in British Library, London, MS Royal 2 B VII (the Queen Mary Psalter) and may or may not be by the same artist (Dennison 1990; cf. Shonk 2016: 179).

later scholarship such as Pearsall (2016: 12) has tended slightly to misrepresent Hibbard Loomis's pioneering paper, perhaps because the misleading term "bookshop" appears in its title. The paper, which was written during World War II when less was known about medieval book production, in fact carefully avoids committing to any specification of the shared location as a single scriptorium, entire neighbourhood, or something in between. The specific term "bookshop" is introduced "[f]or convenience [to mean a] hypothetical lay center where went on, *whether under one roof or not,* the necessarily unified and directed work of compiling, copying, illuminating, and binding any book" (1942, 597; my emphasis). There may, then, on balance, have existed a community of independent lay professionals akin or identical to the one centred on Paternoster Row already in early to mid-fourteenth century London. These professionals did not work together in as unified and directed a fashion as Hibbard Loomis envisioned. They were competitors on the market working together on an *ad hoc* basis, and one such collaborative effort resulted in the Auchinleck manuscript (Shonk 1983, 1985, 2016). This conclusion challenges the notion that London emerged late in the Middle English period as a centre of book production in comparison with the South-West Midlands, East Anglia, and Yorkshire.

It is other, later passages than the one cited which make clear that Hibbard Loomis held translation and versification of texts to have been routine tasks for "bookshops". She further held that the artisans who engaged in these activities with a view to the Auchinleck manuscript introduced modifications to the textual items in the process so as to integrate them with one another. Pearsall and Cunningham (1977: ix–xi) follow suit. However, the many verbal echoes advanced by Hibbard Loomis as evidence of the integrating modifications are a universal characteristic of the romance genre and do not in themselves provide good evidence of close contact between the individuals engaged in the translation and versification activities (cf. Wiggins 2002: 98–102). Parallels of many of the textual items occur individually in other manuscripts and include the verbal echoes. In addition, both Shonk (1981: 34–35) and Mordkoff (1981) argue for translation and versification to have preceded the production of the Auchinleck manuscript.[7]

The distance, stemmatically and chronologically, between the translator-versifiers and the Auchinleck scribes must none the less have been short given that the Auchinleck copy is typically or always the earliest known one. Pearsall (2016) operates in the space between the root of the stemma for the English-language version and the immediate exemplars for the Auchinleck copy of it. He

7 Olson (2012: 101, 103) appears to accept the idea that the translator-versifiers may be identical to the Auchinleck scribes, including Scribe 1 for rewriting *Guy of Warwick* (stanzas).

argues for exemplars – meaning a copy falling somewhere in that space – for some textual items to have been put into circulation by their authors, others to have been specifically commissioned for the compilation of the Auchinleck manuscript, and still others to be the work of minstrels-cum-authors. The metrics presented in Table 5.2 cannot situate in time and space the production of what was at the root of the stemma for the English-language version of any of the individual textual items, as they measure orthographic similarity between the immediate exemplars.

Scribe 1 of the Auchinleck manuscript somehow enjoyed continual access to exemplars written in a mere four hands, although they contained no less than 23 textual items. His access to them must have been continual, since he was able to alternate between the hands. The alternation means either (a) that he obtained the exemplars piecemeal, textual item by textual item, or (b) that exemplars for all the textual items were available to him from the outset. The non-consecutive progress of copying rules out the latter explanation, and the low number of hands strongly suggests nearby sources. So, the likelihood is that the community of book artisans probably did not translate or versify any of the textual items present in the Auchinleck manuscript, but it did copy out the text of these items when they came to hand so as to produce exemplars for them and these exemplars it stocked. The community will have adopted these practices for the production of other manuscripts too. The various scribes may each have kept a repository of their own in their separate workshop and have exchanged exemplars with each other on an as-needed basis. If so, there is no guarantee that exemplars for every textual item necessarily passed through the hands of the *stacionarius* coordinating the scribal work on a manuscript. A scribe commissioned independently to copy one or more textual items into a booklet may have drawn on his own repository or that of a nearby peer for the exemplars for them, like Scribes 3 and 6 of the Auchinleck manuscript possibly did. An exchange of exemplars may plausibly have taken place against payment but there does not survive any evidence in that regard.

4 Type II as an incipient standard

Samuels (1963 [1989: 71]) posited four "incipient standards", which he respectively labelled Types I–IV. One of them, Type I, is not London-based and will be ignored in the present discussion. The other three are London-based and follow each other chronologically. His article repeatedly stressed that there is considerable variation in form within the types, in particular within Type III about which he remarked

(1963 [1989: 71]) that "any form of written standard is conspicuous by its absence", for a fully codified standard language will possess minimum variation in form (Haugen 1966). Samuels thus repeatedly emphasised the incipiency of the types in his article and is reputed to have continued doing so orally throughout his professional life. Much later scholarship has none the less tended to play the incipiency down and has instead portrayed the types as fulfilling more of the criteria for a standard language than Samuels intended and than the evidence warrants. But, what is the actual evidence for Type II?

Samuels (1963 [1989: 70]) advised that the forms of Scribe 1 of the Auchinleck manuscript "may be taken as typical of Type II" and in a footnote listed those of Scribes 1 and 3 as well as six scribes of other manuscripts as defining the type – this association of Scribe 3 with a standardising variety would have been surprising a generation earlier, for Brunner (1933) held him obviously to be a Norman not fluent in English.[8] Hanna (2005: 4–15) updated the list with a few more scribes and manuscripts identified by himself and other scholars. Scribes 1 and 3 are the earliest of them, by as much as half a century in the majority of cases, although allowance must be made for the fact that the vagaries of time have not ensured the survival of much relevant material in fourteenth-century English.

Haugen's discussion implies that selection of orthographic forms to make the basis for a future standard must occur early in the standardisation process (cf. Ayres-Bennett 1994: 55), and the basis for connecting the Type II scribes is a shared core of orthographic forms linguistically localisable to Essex. Internal migration may have brought about a change in the kinds of orthographic forms in use in London, a shift in dialectal composition, that saw Type III succeed Type II. This is what Samuels (1963) proposed to account for the incongruity of Types II and III, for the texts manifesting the latter share a core of orthographic forms linguistically localisable to centrally in the Midlands,[9] all the while that the manuscripts housing them too were produced in London. His article offered the flimsy evidence of fewer than twenty contrastive orthographic forms for a mere twelve items in support of a distinction between Types II and III, which it backed up by stressing how the forms did not exhaust the evidence but were the best representatives. Samuels further held that the shift must have been

8 Runde (2016: 71–72; cf. Runde 2010) notes how Scribe 3 is just as comfortable with English as Scribe 1 and so cannot have been a Norman and, more importantly, how he must have been a translating scribe rather than a *literatim* copying one since his orthography is consistent throughout his stint.

9 Some literature capitalises the word "central" and speak of localisation to the Central Midlands. However, there is no geographic entity or traditional dialect area known as the Central Midlands.

sudden, for the manuscripts manifesting Type II all date from before 1380, whereas those manifesting Type III all date from after that year.

However, there are issues with this narrative. Firstly, there is no strong correlation between these geographical and linguistic localisations, for Ekwall's (1956) survey of toponymic surnames mentioned in London records does not endorse any above-average volume of immigrants from central parts of the Midlands – Wright discusses the perceptual Midlands origin of Standard English in greater detail in Chapter 1. Secondly, Chaucerian verse copied by a single scribe, known as Scribe B, is over-represented in the manuscripts attesting Type III, which makes it a possibility that it is genre that is the strongest of the variables predicting linguistic localisation in the case of Type III.[10] The Type II manuscripts similarly share their genre and in part also their textual items (Hanna 2005: 7).[11] Type IV texts are also united by genre, and where it is end-rhymed verse that Types II and III tend to record, the chief evidence for Type IV is documents.[12] Thirdly,

10 Genre may be the strongest grouping variable for the Type III items, but the argument that the defining manuscripts contain little else but Chaucerian verse copied a single scribe fails to convince. It rests on Horobin and Mooney's (2004) assignment of Trinity College, Cambridge, MS B.15.17 of William Langland's *Piers Plowman* to Doyle and Parkes' (1978) Scribe B, the same scribe who copied National Library of Wales, Aberystwyth, MS Peniarth 392D ('Hengwrt') of Geoffrey Chaucer's *Canterbury Tales* and Huntington Library, San Marino, MS El.26.c.9 ('Ellesmere') of the same poem. They bolster up their palaeographical argument by fitting the *Plowman* manuscript into the chronology of Scribe B's manuscripts established by Samuels (1983) from orthographic forms. It comes first. The orthographic forms, however, are 'long' and 'short' ones such as unabbreviated versus abbreviated THAT, WITH, PER-/PAR-, and PRO-, and glyphs of the grapheme 'h' with and without a cross-stroke. It can be demonstrated statistically that Scribe B selects 'short' forms when he is pressed for time and space (Thaisen 2011), and so it is the manuscripts' production time and physical format (spatiality) that are the salient variables rather than Scribe B's chronological age. In addition, since it is required of a standard that it transcends genres, it may be important that Samuels' list of Type III items includes documents in addition to literary texts. The documents are unspecified ones from Chambers and Daunt (1931), presumably Thomas Usk's appeal against John Northampton, Nicholas Brembre's proclamations, and various London guild returns and wills.

11 Probabilistic modelling presupposes that all training and test text is transcribed according to the same protocol, or the perplexity metrics will be influenced by differences in transcription. This is a methodological limitation and a reason that the paper does not consider non-Auchinleck orthographic forms.

12 Type IV is dubbed "Chancery Standard" after Samuels (1963) but it was no standard employed by the Chancery (Benskin 2004). The first half of the label does not denote the entire national (royal) administration at Westminster as J. Fisher (1977) and J. Fisher et al (1984) appeared to maintain but rather a single department within it. Benskin (2004) emphasised that this department primarily issued documents in Latin and that the first departments to use English, or rather re-introduce this language after the Norman Conquest, were more properly orthographic forms characteristics of Type II persist long after 1380 (Horobin 2003) and are found alongside Type III forms (and even Type IV ones), indicating a more gradual chronological shift than Samuels allows (Horobin 2003; Hanna 2005).

Fourthly, there are examples of London-based authors and scribes who did not select any of the types as their target norm. One of them is the poet John Gower whose orthographic forms have been linguistically localised partly to Kent, partly to Suffolk (cf. Horobin 2003, Mooney and Horobin 2003). Medieval London was a dialectal melting pot or, perhaps rather, patchwork quilt so the presence of a language user whose orthographic forms disagreed with any standardising tendency is not in itself evidence of absent standardisation. However, the examples of such users include scribes demonstrably in close contact with the users of Samuels' Types II and III. Scribe 2 of the Auchinleck manuscript is one, for his orthographic forms linguistically localise him on the Gloucestershire/Worcestershire border (LP 6940) and its Scribe 6 may be another – see below. Yet another is the scribe of both Corpus Christi College, Oxford, MS 198 and British Library, London, MS Harley 7334, both of which are manuscripts of Geoffrey Chaucer's *Canterbury Tales*. This scribe is known as Scribe D after Doyle and Parkes (1978) since he is the fourth of the five hands found in the distribution-copied Trinity College, Cambridge, MS R.3.2 of John Gower's *Confessio Amantis*. Scribe B is the second of those hands, but despite them knowing each other, appearing together in at least one manuscript, and copying similar text-types by the same author, Scribe D's orthographic forms are markedly different from those of Scribe B.

Fifthly, the level of similarity between the orthographic choices made by Scribes 1 and 3 of the Auchinleck manuscript does not in fact exceed that, established by the present analysis, between their choices and those made by the other

the Privy Seal and Signet offices. Moreover, the Chancery cannot have been exclusively situated "at Westminster" because its staff numbers, upwards of 100, certainly exceeded the number of desks that could fit in Westminster Hall. It is rather the case that many clerks had their quarters elsewhere in the London-Westminster area. It has, further, become clear that royal clerks, whether attached to the Chancery or another department, frequently interacted with artisans engaged in the local book trade and sometimes took on writing tasks for other clients. Some were hired on a temporary basis. The clerks' numbers, geographical dispersion within the general London area, and possible temporary attachment to the Chancery cannot have been conducive to anyone imposing norms on them for how to spell in English, let alone for a norm to have developed by more natural means within this specific institution. In line with this contextualisation of Type IV, which is pursued in much greater detail by Stenroos in Chapter 2, it resembles Types II and III in representing a single genre, and Wright (1996) has called attention to how a single-genre variety needs elaboration to be able to satisfy the requirements of a standard that can adequately serve many functions.

scribes. In particular, Scribe 3's 200-line segments do not perplex the models trained on Scribe 1's 200-line segments markedly less than Scribe 5's or Scribe 6's do, nor do Scribe 1's 200-line segments perplex the models trained on Scribe 3's 200-line segments markedly less than Scribe 5's or Scribe 6's do. Scribe 5's segments in fact perplex them the least, albeit they do so by a narrow margin (not shown). Such comparable levels of similarity would be expected only if Scribes 5 and 6 *also* belong to the corpus of Type II scribes. There exists support for this possibility, for (a) *A Linguistic Atlas of Late Medieval English* (McIntosh *et al*, 1986), of which Samuels was one of the editors, linguistically localised the profiles for Scribes 1 (LP 6510), 3 (LP 6500), and 5 (LP 6350) adjacent to one another in the general London area; and (b) Hanna (2000, 2016) proposed on palaeographical criteria that Scribe 6 is identical with Scribe 1, the differences being attributable to a chronological gap between the stints.[13] On the other hand, the linguistic profile for Scribe 6 (LP 7820) belongs in Worcestershire, the perplexity distribution does discriminate Scribes 1 and 6, Wiggins' meticulous comparison of a selected range of orthographic forms convincingly speaks against Scribes 1 and 6 being identical (Wiggins 2004), and Scribe 6's stint is codicologically independent in the manner of Scribe 3's.

Sixthly, any orthographic alignment of Scribes 1 and 3 is unexpected from a codicological point of view. The reason is that the codicology does not suggest that they worked closely together, whereas it does suggest that Scribe 1 worked especially closely with Scribe 2 (cf. Shonk 1983, 1985, 2016), whose linguistic localisation disagrees with his. As Hanna (2016: 217) describes it, Scribe 3 is the only one of Scribes 2–6 "not demonstrably in touch with Scribe 1. Not only is Scribe 3's hand isolated in the book as representing documentary rather than formal

13 While Bliss (1951) was the first to propose identity between Scribes 1 and 6, it is Hanna (2000, 2016) who has developed the argument. The principal palaeographical argument for identity between them is that both scribes employ biting, since biting is a rare feature in early fourteenth-century Textura. Hanna explains other palaeographical differences between them as differences in duct typical of stints produced at different times and for different purposes. The same explanation solves the paradox that the seventh booklet with *Otuel* is written in a western dialect, whereas all other text by Scribe 1 is written in an eastern dialect. Because the booklet was prepared independently, there was no need for its linguistic integration with the rest of the manuscript. Besides, examples of texts with western localisations such as those mentioned in this paper show that such texts were acceptable to a London clientele. *Otuel* could, therefore, be *literatim*-copied from western exemplars. Pearsall and Cunningham (1977: x) find "on the whole convincing" the argument (not discussed by Hanna) from literary clues that *Otuel* and the textual item preceding it, *Roland and Vernagu* may together represent a reworking within the Auchinleck "bookshop" of a single ancestral romance. *Roland and Vernagu* answers to the Scribe 1 first exemplar hand.

training; he appears uniquely estranged from the universal format of the book". It will be recalled that Scribe 3 copied only the third booklet, which is concluded by Scribes 2 and 4 in succession and in which Scribe 1 does not appear. It will also be recalled that the models of Scribe 3's first five 200-line segments have "odd" perplexities; it is these segments which do not adopt the general format of the manuscript, implying an absence of Scribe 1's controlling hand.

Seventhly, there is no support in the perplexity distribution for coincident exemplar hands which could have conditioned Scribes 1's and 3's orthographic forms in the direction of convergence. It is a possibility that Scribes 1 and 3 could have copied from exemplars prepared by one and the same hand in view of how the immediate exemplars were locally produced and locally obtained, even if the present analysis has shown the various texts primarily to record the respective scribes' own forms. There might even, at least theoretically, have been identity between an exemplar hand and an Auchinleck scribe. However, it can be stated with confidence that any support is absent, since no pairing of models and segments corresponding to a Scribe 1 exemplar hand with those corresponding to a Scribe 3 exemplar hand is associated with an appreciably lower perplexity than any other such pairing, including the textual items analysed by the *Atlas*.[14] Those items were *Seynt Mergrete, Seynt Katerine, Guy of Warwick* (couplets), *Sir Orfeo,* and *The Anonymous Short English Metrical Chronicle* for Scribe 1 and *The Seven Sages of Rome* for Scribe 3. Three of the items in the list for Scribe 1 answer to the second exemplar hand that this scribe drew upon according to the results of the present analysis. The first and fourth exemplar hands are represented by one textual item each, and the third exemplar hand by none. The sole item in the list for Scribe 3 answers to the second of the three exemplar hands distinguished for this scribe.

5 Conclusion

Summing up, Samuels investigated texts that certainly are geographically localisable to London since they are housed in manuscripts known on extralinguistic criteria to have been produced there. He was probably in search of reference

14 The two Scribe 5 exemplar hands do likewise not differ noteworthily in perplexity relative to the Scribes 1 or 3 exemplar hands. In addition, the *Atlas* lists as the basis for Scribe 5's LP 6350 the title of *Sir Beves* only but the folios for both *Reinbroun* (fols. 167ff) and *Sir Beves* (fols. 176ff). If *Reinbroun* is included, both exemplar hands discriminated for Scribe 5 are presumably represented in the profile.

texts for the London area for *A Linguistic Atlas of Late Medieval English*, the compilation of which was still far from completed in the early 1960s. Samuels was no doubt aware of how London was a meeting place for texts with all manner of incompatible linguistic localisations, such as Gower's and Scribe D's, but he noticed a tendency for some of the texts to group in respect of the orthographic forms they use for a dozen items: he posited a first class, Type II, the members of which share a linguistic localisation of those orthographic forms to Essex and pre-date 1380, and a second class, Type III, whose members post-date 1380 and share a linguistic localisation to centrally in the Midlands.

Later scholarship has suggested from the membership of not only Types II and III but also Type IV that it is genre that is the true predictor variable that gives rise to their separate linguistic localisations, rather than forms gaining wider currency in the London area and scribes targeting them. Later scholarship has additionally noticed that there exist still other London-produced texts that each question the basis for Types II and III by containing forms characteristic of both and not observing the 1380 boundary date.

If it is unclear or undetermined what variables truly unite the Type II texts so is their relationship with standardisation, apart from their extra-linguistic association with London as the presumed locus of the standardisation process. At the chronological beginning of this process, Haugen's selection and codification stages are tantamount to scribes and other writers beginning to converge in their orthographical representation of lexical items. Whether this tendency toward convergence is better termed "focused variation", "incipient standardisation", or "purging of grosser provincialisms", it is not in evidence in how perplexity is distributed in the Auchinleck manuscript, for the distribution does not group the two Type II scribes against the non-Type II scribes considered separately or in combination. The distribution at best lines up Scribes 1, 3, 5, and 6 against Scribe 2 (with Scribe 4 and his *Battle Abbey Roll* yielding no data) in discrepancy with their respective linguistic localisations.

Middle English is characterised by an unprecedented amount of orthographic variation. A need for scholars to have fixed reference points when addressing this variation might explain why Samuels' types continue to prove remarkably robust, despite evidence undermining them as incipient standards having mounted over the past one or two decades. The evidence presented in this chapter takes, I believe, the discussion past the point of no return. The types may be conclusively laid to rest.

Last, the chapter has discriminated scribes at the levels of both the Auchinleck manuscript and its immediate exemplars, and by this means shown that Scribe 1 copied more than twenty textual items from exemplars written in a mere four hands. This finding aligns well with the proposed existence of a community of book artisans in early to mid-fourteenth century London whose collaboration extended to them exchanging exemplars with one another. It adds to previous scholarship that this community did not simply store exemplars obtained from elsewhere but must also have produced them.

References

Primary sources

The Auchinleck Manuscript, ed. D. Burnley and A. Wiggins (Edinburgh: National Library of Scotland, 2003), http://auchinleck.nls.uk. The transcript is downloadable from the University of Oxford Text Archive: http://ota.ahds.ac.uk/headers/2493.xml.

The Auchinleck Manuscript: National Library of Scotland Advocates' MS 19.2.1. Introduction. D. Pearsall and I. C. Cunningham (London: Scolar Press, 1977).

A Book of London English, 1384–1425, ed. R. W. Chambers and M. Daunt (Oxford: Clarendon Press, 1931).

Kyng Alisaunder, ed. G. V. Smithers, 2 vols, EETS OS 237 (Oxford: Oxford University Press, 1957).

The Seven Sages of Rome (Southern Version), ed. K. Brunner, EETS OS 191 (London: Oxford University Press, 1933).

Secondary sources

Ayres-Bennett, W., 'Elaboration and Codification: Standardization and Attitudes towards the French Language in the Sixteenth and Seventeeth Centuries', in *The Changing Voices of Europe: Social and Political Changes and Their Linguistic Repercussions, Past, Present, and Future*, ed. M. Parry, W. V. Davies and R. Temple. (Cardiff: University of Wales Press, 1994), pp. 53–73.

Benskin, M., 'Chancery Standard', in *New Perspectives on English Historical Linguistics: Volume* II: *Lexis and Transmission*, ed. C. Kay, C. Hough and I. Wotherspoon (Amsterdam: John Benjamins, 2004), pp. 1–40.

Bliss, A. J., 'Notes on the Auchinleck Manuscript', *Speculum* 26 (1951), 652–58.

Bliss, A. J., 'The Auchinleck "St Margaret" and "St Katherine"', *Notes and Queries* 201 (1956), 186–88.

Brinton, L., and A. Bergs, ed. *The History of English: Volume 3: Middle English* (Berlin: De Gruyter Mouton, 2017).

Brunner, K., 'The Middle English Metrical Romances and Their Audience', in *Studies in Medieval Literature in Honour of Albert Croll Baugh*, ed. M. Leach (Philadelphia: University of Pennsylvania Press, 1961), pp. 219–27.

Christianson, C. P., 'Evidence for the Study of London's Late Medieval Manuscript-Book Trade', in *Book Production and Publishing in Britain, 1375–1475*, ed. J. Griffiths and D. Pearsall (Cambridge: Cambridge University Press, 1989), pp. 87–108.

Christianson, C. P., *A Directory of London Stationers and Book Artisans 1300–1500* (New York: Bibliographical Society of America, 1990).
Dennison, L., '"Liber Horn", "Liber Custumarum" and Other Manuscripts of the Queen Mary Psalter Workshops', in *Medieval Art, Architecture and Archaeology in London*, ed. L. Grant, British Archaeological Association Conference Translations 10 (London: British Archaeological Association, 1990), pp. 118–34.
Doyle, A. I., and M. B. Parkes, 'The Production of Copies of the *Canterbury Tales* and the *Confessio Amantis* in the Early Fifteenth Century', in *Medieval Scribes, Manuscripts and Libraries: Essays Presented to N. R. Ker*, ed. M. B. Parkes and A. G. Watson (London: Scolar Press, 1978), pp. 163–210.
Edwards, A. S. G., 'Codicology and Translation in the Early Sections of the Auchinleck Manuscript', in *The Auchinleck Manuscript: New Perspectives*, ed. S. Fein (Woodbridge: York Medieval Press, 2016), pp. 26–35.
Ekwall, Eilert, *Studies on the Population of Medieval London* (Stockholm: Almqvist och Wiksell, 1956).
Fisher, J. H., 'Chancery and the Emergence of Standard English in the Fifteenth Century', *Speculum* 52 (1977): 870–99.
Fisher, J. H., M. Richardson and J. L. Fisher, *An Anthology of Chancery English* (Knoxville: University of Tennessee Press, 1984).
Fisher, M., *Scribal Authorship and the Writing of History in Medieval England* (Columbus: Ohio State University Press, 2012).
Gillespie, A., 'Medieval Books, Their Booklets, and Booket Theory', in *Manuscript Miscellanies, c. 1450–1700*, ed. R. Beadle and C. Burrow (London: The British Library, 2011), pp. 1–29.
Görlach, M., 'The Auchinleck *Katerine*', in *So meny people, longages and tonges: Philological Essays in Scots and Mediaeval English Presented to Angus McIntosh*, ed. M. Benskin and M. L. Samuels (Edinburgh: Middle English Dialect Project, 1981), pp. 211–28.
Hanna, R., 'Booklets in Medieval Manuscripts: Further Considerations', *Studies in Bibliography* 39 (1986), pp. 100–11.
Hanna, R., 'Miscellaneity and Vernacularity: Conditions of Literary Production in Late Medieval England', in *The Whole Book: Cultural Perspectives on the Medieval Miscellany*, ed. S. G. Nichols and S. Wenzel (Ann Arbor: University of Michigan Press, 1996), pp. 37–51.
Hanna, R., 'Reconsidering the Auchinleck Manuscript', in *New Directions in Later Medieval Manuscript Studies: Essays from the 1998 Harvard Conference*, ed. D. Pearsall (York: York Medieval Press, 2000), pp. 91–102.
Hanna, R., *London Literature, 1300–1380*, Cambridge Studies in Medieval Literature 57 (Cambridge: Cambridge University Press, 2005).
Hanna, R., 'Auchinleck "Scribe 6" and Some Corollary Issues', in *The Auchinleck Manuscript: New Perspectives*, ed. S. Fein (Woodbridge: York Medieval Press, 2016), pp. 209–21.
Haugen, E., 'Dialect, Language, Nation', *American Anthropologist* 68 (1966), 922–35.
Hibbard Loomis, L. 'The Auchinleck Manuscript and a Possible London Bookshop of 1330–1340', *Proceedings of the Modern Language Association* 57 (1942), 595–627.
Horobin, S., *The Language of the Chaucer Tradition* (Cambridge: D. S. Brewer, 2003).
Horobin, S. and J. Smith, *An Introduction to Middle English* (Edinburgh: Edinburgh University Press, 2002).

Horobin, S. and L. Mooney, 'A *Piers Plowman* Manuscript by the Hengwrt/Ellesmere Scribe and Its Implications for London Standard English', *Studies in the Age of Chaucer* 26 (2004), 65–112.

Kane, G. and E. Talbot Donaldson, *Piers Plowman: The B version*. (London: Athlone Press, 1975).

Kerby-Fulton, K., L. Olson and M. Hilmo, *Opening Up Middle English Manuscripts: Literary and Visual Approaches*. (Ithaca: Cornell University Press, 2012).

Marshall, H., 'What's in a Paraph? A New Methodology and Its Implications for the Auchinleck Manuscript', *Journal of the Early Book Society* 13 (2010), 39–62.

McIntosh, A., 'The Middle English Poem "The Four Foes of Mankind": Some Notes on the Language and the Text", *Neuphilologische Mitteilungen* 79 (1978), 137–44.

McIntosh, A., M. L. Samuels and M. Benskin, with M. Laing and K. Williamson, *A Linguistic Atlas of Late Mediaeval English*, 4 vols. (Aberdeen: Aberdeen University Press, 1986).

Mordkoff, J. C., 'The Making of the Auchinleck Manuscript: The Scribes at Work', University of Connecticut: PhD thesis (1981).

Olson, Linda, 'Englishing Romance: The Auchinleck Manuscript', in *Opening up Middle English Manuscripts*, ed. K. Kerby-Fulton, L. Olson and M. Hilmo (Ithaca: Cornell University Press, 2012), pp. 99–116.

Pearsall, D., 'The Auchinleck Manuscript Forty Years On', in *The Auchinleck Manuscript: New Perspectives*, ed. S. Fein (Woodbridge: York Medieval Press, 2016), pp. 11–25.

Peikola, M., 'Copying Space, Length of Entries, and Textual Transmission in Middle English Tables of Lessons', in *Scribes, Printers, and the Accidentals of Their Texts*, ed. J. Thaisen and H. Rutkowska (Frankfurt am Main: Peter Lang, 2011), pp. 108–26.

Robinson, P. R., 'The "Booklet": A Self-Contained Unit of Composite Manuscripts', *Codicologica 3* (1980), 49–69.

Runde, E., 'Reexamining Orthographic Practice in the Auchinleck Manuscript through Study of Complete Scribal Corpora', in *Variation and Change in English Grammar and Lexicon: Contemporary Approaches*, ed. R. Cloutier, A. M. Hamilton-Brehm, and W. Kretzschmar, Jr. (Berlin: De Gruyter Mouton, 2010), pp. 265–87.

Runde, E., 'Scribe 3's Literary Project: Pedagogies of Reading in Auchinleck's Booklet 3', in *The Auchinleck Manuscript: New Perspectives*, ed. S. Fein (Woodbridge: York Medieval Press, 2016), pp. 67–87.

Samuels, M. (1963). 'Some Applications of Middle English Dialectology'. *English Studies* 44, 81–94. Cited from *Middle English Dialectology: Essays on Some Principles and Problems*, ed. A. McIntosh, M. L. Samuels and M. Laing (Aberdeen: Aberdeen University Press, 1989), pp. 64–80.

Samuels, M. L., 'The Scribe of the Hengwrt and Ellesmere Manuscripts of the *Canterbury Tales', Studies in the Age of Chaucer* 5 (1983), 49–65.

Shonk, T. A., 'A Study of the Auchinleck Manuscript: Investigations Into the Process of Book Making in the Fourteenth Century, University of Tennessee: PhD thesis (1981).

Shonk, T. A., 'The Scribe as Editor: The Primary Scribe of the Auchinleck Manuscript', *Manuscripta* 27 (1983), 19–20.

Shonk, T. A., 'A Study of the Auchinleck Manuscript: Bookmen and Bookmaking in the Early Fourteenth Century', *Speculum* 60 (1985), 71–91.

Shonk, T., 'Paraphs, Piecework, and Presentation: The Production Methods of Auchinleck Revisited', in *The Auchinleck Manuscript: New Perspectives*, ed. S. Fein (Woodbridge: York Medieval Press, 2016), pp. 176–194.

Stolcke, A., 'SRILM: An extensible language modeling toolkit', in *Proceedings of the 7th International Conference on Spoken Language Processing*, ed. J. Hansen and B. Pellom (Denver: Casual Productions, 2002), pp. 901–904. The toolkit is downloadable from http://www.speech.sri.com/projects/srilm/.

Taylor, A., 'Manual to Miscellany: Stages in the Commercial Copying of Vernacular Literature in England', *The Yearbook of English Studies* 33 (2003), 1–17.

Thaisen, J., 'Gamelyn's Place among the Early Exemplars for Chaucer's *Canterbury Tales*', *Neophilologus* 97 (2013), 395–415.

Thaisen, J., 'A Probabilistic Analysis of a Middle English Text', in *Digitizing Medieval and Early Modern Material Culture*, ed. B. Nelson and Melissa Terras (Tempe Arizona: Center for Medieval and Renaissance Studies, 2012), pp. 171–200.

Thaisen, J., 'Adam Pinkhurst's Short and Long Forms', in *Scribes, Printers, and the Accidentals of Their Texts*, ed. J. Thaisen and H. Rutkowska (Frankfurt am Main: Peter Lang, 2011), pp. 73–90.

Thaisen, J., 'Statistical Comparison of Middle English Texts: An Interim Report', *Kwartalnik Neofilologiczny* 56 (2009), 205–221.

Vaughan, Míċeál F., 'Scribal Corrections in the Auchinleck Manuscript', in *The Auchinleck Manuscript: New Perspectives*, ed. S. Fein (Woodbridge: York Medieval Press, 2016), pp. 195–208.

Wiggins, A., 'Guy of Warwick: Study and Transcription', University of Sheffield: PhD thesis (2002).

Wiggins, A., 'Are Auchinleck Scribes 1 and 6 the Same Scribe?: The Advantages of Whole-Data Analysis and Electronic Texts', *Medium Ævum* 73 (2004), 10–26.

Williamson, K., 'Changing Spaces: Linguistic Relationships and the Dialect Continuum', in *Placing Middle English in Context*, ed. I. Taavitsainen, T. Nevalainen, P. Pahta and M. Rissanen (Berlin: Mouton de Gruyter, 2000), pp. 141–179.

Wright, L., Sources of London English: *Medieval Thames Vocabulary* (Oxford: Clarendon Press, 1996).

Moragh Gordon

6 Bristol <th>, <þ> and <y>: The North-South divide revisited, 1400–1700

1 Introduction

The aim of this chapter is to investigate the distribution of monograph variants <þ>, <y> and digraph <th> in two text-types from Bristol (ordinances and correspondence), and to shed light on when and in what contexts the monograph variants were replaced by <th>. The investigation finds that, unexpectedly, letter-writers used <y> as a minority variant in the function words *the, that, them, this* in Bristol letters of 1548 through to 1711. This is an unexpected finding because Benskin (1982) reported a North-East/South-West distribution distinction with regard to <þ> and <y>, whereby <y> for the dental fricative was supposedly absent from the South – and yet Bristol is a southern city. It looks as though matters were more complex.

Orthographic variation has become an object of study for purposes of localising Middle English texts: *The Linguistic Atlas of Late Mediaeval English*, henceforth *LALME*, which covers the period from 1350 to 1450, includes orthographic variation as a variable to help identify a text's provenance (Benskin et al. 2013 [1982]). *LALME*'s fit-technique operates on the assumption that spellings found in texts of which the scribe's geographical information is known, the so-called anchor texts, can determine the origin of texts of unknown provenance by means of comparison. This approach has its limitations from a historical sociolinguistic perspective (c.f. Stenroos & Thengs 2012). One of the major challenges is that the social context of the scribe, the agent of language variation, is left out of consideration (Benskin et al., 2013 [1982]: pars 2.3.4., 3.1) and as Britain (2008), Kretzschmar (2009) and Stenroos (2016) have argued, the relationship between language and geography is seldom a simplex and unidirectional one and it cannot be assumed that the variation observed in Middle English followed a "regular dialect continuum" pattern (Stenroos 2016: 100). Written language comes with its own conventions that may follow specific distribution channels; in an increasingly late medieval literate society, literacy was a highly sought-after commodity in urban centres and it is likely that scribes moved from different educational centres to larger urban centres for their livelihoods, carrying their dialect with them, whilst picking up new features and writing conventions along the way (Clanchy, 1993; Bevan, 2013; Moran Cruz, 2014; Rees Jones, 2014). There was also a shift in the demand for the type of literacy.

https://doi.org/10.1515/9783110687545-007

With the rise of the urban merchant elite in the fifteenth century, overseas trade expanded, requiring letter-writing skills, as well as more complex record-keeping and administration, which in turn led to the diversification of text-types (Dobson 2000: 280). Merchants and trade guilds were often in charge of urban government and bureaucratic administration, issuing charters and levying fees to control trade and civic life (Coleman 1981: 52; Dobson 2000: 280). As a consequence, administrative texts became increasingly trilingual (Latin, Anglo-French and English), catering for the merchant less-skilled in the Latinate languages (Coleman 1981: 37). The town clerk and recorder, who, amongst other things, were responsible for the keeping of civic records in urban centres, were often influential members, at the pinnacle of what Rees Jones (2014: 220) calls "civic literacy", i.e. the use of records to establish and define urban identity. Recorders were often London lawyers who also functioned as legal advisors in cities elsewhere (Lee 2007: 113). Town clerks were often members of the mercantile elite too, who had been trained at Oxford or the London Inns of Court (Lawson & Silver: 1973; Orme 1989; Baker 1990). Although the recorder and the town clerk may have left the actual writing of documents to locally-schooled scriveners, they were at least aware of what appeared on the page (Bevan 2013: 142–143); for example, many fifteenth-century Bristolian civic records were written by unknown hands but signed by a known recorder or town clerk "[reflecting] evidence of a sort of quality of the work" (Bevan 2013: 142–143).

In the light of this, a scribe can hardly be considered to simply have transported his native dialect unaltered from one place to another, nor can we safely assume that his written language was reflective of his spoken vernacular, even if a scribe remained in his native place. This presents problems in attempting to pinpoint a scribe's origin based on orthographic features. Language is ever-changing under the influence of social factors such as level of formality, gender, and social standing, but also context and the particular cultural conventions and practices tied up with it, that is, the development of text-types and genres (Romaine 1982; Nevalainen 2000a, b; Taavitsainen 2000, 2001; Labov 2001). As Stenroos and Thengs (2012, par. 5) point out, "changes are disseminated along networks of contact, not through the empty countryside", making a wave-like spread of innovations only one model of linguistic change. More than anywhere else, networks of contact concentrated in larger urban centres, meaning that the rate of linguistic variation and change can be expected to have been higher there than in rural areas (Hernández-Campoy 1999, 2003; Hernández-Campoy & Conde-Silvestre 2005; Britain 2010, Britain & Chambers 2013). This results in the problem that dialectal variation in texts from late medieval urban centres is heterogeneous, making it impossible to link features to a single locality. Another complicating factor is that from about the fifteenth century onwards, texts, especially civic records, decreasingly show dialectal features, tending towards a supralocal norm (Stenroos 2016). These texts do not follow variation patterns that can be linked to a linear dialect continuum. However, non-linear patterns are of interest because they can yield insights into the complex relationship between written language, its users and geographical space.

Supralocalisation is "an umbrella term to refer to the geographical spread of linguistic features beyond their region of origin" (Britain 2010: 195). The supralocal character of many of the later fifteenth-century urban texts was the result of levelling of local minority forms and the replacement of local features by others that had a wider currency (Hernández-Campoy & Conde-Silvestre 2005). Regional dialect levelling was part of supralocalisation (Trudgill 1986: 98; Kerswill 2003: 223). This implies that features already present in a wider region became maintained, while more locally-bound forms were lost. As a variety became less regionally-bound and gained a wider currency, it also became open to the adoption of wider supralocal forms that had a national currency (Britain 2010: 195–196). The question is if and how these notions can be applied to orthographic variation and in particular to the replacement of <þ> and variants by <th>, the focus of the present study.

In the Old English period, <th>, <t>, <d>, <ð>, <þ>, and later, a letter-graph similar or identical to <y> were all used to represent the interdental fricatives /θ/ and /ð/ (Stenroos 2004; Laing & Lass 2009). For instance, the initial digraph in *through* could be spelled *trough, drough, ðrough, þrough, and yrough*[1] by Middle English scribes (Stenroos 2006: 14). In the Middle English period, Northern and Southern texts reportedly showed a regionally-bound distribution of spelling variants (McIntosh 1974; Stenroos 2004, 2006). However, between the fifteenth-eighteenth centuries, all variants were gradually replaced by one variant, the digraph <th>, and distinctive local practices disappeared. Stenroos (2004, 2006) has investigated the distribution pattern of the <th> variants in the South in general, but little is known about the development of the form in urban settings. Linguistic innovations may have found their way from urban centre to urban centre in a non-linear fashion, i.e. hopping from one city to another (Nevalainen & Raumolin-Brunberg 2003; Hernández-Campoy & Conde-Silvestre 2005). The time-span 1400–1700 is of interest because it covers the period in which texts become increasingly difficult to localise due to the paucity of specifically local dialect features. During this period Bristol was the most important urban centre in the South West of England and the second most important port town of the

1 This is a somewhat simplified list, as in reality, most of the other graphs in this word had other variants too. Furthermore, the variants of <th> presented here were sometimes also followed by an <h>. This means that spellings like *yhrough* and *þhrough* also ocurred (see Stenroos 2006: 14 for a list of all variants).

country for the later part of the period in terms of size, economic activity and in terms of text production and civic administration. Bristol was also a place towards which people from a wider region gravitated, providing a suitable case study for supralocalisation processes (Carus-Wilson & Lobel 1975; de Vries 1984; Beetham-Fisher 1987; Sacks 1991; Fleming 1996).

2 Historical background of <th> and its variants

Old and Middle English texts display a wide variety of graphs representing dental fricatives, both the voiced variant /ð/ and the voiceless variant /θ/.[2] In the earliest extant texts, which date from the early eighth century, the Roman graphs <d> and <th> were used to represent both sounds, especially in Northern texts. From the late eighth century onwards, *eth* <ð>, which seems to have been introduced by Irish missionaries, and runic *thorn* <þ>, started to appear. Like the other letter-graphs, they were used interchangeably for both voiced and voiceless dental fricatives, although there was a tendency to use <þ> word-initially and <ð> more freely in all positions (Hogg 1992: 76). By the ninth century, <ð> and <þ> came to be preferred over <d> and <th>. The digraph <th> was often maintained in Latin texts, especially in English vernacular names and loan words with a dental fricative (Benskin 1982: 19; Hogg 1992: 77). By the thirteenth century, <ð> had almost completely been replaced by <þ> (Lass 1992: 36). However, the digraph <th> then made a comeback in English vernacular texts and gradually started to replace <þ> (Lass 1992: 36). It is likely that the renewed use of <th> was reinforced by Latin, which had become the main language of administration under Anglo-Norman rule. In the Latin writing tradition, <th> was commonly used for English vernacular names with /θ/ and /ð/, as well as other non-Latin loanwords with dental fricatives (Benskin 1977: 506–507, 1982: 18; Hogg 1992: 77; Lass 1992: 36; Hernández-Campoy & Conde-Silvestre 2015: 25–26).

In the fifteenth century, variation became more complex due to the merging of the letter-graphs <þ> and <y>, which meant that, in some scribes' handwriting, <y> and <th> became indistinguishable (Benskin 1982: 13). <yh>, <ð>, <þh>, <ȝh>, <ȝ>, medial <d>, <dd>, and final/medial <tth>, <tht>, <ȝt> all occurred (Stenroos 2004: 264). The digraph <yh> was only attested in Northern texts, and <ȝ> mostly in texts originating from East Anglia and the East Midlands (Stenroos 2004:

2 It is open to debate whether the contrast between the voiced and voiceless fricatives was phonemic in Old English (Lass 1991–1993; Laker 2009; Minkova 2011), but if there was any contrast this was not reflected in spelling (Lass 1992: 64).

265).[3] There is an added complication with word-medial spellings <d> and <dd>. During the Middle English period, Old English words with intervocalic /d/ came to be pronounced with fricative /ð/ (Lass 1992: 64). This mostly concerned words ending with – *er*, e.g. words such as *father (OE fader), mother (OE modor), gather (OE gaderian)*, originally spelt with the letter <d> and pronounced /d/. This sound change was likely to have been still underway during the fifteenth century. Hence there is a possibility that <d> in word-medial position in Later Middle English texts may reflect actual pronunciation of /d/. According to Stenroos (2004: 264), the occurrence of medial <d> in the fifteenth century is restricted to certain regions, mainly attested in texts from the North East Midlands, the North, the South East and the South West, specifically in the words *whether, either,* and *other*. The question remains whether these <d> spellings reflect pronunciation or whether they are back-spellings.[4] Alternatively, they could also just have been conservative Older English spelling variants of <th> (Stenroos 2004: 264).

McIntosh (1974) and Benskin (1982) established that the variation of the three main variants <th>, <þ> and <y> was conditioned regionally, that is to say, there appeared to be a distinctively Northern system and a distinctively Southern one. Benskin (1982: 14) describes three different ways in which the different variants were used:

I. <þ> and <y> are merged into one graph and cannot be distinguished from each other. This practice typically occurred in texts from the North and parts of the East.
II. <þ> and <y> are two distinct graphs and they are used distinctively to represent /θ/, /ð/ and /j/, /i/ respectively. This system was used in texts originating in the South, the West and the East Midlands.
III. <þ> and <y> are two distinct graphs, but they are used interchangeably to represent both /θ/, /ð/ and /j/, /i/, e.g. *yong* 'young' could be spelled *þong*. This system was found in texts from the border areas where the systems described in (1) and (2) above occurred.

3 In the Bristol texts that are used for the present study, however, there appears to be one token but the text has not been dated, so it will not be included in the overall results: "This here *yhe* mair sherif and gode men" (Recorder's oath, c.15thc, f. 5, Bristol Record Office (BRO): 04719).

4 For example, in some dialects of the sixteenth century, there is spelling evidence for *th*-fronting (the pronunciation of [θ] as [f]). The graphs and <th> both came to represent [f], hence back-spellings like *threvoles* for *frivolous* (Wyld 1936: 291; Milroy 2003: 216). Similarly, <d> spellings for *wether* (*OE hwæðer*), *either* (*OE ǽghwæðer*), *other* (*OE oðar*), could be hypercorrections on analogy with *father* (*OE fader*).

The distribution of the letter-graphs fits with what can be expected of a slow wave-like diffusion of regionally-bound forms, in that there are two distinct dialect areas and a transition zone in which the two different systems meet. However, before 1350, merged <y> as used in system I also occurred in the South (Benskin 1982: 25), so how and when this feature came to be strictly Northern remains an unanswered question. Benskin's (1982: 16) analysis of the regional distribution of the graphs is based on texts that are "markedly local", meaning he did not consider Southern texts that did not contain clearly identifiable local dialect features. The less "markedly local" texts presumably showed more supralocal features. For the purpose of the description of a traditional dialect this may be justifiable, that is, if we accept an idealised homogenous dialect description within a likewise idealised dialect continuum. However, from a variationist perspective, the occurrence of supralocal features as well as local dialect features in one single text is a reality. Whether or not markedly local, the texts are a testimony of the language as it was used and produced at a particular location. It reveals which variables were available to the scribes at that particular place and time. This careful selecting and discarding of data is problematic for the purpose of the study of urban written varieties, as <þ> was used in Northern texts that did not show "markedly local" language according to the system as described in (III) rather than system (I). According to Benskin, this type of non-local usage occurred from the 1440s onwards and was primarily found in legal and administrative texts (Benskin 1982: 25). In other words, legal texts that were considered not clearly dialectal nevertheless reveal patterns of variation and change, which differ from those found in other text-types. As argued earlier, dialectal heterogeneity is inherent to urban centres, especially in the period 1400–1700, when urban civic administration became more complex and record-keeping a more prominent part of a city's administration, thus increasing the demand for skilled scribes who hailed from a wider catchment area (Gordon 2017: Ch. 4). The focus on local dialect features alone cannot provide a realistic picture of the complex linguistic situation in regional centres at the time.

In Northern texts the spread of digraph <th> seems to have been used to represent word-final voiceless dental fricatives, and only later extended to voiceless contexts in other positions, resulting in spellings which corresponded to phonological differences. For example, *think* was spelled with <th>, whereas words with voiced dental fricatives, such as *they, there, them* were spelled with either <þ> or <y> (Benskin 1977: 506–507; Stenroos 2004, 2006).[5] This means that, with

5 Bergs (2013: 250–256) found earlier evidence for pronunciation-related spellings in the Anglo-Saxon *Peterborough Chronicles* (entries 1132–1154 CE), where one scribe in particular

regard to system I), digraph <th> usually indicated a voiceless dental fricative, whereas <y> and <þ> generally represented a voiced dental fricative. In systems II) and III), there was no such phonological distribution and all three variants could occur with either a voiced or a voiceless dental fricative. However, even though the distribution of spelling variants in Southern texts did not reflect phonemic differences, Stenroos (2004: 274) notes that there seem to have been some constraints on the variation of the forms:

A. <th> was used as a capital of lower case <þ>.
B. Although both forms could co-occur in the same text or document, either <þ> was the clear majority form, or vice versa. This might be reflective of a generational change as described by Hernández-Campoy & Conde-Silvestre (2015), i.e. the texts with <þ> as a majority form might be written by older scribes, whereas <th>-full texts are the product of younger scribes, who adopted the innovative form. A note of caution is due here since Hernández-Campoy & Conde-Silvestre (2015) is based on the Paston letters, whereas Stenroos (2004, 2006) looks at other text- types.
C. In some rare cases both variants occur at roughly the same rate, but there may have been lexical conditioning.

As already indicated above, text-type also appears to have been an important factor in relation to the distribution of the forms. Documentary texts, specifically, legal and administrative texts, show rates of <th> higher than those in literary texts (Stenroos 2004: 276). This suggests that the adoption of <th> emerged within a specific group of legally-trained scribes (Benskin 1982; Stenroos 2004: 281). For the present study, which uses ordinances and letters from Bristol, it can be expected that there will be a relatively high rate of <th> in the ordinances since it is known that town clerks and recorders typically had a legal training (Bevan 2013: 82). Civic scribes played an important role in the legal administration of Bristol since they had knowledge of legal language and procedures and are likely to have supervised and trained the scriveners who actually wrote the legal texts (Bevan 2013: 40, 201–3).

Stenroos (2006), based on her study of Southern documentary and literary texts, established that in the fifteenth century, the digraph <th> only occurred as a majority form in certain individual texts. Overall, <þ> remained the majority form up until the end of the fifteenth century (Stenroos 2004: 273–274). Hernández-Campoy and Conde-Silvestre (2015), studying the distribution of <þ> and <th> in

seemed to prefer <th> for the voiced fricative in medial positions. This suggests that scribal practices were geographically diffused, allowing for a wide variety of individual scribal patterns.

the Paston letters (c.1425–1496), describe a transitional stage in which both variants co-occurred, as is to be expected with a change underway. This transitional phase was probably at an advanced stage by around 1425, given that <th> was already the majority variant in letters by that time (Hernández-Campoy & Conde-Silvestre 2015: 27). The change seems to have taken place gradually over the different generations of the Paston family as the older family members showed lower rates of innovative <th> than the younger ones, with increasing rates in succeeding generations (Hernández-Campoy & Conde-Silvestre 2015: 28). Overall, there seems to be evidence to indicate that literary text-types lagged behind in the adoption of <th>, with correspondence in the lead, followed by documentary texts. Over the course of the Early Modern English period, <th> came to replace all other graphs, with <y> spellings in the determiners *ye* and *yat* (Stenroos 2004: 264) the only remnants. The first step of the current study is to investigate how the development of <th> played out in Bristol.

3 Data and method

3.1 Data selection process

In order to trace the distribution and development of <th> in Bristol, a digitally searchable corpus made up of texts from civic records (guild and council ordinances) and letters was created, covering the time-span 1400–1700, as this is the period in which a supralocal written variety developed (Nevalainen 2003). The aim was not to gather texts that were produced by authors born and bred in Bristol, producing authentic Bristolian language, but to capture written language as it was used in Bristol, illustrating the development and diffusion of supralocal forms, and the extent of variation present within the literate community. In the case of civic records, the selection process was straightforward, since it was usually indicated internally that they were written in Bristol and intended for use there. In the case of correspondence, matters were more complicated and only letters whose writers could reasonably be assumed to have lived in the Bristol area at the time of writing and who had connections with people in the city were included. The extent of their connection to Bristol was established on the basis of the content of the letters or on autobiographical information when this was available. In some cases, letters written by Bristolians who temporarily lived elsewhere were used.

3.2 The Bristol data

The corpus of ordinances and letters has been sub-divided into three different sub-corpora that roughly cover the fifteenth, sixteenth and seventeenth centuries (see Table 6.1). The data of Period I includes council and guild ordinances in English contained in the *Little Red Book of Bristol* (henceforth LRB) and the *Great Red Book of Bristol* (henceforth GRB). There also a number of texts in English that could be labeled as petitions rather than ordinances; however, all are brief requests by a given guild for ordinances to be listed in the LRB or GRB, followed by the actual ordinances. Since the format and text style do not differ greatly from the actual ordinances, it was decided to label them as ordinances also. The LRB was written in the fourteenth century and consists of ordinances, memoranda, and miscellaneous notes relating to the town's administration, laws, charters, customs and liberties of the town (Bickley 1900). Most of these texts are in Latin or French, but a substantial portion of the ordinances are written in English, providing the texts analysed here. The GRB is considered to be the successor of the LRB as it contains similar records from a later period.[6] Little is known about the scribes who produced the texts. The ordinances that were composed for the LRB and GRB are likely to have been written by scriveners who were skilled in Latin and French, and who had knowledge of legal procedures. They may have been trained in London at the Inns of Court, but they may also have been trained locally, in Bristol, or another urban centre, in the form of an apprenticeship (Gordon 2017, Ch. 5).

Table 6.1: The three sub-corpora.

time periods	source	word count
period I: 1404–1493	the Great and Little Red Book of Bristol	c. 35,153
period II:1506–1596	the Council Ordinances of Bristol	c. 32,590
period III: 1548–1711	Bristol letter collection	c. 30,975

The data in Period II is taken from council ordinances in a volume that appears to be a continuation of the LRB and GRB, consisting of sixteenth-century guild

6 Both volumes exist in editions (Bickley 1900; Veale 1933) and some folios have also been used by the *Linguistic Atlas of Late Mediaeval English* and the *Middle English Grammar* project (Stenroos et al. 2011). MSS transcriptions were used rather than the printed edition.

and council ordinances.[7] As the latest entry in the GRB is dated 1485 and the first entries in the council ordinance volume do not occur until 1506, a volume containing ordinances of the intermediate twenty-five-year time period may have existed but is now missing. Stanford (1990: xviii) alludes to the possibility that the ordinances with earlier dates in the volume are actually fair copies of earlier entries that were written down later, with evidence that they were copied into the volume before 1570. This may indicate that in the case of the pre-1570 texts, the language was written at a later date than the date given in the text, which has implications for the linguistic analysis.

The data of Period III consists of correspondence from two collections: the Southwell papers and the Ashton Court collection. The Southwell collection contains papers relating to the Anglo-Irishman Robert Southwell (1635–1702), his son Edward I (1671–1730) and his grandson Edward II (1705–1755). The Southwells owned property in Kingsweston, just outside of Bristol (Barnard 2004). The collection consists of ten volumes of which the first two volumes contain letters written in Bristol in the late seventeenth century addressed to the Southwells. The Ashton Court collection contains correspondence by and to the Smythe family, who, starting out as merchants, became wealthy and influential in the Bristol area through land investments and intermarriage with landed gentry and nobility (Bantock 1982; Bettey 1982, 2004). The Ashton Court letters total 88 letters from 1548–1716, but most date from the first half of the seventeenth century. Ten letters from the Southwell collection written in the second half of the seventeenth century form part of the data set. It was common during this period for an amanuensis to write the letter in the name of the person who ultimately signed the text. However, there is no reason to assume that letters from males were written by an amanuensis, as each author appears to be represented by one unique consistent hand, regardless of the time and place they sent their letters from. Quite a few letters of the Ashton Court collection were written by female family members who, given the low literacy rates amongst women at the time, were more likely to have dictated their letters (Cressy 1980). However, it seems that at least one of the most prolific letter writers, Mary Smythe, wrote her own letters, as she made a remark about her handwriting: "I am weary you may ſe by my writing" (Mary Smyth, 30 March 1630s, BRO: ac/c/53). Moreover, all of the women's hands are unique and very different

7 Edited by Stanford (1990), but MSS transcriptions were used rather than the printed edition. For the purpose of this study the council and guild ordinances and memoranda are considered similar enough to be grouped as a single text-type. For a further discussion on why this was deemed appropriate see Gordon (2017, 182,188–193).

from those of any of the men. The women's texts also contain many more phonological spellings, which suggests that the writers of the letters were not formally schooled and were less aware of or concerned about formal spelling norms, something that can be expected if the women indeed wrote the letters themselves.

3.3 Method

The main variants <th>, <þ> and <y> were collected by means of two XML-compatible concordance tools, one of which is available online on the Text Analysis Portal for Research (Rockwell et al. 2005), the other is AntConc 3.3.4. (Anthony 2014).[8] With these tools, word lists were created as well as corresponding word frequencies, from which words with <th>, <þ> and <y> were selected by means of a simple search. The selected words were encoded with the following labels; source/author, year, word, frequency of the word in the corpus, variant (<th>/ <þ>/ <y>), position of the variant (initial/medial/final). Additionally, common abbreviations such as y^{e} for *the*, and y^{t} for *yat* were labelled as abbreviations, as it is known that they continued in use long after <th> had taken over from <þ> and <y> in other contexts (Stenroos 2004, 2006).

4 Discussion and results

As stated above, the material for this study comprises council ordinances (Period I 1404–1493 and Period II 1506–1596) and letters (Period III 1548–1711). Percentages are rounded off to whole numbers. Figures only include statistics of the majority forms <th>, <þ>, and <y>; when minority forms are discussed, numbers and percentages are given.

8 Although the focus is on the competition between the main variants, the variants that Stenroos (2004; 2006) listed as additional minority forms were also considered: <yh>, <ð>, <þh>, <ʒh>, <ʒ>; medial <d>, <dd>; final/medial <tth>, <tht>, and <ʒt>. A preliminary survey of the less common forms revealed that neither <ð>, <ʒ> nor any of the combinations with <ʒ> occurred. The only minority forms were medial <d>, and <tth>.

4.1 Period I: The Little Red Book and the Great Red Book of Bristol 1404–1493

Of the council ordinances in Period I (1404–1496), in total, there were 6,240 words spelled with <th>, <þ> or <y>. The totals of <th>, <þ> and <y> for all texts investigated are shown in Figure 6.1 and are divided into two sub-periods of fifty years (1400–1450 and 1451–1500). For 1400–1450, there were 2,470 words spelled with <th> or <þ>, and for 1451–1500, there were 3,778 <th> and <þ> spellings, and a single instance of <y>. Compared to Stenroos' (2004) observation of the chronological development of <th> in the South in general, it appears that Bristol was relatively early in opting for <th> over <þ>. Whereas <þ> remained the majority form up until the end of the fifteenth century in Stenroos's data (2004: 273–274), the graph in Figure 6.1 below shows that in Bristol, <þ> was a minority form as early as the first half of the fifteenth century, declining rapidly in the second half of the fifteenth century. That being said, it is important to keep in mind that this difference might be text-type related; Stenroos (2004) considered non-documentary texts as well, whereas the present study only includes documentary texts. That text-type may play a role here is substantiated by the fact that the numbers for documentary texts in Stenroos (2004: 277, Figure 10) are more similar to the ones reported for Bristol in Figure 6.1; in the first half of the fifteenth century, the percentage of <th> in Stenroos' (2004) data is close to 60%, and <þ> is around 38%. In Bristol's council

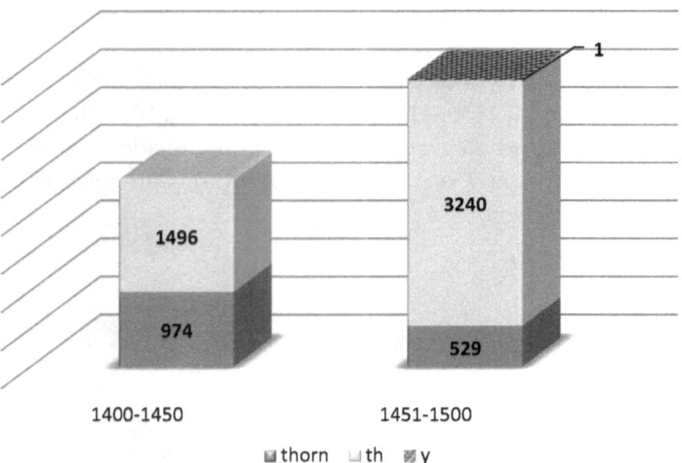

Figure 6.1: Totals of <th> and <þ> distribution in Period I (1404–1493).

ordinances in the first half of the fifteenth century the ratio is 40% for <þ> and 60% for <th>. In the second half of the fifteenth century, the council ordinances of Bristol seem to lag behind Stenroos' (2004) percentages, as Stenroos' (2004) percentage for <th> in documentary texts is almost 100%, whereas for the Bristol data of Period I, the ratio is 15% for <þ> and 85% for <th>. However, despite the apparent lag, Bristol civic records followed a trend similar to other Southern documentary texts, which can be linked to earlier observations that scribes with a legal training may have played a role in the rise of <th> (Benskin 1982, 1992; Stenroos 2004: 281).

Of the minority forms that have not been included in the overall results, the occurrence of medial <d> for present-day <th> spellings are worth mentioning. Even though they are infrequent, they occur in spellings that are different from the ones Stenroos (2004) found in her data (*either, whether, other*). While there was not a single instance of medial <d> in *either, whether*, or *other*, there were four instances for *together* (*OE togædere*) and for *gather* (*OE gad(e)rian*), two for *mother* (*OE–ME modor*), one for *brethern* (*OE brōðor, West Saxon brēþere*), *father* (*OE fader*), and *further* (*OE furðra*). Another medial <d> spelling occurred with *thither* (*OE ðider*) four times.[9] Medial <d> spellings in *mother, father, together, thither* and *gather* may reflect older English pronunciations and/or spellings, but medial <d> found in *further* and *brethern* are not etymological spellings. However, the medial <d> in these cases occurs in the context where the sound change from /d/ to /ð/ took place, that is, /d/ in a postvocalic position followed by a syllabic /r/ or /ər/ (see *OED* (2016) headword 'mother'). The unetymological <d> spellings may be examples of back-spellings, given the low frequencies of the <d> spellings and the more frequent occurrence of <th> and < þ> with postvocalic /d/ and syllabic /r/ or /ər/. The etymological cases of medial <d> would then most likely be fossilised Old English spellings.

There were also eight cases of <tth>, seven of which occurred in one text and in one particular lexical item: *bitth* (third person plural and singular inflection of *to be*). The other instance also occurred in a verb, namely *hatth*. It is possible that <tth> was preferred in verbal inflections. However, all but one of these variants occurs in the first half of the fifteenth century, which suggests that the trigraph was on its way out. In relation to this, *LALME* includes the mapping of variants of *be*, revealing that *bitth* only occurs in the LRB and in no other source surveyed by *LALME*. This may mean that <tth> was a very local writing habit.

9 The Old English spellings are based on the etymological forms that are provided by the *Oxford English Dictionary*.

As Stenroos (2004: 274) points out, during the period 1404–1493 variation in individual texts tended to be restricted, that is to say, either <th> was the majority form, or <þ>. Hence, I consider the distribution patterns in individual documents as opposed to the overall figures for all documents as shown above, although no distinction was made between the different hands, rather, texts were analysed per entry (see Figure 6.2 below). Nonetheless, each document is representative of one instance of a written utterance and each document yields an individual's pattern of usage in that particular document. Of the 37 individual texts that were investigated, the latest text with <þ> as a majority form dates from the 1460s, but texts with <th> as the prevailing form date from as early as 1433. Most of Stenroos' (2004, 2006) observations are confirmed by the data of this study: the texts always have one clear majority form. However, in terms of variability, all the texts that have <þ> as a majority form show rates of <th> that range from 19%–40%, whereas the 27 texts that have <th> as the main form show rates that are close to categorical use, i.e. 15 of the 27 texts have 100% <th>, and a further nine range between 1%–6% of <þ>. Only three <th>-majority texts have a range of <þ> that lies between 23%–40%.

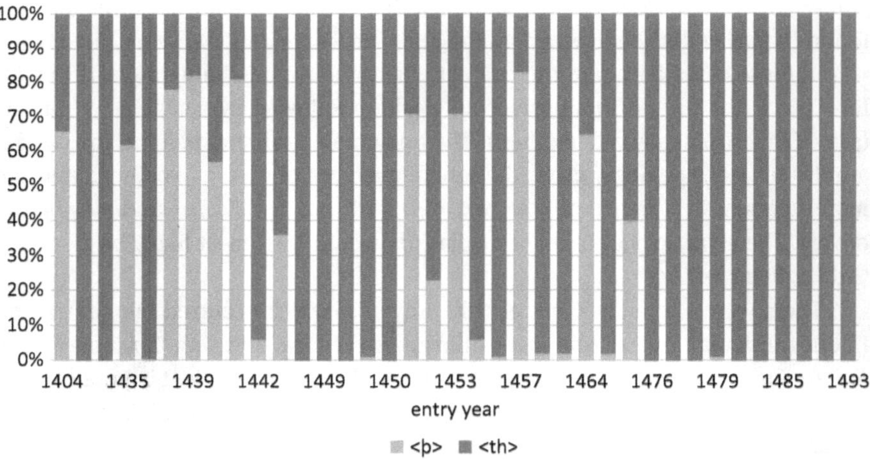

Figure 6.2: Percentages of the individual documents with <þ> or <th> as a majority form.

Based on Hernández-Campoy and Conde-Silvestre's (2015) observations regarding variation and change patterns in the Paston letters c.1425–1496, the onset of the transition stage must have been before the period investigated, since none of the Bristol texts show categorical use of <þ>, whereas <th> is used categorically in quite a few cases. As the Paston data is taken from a different text-type, caution should be heeded here, but it is nonetheless noteworthy that of the 37 Bristol texts, only ten texts have <þ> as the majority form. As demonstrated in Table 6.2 below, the largest percentage of texts with <þ> as the majority form is concentrated in the first half of the century.

Even in the earliest texts, the use of <þ> appears to be lexically conditioned. There was a tendency to use <þ> in function words such as highly frequent determiners *the, that, this*, personal pronouns *they, them, their*, prepositions *with, within, without*, and adverbs *there, therein*; while <th> spellings were used in a greater variety of lexical items, including verbs and content words:

Table 6.2: Distribution of <þ> and <th> in function words and verbs/content words.

	function	verb/content	total
<þ>	98% (1477)	2% (26)	1503
<th>	89% (4222)	11% (514)	4736
total	91% (5699)	9% (540)	6239

In four texts <þ> only occurs once or twice, and all of these occurrences except one appear at the end of a line with a superscript *e*, or were inserted inline when space was lacking. As can be seen in examples (1) and (2) below, <þ> appears to be preferred at the end of a longer line

(1) or Appert. But that they haue An Opyn Place be Syde the high Croſſe of the ſeid Towne of Briſtowe Or In thaire howſis opynlycch and noone oþ^{er} place vppon payn to pay to the vſe of the Comunyalte of Briſtowe (Farrier's ordinance, 1455, f.26, BRO: 04718),

(2) terme foreſaide And that he be no Rebelle of Irelonde nor Alyen But liegeman boren to the Kyng oure souueraign. lorde. And whate man of þ^{e} ſame Craffte do the Contrary of this. and therof conuicted to fore the (Fletcher's ordinance, 1479, f.27b, BRO: 04718)

In these examples the use of <þ> appears to be used for the sake of space. This suggests that some of the scribes of the council ordinances of period I (1404–1493) were aware of a norm and only used the older form in specific situations. As predicted by Stenroos (2004), <y> was extremely rare and only occurred once in a text from 1479, also at the end of a line in the form of an abbreviation.

4.2 Period II: The council ordinances of Bristol 1506–1596

The council ordinance corpus of the period 1506 to 1596 shows little variation with regard to the digraph <th> which was used categorically, with two notable exceptions: there is one occurrence of <y> in a council ordinance from 1560, close to the end of a relatively long line with superscript <e> to represent *the*, and one <þ> in similar circumstances in a document from around 1567 (see Figure 6.3 below):

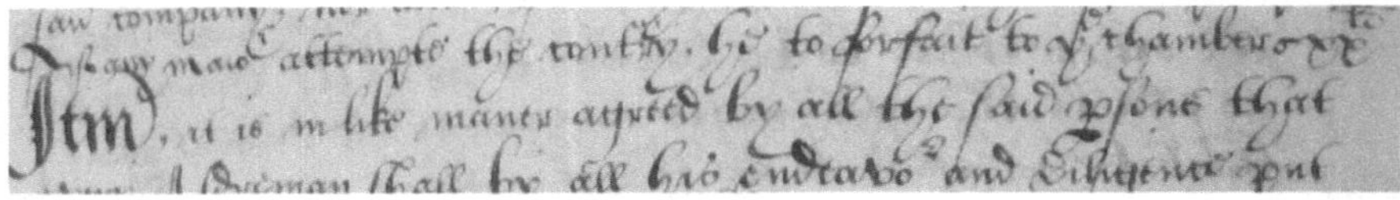

Figure 6.3: <y> crammed in near the end of the line, Ordinance of the Chamberlain, 1560, f.19, BRO: 04272.

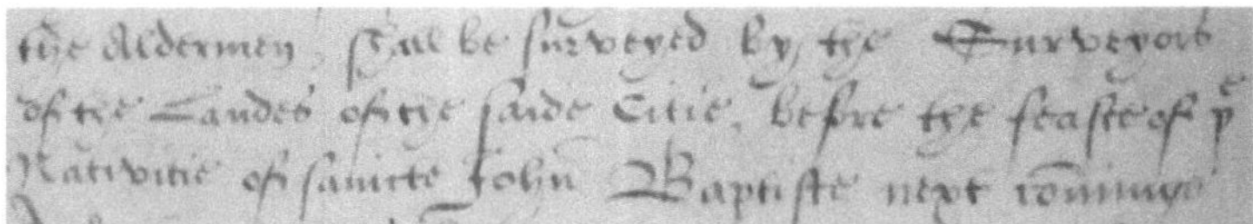

Figure 6.4: <þ> at the end of the 2nd line, Memorandum of tenements, 1568, f.24b, BRO:04272.

The council ordinance volume is a continuation of the ordinances in the LRB and GRB, which contained a wider range of variants. It can only be speculated about why and how <th> variation became so homogenous so rapidly in Bristol's ordinances. As pointed out earlier, it is possible that the earlier entries are fair copies that were entered into the volume considerably later, around the 1570s. It may be that variants were present in the originals but updated by the copier (Stenroos 2004: 276). This would explain why <þ> in Figure 6.4 only occurs in a place where space might have been an issue although, as observed for period I (1404–1493), some scribes tended to maintain <þ> in abbreviated function words, e.g. <þ> with a superscript *e* to represent *the*, with <th> in all other environments. For period II, there are no instances of the digraph in abbreviated function words; the only two abbreviated ones have a monograph.

The single occurrence of <y> is harder to explain. However, as mentioned earlier, there are some undated Bristol civic records that were probably written in the fifteenth century and that have <y(h)> (5 in total) alongside <þ> and <th> as a variant of <th>. This is interesting in the light of Benskin's (1982: 13) claim that <y> as a merger of <þ> typically occurred in the North in Late Middle English (system I), while mixed uses of <y> typically occurred in border areas (system III). Bristol was not situated in a border area or in the North. However, even though we find minority rates of <y> in the Bristol civic records, this is not to such an extent that they are used interchangeably as observed in system III, i.e. there are no examples where <þ> represents <y>. Benskin (1982: 25) claims that <y> was actually also found in the South before 1350, but somehow the variant became restricted to the North in the Later Middle English period. Perhaps Bristol was an area where <y> never completely disappeared. Unfortunately, more informal text-types such as correspondence are scant for the fifteenth and sixteenth centuries, and there do not seem to be any studies that consider the use of <y> in the sixteenth century, which makes it difficult to establish if <y> was actually a retention or a supralocal innovation.

4.3 Period III: The letters 1548–1711

In letters with dates ranging from 1548 to 1711 there is not a single occurrence of <þ>, which is in line Hernández-Campoy and Conde-Silvestre's (2015) finding, as although their corpus of letters precedes mine (c.1425–1504), they found that <þ> was on its way out by the early 1500s as, by that time, only the older generations of the Paston family occasionally used it, whereas some of the younger family members had <th> rates of 100% (2015: 28). The letter-writers from Period III (1548–1711) of the Bristol corpus overlapped with the younger generation of the Pastons. The innovation of <th> among the Bristol letter-writers was on a par with the Paston family's usage, in that the older <þ> form had disappeared by 1548 and <th> was used almost categorically.

However, throughout the period, in Bristol letters of 1548 through to letters of 1711, <y> for <th> is found at 8%. Distribution was restricted: <y> was only used with function words *that, the, this, them* (see Table 6.3 below for the distribution rates of <y> versus <th> in function words).

Table 6.3: <y> vs. <th> in function words *the, that, them, this*.

	<y>	<th>	total
the	20% (219)	80% (888)	1,107
that	13% (56)	87% (371)	427
them	5% (5)	95% (86)	91
this	1% (1)	99% (275)	267
total	15% (281)	85 % (1,620)	1,892

The <y> forms were used by eight authors out of the total of 16 authors that make up the letter corpus. All of the <y> users, except one (Romsey), were members of different generations of the Smythe family. As can be seen in Table 6.4, there is a small timespan overlap with the council ordinances of period II (1506–1596) and John's writings of 1548. <y> is the preferred form in function words *the* and *that* (recall that <y> was extremely rare in the sixteenth-century council ordinances, occurring only once in the form of an abbreviation and in the function word *the*).

Table 6.4: Distribution of <y> in function words amongst the different authors, Period III (1548–1711).

name author		the	that	them	this
John 1548	y	59% (50)	100% (20)	–	10% (1)
	th	41% (35)	–	100% (4)	90% (9)
Elizabeth-1640s	y	1% (2)	1% (2)	–	–
	th	99% (287)	99% (146)	100% (36)	100% (96)
Thomas-1640s	y	42% (99)	43% (30)	25% (5)	–
	th	58% (138)	57% (39)	75% (15)	100% (45)
Thomas jr.-1660s	y	67% (14)	15% (2)	–	–
	th	33% (7)	85% (11)	100% (1)	100% (10)
Romsey 1670	y	1% (1)	1% (1)	–	–
	th	99% (137)	97% (58)	100% (16)	100% (16)
Florence -1680s	y	25% (5)	25% (1)	–	–
	th	75% (15)	75% (3)	–	–
Hugh -1680s	y	92% (12)	–	–	–
	th	8% (1)	–	–	100% (2)
Charles-1710s	y	52% (36)	–	–	–
	th	48% (24)	100% (32)	100% (1)	100% (14)

All in all, the use of <y> receded over the period studied; in later letters the form occurs as a variant only in the definite article *the*. Furthermore, taking the evidence of all periods together, it could be that abbreviations were key in the retention of <y>, and in the earlier periods of <þ> over <th>, with monographs being preferred over digraphs in abbreviated function words. Table 6.5 below provides the figures of abbreviations with an initial or final <th> variant across all periods. This includes superscript abbreviations y^{t}, y^{at}, *þ*^{e}. Period I had only <þ> as a monograph option in abbreviations, while period II had one <y> token and one <þ> token in abbreviations, which are also the only instances of these monographs throughout the period. Period III had only <y> as monographs in the same context. Based on the figures, it appears that in this particular context a monograph was preferred, regardless of text-type. Strikingly, the digraph cases all occur in superscript abbreviations of the word *oth*^{er}. The question remains why and when monograph <y> replaced <þ> in (superscript) abbreviations and why abbreviated forms with <th> variants are rare in council ordinances (the only two cases in the later council ordinances are also monographs).

Table 6.5: Abbreviated forms: digraph <th> versus monographs <y> and <þ>.

time periods	digraph <th>	monograph <y>/<þ>	total
period I: 1404–1493 (LRB and GRB)	7% (11)	93% (143)	154
period II:1506–1596 (council ordinances)	–	100% (2)	2
period III: 1548–1711 (letters)	2% (1)	98% (62)	63
total	5% (12)	95% (207)	219

The historical background of the correspondence authors raises the possibility that <y> was a new, incoming form which had its heyday in correspondence of the seventeenth century. Little is known about Romsey's background, but Table 6.4 reveals that he only occasionally used <y>. Four generations of the Smythes are represented, with John being Thomas' grandfather and Thomas junior, Florence and Hugh's great-grandfather. Elizabeth was Thomas' mother and John's daughter-in-law. Charles was Hugh's son and thus Elizabeth's great-grandchild. Based on the historical background that is known about the Smythe family, Thomas was educated at St. John's College Oxford, after which he returned to Bristol. He was involved in local as well as national politics and lived a geographically mobile life (Bettey 1982, 2004). Less is known about the other family members. However, based on the content of the letters it is clear that they were all quite mobile and had a social network that extended to London and beyond (Bettey 1982, 1992, 2004). This was especially true for John's great-grandsons, but also for John, who was a successful merchant. As can be seen in Table 6.4, it is those men who show high rates of <y>, whereas the women show relatively low rates, with Thomas' sister Mary not using <y> at all. Assuming the women wrote their own letters rather than dictated them, it could be that <y> was part of a supralocal norm, which the women were less subject to. In general, the women had many more phonological spellings and unconventional word boundaries in their letters. This suggests that their literacy schooling was less formal. The <y>-using men have fewer phonological spellings and may have been trained according to specific letter-writing conventions provided by the letter writing manuals that started to make their appearance in the second half of the sixteenth century (Edwards 2009). Alternatively, they could have been schooled by a private tutor, but letter-writing was also part of the curriculum at Oxford (Daybell 2012: 57). It could also be that the level of formality plays a role, as the women's letters are generally addressed to their children (in the case of Elizabeth), or their brother and father (in the case of Mary) and deal with everyday topics. The letters of the men are typically more formal in nature, and, with the exception of Hugh, Thomas and Thomas jr., not addressed to close family members.

5 Conclusion

In the Bristol documents studied, the transition from <þ> to <th> was already underway by Period I (1404–1493). From the earliest texts onwards, <þ> was largely restricted to function words, even in the texts which had <þ> as their majority form, and by the 1470s, <þ> had all but disappeared from the documentary text-type. This development is in line with Stenroos' (2004) findings regarding documentary texts, although Bristol seems to have been slightly more conservative compared to the development of the digraph in Southern documentary texts as a whole. The patterning of the individual texts points towards a generational change. However, occasional single occurrences up until the 1570s suggest that the form had not completely disappeared from the scribes' repertoires. Other minor, perhaps more local, variants (<tth>, <yhe>, <dd>) disappeared from an early period onwards, leading to reduction of variation. Both the adoption of supralocal <th> and the levelling out of other variants suggest that the processes of regional dialect levelling and supralocalisation in orthography were well underway by the second half of the fifteenth century.

The relatively frequent occurrence of <y> in correspondence from the early period onwards is unexpected, since <y> hardly occurs in council ordinances of Period I (1404–1493), or council ordinances of Period II (1506–1596). According to Benskin (1982) and Stenroos (2004), <y> was not a typical Southern form in the later Middle Ages. As is suggested by the single occurrence of <y> in the council ordinances in the 1570s, scribes had knowledge of the graph, which suggests that conscious attempts were made towards orthographic uniformity – it looks as though <y> was acceptable in certain abbreviated function words which were rarely abbreviated in the council ordinances, but with monograph <þ> or <y> rather than digraph <th> when they were. The letter-writers who used <y> were affluent merchants with a loose-knit network that extended over a large geographical area, suggesting that <y> was part of a wider, supralocal writing practice. Although it can only be speculated how the letter-writers were taught to write, it is almost certain that they learned to write in different contexts to those of the scribes who composed the civic ordinances (cf. Fitzmaurice 2002; Nevalainen & Tanskanen 2007; Dossena & Tieken-Boon van Ostade (eds.) 2008).

In sum, this survey reopens Benskin's (1982: 14) division III, which was that <þ> and <y> were used interchangeably to represent <th> only in North/South border areas, Bristol lying far to the south of the country. Both text-type and the distinction between full-spelling and abbreviation seem to have played a role in choice of letter-graphs. The timespan considered here extends beyond Benskin's survey, and so it is not impossible that Bristol <y> was a later, supra-local, innovation, or it may have been a retention of earlier practice.

References

Anthony, L. (2014). AntConc (Version 3.3.4.). Tokyo: Waseda University.

Baker, J. (1990). *The third university of England: The Inns of Court and the common-law tradition*. Colchester: Selden Society.

Bantock, A. (1982). *The earlier Smyths of Ashton Court: from their letters 1545–1741*. Bristol: Malago publications.

Barnard, T. (2004). Southwell, Sir Robert (1635–1702). In *Oxford Dictionary of National Biography* (online ed.). Oxford: Oxford University Press.

Beetham-Fisher, A. L. (1987). *The merchants of medieval Bristol, 1350–1500*. University of Oregon: PhD thesis.

Benskin, M. (1977). Local archives and Middle English dialects. *Journal of the Society of Archivists*, *5*(8), 500–514.

Benskin, M. (1982). The letters <þ> and <y> in Later Middle English, and some related matters. *Journal of the Society of Archivists* *7*(1), 13–30.

Benskin, M., Laing, M., Karaiskos, V., Williamson, K., McIntosh, A., & Samuels, M. L. (2013, [1982]). General introduction, index of sources, Dot Maps. Retrieved from http://www.lel.ed.ac.uk/ihd/elalme/elalme.html

Benskin, M. (1992). Some new perspectives on the origins of Standard written English. In J. van Leuvensteijn & J. Berns (Eds.), *Dialect and standard language in the English, Dutch, German and Norwegian language areas* (pp. 71–105). Amsterdam: Royal Netherlands Academy of Arts and Sciences.

Bergs, A. (2013). Writing, reading, language change-a sociohistorical perspective on scribes, readers and social networks in Britain. In E.-M. Wagner, B. Outhwaithe, & B. Beinhoff

(Eds.), *Scribes as agents of language change* (Vol. 10, pp. 241–260). Boston: Mouton de Gruyter.

Bettey, J. H. (1982). *Calendar of the correspondence of the Smyth family of Ashton Court, 1548–1642*. Gloucester: Bristol Record Society.

Bettey, J. H. (1992). Hugh Smyth of Ashton Court 1530–1581: Somerset landowner, Justice of the Peace and trouble-maker. In T. Mayberry (Ed.), *Proceedings of the Somerset Archaeological and Natural History Society* (Vol. 136, pp. 141–148). Taunton: SAHNS.

Bettey, J. H. (2004). Smyth Family (per. c.1500–1680). In *Oxford Dictionary of National Biography* (Online ed.). Oxford: Oxford University Press.

Bevan, K. L. (2013). *Clerks and scriveners: Legal literacy and access to justice in late Medieval England*. University of Exeter: PhD thesis. Retrieved from https://ore.exeter.ac.uk/repository/handle/10871/10732

Bickley, F. B. (Ed.). (1900). *The Little Red Book of Bristol*. (Vols. 1–2). Bristol: W.C. Hemmons.

Britain, David. (2008). Space and Spatial Diffusion. In J. K. Chambers, P. Trudgill & N. Schilling-Estes (Eds.), *The handbook of language variation and change* (pp. 603–637). John Wiley & Sons doi.org/10.1002/9780470756591.ch24

Britain, D. (2010). Supralocal dialect levelling. In C. Llamas & D. Watt (Eds.), *Language and identities* (pp. 193–204). Edinburgh: Edinburgh University Press.

Britain, D., & Chambers, J. K. (2013). Space, diffusion and mobility. In N. Schilling-Estes (Ed.), *The handbook of language variation and change* (pp. 469–500). Hoboken: Wiley-Blackwell.

Carus Wilson, E. M., & Lobel, D. M. (1975). Bristol. In D.M. Lobel & W.H. Johns (Eds.), *The Atlas of historic towns* (Vol. 2, pp. 1–26). London: The Scholar Press in conjunction with the Historic Towns Trust.

Clanchy, M. T. (1993). *From memory to written record: England 1066–1307* (2nd ed.). Oxford: Wiley-Blackwell.

Coleman, J. (1981). *English literature in history, 1350–1400 medieval readers and writers*. London: Hutchinson.

Cressy, D. (1980). *Literacy and the social order: Reading and writing in Tudor and Stuart England*. Cambridge: Cambridge University Press.

Daybell, J. (2012). *The material letter in Early Modern England: Manuscript letters and the culture and practices of letter-writing, 1512–1635*. Basingstoke: Palgrave Macmillan.

de Vries, J. (1984). *European urbanization 1500–1800*. London: Methuen.

Dobson, B. (2000). General survey 1300–1540. In D. M. Palliser (Ed.), *The Cambridge urban history of Britain* (vol. 1, pp. 271–290). Cambridge: Cambridge University Press.

Dossena, M., & Tieken-Boon van Ostade, I. (Eds.), (2008). *Studies in Late Modern English correspondence: Methodology and data*. Bern: Peter Lang.

Edwards, J. R. (2009). A business education for 'the middling sort of people' in mercantilist Britain. *The British Accounting Review*, *41*(4), 240–255. doi.org/10.1016/j.bar.2009.10.004

Fitzmaurice, S. M. (2002). *The familiar letter in Early Modern English: A pragmatic approach*. Amsterdam: John Benjamins Publishing.

Fleming, P. (1996). The emergence of modern Bristol. In M. Dresser & P. Ollerenshaw (Eds.), *The making of modern Bristol* (pp. 1–24). Tiverton: Redcliffe Press.

Gordon, M. S. (2017). *The urban vernacular of Late medieval and Renaissance Bristol*. Utrecht: LOT.

Hernández-Campoy, J.M. (1999). Geolinguistic models of analysis of the spatial diffusion of sociolinguistic innovations. *Studia Anglica Posnaniensia*, *34*, 7–42. Retrieved from http://ifa.amu.edu.pl.proxy.library.uu.nl/sap/files/34/01hernandez-campoy.pdf

Hernández-Campoy, J. M. (2003). Exposure to contact and the geographical adoption of standard features: Two complementary approaches. *Language in Society*, *32*(2), 227–255. Retrieved from http://www.jstor.org/stable/4169257

Hernández-Campoy, J.M, & Conde-Silvestre, J. C. (2005). Sociolinguistic and geolinguistic approaches to the historical diffusion of linguistic innovations: Incipient standardisation in Late Middle English. *International Journal of English Studies*, *5*(1), 101–134.

Hernández-Campoy, J.M., & Conde-Silvestre, J. C. (2015). Assessing variability and change in early English letters. In A. Auer, D. Schreier, & R.J. Watts (Eds.), *Letter writing and language change* (pp. 14–34). Cambridge: Cambridge University Press.

Hogg, R. M. (1992). Phonology and morphology. In R. M. Hogg (Ed.), *The Cambridge history of the English language* (Vol. 1, pp. 67–167). Cambridge: Cambridge University Press.

Kerswill, P. (2003). Dialect levelling and geographical diffusion in British English. In D. Britain & J. Cheshire (Eds.), *Social dialectology: In honour of Peter Trudgill* (pp. 223–244). Amsterdam & Philadelphia: John Benjamins.

Kretzschmar, jr. W. (2009). *The Linguistics of Speech*. Cambridge: Cambridge University Press.

Labov, W. (2001). *Principles of linguistic change, social factors* (Vol. 2). Hoboken: Wiley-Blackwell.

Laing, M., & Lass, R. (2009). Shape-shifting, sound-change and the genesis of prodigal writing systems. *English Language and Linguistics*, *13*(1), 1–31.

Laker, S. (2009). An explanation for the early phonemicisation of a voice contrast in English fricatives. *English Language and Linguistics*, *13*(2), 213–26.

Lass, R. (1991–1993). Old English fricative voicing unvisited. *Studia Anglica Posnaniensia*, *25–27*, 3–45.

Lass, R. (1992). Phonology and morphology. In R. Lass (Ed.), *The Cambridge history of the English language* (Vol. 3, 1476–1776, pp. 56–186). Cambridge: Cambridge University Press.

Lawson, J., & Silver, H. (1973). *A social history of education in England*. London: Methuen.

Lee, J. M. (2007). *Political communication in early Tudor England: the Bristol elite, the urban community and the crown, c.1471–c.1553*. University of the West of England: PhD thesis.

McIntosh, A. (1974). Towards an inventory of Middle English scribes. *Neuphilologische Mitteilungen*, *75*, 602–624.

Milroy, J. (2003). When is a sound change? On the role of external factors in language change. In D. Britain & J. Cheshire (Eds.), *Social dialectology: In honour of Peter Trudgill* (pp. 209–221). Amsterdam & Philadelphia: John Benjamins.

Minkova, D. (2011). Phonemically contrastive fricatives in Old English? *English Language and Linguistics*, *15*(1), 31–59. doi:10.1017/S1360674310000274

Moran Cruz, J. A. H. (2014). *The growth of English schooling, 1340–1548: Learning, literacy, and laicization in pre-Reformation York diocese*. Princeton: Princeton University Press.

Nevalainen, T. (2000a). Mobility, social networks and language change in Early Modern England. *European Journal of English Studies*, *4*(3), 253–264.

Nevalainen, T. (2000b). Processes of supralocalisation and the rise of Standard English in the Early Modern period. In R. Bermúdez-Otero, D. Denison, R. Hogg, & C. B. McCully (Eds.), *Generative theory and corpus studies. A dialogue from the 10th ICHEL* (pp. 329–371). Berlin & New York: Mouton de Gruyter.

Nevalainen, T. (2003). English. In W. Vandenbussche & A. Deumert (Eds.), *Germanic standardizations past to present* (pp. 127–156). Amsterdam: John Benjamins.

Nevalainen, T. & Raumolin-Brunberg, H. (2003). *Historical sociolinguistics: language change in Tudor and Stuart English*. London: Longman.

Nevalainen, T. & Tanskanen, S.-K. (Eds.), (2007). *Letter Writing*. Amsterdam: John Benjamins.
OED. (2016). mother, n.1 (and int.). *Oxford English Dictionary* (Online ed.). Oxford: Oxford University Press. Retrieved from http://www.oed.com/view/Entry/122640?
Orme, N. (1989). *Education and society in Medieval and Renaissance England*. London: Hambledon Press.
Rees Jones, S. (2014). Civic literacy in later medieval England. In M. Mostert & A. Adamska (Eds.), *Writing and the administration of medieval towns: Medieval urban literacy* (Vol. 27, pp. 219–230). Turnhout: Brepols.
Rockwell, G., Lian, Y., MacDonald, A., & Patey, M. (2005). XML Tools: Word lists. Retrieved from http://taporware.ualberta.ca/~taporware/xmlTools/listword.shtml?
Romaine, S. (1982). *Socio-historical linguistics: its status and methodology*. Cambridge: Cambridge University Press.
Sacks, D. H. (1991). *The widening gate: Bristol and the Atlantic economy 1450–1700*. Berkeley: California University Press.
Stanford, M. (Ed.), (1990). *The ordinances of Bristol, 1506–1598*. Gloucester: Bristol Record Society.
Stenroos, M. (2004). Regional dialects and spelling conventions in Late Middle English: Searches for (th) in the LALME data. In M. Dossena & R. Lass (Eds.), *Methods and data in English historical dialectology 16* (pp. 257–286). Bern: Peter Lang.
Stenroos, M. (2006). A Middle English mess of fricative spellings: Reflections on thorn, yogh and their rivals. In M. Krygier & L. Sikorska (Eds.), *To make his Englissh sweete upon his tonge* (pp. 9–35). Frankfurt am Main: Peter Lang.
Stenroos, M. (2016). Regional language and culture: The geography of Middle English linguistic variation. In T. W. Machan (Ed.), *Imagining medieval English: Language structures and theories, 500–1500* (pp. 100–125). Cambridge: Cambridge University Press.
Stenroos, M., & Thengs, K. V. (2012). Two Staffordshires: Real and linguistic space in the study of Late Middle English dialects. In J. Tyrkkö, M. Kilpiö, T. Nevalainen, & M. Rissanen (Eds.), *Outposts of historical corpus linguistics: From the Helsinki Corpus to a proliferation of resources*. Helsinki: VARIENG. URL: http://www.helsinki.fi/varieng/series/volumes/10/stenroos_thengs/
Stenroos, M. Mäkinen, S. Horobin, & J. Smith (Eds.), (2011). *The Middle English Grammar Corpus* (version 2011.1). Stavanger: University of Stavanger.
Taavitsainen, I. (2000). *Placing Middle English in context*. Berlin: Walter de Gruyter.
Taavitsainen, I. (2001). Changing conventions of writing: The dynamics of genres, text types, and text traditions. *European Journal of English Studies*, *5*(2), 139–150.
Trudgill, P. (1986). *Dialects in contact*. Hoboken: Blackwell.
Veale, E. W. W. (1933). *The great red book of bristol: Text*. Bristol: Bristol Record Society.
Wyld, H. C. (1936). *A history of modern colloquial English*. Oxford: Blackwell

Juan M. Hernández-Campoy

7 <th> *versus* <þ>: Latin-based influences and social awareness in the Paston letters

1 Multilingual England and standard ideology

One of the main complaints by sociolinguists has been the presence of standard and purist ideologies in language history and historiography (see Milroy 2001, 2005, 2012; Hernández-Campoy and Trudgill 2002; Riley 2012; Langer and Nesse 2012), as well as in the reconstruction of prestige patterns (see Sairio and Palander-Collin 2012). The history of languages has traditionally been the history of the national standards, where a standard variety has been equated with the language as a whole, following a unidimensional and unidirectional conceptualization of sociolinguistic and geolinguistic space (see Watts 2000, 2011, 2012; Watts and Trudgill 2002). Even something as abstract as linguists' analyses of linguistic systems have been influenced by a standard-centred ideology and culture as part of a general consciousness (Milroy 1999, 2001), biased by nationalistic beliefs about the histories and origins of languages.

Multilingualism is a phenomenon which is common to the vast majority of the nation-states of the world. Contact-induced changes and codeswitching phenomena are especially predominant in multilingual situations (see Fischer 2013; Klemola 2013; Schendl 2013). English has been a contact-derived language from its earliest stages onwards (Stein 2007; McWhorter 2009; Schreier & Hundt 2013), and invasion and conquest have been the reason for much of the multilingual element. The Norman Conquest, for example, was one of the most significant events in English history, leading to a sociolinguistic situation of multilingualism in medieval England with high-contact among English, French and Latin. According to Schendl (2013), codeswitching and code-alternation between these three languages was a widely-accepted interactional strategy at a textual level in late fourteenth and early fifteenth century England, and thus a reflection of the complex multilingual situation in the literate strata of medieval English society.

2 Multidialectal England and standard ideology

Multilingual England was also multidialectal. In the Middle English period there was no national standard, but rather a mosaic of English dialectal varieties

https://doi.org/10.1515/9783110687545-008

competing with Anglo-Norman French and Medieval Latin. If heteroglossia is the linguistic representation of social, contextual, and/or ideological differences, processes of homogeneization and standardization in language are the culmination of centralization, unification, normalization, regularization, and prescription. As Wright (2013) states, the multilingual as well as the multidialectal situation changed when Standard English began to develop during the fifteenth and sixteenth centuries at the expense of Anglo-Norman, Medieval Latin, and the amalgam of ME dialects (koiné). But even this embryonic Standard was a contact variety, as an outcome of traders from London meeting traders from the rest of the country and from the Continent (see also Wright 1999a, 1999b, 2000a, 2000b, 2001a, 2001b; Kitson 2004).

The development of norms for language usage have traditionally been associated with explicit standardization and overt prescriptivism (Haugen 1966/1997). However, language norms are more likely to result from implicit standardization first, as regular processes of change (mostly regional dialect levelling) that result in supralocalization (Nevalainen 2000, 2003, 2012, 2014), followed by the emergence of a standard ideology (Fisher 1996; Milroy & Milroy 1999; Hope 2000; Nevalainen & Tieken-Boon van Ostade 2006; Spolsky 2012; Pilliere *et al.* 2018). The process of standardization "is shown not to be a linear, unidirectional or 'natural' development, but a set of processes which occur in a set of social spaces, developing at different rates in different registers in different idiolects" (Wright 2000c: 6). As Wright suggests, the first sign of standardization is the reduction in variability as a frequency-based propensity: a change from the use of multiple variants for a given linguistic feature – with what might be a Zipf's Law distribution of 20/80 – to a categorical 100% with no variation. This variant reduction appears as the beginning of standardization because there cannot be subsequent selection without it – even though the feature reduced to by any one writer might not (usually does not) end up in Standard English.

3 Multilingualism and multidialectism in late medieval England

The role of speakers has to some extent been absent in accounts of standardization (Haugen 1966/1997), whereas the individual speaker is a crucial ingredient in the diffusion of linguistic practices and innovations. Both linguistic change and its subsequent diffusion must be assumed to start in speakers themselves: "the drama of linguistic change is enacted not in manuscripts nor inscriptions, but in the mouths and minds of people" (Wyld 1914/1927: 21). As Milroy (1992: 4 and 169) stated, languages without speakers do not change, since "it is *speakers*, and not *languages*, that innovate". Trudgill (1992b: iv) also pointed out that it is speakers who change languages with their everyday use in communicative interaction. At a micro-level of interaction, and from a micro-sociolinguistic point of view, the geographical diffusion of a linguistic innovation has to be thought of primarily in terms of both the innovating individuals and the process of face-to-face interaction (Trudgill 1992a: 76). Providing attitudes are favourable, in face-to-face interaction speakers from different dialect/sociolect backgrounds will accommodate each other linguistically by reducing dissimilarities between their speech models and by adopting each other's features. In fact, "diffusion can be said to have taken place, presumably, on the first occasion when a speaker employs a new feature in the *absence* of speakers of the variety originally containing this feature" (Trudgill 1986: 40).

4 Inter-writer and intra-writer variation

Based on Halliday (1978), Bell (1984: 145) established the distinction between *inter*-speaker (social) and *intra*-speaker (stylistic) variation: "[t]he social dimension denotes differences between the speech of different speakers, and the stylistic denotes differences within the speech of a single speaker". On the one hand, *inter*-speaker variation alludes to social differences amongst groups of speakers reflected in their speech: "[t]he range of variation for particular sociolinguistic variables across the different speakers" (Bell 2007: 90). On the other hand, *intra*-speaker variation refers to stylistic differences in a single speaker reflected in their speech: "[t]he range of variation for particular sociolinguistic variables produced by individual speakers within their own speech" (Bell 2007: 90). This division can be extended to the written level when dealing with corpora of private correspondence, with inter-writer and intra-writer variation. Private correspondence reflects the personal communicative styles of interlocutors in the context of their mutual social relationship and of the situation and purpose of the letter: closer relationship (e.g. kinship, friendship) or more distant (professional, businesslike) (Eckert & McConnel-Ginet 1992; Palander-Collin, Nevala & Nurmi 2009; Kopaczyk & Jucker 2013; Conde-Silvestre 2016). According to Romaine (1998: 18), "personal letters are among the most involved and therefore oral of written genres" within this continuum of communicative immediacy and communicative distance.

4.1 Inter-writer variation and generational change

One of the main principles of stylistic variation in Labov's (1966) Attention to Speech Model establishes that no single speaker is mono-stylistic, though some will have a wider verbal repertoire than others (see also Hernández-Campoy 2016a). Medieval speakers cannot have been fully monolingual, monodialectal or monostylistic. The history of the introduction of the spelling <th> provides an illustration of the multilingual context (with the adoption of a form entering from the continent) and multidialectal situation (its diffusion through prestige texts). This variable is a sign of contact-induced change which started in multilingual England but which was completed in what had become a far more monolingual England. During the Old English period, the Anglo-Saxons used an alphabet of runes. The early Christian missionaries introduced the Roman alphabet when they brought Christianity, literacy and European culture to England during the early seventh century A.D. (Upward & Davidson 2011). The adoption of the Roman alphabet at the expense of the Runic one was rapid except for a few letters that did not have an equivalent in Latin and thus prevailed until the end of the Middle Ages: 'wynn' ƿ (> *uu/w*), 'eth' ð (> *th*), 'yogh' ʒ (> *y/j/g*), and 'thorn' þ (> *th*). As Millward & Mayes (1996/2012: 84) point out, "Christianization is an important landmark in the history of the English language because it brought England and English speakers into the only living intellectual community of Europe, that of the Latin Church. England immediately adopted the Latin alphabet, and English was soon being written down extensively". In the late Middle English period, the adoption of the Roman digraph <th> was therefore a contact-induced change in English writing, and thorn was a relic grapheme resisting continental orthographic influence. The progressive adoption of the new orthographic variant <th> at the expense of the old runic <þ> was a slow process (Scragg 1974: 10; Benskin 1977: 506–507; 1982: 18–19; Lass 1992: 36; Hogg 1992: 76–77; Stenroos 2004, 2006; Bergs 2007; Conde-Silvestre & Hernández-Campoy 2013).

þing > thing *broþer > brother* *comeþ > cometh*

Use of <th> was attested in the Anglo-Saxon period, predominantly in the spelling of vernacular names in Latin texts, but it was reintroduced in the twelfth century through Anglo-Norman scribes (Benskin (1982: 19). In this context of continental magnetism, the presence of the digraph <th> in both Latin and Biblical texts acted as an external prestigious norm that triggered the *actuation* of this orthographic change, so that the Roman-based form became popular during the fifteenth century operating as a socially conscious choice (Stenroos 2004, 2006; Bergs 2007;

Jensen 2012; Conde-Silvestre & Hernández-Campoy 2013). This process inevitably took place in connection with social and stylistic factors, diffusing along the social space in careful and conscious styles, acquiring overt prestige and becoming part of the accepted linguistic norm, as a typical Labovian 'change from above' (Hernández-Campoy, Conde-Silvestre & García-Vidal 2019).

This nature of <th> is something that can be observed in the *Paston Letters* in speaker's sociolinguistic variation at the level of interpersonal communication.[1] This collection of private correspondence with 422 authored documents written from 1425 to 1503 by 15 members belonging to four different generations of a Norfolk minor gentry family constitute an illustration of the gradual replacement of the runic symbol <þ> with the Roman-based <th> (Figure 7.1).[2] For the purpose of our study, the informants observed were five male members of this family, born between 1436 and 1459, and about whom we have extensive biographical information: John I, William II, John II, John III and William III. According to Davis (1971), these ones are the only authors whose letters were actually autographed among the 15 members of the family, given the widespread illiteracy characteristic of those historical periods and their resulting use of scribes and dictation (Orme 1973, 1984, 2006; Cressy 1980; Graff 1981; O'Day 1982; Bergs 2005; Hernández-Campoy 2016b; Cutillas-Espinosa & Hernández-Campoy fc).[3] Literacy attainment in the late Middle Ages and the Early Modern period of

1 The data used for the present study are based on epistolary documents drawn from the electronic edition of the *Paston Letters* (first part), currently available online from the Corpus of Middle English Prose and Verse at the University of Michigan (http://quod.lib.umich.edu/c/cme/paston/ [accessed on June 30, 2019]) and the University of Oxford Text Archive (https://ota.oucs.ox.ac.uk/headers/1685.xml/ [accessed on June 30, 2019]).

2 Since both the topic and the corpus data ultimately rest on manuscript evidence, palaeographical aspects might come into consideration. Scribes were prone to dittographies, mistakenly repeating graphs within a given word. There could also be scribal calculations of writing space and the graphic environment where the graph was supposed to stand to be taken into account. In this way, the choice of the variants for an orthographic variable like (TH) might not have been so much conditioned by socio-demographic factors. Rather, as demonstrated by Meyer's Laws, because of his ductus, a scribe could have been partial to selecting single letters over digraphs at the end of the line for mere writing space reasons. However, these scribal practices may be dismissed in the Paston letters observed since only sent letters were scrutinised for the present study, and not drafts, where they might have been more likely. Additionally, as discussed later, most Paston members used as informants for this study did not use secretaries to write their letter under dictation.

3 In historical sociolinguistic research, authorship constitutes one of the most controversial socio-demographic issues in its methodology since data skewing can lead to wrong conclusions on patterns of sociolinguistic behaviour (see Bergs 2015; Hernández-Campoy 2016b; Cutillas-Espinosa & Hernández-Campoy fc). It is well-known that many of the Paston letters

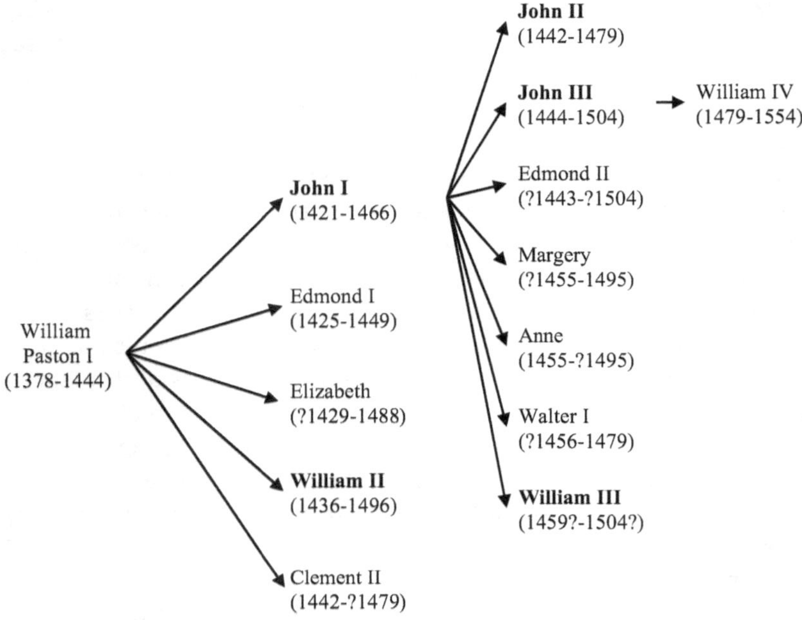

Figure 7.1: Paston family and members observed for this study (in bold).

were autographed, but others were dictated and written by a secretary due to the authors' illiteracy (see Davis 1954, 1965, 1971; Cressy 1980; Bergs 2005, 2015). Here, the question of authorship and scribes does not play such an important role in intra-speaker variation as in inter-speaker variation given that the object of observation is the reaction towards different social class/rank groups resulting from the social impact of the letter recipient (addressee) upon the addresser's upward/downward/symmetrical accommodation through their linguistic behaviour. Additionally, the impact of verbatim dictation or just instructions to the scribe for the draft composition is an open question, since we do not know whether dictated letters represent the language preferences and practices of the authors or those of the secretaries, or both, with some kind of intertextuality. Being experts in language and appropriate language use, and fully aware of both the discursive and social practices of the time in written correspondence, it might also even be the case that scribes used the language which they thought was appropriate for a certain kind of author; and the criteria for what the scribe thought the author should sound like must represent the socio-cultural image or ideal that society held at that time regarding certain people and authors (see Davis 1967, 1971; James 1996; Bergs 2015: 131). Finally, although the informants used for this study wrote their own letters (autographs, except in some cases in John Paston I), their few scribal ones are not statistically significant ($p \geq 0.05$) in both individual and overall results.

England was inextricably linked to social position, as well as to social conventions (gender) and locality. According to Cressy (1980: 141–177), 10% of the male and 1% of the female population was literate (in a total population that was no more than 2,000,000), but it was much higher in London.

As examined in Hernández-Campoy (2020), analysis of the relative frequencies of the variable (TH) in the letters of these five male Paston informants suggests a distinctive pattern of linguistic behaviour over their lifetimes tending to an S-curve, which suggests that this was a change in progress, showing as it does the characteristics of a generational change (Figure 7.2). At the level of inter-speaker variation, their differences are significant at $p < 0.01$ ($\chi^2 = 291.799$; df = 4).

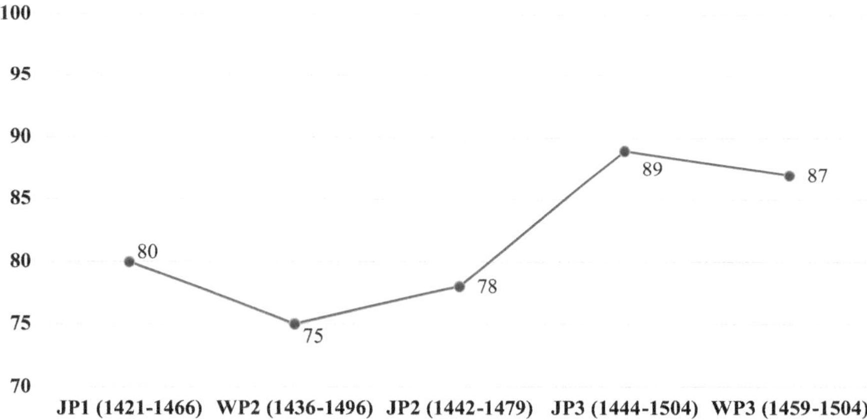

Figure 7.2: Evolution in frequencies for the form <th> in five male members of the Paston family.

A trend study of two time-cohorts from letters written between 1460–1465 and 1480–1485, separated by some twenty years, provides a picture of how these Pastons members behaved with regard to use of the new form <th> (see Hernández-Campoy 2020). Figure 7.3 exhibits similar age-based differences in the use of the innovating variant in both time-cohorts, but with higher frequencies in the second (1480–1485), i.e., much closer to 100%. The comparison of total scores for <th> in 1460 and 1480 is statistically significant at $p < 0.01$ ($\chi^2 = 40.1774$; df = 1), confirming that the differences are relevant and following a positive monotonic pattern.

Individual comparisons inter-groups also suggest the existence of significant variation between them at $p < 0.01$, which means that, interestingly, something was going on within the local community: there is a slow but steady progress in the use of the innovative variant suggesting an age-based pattern

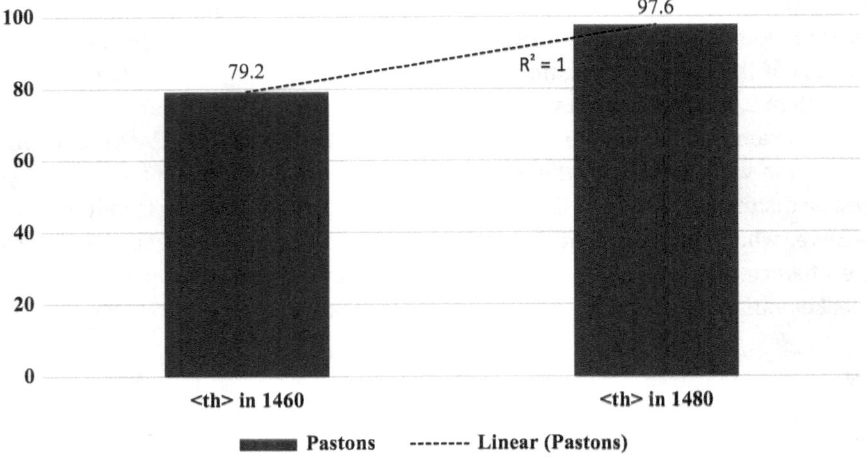

Figure 7.3: Innovative variant <th> in 1460 and 1480 in the Paston family.

for generational change. In this kind of language change, each successively younger generation employs the new form more than the previous one. Quantitatively, this is reflected through the presence of similar age-based differences in the use of the innovating variant per group, but progressively with higher frequencies, i.e., becoming much closer to 100%. The driving force for the change seems to be the same after two decades, in the direction of the ongoing process taking place generation after generation (see Hernández-Campoy, Conde-Silvestre & García-Vidal 2019; and Hernández-Campoy 2020).

4.2 Intra-writer variation and addressee design

The observation of intra-speaker patterns of variation is crucial in detecting and accounting for change in progress, given the omnipresence of style-shifting in language production (Labov 1966; Wagner & Buchstaller 2018). In fact, linguistic change interacts with changing patterns of diaphasic variation, since the stylistic range of a given language is one of the sociolinguistic mechanisms most sensitive to social change (Ure 1982: 7). The creation of speaker identity, image projection and rhetorical stance, for example, are stylistic determinant factors in sociolinguistic malleability across an individual's lifespan, being sensitive to age-specific stages and moment-by-moment interactional socio-communicative situations (Eckert & Rickford 2001; Coupland 2007; McCrae & Costa 2008; Rickford & Price 2013; Hernández-Campoy 2016a; Hernández-Campoy &

García-Vidal 2018a, 2018b). The *Paston Letters* illustrate the way a network of fifteenth-century letter-writers exploited the indexical nature of variable (TH) as a mechanism for constructing social meaning and social positioning through stylistic choice. This is a correlation of a contact-induced change resulting from a formerly multilingual situation, with the acceptance of the foreign orthographic digraph adopted by the Standard variety, at a time when supralocalization processes could be said to have been imposing certain 'norm-enforcing' practices.

As seen macroscopically, the situation of variability between the innovation <th> and the conservative form <þ> was a sign of language change in progress through generational waves. During the Pastons' period of private letters preserved (1425–1503), fluctuation between both forms was still taking place, as intermediate stages of variability between the categorical use of the conservative form (<þ>) and the categorical use of the innovative one (<th>). TH was therefore a sociolinguistic variable at that time with indexical meaning, where both <þ> and <th> spelling variants constituted different ways of saying the same thing, although with different social significance. Yet, cross-sectionally and microscopically (Palander-Collin, Nevala & Nurmi 2009), observing the Pastons' sociolinguistic behaviour allows us to account for the divergent written practices of these Paston members throughout their lifetimes.[4] John Paston I (1421–1466), for example, was educated at Trinity Hall and Peterhouse in Cambridge and the Inner Temple in London. As a lawyer, he became Justice of Peace for Norfolk (1447, 1456–1457 and 1460–1466), Knight of the Shire (1455), and MP for Norfolk (1460–1462). John I married Margaret Mautby and inherited the family estates and wealth. His multiplex social networks are reflected in the amount and social array of addressees found in his private correspondence preserved (written between 1440 and 1469)[5]: higher (Royalty and Nobility), equal (his Wife and Minor Gentry people), and relatively lower (Legal Professionals). As shown in Hernández-Campoy & García-Vidal (2018b), with an average of

4 *HiStylVar* Project (2015–2017: 'Sociolinguistic Models of Stylistic Variation in English Historical Correspondence Corpora'), in collaboration with Juan Camilo Conde-Silvestre, Tamara García-Vidal, and Belén Zapata-Barrero, whose aim was the exploration of the motivations and mechanisms for stylistic variation in 15th-18th century historical corpora of English written correspondence by applying and thus testing the validity of current theoretical models of intra-speaker variation.

5 The classification of context types was based on seven profiles of addresses consistently found in the corpus of letters: Royalty, Nobility, Legal Professionals, Clergy, Minor Gentry, Relatives and Partner (wife/husband), which provided us with a measure of the multiplexity (situation: uniplex/multiplex) and density (connections: loose-knit/dense) of our informants' social networks, and subsequently an effect of interpersonal relations on language choice and use.

80% in 'standardness' (2007/2507),[6] John I exhibits a high level of variability ($\bar{x}$ = 87.26 and σ = 76.86), which is conditioned by the socially-diverse range of recipients found in his private letters. As an example of Bell's (1984) Audience Design (in the form of Recipient or Addressee Design here), his sociolinguistic behaviour exhibits unambiguous adjustments in the use of the prestige-innovating variant <th> organised through both upward and downward accommodation patterns depending on the relative status of addressees (Figure 7.4): 100% when addressing Royalty, 97% with Nobility, 82% with his Wife, 74% with other Minor Gentry interlocutors, and 73% with Legal Professionals.

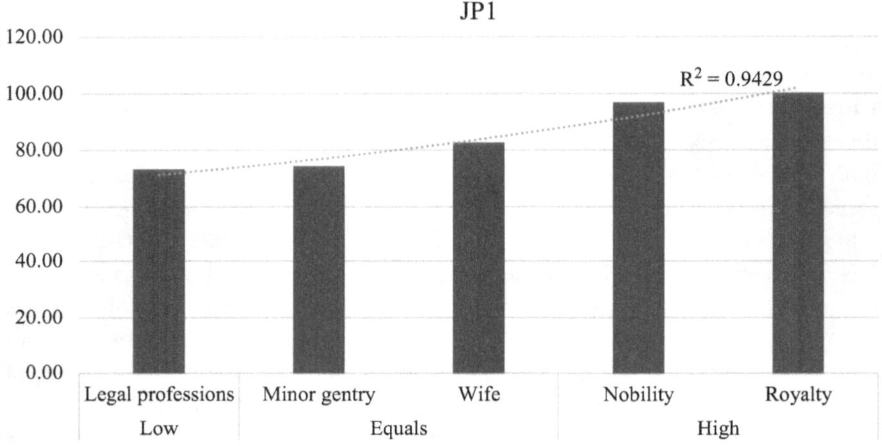

Figure 7.4: Correlation of variable (TH) and letter recipients in John I.
Source: Adapted from Hernández-Campoy & García-Vidal (2018b).

The Pearson correlation coefficient (Cantos 2013: 58–63) indicates that the use of the innovative form <th> and the status of letter recipients are very strongly correlated, showing a monotonic increasing relationship between John I's styles and his audienceship (ρ = 0.9429). This means that there is a socio-stylistic function here governed by a predictive model of dependency between variables in implicational scale: the higher the social rank, the higher the frequencies of the prestige variant <th>, and vice versa.

6 Assuming, as stated above, that it was still an embryonic form of the Standard English variety, or proto-standard, that developed during the 15th century and later fixed and codified (Wright 2000c, Benskin 2004).

John Paston III (1444–1504) was John I's second oldest son and served as MP for Norwich (1485–86), sheriff of Norfolk and Suffolk, 'councillor' to the Earl of Oxford, and Knight of the Shire (1487). Like his father, John III (89% standard) was also a highly mobile member in the family – often travelling throughout the country and abroad in the service of the Duke of Norfolk – with a multiplex social network and diverse recipients in his epistolary interaction, as echoed in his style-shifting practices. He married Margery Brews first and, after her death, Agnes Morley of Glynde. Like his father, his socio-historical background reflects a multiplex social network and diverse audienceship in his epistolary interaction preserved (written between 1461 and 1503). Similarly, as Figure 7.5 shows, John III's attunement practices also seem to be based on addressee design.

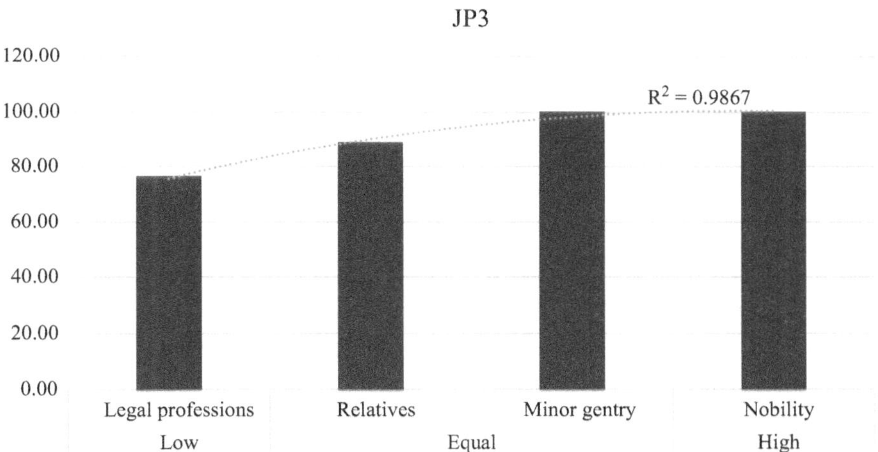

Figure 7.5: Correlation of variable (TH) and letter recipients in John III.
Source: Adapted from Hernández-Campoy & García-Vidal (2018b).

The Pearson correlation coefficient also indicates that the use of the innovative form <th> and the status of letter recipients are very strongly correlated, showing a monotonic increasing relationship between John III's styles and his audienceship ($\rho = 0.9867$). Both John I and John III exhibit a significant monotonic relationship between their styles and the social rank of recipients, though at different degrees of homogeneity and frequencies in their respective variation patterns.

William Paston II (1436–1496) was William I's third son. He studied at Cambridge and married Lady Anne Beaufort, daughter of the Duke of Somerset. From 1450 onwards he frequently travelled to London, where he acted as MP for various constituencies (Newcastle under Lyme and Bedwyn, Wiltshire). Although his use of the variable (TH) also denotes differences in the status of his letter recipients, his frequencies are more homogeneous and constant (Figure 7.6).

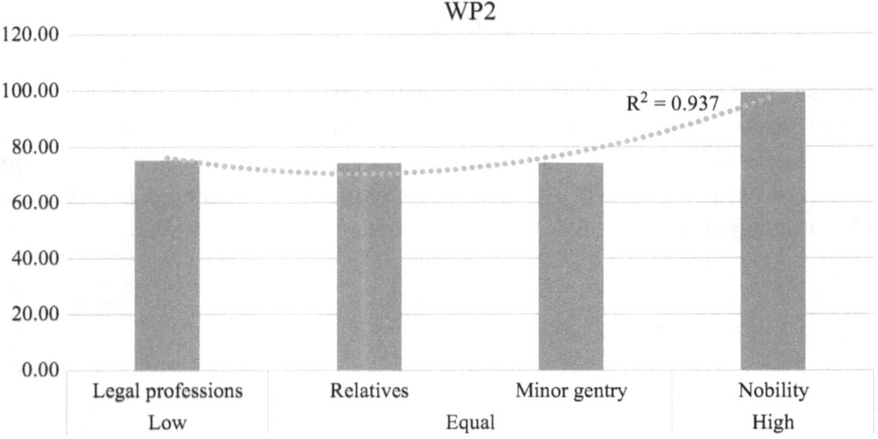

Figure 7.6: Correlation of variable (TH) and letter recipients in William II.

The Pearson correlation coefficient for William II behaviour also indicates that the use of the innovative form <th> and the status of letter recipients are very strongly correlated, showing a monotonic increasing relationship between William II's styles and his audienceship ($\rho = 0.9299$).

These Paston informants, therefore, exhibit accommodative competence and use of multiple voices with *upward/downward* accommodation depending on the relative sociolinguistic status of their letter recipients (audience), and given the multiplicity and complexity of their social networks and their communicative and relational interactions, an extensive accommodative competence when addressing their correspondents according to rank (wife, royalty, nobility, minor gentry, legal professions), making attunements according to situation and social profile. Inferential statistics through a non-parametric Pearson's Chi-square test of significance (Cantos 2013: 75–80) confirms that the different sociolinguistic practices in these Pastons' results when addressing different social-ranked recipients did not occur by chance: the relationship is significant at $p < 0.01$ in the four cases.

As these results on inter-writer and intra-writer variation suggest, although the process of standardization did not affect all individuals at the same time, and was not extended to all linguistic features with the same intensity (see Hernández-Campoy & Conde-Silvestre 1999), it gradually advanced in a stable and persistent direction. Together with a process of prestige-norm focussing, the standard began to be associated with the idea of suitability. The early development of the concept of a standard resulted, therefore, in the substitution of linguistic marks of speakers' regional origins by indicators of their social extraction, or, in sociolinguistic terms, in the replacement of *dialects* by *sociolects*. The use of the incipient standard became widespread among members of the upper-middle classes and started to function effectively in the domains formerly associated with French and Latin (law, government, administration, literature and education).

4.3 Intra-writer variation and writer design

As shown in Hernández-Campoy & García-Vidal (2018a), John II appears as the member of the Paston family who instrumentalised the indexical nature of <þ> and <th> following a more proactive agency in use as a case of speaker design (Coupland 2007; Hernández-Campoy 2016a). By being socially aware of the prestige of a continental innovation in a change from above, John II used this new linguistic form as a resource for identity construction, representation, and social positioning. He made use of this linguistic resource for the the construction of rhetorical stance and projection of identity performatively in order to achieve a particular aim through the instrumentalization of an orthographic feature in his language production: <th> versus <þ>.

As stated earlier, the Pastons were a privileged minor-gentry family, and their historical context was the framework of the War of the Roses between 1455 and 1487. They found themselves embroiled in different struggles during the civil war, such as the Siege of Caister – triggered by the disputes with the Duke of Norkolk and the Duke of Suffolk about the ownership, at that time held by the Pastons (Davis 1954, 1971; Richmond 1990, 1996; Barber 1986/1993; Bennett 1995; Gies and Gies 1998; Bergs 2005; Ibeji 2011). Taking advantage of this time of war, the Duke of Norfolk seized Caister Castle in 1469, besieging it for two months. The Castle was then surrendered to the Duke, who took the rents of the manor until c.1476. Sir John Paston II (1442–1479), the eldest son of John I and, from the internal evidence of his correspondence, a 'gentleman of leisure', or *bon vivant*, interested in books, tournaments and love affairs (Barber 1986/1993: 20; Bergs 2005: 66; his political career makes of him a highly social and geographically mobile character) asked King Edward IV in 1475 to intervene and help his family in this matter, affecting what they claimed to be their inheritance: the manor of Caister Castle. Interestingly, despite exhibiting a mostly standard characterization (77%) in his letters, and, like his father, also a graded style-shifting with different verbal attunements based on audienceship (100% with nobility, 79% with Clergy, 91% with other minor gentry interlocutors, 74% with relatives, 89% when addressing legal professionals), surprisingly, he was just 33% standard when addressing royalty (see Figure 7.7).

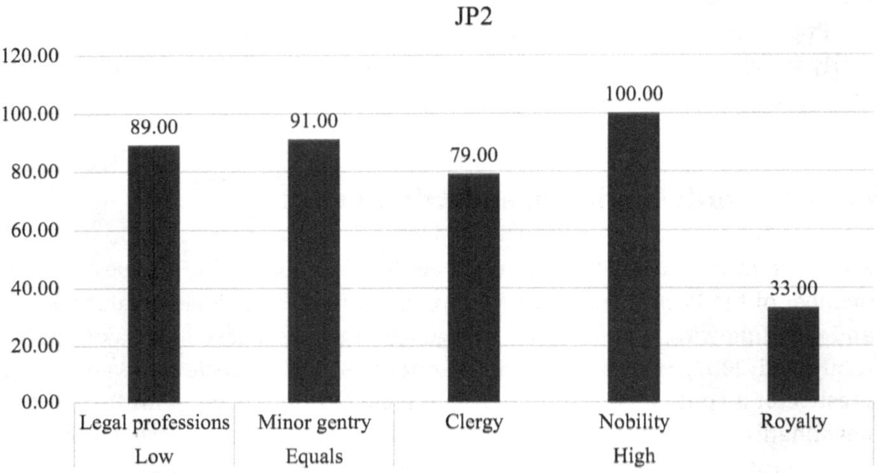

Figure 7.7: Correlation of variable (TH) and letter recipients in John II.
Source: Adapted from Hernández-Campoy & García-Vidal (2018a).

In fact, statistically, there is no clear tendency. The Pearson correlation coefficient does not suggest a meaningful relationship between the use of the innovative form <th> and the status of letter recipients, with a ρ-index far from 1.

The explanation provided by Hernández-Campoy and García-Vidal (2018a) to his sociolinguistic behaviour when addressing the King – violating expectations not only for rank and audienceship but also for stylistic variation principles at only 33% standard – is based on the socio-constructionist Speaker Design Theory (see Coupland 2007; Hernández-Campoy 2016a). In the form of Writer Design here, this deliberate and proactive underuse of the proto-standard form by Sir John II, instead using <þ>, may be understood as a conscious and deliberate case of *hyper-vernacularization*: an inappropriate performance; that is, unlike hyperdialectism, it refers to the use of non-standard forms correctly (without faulty analysis) though inappropriately, according to socio-demographic and/or stylistic parameters, and whose counterpart would be *hyper-standardization* (hypercorrection) (see Cutillas-Espinosa, Hernández-Campoy and Schilling-Estes 2010). John II was surely pursuing a communicative effect and some kind of stylistic colouring through the instrumentalization of vernacularity in his written correspondence with the King. Despite being averagely anchored to a supra local sociolinguistic practice in epistolary communication (78% standard), his verbal behaviour with the King (only 33% standard) suggests that he was somehow being performative and overtly embracing some kind of authenticity – in the socio-constructionist conception[7]– with his shifting to a more casual style through the use of the conservative form <þ>. His father (John I) was sociolinguistically conventional when addressing royalty (100% standard). Nevertheless, John II wanted to be different, but also consciously taking advantage of his personal relationship and previous shared experience with the monarch (see Bergs 2005: 66). With his hyper-vernacular behaviour, John II used the non-standard feature <þ> to achieve a specific effect. The unexpected use of a vernacular form, with downward rather than upward accommodation, indicates that John II was not shifting his epistolary language production in reaction to formality and audienceship. Rather, he used an almost obsolete dialectal feature to project a low-profile, ordinary persona, a weak image and downward social mobility (reminding the King of the Pastons' humble origins) in pursuit of his petition: the defencelessness situation of his family against the power and strength of the Duke of Norfolk.

5 The prestige of the norm and the norm of prestige

Although the selection of the variety of English to become the national standard mostly came after 1500, the embryonic stages of standardization arose with the initial focussing of the English linguistic community through the development of some degree of agreement about norms of usage. As shown in Hernández-Campoy (2008), the 'Memorandum on French Grammar' written by William Paston II between 1450 and 1455 denotes the awareness of linguistic norms of usage within the

7 In Labov (1972), authenticity was understood as a synonym for 'prototypical': the unselfconscious, everyday speech produced by spontaneous speakers of pure vernacular (see also Bucholtz 2003: 398; and Hernández-Campoy 2016a: 175–176). However, in recent socio-constructionist views, the 'authentic' speaker refers to a sociolinguistic positioning in society imbued with social meaning within an implicit theory of identity (Bucholtz 2003, 2009; Eckert 2003; Coupland 2003, 2007, 2010; Guy and Cutler 2011; Johnstone 2014). The authentic speaker currently appears as an unexpected (non-idiosyncratic) identity assumed in verbal practice creatively, as different studies have found in media communication at the level of celebrities, politicians, TV/radio presenters, singers, etc. (see Hernández-Campoy and Cutillas-Espinosa 2012).

framework of an emergent national standard and in the context of competence in a second language. At a linguistic level, this document provides a description of the incipient standard English grammar of the late Middle English period when contrasting it with French: a particular variety of French and a particular one of English, and not others, as the accepted referents for both languages. At a sociolinguistic level, this memorandum constitutes a crucial piece evidence of the *norm-usage* dichotomy and the *overt/covert* prestige motivations conditioning the social psychology of late Middle English society and, consequently, the users' sociolinguistic behaviour with a contradictory practice.

This contradictory sociolinguistic practice through the awareness of growing new prestige patterns in this period can be illustrated with the quantitative and qualitative analysis of William II's Memorandum. When describing the verb conjugation system of the English language of the 1450s, for example, he referred to the present, past, future, conditional and compound tense morphological constructions. But he did not make any explicit mention of the mood distinction (indicative vs. subjunctive), despite using subjunctive constructions and forms 16% of the time in his writing. The fact of omitting the morphology of subjunctive constructions may be taken as a clue that mood was losing relevance at the time. Of those 16% of subjunctive constructions, William II used a subjunctive form 100% of the time, while the emerging levelling to indicative form, as the reflection of a mood neutralization tendency, is not present in his writing practices (0%). The omission of mood morphology in the description of English in William's 'Memorandum on French Grammar' as a standard-centred ideology versus his use of subjunctive forms in subjunctive contexts is thus a contradictory sociolinguistic behaviour. This contradictory behaviour may be understood as a symptom of the process of mood instability due to the encroachment of the indicative form on the expected subjunctive contexts and the subsequent confusion, linguistic insecurity and hypercorrection consequences.

But in William Paston II's verbal practice, his adoption of the incipient national Standard was not full, despite his proficiency and, crucially, public acceptance of this variety – as shown in his Memorandum. The use of past *be* forms (#116 instances) in his 33 letters and notes written between 1436 and 1496 (15,418 words) shows, for example: (i) both indicative (#98; 84%) and subjunctive (#18; 16%) constructions; (ii) not only *was* and *were* forms but also non-standard spelling ones such as *wer* (#2 instances), *war* (#3) and *ware* (#6) for *were*; (iii) orthographic variants such us the use of the *were* form (#5) meaning the relative adverb *where*; and iv) cases of the typically non-standard levelling to *were* in clauses with singular subject (both *he/she/it* forms and singular Noun Phrases, but not in Existentials) in both positive and negative polarity. The study of his use of the spelling variables (TH), (SHOULD) and (WHICH) in his Memorandum specifically also confirms his adherence to a non-standard practice: 58% use of TH standard spelling forms, only 11% in SHOULD and 0% in WHICH.

This means that, at least in his written practices, there is a predominance of features that were not those that ended up in the standard variety – as is typical of the supralocalisation period. In many ways, William II seems to be more favourably disposed towards: (i) assuming the role of the national Standard as the English language in interlanguage English-French comparisons; (ii) overtly aiming for the forms which enjoyed prestige in the speech community; and (iii) overreporting himself in the direction of the prestige model despite his non-standard usages. The *norm* versus *usage* dilemma for the incipient Standard English may be seen here: expectations on what the language norms should be versus actual usage in performance.

6 Conclusion

Multilingualism and multidialectalism are the breeding-ground for socio-psychological phenomena such as 'attitudes' and factors such as 'prestige'. The standard-centred ideology constitutes a consciousness status that has predominated in linguistic descriptions, management and research orientation. As a result, the history of languages has traditionally been the history of standards and the heteroglossic situation of late medieval England has been disregarded. As seen here, the *Paston Letters* illustrate the awareness of the growing *norm/usage* dilemma and the new standard-ideology, where 'prestige' and 'attitude' contributed to the generalization of a foreign orthographic digraph adopted by the incipient Standard variety as a contact-induced process – at a time when supralocalization developments were imposing 'norm-enforcing' practices. These epistolary writers instrumentalised the late medieval heteroglossia to construct and project social meaning through inter- and intra-speaker variation, playing with the indexical nature of linguistic features in process of ongoing change by means of recipient-based and speaker-based stylistic choice.

References

Barber, R. (ed.), (1986/1993). *The Pastons. A Family in the Wars of the Roses*. Woodbridge: The Boydell Press.

Bell, A. (1984). Language Style as Audience Design. *Language in Society* 13. 145–204.

Bell, A. (2007). Style in Dialogue: Bakhtin and Sociolinguistic Theory. In: R. Bayley (ed.), *Sociolinguistic Variation: Theories, Methods, and Applications*. Cambridge: Cambridge University Press, 90–109.

Bennet, H.S. (1995/1990). *The Pastons and their England: Studies in an Age of Transition*. Cambridge: Cambridge University Press.

Benskin, M. (1977). Local archives and Middle English dialects. *Journal of the Society of Archivists* 5(8): 500–514.

Benskin, M. (1982). The letters <þ> and <y> in later Middle English, and some related matters. *Journal of the Society of Archivists* 7: 13–30.

Benskin, M. (2004).Chancery Standard. In: C. Kay, C. Hough & I. Wotherspoon (eds.), *New Perspectives on English Historical Linguistics II: Lexis and Transmission*. Amsterdam/ Philadelphia: John Benjamins, 1–40.

Bergs, A. (2005). *Social Networks and Historical Sociolinguistics: Studies in Morphosyntactic Variation in the Paston Letters (1421–1503)*. Berlin: Mouton de Gruyter.

Bergs, A. (2015). Linguistic Fingerprints of Authors and Scribes. In: A. Auer, D. Schreier & R. Watts (eds.), *Letter Writing and Language Change*. Cambridge: Cambridge University Press, 114–132.

Bergs, A. (2007). Spoilt for choice? <The> problem < þe> in <Đe> Peterborough Chronicle. In: A. Bergs & J. Skaffari (eds.), *The Language of the Peterborough Chronicle*. Bern: Peter Lang, 45–56.

Britain, D. (ed.)(2007). *Language in the British Isles*. Cambridge: Cambridge University Press.

Bucholtz, M. (2003). Sociolinguistic Nostalgia and the Authentication of Identity. *Journal of Sociolinguistics* 7: 398–416.

Bucholtz, M. (2009). From Stance to Style: Gender, Interaction, and Indexicality in Mexican Immigrant Youth Slang. In A. Jaffe (ed.), *Stance: Sociolinguistic Perspectives*. Oxford: Oxford University Press, 146–170.

Cantos, P. (2013). *Statistical Methods in Language and Linguistic Research*. Sheffield: Equinox Publishing.

Conde-Silvestre, J.C. (2016). A 'third-wave' historical sociolinguistic approach to late Middle English correspondence: Evidence from the Stonor Letters. In: C. Russi (ed.), *Current Trends in Historical Sociolinguistics*. Warsaw/Berlin: Open De Gruyter, 46–66.

Conde-Silvestre, J.C. & J.M. Hernández-Campoy. (2013). Tracing the generational progress of language change in fifteenth century English: the diffusion of <th> in the Paston Letters. *Neuphilologische Mitteilungen* 114(3): 279–299.

Conde-Silvestre, J.C. & J.M. Hernández-Campoy. (2015). Assessing Variability and Change in Early English Letters. In: A. Auer, D. Schreier & R. Watts (eds.), *Letter Writing and Language Change*. Cambridge: Cambridge University Press, 14–34.

Coupland, N. (2003). Sociolinguistic Authenticities. *Journal of Sociolinguistics* 7(3). 417–431.

Coupland, N. (2007). *Style: Language Variation, and Identity*. Cambridge: Cambridge University Press.

Coupland, N. (2010). The authentic speaker and the speech community. In C. Llamas and D. Watt (eds.), *Language and Identities*. Edinburgh: Edinburgh University Press, 99–112.

Cressy, D. (1980). *Literacy and the Social Order: Reading and Writing in Tudor and Stuart England*. Cambridge: Cambridge University Press.

Cutillas-Espinosa, J.A. & J.M. Hernández-Campoy. (forthcoming). Historical Sociolinguistics and Authorship Elucidation in Medieval Private Written Correspondence: Theoretical and Methodological Implications for and from Forensic Linguistics.

Cutillas-Espinosa, J.A., J.M. Hernández-Campoy & N. Schilling-Estes. (2010). Hyper-vernacularisation in a Speaker Design Context: A Case Study. *Folia Linguistica* 44: 1–22.
Davis, N. (1954). The Language of the Pastons. In James A. Burrow (ed.), *Middle English Literature: British Academy Gollancz Lectures*. Oxford: Oxford University Press, 45–70.
Davis, N. (1965). The Language of the Pastons. *Proceedings of the British Academy* 40: 119–144.
Davis, N. (1967). Style and Stereotype in Early English Letters. *Leeds Studies in English* 1 (n.s): 7–17.
Davis, N. (ed.), (1971). *Paston Letters and Papers of the Fifteenth Century*. Oxford: Clarendon.
Dossena, M. & G. Del Lungo Camiciotti. (eds.), (2012). *Letter Writing in Late Modern Europe*. Amsterdam/Philadelphia: John Benjamins.
Dossena, M. & I. Tieken-Boon van Ostade. (eds.), (2008). *Studies in Late Modern English correspondence: Methodology and Data*. Bern: Peter Lang.
Eckert, P. (2003). Elephants in the Room. *Journal of Sociolinguistics* 7(3). 392–397.
Eckert, P. (2018). *Meaning and Linguistic Variation: The Third Wave in Sociolinguistics*. Cambridge: Cambridge University Press.
Eckert, P. & S. McConnell-Ginet. (1992). Think practically and look locally. Language and gender as community-based practices. *Annual Review of Applied Linguistics* 21: 461–490.
Eckert, P. & J. Rickford. (eds.), (2001). *Style and Sociolinguistic Variation*. Cambridge: Cambridge University Press.
Fisher, J. H. (1996). *The Emergence of Standard English*. Lexington, KY: University of Kentucky Press.
Fischer, O. (2013). The role of contact in English syntactic change in the Old and Middle English periods. In D. Schreier & M. Hundt (eds.), *English as a Contact Language*. Cambridge: Cambridge University Press, 18–40.
Gies, F. & J. Gies. (1998). *A Medieval Family: The Pastons of Fifteenth-Century England*. New York: Harper Collins Publications.
Graff, H.J. (ed.), (1981). *Literacy and Social Development in the West: A Reader*. Cambridge: Cambridge University Press.
Guy, G.R. & C. Cutler. (2011). Speech Style and Authenticity: Quantitative Evidence for the Performance of Identity. *Language Variation and Change* 23(1): 139–162.
Halliday, M.A.K. (1978). *Language as Social Semiotic: The Interpretation of Language and Meaning*. London: Edward Arnold.
Haugen, E. (1966/1997). Dialect, language and nation. In: J.B. Pride and J. Holmes (eds.), *Sociolinguistics*. Harmondsworth: Penguin, 97–112.
Hernández-Campoy, J.M. (2008). Overt and Covert Prestige in Late Middle English: A Case Study in East Anglia. *Folia Linguistica Historica* 29: 1–26.
Hernández-Campoy, J.M. (2016a). *Sociolinguistic Styles*. Malden: Wiley-Blackwell.
Hernández-Campoy, J.M. (2016b). Authorship and Gender in English Historical Sociolinguistic Research: Samples from the *Paston Letters*. In: C. Russi (ed.), *Current Trends in Historical Sociolinguistics*. Warsaw/Berlin. Open De Gruyter, 108–142.
Hernández-Campoy, J.M. (2020). Corpus-based Individual Lifespan Change in Late Middle English. In: K.V. Beaman & I. Buchstaller (eds.), *Language Variation and Language Change across the Lifespan: Theoretical and Empirical Perspectives from Panel Studies*. London/New York: Routledge.

Hernández-Campoy, J.M. & J.C. Conde-Silvestre. (1999). The social diffusion of linguistic innovations in 15th century England: Chancery spellings in private correspondence. *Cuadernos de Filología Inglesa* 8: 251–274.
Hernández-Campoy, J.M. & J.C. Conde-Silvestre. (2012). *The Handbook of Historical Sociolinguistics*. Malden: Wiley-Blackwell.
Hernández-Campoy, J.M., J.C. Conde-Silvestre & T. García-Vidal (2019). Tracing Patterns of Intra-Speaker Variation in Early English Correspondence: A Change from Above in the *Paston Letters*. *Studia Anglica Posnaniensia*, 54: 1–27.
Hernández Campoy, J.M. & J.A. Cutillas-Espinosa. (eds.) (2012). *Style-Shifting in Public: New Perspectives on Stylistic Variation*. Amsterdam/Philadelphia: John Benjamins.
Hernández-Campoy, J.M. & T. García-Vidal. (2018a.) Persona Management and Identity Projection in English Medieval Society: Evidence from John Paston II. *Journal of Historical Sociolinguistics* 4(1): 1–31.
Hernández-Campoy, J.M. & T. García-Vidal. (2018b.) Style-shifting and accommodative competence in late Middle English written correspondence: Putting Audience Design to the test of time. *Folia Linguistica Historica* 39(2): 383–420.
Hernández-Campoy, J.M. & P. Trudgill. (2002) Functional Compensation and Southern Peninsular Spanish /s/ Loss. *Folia Linguistica Historica* XXIII: 141–167.
Hogg, R. (1992). Phonology and morphology. *The Cambridge History of the English Language. Vol 1: The Beginnings to 1066*, 67–167. Cambridge: Cambridge University Press.
Hope, J. (2000). Rats, bats, sparrows and dogs: Biology, linguistics and the nature of Standard English. In: L. Wright (ed.), *The development of Standard English 1300–1800*. Cambridge: Cambridge University Press, 49–56.
Ibeji, M. (2011). Paston Family Letters. BBC webpage: http://www.bbc.co.uk/history/british/middle_ages/pastonletters_01.shtml
Jaffe, A. (ed.), (2009). *Stance: Sociolinguistic Perspectives*. Oxford: Oxford University Press.
James, D. (1996). Women, men and prestige speech forms: A critical review. In: Victoria L. Bergvall, Janet M. Bing & Alice F. Freed (eds.), *Rethinking Language and Gender Research: Theory and Practice*. London: Longman, 98–125.
Jensen, V. (2012). The consonantal element (th) in some late Middle English Yorkshire texts. In J. Tyrkkö, M. Kilpiö, T. Nevalainen & M. Rissanen (eds.), *Outposts of Historical Corpus Linguistics: From the Helsinki Corpus to a Proliferation of Resources. Studies in Variation, Contacts and Change in English* (vol. 10). Helsinki: Research Unit for Variation http://www.helsinki.fi/varieng/series/volumes/10/jensen/[17/6/2018]
Johnstone, B. (1996). *The Linguistic Individual: Self-expression in Language and Linguistics*. New York: Oxford University Press.
Johnstone, B. (2014). "100% Authentic Pittsburgh": Sociolinguistic authenticity and the linguistics of particularity. In V. Lacoste, J. Leimgruber and T. Breyer (eds.), *Indexing Authenticity: Sociolinguistic Perspectives*. Berlin: De Gruyter, 97–112.
Kitson, P. (2004). On margins of error in placing Old English literary dialects. In: M. Dossena and R. Lass (eds.), *Methods and Data in English Historical Dialectology*. Bern: Peter Lang, 219–239.
Klemola, J. (2013). English as a Contact Language in the British Isles. In: D. Schreier & M. Hundt (eds.), *English as a Contact Language*. Cambridge: Cambridge University Press, 75–87.

Kopaczyk, J. & A. Jucker. (eds.), (2013). *Communities of practice in the History of English*. Amsterdam/Philadelphia: John Benjamins.
Labov, W. (1966). *The Social Stratification of English in New York City*. Washington D.C.: Center for Applied Linguistics.
Labov, W. (1972). *Sociolinguistic Patterns*. Philadelphia: University of Pennsylvania Press.
Langer, N. & A. Nesse. (2012). Linguistic Purism. In: J.M. Hernández-Campoy & J.C. Conde-Silvestre (eds.), 607–625.
Lass, R. (1992). Phonology and morphology. In: R. Lass (ed.), *The Cambridge History of the English Language. Vol 2: 1066–1476*. Cambridge: Cambridge University Press, 23–156.
McCrae, R. & P. Costa. (2008). Empirical and theoretical status of the five-factor model of personality traits. In: G. Boyle, G. Matthews & D. Saklofske (eds.), *Sage Handbook of Personality Theory and Assessment: Vol 1 Personality Theories and Models*. Los Angeles: Sage, 273–294.
McWhorter, J. (2009). *Our Magnificent Bastard Tongue: The Untold History of English*. New York: Gotham Books.
Millward, C.M. & M. Mayes. (1996/2012). *A Biography of the English Language*. Boston: Wadsworth.
Milroy, J. (1992). *Language Variation and Change. On the Historical Sociolinguistics of English*. Oxford: Blackwell.
Milroy, J. (1999). The consequences of standardisation in descriptive linguistics. In: T. Bex & R.J. Watts (eds.), *Standard English: The Widening Debate*. London: Routledge, 16–39.
Milroy, J. (2001). Language ideologies and the consequences of standardization. *Journal of Sociolinguistics* 5 (4): 530–555.
Milroy, J. (2002). The legitimate language: giving a history to English. In: R. Watts & P. Trudgill (eds.), *Alternative histories of English*. London: Routledge, 7–25.
Milroy, J. (2005). Some effects of purist ideologies on historical descriptions of English. In: N. Langer & W.V. Davies (eds.), *Linguistic purism in the Germanic languages*. Berlin & New York: Walter de Gruyter, 324–342.
Milroy, J. (2012). Sociolinguistics and Ideologies in Language History. In: J.M. Hernández-Campoy & J.C. Conde-Silvestre (eds.), 571–584.
Milroy, J. & L. Milroy. (1999). *Authority in language: Investigating standard English*. London: Routledge.
Nevalainen, T. (2000). Processes of supralocalisation and the rise of standard English in the Early Modern period. In R. Bermúdez-Otero, D. Denison, R.M. Hogg & C.B. McCully (eds.), *Generative theory and corpus studies: A dialogue from 10 ICEHL*. Berlin & New York: Mouton de Gruyter, 329–371.
Nevalainen, T. (2003). English. In: A. Deumert & W. Vandenbussche (eds.), *Germanic standardizations: Past to present*. Amsterdam: John Benjamins, 127–156.
Nevalainen, T. (2012). Variable focusing in English spelling between 1400 and 1600. In: S. Baddeley & A. Voeste (eds.), *Orthographies in Early Modern Europe*. Berlin/Boston: De Gruyter Mouton, 127–165.
Nevalainen, T. (2014). Norms and usage in seventeenth-century English. In: G. Rutten, R. Vosters and W. Vandenbussche (eds.), *Norms and Usage in Language History, 1600–1900. A sociolinguistic and comparative perspective*. Amsterdam/Philadelphia: John Benjamins, 103–128.
Nevalainen, T. & H. Raumolin-Brunberg. (2003). *Historical Sociolinguistics. Language Change in Tudor and Stuart England*. London: Longman Pearson Education.

Nevalainen, T. & I. Tieken-Boon van Ostade. (2006). Standardisation. In: R. Hogg & D. Denison (eds.), *A History of the English Language*. Cambridge: Cambridge University Press, 271–311.

O'Day, R. (1982). *Education and Society 1500–1800. The Social Foundations of Education in Early Modern Britain*. London and New York: Longman.

Orme, N. (1973). *English Schools in the Middle Ages*. London: Methuen.

Orme, N. (1984). *From Childhood to Chivalry: The Education of the English Kings and Aristocracy, 1066–1530*. London & New York: Methuen.

Orme, N. (2006). *Medieval Schools: From Roman Britain to Renaissance England*. New Haven, Conn., and London: Yale University Press.

Palander-Collin, M., M. Nevala & A. Nurmi. (2009). The Language of Daily Life in the History of English. Studying how Macro Meets Micro. In: A. Nurmi, M. Nevala & M. Palander-Collin (eds.), *The Language of Daily Life in England (1400–1800)*. Amsterdam/Philadelphia: John Benjamins, 1–23.

Pilliere, L., W. Andrieu, V. Kerfelec and D. Lewis. (eds.), (2018). *Standardising English: Norms and Margins in the History of the English Language*. Cambridge: Cambridge University Press.

Rickford, John and Mackenzie Price. (2013). Girlz II women: Age-grading, language change and stylistic variation. *Journal of Sociolinguistics* 17(2): 143–179.

Richmond, C. (1990/2002). *The Paston Family in the Fifteenth* Century *(vol. 1): The First Phase*. Cambridge: Cambridge University Press.

Richmond, C. (1996). *The Paston Family in the Fifteenth Century (vol. 2): Fastolf's Will*. Cambridge: Cambridge University Press.

Riley, K. (2012). Language Socialization and Language Ideologies. In: A. Duranti, E. Ochs and B.B. Schieffelin (eds.), *The Handbook of Language Socialization*. Malden: Wiley-Blackwell, 493–514.

Romaine, S. (1998). Introduction. In: S. Romaine (ed.), *The Cambridge History of the English Language*. Vol. IV: 1776–1997. Cambridge: Cambridge University Press, 1–56.

Sairio, A. & M. Palander-Collin. (2012). The Reconstruction of Prestige Patterns in Language History. In: J.M. Hernández-Campoy & J.C. Conde-Silvestre (eds.), 626–638.

Schreier, D. & M. Hundt. (eds.), (2013). *English as a Contact Language*. Cambridge: Cambridge University Press.

Schendl, H. (2013). Code-Switching in Late Medieval Macaronic Sermons. In: J.A. Jefferson and A. Putter (eds.), *Multilingualism in Medieval Britain (c. 1066–1520): Sources and Analysis*. Turnhout: Brepols, 153–170.

Scragg, D. (1974). *A History of English Spelling*. Manchester: Manchester University Press.

Spolsky, B. (2012). What is language policy? In: Bernard Spolsky (ed.), *The Cambridge Handbook of Language Policy*. Cambridge: Cambridge University Press, 3–15.

Stein, R.M. (2007). Multilingualism. In: P. Strohm (ed.), *Middle English*. Oxford: Oxford University Press, 23–50.

Stenroos, M. (2004). Regional dialects and spelling conventions in late Middle English. Searches for (th) in LALME data. In: M. Dossena & R. Lass (eds.), *Methods and Data in English Historical Dialectology*. Bern: Peter Lang, 257–285.

Stenroos, M. (2006). A Middle English mess of fricative spellings: reflections on thorn, yogh and their rivals. In: M. Krygier & L. Sikorska (eds.), *To Make his English Sweete upon his Tonge*. Frankfurt a. Main: Peter Lang, 9–35.

Taavitsainen, I. (2000). Scientific language and spelling standardisation 1375–1550. In: L. Wright (ed.), *The Development of Standard English, 1300–1800: Theories, Descriptions, Conflicts*. Cambridge: Cambridge University Press, 131–154.
Trudgill, P. (1986). *Dialects in Contact*. Oxford: Blackwell.
Trudgill, P. (1992a). Dialect Contact, Dialectology and Sociolinguistics. In: K. Bolton & H. Kwok (eds.), *Sociolinguistics Today: International Perspectives*. London: Routledge & Kegan Paul, 71–79.
Trudgill, P. (1992b). Editor's Preface. In: J. Milroy (1992), *Language Variation and Change. On the Historical Sociolinguistics of English*. Oxford: Blackwell, vi-vii.
Upward, C. & G. Davidson. (2011). *The History of English Spelling*. Malden: Wiley-Blackwell.
Ure, J. (1982). Introduction: Approaches to the Study of Register Range. *International Journal of the Sociology of Language* 35: 5–23.
Wagner, S.E. & I. Buchstaller (eds.), (2018). *Panel Studies of Variation and Change*. New York: Routledge.
Watts, R.J. (2000). Mythical strands in the ideology of prescriptivism. In: L. Wright (ed.), *The development of Standard English 1300–1800: Theories, descriptions, conflicts*. Cambridge: Cambridge University Press, 29–48.
Watts, R.J. (2011). *Language myths and the history of English*. New York: Oxford University Press.
Watts, R.J. (2012). Language Myths. In: J.M. Hernández-Campoy & J.C. Conde-Silvestre (eds.), 585–606.
Watts, R.J. & P. Trudgill (eds.), (2002). *Alternative histories of English*. London: Routledge.
Wright, L. (1999a). Mixed-language business writing: five hundred years of codeswitching. In: E.H. Jahr (ed.), *Language Change: Advances in Historical Sociolinguistics*. Berlin: Mouton de Gruyter, 99–118.
Wright, L. (1999b). Middle English variation: the London English guild certificates of 1388/9. In: E.H. Jahr (ed.), *Language Change: Advances in Historical Sociolinguistics*. Berlin: Mouton de Gruyter, 169–196.
Wright, L. (2000a). Bills, accounts, inventories: Everyday trilingual activities in the business world of later medieval England. In: D. Trotter (ed.), *Multilingualism in Later Medieval Britain*. Cambridge: D. S. Brewer, 149–156.
Wright, L. (2000b). Social context, structural categories and medieval business writing. *Bilingualism: Language and Cognition* 3(2): 124–125.
Wright, L. (ed.), (2000c). *The Development of Standard English 1300–1800: Theories, Descriptions, Conflicts*. Cambridge: Cambridge University Press.
Wright, L. (2001a). Some morphological features of the Norfolk guild certificates of 1388/9: an exercise in variation. In: P. Trudgill and J. Fisiak (eds.), *East Anglian English*. Woodbridge: D. S. Brewer, 79–162.
Wright, L. (2001b). The role of international and national trade in the standardisation of English. In: I. Moskowich-Spiegel Fandiño, B. Crespo-García, E. Lezcano-González and B. Simal-González (eds.), *Re-interpretations of English; Essays on Language, Linguistics and Philology*. A Coruña: University of A Coruña, 189–207.
Wright, L. (2013). The contact origins of Standard English. In D. Schreier & M. Hundt (eds.), *English as a Contact Language*. Cambridge: Cambridge University Press, 58–74.
Wyld, H.C. (1914/1927). *A Short History of English*. London: John Murray (3rd Edition).

Terttu Nevalainen

8 Early mass communication as a standardizing influence? The case of the Book of Common Prayer

> Together with the King James Version of the Bible and the works of Shakespeare, the Book of Common Prayer has been one of the three fundamental underpinnings of modern English.
>
> (*Wikipedia*)

1 Introduction

The Early Modern period (1500–1700) represents a transition from a mostly oral to a semiliterate society. In the 16th century, an overwhelming majority of the English people could not sign their names, let alone write (Cressy 1980: 175–177). In the course of the 17th century, literacy rates increased especially among the higher social orders and in towns, notably in London, but a high degree of illiteracy prevailed much longer in rural areas, and among the lower social ranks and women in general. Despite being unable to write or having little use for this technical skill in their daily lives, many people had acquired some ability to read. Yet, although the available reading matter became more plentiful with time and contained popular literature such as almanacs, the only book people living in the countryside typically owned was the English Bible (Lancashire 2012: 642).[1]

In its different forms, religion exerted a major cultural influence on people's lives in Early Modern England. Since church attendance on Sunday and holy days was made compulsory by the Act of Uniformity first passed in 1549, "the entire churchgoing population ... heard, read, and repeated after the priest the English language of the Prayer Book, including substantial readings from the Bible, at least once a week" (Long 2007: 68). Part of the liturgical reform of the Reformation, the vernacular was substituted for the traditional Latin as the language of public worship and of the Bible in the early 16th century.

1 For further discussion and references, see e.g. Nevalainen & Raumolin-Brunberg (2017: 34–35, 40–42).

Note: I would like to thank the two anonymous reviewers and the volume editor for their most useful and constructive feedback on the first version of this chapter.

https://doi.org/10.1515/9783110687545-009

We may argue that, published in the Book of Common Prayer (BCP), the English liturgy represents mass communication *par excellence*, as it involves a "process by which a person, group of people, or large organization creates a message and transmits it through some type of medium to a large, anonymous, heterogeneous audience" (Pearce 2009: 623). In the case of the BCP, all these creator categories are responsible for producing the text: the church as an organization, the groups of compilers and revisers of the text, and the individual minister transmitting it to the congregation. The publication of the Book of Common Prayer was an innovation in the mid-16th century in that it brought together the various rites and services of the Church in a single book, as well as provided "a single order of public worship to be followed uniformly in churches throughout the country" (Brook 1965: 17). In proportion to its receivers, it emerges as one of the most representative texts, if not the most representative text, in the Early Modern English period (EModE).

The receiver-based model of text representativeness comes from Leech (2007), who discusses it in the context of the balance and representativeness of linguistic corpora. He writes:

> I maintain that the representation of texts should be proportional not only to their initiators, but also to their receivers. After all, decoding as well as encoding is a linguistic activity. [. . .] I propose, therefore, that the basic unit to be counted in calculating the size of a given textual universe is not the text itself, but an initiator – text – receiver nexus, which we can call an *atomic communicative event* (ACE). When a radio programme is listened to by a million people, there is only one text, but a million ACEs. (Leech 2007: 138)

Continuing Leech's argument, we can say that without decoding there is no linguistic influence. The overarching research question addressed in this chapter is precisely that: to what extent is it possible to detect the impact of liturgical language on the mainstream usage of the period and, ultimately, on the English language at large, as suggested by the Wikipedia quote in the epigraph? More specifically, how can a linguist approach empirically the question of the direction of linguistic influence over time (a) from liturgical language to general usage and, *vice versa*, (b) from general usage to liturgical language? The first alternative is raised in the context of standardization and the consolidation of liturgical registers in the vernacular, but it is of course the second that must have provided the structural foundation for the use of English in liturgical functions in the first place.

These questions have been addressed in general terms in work that approaches language and religion as a sociolinguistic field of study. Beginning with language choice, Crystal (1990: 122) notes that "indeed, no imposed linguistic change has ever affected so many people at once as when Latin was replaced by the vernacular in Roman Catholic Christianity". A particular area of sociolinguistic interest is "the way in which the language of the sacred writings affects later forms of language" (Samarin 1987: 13). Enlarging on the impact of liturgical language on the vernacular, Darquennes and Vandenbussche (2011: 7) argue that "[i]t is commonly known that translations of holy scriptures triggered and influenced processes of standardization in many languages". The authors support their argument by referring to the contributions in Deumert and Vandenbussche (2003) on individual Germanic languages which discuss the standardizing influence of the Bible and liturgy on various levels of language ranging from spelling and lexis to morphology and syntax. Emanating from the religious domain, such standardizing changes diffuse from outside the speech community and represent, in sociolinguistic terms, change from above. By contrast, liturgical and biblical language following and being influenced by the current usage of the speech community would represent the opposite kind of process, change from below (see e.g. Labov 2007: 346; and for an application to Biblical Hebrew, Kim 2013: 89–94).

This chapter is organized as follows. Section 2 sets the scene by discussing the issue of alleged conservativeness of language use in the religious domain in the Early Modern period. The Book of Common Prayer and its sources and revisions are introduced in section 3. Section 4 approaches the research questions outlined above empirically by comparing a number of grammatical features in the two major Early Modern editions of the Book of Common Prayer published a hundred years apart. Section 5 returns to the influence of liturgical language as a form of mass communication, and the concluding remarks in section 6 assess the major findings of the study.

2 The language of religion and "changing linguistic habits"

In his discussion of the topic, Crystal (1990: 132) makes the broad generalization that "[l]iturgical language, as religious language generally, typically looks backwards, not forwards". He supports this statement by listing a number of grammatical and lexical features that until quite recently represented the liturgical linguistic norms in much of the English-speaking world. These include, for example, function words and inflections (*thou, thee, ye, art, wilt, unto, -(e)th, -(e)st, spake, brethren*, etc.), imperative or subjunctive verbs with the subject expressed (*go thou, do we sit, glory be to the Father, praise be*), as well as distinctive idioms (*who livest and reignest, through the same Jesus Christ*) (Crystal 1990: 122–123).

The features Crystal lists are characteristic of Early Modern English religious prose, and liturgical prose in particular, which is also traditionally described as conservative and resistant to linguistic innovation and change (e.g. Brook 1965: 107). Kohnen, Rütten and Marcoe (2011) acknowledge this generalization, but go on to show that that is not the case for all religious registers: in many respects, prayers, catechisms, sermons and religious biographies reflect changes in the language over time.

The situation is more intricate for the liturgical genres that are consciously modified over time. Although religious texts such as the 1611 King James Bible and the 1662 edition of the Book of Common Prayer may be characterized as linguistically conservative, this does not hold for their predecessors, early 16th-century Bible translations and the first editions of the Book of Common Prayer. Their translators and compilers were faced with a two-fold challenge: at the time, it was important to show that the vernacular was suitable for the Scriptures, but it was equally important to make the Bible and liturgical language understandable to the common people both at church and at home. This was the stated aim of William Tyndale (1494–1536), the first English translator of the New Testament from the Greek original, to whose work the subsequent Bible translations in the Early Modern period are heavily indebted (Barber 1997: 55–56, Lancashire 2012: 642).

In particular, morpho-syntactic features that were archaic in the 17th century were not necessarily so a century before. These include such typical southern verbal forms as the third-person present indicative suffix -(*e*)*th* (as opposed to -(*e*)*s*) and the present indicative plural *be* (as oppose to *are*). As to pronouns, the traditional subject form *ye* was current, as was the use of the relative pronoun *which* with human antecedents. In personal correspondence, for example, the forms -(*e*)*s*, *are*, and subject *you*, which all came to be generalized in the language, were still variable in the mid-16th century, while *ye* and *you* had replaced the second person singular *thou* in most contexts (Nevalainen 2000, 2006). The following three examples (1–3) come from letters that John Johnson (b. 1514), a wool merchant active in the City of London and Calais, wrote to his wife in 1545 and which reveal a range of variation common at the time both at the individual level and at the level of the community at large.[2]

(1) Your yong jentleman, Mr. Prat, **hathe** complayned by his lettre to his mother that he **lackythe** bothe meat and drycke, as well his brekefastes,

2 CEEC = *The Corpus of Early English Correspondence*. Compiled by Terttu Nevalainen, Helena Raumolin-Brunberg; Samuli Kaislaniemi, Mikko Laitinen, Minna Nevala, Arja Nurmi, Minna Palander-Collin, Tanja Säily & Anni Sairio, Department of Languages, University of Helsinki. http://www.helsinki.fi/varieng/CoRD/corpora/CEEC/. The letter collections included are listed with their references, e.g., in Nevalainen & Raumolin-Brunberg (2017).

as also at meles not sufficient. (CEEC, John Johnson to Sabine Johnson, 1545; JOHNSON 250)

(2) All your menservauntes have bene of counsaill with hym, for they **be** of no les opynion, declaring that your breid is not good ynoghe for dogges, and drincke so evill that they cannot drinck it, but **ar** fayn when they go into the towne to drincke to their dynnars. (CEEC, John Johnson to Sabine Johnson, 1545; JOHNSON 250)

(3) Yf **ye** knowe they complayn with cawse, I praie **you** se it amendyd: (CEEC, John Johnson to Sabine Johnson, 1545; JOHNSON 250)

John Johnson uses the southern -*(e)th* variant in the third-person singular present indicative (1). His use of the indicative plural of *be* is variable, and he alternates between *be* and *are* in the same context (2). The interpretation of the second-person pronoun in (3) is ambiguous: if "I praie you" is parsed as a clausal unit, *you* is the object form, but if "you se it amended" is analysed as a clause, *you* becomes the subject form. Such ambiguous contexts may have contributed to the change from *ye* to *you* in the subject function at the time (Nevalainen & Raumolin-Brunberg 2017: 60–61).

The three linguistic variables illustrated in (1) – (3) were among those focused on by Kohnen, Rütten and Marcoe (2011), who found that the religious registers they studied adopted the incoming forms with time, although their rates of change varied. There were also features such as the second-person singular pronoun *thou*, characteristic of liturgical language, which persisted in these registers and continued to be used, for example, in prayers throughout the EModE period. Interestingly, the authors show (in their Figure 3) that an increasing proportion of all *thou*-forms in catechisms, sermons and religious biographies did not represent primary use but occurred in Bible quotations and addresses to God, in invocations or short prayers, inserted into the text.

In her comprehensive study of the BCP, Brook (1965) nevertheless maintains that the religious language of the BCP and the Bible is *sui generis*, adhering to its own standards:

> The rough alternation between the issue of revised editions of the Book of Common Prayer and revised translations of the Bible may have helped to establish a standardised 'religious' usage, common to both books, kept alive by tradition in the face of changing linguistic habits. (Brook 1965: 107)

She suggests that this religious usage can be seen most clearly in the forms of verbs and pronouns. However, focusing on the BCP, "changing linguistic habits" were in fact given as one of the reasons that necessitated its 1662 revision (Figure 8.1). The question then becomes how far-reaching were these changes and what kinds of linguistic choices were made regarding ongoing linguistic change?

3 The Book of Common Prayer: An overview

3.1 Brief history and popular reception

The first edition of the Book of Common Prayer was published under Edward VI, England's first Protestant monarch, in 1549, and it was reissued with some doctrinal alterations in 1552. This edition was enforced by the 1552 Act of Uniformity, only to be repealed the following year by Mary I, Edward's Catholic successor. The 1552 Book was reissued basically unaltered under Elizabeth I in 1559. The extract in (4) from a letter sent in 1574 by Bishop Parkhurst of Norwich to William Maister, his diocesan chancellor, details the hierarchical network of church officials involved in securing that the order of the Book of Common Prayer was duly observed in parishes.

(4) Mr. Chancelor, for the better execucion of the seruice comitted to vs by the justices toching the reformacion of such persons as shalbe found any waye to disobey the order of the **booke for the forme of common prayer** and admynistracion of the sacramentes, yt is thought verey necessarye that comandement be sent to my archdeacons and their mynisters that they and every of them in ther seuerall circuites do geue in chardge to the clergie and the questmen to present before them betwene this and the first weke in Lent, viz. before the first of March next, the names and surnames of all such persons as dwelling in their seuerall parishes be negligent, obstinate, or any other enemies or hinderers of her Majestie's procedinges, contrarye to **the said boke** and the statute prouided in that behalfe. (CEEC, John Parkhurst to William Maister, 1574; PARKHURST 226–227)

Some glimpses of the popular reception of the Book can be caught, for example, in *ego* documents such as diaries and personal correspondence. In a letter addressed to Sir Robert Cecil in 1601, Sir John Harington complains that he has not been offered the commission of colonel in the county of Somerset that he applied for because he was thought to be "backward in religion". In the extract

THE BOOK
OF
Common-Prayer
And Adminiſtration
Of the
SACRAMENTS,
AND OTHER
RITES & CEREMONIES
Of the CHURCH,
According to the Uſe
Of the
CHURCH of ENGLAND;
Together with the
PSALTER or PSALMS
OF
DAVID,
Pointed as they are to be Sung
or Said in CHURCHES:
And the
FORM & MANNER
OF
Making, Ordaining, & Consecrating
OF
BISHOPS, PRIESTS,
AND
DEACONS.

LONDON,
Printed by His Maties Printers.
Cum Privilegio.
MDCLXII.

D. Loggan sculp.

Figure 8.1: The 1662 Book of Common Prayer (Church of England; public domain, https://commons.wikimedia.org/w/index.php?curid=50893180).

in (5), Harington, a poet and courtier, appeals to his adherence to the Book of Common Prayer as proof to the contrary, and goes on to boast that he in fact has a better command of the Articles of the Creed and the Catechism than his young rival.

(5) I protest before god to yowr honor I ame no papist neyther in lyfe or thowght, I allow and use **the book of common prayer**, which many of owr forward men doe not, I beleeve 12 articles of the creed and they beleeve skant 11. and thowgh yt ys unusuall in Choyce of a Collonell to examin him by his Catachysme, yet yf I cannot geve accownt of both dutyes better then my ryvall can of eyther, let me loose all place and all good opinion. (CEEC, John Harington to Sir Robert Cecil, 1601; HARINGTON 88)

During the Interregnum (1642–60) the Book of Common Prayer was banned, but it continued to be used by most churches. A new, revised edition of the Book was completed after the Restoration in 1661, enforced by and printed together with the Act of Uniformity in 1662 (see Figure 8.1).[3]

All the clergy had to accept this revised Prayer Book by St. Bartholomew's Day, 24 August 1662. Some dissenting reactions to it were recorded by Samuel Pepys in his diary, quoted in (6) and (7).[4] Pepys himself steered a middle course in matters of religion, disliking both Puritan extremism and strongly authoritarian clergy, but observed most practices required of an Anglican: he attended his home parish "with a moderate regularity", said grace before and after meals and conducted Sunday prayers at home (Latham 1983: 351).

(6) He told me **the new service-book** (which is now lately come forth) was laid upon their deske at St. Sepulchre's for Mr. Gouge to read; but he laid it aside, and would not meddle with it: and I perceive the Presbyters do all prepare to give over all against Bartholomew-tide. (10 August 1662)

(7) Among other things they tell me that there hath been a disturbance in a church in Friday Street; a great many young people knotting together and crying out "Porridge"[5] often and seditiously in the church, and took **the**

3 For further details, see e.g. Brightman (1921), Brook (1965), Cummings (2011), and Swift (2013). The Wikipedia article traces the history of the BCP to the present. https://en.wikipedia.org/wiki/Book_of_Common_Prayer#1662.

4 My quotes come from the online edition of *The Diary of Samuel Pepys* at https://www.pepysdiary.com/.

5 A nickname given to the Prayer Book by the Dissenters.

Common Prayer Book, they say, away; and, some say, did tear it; but it is a thing which appears to me very ominous. I pray God avert it. After supper home and to bed. (24 August 1662)

The Book of Common Prayer is estimated to have gone through over 500 editions and sold up to a million copies between 1549 and 1729 in English alone (Cummings 2011: x, Swift 2013: 32). As appears from Pepys's diary entry in (8), the Book was also published in French (as well as in Latin and Welsh), and in a large variety of print formats from folio to octavo, and in black letter and Roman type.

(8) At last I rose, and with Tom to the French Church at the Savoy, where I never was before – a pretty place it is – and there they have **the Common Prayer Book** read in French, and, which I never saw before, the minister do[th] preach with his hat off, I suppose in further conformity with our Church. (28 September 1662)

Swift (2013: 30–31) remarks that the BCP was cheaper than the Bible, and specifies that, in 1549, a royal proclamation set its cost "at 2 shillings and 2 pence with no binding, 3 shillings and 3 pence bound in sheepskin, and 4 shillings in calves' leather"; by the end of the century its price had come down to about 10 pence – at the time people could buy a Shakespeare Quarto for a sixpence and the cheapest theatre ticket for a penny.

3.2 Sources and revisions

The principal author and compiler of the Edwardine Books of 1549 and 1552 was Archbishop Thomas Cranmer. With some revisions, the 1552 Book prevailed as the Anglican service book well into recent times: it was not until the late 20th century that a complete revision of the Anglican service was approved and came into use.

Cranmer's original work entailed the substitution of the vernacular for the traditional Latin. There were several modes of compilation: translations, mainly from Latin; adaptations of vernacular and non-vernacular sources; and fresh compositions. Different styles were needed for oral delivery and reading, and the different components of the BCP. For example, when devising the vernacular form for the Collect, a short formulaic prayer that sets the theme for the occasion to be observed, Cranmer provided a powerful English model for the classical periodic construction (Adamson 1999: 590–591, Ferguson 1976: 102, Brook 1965: 128–137, Prins 1933: xi–xiv; for further discussion, see section 5).

Cranmer translated Latin old rites into English, making adjustments befitting the requirements of the theology of the Reformation (Long 2007: 66). Swift (2013: 32–33) notes that the Book of Common Prayer was partly based on Cranmer's 1538 Latin breviary, which prescribed the daily prayers, psalms, and readings from the Bible, to be recited at canonical hours. It was modelled on an earlier breviary commissioned by Pope Paul III and written by the Spanish cardinal Francisco de Quinones. On the other hand, reformed continental influences, notably the Lutheran ritual, provided direct and indirect input into the first English BCP, for example, in the vernacular English Primers published in the 16th century (Brook 1965: 18–19; for details, see Brightman 1921: Introduction). Brook (1965: 76–79) also discusses the impact on Cranmer of pre-Reformation works, including vernacular versions of the Lord's Prayer and Creed, and medieval vernacular books of devotion intended for private use.

The single most significant subsequent revision of the Prayer Book was ultimately the work of a group of eight Anglican bishops. This solution was adopted when the conference summoned by the King in 1661 to discuss revision, consisting of bishops and Presbyterian clergy, had failed to reach an agreement (Brook 1965: 31–32). As stated in the Preface to this edition, composed by Robert Sanderson, Bishop of Lincoln, one of the major aims of the undertaking was linguistic:

> That most of the alterations were made [...] for the more proper expressing of some words or phrases of antient vsage, in terms more suteable to the language of the present times; and the clearer explanation of some other words and phrases that were either of doubtfull signification, or otherwise liable to misconstruction.
>
> (Preface to the 1662 BCP; Brightman 1921, vol. 2: 31–33)

Later critics maintain that this modernization project largely failed. Cummings (2011), for one, remarks that the 1662 edition was a consciously backward-looking book not only in its appearance – printed in black letter and preserving the ornamental initial letters of the early editions – but also linguistically. He argues that although some grammatical and lexical changes were made, "more often, with a linguistic historical consciousness that is remarkable, it preserved and even revelled in the archaic feel of an English language now a hundred years old" (Cummings 2011: xv). Similar linguistic conservatism is also attributed to the 1611 King James Bible, which provides the biblical material in the 1662 Book (Brook 1965: 106). Griffith-Jones (2013: 69) notes that the King James Bible was oddly archaic even in 1611; according to Crystal (2003: 59), some 80% of the text shows the influence of William Tyndale's early 16th-century translations.

Several initiatives for a new revision were made over the years. In 1689, Humphrey Prideaux, later the Dean of Norwich, pointed out the negative effects of linguistic change on the worship of God:

> For the language in which it is wrote being constantly on fluxu [*sic*], as all other living languages are, in every age some words that were in use in the former grow obsolete, and some phrases and expressions formerly in grace and fashion, thorough disuse become uncouth and ridiculous, and always to continue these in our Liturgy without correction, would be to bring a disparagement upon the whole, and expose to contempt the worship of God among us. (Prideaux 1834: 52–53)

Prideaux's proposal was not acted upon, and the 1662 version prevailed.

4 Linguistic variation: A comparison of the 1552 and 1662 books

4.1 Material

The Wikipedia quotation at the beginning of this chapter refers to the many expressions going back to the Book of Common Prayer and allusions made to it that have left their mark on the use of the English language. Fewer claims have been made about the grammatical influence of the Book. There have been many reprints and reissues over the centuries, but any early grammatical impact on or indebtedness to the emerging mainstream usage can best be seen by comparing the two most influential EModE editions, those of 1552 and 1662.

As discussed in Nevalainen (2000), the diffusion of individual linguistic features into mainstream use can vary from a few decades, as with the subject form *you*, to some hundreds of years, as in the case of the indicative plural *are*. The linguistic alterations made to the 1662 edition of the BCP deviate from ordinary linguistic change in that they took effect immediately because they were implemented consciously on grounds that the existing expressions were no longer "suteable to the language of the present times". This situation makes it possible to observe the different kinds of change in highly stable environments.

For the purposes of this study, Brightman's parallel-text edition (1921) is used. Aiming at scholarly accuracy, it provides the sources and texts of the two editions analysed below. Brightman states: "throughout, I have endeavoured here to reproduce *verbatim*, *litteratim* and *punctatim*, and even with their misprints, the texts of the Whitchurche issues of the books of 1549 and 1552, and the text of the Book Annexed of 1661, omitting only the Psalter" (1921: Preface p. iv). The quantitative part of my study in sections 4.2 and 4.3, drawing on the analyses in Nevalainen (1987 and 1991), includes all the non-biblical matter shared by the two versions in Brightman's edition and subject to revision in 1661.[6]

My analysis divides the BCP material into two register categories, the Prefaces and Rubrics, on the one hand, and the Prayers and Orders of Service, on the other. As discussed by Brook (1965: 121–147, 172–191), they are fundamentally different in that the Prefaces and Rubrics were intended to be read rather than to be spoken and heard, whereas the opposite was the case with the Prayers and Orders of Service. There is naturally a good deal of stylistic and register variation within these two major categories, but the basic distinction is crucial for trying to determine the language that reached the widest possible public at the time. It is therefore primarily the Prayers and Orders of Service that are the focus of interest in the following sections. Overall, the processes implemented in the 1662 Book can be divided into those aimed at consolidating register usage (4.2), and those representing linguistic modernization proper (4.3).

4.2 Consolidating register usage

The linguistic revision carried out in 1661 was not uniform across the BCP but it also maintained, enforced and, ultimately, created genre and register differences. This was achieved by a conscious retention or regularization of certain features that were current in the mid-16th century, bypassing any changes that they had undergone in general use by the mid-17th century. This aspect of the revision can therefore be thought of as a process of register harmonization from above rather than one of linguistic modernization from below.[7]

6 Stevenson (2006: 137–138) notes that "anyone wanting to know about the origins and development of the English Prayer Books and their many derivatives has to study Brightman", and specifies that, in Brightman, "it is also possible to see the many editorial changes made for the 1662 book". Marshall (1990) and some facsimiles available in the Early English Books Online (EEBO) collection were consulted for further information on the editions and their reissues. See https://eebo.chadwyck.com/home.

7 In his sociolinguistic study of Biblical Hebrew, Kim (2013: 95) distinguishes between stylistic changes from above and natural and largely irreversible linguistic ones from below.

4.2.1 Second-person pronouns *thou* and *ye*

Register differences were maintained and consolidated in the 1662 Book by the retention, particularly in prayers, of the second-person singular pronoun *thou* with reference to the Deity (Barber 1997: 153–154, Brook 1965: 53–54). As noted in section 2, *thou* was consistently used in the corpus of Early Modern English prayers compiled by Kohnen, Rutten and Marcoe (2011), and it continued to appear to some extent with a singular referent especially in Bible quotations and prayer sections in the other religious genres they studied.

The use of *thou* and *thee* also sustained the second-person singular possessive determiners *thy* and *thine*, which in the early 16th century were used much in the same way as the indefinite article in Present-day English still is: the long form precedes nouns that begin with a vowel and the short one those that begin with a consonant. The same pattern was followed by the determiners *my* and *mine*. The extension of the short form to both prevocalic and preconsonantal contexts stabilized in personal correspondence by the end of the 16th century (Nevalainen & Raumolin-Brunberg 2017: 61 –62). As illustrated by Brook (1965: 56), typical mid-16th-century variability is shown by the two Edwardine Books, but the older usage was often adhered to in the 1662 version, as in (9) and (10).

(9) O Lord correct me, but with iudgement, not in **thine** anger, lest thou bring me to nothing. (1662, The Order for Morning Prayer, 129).

(10) O Lord save **thy** people: and bless **thine** heritage. (1662, Mattins, 139)

Unlike the use of *thou* in prayers, the traditional subject form *ye* already varied with *you* in the 1552 book and its 1549 predecessor; in personal communication, the change to *you* ran its course in the 16th century (Nevalainen & Raumolin-Brunberg 2017: 60–61). Brook (1965: 55–56) finds that, in the 1549 and 1552 Books, the extension of *you* to the subject function occurs in the more conversational, less formally liturgical passages, for example, in the Exhortations at Baptism and in the Catechism, and that in most of these cases the 1662 Book reverts to the traditional subject form *ye*. The examples in (11) from the Communion illustrate this retrograde change being made hand in hand with modernization: the 1662 Book changes the southern indicative plural form *be* to *are* (see section 4.3.1) in a sentence where it consciously alters the incoming subject form of the 1552 Book, also accurately followed in its 1559 reissue, to *ye*.

(11a) When God calleth you, bee **you** not ashamed to saye **you** wyll not come? (1552, Communion)

(11b) When God calleth you, bee **you** not ashamed to saye **you** wyll not come? (1559, Communion)[8]

(11c) When God calleth you, are **ye** not ashamed to say **ye** will not come? (1662, Communion)

The examples in (11) also illustrate another conservative feature that was largely retained in the 1662 Book: the third-person singular present indicative suffix -*e*(*th*) in *calleth*. In other religious genres the incoming -(*e*)*s* is adopted later and more slowly than, for example, in personal letters – this is the case especially in prayers and catechisms – but in none of the religious genres studied by Kohnen, Rutten and Marcoe (2011; Table 2) does the outgoing form prevail as the exclusive alternative.

4.2.2 Affirmative periphrastic *do*

The use of *do* periphrasis in affirmative statements presents an interesting case for the present study as major developments took place in general use between the publication of the two editions of the BCP. Affirmative periphrastic *do* picked up in the 16th century and was popular in both emphatic and non-emphatic functions, and in formal as well as in informal contexts, but then underwent a rapid decline in the 17th century (Nurmi 1999, Warner 2012). It was partly subject to revision in the 1662 Book but, besides omissions, there were also contexts to which the auxiliary was added (Nevalainen 1991).

The vast majority of the 116 instances of affirmative periphrastic *do* found in 1552 were retained in the 1662 Book, which returned altogether 114 occurrences. Eleven of the 1552 instances were deleted, and nine new ones added. All the additions were made to the Prayers and Orders of Service. The majority (seven out of nine) occurred with second-person singular subjects and in the past tense, as in (12).

(12) O Almighty God, who by thy blessed Son **didst** call Matthew from the receipt of custome to be an Apostle ... (1662, Collects, Holy Days, 619)

8 *The booke of common praier, and administration of the sacramentes, and other rites and ceremonies in the Church of Englande*. Londini in officina Richardi Iugge, & Iohannis Cawode, 1559. This version of the BCP, reissued under Queen Elizabeth in 1559, was essentially the same text as the 1552 Book.

However, this context did not automatically trigger the use of *do*. The case in (13), for example, adopts the earlier 1552 (and 1549) verb form unaltered.

(13) Almighty God, who **calledst** Luke the Physician, whose praise is in the Gospel, to be an Evangelist . . . (1662, Collects, Holy Days, 625)

A notable difference between (12) and (13) is the material intervening between the subject (*who*) and the verb. It is one of the syntactic environments that often appears to have prompted the use of *do*. Comparing (14) and (15), we find that the deletion of *do* in (15) occurs in a context similar to (13), with no separation of the subject and the verb.

(14) ALmightye God, whyche **doest** see that we haue no power of oure selues to helpe oure selues: (1552, Collect, Second Sunday in Lent, 299)

(15) Almighty God, who **seest** that we have no power of our selves, to help our selves: (1662, Collect, Second Sunday in Lent, 299)

In four of the additions, a present perfect of the verb in the 1552 Book, as in (16), was replaced by a simple past tense form of *do* in the 1662 edition (17).

(16) LOrd almightie, which **hast indued** thy holy Apostle Barnabas, with singuler giftes of thy holy gost: (1552, Collect, Holy Days, 589)

(17) O Lord God Almighty who **didst** endue thy holy Apostle Barnabas with singular gifts of the holy Ghost: (1662, Collect, Holy Days, 589)

In both Books, periphrastic *do* typically appears in a subordinate clause with a second-person singular subject and in the past tense. A typical context for both the retention and addition of *do* is the Collect. In general, the use of affirmative *do* is syntagmatically more marked than that of the simple finite verb in the Prayer Book.

Looking at the religious domain more broadly, Nevalainen (1991: 305, 313–316) found that the use of affirmative periphrastic *do* peaked in the early 17th century both in the Bible extracts and sermon texts included in the Helsinki Corpus of English Texts (HC). These observations support Brook (1965: 110), who notes that periphrastic *do* is more common in the Authorized Version than in the Prayer Book. The study also shows that the use of *do* was on average more contextually constrained in the BCP than in the Bible extracts, where it in turn proved more constrained than in the sermon texts. As discussed above, in the 1662 Book, new instances of *do* were only added to heavily circumscribed contexts.

4.3 Linguistic modernization

4.3.1 Indicative plural of *be*

As shown above, the 1662 revision did not aim in every respect to present a rendition of the BCP in contemporary 17th-century English. However, there were some areas of grammar where this appears to have been the aim. One of them is the change of the traditional southern indicative plural form *be* to the originally northern form *are*, a process largely completed in the south by the turn of the 17th century (Nevalainen 2000). The usage was still variable in the 1552 Book as, for example, in the identical contexts in (18).

(18) Likewise the same saincte Paul (writing to the Colossians) speaketh thus to al men that **be** maried. [. . .] Heare also what sainct Peter thapostle of Chryste, which was hymselfe a maried man sayeth vnto all men that **are** maried. (1552, Matrimony, 813)

Table 8.1 compares the two editions showing the relative frequencies of these variant forms in the same non-biblical contexts but separating the Prefaces and Rubrics from the Prayers and Orders of Service. The use of the incoming form is quite evenly distributed in the 1552 Book in the two text categories analysed: it is found in about one third of the cases in both. In the 1662 edition *are* is the predominant form with an average 80% frequency but a small though statistically significant difference between the two text categories: *are* is introduced less frequently to the Prefaces and Rubrics than to the other non-biblical matter in the Book, i.e. the Prayers and Orders of Service.

Table 8.1: Distribution of *be* and *are* in the two editions according to text function.

Text function	BCP 1552		Total N	BCP 1662	
	are	*be*		*are*	*be*
Preface/Rubric	16 (35%)	30 (65%)	46 (100%)	32 (70%)	14 (30%)
Prayer/Order of service	36 (32%)	75 (68%)	111 (100%)	93 (84%)	18 (16%)
Total	52 (33%)	105 (67%)	157 (100%)	125 (80%)	32 (20%)

Example (11), above, shows how *are* is introduced into the Communion context in the 1662 Book, whereas example (19) illustrates the retention of *be* in a Preface.[9]

(19) It is also more commodious; both for the shortness thereof, and for the plainness of the order, and for that the rules **be** few and easy. (1662, Preface, 37)

Certain linguistic contexts favour the use of *are* as opposed to *be*. In both Books, *are* is typically introduced to main clauses; in the 1662 edition, it always accompanies zero subjects, and it is strongly favoured in negative contexts and when the verb is used in the auxiliary function. The latter two features co-occur with *are* in the second subclause in (20), while *be* is found in the first, where the verb occurs as a copula in an affirmative clause (Nevalainen 1987: 308–310).

(20) Almighty God unto whom all hearts **be** open, all desires known, and from whom no Secrets **are** hid: (1662, Communion, Collect for Purity, 641)

4.3.2 Subject relative pronouns *which* and *who*

A comparison of the two BCP editions in examples (12) to (17) shows that the use of the relative pronoun *which* with reference to the Deity in 1552 had been changed to *who* in 1662. There is a strong indication that the introduction of *who* as a subject relativizer was a Late Middle English innovation, which appeared in the closing formulas of English family letters in the 15th century. Rydén (1983: 127) traces its first attestation back to a letter written by William Paston I in 1426 (see 21).[10] Other early instances can also be found in the first half of the 15th century, as in (22).

(21) I submitte me and alle þis matier to yowr good discrecion, and euere gremercy God and ye, **who** euere haue you and me in his gracious

9 The excerpt reproduces the Preface of the first Edwardine Book, which retained *be* in this context but also included *are* in the preceding context: "Rules *are* here set forth; which, as they *are* few in number, so they *are* plain, and easie to be understood"; these instances were replicated in the subsequent editions.

10 For further discussion on the rise of *who*, see e.g. Bately (1965), Romaine (1982), Fischer (1992: 300–301), Nevalainen & Raumolin-Brunberg (2002), Bergs (2003), and Nevalainen (2012).

gouernaunce (William Paston I to William Worstede, John Longham, and Piers Shelton, 1426)

(22) I kan no more, but Almyȝty God be owre good lorde, **who** have ȝow euer in kepyng. (CEEC, Agnes Paston to John Paston I, 1440s; PASTON I,30)

Rydén further suggests that obvious models for the introduction of *who* into English in these contexts were letters written in French in the 14th and 15th centuries. Following the medieval principles of the art of letter-writing (*ars dictaminis*), letters and documents typically ended in a closing formula, with a relative clause appended to a word denoting the Deity (Nevalainen 2001). The examples in (23) and (24) come from the Stonor family letters, cited in Rydén (1983: 131).

(23) mais je pri a la Trinite **qe** vous doigne bone vie et sauntee de corps a long durre (Nicholas Cowley to Edmund Stonor, c. 1365)

(24) A dieu, **qe** vous garde (Margaret, Countess of Devon, to Edmund Stonor, c. 1380)

The letter-closing expressions also resemble Latin formulas at the end of late medieval sermons intended for delivery to lay audiences, as in (25) and (26) (Rydén 1983: 131). Rydén suggests that these formulas with *qui* may have served as one model for the expressions found in English family letters. They would have been familiar to a large number of churchgoers.

(25) To be whiche blisse brynge vs he þat for vs died on Rode Tre, **qui** cum Patre et Spiritu Sancto viuit et regnat (Ross 1940, sermon no. 14)

(26) þat we may com to þat place graunte vs he þat for vs died in Rode Tree. Amen. **Qui** cum Patre et Filio et Spiritu Sancto regnat, Deus per infinitatem (Ross 1940, sermon no. 37)

A third likely source of influence were the native interrogative and generalizing *wh*-forms, which Bergs (2003: 105), for one, argues could have provided an easy extension of the relative paradigm to the subject relative function as well. These sources are also considered possible contributing factors by Nevalainen and Raumolin-Brunberg (2002: 111). The fact remains that the context in which the relative pronoun *who* begins to appear at any regularity is the closing formulas in English family letters in the 15th century.

It is noteworthy, as Rydén (1983: 128–130) points out, that throughout the 15th century, the *wh*-forms *which* and *the which* were also available as alternative forms in English epistolary formulas, whereas the subject relative *that* apparently was not. The reason he suggests is that it could not be used in a non-restrictive function as required by the Deity formula.

It took some hundred years for anaphoric *who* to be established outside letter formulas and to diffuse from personal names to common nouns, and from non-restrictive to restrictive relative clauses. In the early 16th-century data, (*the*) *which* was still the majority *wh*-relativizer, whereas *who* only appeared in some 30% of the over 4,500 cases studied by Rydén (1966).

These findings are corroborated by the 1552 Book, where *who* also appears in about one third of the cases, and in nearly all of them in non-restrictive relative clauses (Table 8.2). The distribution of the two forms has become diametrically opposite in the 1662 Book, where the incoming *who*-form represents over 90% of the cases, and the use of *which* is largely confined to restrictive relative clauses. The 1662 Book changes *which* to *who* in practically all non-restrictive relative clauses, as for example in (29), below. For similar cases, see those in (12) to (17).

Table 8.2: Diffusion of *who* in the two editions of the BCP.

RC type	**BCP 1552**		**Total N**	**BCP 1662**	
	who	***which***		***who***	***which***
Non-restrictive	54 (33%)	109 (67%)	163	160 (98%)	3 (2%)
Restrictive	2 (9%)	20 (91%)	22	12 (55%)	10 (45%)
Total	56 (**30%**)	129 (**70%**)	185	172 (**93%**)	13 (**7%**)

A typical context for *which* in the 1552 BCP is the invocation in the Collect, as in (27); this Collect also includes an instance of the minority form *who* with reference to the Deity in the formulaic ending. Both these relativizers correspond to the Latin *qui* in the Gregorian Rite in (28) and appear in non-restrictive relative clauses. A major difference between the two English pronouns is that *which* is used with a second-person antecedent, and *who* with a third-person one, exactly as in the letter-closing formulas in (21) and (22). This difference is taken as an indication that the diffusion of the subject relative *who* reversed the natural Noun Phrase Accessibility Hierarchy and was a conscious process (e.g. Romaine 1982: 212–213).

(27) God, **which** as vpon this daye hast taughte the heartes of thy faythfull people, by the sendinge to thē light of thy holy spirite: Graunte vs by the same spirite to haue a right iudgement in all thinges, & euermore to reioyce in his holy comforte, through the merites of Christ Iesu oure Sauioure: **who** lyueth and reygneth with thee in the vnitie of the same spirite, one GOD worlde wythout ende. (BCP 1552, Whitsunday, Collect, 443)

(28) Deus **qui** hodierna die corda fidelium sancti spiritus illustratione docuisti: da nobis in eodem spiritu recta sapere et de eius semper consolatione gaudere. Per [dominum nostrum iesum christum filium tuum **qui** tecum viuit et regnat] in vnitate [eiusdem spiritus sancti deus per omnia secula seculorum.] (*Sacramentarium Gregorianum* 90; Brightman, 442)

(29) God, **who** as at this time didst teach the hearts of thy faithfull people by the sending to them the light of thy holy spirit: Grant us by the same Spirit to have a right Iudgement in all things, and evermore to reioyce in his holy comfort through the merits of Christ Iesus our Saviour, **who** liveth and reigneth with thee in the Vnity of the same spirit, one God world without end. (BCP 1662, Whitsunday, Collect, 443)

The distinction of Prefaces and Rubrics as opposed to Prayers and Orders of Service emerges with the relative pronouns as well: none of the seven instances of *which* with human antecedents in the Prefaces and Rubrics were changed in the 1662 edition; see (30).

(30) And every man **which** is to be admitted a Priest shall be full foure and twenty years old. (1662, Making of Deakons, Preface, 931)

However, *who* has the advantage of being confined to human antecedents, as opposed to *which* and *that*, which do not make the human/non-human distinction. In the second half 17th of the century, the use of *which* with human antecedents had become extremely rare even in restrictive relative clauses in the language community at large (under 5% of the cases; Ball 1996, Nevalainen 2012). Here the BCP usage is up to date if we exclude the Prefaces and Rubrics from the account.

4.3.3 Inconspicuous innovation

Certain grammatical features that underwent some revision in the 1662 BCP have not attracted extensive long-term studies. A case in point is the distribution of the definite article. There were various "omissions" of the definite article in the early versions of the BCP, attributed to Latin influence by Brook (1965: 154–155), but which were subsequently supplied in the 1662 edition. However, it is difficult to distinguish any foreign influence from native constructions undergoing change at the time, including the use of a definite article determiner in a noun phrase consisting of an abstract noun complemented or modified by an *of*-phrase.[11] The pattern is illustrated by the cases in (31) and (32). Here the source that the 1552 version was modelled on is more likely to be German (33) than Latin, in which case the zero article in (31) represents native English variation rather than direct Latin influence.

(31) Almightie and euerlasting God, heauenly father, we geue thee humble thankes, that thou haste vouchsafed to call vs to [Ø] knowledge of thy grace and fayth in thee. (1552, Public baptism, 733)

(32) Almighty and everlasting God, heavenly Father, we give thee humble thanks that thou hast vouchsafed to call vs to **the** knowledge of thy grace and faith in thee (1662, Public baptism, 733)

(33) *Source*: Almechtiger Gott, himlische Vatter, wir sagen dir ewigs lob vnnd danck, das du vns zü **dieser** erkandnuss deiner gnaden vnd glauben an dich, so gnediglich berüffen hast. (Hermann of Cologne, *Simplex ac pia deliberatio*, p. 732)

5 Discussion

Discussing approaches to the effects of mass communication, Pearce (2009: 623–624) distinguishes three major paradigms. The first paradigm claims that mass media have a powerful, immediate and direct impact on their target audience, whereas the second, minimalist or limited effects paradigm, argues that mass media tend to reinforce existing behaviours rather than change them. Finally, the third paradigm presents the idea that the effects of mass communication are long-term and cumulative. It is the third approach that according to Pearce is generally supported today. Reinforced by weekly church attendance, the form and content of the Book of Common Prayer could no doubt exert all

11 For further discussion of early 16th-century usage, see Raumolin-Brunberg (1991: 173–185) and the references given there.

three kinds of effect depending on the circumstances but, over time, the effects have no doubt been long-term and cumulative. An important contributing factor, the spoken modalities of the liturgy contain essential elements of interpersonal communication, where the source and the receiver are individuals and the channel is face-to-face, although the communication itself is public and typically one-to-many rather than one-to-one (Crystal 1976, Pearce 2009: 623).

The use of the vernacular in liturgy became one of the cornerstones of the English Reformation. The Reformation period is also of linguistic consequence in that the social and economic changes that it brought about coincided with a population boom in London, which may have precipitated ongoing processes of linguistic change such as the rapid rise of the subject form *you* in the capital in the mid-16th century (Nevalainen 2000). However, besides changes in local norms, the period coincided with a supralocal competition of norms between traditional southern forms and some incoming originally northern ones, which collided in cases such as the verbal *-s*. The examples in (1) to (3) by the London merchant John Johnson suggest that the southern forms dominated in the 1540s, and that the choices made by the compilers of the BCP largely followed the then-current southern practice. Comparing Johnson's usage with the members of his social network and the community at large shows that, apart from his conservative use of *ye/you*, he was linguistically a middle-of-the roader, neither particularly conservative nor progressive (Nevalainen & Raumolin-Brunberg 2017: 218–222). The same observation applies to many linguistic choices made in the 1552 Book of Common Prayer, including the variation between the subject forms *ye* and *you* (Brook 1965: 53ff.).

A similar comparison of the 1662 edition of the BCP shows a more varied picture. Bringing up to date the use of forms such as the subject relative pronoun *who* and the indicative plural *are*, which had been established outside the religious domain during the hundred years that separate the two editions of the BCP, the revisers fulfilled their promise to modernize the expression of the BCP. Certain other features that were no longer in current use at the time were nevertheless retained – or even retroactively regularized. However, as shown by the empirical studies in section 4, this generalization needs to be qualified: the BCP consists of several subgenres and registers. Some of them, such as the Collects, originally translated and formulated by Cranmer, retain their specific linguistic features. The findings show, furthermore, that certain sections of the BCP, such as Prefaces and Rubrics, which were not intended for oral delivery, did not undergo a systematic modernization.

The inherent hybridity of the reformed liturgy complicates a direct answer to the question of the potential impact of the liturgical language on the general public and *vice versa*. One thing is clear: the changes made to the language of the BCP, including the retroactive ones, helped consolidate the liturgical register status of these features and constructions. The modernization of certain expressions in 1662 may have contributed to the final stages of the codification of these forms as part of standard English, while the register characteristics and stylistic variability of liturgical language were in part maintained with forms and constructions no longer in general use (e.g. Griffith-Jones 2013: 81). For example, the second-person singular pronoun *thou*, accompanied by the verbal inflection in -*(e)st*, remained a hallmark of liturgical language for centuries.

A good example of the slow process of modernization is the Collect. Ferguson (1976: 102–103) discusses its complex syntactic structure, which is encapsulated in the formula: Invocation (+ Basis) > Petition (+ Purpose) + Ending. The Invocation was presented in the second-person singular, which could prompt the insertion of *do* for ease of pronunciation in the Basis, which was typically introduced by a relative clause (34).

(34) O God, **whych** by the leadinge of a starre **dyddest** manyfeste thy onely begotten sonne to the Gentyles: Mercyfully graunt, that we **which** know **thee** now by fayth, may after this lyfe haue the fruicion of **thy** glorious Godhead, through Christ our Lorde. (1552, Collects, Epiphany, p. 249)

The 1662 Book modernized the relative pronoun but preserved the auxiliary *do* and inflected forms of *thou*. Although the perception of these linguistic features must have changed over the one hundred years that separates the two Books, there were segments of the population that in their daily life continued to use some of the archaic features found in the religious domain. These include the second person singular *thou*, which could be used in family correspondence by parents addressing their children or a husband addressing his wife well into the 18th century. This was also the case with those members of the clergy who continued to use -*th* forms in verbs such as *hath* (for *has*) longer than members of other social groups. Examples such as these from Nevalainen et al. (2018) show that linguistic elements associated with liturgical language could continue life in general usage.

Returning to the Collect, it was not until the late 20th century that both the structure and grammar were changed to better correspond to Present-day usage; lexical changes are also in evidence. The version in (35) comes from the American Book of Common Prayer for the Episcopal Church from 1979.

(35) O God, by the leading of a star **you** manifested **your** only Son to the peoples of the earth: Lead us, **who** know you now by faith, to your presence, where we may see **your** glory face to face; through Jesus Christ our Lord,

> **who lives** and **reigns** with **you** and the Holy Spirit, one God, now and for ever. *Amen.* (Collects, Epiphany; Marshall 1990: 1979 II.)

The late 20th-century revision of the Anglican service greatly reduced the distinctiveness of liturgical language. Crystal (1990) argues that in this context the discussion of language change ought to transcend the linguistic surface level and be defined at a deeper level of an aggregate of functions such as informative, identifying, expressive, performative, historical, etc. He sums up his argument by saying that "[a]lthough many of the low-level formal features of this variety have disappeared (the distinctive word-endings, grammatical words and so on), the major functional choices and contrasts in the language have been preserved and remain as distinctive as ever" (1990: 138).

6 Conclusion

The 1552 edition of the BCP represented the grammatical practice and linguistic variability of the language community in the mid-16th century, and this form of language provided the foundation for the Anglican liturgy for a long time to come. The linguistic modernization of the 1662 BCP was conservative, consolidating, for example, formulaic registers with grammatical elements such as *thou* and the concomitant use of affirmative periphrastic *do*. Reflecting the southern origins of biblical language, the third-person present indicative suffix -(*e*)*th* was also preserved in the BCP. Among the features that underwent modernization, the southern present indicative plural *be* was mostly changed to the incoming *are* in the revision. This change had been completed in general use in the south earlier than that of verbal -*s*, and may therefore have been incorporated in the 17th-century revised edition more readily than the other verbal process.

Brook (1965: 34) summarizes the notion of 'Prayer-Book English' by saying that it is "a sixteenth-century liturgical vernacular with a seventeenth-century overlay". During the one-hundred-year period that separates the two Books, the popular perception of the contemporaneity of the text must have changed accordingly. However, some of the distinct grammatical features of liturgical language also persisted into the 18th century in literary and popular use. Although the BCP may not have exerted a formative standardizing influence on Early Modern English grammar at large, it made a long-term, cumulative impression on the register perception of the language community and so, in words of Cummings (2011: xv), came "to embody a site of deep social memory".

References

Adamson, Sylvia (1999). Literary language. *The Cambridge history of the English language, Vol. 3, 1476–1776*, ed. by Roger Lass, 539–653. Cambridge: Cambridge University Press.

Ball, Catherine (1996). A diachronic study of relative markers in spoken and written English. *Language Variation and Change* 8: 227–258.

Barber, Charles (1997). *Early Modern English*. 2nd ed. (1st ed. 1976.) Edinburgh: Edinburgh University Press.

Bately, Janet (1965). *Who* and *which* and the grammarians of the 17th century. *English Studies* 46: 245–250.

Bergs, Alexander T. (2003). What if one man's lexicon were another man's syntax? A new approach to the history of relative *who*. *Folia Linguistica Historica* 24(1–2): 93–110.

Brightman, F. E. (1921) *The English Rite, being a synopsis of the sources and revisions of* The Book of Common Prayer. 2 vols. Second, revised edition. London: Rivingtons.

Brook, Stella (1965). *The language of* The Book of Common Prayer. London: Deutsch.

Cummings, Brian (2011). *The book of common prayer: The texts of 1549, 1559, and 1662*. Oxford: Oxford University Press.

CEEC = The Corpus of Early English Correspondence. 1998. Compiled by Terttu Nevalainen, Helena Raumolin-Brunberg; Jukka Keränen, Minna Nevala, Arja Nurmi & Minna Palander-Collin. Helsinki: Department of English, University of Helsinki.

Cressy, David (1980). *Literacy and social order*. Cambridge: Cambridge University Press.

Crystal, David (1976). Nonsegmental phonology in religious modalities. *Language in religious practice*, ed. by William J. Samarin, 17–25. Rowley MA: Newbury House.

Crystal, David (1990). Liturgical language in a sociolinguistic perspective. *Language and the worship of the church*, ed. by David Jasper & Ronald C. D. Jasper, 120–146. Basingstoke: Macmillan.

Crystal, David (2003). *The Cambridge encyclopedia of the English language*, 2nd ed. (3rd ed. 2019). Cambridge: Cambridge University Press.

Darquennes, Jeroen & Wim Vandenbussche, eds. (2011). Language and religion as a sociolinguistic field of study: Some introductory notes. *Sociolinguistica* 25: 1–11.

Deumert, Ana & Wim Vandenbussche, eds. (2003). *Germanic standardizations: Past to present*. Amsterdam & Philadelphia: Benjamins.

Ferguson, Charles A. (1976). The collect as a form of discourse. *Language in religious practice*, ed. by William J. Samarin, 101–109. Rowley MA: Newbury House.

Fischer, Olga (1992). Syntax. *The Cambridge history of the English language*, Vol. 2, ed. by Norman Blake, 207–408. Cambridge: Cambridge University Press.

Griffith-Jones, Robin (2013). The King James Bible and the language of liturgy. *The King James Version at 400: Assessing its genius as Bible translation and its literary influence*, ed. by David G. Burke, John F. Kutsko & Philip H. Towner, 69–86. Atlanta: Society of Biblical Literature.

Kim, Dong-Hyuk (2013). *Early Biblical Hebrew, late Biblical Hebrew, and linguistic variability: A sociolinguistic dating of biblical texts*. Leiden & Boston: Brill.

Kingsford, Charles Lethbridge, ed. (1919). *The Stonor letters and papers 1298–1483*. Vols. I–II. Camden Society Third Series 29, 30. London: The Royal Historical Society.

Kohnen, Thomas, Tanja Rütten & Ingvilt Marcoe (2011). Early Modern English religious prose – A conservative register? *Methodological and historical dimensions of Corpus Linguistics* (Studies in Variation, Contacts and Change in English 6), ed. by Paul Rayson, Sebastian Hoffmann & Geoffrey Leech. Helsinki: VARIENG. http://www.helsinki.fi/varieng/series/volumes/06/kohnen_et_al/

Labov, William (2007). Transmission and diffusion. *Language* 83(2): 344–387.

Lancashire, Ian (2012). Early Modern English: Lexicon and semantics. *English historical linguistics: An international handbook*, Vol. 1, ed. by Alexander Bergs & Laurel Brinton, 637–652. Berlin: De Gruyter Mouton.

Latham, Robert, ed. (1983). *The Diary of Samuel Pepys*, Vol. 10: *Companion*. Berkeley & Los Angeles: University of California Press.

Leech, Geoffrey (2007). New resources, or just better old ones? The Holy Grail of representativeness. *Corpus Linguistics and the Web*, ed. by Marianne Hundt, Nadja Nesselhauf & Carolin Biewer, 133–149. Amsterdam: Rodopi.

Long, Lynne (2007). Vernacular Bibles and prayer books. *The Oxford handbook of English literature and theology*, ed. by Andrew W. Hass, David Jasper & Elisabeth Jay, 54–78. Oxford. Oxford University Press.

Marshall, Paul V. (1990). *Prayer Book parallels: The public services of the Church arranged for comparative study* (Anglican liturgy in America, Vol. 2). New York: *The Church Hymnal Corporation*.

Nevalainen, Terttu (1987). Change from above: A morphosyntactic comparison of two Early Modern English editions of *The Book of Common Prayer*. *Neophilologica Fennica* (Mémoires de la Société Néophilologique de Helsinki XLV), ed. by Leena Kahlas-Tarkka, 295–315. Helsinki: Société Néophilologique.

Nevalainen, Terttu (1991). Motivated archaism: The use of affirmative periphrastic *do* in Early Modern English liturgical prose. *Historical English syntax* (Topics in English Linguistics 2), ed. by Dieter Kastovsky, 303–320. Berlin & New York: Mouton de Gruyter.

Nevalainen, Terttu (2000). Processes of supralocalisation and the rise of Standard English in the Early Modern period. *Generative theory and corpus studies: A dialogue from 10 ICEHL* (Topics in English Linguistics 31), ed. by Ricardo Bermúdez-Otero, David Denison, Richard M. Hogg & C.B. McCully, 329–371. Berlin and New York: Mouton de Gruyter.

Nevalainen, Terttu (2001). Continental conventions in early English correspondence. *Towards a history of English as a history of genres* (Anglistische Forschungen 298), ed. by Hans-Jürgen Diller & Manfred Görlach, 203–224. Heidelberg: Universitätsverlag C. Winter.

Nevalainen, Terttu (2006). Mapping change in Tudor English. *The Oxford history of English*, ed. by Lynda Mugglestone, 178–211. Oxford: Oxford University Press.

Nevalainen, Terttu (2012). Reconstructing syntactic continuity and change in Early Modern English regional dialects: The case of *who*. *Analysing older English*, ed. by David Denison, Ricardo Bermúdez-Otero, Christopher McCully & Emma Moore, with the assistance of Ayumi Miura, 159–184. Cambridge: Cambridge University Press.

Nevalainen, Terttu, Mikko Laitinen, Minna Nevala & Arja Nurmi (2018). From nearing completion to completed. *Patterns of change in 18th-century English: A sociolinguistic approach*, ed. by Terttu Nevalainen, Minna Palander-Collin & Tanja Säily, 251–254. Amsterdam & Philadelphia: John Benjamins.

Nevalainen, Terttu & Helena Raumolin-Brunberg (2002). The rise of the relative *who* in Early Modern English. *Relativisation on the North Sea Littoral* (LINCOM Studies in Language Typology 7) ed. by Patricia Poussa, 109–121. Muenchen: LINCOM Europa.

Nevalainen, Terttu & Helena Raumolin-Brunberg (2017). *Historical sociolinguistics: Language change in Tudor and Stuart England*. 2nd ed. London: Routledge.
Nurmi, Arja (1999). *A social history of periphrastic* do. Mémoires de la Société Néophilologique de Helsinki 56. Helsinki: Société Néophilologique.
Pearce, Kevin J. (2009). Media and mass communication theories. *Encyclopedia of communication theory*, ed. by Stephen W. Littlejohn & Karen A. Foss, 623–627. Los Angeles, CA & London, UK: SAGE Publications.
Prideaux, Humphrey ([1689] 1834). *A letter to a Friend on the Convocation of 1689, recommending a revision of the Liturgy*, ed. by Rev. C.N. Wodehouse. Norwich: John Stacy & London: Longman, Rees, Orme, Brown, Green & Longman.
Prins, A.A. (1933). *The Booke of the Common Prayer, 1549: An enquiry into its language (phonology and accidence), with an introductory note about its composition and origin*. Amsterdam: M. J. Portilelje.
Raumolin-Brunberg, Helena (1991). *The noun phrase in early sixteenth-century English: A study based on Sir Thomas More's writings* (Mémoires de la Société Néophilologique de Helsinki 50). Helsinki: Société Néophilologique.
Romaine, Suzanne (1982). *Socio-historical linguistics: Its status and methodology*. Cambridge: Cambridge University Press.
Ross, Woodburn O. (1940). *Middle English sermons*. Early English Text Society, O.S. 209. Oxford: Oxford University Press.
Rydén, Mats (1966). *Relative constructions in early sixteenth century English*, Uppsala: Almqvist & Wiksell.
Rydén, Mats (1983). The emergence of *who* as relativizer. *Studia Linguistica* 37(2): 126–134.
Samarin, William J. (1987). The language of religion. *Sociolinguistics: An international handbook of the science of language and society*, Vol. 1, ed. by Ulrich Ammon, Norbert Dittmar & Klaus J. Mattheier, 85–91. Berlin & New York: de Gruyter.
Stevenson, Kenneth (2006). The Prayer Book as 'sacred text'. *The Oxford guide to the Book of Common Prayer: A worldwide survey*, ed. by Charles Hefling & Cynthia Shattuck, 133–139. Oxford & New York: Oxford University Press.
Swift, Daniel (2013). *Shakespeare's common prayers:* The Book of Common Prayer *and the Elizabethan age*. Oxford: Oxford University Press.
Warner, Anthony (2012). Early Modern English: Periphrastic DO. *English historical linguistics: An international handbook*, Vol. 1, ed. by Alexander Bergs & Laurel Brinton, 743–756. Berlin: De Gruyter Mouton.

Part 2: **The revised version**

Alpo Honkapohja and Aino Liira

9 Abbreviations and standardisation in the *Polychronicon*: Latin to English and manuscript to print

1 Introduction

Abbreviations were an integral part of the writing systems used in the Middle Ages. They were used both to conserve precious writing materials and to alleviate "the labour of writing Latin" (Hector 1958: 37). Proof of how widespread and sophisticated the Latin system had become is that the most comprehensive reference work for medieval Latin abbreviations by Adriano Cappelli (1990 [1899]) contains some 14 000 abbreviations. When vernacular languages like English and Anglo-Norman French began to be written down, the system of abbreviation was applied to them, partly modelled after Latin, partly inventing new abbreviations. The system was especially important in a multilingual society, as abbreviations can be language-independent. Towards the end of the Middle Ages the number of abbreviations began to decrease, simultaneously with technological innovations in book production and the emergence of English in a new nationwide function.

The gradual disappearance of the abbreviation and suspension system is linked to the technological developments in book production. As parchment began to be replaced by a cheaper material, paper, and the printing press made it possible to produce multiple copies with ease, the two main needs for using an abbreviation and suspension system lost their importance. The system was eventually abandoned in printed books, although it continued in handwriting used for personal letters and notes, and legal writing (Hector 1958: 28, 38; Kytö, Grund and Walker 2011). Furthermore, a decrease in the use of abbreviations took place at the same time as vernacular English was gaining ground from Anglo-Norman French and even Latin, and a new written standard for English was beginning to emerge. The details of this gradual change, however, remain largely uncharted.

Our aim in this chapter is to help build a foundation for the timeline and reasons of the loss of the abbreviation system. By quantitatively studying changes in the abbreviations and variation across copies of a single work, Ranulph Higden's

Note: We would like to thank Jane Roberts and two anonymous reviewers for their comments. Their feedback led to a much improved article. We are also thankful to Sara Norja for proofreading and Laura Wright for editing the article and making a number of helpful suggestions. All remaining mistakes are our own.

https://doi.org/10.1515/9783110687545-010

Polychronicon, we hope to provide a descriptive outline for the reduction in their numbers and the changes in the system concurrent with changes in written language. We ask what happened to the system of abbreviation with the rising vernacular written standard on the one hand, and with the new technologies of paper and printing on the other. Our analysis is divided into four sections, the first of which focuses on the proportion of abbreviated words in Latin and English in the data. The second section establishes a picture of the abbreviation types that disappeared first and the kinds of words in which abbreviations survived the longest. In the third section, we examine the effects of technological aspects of book production, such as right-margin justification in double column layouts, on the abbreviation system. Finally, the fourth section compares the reduction of abbreviations and the reduction of spelling variants in general.

Our findings show that the rate of the disappearance was different in Latin and English, and that different abbreviation types disappeared at different rates. While there was a major reduction in the use of abbreviations in large *de luxe* manuscripts like the *Polychronicon*, our data show only minor reduction in spelling variants. Moreover, the density of some abbreviation types actually increases in printed books due to the emergence of a standard set of abbreviations used by early modern printers. Abbreviations were used for line justification, among other purposes, and they seem to have survived the longest in this function. The results thus show that the medieval abbreviation and suspension system underwent both qualitative and quantitative changes. These changes happened early in the standardisation process, but many of the usages survived up to early printed books and later.

2 The emergence of a written standard and the loss of abbreviations: Previous work

The loss of the medieval abbreviation and suspension system in English has, by and large, not been described from the point of view of standardisation and with the quantitative precision of corpus linguistics. Diachronic developments are mainly treated by concise and imprecise statements in palaeographical handbooks. For example, Petti (1977: 22) notes that "[t]he general pattern in English literary manuscripts was one of gradual reduction, so that by the Renaissance, abbreviations were of modest proportions and, in any case, more abundant in drafts than in formal copies, where the practice was hardly more extensive than in printed books". What we do not know is how exactly this change proceeded.

This is, however, not to say that there has not been any quantitative work at all. We now have some corpus resources which encode suborthographic phenomena, including abbreviations, in a way that can be studied quantitatively.[1] A handful of studies[2] have made use of them, proving that studying them can yield interesting results. Two corpus studies overlap with our period. Shute (2017a, 2017b) touches upon abbreviations as a part of her quantitative study of spelling variation in Caxton, noting that they are statistically more likely to occur close to the right margin. Smith (2019) gives a diachronic account of one common abbreviation in the *Linguistic Atlas of Older Scots* (LAOS). Moreover, there have been some interesting discoveries in French scholarship (see, e.g., Hasenohr 2002; Camps 2016; Stutzmann et al. 2018). All of these will be discussed in sections 4.1, 4.2 and 4.3 below. However, with respect to English, an overall quantitative account of the gradual disappearance of many abbreviations between ca. 1350 and 1500 is lacking. We do not know how it lines up with the emergence of the English vernacular as the main language of written communication.

The development of a written standard for English is a process whose broad outlines are known, but the causes and exact mechanisms are incompletely understood and have recently been opened up for new discussion. The broad outlines are that post-conquest England, between 1066 and c. 1350, was a trilingual society in which all educated language users knew Latin and Anglo-Norman French (cf., e.g., Ingham 2012). English may have been the primary spoken

1 The few corpora that encode abbreviations in a way that enables applying quantitative methods include texts made available by the Medieval Nordic Text Archive (MENOTA), a network of libraries, archives and research departments of Old Icelandic, Old Norwegian and Old Swedish Texts. In English studies, corpora that encode abbreviations include the Edinburgh resources, LAEME (see Laing 2013) and LAOS, as well as the Middle English Grammar Corpus (MEG-C) and Middle English Local Documents (MELD) corpora compiled at the University of Stavanger, and the digital edition *An Electronic Text Edition of Depositions 1560-1760* (Kytö, Grund & Walker 2011). Recently Stutzmann et al. (2018), as a part of the HIMANIS network, have applied Handwritten Text Recognition to a large corpus of French administrative texts from the 14th and 15th centuries; the resulting corpus allows retrieval of both abbreviated and unabbreviated forms through a plain text search. None of these resources has been used exhaustively for the study of abbreviations.

2 Wright has studied abbreviations in English/Anglo-Norman/Latin mixed-language documents, with small datasets that a single scholar can handle manually (see, e.g., Wright 2000, 2011 and 2013). Two recent Dutch PhD dissertations (ter Horst 2017 and Stam 2017) have investigated similar multilingual phenomena using corpora, focusing on Latin and Irish. Kestemont (2015) studied scribal profiles, including abbreviations, using a stylometric approach in the letter collection of the Middle Dutch mystical female poet Hadewijch. Other discoveries were made by Rogos (2012), who focused on late Middle English literary manuscripts, noting that word-final characters alternate with graphic sequences rather than substitute them.

language for most of the population, but written English reflected the local dialect and was frequently mixed with Latin and Anglo-Norman in documents (cf., e.g., Wright 2002). The change began in the fifteenth century when English was increasingly used as the language of writing. This led to a loss of much of its variation and a new written standard eventually emerged.

There is, however, no single accepted explanation for what led to the emergence of a new written vernacular standard. A very influential account was written by Samuels (1983 [1963]), who proposed that the development towards standardization for written English can be divided into four Types. The last of these is the so-called "Chancery" standard, according to which a department of Royal administration provided the model for the written standard of English. This idea was developed further by Fisher (1977, 1979, 1996), but his strong claims have been decisively dismantled by Benskin (2004) and Wright (2000), who have shown Fisher's work to be lacking theoretically and selective in its use of data (see also chapters 1 and 2 in this book). Neither Samuels (1983 [1963]) nor Fisher take abbreviations into account, but interestingly, Samuels, in a later article (1983), discusses the frequencies of a few common abbreviation types in two manuscripts of the *Canterbury Tales*, mentioning diachronic developments in reference to his types.[3] His findings and views will be discussed in more detail in sections 4.1 and 4.2 below.

While the theory of a Chancery standard has been very influential, and is often still the view found in many textbooks, recent work on standardisation has moved in a more sociolinguistic direction (see, e.g., Deumert and Vandenbussche 2003; Nevalainen and Tieken-Boon van Ostade 2006). Since the present study seeks to situate the loss of abbreviations, on the one hand, in the external context of book production, and on the other hand in linguistic change, it too can be described as sociolinguistic. The linguistic framework is based mainly on ideas proposed by Wright (2013), who calls attention to simplification caused by dialect contact (2013: 71) as a potential explanation for the loss of variety, and examining variation from the point of view of a complex system (2013: 64–66).

The view of variation promoted by Wright is informed in particular by the "linguistics of speech" approach proposed by Kretzschmar (2009, 2015; Kretzschmar & Stenroos 2012). According to this approach, language, when examined through big enough data, behaves like a complex system. A complex system refers to the kind of systems that display self-organised patterns, such as those described for contemporary biology and economics (Kretzschmar and Stenroos 2012: 112). Variation

3 The article is written as a response to critique by Ramsey (1982), who claims that the Hengwrt and Ellesmere manuscripts of the *Canterbury Tales* were copied by different scribes.

in historical linguistic data is a "result of the interplay of historical and cultural forces to which language is always subject", and this interplay is characterised by "the massive interaction of speakers and writers over time, as a complex system from which the regularities of our language emerge" (Kretzschmar and Stenroos 2012: 112). Thus written Middle English can be expected to show variation characteristic of a complex system and standardisation can be seen as gradual reduction of this variation.

From the point of view of the linguistics of speech, the development of a written standard forces unnatural uniformity on the natural variability of language. According to Wright, "[t]here is nothing 'natural' about this process of reduction" (2013: 65). Naturally occurring language data, especially speech data, will show a characteristic complex distribution in which a few variants are very common, but there will be a long tail of many uncommon variants (see, e.g., Kretschmar and Stenroos 2012). When languages change, the relative frequency of variants changes in proportion to one another (Kretzschmar and Stenroos 2012). The process that most characterises the fifteenth century is not selection, but rather a whittling down of variants, or *elimination*. "The actual whittling-down process to one supreme variant used by everybody happened well after 1500, and thus after the period of 'Chancery Standard'" (Wright 2013: 65–66). The type of English written by London Bridge clerks in 1501–1502, which has a reduced number of spelling variants per scribe, but still a large pool of variants and different dominant forms compared to ones that eventually became selected, Wright calls *proto-standard English* (2013: 64). It is this kind of gradual elimination of variation into proto-standard English that we expect to see in our present data.

However, applying the linguistics of speech approach to abbreviations is not entirely straightforward, as its claims are mainly based on spoken data. In a non-standardised written culture such as Middle English between 1066 and 1350, it can be expected to influence written texts (cf. Kretzschmar and Stenroos 2012), even if writing may be somewhat conservative and there is no one-to-one correspondence between sounds and spellings. Less clear is how directly a linguistics of speech approach can be applied to writing systems and orthographic features. Abbreviations, in particular, are an interesting orthographic feature: On the one hand, they are a device developed to save time and space (Petti 1977: 22) and can thus be expected to be conditioned by the physical properties of the handwritten and printed space (Varila 2016; Shute 2017a; Tyrkkö 2017). On the other hand, they are legitimate spelling variants of their own that were part of the pool of variants available to writers of Middle and Early Modern English (Lass 2004; Driscoll 2009; Rogos 2012).

The fifteenth century, which saw the initial stages of a new written standard for English, also saw major developments in written culture. The most famous one is, of course, the printing press, but there were also other developments, including the less sudden but equally important paper revolution, which made manuscript books more affordable to a middle-class audience and promoted functional literacy, such as account-keeping, among merchants (see, e.g., Lyall 1989; Da Rold 2011; Robinson 2014; and Honkapohja 2017: 23–24). It would also be possible to see the loss of abbreviations in terms of shared practices of the scribal community and changes in the copying process. This type of visual pragmatics approach, utilised for the *Polychronicon* by Carroll et al. (2013), correlates the co-occurrence of particular visual elements of the manuscript or printed page with meaning-making processes (see also Liira 2020: 274, 276). Nevertheless, because the focus of this chapter and book is on standardisation and multilingualism, we will only take material text into account in a somewhat limited manner: script, one- vs. two-column layout and the effect of line breaks are discussed in section 4.3.

As we are examining standardisation within a theoretical framework in which elimination of spelling variation is central, and basing it on studies which lead us to expect reduction in the course of the fifteenth century, it is worth asking whether abbreviations disappear at the same time as other variation. Is their disappearance related to these same processes, or is their gradual abandonment a separate process? This chapter seeks to answer these questions in addition to providing a diachronic outline for the gradual elimination of abbreviations from the late fourteenth century to the early sixteenth century. The *Polychronicon* provides a very good point of comparison for this, as it was consistently popular throughout the period. Our study takes into account both Latin and English, as well as manuscripts and early printed editions.

3 Data

3.1 The *Polychronicon*

Ranulph Higden's (OSB; d. 1364) *Polychronicon* is a universal chronicle divided into seven books, the first of which presents geographical information about the known world while the other six books narrate the history of the world from the biblical creation to Higden's own time. Higden continued revising the *Polychronicon* throughout his life: three distinct versions have been identified, and the intermediate version ending at 1342–1346 is found in the majority of the copies (Waldron 2004: xiii). The intermediate version of the chronicle was translated from the original Latin into Middle English by John Trevisa (fl. 1342–1402). The translation was requested by Trevisa's patron Sir Thomas

Berkeley, and it was finished in 1387 according to the translator's colophon. While Higden had composed his chronicle for a clerical audience, the readers of the English *Polychronicon* were presumably both aristocrats and clergy (Shepherd 1999: 31; see also Beal 2012: 68). Despite its universal theme, Higden's chronicle is heavily focused on the British and Irish Isles, and the translation reflects a wider interest in both vernacular literature and national history at this time (Matheson 1984: 209; Given-Wilson 2004: 139–140).

The English *Polychronicon* survives in fourteen manuscripts while the Latin manuscripts number over 120 (Waldron 2004: xiii). The English text was first printed by William Caxton in 1482 and again by Wynkyn de Worde and Peter Treveris, in 1495 and 1527, respectively. The work thus remained popular for over two centuries. It is particularly suitable for the study of standardisation as it covers the period which saw two remarkable changes in book production: the emergence of a new vernacular standard and the introduction of paper and printing. This provides an excellent starting point for a parallel corpus, allowing a comparison of spelling features across passages that are textually close to each other (cf. McIntosh, Samuels, and Benskin 1986: 2.1.3.). Waldron (1991: 67) has noted that "[w]hen the manuscripts of Trevisa's Middle English version of the *Polychronicon* have been fully transcribed and collated, they will yield (it can be safely said) a good deal of information on scribal attitudes to the language of the text being copied and on movements towards standardization in the written forms of English".[4] For this reason, we selected copies of the *Polychronicon* for our quantitative study of the development of a supra-regional standard of written English.

3.2 The corpus

We sampled a selection of *Polychronicon* manuscripts for the present study, choosing one Latin manuscript, nine English manuscripts and the three early printed editions. Three aims guided the selection: to have at least two manuscripts from each 25-year period, to maximise the number of different scribes, and to select manuscripts from different parts of the stemmatological tree. Hu (Glasgow, University Library MS Hunter 223) was selected as the Latin manuscript for our corpus, as Waldron (2004: xviii) notes that Trevisa must have used a copy similar to this manuscript as his source text. The oldest extant manuscripts of the English translation, M (Chetham's Library MS Mun.A.6.90)

4 Steps towards this full collation have been taken by Waldron in his edition of Book 6 of the *Polychronicon* (2004).

and C (British Library MS Cotton Tiberius D.vii), were likely copied in the Berkeley area and are thus closest to the translator's original copy, now lost, in both date and language. A completely even representation turned out not to be possible, as the third quarter of the fifteenth century is only represented by one manuscript, T.[5] Moreover, the section selected for our corpus in the two earliest manuscripts, C and M, was copied by the same scribe. To balance the selection we also added a second manuscript from "Scribe Delta" into the second period.

The manuscripts and printed editions used for the present study are briefly described below; for more extensive descriptions, see Waldron (2004: xviii–xxxvii) and Liira (forthcoming 2020).[6] Figure 9.1 shows how the ones that were selected for the corpus are related to each other according to Waldron's stemmas.

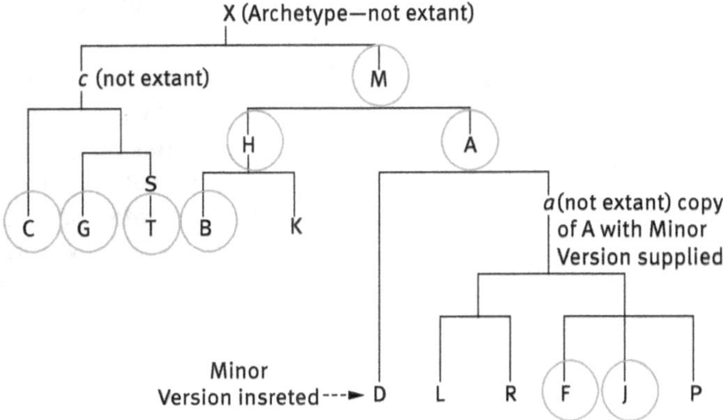

Figure 9.1: Selection of manuscripts based on stemmatological tree (Waldron 2004: xxiii, reproduced with permission).

Latin manuscript

s. xiv

Hu Glasgow MS Hunter 223

325 x 215 mm, single-column layout

Single hand, Anglicana Formata

5 There is some fluctuation in the dating of MS B: Waldron (2004) dates it to xv^{med} but Mooney, Horobin & Stubbs (2011) to 1450–1475, following Dutschke (1989: 683), which would make it contemporary with MS T. Our findings, interestingly, suggest an earlier dating or perhaps simply conservative scribes.

6 The manuscript sigla used in this article are Waldron's; the sigla for the printed editions are ours.

English manuscripts

s. xiv/xv
C London, British Library MS Cotton Tiberius D. vii (vol. 1)
Current size (inlaid) 380 x 280 mm, single-column layout
Single hand in vol. 1, Anglicana Formata: Hand 1, “The Polychronicon Scribe” (1–169r)

M Manchester, Chetham’s Library MS Mun.A.6.90
350 x 265 mm, single-column layout
Single hand, “The Polychronicon Scribe”, Anglicana Formata

s. xv^{in}
H London, British Library MS Harley 1900
350 x 240 mm, single-column layout
Single hand, Anglicana Formata

s. xv^{1}
A London, British Library MS Additional 24194
420 x 290 mm, two-column layout
Single hand, “Delta”, Anglicana Formata

F Tokyo, Senshu University Library MS 1 (olim Oslo/London Schøyen Collection MS 194)
420 x 285 mm, two-column layout
Single hand, “Trevisa-Gower Scribe”, Anglicana Formata with some Textualis forms

J Cambridge, St John’s College MS 204 (H.1)
395 x 300 mm, two-column layout
Single hand, “Delta”, Anglicana Formata

s. xv^{med}
B San Marino, Huntington Library MS HM 28561
380 x 275 mm, two-column layout
Four hands, two in the Polychronicon: Hand 1 (ff. 1–78r), Anglicana Formata and Secretary; Hand 2 (ff. 123v–319v), Secretary; the two alternating ff. 78–123r.

G Glasgow, University Library MS Hunter 367
260 x 255 mm, two-column layout
“Possibly three different hands, but could be one scribe” (Mooney, Horobin, and Stubbs 2011), Anglicana with some Secretary/continental forms

s. xv^3
T Princeton, University Library MS Taylor 6
460 x 310 mm, two-column layout
Single hand, the "Hooked-g Scribe", Bastard Secretary

English printed eds
Cax Caxton, William (Westminster, 1482), STC 13438[7]
2°, single-column layout, Type 4:95B[8]

Wor De Worde, Wynkyn (Westminster, 1495), STC 13439
2°, two-column layout, Type 4:96G[9]

Tre Treveris, Peter (Southwark, 1527), STC 13440
2°, two-column layout

For our corpus, we selected a passage in Book 1, within chapters 1–7. This passage was chosen to maximise the amount of Latin, as it contains a list of Higden's references, copied in Latin even in the English manuscripts. In addition to the list of authorities, Latin occurs, for instance, in chapter titles and headings, and in the frequent source references in the running text. See Table 9.1 for the word count in English and in Latin in each transcribed and tagged corpus sample.

3.3 Encoding

We use a corpus-based approach with the intention of describing how abbreviations are reduced in the present corpus of 13 samples taken from the *Polychronicon*. To enable the quantitative analysis, a number of important divisions were annotated in the data: language, headings, line breaks, word divisions as well as both abbreviations and their expansions. The system of encoding was based on TEI P5 XML. However, to facilitate the encoding, the manuscript and printed witnesses were transcribed in MS Word, adding preliminary mark-up, which was converted to TEI XML using the scripts in the OxGarage web service. This was processed by running the automatically converted XML through a number of XSLT scripts which converted the automatically created tags into more semantically justified ones (cf. also Cummings 2009: 309–312).

7 Designated K by Waldron (2004).
8 BMC 11: 127.
9 BMC 11: 195.

Table 9.1: Corpus and word count.

MS/ed	Date	Word count	English	Latin	Percent of Latin
Hu	s. xiv	2112		2112	100%
C	s. xiv/xv	2828	2474	354	12.52%
M	s. xiv/xv	2861	2488	373	13.03%
H	s. xv^{in}	2871	2497	374	13.03%
A	s. xv^{1}	2744	2391	353	12.86%
F	s. xv^{1}	2851	2471	380	13.33%
J	s. xv^{1}	2812	2447	365	12.98%
B	s. xv^{med}	2842	2489	353	12.42%
G	s. xv^{med}	2730	2417	313	11.47%
T	s. xv^{3}	2804	2440	364	12.98%
Cax	1482	2854	2491	363	12.72%
Wor	1495	2865	2482	383	13.37%
Tre	1527	2832	2458	374	13.2%
Total		**36006**	**29545**	**4349**	**12.08%**

TEI XML is well-suited for this type of study as it provides tags for all the features we wanted to study. As the aim is to take multilingualism into account, sections in Latin were tagged as <foreign lang="Lat">. The <foreign> tag "identifies a word or phrase as belonging to some language other than that of the surrounding text" (TEI Guidelines 3.3.2.1). Line breaks were tagged as <lb/>, marking "the beginning of a new (typographic) line in some edition or version of a text" (TEI Guidelines 3.10.3). Headings and marginal comments were indicated by <seg>-tags, which indicate any kind of segment (16.3), and the specific type of division was specified by attributes.

Each word was tagged inside <w> tags. If a word does not contain an abbreviation, the encoding is simple: <w>word</w>. Our definition of words is based on editorially identified word divisions. According to the TEI P5 Guidelines, <w> represents "a grammatical (not necessarily orthographic) word" (TEI Guidelines 17.1). The words were tagged according to what we considered to be separate words in transcription. The transcription is thus semi-diplomatic: it mainly follows the manuscript, but makes occasional editorial normalisations of word division. Words such as *shalbe* were annotated as two separate words <w>shal</w><w>be</w>, and words such as *not withstandynge* as one word <w>not withstandynge</w>, regardless of where the scribes and typesetters left a space. Word token counts in the analysis are based on the numbers of <w> tags identified in the transcription.

The most important part of the tagging is the need to annotate both the abbreviations and their expansions. The TEI P5 Guidelines provide mechanisms which allow precisely this. The system for encoding used in this study is represented in detail in Honkapohja (2013) and discussed in Honkapohja (2018: 246–248),[10] but we will present it here using one example, *þꝰfore* 'therefore'. In its XML format the word looks like this:

```
<w>
<choice>
<abbr>Þ<am>hook</am>fore</abbr>
<expan>Þ<ex>er</ex>fore</expan>
</choice>
</w>
```

The possibility of including both the abbreviated and expanded form is enabled by <choice> tags, which are used for every abbreviated word. The tag "groups a number of alternative encodings for the same point in a text" (3.4). Within the <choice> structure, the two alternative encodings are marked with <abbr> (abbreviation), which "contains an abbreviation of any sort" and <expan> (expansion), which "contains the expansion of an abbreviation" (3.5.5). There are also specific tags for encoding abbreviations and expansions within these alternative structures. The <am> (abbreviation marker) tag is used inside the <abbr> tag, marking "a sequence of letters or signs present in an abbreviation which are omitted or replaced in the expanded form of the abbreviation" (TEI Guidelines 11.3.1.2).[11] Similarly, inside the <expan> tags, an <ex> (editorial expansion) is used to annotate "a sequence of letters added by an editor or transcriber when expanding an abbreviation" (TEI Guidelines 11.3.1.2). The tagging of abbreviations, Latin sections, line breaks and individual words enabled us to carry out the quantitative analyses presented in the following section.

---

10 See also Cummings (2009), Driscoll (2009) and Stutzmann (2014) for the application of similar systems of encoding.

11 Because the aim of the paper was a corpus study and not displaying the abbreviations, we used names for all of them (e.g. hook).

4 Results and analysis

The natural starting point for studying the disappearance of abbreviations and suspensions is to provide descriptive statistics on how much they were used. While the higher number of abbreviations in Latin compared to the vernacular is often noted (Hector 1958: 36–37; Hasenohr 2002: 82–83; Laing 2013: 3.4.5.1), there are not many quantitative studies which would give us exact numbers; these would be useful for giving us some indication of what to expect. There are, however, a couple of recent studies. Stutzmann et al. (2018) report ca. 60% for Latin and 30% for French in a corpus comprising registers and formularies connected to the French royal chancery in the fourteenth and fifteenth centuries. Honkapohja (2018: 250–251) finds a mean abbreviation density of 34.8% for Latin recipes and a mean density of 9.2% in Middle English in medical texts copied ca. 1450–1490. These figures give some indication of what to expect with roughly contemporaneous data. However, it has to be noted that they represent different genres: administrative texts and medical treatises and recipes. Neither of the studies are structured diachronically.

4.1 Abbreviation density

Firstly, we calculated the abbreviation densities for the manuscripts and printed editions. These were counted by dividing the number of abbreviated words (<abbr> tags) by the word count (<w> tags). Figures 9.2, 9.3 and 9.4 display the abbreviation densities in chronological order. They reveal major differences between Latin and English frequencies, and a different rate of disappearance.

The most immediately striking aspect of the results displayed in Figure 9.2, which shows the combined abbreviation density of Latin and English, is how much more frequent abbreviation is in Latin than it is in Middle English. This is precisely what manuscript scholars are well aware of, but which has only rarely been quantified. In the *Polychronicon* manuscripts, more than half of the words, 55.49%, are abbreviated in the Latin Hu, whereas the two most heavily abbreviated English manuscripts, H and F, only abbreviate between 20 and 30% of the words: 26.82% and 23.36%, respectively. The figures for both Latin and Middle English are slightly lower than those reported by Honkapohja (2018) or Stutzmann et al. (2018). The likely explanations are genre and grade, as the *Polychronicon* manuscripts are *de luxe* productions, whereas Honkapohja examined medical texts and Stutzmann et al. administrative documents. Abbreviations were used more in less important and more utilitarian and workmanlike texts and copies (Roberts 2005: 9–12; Kopaczyk 2011: 95).

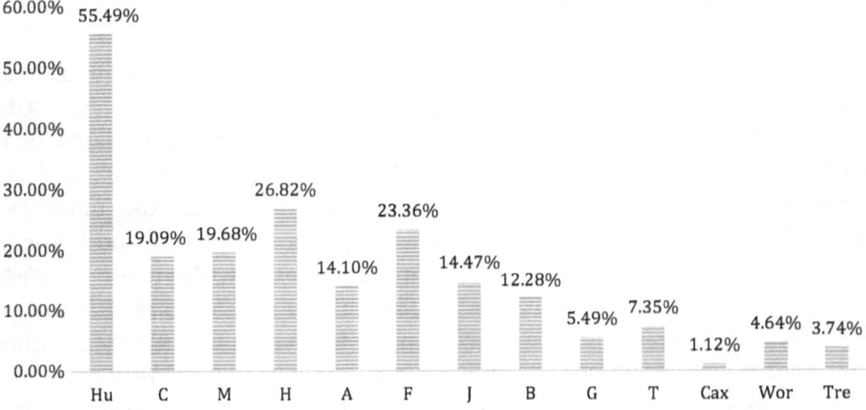

Figure 9.2: Abbreviation density, English and Latin combined.

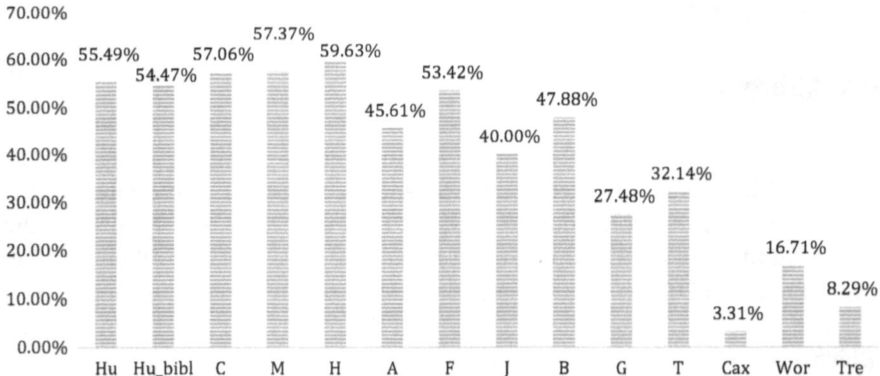

Figure 9.3: Abbreviation density, Latin.

The *Polychronicon* corpus is, however, able to provide us with a diachronic view to these developments. The other English manuscripts copied before the mid-fifteenth century (C, M, A, J) contain between 10 and 20% abbreviated words. The overall density drops close to 10% and below in the three manuscripts copied in the mid- to late fifteenth century (B, G, T), and below 5% in early printed books (Cax, Wor, Tre). There is, however, some variation between copies contemporary to each other, as the s. xv^3 manuscript T contains more abbreviations, 7.35%, than the s. xv^{med} manuscript G, in which the density is 5.49%. Even more surprisingly, the lowest number of abbreviations is used by Caxton, whereas their number is

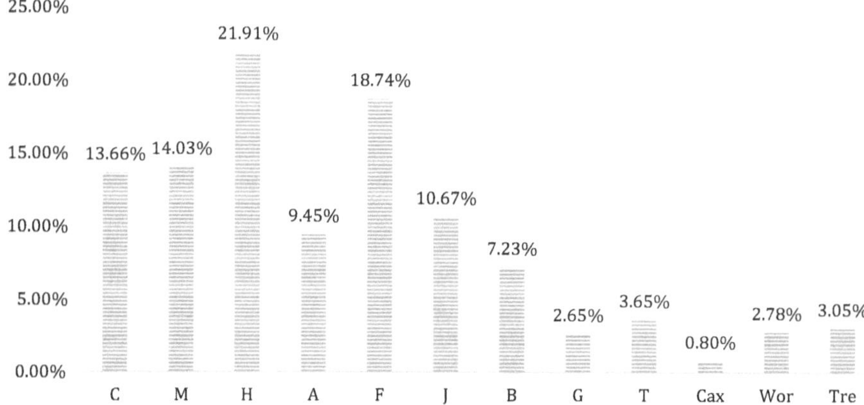

Figure 9.4: Abbreviation density, English.

higher in the two later printed books, De Worde and Treveris. These differences show that while there is a general downward trend, the reduction of abbreviations varied based on the preferences and practices of scribes and typesetters.

Looking at abbreviation densities for only the Latin sections reveals higher density, less variation and a slower decrease. These are illustrated by Figure 9.3. More than half of Latin words are abbreviated in all but two manuscripts (A and J) copied before 1425. Moreover, abbreviation density remains at least 25% even in the later manuscripts. MS B from the mid-fifteenth century still contains 53.42% of abbreviated words and G and T contain 27.48% and 32.14%, respectively. This shows that the scribes copying both languages retained the abbreviation and suspension system for Latin much longer than they did for the vernacular. A likely reason for the large amount of abbreviation in Latin is that in the present data it is used in paratextual elements as well as bibliographical information. For example, Stam (2017: 79, paraphrasing Tristram 1997) lists the economical nature of the Latin abbreviation system as one of the reasons for using Latin. Consequently, the present figures are likely to show the importance and practicality of the highly developed Latin abbreviation system in citations and headings.

What is particularly striking is that the Latin manuscript (Hu) no longer stands out as the most heavily abbreviated witness. The abbreviation density of Hu is actually lower than in three out of the four earliest English manuscripts (C, M, H). The density is lower regardless of whether the point of comparison is the entire text (Hu) or solely the sections and headings that are in Latin in all manuscripts (Hu_bibl). The abbreviation density for Hu_bibl is even slightly lower (54.47%) than the entire sample (Hu: 55.49%). This indicates that the Latin abbreviation and suspension system remained in use at least until 1425, and that, unlike in English, the decrease in density remained moderate even later in the century.

In English, the abbreviation density shows a sharper contrast between the practices of individual scribes and drops below 5% after the mid-fifteenth century. Figure 9.4 displays the abbreviation density of all the Middle English in the present data. It shows a gradual reduction that happens earlier than in Latin, but also major differences in the abbreviation profiles of individual scribes. The work of the two heavily abbreviating scribes (H, 21.97%, and F, 18.74%), in particular, stands out as they abbreviate twice as many words as the other scribes active before 1425 (C, M, A, J). Another striking feature is that the slightly later H contains several more abbreviations than the two earliest, C and M, which according to Waldron (2004: xxxix) are close to Trevisa's archetype. It has to be noted, though, that C and M both represent the work of one scribe, "The Polychronicon Scribe", as do A and J, copied by "Scribe Delta" (see section 3.2 above). It would thus appear that individual scribes largely vary in their use of abbreviations and that the abbreviation densities of scribes are fairly similar across different manuscripts they have copied. In order to understand what constitutes variation in the work of various scribes, it is necessary to look closer at which words different scribes abbreviate and which they expand.

The higher abbreviation density of the heavily abbreviating scribes, H and F, can be explained partly by their propensity to use abbreviations for frequent function words and partly by their frequent use of two general signs of abbreviation, the macron (for a nasal *frō* 'from', *secōd* 'second') and the hook (for <er>, <re> or <e>: *ʒer*^{9} 'year', *man*^{9} 'manner', *þ*^{9}*fore* 'therefore'). Table 9.2 shows the ten most frequent abbreviated words in four early manuscripts, which makes it possible to compare the practices of H and F with the less enthusiastically-abbreviating M and A. Abbreviations for small grammatical words such as & 'and' and *þ*^{t} 'that' are very high in all of the earlier manuscripts, and constitute the top two in three of the manuscripts (M, H, F). However, the scribes of H and F tend to abbreviate two additional function words, 'from' (H: 41 tokens, F: 14 tokens) and 'in' (H: 14 tokens, F: 9 tokens), which contributes to their higher abbreviation density. Manuscript A already has a much lower percentage of the ampersand (36 tokens) in comparison with the other three pre-1425 manuscripts (142, 142, 168).

Lexical words also get abbreviated and some types of abbreviation are applicable to many different words. The heavily abbreviating H and F scribes also have a number of abbreviations which both use frequently, but other scribes normally spell out, such as abbreviating 'Christ' with a superscript (H: 9 tokens, F: 12 tokens, interestingly, the Hu scribe uses Nomina Sacra based abbreviations for all of these, but the practice is completely different in the English tradition). Two abbreviations in particular, the macron and the hook, are used productively

Table 9.2: The ten most frequently abbreviated English words in the early manuscripts.

Chetham (M)		Harley (H)		Tokyo (F)		Add 24194 (A)	
& 'and'	142	& 'and'	142	& 'and'	168	& 'and'	36
þ^{t} 'that'	38	þ^{t} 'that'	52	þ^{t} 'that'	23	þ^{e} 'the'	18
vnd^{r} 'under'	11	frō 'from'	41	frā 'from'	14	secoūde 'second'	10
her^{9} 'here'	6	ī 'in'	14	all^{9} 'all'	12	oþ^{9} 'other'	7
diu^{9}sce 'diverse'	5	ʒer^{9} 'year'	10	c^{i}st 'christ'	12	ꝑtie^{s} 'parties'	6
frā 'from'	5	vnd^{9} 'under'	10	ī 'in'	9	þ^{9}fore 'therefore'	6
man^{9} 'manner'	5	c^{i}st 'christ'	9	secōd 'second'	9	acoūted 'accounted'	5
oþ^{9} 'other'	5	oþ^{9} 'other'	8	man^{9} 'manner'	6	seuē 'seven'	5
ꝑtyes 'parties'	5	bygȳnȳg 'beginning'	7	oþ^{9} 'other'	6	seuēþ 'seventh'	5
þ^{9}fore 'therefore'	5	ꝑties 'parties'	6	ꝑties 'parties'	6	acoūteþ 'accounts'	4

and can thus contribute to a higher abbreviation density. The H and F scribes, for example, use the hook in words like *ʒer^{9}* 'year' (H: 10 tokens) and *all^{9}* 'all' (F: 12 tokens), and the macron in words like *bygȳnȳg* 'beginning' (H: 7 tokens). However, these abbreviations do not affect the overall density as much as the frequent function words. Scribe Delta (A and J), who is the least abbreviating scribe before 1425, uses the macron very frequently, abbreviating numerals such as *secoūde* 'second' (10), *seuē* 'seven' (5) and *seuēþ* 'seventh' (5) and verbs *acoūted* 'accounted' (5), *acoūteþ* 'accounts' (4). Nevertheless, his lower frequency of using the ampersand (36) and omission of *þ^{t}* 'that' brings the overall density down. Consequently, because of their frequency, function words constitute a major part of an individual scribe's abbreviation repertoire. By the mid-fifteenth century, the scribes copying the English *Polychronicon* were usually expanding them.

The habit of the later scribes of spelling out function words becomes striking when one moves to the manuscripts copied in the latter half of the fifteenth century. The majority of abbreviations in Table 9.3, which shows abbreviations from the three manuscripts dated to the mid- to late fifteenth century, are lexical words. There is one exception, since the scribe of T uses the ampersand

Table 9.3: The ten most frequently abbreviated words in the late manuscripts.

San Marino (B)		Hunter 367 (G)		Taylor (T)	
age^{s} 'ages'[12]	34	eu^{9}ych 'every'	4	& 'and'	57
oþ^{9} 'other'	9	t^{a}nsmig^{a}cioun a 'transmigration'	4	comoū 'common'	2
ꝑties 'parties'	6	abrah^{a}m 'Abraham'	3	sūme 'some'	2
sōme 'some'	6	man^{9} 'manner'	3	Abrah^{a}m 'Abraham'	1
Man^{9} 'manner'	5	mē 'men'	3	accoūt 'account'	1
Ryu^{9} 'river'	5	descripcioū 'description'	2	Cesar^{9} 'Caesar'	1
diu^{9}se 'diverse'	4	incarnacioū 'incarnation'	2	comoū 'common'	1
eu^{9}ech 'every'	4	Isrł 'Israel'	2	correccioū 'correction'	1
secūde 'second'	4	ꝓporcioū 'proportion'	2	cūnyng 'cunning'	1
t^{a}nsmigracion 'transmigration'	4	sūme 'some'	2	deꝑted 'departed'	1

frequently (57 tokens). It is this frequency that causes the slight increase in abbreviation density from the mid-fifteenth century to the third quarter (see Figure 9.4 above). If one does not take the ampersand into consideration, there is a steady reduction in abbreviation counts. The frequencies of words making it to the list are also generally lower. The only other abbreviated word with more than ten tokens for this period is the practice of the B scribe to abbreviate 'ages' with a superscript <s> (34 tokens). The frequencies of abbreviated lexical words, in contrast, do not experience a rapid drop but rather a slow and steady reduction as the century progresses. Thus, the major drop in the abbreviation density is caused by the fact that scribes cease to use the abbreviated forms of function words. Surprisingly, they do experience a small-scale renaissance in the early printed books (see Table 9.4).

12 Strictly speaking the form *age^{s}* is not an abbreviation as it does not shorten the word. It does, however, serve the function of saving space.

Table 9.4: The most frequently abbreviated English words in the early printed books.

Caxton (Cax)		**De Worde (Wor)**		**Treveris (Tre)**	
& 'and'	10	& 'and'	34	y^{e} 'the'	19
acoūted 'accounted'	1	y^{e} 'the'	13	& 'and'	13
acoūten 'account'	1	y^{t} 'that'	6	y^{t} 'that'	4
circūsicōn 'circumcision'	1	acoūte 'account'	2	acoūted 'accounted'	2
venemo9 'venomous'	1	acoūted 'accounted'	2	foūdē '[was] found'	2
		foūden '[was] found'	1	mē 'men'	2
		Gouernȳge 'governing'	1	Whā 'when'	2
		Normās 'Normans'	1	wōdres 'wonders'	2
		ꝓuynce 'province'	1	wrytē 'write'	2
		quātyte 'quantity'	1	acountē 'account'	1

Table 9.4 shows two developments. On the one hand, there is a further reduction in the types and density for abbreviations of lexical words; on the other, a small "standard" set of abbreviations has emerged. This small set of popular types used by the printers comprises the ampersand (&) and the superscript abbreviations *y*^{e} 'the' and *y*^{t} 'that'. We will refer to it as the Standard Printer Set of Abbreviations (henceforth SPSA). The higher abbreviation density of De Worde and Treveris compared to Caxton is largely explained by the absence of two items from SPSA, as Caxton only uses the ampersand. Other types of abbreviations are still used occasionally. All of the typesetters sometimes abbreviate a nasal with the macron. The macron, too, is used by De Worde and Treveris slightly more often. Moreover, all still make occasional use of Latin abbreviations for Romance loan words, such as *venemo9* 'venomous' by Caxton or *ꝓuynce* 'province' by De Worde.[13] This indicates that they did have these types as a part of their printing sets, even if they were not used very frequently.

Interestingly, two of the abbreviations which later became part of the SPSA, *þ*^{t} 'that' and *w*^{t} 'with' (which is not used by the scribes in the present *Polychronicon* data), are discussed by Samuels (1983), who observes their

13 De Worde also uses the 9 '-us' abbreviation for a number of Latin words, including personal names: *Methodi9* 'Methodius', *Marian9* 'Marianus'.

frequencies in connection with Types II and III of London English and diachronic change between 1400 and 1420. His data consist of samples from one scribe, known as scribe B (cf. Doyle and Parkes 1978), perhaps to be identified as Adam Pinkhurst (cf. Mooney 2006), who copied the two earliest *Canterbury Tales* manuscripts.[14] Samuels examines the proportion of *þ*^{t} and *that* used by the scribe in the stints he contributed to three manuscripts.[15] He notes far fewer uses of the abbreviated form in the latest manuscript, and explains this with changes in the scribal habits of scribe B (Samuels 1983: 51). The scribe was adapting to changes of spelling fashions in London, which had "only recently undergone a complete metamorphosis [...] from type II to type III" (1983: 53). This change happened in 1400–1420 and "was crucial for the development of Standard English, for it was from the competing and changing fashions in spellings at this time that the new written standard was to evolve" (1983: 53). One of the changes Samuels mentions was an overall move away from thorn, which is also reflected in the abbreviated form, as "*þ* was obsolescent in London by this period and being replaced by *th*" (1983: 59).[16]

Even though the change happens slightly later, our data is generally in line with Samuels' observations. The proportion of *þ*^{t} does decrease sharply after the early fifteenth century, so it appears that there was a shift in fashion of the practices of scribes contributing to these types of *de luxe* books. The copyists of M, C, H and F (see Table 9.9 below) use it as the major form; others as a minor form, probably when the constraints of space require it. Nevertheless, the abbreviated forms did not disappear completely, and they survived into printed books, which shows that they were still part of the repertoire. In addition to their appropriation by early printers, abbreviations like *y*^{e} 'the' and *y*^{t} 'that' were used in correspondence centuries later. Our results also show that it is necessary to look at how the frequencies of different abbreviation types developed diachronically, which will be the focus of the next section.

14 For criticism of Mooney's identification, see Roberts (2011) and Warner (2015, 2018). For a different account of spellings, see Thaisen (2011), who discusses his short and long variants in terms of space.

15 These are the "Hengwrt Chaucer" Peniarth MS 392D, the "Ellesmere Chaucer" Huntington Library, in San Marino, California (EL 26 C 9), and a copy of Gower in Cambridge, Trinity College, MS R.3.2.

16 Thaisen (2011: 84) attributes this variation purely to constraints of time and space. Samuels (1983: 58–59) also notes a shift in the proportions of & and *and* in favour of the expanded variant.

4.2 Abbreviation types

Developments in frequencies of abbreviation types have been the subject of a few interesting discoveries, but these have mainly focused on a few individual types. The view in palaeographical handbooks is that abbreviating in the vernacular never was as common as in Latin. Both Hector (1958) and Petti (1977: 22) note that the Latin system reached its most elaborate form by the twelfth century and then began to decrease. According to Hector (1958: 28): "After about 1200 no new abbreviations were introduced into the writing of Latin, and during the later Middle Ages some of those that had formerly been in regular use were gradually discarded". He, however, does note their presence in Latin documents after 1500 (1958: 38). The English system was based on the Latin one from the beginning. For example, Hector (1958: 37) says that it was applied to native proper names in Latin documents and "when archives came to be written in English language there was thus already established a tradition". Petti (1977: 22) notes a general pattern of reduction, but also survival to the Renaissance in formulaic uses.[17] The expected overall picture is one of gradual reduction.

Nonetheless, there are some results which point to exceptions to this overall trend. One of these is identified by Samuels (1983), who, in contrast to his proposed drop in frequencies for *þ*^{t}, notes that the frequencies of some abbreviations actually increase. These include a shift from expanded <er> to abbreviated ꝰ 'er', "from *h* to crossed *h* [...] and *d* to tailed *d*" (58) as well as from *with* to *w*^{t}. Thus, according to him, the move from Type II to III by 1420 also involved an increase of a few common types of abbreviation. These observations are supported by recent work on Older Scots and continental French.

The Older Scots results are presented by Smith (2019: 202–203, 208), who studied the use of a single abbreviation, the final loop ƒ for '-is' plural in legal documents from 1380 to 1500 in the *Linguistic Atlas of Older Scots* (LAOS). Smith suggests that "as vernacular writing became more common, scribes began to use more 'shorthand' features" (2019: 208). Moreover, she notes that scribes from densely populated Lowland repositories of Scotland use it more than ones in more peripheral areas.

Similar developments in which some abbreviations increase in frequency have been noted by French scholars, who have elaborated them into a hypothesis. French scholarship on abbreviations consists of observational work by

17 Parkes (2008 [1969]: preface), which would be the most directly relevant source for the Anglicana and Secretary hands in the present study, does not discuss abbreviations due to "limitations of space".

Bozzolo et al. (1990), Careri et al. (2001), Hasenohr (2002) and Careri et al (2011). Their observations are studied quantitatively using a small corpus of manuscripts of *La Chanson d'Otinel* by Camps (2016). The French account of Latin abbreviations is essentially in line with Hector (1958) and Petti (1977). The number of abbreviations in Latin multiplied up to the twelfth-century renaissance, which saw an expansion of written culture outside monasteries, and even a new scholastic way of reading and writing, which differed from the slow meditative reading practised in monasteries (Hasenohr 2002: 81–82). In contrast, vernacular romance manuscripts copied in the twelfth century lack abbreviations almost completely (2002: 81–82).[18] But whereas the density and type count of Latin abbreviations gradually decreased after the twelfth century, the vernacular abbreviation system grew increasingly independent of it in a process that can be labelled *francisation* 'Frenchisisation' (Camps 2016: cclix).

It seems likely that a similar process took place in English, which explains the developments noted by Samuels (1983) and Smith (2019). Some parts of the abbreviation system, such as the hook ꝰ for <er, re, e> or final loop ꝭ for plural <is, ys, es> proved useful for vernacular copyists. As scribes became increasingly fluent in using them and more and more vernacular texts were copied, their frequency increased. If this kind of process is found to take place it could be labelled "Anglicisation" or maybe just "vernacularisation" of the abbreviation system. But what kind of developments can we observe for various abbreviation types in the *Polychronicon* corpus?

In order to study how the frequencies of various abbreviations change over time, we will apply a type of diagram commonly used in variationist sociolinguistics: the S-curve. The S-curve is useful in illustrating how the variant forms of a linguistic variable change diachronically (see, e.g., Kroch 1989; Labov 1994: 65–67; Kretzschmar and Stenroos 2012; Nevalainen 2015). To compare mean frequencies, the twelve English samples were divided into four periods, each consisting of three manuscripts/books.[19] Mean frequencies were counted for each period.

18 This corresponds to what Laing (2013: 3.4.5.1) notes for the *Linguistic Atlas of Early Middle English* (LAEME).

19 This division has some problems: Firstly, the two first sub-periods have three manuscripts, but each period represents the output of only two scribes. However, both of them also contain one outlier, that is, a manuscript containing exceptionally many abbreviations, which balances them out. Secondly, the third sub-period is longer than the others, covering 50 years. However, in here the results do provide some useful generalisations. The B scribe is considerably more conservative than the G scribe, even though Waldron (2004) dates both of these manuscripts to s. xv^{med}. On the whole, this division into sub-periods did provide some significant results using the s-curve.

Early manuscripts: M, C, H
1400–1425: F, A, J
1425–1475: B, G, T
Printed books (1484–1527): Cax, Wor, Tre

To keep the number of variables manageable, the abbreviation types were grouped into six categories:[20] (1) the ampersand (&), (2) the macron (*circūsicōn* 'circumsicion'), (3) the hook (*euꝰych* 'every'), (4) other brevigraphs (*ꝓuynce* 'province', *ꝑtie*^{s} 'parties'), (5) superscripts (*þ*^{t} 'that', *abrah*^{a}*m* 'Abraham'), (6) the strikethrough (crossing the ascender in certain letters such as ħ or ł, sometimes indicating a final <e>, sometimes otiose). The reason for treating the macron and the hook on their own is their high frequency. These two abbreviations could be highly productive: together with the ampersand, these abbreviations represent much more than half of all the abbreviations in the data. On the other hand, there are numerous other brevigraphs, which is an umbrella term for Latin-based abbreviations which sometimes resemble the letters they replace and sometimes have an apparently arbitrary shape (Petti 1977: 23). As there are several fairly low frequency brevigraphs, treating them as separate would only show too many very low frequency items to be of use. Superscript abbreviations cause the same problem. Moreover, as they are part of the Latin alphabet, they are an open-ended category, which can lead to a high number of types. Consequently, these six categories treat categories 1 to 3 as individual types, while categories 4–6 are amalgams of several less frequent types. Together they offer an illuminating overview of the diachronic developments that took place from the late fourteenth to the early sixteenth century.

The S-curves reveal how the slower decrease, evident in the density diagrams, progresses with respect to abbreviation types. Figures 9.5 and 9.6 illustrate how these take place. In English, there is a major overall decrease between the second period and the third period (after 1425). In Latin, however, all types remain fairly frequent even in the final manuscript period (1425–1475), but there is a drop in the frequencies of all types except brevigraphs and macrons.

Some abbreviation types show a surprising increase in the early period. One of these is the macron, which actually increases in English from the first period to the second. There are two possible explanations for this. One is related to

20 These categories are based on a system of taxonomies that can be found in many palaeographical handbooks. The system was first introduced by Chassant ([1845] 1970), and very influential versions of it are presented by Cappelli (1990) and Petti (1977). For an account of various abbreviation categories as well as their treatment in handbook literature, see Honkapohja (2013: sections 1 to 4).

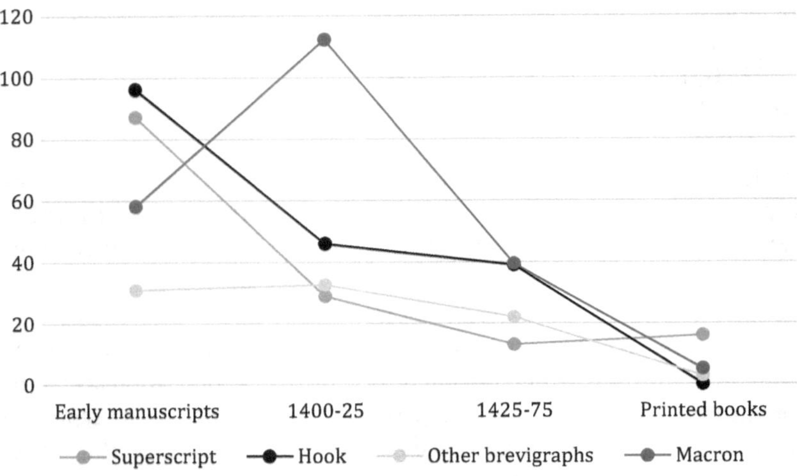

Figure 9.5: Diachronic changes in mean number of abbreviation types in English.[21]

Frenchisisation. Camps (2016: cclix) notes that, while there is a drop in the diversity of abbreviation types after the twelfth century, the density of a few common abbreviation types, especially the macron, may increase both in Latin and French. If an increase in the use macron in English in this period is corroborated by other studies we could indeed speak of the "Anglicisation" or "vernacularisation" of the abbreviation system. On the other hand it has to be kept in mind that our corpus is fairly small and the same developments could also simply be due to scribal preferences.

Indeed, there is support for the explanation that the reason can be found in scribal preferences. The "Polychronicon Scribe" of C and M does not use the macron very much, whereas "Scribe Delta" (A and J) and the "Trevisa-Gower Scribe" (F) both use it frequently (see Table 9.2). A similar jump can be observed also for the parts that are in Latin, as the mean number of macrons and hooks increases from Hu to the early English manuscripts. This is because the "Polychronicon Scribe" uses the macron for Latin, although he does not use it for English. Moreover, he and the Harley scribe (H) make much use of the convention of writing Latin endings in superscript. These increases are consistent

21 The figure omits two categories: ampersand and strikethrough. For ampersand, see Figure. 9.7. Strikethrough, on the other hand, is very infrequent: the mean numbers are (4.3333, 3.3333, 1.666667, 0).

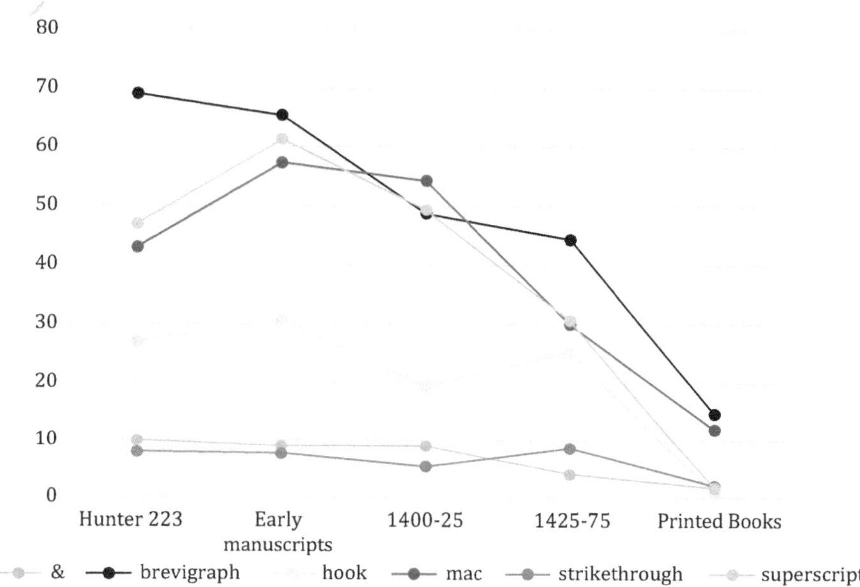

Figure 9.6: Diachronic changes in mean number of abbreviation types in Latin.[22]

with the fact that the abbreviation density for Latin is higher in English manuscripts before 1425 than in Hu (see Figure 9.3 above).

Both English and Latin abbreviation repertoires experience change and reduction from manuscript to print. All types of abbreviation are present in the third period, but the repertoire of abbreviations is much reduced in printed books. In addition to the macron, which is sometimes used in both languages, there are two specific developments for English and Latin. In Latin the main type of abbreviations that remain in use are brevigraphs. In English, the emergence of SPSA causes a slight increase for superscript abbreviations from late manuscripts to printed books.

Figure 9.7 illustrates the mean density of abbreviating 'and', 'the' and 'that' in an S-curve. It shows how, in the early period, both & 'and' and y^t 'that' are the major variant, used more than 70 per cent of the time. The development partly corresponds with what Samuels mentions of the use of the abbreviated form of 'that' in two *Canterbury Tales* manuscripts. However, our results do not support his idea that y^t is caused by the shift from thorn to <th> taking place

22 For the sake of comparison we used only the part of Latin that is in Latin even in the English MSS.

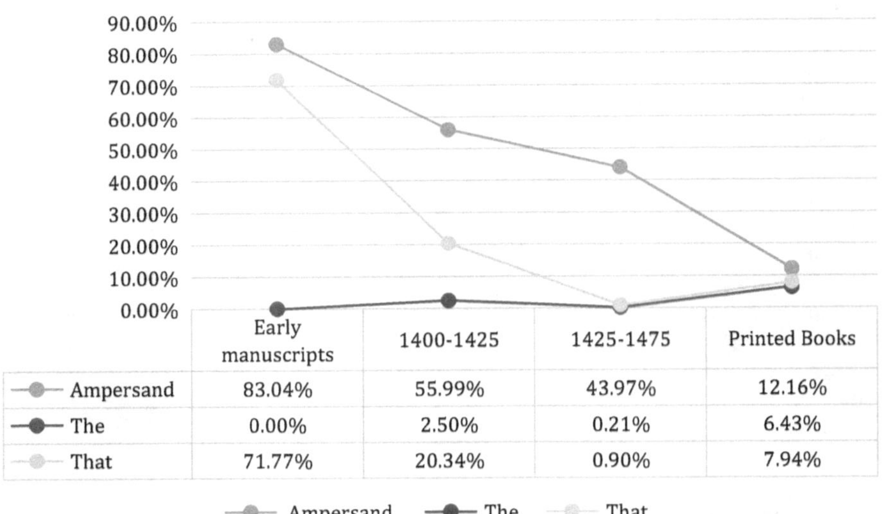

	Early manuscripts	1400-1425	1425-1475	Printed Books
Ampersand	83.04%	55.99%	43.97%	12.16%
The	0.00%	2.50%	0.21%	6.43%
That	71.77%	20.34%	0.90%	7.94%

Figure 9.7: Mean density of three SPSA abbreviations.

between 1400 and 1420. In the *Polychronicon* corpus, spellings with thorn remain the majority form until manuscript witnesses G and T, which are from the middle of the century (see Table 9.5 for 'the' and Table 9.9 for 'that'), whereas a drop in the number of the abbreviated forms happened by 1425.

The proportion of abbreviating 'and' shows a fairly steady decrease up to printed books, in which the word is still abbreviated 12.16% of the time. The two thorn-based abbreviations are not quite as frequent, partly because Caxton does not use them (see Table 9.4 above), but both show the interesting development in which the mean frequency of the abbreviated forms increases with printing. The superscript variant of the definite article, *y^e^*, is a particularly interesting case as it is not abbreviated by the scribes of the early manuscripts and only once between 1425 and 1475, but is clearly part of the repertoire of the typesetters of De Worde (13 tokens) and Treveris (19 tokens). To shed light on what is causing this curve, we will next examine the actual forms.

Table 9.5 shows the distribution of spellings for the definite article. It clearly deviates from the expected development in which a gradual elimination of variants takes place. The two early scribes, H and M, are completely consistent in spelling the word expanded and with an initial thorn: *þe*. However, the scribes working in the next period, 1400–1425, use several spelling variants, including as many as four different ones used by the scribes of F and J. Nevertheless, abbreviations of the definite article remain the minority form, as only one scribe (A) abbreviates the word more than ten times

Table 9.5: Distribution of variants of 'the'.

Early manuscripts	**M**	**þe**	**235**						
	H	þe	242						
1400–1425	A	þe	219	þ^{e}	18	the	3		
	F	þe	215	the	20	þ^{e}	5	þþe	2
	J	þe	223	þ^{e}	7	the	7	þhe	1
1425-1475	B	þe	243						
	G	the	238						
	T	the	227	þ^{e}	1				
Printed Books	Cax	the	253						
	Wor	the	246	y^{e}	13				
	Tre	the	220	y^{e}	19				

(18 tokens). The next period, 1425–1475, sees a step toward standardisation and the emergence of <th> spellings, but only a single token of the abbreviated variant. However, De Worde and Treveris make occasional use of the abbreviation as an alternative to the already modern spelling. In Latin manuscripts, a bigger set of abbreviations remained in use.

One of the characteristic features of the Latin abbreviation system were the so-called brevigraphs, many of which first emerge in the fifth and sixth centuries (cf. Lindsay 1915: 3; Hasenohr 2002: 80). A number of brevigraphs were also applied to English, such as the ubiquitous hook, as well as ꝓ 'pro' and ꝑ 'per/par', which were useful for Romance loan words such as *proporcion*, *profit*, *departed*, *persones*. However, the number of brevigraphs used for English was no match for the great range of variety found in Latin. Figure 9.8 below shows the mean number of brevigraphs (other than hook), for each period, in English and Latin.[23] Despite the ten times higher word count for English in our data, these types of abbreviations are more common in Latin. They also remain in use by early printers, especially in Latin but occasionally also in English.

Two printers, De Worde and Treveris, use brevigraphs for the Latin bibliographical section. Figure 9.9 shows the brevigraphs and macrons used by

23 The Latin point of comparison is with Hu_bibl, that is, the part that remains in Latin in the English translations.

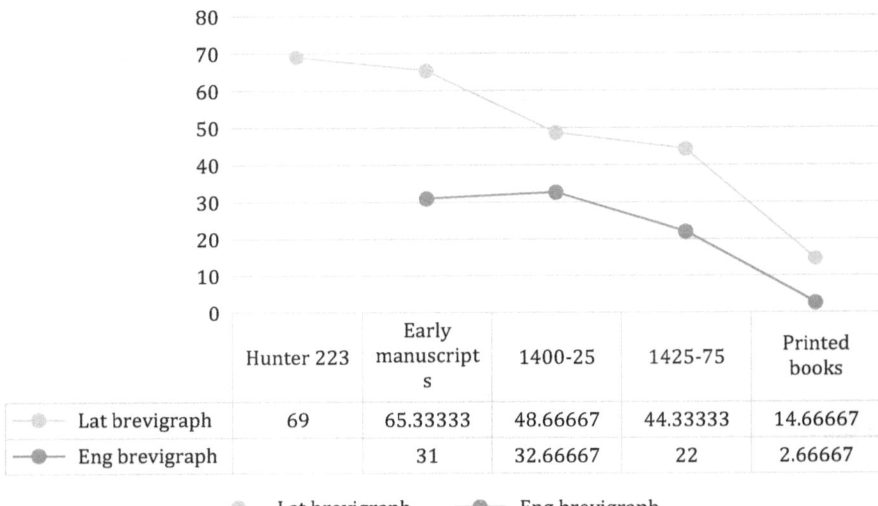

	Hunter 223	Early manuscripts	1400-25	1425-75	Printed books
Lat brevigraph	69	65.33333	48.66667	44.33333	14.66667
Eng brevigraph		31	32.66667	22	2.66667

Figure 9.8: Diachronic changes in mean number of brevigraphs.

Figure 9.9: Latin abbreviations used by Caxton and De Worde (Left: *The Polychronicon*, William Caxton, 1482 (STC 13438). © British Library Board (G.6011-12, f. 7r). Image published with permission of ProQuest. Further reproduction is prohibited without permission. Right: *The Polychronicon*, Wynkyn De Worde, 1495 (STC 13439). © British Library Board (C.11.b.2., f. 5r). Image published with permission of ProQuest. Further reproduction is prohibited without permission. Images produced by ProQuest as part of *Early English Books Online*. www.proquest.com.).

Caxton and De Worde. Perhaps surprisingly, De Worde uses them very frequently. Individual examples such as the Latin word *triptita* 'three-part' (illustrated in the figure) and the word *venemo9* 'venomous' (see Table 9.4 above) reveal, however, that these symbols were included in Caxton's printing type sets. It is possible that De Worde uses more abbreviations because of the two-column layout. Therefore, we will next investigate the effects of material limitations on abbreviation frequencies.

4.3 Developments in book production

One of the major questions this study aims to answer is how far the abbreviations were conditioned by technology and how far by standardisation, as the fifteenth century also saw the so-called paper revolution, which made book production cheaper and thus may have reduced the need for abbreviation. There are also changes in the *mise-en-page*, since some of the manuscripts have a double-column layout and some a single-column one. Moreover, there is a shift from Anglicana hands to Secretary hands. The purpose of this section is to examine these changes.

The first change to be discussed is paper. The English versions of the *Polychronicon* are high-grade manuscripts, and continue to be copied on parchment until the late fifteenth century. None of the manuscript copies included in this study is on paper, whereas all of the three printed books (Cax, Wor and Tre) are. The major reduction for English abbreviations happens from the first quarter of the fifteenth century to the mid-fifteenth century (see Figures 9.4 and 9.5) and the major reduction of Latin abbreviations from manuscripts to print (see Figures 9.3 and 9.6). While the present data do not allow us to draw conclusions of the influence of writing support (as opposed to the influence of print technology), it would appear that the switch from parchment to paper is not an important dividing line, as the number of English abbreviations begins to decline in the manuscripts copied on parchment.

The second change comes with the script used to copy the body of the text. The majority of the manuscripts in the data are copied in varieties of the Anglicana script, mainly Anglicana formata, which was a common book script used in fourteenth-century England (see Parkes 2008 [1969]: xvii). The manuscripts dating from the period 1425–1475 display Secretary or Secretary-influenced hands: B has two scribes working on the *Polychronicon*, one of whom writes Anglicana and Secretary, the other Secretary. G is copied in Anglicana with some Secretary forms. T is copied in Bastard Secretary, a script which mixes Secretary with Textura influences in the style of the French Bastarde script (Parkes 2008 [1969]: xxi). The choice of script depends on the preferences of the commissioner and the scribe, but also the current fashion. The higher abbreviation frequencies seem to correlate with Anglicana. With the limited data it is difficult to say, however, if the script is a deciding factor or if the low frequencies attested in the Secretary manuscripts are due to a general decrease in the number of abbreviations in this period.[24]

A general question is whether abbreviations are simply used to save space, as this was always one of the main reasons to use an abbreviated variant instead of spelling the word out (see Samuels 1983: 59; Thaisen 2011: 84). Petti (1977: 22) notes that abbreviation could also be used "for keeping lines of writing of equal length, rather like 'justifying' in printing". If they are used for this purpose, one would expect them to be more frequent closer to the right margin. Indeed, Shute (2017a) discovered that early modern printers used abbreviations as one of two main strategies for right-margin justification: that is, when they needed to fit a word on a page, they could use an abbreviation to make it fit (see also Camps 2016: ccli–ccliii).

In order to investigate whether we can reproduce the effect discovered by Shute, we calculated the proximity of <am> tags to <lb> tags that signify a line break. Each line was divided into five bins. The bins were summed up.[25] If abbreviations were used for justification, we would expect the number in the rightmost bin to be significantly higher than others. If they were not, then the variation would not likely be statistically significant.

The results reveal that right-margin justification is an important conditioning factor in manuscripts, too, but also that it does not apply all the time (see tables 9.6 and 9.7). In most cases, the number of abbreviations is highest in the rightmost bin (see Figures 9.10 and 9.11). However, neither Latin nor English shows large enough differences to be statistically significant for the four earliest manuscripts (Hu, C, M, H). The differences become overwhelmingly significant in English manuscripts dated to the first quarter of the fifteenth century. This change corresponds with the change to a two-column layout (see Table 9.7). With regard to the manuscripts from the latter half of the century and the early printed books, the results are less clear. The results are not statistically significant for T or, perhaps surprisingly, Wor. However, the token counts for printed books are so much lower for the later period that the element of random chance cannot be ruled out. In Latin, the differences are not statistically

24 A similar question can be raised regarding the printed books: to what extent do characteristics such as the size of a typeface influence the compositors' abbreviation practices, in addition to the obvious limitations imposed by the selection of types? Pursuing this question is, unfortunately, outside the scope of the present study.

25 For this calculation, abbreviations that were part of headings or marginal headings were omitted, which means that the numbers are slightly lower than the ones reported in overall counts. In addition, a number of exceptionally short or long lines were omitted.

Table 9.6: Right margin justification, Latin.

MS	Date	Matr	Cols	bin 1	bin 2	bin 3	bin 4	bin 5	p-value	
Hu	s. xiv	parch	one	244	255	282	258	303	0.076738	NO
C	s. xiv/xv	parch	one	25	33	34	32	35	0.740386	NO
M	s. xiv/xv	parch	one	29	30	32	32	34	0.975033	NO
H	s. xv(in)	parch	one	42	47	57	43	60	0.245256	NO
A	s. xv(1)	parch	two	18	22	27	30	27	0.453781	NO
F	s. xv(1)	parch	two	34	26	22	35	32	0.381171	NO
J	s. xv(1)	parch	two	16	19	26	16	23	0.419709	NO
B	s. xv(med)	parch	two	22	30	25	29	38	0.277467	NO
G	s. xv(med)	parch	two	12	10	13	13	20	0.378859	NO
T	s. xv(3)	parch	two	12	10	14	15	19	0.511199	NO
Cax	1482	paper	one	0	0	2	4	5	0.0053	**YES**
Wor	1495	paper	two	8	11	10	11	16	0.540058	NO
Tre	1527	paper	two	2	6	5	4	14	0.008399	**YES**

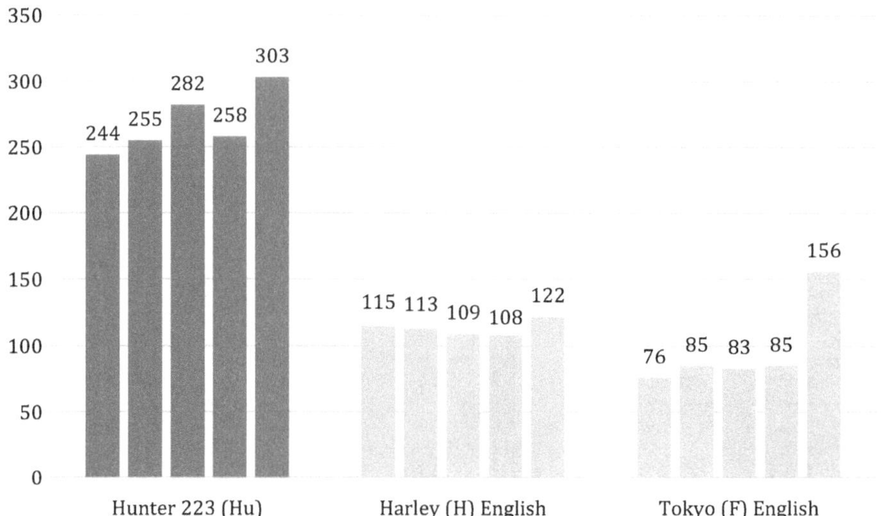

Figure 9.10: Right margin justification in three early manuscripts.

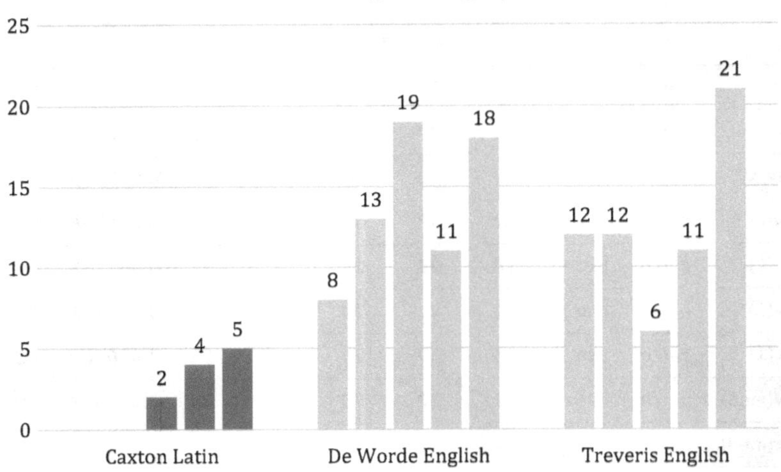

Figure 9.11: Right margin justification in three early printed books.

Table 9.7: Right margin justification, English.

MS	Date	Matr	Cols	bin 1	bin 2	bin 3	bin 4	bin 5	p-value	
Hu	s. xiv	parch	one							
C	s. xiv/xv	parch	one	64	59	55	55	61	0.904595	NO
M	s. xiv/xv	parch	one	34	26	40	38	33	0.490888	NO
H	s. xv(in)	parch	one	115	113	109	108	122	0.893628	NO
A	s. xv(1)	parch	two	34	34	35	50	80	6.26E-08	**YES**
F	s. xv(1)	parch	two	76	85	83	85	156	3.25E-09	**YES**
J	s. xv(1)	parch	two	45	48	40	53	85	9.97E-05	**YES**
B	s. xv(med)	parch	two	28	30	43	29	55	0.004758	**YES**
G	s. xv(med)	parch	two	15	10	11	18	16	0.511199	NO
T	s. xv(3)	parch	two	13	14	20	13	28	0.047464	**YES**
Cax	1482	paper	one	3	3	7	2	6	0.34538	NO
Wor	1495	paper	two	8	13	19	11	18	0.178522	NO
Tre	1527	paper	two	12	12	6	11	21	0.050751	NO

significant, except in the early printed books – even though the right hand bin is always the biggest (see Table 9.6).

The fact that abbreviations are most frequent in the rightmost bin, but the difference in the earlier manuscripts is so small that it could be due to random chance, suggests that while the economy of space was always an important conditioning factor for abbreviating, there were also other reasons to use them in the fourteenth century. When the abbreviation and suspension system began to fall out of use, these results seem to suggest that it still continued to be used for line justification purposes. Shute's results suggest that the system was adapted to this end by the early printers (cf. Shute 2017a). The genre may also affect the results, since the two-column layout in *de luxe* quality required the scribes to produce very even margins; to achieve this they used the abbreviations as a justification device in the manner noted by Petti (1977:22).

From the point of view of standardisation, however, our results suggest that, as the system began to disappear, the function of justification was among the last to survive, as this use was appropriated by early printers. One major question remains, however: Was the disappearance of abbreviations an independent process or did the abbreviations disappear as a part of the elimination of spelling variations? In the next section, we compare how abbreviation density corresponds with spelling variation.

4.4 Spelling variation

The final topic we examine in this study is how the reduction in the number of abbreviations corresponds with reduction in the number of English spellings. The main research question here is whether we are dealing with two sides of the same phenomenon or two separate phenomena. This is important, as our theoretical framework presumes gradual elimination of variation in the course of the fifteenth century towards proto-standard English. Moreover, statistical approaches require independent populations to establish that the observed reduction in abbreviation (sections 4.1 and 4.2) is not simply a by-product of an overall drop in variation at this point. A secondary research question is to determine whether the spelling variants data are distributed as in a complex system.

In order not to confuse the two figures into the same data, we performed the counts twice, both including and excluding the abbreviations. The reason for this approach was that on the one hand several scholars argue that the abbreviated spellings should be treated as legitimate spelling variants of their own (Lass 2004; Driscoll 2009; Rogos 2012). On the other hand, we would not be dealing with two independent samples if reduction in abbreviations showed as reduction of spelling variants or vice versa, which might potentially confound the results.

When making the decision, we followed the following "rules". Words like *euꝰech*, *euꝰeche*, *euꝰiche*, *euꝰyche* 'every' have four spelling variants with abbreviation and four without abbreviation, because the variation is not caused by the abbreviation. Words like *grace*, *g*^{a}*ce* 'grace' have two variants including abbreviation, but only one excluding it. Words like *hundred*, *huđrid* ('hu(n)drid') have two variants including abbreviation and two variants excluding abbreviation, because even though there is both an abbreviated and an expanded form, there is also variation of the graphs and <e>. Finally, the words *hert*, *herte* were counted as having two including abbreviation and two variants excluding abbreviation, even though neither of the forms is abbreviated. Capital letters were not counted as spelling variants, but the doubling of letters (*ffrom*, *from*) was counted even when it represents a larger initial or a *littera notabilior*. The reason for this is that it can in other instances be a significant spelling variant, and we try to avoid exercising too much editorial interpretation. To keep morphological variation separate from orthographic variation, the singular and plural of each word were counted as separate words (*age* and *ages* = two different words) as were different verb forms. The results are shown in Figures 9.12, 9.13 and 9.14.[26]

Regardless of whether one counts abbreviation characters as variants or not, the results show a much slower reduction for spelling variation than for abbreviations. Figures 9.12 and 9.13 display the average number of spelling variants per words with two or more tokens, excluding abbreviation and including abbreviation. Figure 9.14 illustrates the same data using a different method of calculation: it shows the number of words in each manuscript that have three or more spelling variants, both including and excluding variation. These tables reveal that, while the proportions may vary, the relative amount of spelling variation stays the same between the various witnesses.

There is no decrease from the early manuscripts to the mid-fifteenth century. It could even be argued that there is a slight increase, as the two early scribes, H and the "Polychronicon Scribe", spell very consistently. The scribe of H in particular is the most consistent speller before early printed books, especially excluding abbreviations. The impression of a slight increase is augmented by the fact that one of the scribes in the 1400–1425 period, F, stands out as using more spelling

26 The Cotton manuscript, C, was not included in this part of the study, because it was considered too damaged to provide reliable evidence for spelling variation.

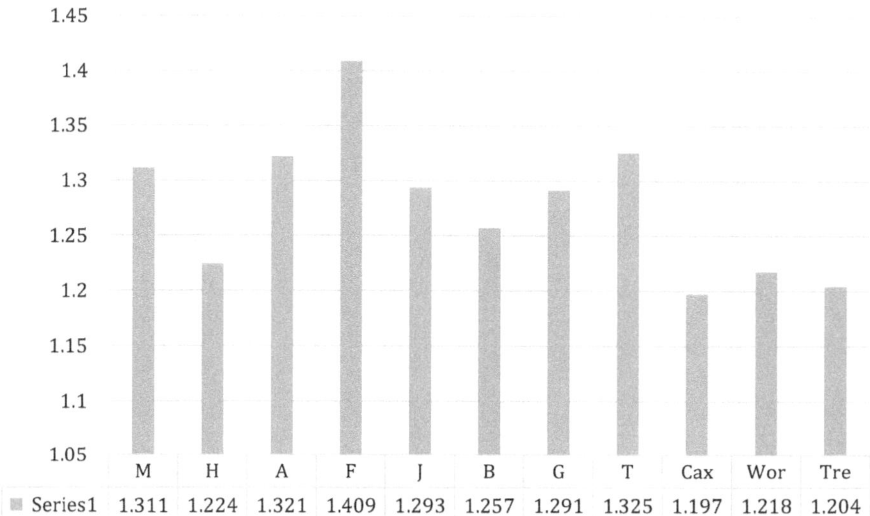

Figure 9.12: Average number of spelling variants excluding abbreviations.

variants by three out of four ways for calculating spelling variation, and as using the second highest number of variants (see Figure 9.14) after scribe A. There is, however, a slight drop from manuscript to print.

The secondary research question is to find out whether spelling variants of individual words are distributed as predicted by the linguistics of speech. To recapitulate, if this was the case, one would expect to find "a few very common variants, many uncommon variants" (Kretzschmar and Stenroos 2012). More specifically, we would expect the distribution to follow the so-called A-curve. When applied to scribal data, one would expect "that clerks wrote a majority form for a given feature, a substantial minority form, and then a tail-off of several minority forms at very low rates" (Wright 2013: 64). Moreover, we would expect some reduction towards a proto-standard form.

The results do reveal an A-curve distribution for some words, but there are major differences in the number of spelling variants for individual words (see Table 9.8). Some words are spelled very consistently even in the earliest manuscripts, some have varied forms in early printed books. A good example of consistency is how the preposition 'of' is spelled entirely consistently already in the earliest manuscript witnesses (see also 'the' in Table 9.5).[27] To some extent this is

27 The spelling with a double in MS G almost certainly indicates a *littera notabilior*.

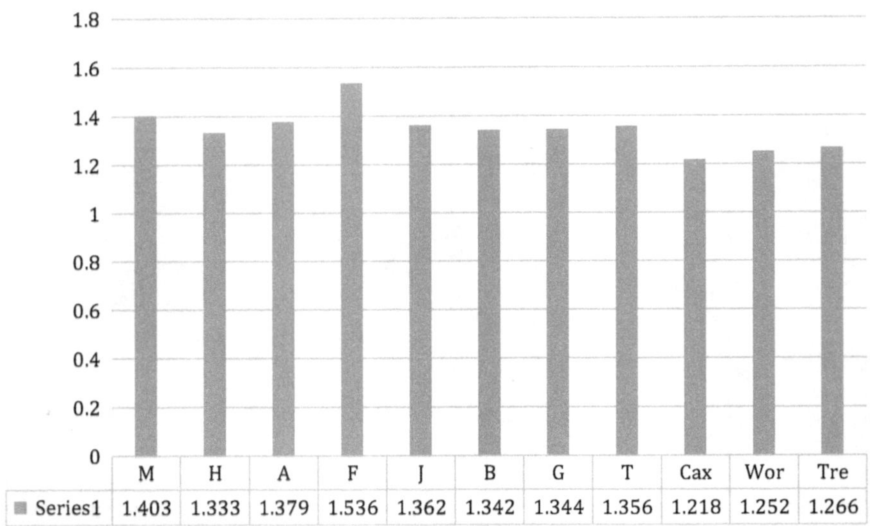

Figure 9.13: Average number of spelling variants including abbreviations.

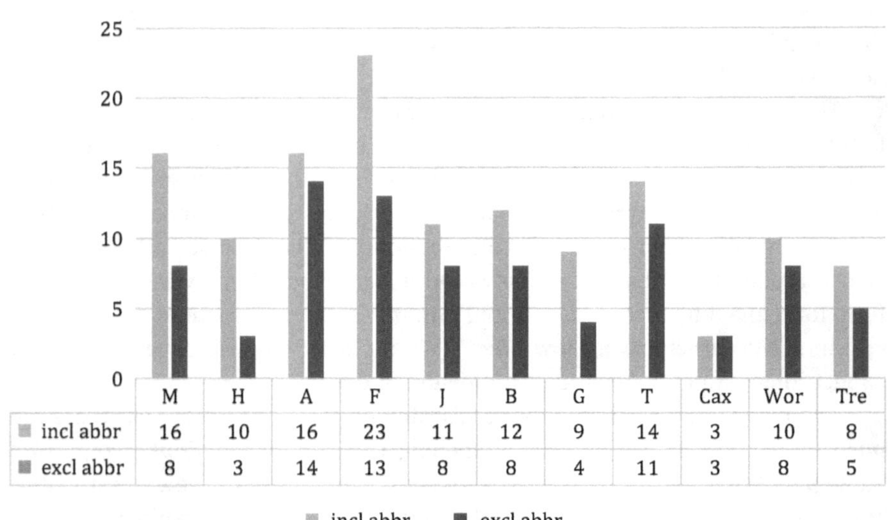

Figure 9.14: Number of words with three or more spellings.

Table 9.8: Spelling variants for 'of' and 'from'.

		OF		FROM						
Early manuscripts	M	of 163		fram 35	frā 4	f^{a}m 2	ffram 2	fra91		
	H	of 166		frō 39	from 2	ffrō 1	ffrom 1	fro 1		
1400–1425	A	of 157		from 29	fram 9	frō 3	ffram 1	ffrom 1	fro 1	
	F	of 162		from 24	frō 10	fram 5	frā 3	fro 1	ffrom 1	ffrō 1
	J	of 160		from 35	frō 3	fro 2	fram 1			
1425–1475	B	of 165		from 39	ffrom 2	frō 2	fro 1			
	G	of 158	Off 1	from 24	fro 18	frō 1				
	T	of 161		from 25	fro 16	frō 1				
Printed books	Cax	of 170		fro 32	from 10	ffrom 1	ffro 1			
	Wor	of 169		fro 33	from 11					
	Tre	of 161		fro 32	from 7	frome 3				

what one would expect, as some studies suggest that very frequent words are likely to have fewer variants (Evans 2012; Shute 2017b: 113). However, there are also fairly frequent function words that do exhibit variation, which follows the expected A-curve pattern. A good example of these is the preposition 'from', as it still has two variant spellings used by all printers *fro* and *from*, and an additional variant *frome* used by Treveris. On top of that, the word is often abbreviated with a macron or spelled with a double initial. If one includes these in the count, the distribution of variants resembles the characteristic A-curve found in complex systems still in early printed books. It is thus clear that reduction of variation does not happen at the same rate for these two words.

While words can retain spelling variants, many individual spellings show developments towards proto-standard forms. Table 9.9 illustrates two cases which go through qualitative changes towards forms that are closer to eventually standard variants: 'that' and 'to be', 3rd person plural. The scribal forms for 'that' show how thorn is replaced by <th>, starting in the mid-fifteenth century (G and T). As we know, this was a gradual change subject to variation, which could be conditioned by such factors as text type or recipient (see chapters by Hernández-Campoy and Gordon in the current volume). The date of the change in our current data corresponds roughly to what one would expect. What is interesting for

Table 9.9: Spelling variants for 'that' and the verb 'to be'.

		THAT		**TO BE, 3rd person pl**	
Early manuscripts	M	þ^{t} 37	þat 23	buþ 9	
	H	þ^{t} 52	þat 12	beþ 9	
1400–1425	A	þat 54	þ^{t} 2	beeþ 7	beþ 1
	F	þat 34	þ^{t} 23	beþ 9	
	J	þat 57	þ^{t} 1	beeþ 8	beþ 1
1425–1475	B	þat 60	þ^{t} 2	biþ 6	beþ 3
	G	that 54	þ^{t} 1	beth 5	ben 3
	T	that 54	þat 2	ben 9	beth 1
Printed books	Cax	that 65		ben 9	
	Wor	that 59	y^{t} 6	ben 8	
	Tre	that 57	y^{t} 4	ben 7	

our research questions is that a major drop in abbreviation frequencies happens earlier than change from thorn to <th> in all classes of words.

Spellings with thorn lingered longer in function words (see, e.g., Gordon: 206). In the present data thorn is replaced by <th>, word-initially, in 'that' and, word-finally, in forms of 'to be'. However, the drop in frequency of the abbreviated spelling occurs right after 1400. In the two earliest manuscripts (M and H), the abbreviated spelling, *þ*^{t}, is the major variant. In later manuscripts (A, F, J, B, G), it is used as an occasional minor variant. These manuscripts are the ones in which margin justification is highly significant, so it is very likely that the scribes use it when they need to save space. The scribe of T in the third quarter of the fifteenth century does not use the abbreviated form, but spells the word twice with thorn as a minor variant to the Present-Day English spelling *that*. The abbreviated form, however, becomes part of the SPSA leading to the familiar situation in which *y*^{t} is an occasional variant for *that*, for example, when right-margin justification demands it.

The forms used for the third-person plural of 'to be' show an even clearer development from regional to proto-standard. The earliest scribe (M) spells the word *buþ*, which is likely close to Trevisa's own form (cf. Waldron 1991). It gets replaced by the Southern *-th* paradigm and eventually the Midland paradigm *-en*. This is proto-standard English and the same form as observed by Wright (2013) for London Bridge clerks. It is not the form that eventually became standard (*are*). There is also the change from thorn to <th>. The Midland spellings first appear in G in the mid-fifteenth century as a minor variant (*beth* 5, *ben* 3). In T, they are already the major variant (*ben* 9, *beth* 1), and in the printed books the sole variant. Based on this evidence, it therefore appears that there is both quantitative and qualitative development towards proto-standard English in the latter half of the fifteenth century. The change progresses at a different rate for different words, as some words still retain variation in printed books.

The overall conclusion is that abbreviation decreases faster than spelling variation, and thus these two processes are separate. Figures 9.15 (a) and (b) give an overall impression of the rate of change for the reduction of spelling variation and abbreviation. If anything there is a slight increase in variation from the earliest English manuscripts to the mid-fifteenth century. The fourteenth-century professional scribes wrote in a consistently spelled local dialect, and the number of variants used by an individual scribe was not bigger than for scribes writing in the mid- or late fifteenth century – we did not find quantitative evidence of reduction of variation before a slight drop towards the early printed books.

It is possible that the increase from early manuscripts to ones copied between 1400–1425 can be explained by the differences between regional variants and a London melting pot. The earliest manuscripts of the *Polychronicon* are

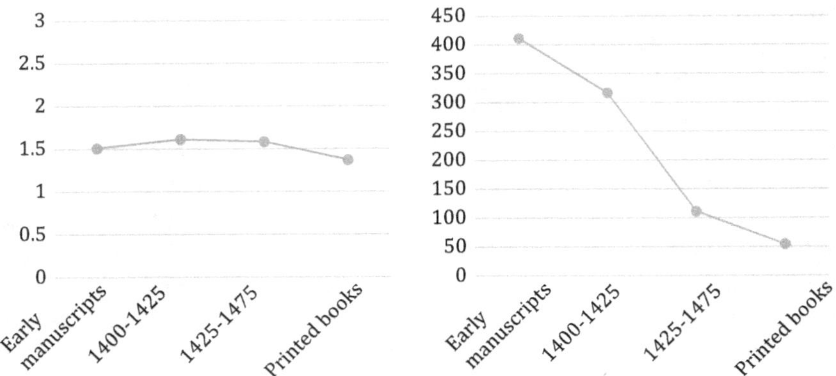

Figures 9.15 (a) and (b): Mean abbreviations and mean spelling variants. S-curves for the reduction of spelling variants, reduction of abbreviations in Middle English.

copied in a Gloucestershire dialect close to Trevisa's own. Moreover, as Waldron (1991: 67) points out, Trevisa and his patron Sir Thomas Berkeley appear to have hoped for the work to contribute to lay education, and the example of King Alfred's educational program is invoked in Trevisa's *Dialogue between a Lord and a Clerk*, which comments on the translation work. Perhaps an educational aim would have contributed some uniformity to spelling. The later copies, on the other hand, are copied in varieties closer to London, which was a major commercial hub, in which "both provincial sellers and foreign buyers interacted" (Wright 2013: 68). As a result, its language was "an urban amalgam drawing on non-adjacent dialects" (Kitson 2004: 71). If this is true, the pool of variants available to the early fifteenth-century London scribes would be slightly more extensive than that available to provincial ones. But as our data are fairly limited, it is impossible to conclude this with certainty.

5 Discussion and conclusions

This chapter has presented a quantitative look at the reduction of abbreviation with the arrival of standardisation, and provided outlines on the rate of disappearance for the abbreviation and suspension system. We uncovered a number of promising results that need to be examined with other data in different genres. It remains to be seen how many of our discoveries are specific to high-end manuscripts such as copies of the *Polychronicon*, and how many are typical of abbreviations in other types of texts.

The data from the *Polychronicon* show that in English the reduction happens between the late fourteenth and mid-fifteenth century, while the scribes continue to use abbreviations in Latin until the third quarter of the fifteenth century. There is, however, a great deal of variation in the rate with which individual abbreviation types disappear. In the early copies, small function words strongly contribute to the raw abbreviation density. Moreover, a few popular types of abbreviation, the macron and the hook in particular, could be applied to many different types of words and their overall frequency fluctuates depending on individual scribal preferences. As soon as scribes begin to spell small function words and stop using the hook, the number of abbreviations decreases rapidly. Brevigraphs, on the other hand, remain more constant, showing a slow and steady decrease. They are always more common in Latin and are still used by the later printers.

The quantitative approach also reveals that although the trend is towards less use, the process was not always one of decrease. There is a general increase in the abbreviation density from Caxton to the two later printers, which may be related, on the one hand, to the small but commonly used set of abbreviations favoured by the printers, here called the SPSA. The SPSA forms must have been part of the pool of variants in proto-standard English in other works at the time, as they are all very common types, but the later manuscript copies of the English *Polychronicon* do not contain these abbreviations. According to the linguistics of speech approach, variation consists of change of frequency of items, so this is likely to be a shift in the "ratios of a given feature" in favour of "a feature found in a majority elsewhere" (cf. Wright 2018: 348) rather than disappearance as such. As our 3000-word samples are fairly small, it is also possible that they exist as low frequency minor variants and a bigger sample from these manuscripts would uncover a handful of tokens. Nevertheless, the present results show that the SPSA were not used by professional scribes responsible for mid- to late fifteenth-century manuscript copies of the *Polychronicon*.

Our study also found one conditioning factor for abbreviations from the mid-fifteenth century to printing. Abbreviations tend to be more common closer to the right margin. When the abbreviation and suspension system began to fall out of use, it remained in use as an alternative when the scribes were pressed for space and needed to produce a neat right-margin justification. Yet our study reveals that even though the majority of abbreviations occur near the right-hand margin, the difference is not statistically significant for either the early period or the printed editions. This means that, even though abbreviations were partly motivated by the need to save space, there were also other uses for the abbreviation system.

Finally, our study suggests that although both abbreviation and spelling variation eventually disappeared, the processes were separate. The loss of abbreviations happens earlier than the loss of spelling variation. Our data show only a slight reduction in the number of variants towards early printed books; the idea of one word, one spelling was still not the norm. Qualitatively, we did uncover changes towards proto-standard spellings, even if, from a wider perspective, they can be explained by shifting ratios in a complex repertoire of forms available at the time. It is not completely certain to which events this corresponds. Multilingual systems of accounting were still in use at the time (cf. Wright 2018: 352; Alcolado Carnicero 2013: 217). The writing support in all of the manuscripts is parchment. One possibility is the shift from Anglicana to Secretary scripts, as in our data manuscripts copied in Secretary have a lower abbreviation density than ones copied in Anglicana. Whatever the reason, it would appear that professional scribes, working on *de luxe* commissions like these *Polychronicon* copies, were mainly expanding their function words by the mid-fifteenth century, whereas their language only shows a shift towards proto-standard spellings after the mid-fifteenth century.

This chapter has described what happened to abbreviations in a single work from the late fourteenth to the early sixteenth centuries. There are, of course, many things it did not cover. These include some of the more multilingual sources of the time. The medieval abbreviation and suspension system has been linked to hiding morphological endings in a multilingual society. Abbreviations could function as visual diamorphs, that is, language independent elements which can potentially be expanded in several languages, including Latin, English and Anglo-Norman French. This usage is mentioned already by Hector (1958: 37), who notes that English proper names in Latin documents could be "terminated by a mark of suspension to preserve the fiction that they were declinable Latin words". The phenomenon is investigated further by Wright, who notes it has the effect of suppressing morphological endings and highlighting stems in mixed-language writing (Wright 2011; ter Horst and Stam 2018: 223–242). The functions of abbreviations as visual diamorphs in highly mixed-language data remain yet to be described quantitatively.

Another feature which should be subject to more quantitative work is whether there is a gradual adoption of certain features into the vernacular. This process is known as "Frenchisisation" in French philological traditions since the 1990s. There are also other interesting ideas and results; for example, according to Hasenohr (2002: 88–90; see also Camps 2016: ccl) the application of the Latin abbreviations to French seems to originate in the Anglo-Norman speaking territories of the Angevin empire and from there spread to the rest of France. Even though French and English scholarly traditions do not always interact much, manuscript abbreviations are an area in which much could be gained from such interaction.

To conclude, much of the elaborate system of abbreviations that developed over centuries of handwritten book production gradually fell out of use, which indeed largely happened during the period studied in the present chapter. Nevertheless some parts of it continued in use and have become parts of standardised language. Standardisation is applied, for example, in the form of a rule, which states that "contractions, where the last letter of the abbreviation is also the last letter of the word, should not be followed by a point, whereas suspensions should. [...] One should thus write 'Mr', 'Mrs' [...] but 'Feb.', 'Rev.' etc." (Driscoll 2002). Moreover, some abbreviations which were used in the Middle Ages continue to be used in Present-Day English. Two especially common ones are & and *etc.* The latter has even expanded from Latin manuscript culture to spoken language. Abbreviated Latin was especially important for bibliographic references, and these are among the ones that have survived. It is telling that abbreviations such as *cf.*, *et al.*, *e.g.*, *ibid.* or *viz.* are still used in the academic register today, even if some of them are stylistically old-fashioned. Thus even though most of the medieval abbreviation and suspension system is long gone, parts of it are still with us and show no signs of imminent disappearance.

References

Alcolado Carnicero, José Miguel. 2013. Social networks and mixed-language business writing: Latin/French/English in the wardens' accounts of the Mercers' Company of London, 1390–1464. University of Castilla-La Mancha: PhD thesis.

Beal, Jane. 2012. *John Trevisa and the English Polychronicon* (Medieval and Renaissance Texts and Studies 437). Tempe, AZ: ACMRS.

Benskin, Michael. 2004. Chancery standard. In Christian Kay, Carole Hough, & Irené Wotherspoon (eds.), *New perspectives on English historical linguistics*, vol. 2, 1–40. Amsterdam: John Benjamins.

BMC 11 = Hellinga, Lotte & George D. Painter. 2007. *Catalogue of books printed in the XVth century now in the British* Library. *BMC Pt. 11: England*. 't Goy-Houten: HES & De Graaf.

Bozzolo, Carla, Dominique Coq, Denis Muzerelle & Ezio Ornato. 1990. Les abréviations dans les livres liturgiques du XVe siècle: pratique et théorie. In Manuel C. Díaz y Díaz (ed.) *Actas del VIII Coloquio Internacional de Paleografia Latina* (Estudios y Ensayos 6), 17–27. Madrid: Joyas Bibliograficas.

Camps, Jean-Baptiste. 2016. *La Chanson d'Otinel Édition complète du corpus manuscrit et prolégomènes à l'édition critique*. University of Paris Sorbonne: PhD thesis.

Cappelli, Adriano. 1990 [1899]. *Lexicon abbreviaturarum dizionario di abbreviature latine ed italiane*. Milano: Hoepli.

Careri, Maria, Christine de Saint-Pol Ruby & Ian Short. 2011. *Livres et écritures en français et en occitan au XIIe siècle: catalogue illustré*. Rome: Viella.

Careri, Maria, Genevieve Hasenohr, Françoise Féry-Hue, Françoise Gasparri, Gilette Labory, Sylvie Lefèvre, Anne-Françoise Leurquin & Christine Ruby. 2001. *Album de manuscrits français du XIIIe siècle*. Rome: Viella.

Carroll, Ruth, Matti Peikola, Hanna Salmi, Mari-Liisa Varila, Janne Skaffari & Risto Hiltunen. 2013. Pragmatics on the page: Visual text in late medieval English books. *European Journal of English Studies* 17. 54–71.

Chassant, L-A. 1970 [1845]. *Dictionnaire des abréviations latines et francaises usitées dans les inscriptions lapidaires et métalliques, les manuscrits et les chartes du moyen âge*. Hildesheim: Georg Olms Verlag.

Cummings, James. 2009. Converting Saint Paul: A new TEI P5 edition of The Conversion of Saint Paul using stand-off methodology. *Literary and Linguistic Computing* 24(3). 307–317.

Da Rold, Orietta. 2011. Materials. In Alexandra Gillespie & Daniel Wakelin (eds.), *The production of books in England, 1350–1500*, 12–33. Cambridge: Cambridge University Press.

Deumert, Ana & Wim Vandenbussche (eds.), 2003. *Germanic standardizations: Past to present*. Amsterdam & Philadelphia: Benjamins.

Doyle, A. I. & M. B. Parkes. 1978. The production of copies of the *Canterbury Tales* and the *Confessio Amantis* in the early fifteenth century. In M. B. Parkes & Andrew G. Watson (eds.), *Medieval scribes, manuscripts & libraries: Essays presented to N. R. Ker*. London: Scolar Press.

Driscoll, Matthew J. 2002. Stray thoughts on abbreviations in some modern European languages. In Jonna Louis-Jensen & Ragnheiður Mósesdóttir (eds.), *Grace-notes played for Michael Chesnutt on the occasion of his 60th birthday, 18 September 2002*. Copenhagen: Det Arnamagnæanske Institut. http://www.driscoll.dk/docs/thoughts.html (accessed 7 January 2019).

Driscoll, Matthew. 2009. Marking up abbreviations in Old Norse-Icelandic manuscripts. In Maria Grazia Saibene & Marina Buzzoni (eds.), *Medieval texts – contemporary media: The art and science of editing in the digital age*, 13–34. Pavia: Ibis.

Dutschke, C. W. 1989. *Guide to medieval and renaissance manuscripts in the Huntington library*, vol 2. San Marino, CA: Huntington Library.

Evans, Melanie. 2012. A sociolinguistics of early modern spelling? A case study of Queen Elizabeth I. In Jukka Tyrkkö, Matti Kilpiö, Terttu Nevalainen & Matti Rissanen (eds.), *Outposts of historical linguistics: From the Helsinki Corpus to a proliferation of resources* (Studies in Variation, Contacts and Change in English 10). Helsinki: VARIENG. http://www.helsinki.fi/varieng/journal/volumes/10/evans (accessed 7 January 2019).

Fisher, John H. 1977. Chancery and the emergence of standard written English in the fifteenth century. *Speculum* 52. 870–899.

Fisher, John H. 1979. Chancery standard and modern written English. *Journal of the Society of Archivists* 6. 136–144.

Fisher, John H. 1996. *The emergence of Standard English*. Lexington: University Press of Kentucky.

Given-Wilson, Chris. 2004. *Chronicles: The writing of history in medieval England*. Hambledon & London & New York: A&C Black.

Hasenohr, Geneviève. 2002. Écrire en latin, écrire en roman: réflexions sur la pratique des abréviations dans les manuscrits français des XIIe et XIIIe siècles. In Michel Banniard (ed.), *Langages et peuples d'Europe: cristallisation des identités romanes et*

germaniques (VIIe–XIe siècle), 79–110. Toulouse-Conques: CNRS, Université de Toulouse-Le Mirail.
Hector, Leonard Charles. 1958. *The handwriting of English documents*. Ilkley: Scolar Press.
HIMANIS 2018. https://www.himanis.org/ (accessed 31 July 2018).
Honkapohja, Alpo. 2013. Manuscript abbreviations in Latin and English: History, typologies and how to tackle them in encoding. In Anneli Meurman-Solin & Jukka Tyrkkö (eds.), *Principles and practices for the digital editing and annotation of diachronic data* (Studies in Variation, Contacts and Change in English 14). Helsinki: VARIENG. http://www.helsinki.fi/varieng/series/volumes/14/honkapohja/ (accessed 7 January 2019).
Honkapohja, Alpo. 2017. *Alchemy, medicine, and commercial book production* (Texts and Transitions 9). Turnhout: Brepols.
Honkapohja, Alpo. 2018. 'Latin in Recipes?' A corpus approach to scribal abbreviations in 15th-century medical manuscripts. In Päivi Pahta, Janne Skaffari & Laura Wright (eds.), *Multilingual practices in language history: English and beyond*, 243–271. Boston & Berlin: De Gruyter.
Horst, Tom ter. 2017. *Codeswitching in the Irish-Latin Leabhar Breac: Mediæval homiletic culture*. University of Utrecht: PhD thesis.
Horst, Tom ter & Nike Stam. 2018. Visual diamorphs: The importance of language neutrality in code-switching from medieval Ireland. In Päivi Pahta, Janne Skaffari & Laura Wright (eds.), *Multilingual practices in language history*, 223–242. Boston & Berlin: De Gruyter.
Ingham, Richard. 2012. *The Transmission of Anglo-Norman: Language history and language acquisition*. Amsterdam: Benjamins.
Kestemont, Mike. 2015. A computational analysis of the scribal profiles in two of the oldest manuscripts of Hadewijch's letters. *Scriptorium* 69. 159–175.
Kitson, Peter. 2004. On margins of error in placing Old English literary dialects. In Marina Dossena & Roger Lass (eds.), *Methods and data in English historical dialectology* (Linguistic Insights: Studies in Language and Communication 16), 219–239. Bern: Peter Lang.
Kopaczyk, Joanna. 2011. A V or not a V? Transcribing abbreviations in seventeen manuscripts of the 'Man of Law's Tale' for a digital edition. In Jacob Thaisen & Hanna Rutkowska (eds.), *Scribes, printers, and the accidentals of their texts* (Studies in English Medieval Language and Literature 33), 91–106. Frankfurt: Peter Lang.
Kretzschmar, William A., Jr. 2009. *The Lingsuistics of Speech*. Cambridge: Cambridge University Press.
Kretzschmar, William A., Jr. 2015. *Language and Complex Systems*. Cambridge: Cambridge University Press.
Kretzschmar, William A., Jr. & Merja Stenroos. 2012. Evidence from surveys and atlases in the history of the English language. In Terttu Nevalainen & Elizabeth Closs Traugott (eds.), *The Oxford handbook of the history of English*. Oxford & New York: Oxford University Press.
Kroch, Anthony. 1989. Reflexes of grammar in patterns of language change. *Language Variation and Change* 1(3). 199–244.
Kytö, Merja, Peter Grund & Terry Walker. 2011. *Testifying to language and life in early modern England: Including CD-ROM: An electronic text edition of depositions 1560–1760* (ETED). Philadelphia: Benjamins.
Labov, William. 1994. *Principles of linguistic change: Internal factors*. Oxford: Blackwell.

Laing, Margaret. 2013. *A linguistic atlas of early Middle English, 1150–1325*, version 3.2. Edinburgh: The University of Edinburgh. http://www.lel.ed.ac.uk/ihd/laeme2/laeme2.html (accessed 7 January 2019).
LAOS = Williamson, Keith. 2008. A linguistic atlas of Older Scots, Phase 1: 1380–1500. The University of Edinburgh. http://www.lel.ed.ac.uk/ihd/laos1/laos1.html (accessed 7 January 2019).
Lass, Roger. 2004. Ut custodiant litteras: Editions, corpora and witnesshood. In Marina Dossena & Roger Lass (eds.), *Methods and data in English historical dialectology* (Linguistic Insights: Studies in Language and Communication 16), 21–48. Bern: Peter Lang.
Lindsay, Wallace Martin. 1915. *Notae latinae: An account of abbreviation in Latin MSS of the early minuscule period*. Cambridge: Cambridge University Press.
Liira, Aino. 2020. Paratextuality in manuscript and print: Verbal and visual presentation of the Middle English *Polychronicon*. (Annales Universitatis Turkuensis B512). University of Turku: PhD thesis. http://urn.fi/URN:ISBN:978-951-29-8058-1 (accessed 22 May 2020).
Lyall, Roderick J. 1989. Materials: The paper revolution. In Jeremy Griffiths & Derek Pearsall (eds.), *Book production and publishing in Britain, 1375–1475*, 11–30. Cambridge: Cambridge University Press.
Matheson, Lister M. 1984. Historical prose. In A. S. G. Edwards (ed.), *Middle English prose: A critical guide to major authors and genres*, 209–248. New Brunswick, N.J: Rutgers University Press.
McIntosh, Angus, M. L. Samuels & Michael Benskin. 1986. *A linguistic atlas of late mediaeval English*, vol 1. Aberdeen: Aberdeen University Press.
MEG-C = Stenroos, Merja, Martti Mäkinen, Simon Horobin & Jeremy Smith. 2011. The Middle English Grammar Corpus, version 2011.1. University of Stavanger. https://www.uis.no/research/history-languages-and-literature/the-mest-programme/the-middle-english-grammar-corpus-meg-c/ (accessed 7 January 2019).
MELD = Stenroos, Merja, Kjetil, V. Thengs & Geir Bergstrøm (2017–). A Corpus of Middle English Local Documents, version 2017.1. University of Stavanger. www.uis.no/meld (accessed 7 January 2019).
MENOTA = Medieval Nordic Text Archive. http://www.menota.org/EN_forside.xhtml (accessed 7 January 2019).
Mooney, Linne. 2006. Chaucer's scribe. *Speculum* 81. 97–138.
Mooney, Linne, Simon Horobin, & Estelle Stubbs. 2011. Late medieval English scribes. https://www.medievalscribes.com (accessed 7 January 2019).
Nevalainen, Terttu. 2015. Descriptive adequacy of the S-curve model in diachronic studies of language change. In Christina Sanchez-Stockhammer (ed.), *Can we predict linguistic change?* (Studies in Variation, Contacts and Change in English 16). Helsinki: VARIENG.
Nevalainen, Terttu & Ingrid Tieken-Boon van Ostade. 2006. Standardisation. In Richard Hogg & David Denison (eds.), *A history of the English language*, 271–311. Cambridge: Cambridge University Press.
OxGarage. http://www.tei-c.org/oxgarage/ (accessed 7 January 2019).
Parkes, M. B. 2008 [1969]. *English cursive book hands 1250–1500*. Aldershot/Burlington,VT: Ashgate.
Petti, Anthony G. 1977. *English literary hands from Chaucer to Dryden*. London: E. Arnold.
Ramsey, Roy Vance. 1982. The *Hengwrt* and *Ellesmere* manuscripts of the *Canterbury Tales*: Different scribes. *Studies in Bibliography* 35. 133–154.

Roberts, Jane. 2005. *Guide to scripts used in English writing up to 1500*. London: British Library.
Roberts, Jane. 2011. On giving Scribe B a name and a clutch of London manuscripts from c. 1400. *Medium Aevum* 80(20). 247–270.
Robinson, Pamela. 2014. Materials: Paper and type. In Vincent Gillespie & Susan Powell (eds.), *Companion to the early printed book in Britain, 1476–1558*, 61–74. Cambridge: Boydell & Brewer.
Rogos, Justyna. 2012. Isles of systemacity in the sea of prodigality? Non-alphabetic elements in manuscripts of Chaucer's 'Man of Law's Tale'. https://www.isle-linguistics.org/assets/content/documents/hogg/rogos2012.pdf (accessed 7 January 2019).
Samuels, Michael. 1983 [1963]. Some applications of Middle English dialectology. In Angus McIntosh, Michael Samuels & Margaret Laing (eds.), *Middle English Dialectology: Essays on some principles and problems*, 81–94. Aberdeen: Aberdeen University Press.
Samuels, Michael. 1983. The scribe of the *Hengwrt* and *Ellesmere* manuscripts of the *Canterbury Tales*. *Studies in the Age of Chaucer* 5. 49–65.
Shepherd, Stephen. 1999. John Trevisa, *Dialogue between the Lord and the Clerk on translation* (extract) and *Epistle to Thomas, Lord Berkeley*, on the translation of Higden's *Polychronicon*. In Jocelyn Wogan-Browne, Nicholas Watson, Andrew Taylor & Ruth Evans (eds.), *The idea of the vernacular: An anthology of Middle English literary theory, 1280–1520*, 130–138. University Park, PA: The Pennsylvania State University Press.
Shute, Rosie. 2017a. Pressed for space: The effects of justification and the printing process on fifteenth-century orthography. *English Studies* 98(3). 262–282.
Shute, Rosie. 2017b. A quantitative study of spelling variation in William Caxton's printed texts. University of Sheffield: PhD thesis.
Smith, Daisy. 2019. The predictability of {S} abbreviation in Older Scots manuscripts according to stem-final *littera*. In Rhona Alcorn, Joanna Kopaczyk & Benjamin Molineaux (eds.), *Historical dialoctology in the digital age*. Edinburgh: Edinburgh University Press.
Stam, Nike. 2017. *A typology of code-switching in the Commentary to the* Félire Óengusso. University of Utrecht: PhD thesis.
Stutzmann, Dominique. 2014. Conjuguer diplomatique, paléographie et édition électronique : les mutations du XIIe siècle et la datation des écritures par le profil scribal collectif. In Antonella Ambrosio, Sébastien Barret & Georg Vogeler (eds.), *Digital diplomatics: The computer as a tool for the diplomatist?* (Archiv für Diplomatik, Schriftgeschichte, Siegel- und Wappenkunde 14), 271–290. Vienna/Cologne: Böhlau.
Stutzmann, Dominique, Christopher Kermorvant, Enrique Vidal, Sukalpa Chanda, Sébastien Hamel, Joan Puigcerver Pérez, Lambert Schomaker & Alejandro H. Toselli. 2018. Handwritten text recognition, keyword indexing, and plain text search in medieval manuscripts. Paper presented at Digital Humanities 2018 conference, Mexico City, 26–29 June. https://dh2018.adho.org/handwritten-text-recognition-keyword-indexing-and-plain-text-search-in-medieval-manuscripts/ (accessed 7 January 2019).
TEI consortium. 2013. TEI P5: Guidelines for electronic text encoding and interchange. http://www.tei-c.org/Vault/P5/2.4.0/doc/tei-p5-doc/en/html/ (accessed 7 January 2019).
Thaisen, Jacob. 2011. Adam Pinkhurst's short and long forms. In Jacob Thaisen & Hanna Rutkowska (eds.), *Scribes, printers, and the accidentals of their texts* (Studies in English Medieval Language and Literature 33), 73–90. Frankfurt: Peter Lang.
Tristram, Hildegard. 1997. Latin and Latin learning in the Táin Bó Cuailnge. *Zeitschrift für celtische Philologie* 49–50. 847–877.

Tyrkkö, Jukka. 2017. New methods of bringing image data into historical linguistics: A case study with medical writing 1500–1700. *Studia Neophilologica* 89, suppl. 1. 90–108.
Varila, Mari-Liisa. 2016. *In search of textual boundaries: A case study on the transmission of scientific writing in 16th-century England* (Anglicana Turkuensia 31). University of Turku: PhD thesis.
Waldron, Ronald. 1991. Dialect aspects of manuscripts of Trevisa's translation of the *Polychronicon*. In Felicity Riddy (ed.), *Regionalism in late medieval manuscripts and texts: Essays celebrating the publication of A Linguistic Atlas of Late Mediaeval English.* Cambridge: D. S. Brewer.
Waldron, Ronald. 2004. *John Trevisa's translation of the 'Polychronicon' of Ranulph Higden, Book VI: An edititon based on British Library MS Cotton Tiberius D.VII* (Middle English Texts 35). Heidelberg: Winter.
Warner, Lawrence. 2015. "Scribes Misattributed: Hoccleve and Pinkhurst". *Studies in the Age of Chaucer* 37: 55–99.
Warner, Lawrence. 2018. *Chaucer's Scribes. London Textual Production 1384-1432*. Cambridge: Cambridge University Press.
Wright, Laura. 2000. *The development of Standard English, 1300–1800*. Cambridge: Cambridge University Press.
Wright, Laura. 2002. Standard English and the lexicon: Why so many different spellings? In Mari C. Jones & Edith Esch (eds.), *Language change: The interplay of internal, external and extra-linguistic factors*, 181–200. Berlin & New York: Mouton de Gruyter.
Wright, Laura. 2011. On variation in medieval mixed-language business writing. In Herbert Schendl & Laura Wright (eds.), *Code-switching in early English*, 191–218. Göttingen: De Gruyter.
Wright, Laura. 2013. The contact origins of Standard English. In Daniel Schreier & Marianne Hundt (eds.), *English as a contact language* (Studies in English Language), 58–74. Cambridge: Cambridge University Press.
Wright, Laura. 2018. A multilingual approach to the history of Standard English. In Päivi Pahta, Janne Skaffari & Laura Wright (eds.), *Multilingual practices in language history: English and beyond*, 339–358. Boston & Berlin: De Gruyter.

Herbert Schendl

10 William Worcester's *Itineraria*: mixed-language notes of a medieval traveller

1 Introduction

One of the factors that strongly influence the nature of medieval language-mixing and code-switching is the variable 'text-type'. There are obvious differences in the multilingual practices found between various types of sermons, letters, medical texts and various literary genres, such as drama or verse. Particularly complex are the patterns of language-mixing in administrative texts, such as business accounts or wills, which have been extensively studied in recent years, see particularly Wright (2010, 2011) and Trotter (2011). The present paper looks at a medieval text that shows a range of multilingual practices including many of those typical of administrative texts, namely William Worcester's *Itineraria*. This is a collection of travel notes and descriptions, dating from the late 15th century and predominantly written in the kind of medieval mixed-language usually found in the text-type of accounts and inventories, consisting of a Medieval Latin matrix, plus a high frequency of English and some French material. Switches range from single words to monolingual English paragraphs and sub-texts. For a better understanding of Worcester's linguistic practices in the newly emerging text-type of travel notes and descriptions of England's towns and its countryside, a brief look at its author's biography may be helpful, since this provides a number of important social variables which may help to better understand his linguistic usage.[1]

William Worcester was born in Bristol in 1415, studied in Oxford and entered the service of Sir John Fastolf in 1436, whose secretary he remained till Fastolf's death in 1459. In this capacity, Worcester fulfilled a wide range of functions, such as managing parts of Fastolf's property and carrying out numerous business transactions. He travelled extensively both in Britain and France, where Fastolf had stayed from 1412 to 1439 and also possessed some property. Furthermore, Worcester carried out historical research in archives and libraries mainly to support some of Fastolf's lawsuits, and increasingly

1 For details on Worcester's life and writings see McFarlane (1957/1981) and Orme, *Worcester*, and Broadway (2015).

https://doi.org/10.1515/9783110687545-011

developed very broad antiquarian and topographical interests, especially in history, geography and archaeology, but also in astronomy, medicine and languages. After Fastolf's death, Worcester was for more than ten years involved in a legal case about Fastolf's will (involving John Paston) and finally received a small property and enough money to retire to Pockthorpe, today part of Norwich.

Worcester was trilingual in English, Latin and French, and produced or was involved in the production of original texts and translations, such as *The Boke of Noblesse* (1451) and a translation of Cicero's *De senectute* from French as well as some now lost manuscripts on history and genealogy (see Orme, *Worcester*, and Broadway (2015) for further details). Most importantly, however, Worcester left extensive travel notes and descriptions from a number of journeys which he undertook for pleasure and out of antiquarian interest in the last years of his life, from late 1477 to 1480. These notes are written in Worcester's own hand and are preserved in Cambridge, Corpus Christi College, MS 210, a manuscript listed under the title *Itineraria*. It has been edited in two separate parts, namely the detailed description of medieval Bristol from the year 1480 edited by Neale (2000), which will be referred to as *Bristol* (abbreviated *Br*), and the travel notes from the various other journeys edited by Harvey 1969 as *Itineraries* (abbreviated *It*), both with translations into modern English.[2]

The longest of Worcester's journeys was in 1478, leading from Norwich via London and Bristol to St Michael's Mount, Cornwall, and Tintern Abbey, Wales. This was followed by a second journey to London and Walsingham Priory in 1479, and his last one in 1480 was from Norwich to Oxford, Cirencester, Glastonbury and Wells, with an extended stay of almost a month at his sister's house in Bristol. Worcester's notes were made on loose narrow sheets of paper (approximately 12x8 inches) which would fit into the saddlebag of his horse while travelling. The notes are spontaneous, informal products frequently written "in conditions which most of us would now find unbearably crude" (Harvey 1969: xvi). These "hasty notes, mostly written on the spot" (Neale 2000, cover text) are frequently "scrappy and unorganized" (Hoskins 1984: 18), evidently with little or no revision. This is also mirrored in the partly chaotic layout of the sheets of paper. However, Worcester's handwriting reflects the circumstances under which an entry was written: either "neat, careful extracts from a

2 The manuscript comprises 332 pages and is accessible online at https://parker.stanford.edu/parker/catalog/mp810zm2076. For a description of the manuscript see Harvey (1969: xviii-xx). The references following the quoted examples give the page number of the respective edition immediately after the abbreviated title (e.g. '*Br* 12'), while the abbreviation 'pg' is followed by the page number of the manuscript.

chronicle in a church, or almost illegible notes as he stood on the spot" (Neale 2000: viii). Worcester seems to have planned to use some of these notes for later projects, but the notes themselves were not directly intended to be used by other people. All of this makes the *Itineraria* a particularly valuable document of late medieval writing in what was to become a new text type combining travel accounts, topographical writing and local history.

Worcester noted down whatever he found interesting: information on towns and villages, particularly the form and dimensions of roads and streets, features of the architecture and dimensions of buildings, and a mixture of historical and religious information which he found in archives, churches and libraries, or got from conversations with people en route. He describes features of natural history such as landscape, rivers, and flora and fauna. Because of this manuscript, Worcester has variously been called the founder of local topography, the first antiquary and even the first English archaeologist (Harvey 1969: xii; Hoskins 1984: 18). For Harvey, Worcester represents "that particular blend of interests . . . which has ever since been an outstanding characteristic of the English approach to antiquity" (Harvey 1969: x).

The detailed description of the buildings and streets of Bristol dating from 1480 is on the whole better structured than most of the notes from his other travels, as it is the result of his longer stay with his sister, but the whole text shows the same main linguistic features. The linguistic aspects of Worcester's multilingual text have so far not been discussed in any detail, though Harvey, the editor of the *Itineraries*, made some positive comments on Worcester's Latinity in his introduction, at a time when medieval Latin and language-mixing were generally considered negatively. He describes (1969: xvi) the language of the manuscript as "the heavily anglicized Latin of fifteenth-century business" and stresses that Worcester's medieval Latin should not be judged from the point of view of classical scholarship. However, there is much more to be said about Worcester's language in the context of recent studies in historical code-switching and medieval language mixing.

2 The language of Worcester's *Itineraria*: general remarks

The present paper will discuss selected aspects of the language of the whole *Itineraria*, that is, both of the *Itineraries* and the *Bristol* part of the notes. The text is predominantly written in Medieval Latin with a large amount of inserted Middle English and some Anglo-Norman French material, ranging from single words and phrases to clauses and sentences; that is, in the kind of mixed-language more commonly found in business accounts, inventories and testaments of the period. There are also paragraphs and lists in monolingual Latin, and, though less frequent, in monolingual (or almost monolingual) English, and there are also a few words in Italian.[3] That is, there is a wide range from codeswitching to language-mixing, generally from Medieval Latin to English but also from English to Medieval Latin. The Anglo-Norman French material is, however, restricted to a small number of entries.

In Worcester's Medieval Latin, incomplete or verbless clauses and sentences as well as false concords are frequent. For Harvey, Worcester's Latin "was losing its strict grammar, its genders, its inflexions [and] it was gaining a new vocabulary adequate to meet contemporary needs" (Harvey 1969: xvi), but it would be more appropriate to see it as mixed-language. For the present paper it is particularly interesting that the *Itineraria* shows many of the typical features of medieval multilingual administrative texts, though Worcester's notes as a whole – in spite of a some lists and account-like entries – do not belong to the text-type 'administrative texts', but rather represent the text-types 'travel account', 'topography' and 'local history', which were to develop more fully in the sixteenth century. Worcester's use of the mixed-language system outside the domain of administrative texts is evidence of its wider use by people familiar with it from their professional training, shedding some new light on the relevance of this type of mixed-coding for the development of English.

The language of medieval mixed-language administrative texts represents in Wright's words a "linguistic code [which] was governed by principles that were specific to itself" (Wright 2010: 130–131), namely:

- "do not write in monolingual Medieval Latin or Anglo-Norman, but include English nouns, stems of verbs, adjectives and *-ing* forms, variably (. . .)
- calque Romance nouns with English nouns (e.g. the words *gigantem* and *giant* . . .)
- use both Germanic and Romance word-orders (. . .)
- variably apply number concord within the noun phrase (e.g. *ꝑ le gynnes* and also *ꝑ leȝ gynnes*, 'for the gins' . . .)

3 While long passages of monolingual Latin are frequent in both parts (sometimes with inserted vernacular place names), longer monolingual English passages are relatively rare: in the *Bristol* part, they amount to a total of about five pages of monolingual English (printed edition between *Br* 22 and *Br* 28, *Br* 130, 222, 236); in the *Itineraries*, some predominantly monolingual passages ranging from four to 20 lines in the printed edition are found on *It* 34, 66–68, 76, 330.

- use a multiplicity of suffixes to indicate verbal nouns (. . .)
- visually merge any material that can be merged with the abbreviation and suspension system, but do it variably (e.g. the Latin word *carpentarius* and the English word *carpenter* . . .)
- use *le* to qualify a vernacular noun
- be categorical about variation." (Wright 2010: 130–131; also Wright 2011: 200–207)

The present paper will mainly focus on five of Wright's above features frequently found in Worcester's text, namely (i) its multilingual nature, with its mixture of Latin, English and some French; (ii) the use of forms of *le* to indicate the switch from Latin to words of English or French etymology; (iii) variable number concord within the noun phrase; (iv) variable use of largely synonymous Romance and English nouns; (v) the categoriality of variation.[4] Romance and Germanic word order, abbreviations and suspensions as well as the different suffixes of verbal nouns also occur in the manuscript, but they will not be analysed systematically here .

The short passage under (1) from the *Itineraries* shows some typical language-mixing in the text its wider context.

(1) Insƚa prestholm ꝑxīa jnsƚa anglesey p̄ dj̄ miliar’ de anglesey in orientƚi ꝑte anglesey & ibi crescūt cunicƚi . & ßpentes addyrs snakes Gullys mewys cormorantes / Et arbores voc’ elders . / Et est capella ibi in medio jnsƚe edificata . / et est longitudīs . dīdij miliar’ & latitudīs vni^9 qr^{a}ƚij miliaris nō est popƚata . / distat a le maynlond . c^{i}ca spaciū duoꝝ arcuū voc’ bowshottys . Et est ibi vnū bay ꝑ nauibʒ saluandīs in le northsyde jnsƚe voc’ le Rounde table / et est portus in dcā jnsƚa voc’ math haver /. (*It* 134, 136, pg 70)
'The island of Priestholm lies close to Anglesey, half a mile off on the east side of Anglesey, and there live rabbits and serpents, adders, snakes, gulls, mews, cormorants, and trees called elders. There is a chapel built in the middle of the island, and its length is half a mile and its width a quarter of a mile. It is not inhabited. It lies about two bowshots from the mainland. On the north side of the island is a long bay for the safe riding of ships called the Round Table, and a harbour in the island called Math Haver.'

4 This paper is not only much indebted to Laura Wright's work on mixed-language administrative texts, but particularly also to her transcription of the quoted examples from Worcester's manuscript. She has also pointed out a number of ambiguous or unclear readings which were silently expanded by the editors of the text. Such ambiguous examples have been excluded from the statistics given here.

As illustrated in (1), most place names in the manuscript are used in their vernacular form such as *Prestholm* and *Anglesey*, while those of larger cities or towns like London, Norwich and Bristol vary between English and Latin forms (see example 32). The enumeration of the animals living on the island starts with the Latin form *cuniculi* ('rabbits'), while the immediately following form *serpentes* is ambiguous, and could either represent the plural of Latin *serpens* or of English *serpent* (cf. DMLBS and MED).[5] The next four animal names *addyrs, snakes, gullys,* and *mewys*, are English forms, possibly triggered by the ambiguous form *serpentes*, while *cormorantes* is again ambiguous (cf. DMLBS s.v. *cormorans* and MED s.v. *cormeraunt*) and possibly triggers the switch back to Latin *et arbores vocate*. After these three Latin words, another switch into English follows (*elders*), preceded and flagged by the frequently used Latin vo*c*ate. Next follows the mixed prepositional phrase *a le maynlond* with the article *le* following the Latin preposition *a* ('from') and flagging the switch to the following English noun, a pattern frequent in administrative texts.[6] The next English switch *bowshottys* is again flagged by Latin vo*c*ꝰ, while the following single-word switch *bay* is preceded by *vnum*, which like all numerals excludes the use of *le* before an English noun.

After this brief overview, a selected number of linguistic features will be discussed in more details, starting with the article *le*, which is perhaps one of the most obvious features of medieval administrative texts.

3 AN *le* – forms, functions and variation

The forms and functions of the originally Anglo-French article *le* have received much attention in research into the administrative mixed-language code (Trotter 2010, Wright 2011, Ingham 2018). Both Trotter (2010: 60) and Wright (2010: 131) proposed that the main function of *le* in such texts is to mark a switch from Latin to the vernacular (i.e. either English or French), while Ingham (2018: 327) emphasizes the likely origin of this construction in earlier spoken code-switching

---

5 Such written forms which belong to more than one code are called "visual diamorphs" by Wright (2011: 203), who has proposed a further classification of visual diamorphs (2011: 194–195), with <-*es*> being a 'bound morpheme' visual diamorph. Wright's research has particularly focused on visual diamorphs resulting from the medieval system of abbreviation and suspension marks. The role of visual diamorphs in triggering code-switching in medieval Irish texts is emphasized in ter Horst & Stam (2018). For Woolard's similar notion of "bivalent elements" see Gardner-Chloros (2009: 108).

6 *In* (cf. *in le northsyde jnsule*) like *de* and *et* are 'function word' visual diamorphs in the trilingual situation of medieval England (Wright 2011:194).

with French. For a late medieval text like Worcester's, the interpretation advanced by Trotter and Wright seems convincing and is supported by the present data.

As shown in Table 10, the clearly predominating form before morphologically singular vernacular nouns in both parts of the text is *le*, with 210 occurrences in the *Itineraries* and 283 in the *Bristol* part of the manuscript, amounting to 98.5% of all singular article forms, while *la* only accounts for 1%, with a single instance of the form in the *Itineraries* and five in *Bristol*; furthermore, there is a single instance of *les* before a Latin singular noun in *Bristol* (see below). These figures include all instances of *le* forms in the slot before singular nouns, irrespective of syntactic and semantic aspects of the noun phrase. The high frequency of *le* in *Bristol* is partly due to the regular reference to the two main streets of medieval Bristol, *The Key* (*Quay*) and *The Back*, which are predominantly used with *le* (*le Bak* 55 instances against 7 without article[7]; *le Key* 45 instances against 5 without[8]). In a clear majority of instances, *le*/*la* is followed by a single noun (*It* 63%, *Br* 84%), while complex noun phrases are less frequent, particularly in *Bristol*. Forms of the article are very frequent in mixed-language prepositional phrases of the type [Latin preposition + *le*/*la*/*les* + English/French noun]: of the 235 instances of *le*/*la*/*les* in the *Itineraries*, almost half (115, i.e. 49%) occur in prepositional phrases, while in *Bristol* this percentage is as high as 72%, with 231 instances. In both parts, *de* is by far the most frequent preposition (*It* 40 instances, *Br* 117)

Table 10: Absolute and relative frequencies of *le*/*la*/*les* in the *Itineraries* (*It*) and *Bristol* (*Br*) as well as in the total text (Nsg = noun in singular; Npl = noun morphologically marked plural).[9]

	le+Nsg		la+Nsg		les+Nsg		Tot. le/la/les Nsg		les+Npl		le+Npl		Tot. le(s+Npl	
	abs	%	abs	%	abs	%	abs	%	abs	%	abs	%	abs	%
It	210	99,5	1	0,5	0	0	211	100	14	58	10	42	24	100
Br	283	98	5	1,5	1	0,5	289	100	16	53	14	47	30	100
Total	493	98,5	6	1	1	0,5	500	100	30	56	24	44	54	100

As for semantic class, forms of *le* occur in the *Itineraries* particularly with nouns denoting features of landscape, directions or the cardinal points, as well as

7 Neale (2000) consistently uses capitalized *Le Key* and *Le Back* to refer to these streets and these are also the forms used in Jacobus Millerd's map of Bristol from 1673; present-day spelling *Quay* will be used in this paper.

8 In the English parts of the text, *the bak*(*k*) occurs 4 times, against a single occurrence without article. For the latinized forms *keya*(*m*), *bakkam* see the discussion of examples (23) to (25) below.

9 Percentages rounded. The cases of single occurrence of a type are actually below the 0.5% given in the table.

professions, but less so before place-names, although its use is highly variable as the following examples illustrate. In the *Bristol* section, forms of *le* tend to occur with nouns denoting specific natural or man-made locations (e.g. *le narrow sea*, *le pillory*), while they are rare before street names as in *prope Highstreet* 'near Highstreet' (except for *le Key* and *le Bak*).

(2) patria vocata le Skye (*It* 4, pg 231)
'the land called Skye'

(3) Robtꝰ wyse le ffuller de Southwork manēs infra le spytell . ꝑpe watkyn keruer (*It* 42, pg 35)
'Robert Wise the fuller of Southwark, dwelling within the spittle near Watkin the carver'

(4) It' granariū ^{16} equi . et 30 vacce cū le storehows m̓cādiʒaꝶ (*It* 48, pg 11)
'Item the granary 16 horses and 30 cows with the storehouse of goods'

(5) It' le byldyng de le jnner Court edificat' cū bryke (*It* 48, pg 11)
'Item the building of the Inner Court built with brick'

(6) & jacet in ~~mare~~ le narow see ꝑ ^{circa} .15. miliaria (*It* 110, pg 27)
'and it lies in ~~sea~~ the narrow sea by about 15 miles'

Ship names are regularly preceded by *le* (*It* 10 instances, *Br* 5), such as *le mary Radclyff, le Galyot, le Cateryn* (*It* 132, pg 19) and so are a small number of personal names like *hugo le Ris, Joħes le veylle* (*It* 56, pg 51); *walteꝶ le/goode* (*It* 104, pg 45). On the other hand, *the* and *a(t)* occur in some instances of a church and street name where *le* was adopted later (see the discussion of similar cases in Wright 2010: 136–137).

(7) de vico seynt marye the Porte strete (*Br* 40, pg 101) . . . vocata Seynt marye a port / et iacet in vico seynt Marye at port (*Br* 200, pg 162)
'of the street of Saint Mary the Port Street . . . called Saint Mary a Port, and it lies in the street of Saint Mary at Port'

As shown in Table 10, the form *la*, which by this time no longer indicated feminine grammatical gender (Wright 2010: 136) is extremely rare, with just a single unambiguous instance in the *Itineraries*[10] and five in the *Bristol* part, sometimes varying with *le* before the same lexical item, as with *la/le weer(e* ('weir'), see (8).

(8) vs⁹ la meere (*It* 292, pg 216)
'towards the Mere'

p lat⁹ vici de la weer (*Br* 50, pg 103)
'beside the broad street of the Weir'

ad finē vie vltra le weere (*Br* 6, pg 88)
'to the end of the road beyond the Weir'

The overall predominance of *le* over *la* at 99% is also underlined by the following passage, in which the visual diamorph *dameselle* (a borrowing from French into English)[11] occurs before some unambiguous French words such as *vng fause homme* (while *de Digeon* and *clerk* are visual diamorphs – borrowings like this one are the third type in Wright's (2011: 195) classification of visual diamorphs). In this partly French context one might have expected *la*, the feminine form of the French article, to be the obvious choice, but evidently *le* was by then the default choice before a vernacular noun in a mixed-language context even for Worcester, who was proficient in French.

(9) md qd mulier quedā voc le dameselle d dgeon . & vng fause hom̄e clerk fecit fabricari falsas lrâs̄ (*It* 4, pg 78)
'Memorandum that a certain woman called the damsel of Dijon and a false male clerk had fabricated false letters'

As for the use of *le* forms before nouns morphologically marked for plural, the use of the plural form *les* and of the singular *le* is rather similar in the two parts, with a small predominance of *les* over *le* (*It* 58%, *Br* 55%, see Table 10). This agrees with Wright's (2010: 131) finding for administrative texts that "number concord within the noun phrase" is variable. In Worcester's text, there is sometimes variation

10 Harvey's transcription *en la Peke* 'in the Peak' (*It* 166) is not clearly supported by the manuscript reading (pg 227) which is ambiguous between <a> and <e> and therefore not included in the count.

11 See AND s.v *dameiselle* and MED s.v. *damisele* with numerous, partly overlapping spelling variants. A few lines after the above quotation, the English/French part is taken up by the Latin 'et fals⁹ cl̄ic⁹ ⁹uict⁹ ~~eū~~ accusabat abbatē de verseilles ... Ir q dicta damicella de dygeon fuit in vno engyn posita' (*It* 4, pg 78) 'and the false clerk upon conviction accused the Abbot of Versailles ... Item that the said Damsel of Dijon was placed on the rack'.

between the two forms even within a few lines and with the same word-form. The fusion of preposition and plural article occurs only once with the form *dez*, see the last example under (10).

(10) fecit lejustes (*It* 220, pg 278)
'and jousted'

fecit leʒ justes (*It* 220, pg 278)
'and jousted'

Groghy Rupis vocaɾ' leʒ Shotes (*It* 76, pg 66)
'Gruggy Rock called the Shoots'

le Rokȩ voc' Trogy anglice le Shotes (*It* 134, pg 69)
'the rock called Gruggy, in English the Shoots'

de leʒ hauyns (*It* 32, pg 37)
'of the havens'

Donet Ballok <~~seoe~~> dn̄s deʒ isles (*It* 6, pg 231)
'Donald Ballok Lord of the Isles'

Trotter (2010) and Wright (2010) state that *le* indicates a switch from Latin to the vernacular (i.e. either English or French), but Wright (2011: 202) lists some exceptions to this rule from a will from 1425, where *le* also occurs before a restricted class of Latin nouns, namely weights and measures. In Worcester's text, the originally rather categorical rule has become even more variable, with five instances of *le(s* occurring before a Latin noun (though with an English modifying place name or general noun following the Latin).[12] Four of the five instances occur in the *Bristol* part of the manuscript. Since this is a rather unusual and undocumented use, all instances will be quoted here.

(11) Rye pat^{r}a ditissiā v̓s^{9} le pat^{r}am Polelond
Revel . est pat^{r}a ditissiā v̓s^{9} patriā pole (*It* 192, pg 237)
'Riga an extremely rich province towards the country of Poland, Revel (Tallinn) an extremely rich country towards the country of Poland'

(12) ab extrēa banci aque auene ꝑpe le domū de Roꝑscrafft (*Br* 2, pg 87a)
'from the furthest bank of the water of Avon near the Ropemakers' Hall'

---

12 Two examples of *le* and *la* in Neale's edition (*la dicti marisci*, *Br* 2; *versus le aquam de Avyn*, *Br* 100) have been omitted from the count, since the manuscript is either blotted or we disagree with Neale's transcription.

(13) *p* le magnū gardinū & Orchard . m^ar^rkyswiłłi^a maiore q^o^nd (*Br* 110, pg 124)
'past the great garden & orchard of Mark William, formerly mayor'

(14) que Incipit in *p*te boriali Ecclīe scī Nichī de le porta ei[9] siue de fine hygh-strete (*Br* 126, pg 128)
'which begins on the northern side of the church of St Nicholas from its door or from High Street end'

In spite of the high frequency of *le*, there is also some variation with competing forms and constructions, without any obvious functional differences. The most frequent of these is the 'zero article', i.e. the absence of *le*, which often occurs in more or less identical constructions and even in close vicinity to *le*, see the following examples with pairs like *le pleyn* vs *pleyn*, *le fuller* vs *keruer*, and *mersh strete* vs *le Mershstrete.*

(15) Castellū de yember^r^y su*p* le pleyn de salysbery dirutū . . . Castełł yenderber^r^y dirut sup pley<n> . . . Castełł yenderberye / su*p* le pleyn ^dirut^ de salysbery (*It* 140, pg 31)
'Castle Yembury on Salisbury Plain in ruins . . . Castle Yenderbury in ruins on the Plain . . . Castle Yenderbury on Salisbury Plain in ruins'

(16) Robt[9] wyse le ffuller de Southwork manēs infra le spytell *p*pe watkyn keruer (*It* 42, pg 35)
'Robert Wise the fuller of Southwark dwelling within the spittle near Watkin carver'

(17) vsqȝ *p*xiam crucē de marblestone vs[9] norwicū . . . It'a dcā cruce voc' ^de^ le marblestone vsqȝ crucē de ligno (*It* 254, pg 322)
'to the nearest cross of marble towards Norwich . . . Item at the said cross called of marble to the wooden cross'

(18) de le key vs[9] mersħstrete . . . de le key eīdo *p* alterā *p*tē Ecclīe scī Stephani *p* le northħ dore vsqȝ le mershstrete (*Br* 20, pg 91)
'from the Quay towards Marsh Street . . . from the Quay going by the other side of the church of St Stephen by the north door as far as the Marsh Street'

Variation between *le* and *the* before an English noun as in (19) is rare, while the indefinite article *a* is more frequent, sometimes after *anglice* or *vocatum* and referring to a preceding noun phrase with *le*, see (20) and (21).

(19) Iᵗ the fermorye chyrch ^{9}tiȝ in longitu$^{d\bar{n}}$. 34 . virgas (*It* 58, pg 8)
'Item the infirmary church is 34 yards long'
Iᵗ le ffermory ^{9}tiȝ . ~~60~~+ . 60 . stteppys meos (*It* 58, pg 8)
'Item the Infirmary is 60 of my steps'

(20) le Slope in Cristm^{a}strete Gradus anglice a slepe sƀt^{9} archus (*Br* 72, pg 110)
'The Slip in Christmas Street a stairway in English a slip under the arch'

(21) longitudo de le Sl<e>p anglice a steyre de lapidibȝ ad ~~ke~~ fundū aque de le bakę ... altitudo de fūdo aque Abone ad fine d<> gradus anglic^{e} a steyr ^{9}tiêt c^{r}ca . 7 . brachia (*Br* 124, pg 128)
'the length of the Slip in English a stair of stones to the ~~ke~~ bottom of the water at the Back ... the height from the bottom of the river Avon at the end of the said stairway in English a stair contains about 7 fathoms'

(22) Domus & hospiciū ... $^{\text{vocat<ū>}}$ $^{\textbf{a cloth halle}}$ (*Br* 146, pg 136)
'A house and lodging ... called a cloth hall'

In a number of instances in the *Bristol* part prepositional phrases of the form [Latin preposition + non-Latin root + Latin inflection] occur instead of the predominating pattern [Latin preposition + *le*(*s*) + vernacular noun]. The former construction was the "older way of expressing a prepositional phrase in mixed-language texts" (Wright 2011: 200); from the early fifteenth century the construction with *le* became increasingly more common. Worcester clearly prefers the newer construction and the restriction of the older construction to the Bristol streetnames *Key* (8 tokens) and *Bakk* (1 token) may reflect Worcester's age (about sixty-five at the time of writing) and be a relic construction from his school days in Bristol, i.e. it may be linked to the sociolinguistic variable 'age'. Note the variation between the two variant constructions with the same sentence in (24), and the same lexical item in (25).

(23) d<e> le customhous + ad keyā . et de keyā ad le post <?> showtes[13] (*Br* 70, pg 110)
'from the customhouse + to the Quay and from the Quay to the post (?for) shouts'

13 Letter-graphs in angle brackets are blotted; there is a line separating marginalia from main text running between the <w> and <t> of 'showtes'. A shout was a type of river boat.

(24) longitudo vici le Bakk . . . ꝑ longā keyam coram aquā (*Br* 2, pg 87)
'the length of the Back street . . . by the long quay fronting the water'

(25) introit⁹ ad le bakę (*Br* 6, pg 87)
'the entry to the Back'
sic eundo vsqȝ ad bakkam sc̄i augustī (*Br* 46, pg 102)
'thus going as far as St Augustine's Back'[14]

4 Lexical variation

Lexical variation is a pervasive feature of Worcester's text and appears in very different forms, sometimes crossing and blurring language boundaries in ways which make decisions difficult for the modern analyst. It occurs between equivalent terms in the two dominant languages in the text, with or without etymological or derivational relation, but also between different (near-) synonyms of the same language. And, in a wider sense, there is variation in regard to the switch of languages used within a lexical syntagma or compound. All these different types will be briefly illustrated and discussed in this section.

Worcester's use of derivationally related Romance and English words resembles that regularly found in adminstrative mixed-language documents (Wright's 'calques', see 2010: 130), with pairs such as *porter* and *portario*, *manor* and *manerium*, *corner* and *cornerium* or *condyt* vs *conductus* illustrated in the quotations below. Further instances are e.g. *in fforest Dartemore . . . in dcā fforesta* (*It* 26, pg 23), *abbathiā de Tyntern* vs *Tyntern abbey* (*It* 36, pg 61).

(26) vbi in pʳncipio est ymago hoīs & vocatᵉʳ le porter & oꝑtet petere licenciā a portario ad jntranđ aulā (*It* 290, pg 213)[15]
'where to begin with is the image of a man called the porter & one must ask leave of the porter on entering the hall'

(27) cū Epcī wyntoīe apđ walthmᵃʳ maner (*It* 254, pg 321)
'with the Bishop of Winchester at Waltham Manor'

14 *St Augustine's Back* is given as a street name in Millerd's 1673 map of Bristol. This fact and the parallel construction *keya(m)* alternating with *le key* for the street name make this interpretation more likely than that as an adverbial 'at the back of' (a meaning which is elsewhere expressed by *a retro (de)*, see (34)).

15 See DMLBS s.v. *portarius* [LL], *porterius*; MED s.v. *porter* n.; AND s.v. *porter*[1].

a portu manerij ffayrechyldes (*It* 254, pg 322)[16]
'from the gate of the manor of Fairchilds'

(28) vsqȝ Corneriū magnu^m ī p^incipio de le key Bristoll (*Br* 6, pg 88)
'as far as the main corner at the beginning of the Quay of Bristol'

a le gr^aunt Corner place ꝑpe Incepcōȝ de le key . . . <I*t*> A cornerio incipiēte (*Br* 158, pg 151)[17]
'at the great corner place near the beginning of the Quay . . . Item beginning at the corner'

vsqȝ le corner sctī magni sunt / 260 /. stepꝑ (*It* 152, pg 85)
'to the corner of St. Magnus there are 260 steps'

(29) partis de le key vbi vn⁹ Condyt scituatur . . . partis de le key vbi in medio . vn⁹ conduct⁹ aque de petra frestone scituat^r (*Br* 128, pg 128)[18]
'the part of the Quay where a conduit is situated . . . the part of the Quay where in the middle a water-conduit of freestone is situated'

Variation between Latin and English forms of place-names of major towns and cities is also frequent, but not with minor towns or villages, where the English forms are regularly used.

(30) lati^do pontis Bristoll (*Br* 204, pg 163)
'the width of Bristol Bridge'

vie ad Bristow brygge (*Br* 212, pg 166)
'the road going to Bristol Bridge'

equitaui . . . vsqȝ Norwych de londoñ . . . de norwico vsqȝ london . . . de london vsqȝ Oxonford . . . de Oxonia (*Br* 220, pg 174)
'I rode . . . to Norwich from London . . . from Norwich to London . . . from London to Oxford . . . from Oxford'

16 See DMLBS s.v. *manerium*, *~ius*, *~ia* [AN *maner* < manere], attested since late 11th c.; MED s.v. *manor*, attested since c 1300. The two word-forms in the above quotation are clearly differentiated in the manuscript; furthermore, the position of *maner* and *manerij* in regard to the respective place names also differentiates the two forms.

17 See DMLBS s.v. 2 *cornarius*, regularly attested since 12th c.; MED s.v. *corner* attested since late 13th c.

18 See DMLBS s.v. 2 *conductus* 2, attested since late 11th c.; MED s.v. *conduit* n., 1(a), attested since late 14th c.; AND s.v. *conduit*[1].

sicut itur londonĵs (*Br* 224, pg 176)
'as one travels to London'

The pair *domum custume* and *customhous* in (31), on the other hand, should be classified as a loan translation. In (32), Latin *portu(m* and English *port* are etymologically related, while the two synonymous pairs in each language (*portu(m – hamonem, havyn – port*) are not.

(31) extendēdo ad domū custume[19] Regę . . . ex t^i^bȝ ꝑtibȝ de le customhous + ad keyā (*Br* 70, pg 110)
'extending to the King's customhouse . . . along three sides of the customhouse + to the Quay'

(32) & cadit jn portu Otyrmouth havyn (*It* 18, pg 16)
'and it falls into the harbour of Ottermouth haven'

ex alťa ꝑte aque de le havyn de ffowey (*It* 22, pg 18)
'on the other side of the water of the haven of Fowey'

& cadit in mari apđ portum siue hamonē[20] de Appu^a^ldore / port (*It* 26, pg 23)
'and falls into the sea at the harbour or bay of Appledore port'

Except possibly for *hamonem*, all synonymous and equivalent nouns discussed above were well attested by Worcester's time. However, Worcester also seems to have created new synonyms to complement existing lexemes, as in *panellas glasitas* (*It* 54, pg 8), *panas glasatas* (*It* 60, pg 5); according to the *Dictionary of Medieval Latin from British Sources* both of these are derived from Middle English *pan(e* and *glasen* respectively and only attested from Worcester.[21] Worcester used the new formation *glasatas* (with variant spellings) even next to the synonymous Latin *vitreatus*.[22] It is noteworthy that Worcester also used the English plural forms *panes*, *panys* alongside his

19 See DMLBS, s.v. *custuma* 4 and 5.

20 See DMLBS, s.v. *hamo* 'hook, bay', where the quotation from Worcester is the only instance given. Worcester uses the word a few times.

21 See DMLBS, s.v. *pana* [ME pane, OF pan] 2 & 3: "panel of glass, section of window, frame" and s.v. *glasare* [ME glasen] "to fit with glass, glaze". Evidently, first attestations in historical dictionaries have to be treated with caution.

22 See DMLBS s.v. *vitreare*.

new formation *panas*, but equally alongside the (near-) synonyms *panellas*,[23] see (33), and *pagettas*.[24]

(33) Et hēt .8.to panas (*Br* 132, pg 130) . . . Et qlīt fenestra hēt .5. panes. altīs .12. pedū . . . & hēt .5. panys . . . q̂liȝ fenestra nō hēt ~~v~~ nisi .4. ~~panellas~~ panellas vitreatas (*Br* 136, pg 130)
'And it has 8 panes . . . and each window has 5 panes 12 feet high . . . and it has 5 panes . . . each window has only ~~v~~ 4 glazed ~~panels~~ panels'

An illustration of Worcester's extensive lexical variation is the next passage which, over a couple of pages, shows a range of linguistic choices, both paradigmatic (lexical) and syntagmatic (syntactic), to refer to the notion of '(old) market'. This results in different types of syntagmas, partly with different word-order, from monolingual noun phrases like English *Old Market* and Latin *mercato antiquo* or *veteri*(s) *mercato*, to the mixed-language noun phrase *antiquo market*. A special case is *le veyle market . . . via lapidea . longa & lata vocata le veile m^{a}rket* (*Br* 110, pg 124), since neither the *Middle English Dictionary* nor the *Oxford English Dictionary* have an entry or cross reference to *veile* or *veyle* ('old'), while it is listed as headword in the *Anglo-Norman Dictionary*. On the basis of this lexicographical evidence and Worcester's competence in French, *veile/veyle* should be classified as French, though one cannot rule out that *veyle/veile* formed part of the author's 'English' lexical repertoire. The forms without modifying adjective range from *le Market*(*t*) and *Market* to *Mercato*. There is no functional difference between the different variants. They support the claim that extensive variation is a defining feature of the mixed-language administrative code. (Note also the variation between *ex t^{a}nsuerso* and *le travers* 'across' in *Br* 110, pg 124.)

(34) via lōga in posteriori ꝑte a retro vie de old market vsqȝ Laffordysyate . via posterior ex ꝑte meridio^{li} a retro de antiquo market Incipiēdo a porta p^{i}ma Castri Bristoll̄ . . . in meridio^{li} de *le* crosse in mercato ꝑdc̄o . . . et sic ꝯtinue eūdo a retro gardina tentoꝝ in mercato antiquo / vsqȝ ad murū Eccl̄ie

23 See DMLBS s.v. *panellus* (with reference from *panella*), with different attested meaning; in sense 6 "frame, light" only attested from Worcester!

24 See DMLBS s.v. *pagetta* "window, light, pane of glass", with no information on etymology or related form. The only quotation there is from Worcester. There are at least two instances in the *Itineraria*, see especially *ꝯtīet .5. ł .6. pagettas anglice panys* (*It* 116, pg 15) 'has 5 or 6 lights in English panes'.

occide/tale ... hospitlē dom⁹ cū capella in ~~veteris~~ veteris m̃cato ꝑpe laffordys//yate (*Br* 106, pg 123)
'the long road in the back side behind the road of Old Market as far as Lawford's Gate. The back road on the south side behind Old Market, beginning from the main gate of Bristol Castle ... on the south of the cross in the aforesaid market ... and so continuing going behind the gardens of the buildings in Old Market, as far as to the west church wall ... The hospital building with chapel in ~~Old~~ Old Market next to Lawford's Gate'

le markett weyes v^r^s⁹ laffordyate Via ^lōga^ nō edificata in ~~pte~~ al'ra ꝑte boriali de le m^a^rket place in ꝑochia sctī philippi ... Et ex t^a^nsuerso vie veīete de le veyle market vsqꝫ aquā ad Erlesmedew ꝑ le grun^a^t Orchard markys wiliā ... ad viam de markett ꝑpe laffordysyate ... directe ꝑ le travers de dcī market ... de illa p^i^ori ve^ne^lla . ex t^a^nsuerso de le market (*Br* 110, pg 124)
'the market ways towards Lawford's Gate. The long unpaved road on the other ~~side~~ northern side of the market place in the parish of St Philip ... and across the road coming from the Old Market as far as the water at Earlsmead by the great orchard of Mark William's ... to the market road near Lawford's Gate ... directly opposite the said market ... from that previous lane opposite the Market'

Via lapidea . longa & lata vocata le veile m^a^rket a p^i^ncipio alte crucis (*Br* 112, pg 124)
'The long and broad stone-paved road called the Old Market from the beginning at the tall cross'

Via ^longa^ a dcā cruce ... vocata le market ... latitudo dcē vie de mercato ⁹tinet ... (*Br* 122, pg 127)
'The long road from the said cross ... called the Market ... The width of the said Market road measures ...'

Capella hospit'is stē trinitatis in veteri m̃cato anglice old Mrket (*Br* 150, pg 138)
'The chapel of Holy Trinity hospital in the Old Market in English Old Market'

More complex are morphologically and etymologically related synonyms like *ala* – *ela* – *ele* ('aisle, wing; *pl.* transept') and *spera* – *spere* ('spire'). While some of the word-forms of these lexemes are unambiguous Latin or English, there are also forms which, in isolation, are visual diamorphs, though they are partly disambiguated by the syntactic slot in which they occur. However, a small number of problematic cases remain, which will be discussed in more detail below.

Worcester uses a variety of word-forms to refer to church aisles, such as *alas*, *elaꝝ*, *ele*, *elys*. Forms of *al* – as in *cū vna ala* (*It* 172, pg 264), *vlt^{a} Alas* (*It* 286, pg 210), *alaꝝ* (*It* 298, pg 217), are clearly Latin, and so are those of *el-* with an unambiguous Latin suffix such as <–*a*, – ꝝ> as in *Elea* (*It* 226, pg 263) or *duaꝝ elaꝝ* (*It* 280, pg 224).[25] However, the existence of the Middle English lexeme *ele* causes problems of interpretation since some *el-* forms are potential candidates for visual diamorphs.[26] Since medieval Latin <–*e*> is a regular spelling for classical Latin <–*ae*>, many noun forms in <–*e*> qualify as a Latin genitive or dative. When such forms occur in Latin clauses in a syntactic slot that requires a singular genitive, as is often the case with *ele*, an interpretation as Latin might arguably be preferable, especially in combination with a premodifying adjective with the same case ending as in (35), though their formal identity with English forms still causes them to be visual diamorphs.

(35) longi^{do} noue ele in ꝑte meridionali (*It* 226, pg 263)
'The length of the new aisle on the south'

Itē sūt meridionale ꝑte Ele # .7. ffenestre (*It* 226, pg 263)
'Item on the south side of the Aisle are 7 windows'

lati^{do} dicte Ele ꝰtīet .8. virgas . . . qđ dcā Ela extendit᷑ (*It* 226, pg 263)
'the width of the said Aisle is 8 yards . . . that the said Aisle extends'

In the compound *Crosse Ele* 'transept',[27] the interpretation of *ele* as English is supported by the preceding article *le* (see *It* 60, pg 5 for the variant form *le Crosse yle*).

(36) It᷑longitude le Crosse Ele ꝰtinet . . . 120 . stepp̄ (*It* 50, pg 7)
'The length of the Transept is . . . 120 steps'

Before discussing the remaining word-forms of *el*–, a brief excursion into an aspect of medieval spelling is appropriate. As Wright has pointed out in a recent paper, "orthographical convention served to create an integrated multilingual text, but also to keep Middle English and Anglo-Norman on the one hand

25 See DMLBS s.v. *ala* [CL], 5. aisle: "**a** of a church", also with cross-reference from *ela* to "v. 1. *ala* (4a)"; the only quotation under *ala* with a form of *ela* is from Worcester (*elarum*).

26 See MED s.v. *ēle* n(2). The Anglo-French form *ele* (see AND s.v. *ele*[1] 'wing'), another potential candidate for visual diamorphs, can be disregarded here.

27 See MED s.v. *ēle* n(2), 2. "a wing of the transept (cp *cross ele*, under *cross*)", and s.v. *cros* n 9b "one side of the transept of a cruciform church; in pl., the transept".

distinct from Medieval Latin on the other" (Wright 2017: 282). In her corpus of late 14th century cathedral accounts, <y> was "rarely if ever used" in medieval Latin words such as *clavis*, *tegƚis*, while in Anglo Norman and English words "both and <y>" were used (2017: 282). This still seems to apply to some extent for Worcester's text, where <y> is regularly used in the English inflectional suffixes <–ys> and <–yth> (besides *-es* and *-eth*), while <y> does not occur in Latin suffixes, where <i> is the regular choice; <–es>, however, occurs in both English and Latin, see example (1) above.[28] On the basis of this orthographical distribution, the form *elys* in (37) to (40) can be classified as English. In (41), the article *le* before *Elis* points to an English form (but see the exceptions to this rule discussed in section 3), though <–is> has not been found in an unambiguous English inflectional suffix in the text. Thus a certain amount of ambiguity remains, which may reflect Worcester's linguistic awareness better than a rigid classification.

(37) nauis Eccƚie cū duabꝫ Elys . c^{i}ca . 46 . steppys meis (*It* 52, pg 7)
'the nave of the Church with two Aisles about 46 of my steps'.

(38) lati^{do} Eccƚie cū Elys & brachijs dcē Eccƚie ^{9}tiꝫ . 50 . steppys de mea mēsura (*It* 80, pg 54)
'The width of the Church with the Aisles and transepts of the said Church is 50 steps of my measure'

(39) lōgi^{e} navis Eccƚie . ^{9}tiet . 98. stepp̄ lati^{do} navis Eccƚie cū .2. Elys ^{9}tiêt . 50. stepp̄ (*It* 148, pg 56)
'the length of the nave of the Church is 98 steps the width of the nave of the Church with two Aisles is 50 steps'

(40) latitudo navis Eccƚie cū duabꝫ Elys (*It* 154, pg 86)
'The width of the nave of the Church with two Aisles'

(41) et queƚit fenestra in le Elis Eccƚie (*It* 116, pg 15)
'and each window in the Aisles of the Church'

---

28 There is a single occurrence of the spelling *cadyt* in *Wye cadyt* (*It* 70), which might be due to the preceding river name *Wye*. Otherwise *cadit* is the regular form. See also the distinction between <i> and <y> in *cū fenestris & vanys* (*It* 50, pg 12) 'with windows and vanes' (quoted as (48) below).

Very similar to *ela/ele* is the distribution of *spera/spere* 'spire', with 17 occurrences of different word-forms in the *Bristol* part. Ten of these have an unambiguous Latin inflection (*spera, speram*), five forms of *spere* are visual diamorphs, but like the *ele* forms, occur in a Latin syntactic slot which requires the genitive singular. Only two instances are English word-forms, namely *le spere* and *spere* in a monolingual English sentence, see (43) and (44).[29]

(42) ī ꝑxu^{m} ad ligād̹ ꝑpam que quidē ꝑpa stat modo vlt^{a} ~~100~~ 100. pedes (*Br* 72, pg 111)
'tying closely together the spire which spire now stands more than 100 feet'

(43) alti^{do} de le spere (*Br* 132, pg 130)
'the height of the spire'

Spere altitudo (*Br* 190, pg 158)
'the height of the spire'

(44) How many onche . doth the spere of trinite chyrcħ of norw^{c} . . . (*Br* 132, pg 130)

To sum up, *ela/ele* and *spera/spere* not only have a similar phonological form, but also a similar distribution of unambiguous Latin forms, potential visual diamorphs in a Latin singular genitive slot and only a small number of unambiguous English forms, partly preceded by *le*.

The above discussion has raised the issue of general nouns which are potentially visual diamorphs in isolation, yet potentially disambiguated by syntactic position. This is, however, is not always possible, as for instance in constructions like the prepositional phrase *pre fame*, which could either be monolingual Latin (*fame* as ablative of *fames*) or a mixed Latin + English prepositional phrase (see MED s.v. *fame* n.(2) 'famine' with a single quotation from "a1500 (?c1424)"). The same ambiguity exists in the frequent cases where terms of social status and profession follow a personal name and where both

29 See DMLBS s.v. 2 *spira* [ME spire < AS spir] "1. Tall plant, reed or palm" (also with <e> spelling); 2. spire. All five instances in this meaning are from Worcester (including that from 'Dallaway') and are the variant with <e>. OED s.v. *spire* has first attestations of the meaning 'spire' (under 8.) from around 1600, and a reference to OED s.v. *spear* n.^{2}, †1. "A spire of a church", with first attestation from Worcester [alias 'Botoner'], the next from 1509, with comment "Irregular variant of spire n.". – Worcester also gives synonyms *Turris & spera siue pinacm̄* (*Br* 184, pg 156) and *Turris & spera . siue le broche* (*Br* 190, pg 158).

unambiguous Latin and English word-forms are also attested, such as *ab̄b̄* ('abbot', *It* 74, pg 81) or *march^a^nt* ('merchant', *Br* 252, pg 201).

(45) & mortl̄itas p̄ fame & jnumdacō pluuie (*It* 178, pg 331)
'and death from famine and floods of rain'

(46) ^beata^ mg^a^areta m^a^rtir occisa in lytillwood (*It* 228, pg 263)[30]
'St Margaret martyr was killed in Littlewood'

(47) dn̂s Radı̄s Bygot Rector de Trunch̄ (*It* 226, pg 268)[31]
'Sir Ralph Bygot, Rector of Trunch'

On the syntagmatic level, monolingual versus multilingual constructions often show variation by changing language, as in coordinated nouns and noun phrases such as *de bryke & mearemio* 'of brick and timber' (*It* 48, pg 11), in syntactic groups like *crucē de marblestone* 'cross of marble' (*It* 254, pg 322) and, rarely, in combinations such as . 3 . *pastella venyson* 'venison pasties' (*It* 264, pg 173).[32]

(48) an Oryell̄ cū fenestris & vanys de auratę (*It* 50, pg 12)
'an Oriel with windows and vanes of gilt'

(49) sunt de villis ^& **havyns** de^ Tynby (*Br* 146, pg 136)
'they are from towns and havens of Tenby'

(50) vacue de planchers & cooptura (*Br* 240, pg 197)
'stripped of floors and ceilings'

(51) p le magnū gardinū & Orchard . m^a^rkyswilliā (*Br* 110, pg 124)
'by the great garden and orchard of Mark William'

(52) tribȝ . robis . de auro . de purpyr̄ & de perseblewe (*It* 48, pg 11)
'three robes of gold, of purple and of perse [dark] blue'

(53) arbores & mastys de vyrre (*It* 22, pg 92)
'poles and masts of fir'

30 See DMLBS s.v. *martyr* (with cross-reference from *martir*) and MED s.v. *martir*.

31 See DMLBS s.v. *rector*, MED s.v. *rectour*, with <o> spellings from 15th c and before.

32 *pastella venyson* can be seen as a contact formation, combining Romance word-order with Germanic direct contact position, i.e. without connecting preposition *de*.

ibi crescūt arbores de ebete voc mastys p nauibȝ (*It* 134, pg 69)[33]
'there grow fir trees called masts for ships'

(54) crucē de marblestone . . . crucē de ligno (*It* 254, pg 322)
'cross of marble . . . cross of wood'

(55) ad viam de markett (*Br* 110, pg 124)
'to Market Street'

vie de Mercato (*Br* 122, pg 127)
'Market Street'

le markett weyes . . . le m^a^rket place (*Br* 110, pg 124)
'the market ways . . . the market place'

(56) a steyre de lapidibȝ (*Br* 124, pg 128)
'a stairway of stones'

(57) orchard de fructibȝ (*It* 296, pg 211) 'fruit orchard'

In the following two examples, the coordinated second nouns are potential visual diamorphs, but seem to be disambiguated by the syntactic construction, i.e. both *pasture* and *fame* being inflected forms of *pastura* and *fames* parallel to the preceding *prati* ('of the meadow') and *gladio* ('by the sword').

(58) It valor p^a^ti & pastur p a^m^ (*It* 56, pg 51)
'Item the value of the meadow and pasture per year'

(59) vndecies centena milia Judeoꝝ gladio & fame perieꝝt (*Br* 192, pg 159)
'eleven times a hundred thousand Jews perished by the sword and of starvation'

5 Conclusion

Worcester's travel notes provide important evidence for the study of medieval multilingualism for a number of reasons. They are written in a mixture of medieval Latin, English and some French, and show many if not most of the

33 See DMLBS s.v. *abies* [CL] 'fir', with this quotation from Worcester as a variant form.

linguistic features typical of the mixed linguistic code of medieval administrative texts, though the notes are closer to a different text-type, namely the kind of topographical and antiquarian travel accounts emerging in the late medieval and early modern periods. They were written on single sheets of paper mostly on the spot and in haste during his journeys and thus represent mainly spontaneous, unmonitored language. Different to many other medieval texts, we also know a great deal about the author's life, education, professional career and personal interests and reading, but also his multilingualism in English, Latin and French. This information enables us to establish some important sociolinguistic variables, particular those of 'age', 'education' and 'profession'.

As in the majority of administrative multilingual texts, the most pervasive feature is variation, which is apparent on various linguistic levels, mostly lexical, but also morphological and orthographic. Among the obvious features is Worcester's extensive use of the article *le/la/les*, which resembles in many ways that of administrative texts, though some loosening of earlier restrictions is noticable, such as the occurrence of the form before Latin word-forms and the variation with forms of the English indefinite article. Lexical variation occurs in a number of different forms, both on the paradigmatic level of words and on the syntagmatic levels of combination of words. Among these is the co-occurrence of etymologically and semantically related Romance and English lexemes, and the role of visual diamorphs on the level of function words, bound morphemes and lexical words. A noteworthy aspect is Worcester's apparent lexical creativity which is reflected in a number of words, word-forms or meanings only or for the first time attested in Worcester's *Itineraria*, though these often only add another synonym to the lexical inventory of late Middle English.

Worcester's multilingual practices cover a range of different forms. There are some stretches of monolingual Latin and, to a lesser extent, English, but mixed-language is far more frequent. The presence of some French text testifies Worcester' trilingualism. Many passages can be classified as code-switches in the traditional sense of the term, but a great number of single-word 'switches' show a very intimate fusion of Latin and English, whose major function seems to be to establish the multilingualism of the text. Creating a new Latin derivation from English as in *pana* and then using *panas* and *panys* in close proximity and with two other lexical innovations, *pagettas* and *panellas*, can neither be explained by lexical necessity or by stylistic reasons, especially not in a widely unmonitored text largely written on the spot and in haste. For Worcester the use of the administrative mixed-language code was evidently a default option for note-taking which he had acquired over decades of professional life and in which he was very much at ease. His use of this system in a new text-type might indicate that this system was used more widely than assumed so far, at least by people familiar with it from their professional training. This provides a further argument for the relevance of this type of mixed-coding for the development of English.

As for the sociolinguistic variables mentioned above, the variable 'age' (apart of the variable 'profession') may be relevant for Worcester's restricted use of the older construction *ad keyā* (instead of *ad le key*) as being a relic form from his youth, while his high fluency of the mixed code towards the end of the fifteenth century may reflect his advanced age at the time of his writing, a period when even "the most laggardly, conservative institutions had finally tipped over into monolingual English" (Wright 2018: 344).

References

Primary texts

Harvey, John H. (ed.). 1969. *William Worcestre: Itineraries*. London: Clarendon Press.
Neale, Frances (ed.). 2000. *William Worcestre: The topography of medieval Bristol*. Bristol: Bristol Record Society.
Nichols, J. G. (ed.). 1860. *William Worcester, The Boke of Noblesse, addressed to King Edward the Fourth on his Invasion of France in 1475*. London: Roxburghe Club.
Facsimile of CCCC MS 210: <https://parker.stanford.edu/parker/catalog/mp810zm2076>

Secondary literature

AND = Stone, Louise W. – T.B.W. Reid – William Rothwell (eds.). 1977–1992. *The Anglo-Norman Dictionary*. London: MHRA. http://www.anglo-norman.net/.
Broadway, Jan. 2015. "The afterlife of William Worcestre". Paper given at the symposium 'William Worcestre 1414–2015: the Legacy of an Early English Topographer'. Bristol, 31 October 2015. Online: <http://xmera.co.uk/Worcestre.pdf>
DMLBS = Dictionary of Medieval Latin from British Sources. Ronald E. Latham, David R. Howlett et al. (eds.). 1975–2013. Oxford: The British Academy & Oxford University Press. http://logeion.uchicago.edu/lexidium/.
Gardner-Chloros, Penelope. 2009. *Code-switching*. Cambridge: Cambridge University Press.
Hoskins, W.G. 1984. *Local history in England*. 3rd ed. London: Routledge.
Ingham, Richard. 2018. "Medieval bilingualism in England: On the rarity of vernacular code-switching". In Päivi Pahta, Janne Skaffari and Laura Wright (eds.). *Multilingual practices in language history: English and beyond*. Berlin: de Gruyter, 39–59.
McFarlane, K.B. 1957. "William Worcester: A preliminary survey". In J. Conway Davis (ed.). *Studies presented to Sir Hilary Jenkison*. London, 196–212; reprinted in McFarlane, K.B. (ed.). *England in the fifteenth century*. London: The Hambledon Press 1981, 199–224.
MED = Middle English Dictionary Online. http://quod.lib.umich.edu/m/med/.
OED = Oxford English Dictionary Online. http://dictionary.oed.com/.
Orme, Nicholas, "Worcester [Botoner], William (1415–1480x85)". In *Oxford Dictionary of National Biography*". online: https://doi.org/10.1093/ref:odnb/29967.

ter Horst, Tom and Nike Stam. 2018. "Visual diamorphs: The importance of language neutrality in code-switching from medieval Ireland". In Päivi Pahta, Janne Skaffari and Laura Wright (ed.). *Multilingual practices in language history: English and beyond*. Berlin: de Gruyter, 223–242.

Trotter, David. 2010."Bridging the gap: The (socio)linguistic evidence of some medieval English bridge accounts". In Richard Ingham (ed.). *The Anglo-Norman language and its contexts*. Woodbridge: York Medieval Press, 52–62.

Trotter, David. 2011. "Death, taxes and property: Some code-switching evidence from Dover, Southampton, and York". In Herbert Schendl and Laura Wright (eds.). *Code-switching in Early English*. De Gruyter Mouton: Berlin/ Boston, 155–189.

Wright, Laura. 2010. "A pilot study on the singular definite articles *le* and *la* in fifteenth-century London mixed-business writing". In Richard Ingham (ed.). *The Anglo-Norman language and its contexts*. Woodbridge: York Medieval Press, 130–142.

Wright, Laura. 2011. "On variation in medieval mixed-language business writing". In Herbert Schendl and Laura Wright (eds.). *Code-switching in Early English*. De Gruyter Mouton: Berlin/ Boston, 191–218.

Wright, Laura. 2017. "On non-integrated vocabulary in the mixed-language accounts of St Paul's Cathedral, 1315–1405". In Richard Ashdowne and Carolinne White, (eds.). *Latin in Medieval Britain. Proceedings of the British Academy* 206. London: British Academy, 272–298.

Wright, Laura. 2018. "A multilingual approach to the history of Standard English". In Päivi Pahta, Janne Skaffari and Laura Wright (eds.). *Multilingual practices in language history: English and beyond*. Berlin: de Gruyter, 339–359.

Philip Durkin

11 The relationship of borrowing from French and Latin in the Middle English period with the development of the lexicon of Standard English: Some observations and a lot of questions

1 Introduction

The role of lexical borrowing from Anglo-Norman and (British) medieval Latin in the development of modern standard English is a topic that is very difficult to address for a number of interconnected reasons, among which three stand out as particularly problematic: firstly, "standard English" is a difficult concept, and identifying even the outline of its historical development even more so (see Introduction to this volume); secondly, the volume of Anglo-Norman and medieval Latin borrowings in modern English is so vast that all generalizations must be approached with caution, and examples chosen carefully and (ideally) in a principled way; thirdly, our tools for assessing questions of word frequency in earlier periods of English, especially on a comparative basis across different forms of discourse, are still at a very rudimentary stage of development.

This chapter will look first at some things that can be established with reasonable confidence about the composition of the lexicon of modern published English written discourse, and especially about the composition of its high-frequency vocabulary, taking this to be the core of the lexicon of Standard English today. It will then look at what some relatively simple, dictionary-derived information about language of immediate origin and date of first attestation in English suggests about the key periods for those borrowings that have most profoundly affected the high-frequency vocabulary of modern standard English written discourse. It will then examine how such data has been connected with standard, handbook accounts of the 'Rise' or 'Resurgence of English', and also at how more recent research problematizes such accounts. The main focus will be on borrowings from Anglo-Norman, although borrowings from (British) medieval Latin will also be considered, particularly the large contribution to the high-frequency vocabulary of modern English made by words that probably show some input from both of these sources (i.e. words borrowed partly from Anglo-Norman and partly

https://doi.org/10.1515/9783110687545-012

from Latin). The chapter ends with an attempt to establish some programmatic questions for further investigation of these issues.

2 Words of French and Latin origin in the lexicon of modern published English written discourse

If we start from the perspective of contemporary English (i.e. a teleological perspective) it seems obvious that lexical borrowing from French and Latin during the Middle English period has had an enormous impact on the lexicon of modern published written English, albeit with many centuries of selection of particular lexical items for the conventional realization of particular meanings intervening.

If we start out from considering effects on the lexicon as a whole, among the approximately 275,000 headword entries in the full *Oxford English Dictionary*, roughly one third are words borrowed from other languages (i.e. loanwords, excluding loan translations or calques); even if this survey is extended to include the approximately 600,000 lexemes in the *OED* (including compounds and derivatives nested under other headwords), the proportion of loanwords remains high, at approximately one sixth of all lexemes. (Of course, even the *OED*'s huge wordlist is selective: anyone who has expertise in a particular specialist field, such as a scientific discipline, a profession or trade, or a hobby, is likely to find that only a part of the specialist vocabulary of that field is reflected in even the largest dictionary wordlist.) Roughly 75% of those loanwords have either Latin or French (or both) as their language of immediate origin. (See analysis in Durkin (2014) 22–9.)

However, a simple numerical analysis like this neglects the fact that many lexemes in the *OED* are very rare, and also ignores the many lexemes that have been derived from words that have been borrowed from other languages. In an attempt to get around both of these issues, the still valuable overview in Scheler (1977: 70–74) presents data (drawn from Finkenstaedt *et al.* 1973) based on the more selective wordlist of the *Shorter Oxford English Dictionary* (first edition), the still more selective, learner-oriented wordlist of the *Advanced Learner's Dictionary of Current English* (1963 edition), and a basic vocabulary list, the *General Service List of English Words*. Grouping together (somewhat approximately) compound and derivative lexemes under their etymological parents, this presents a striking picture of Latin- and French-derived lexis in English, with these making up more than 50% of the lexis of the *SOED* and *ALD*, and not far below 50% (and still slightly more in total than all words of inherited origin) even in the basic vocabulary of the *GSL*. While the percentage of Latin-origin words drops significantly in the more selective wordlists, that from French actually increases somewhat. Table 11.1 summarizes this data.

Table 11.1: Three main sources of words in the wordlists of the *Shorter Oxford English Dictionary* (first edition), the *Advanced Learner's Dictionary of Current English* (1963 edition), and the *General Service List of English Words*; after Scheler (1977) 72.

	SOED **(%)**	***ALD*** **(%)**	***GSL*** **(%)**
Inherited:	22.2	27.43	47.08
French:	28.37	35.89	38.2
Latin:	28.29	22.05	9.59

Such totals are not linked to the date at which words were borrowed into English, and therefore leave many key historical questions hanging. A step towards a diachronic perspective may be obtained by correlating dictionary data on language of origin with the date of first attestation of each lexical item. Figure 11.1 (reproduced from Durkin 2014) takes data from the parts of the revised edition of the *OED* so far published (in order to ensure consistency of approach). Here, borrowing of words from Latin appears to show two peaks, one in Early Modern English, the other in the nineteenth century. Borrowing from French appears reasonably steady from the early fourteenth century to the early nineteenth century. Only those words identified as probably showing input from both Latin and French (or, in some cases, from either of those sources) show significantly more borrowing in the Middle English period than later.[1] However, this picture fails to take into account two important factors: the rate at which new words of any origin are first recorded is not constant (at least, as reflected by *OED*'s data); also, words differ greatly in their frequency of use. The first of these issues may to some extent be obviated by looking at words of Latin and French origin as a proportion of all words first recorded in

1 On the criteria by which these categories are distinguished see detailed discussion in Durkin (2014) 236–249. To generalize very broadly, borrowings of words directly from French (and ultimately from Latin) are most often identified on the basis of sound changes shown by the word stem in French that are shared by the English borrowing; borrowings from Latin alone or more often identified on the basis that classicizing forms of the same word are very rare or differ in meaning in French; while borrowings showing input from both languages are typically identified on the basis of both languages showing heavy attestation of formally viable word forms in a range of meanings corresponding to those of the English borrowing.

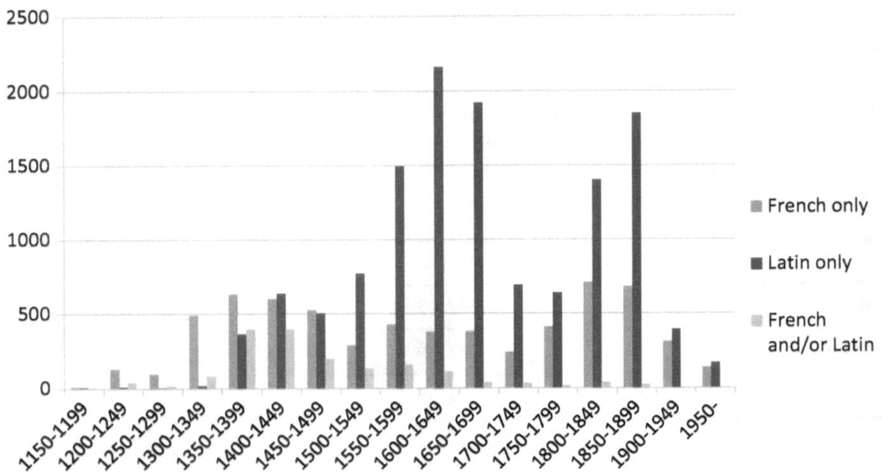

Figure 11.1: Loanwords from French, Latin, and French and/or Latin in parts of OED3 so far completed, arranged chronologically (reproduced from Durkin (2014) 33).

century, as in Figure 11.2. Here, the prominence of French loanwords in the Middle English period stands out immediately; when their totals are combined, borrowings from French and Latin make up more than 40% of all new words throughout the period from 1300 to 1500.

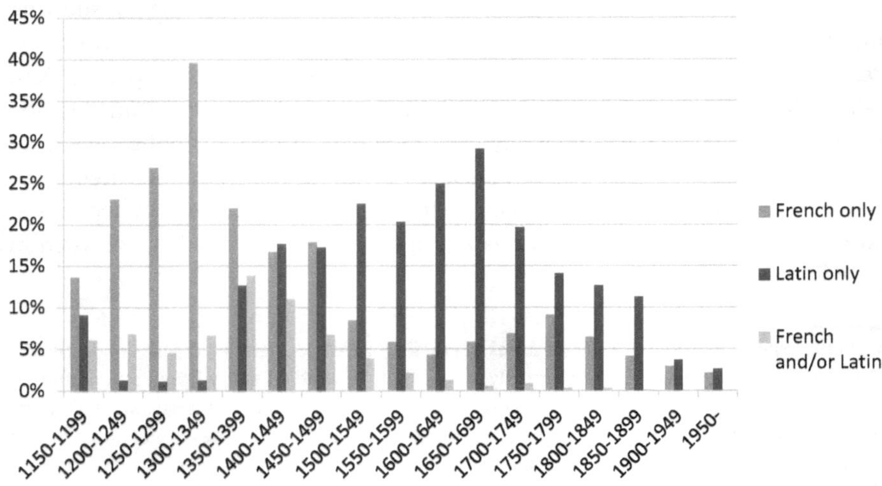

Figure 11.2: Loanwords from French, Latin, and French and/or Latin as a proportion of all new words, as reflected by parts of *OED3* so far completed (reproduced from Durkin (2014) 35).

Still, this data does not take account of differences in the frequency of use of individual words. One, explicitly teleological, approach is to look at what the most frequent words are in modern English, and to examine their etymological origin and date of first attestation. If our interest is in the development of the lexicon of Standard English, then, in a very long-term perspective, a reasonable starting point can be found in the high-frequency vocabulary of modern English, as reflected by a corpus. Durkin (2014: 34–40) takes the 1000 most frequent items in the *British National Corpus*,[2] and looks at the language of origin and date of first attestation given for each of these in the *OED*. Figure 11.3 and Appendix 1 revisit this data (updated as entries have since been updated in the ongoing revision of the *OED*).[3] Attempting an empirical approach such as this in examining very long-term lexical change foregrounds many difficult issues, such as: any high-frequency list will reflect any biases and shortcomings in the corpus from which it is derived (although here the bias of the *BNC* towards formal published writing from Britain becomes a virtue if our primary interest is in the lexis of the standard language)[4]; some of the high-frequency words are not directly borrowed words but are formed from them (although these make up a very small proportion of the total here, and hybrids such as *perhaps* are very rare); lexical histories are frequently complex, and modern-day frequencies can reflect semantic developments long after the period of borrowing (as e.g. *computer* or *test* – although see section 3.3 on the surprising history of *carry*, where semantic change in English seems closely tied to the circumstances of the word's initial borrowing). On the other hand, a method that forces one to foreground such issues can be helpful in highlighting the difficulties of making generalizations

---

2 Using the frequency list by Leech et al.: see Leech et al. (2001) and also http://ucrel.lancs.ac.uk/bncfreq/ (data derived from http://ucrel.lancs.ac.uk/bncfreq/lists/1_1_all_alpha.txt). As will be seen from Appendix 1, items are separated by word class, and a few of the items are phrases used prepositionally; *used to* is listed separately from *use*, which for present purposes usefully highlights its impact on the repertoire of function words in modern English. Etymologically distinct homonyms are not distinguished in this frequency list, and pragmatic decisions have therefore had to be made in the analysis given here; the most problematic cases are all footnoted in Appendix 1. I have removed proper names from the list, and forms derived from these such as *European* or *American*, promoting the next items in the rank order in to maintain the total at 1000 (see further Durkin (2014) 36 n.5).

3 Appendix 1 thus supersedes the data at http://fdslive.oup.com/www.oup.com/booksites/uk/booksites/content/9780199574995/Exploring%20loanwords%20among%20high-frequency%20vocabulary.pdf

4 One item particularly indicative of the bias of the *BNC* towards current affairs and politics, especially via newspapers, is the inclusion of *hon.* for *honourable* (primarily reflecting its formal use in the UK parliament). For the statistically very similar results found when the same exercise is run on other corpora see Durkin (2014) 38–9.

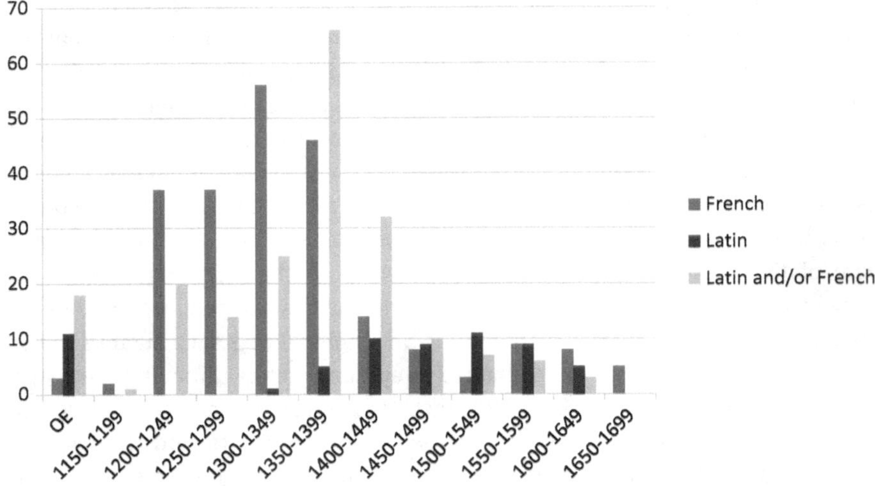

Figure 11.3: Totals of loanwords from French, Latin, and French and/or Latin in the 1000 most frequent items in the *British National Corpus*, arranged chronologically.

about lexical history; in particular, as will be investigated more in section 3.1, an empirically-derived set of words is extremely helpful in holding up to scrutiny generalizations about the lexical fields and registers typically affected by medieval borrowing.

Bearing these cautions in mind, it is nonetheless striking that this exercise suggests that among these most frequent words in modern use, just under 50% are borrowings from French or Latin or both (or, in a few cases, are formed within English from words of this origin); borrowings from all other languages combined contribute only 4% of the items in this list (the remaining words being derived from the inherited Germanic lexis of Old English). If we then ask when these words entered English, Figure 11.3 presents an equally striking picture: the vast majority of these words have first attestations during the Middle English period. Only borrowings from Latin alone buck this trend, but they are hugely outnumbered by those from French alone and from French and/or Latin. Those identified as from French alone (usually on grounds of word form) are first attested mostly in the thirteenth and fourteenth centuries; those that could be from French or Latin (and in very many cases probably show some input from each language) show a huge spike in the late fourteenth century. The high-frequency vocabulary of contemporary written English thus appears to show a much more marked impact from late Middle English borrowing from French and Latin than is shown by the lexicon as a whole.

Looking at frequency in modern English mapped against date of first attestation of course runs the risk of creating a false impression that these words have been part of the high-frequency vocabulary of English for all of their history. What limited data is currently available suggests (unsurprisingly) that the general picture is rather different, with gradually increasing frequency of use over time much more the norm. Compare Durkin (2014: 336–40), where analysis of the most frequent spelling forms (examined rather than lemmatized forms for reasons of practicality) in the Middle English and Early Modern English components of the *Helsinki Corpus* compared with the *BNC* suggests that of those spelling forms (*c*1000) which show a frequency of 0.01% or higher, only 7% are words borrowed from French or Latin in the Middle English component, 19% in the Early Modern English component, but 38% in the *BNC*. Thus, the incidence of words of French or Latin origin in high-frequency use appears to show a gradually ascending curve (a finding supported by more detailed examination of fifteenth- and sixteenth-century data along similar lines). However, individual word histories sometimes buck such general trends, as will be seen in section 3.3 in a close examination of the history of *carry* in English.

3 Connecting this data with narratives about the development of standard English

3.1 Traditional accounts

In many handbooks and histories of English the account given of the history of lexical borrowing from French and Latin in Middle English is closely bound up with the account given of the spread of English to a wider variety of variously 'official' written and spoken functions at the expense of Anglo-Norman or Latin, as well as the increasing use of English as a literary language. Often an account of lexical borrowing is presented side-by-side with an account of what is identified as the 'reestablishment' or 'resurgence' of English, especially in the decades following the Black Death. Perhaps most influential are two consecutive chapters (6 and 7) in Baugh and Cable (2012 [ed. 1 1951]); another recent elaborated account directed to more advanced students and scholars is in Miller (2012). Miller presents a set of examples of French loanwords illustrating "Cultural spheres of French loans", divided into "government", "law", "military", "art and architecture", "religion", "literacy and education", "description" (chiefly adjectives), "social/cultural terms", and "culinary and dining" (Miller 2012: 164–7), followed shortly afterwards by a section headed "The resurgence of English" in which 22 numbered "factors traditionally adduced as contributing to the survival of English together with those hailed as evidence for its resurgence" are listed, among the latter being the landmarks usually noted as showing the spread of English in official functions, such as in the law courts and parliament (Miller 2012: 168–71). Miller's account is careful and nuanced, but one suspects that the positioning of "government" and "law" at the head of the list of examples of borrowing from French is motivated by the assumption that these are closely connected with the narrative of the replacement of Anglo-Norman by English in official functions; similarly, Baugh and Cable present, in this order, "governmental and administrative words", "ecclesiastical words", "law", "army and navy", "fashion, meals, and social life", "art, learning, medicine", and (somewhat later) "popular and literary borrowings". Further, the actual examples provided in these lists (and those in nearly all other handbooks and histories) are those that have been selected by the authors, and accreted from many generations of similar accounts, as being taken to be important, salient, and illustrative of these categories. However wary each scholar is of the danger of fitting the examples to the categories rather than vice versa, such dangers are ever-present in an area where the sheer volume of borrowings means that only a very few examples can be presented.

Another widespread (almost pervasive) approach is to consider French and Latin loans in the context of the development of stylistic registers, with vocabulary of native origin forming the core of the everyday, frequently low-status register, while Romance- or Latin-derived near or full synonyms form a higher-status register (subsequently, with the growth of standardization, feeding into the 'neutral' register acquired through formal education). Thus pairings such as *hearty* and *cordial*, *begin* and *commence*, *hide* and *conceal* are pointed to.[5] A more elaborate version identifies instances where there appears to be a three-fold layering of native, French-derived, and Latin-derived words, with the Latin-derived as the most formal, as e.g. *kingly*, *royal*, and *regal*, or *ask*, *question*, and *interrogate*.[6] This process is frequently labelled as 'layering'; especially in a continental European tradition, it is often presented alongside the identification of the vocabulary of modern English as being relatively 'dissociated', as for instance in the lack of formal relationship between semantically related terms as the noun *hand* and the adjective *manual* (where native *handly* and *handy* have, rather than

5 These examples are taken from Hughes (2000) 120. Hughes in fact stands out among such commentators for the clear statement he makes that many actual examples do not conform to this pattern: "it is important to realise how comprehensively the new French vocabulary displaced basic terms for ordinary things" (Hughes 2000: 120–121).

6 These examples are taken from Crystal (2004) 188–9.

becoming lower-status alternatives to *manual*, instead shown in the one case complete loss and in the other semantic specialization).[7]

Clearly, there is some truth in all of this, and probably a great deal of truth. It can be instructive though to pay attention to the many loanwords that do not fit either of these patterns (belonging to particular semantic domains, or employment in layering relationships) at all well. It is here that an empirically-derived set of significant loanwords may be particularly useful in testing assumptions. In this context we may therefore return in a little more detail to the loanwords among the 1000 most frequent words in present-day published written English as reflected by the *BNC*. These are listed in full in Appendix 1. These words that have ultimately attained the greatest degree of currency in modern English provide an interesting group for testing some of the assumptions about semantic groupings among Middle English loans. Here, we can find words that fit fairly easily into some of the traditionally identified semantic categories, such as law, government, or administration (or, very often, straddling all of these), such as *appeal*, *authority*, *court*, or learning and science, such as *chapter*, *degree*, or *science*; others point interestingly to the importance of adding business and business administration alongside law and government, such as *account*, *charge*, or *price*. Very large numbers of words though do not fit into such categories, such as *arrive*, *carry*, *catch*, *enjoy*, *enter*, *fine* (adjective), *large*, *remain*, *suppose*, *sure*, *very*. In some of these instances considering 'layering' is useful in suggesting oppositions still in play between less and more formal lexical choices, such as (probably) native *big* beside borrowed *large*, *think* beside *suppose*, *go in* beside *enter*, *stay* versus *remain*. Viewed specifically in terms of the development of a standard variety, the more formal item in such oppositions retains association with language acquired in the schoolroom and through reading and education, as opposed to in the colloquial usage of the home. In other cases, though, it is difficult to identify such layering phenomena. In understanding the histories of these lexical items a key desideratum is tracing the history of such oppositions, and in particular identifying how often items which now appear to be stylistically neutral may previously have been more stylistically marked. A detailed examination of *carry* in section 3.3 suggests that at least some items spread to general use even in basic meanings remarkably quickly, and in histories that may bypass oppositions of learned versus everyday entirely.

7 This use of *dissociation* (German *Dissoziation*) originated in Leisi (1955).

3.2 Approaches centred on examining the effects of bi- and multilingualism

Over the past two decades, a great deal of important work has placed a new emphasis on viewing the development of the Middle English lexicon in the light of bilingualism and trilingualism throughout the Middle English period.[8] Additionally, long overdue attention has begun to be paid to the multilingual, Latin-matrix document keeping that dominated in many areas of business life and day-to-day administration in later medieval England. In such documents, the grammatical frame is provided by Latin, albeit often very heavily abbreviated employing the conventional system of marks of suspension, so that most of the distinctive Latin inflectional morphology is represented only by a series of marks indicating where the relevant endings are to be supplied by the reader; very often, a high proportion of the content words (especially nouns) show stems of vernacular, not Latin, origin, without Latin inflectional endings (not even as represented by an abbreviation); hence, they appear to be vernacular items embedded in context where (heavily abbreviated) Latin provides the frame; determining which vernacular, Anglo-Norman or English, such items belong to is often impossible.[9]

Thus, put very crudely, we have moved from a position where a central question posed was "which new words did English speakers need as English came to be used in new (or revived) functions?", to one where this (still valid) perspective is complemented and enriched by considering how long-lasting functional multilingualism may have informed and shaped the lexical choices made by speakers and writers in each language. The ambiguity of language identity in multilingual record keeping brings into particularly sharp focus the question of how far less common content vocabulary may have been demarcated into different 'languages' at all; if the word for 'cinnamon' in Anglo-Norman is *cinamome* (or *cinamone*, etc.), in Middle English is *cinamome* (with similar spelling variants), and in Latin is *cinnamōmum*, the question of 'translation' from one language to another is reduced to knowledge of the usual grammatical behaviour of the identical word stem in each language. This example comes from the lexical field of spices and traded goods, but we may find similar patterns in fields such as handcrafts and tools, with for instance the carpenter's plane being in Anglo-Norman

---

8 A good deal of the most significant work appears in three edited collections, Trotter (2000), Ingham (2010), and Schendl and Wright (2011).

9 See the foundational work by Wright (1996), and among more recent work especially Wright (2010) and Trotter (2010) on the frequent use in such texts of the French definite article *le* before vernacular items, regardless of whether they belong to Anglo-Norman or Middle English.

plane, in Middle English *plane*, and in Latin *plana*. Closer to the lexical core of each language, it is difficult to avoid the conclusion that performance in each language was influenced by the speaker's use of each of the other languages; switch in the language that is conventionally used in a particular context remains an event of huge importance, but one best seen in the context of the multilingual practice of the individuals concerned.

A particularly interesting approach to some of the issues examined in section 3.1 based in the study of multilingualism is provided by Ingham (2012), who considers side-by-side the (limited) evidence concerning elementary school education in medieval England and the internal evidence provided by Anglo-Norman as a grammatically consistent language variety of which its users had clear mastery. Ingham suggests that until the mid fourteenth century (male) pupils destined for a largely Latin-medium grammar school education typically first learned Anglo-Norman at 'song schools', probably between the ages of five and seven, thus acquiring a near-native-like command of Anglo-Norman, which then served as the medium through which they acquired Latin. For generations of students of the history of the English language, this will chime immediately with the comments in John Trevisa's late-fourteenth-century translation of Ranulf Higden's *Polychronicon* on the changes in grammar school education in the decades following the Black Death.

Building on this work, Ingham (2018) considers the likely effects of functional multilingualism and such early-acquired facility in Anglo-Norman on the lexical practice of a particular group who were required to make frequent use of each of the languages of medieval England, namely clergy preaching in English. Ingham suggests that consideration of the English of this English-speaking but French-educated group helps explain how so much 'general' vocabulary like *branch*, *strife*, or *beast* entered English from French. A scenario such as this may also help explain rather more of the examples considered in section 3.2 that are problematic for more traditional accounts. More generally, if very early acquisition of Anglo-Norman was the gateway to learning Latin for a large tranche of that subset of the population who were literate, we may see implications for lexical borrowing in many different semantic fields, as well as for phenomena such as stylistic layering that have long been identified.

Other recent work highlights the impact of Anglo-Norman borrowing also on the everyday terminology of working life. For instance, Sylvester (2018), drawing on the work of the *Bilingual Thesaurus of Middle English and Anglo-Norman* project, suggests that in, for instance, the vocabulary of building, the impact of borrowed vocabulary is most marked at the superordinate and basic levels, not at the (intervening) hyponymic level, "suggest[ing] a resistance to the imported French vocabulary not at the lowest section of the social stratum, but rather by the class of skilled workers" (Sylvester 2018 262). On spoken and written Anglo-Norman in agricultural contexts compare Ingham (2009) and Rothwell (2010).

3.3 Considering the effects of borrowing on areas of the basic vocabulary

Another valuable window into the wide variety of contexts of lexical contact between Anglo-Norman and Middle English is afforded by a close investigation of some aspects of change affecting areas of the basic vocabulary. One such case is change in the set of kinship terms in Middle English. As has been frequently investigated, Middle English appears to show a shift from a from a bifurcate-collateral system of kinship relations (with focus on the patrilinear extended family) to a lineal one (with focus on the new family formed by a husband and wife on marriage).[10] Most striking here is the structural change seen in the replacement of the reflexes of Old English *fædera* 'paternal uncle' and *ēam* 'maternal uncle' by the single term *uncle* 'uncle', borrowed from French (probably specifically Anglo-Norman), and similarly the replacement of the reflexes of Old English *faðu* 'paternal aunt' and *mōdrige* 'maternal aunt' by borrowed *aunt* 'aunt'. The introduction of the prefix *grand-* has appeared a minor and unremarkable instance of further lexical influence from Anglo-Norman on the set of kinship terms in English: Old English had terms of the type *ealde-fæder* 'grandfather', literally 'old father', which were superseded in Middle English by terms of the type *grandsire* or *grandfather* (and *grandame* or *grandmother*), in which Romance-derived *grand-* acts as a modifier where native *eald* had earlier played the same role. However, closer inspection of the surviving evidence throws up some considerable surprises in this apparently very simple story: this use of *grand-* is found in English from the early thirteenth century, nearly two centuries before the borrowing of the simplex adjective *grand*; furthermore, formations of this type appear rather thicker on the ground in Middle English than in continental Old and Middle French, where the older synonyms *aieul* 'grandfather' and *aiuele* 'grandmother' continued in common use. Most strikingly of all, the types in *grand-* are not found at all in surviving Anglo-Norman materials, where *aiel* and *aiele* remain the norm. The English evidence shows the *grand-* types in a variety of different text types, and these appear the default Middle English terms for 'grandfather' and 'grandmother'. The natural assumption is

10 See Fischer (2002), drawing on Anderson (1963) and Goody (1983).

that they must have been borrowed from Anglo-Norman in contexts of everyday communication, rather than literary or legalistic importations from across the Channel, particularly since *aiel* is the default term in Anglo-Norman legal use. But if so this must indicate a seam of use in Anglo-Norman that shows no trace in our surviving records: in particular, it is highly suggestive that Middle English may have been receptive to a register of colloquial or family-based lexis in Anglo-Norman that is poorly reflected by the surviving written evidence. This is particularly remarkable when we consider that the initial borrowing is likely to have been between the Anglo-Norman and Middle English lexicons of bilingual individuals, whose Anglo-Norman written praxis was nonetheless resistant to this colloquial lexis.[11]

Defining what constitutes 'basic' vocabulary is notoriously difficult. One recent approach has produced a 100-item meaning list (the Leipzig-Jakarta List of Basic Vocabulary) on the basis of extensive cross-linguistic work, the words normally realizing these 100 basic meanings being taken to be particularly resistant to borrowing (on the basis that, in a large cross-linguistic comparison, these meanings are less often realized by a borrowed word than other meanings are).[12] *Carry* stands out among the French borrowings among the 1000 most frequent words in the *BNC* in that it is also the usual realization in modern English of a meaning from this 100-item Leipzig-Jakarta List of Basic Vocabulary.[13] The word was borrowed into English before the end of the fourteenth century (perhaps significantly earlier than this, although there is no earlier evidence of its use in English).[14] Its etymon is Anglo-Norman *carrier* (also *charier*; continental Old French, Middle French *charrier*), which has as its core meaning 'to transport by cart'. In Middle English the word's most frequent meaning (based on a survey of all quotations in which the words appears in all entries in the *Middle English Dictionary*) appears to have been 'to transport (goods, merchandise, materials, produce, animal feed, etc.) in bulk (especially by cart, by pack animal, by boat, etc.)'; this frequently occurs in business records and administrative documents, but also in many other contexts where transportation (largely of goods) by cart is discussed. Other closely related meanings that are frequently found (and also found in French, but no so often) relate to the transportation of people

11 For more detailed discussion of this example see Durkin (2019).

12 See Haspelmath and Tadmor (2009) and also https://wold.clld.org/.

13 The other French loans in this 100-meaning list are *cry* (which innovated the relevant meaning 'to weep' within English), *soil* (which continues to vary with *earth*, *ground*, and *dirt* in this meaning in different varieties and registers), and (more doubtfully) *crush* (which is of uncertain etymology).

14 See detailed discussion in Durkin (2018), which the discussion of *carry* given here summarizes.

(or sometimes specifically dead bodies) by people or animals, or in carts, litters, etc. But we also find that 20% of instances relate to bearing things other than people from one place to another, typically by hand. This broadened meaning, in which *carry* has found its niche in the vocabulary of modern English, appears to have been innovated in English, apparently at more or less the same time that the word was borrowed: certainly, there is no clear evidence for the existence of this meaning in Anglo-Norman or continental French. The obvious competitor in this meaning is *bear*. Tracing this competition diachronically is extremely challenging: what we ideally want is to know is how often both *carry* and *bear* occur in just this meaning (separating out the many other established uses of the high-frequency word *bear*) in consecutive chronological slices of data, before we get onto other important questions of whether there are trends in particular text types, registers, etc. However, preliminary investigation in Durkin (2018) suggests that in the writings of Chaucer there are 25 examples of *carry*, and more than half of these show the meaning that was apparently a new innovation in English, 'to transfer/carry (something, especially in one's hands)'; furthermore, while use of *bear* in this meaning appears to be more frequent in Chaucer, it is only by a margin of approximately 2:1. (Examination of other major late Middle English writers for whose works concordances exist presents fewer instances of either verb in the relevant meanings, but does not contradict this picture substantially.) Thus, close inspection of the early history of *carry* presents a number of interesting points:

- It appears to have spread from specialized, technical use to more general use, but from the workaday world of bulk transportation of goods rather than from a more rarefied sphere of intellectual life.
- Use in the generalized basic meaning 'to transfer/carry' appears to show an innovation within English, that seems to have occurred remarkably soon after the word's borrowing.
- Within the first few decades of the word's recorded existence in English, we find that in a major (and voluminous) writer *carry* appears already to be a near rival of *bear* in this basic meaning.

It may perhaps be the case that words with core meanings occurring with high frequency are likely to show atypical trajectories. It may also perhaps be the case that a rapid advance of *carry* at the expense of *bear* was connected with the native word showing extensive polysemy, including a number of high-frequency meanings ('have about or on one's person as a mark or attribute', 'give birth to', 'tolerate', etc.). However, it is nonetheless striking how far *carry* departs from an assumption of diffusion of Romance lexis from the language of learning and the learned, or from the language of the highest social classes: instead, it appears more likely that it showed rapid generalization from (relatively) specialized use in the technical vocabulary of a trade to general use in the everyday lexicon.

4 Some possible directions for further investigation

This chapter has attempted to highlight some of the aspects of Middle English borrowing from Anglo-Norman and Latin that are neglected in most introductory accounts of the history of English, in order to sketch what might be involved in providing a more fully rounded account of this enormous topic. A focus on the role of such lexis in the development of standard English is particularly useful for the questions it poses about the principal lens through which later Middle English borrowing is typically viewed. Specifically, how much are we losing from the overall picture as a result of the customary focus on the development of new registers in law, government, etc., with the assumptions this brings with it about subsequent diffusion of lexis to more general use? Related to this latter point, how useful is the customary focus on stylistic effects of layering, identifying instances where the new vocabulary occupies a niche as the stylistically high variant in opposition to semantically overlapping native terms?

The examples and studies surveyed here suggest that these time-honoured perspectives are only part of a much richer and more varied history, where borrowing from Anglo-Norman (and even Latin) affected the everyday lexis of many areas of life, including the terminology of such areas as handcrafts, farming, and everyday trade and commerce. Borrowings that are stylistically relatively high may owe as much or more to the close involvement of functional multilingualism with the acquisition and practice of literacy, than to the terminological expansion of particular specialist fields as the conventional functions in which English was employed grew.

Finally, it may be a useful exercise to consider at least briefly some of the research approaches that could shed further light on these questions, although all would make considerable demands in research time and resources. Inevitably, both onomasiological and semasiological approaches suggest themselves, tracking the trajectories show by specific words over time (especially in their changing frequency of use, and the competition they show with other words of overlapping meaning), and examining the changing shape of particular word fields over time.

The *Historical Thesaurus of the Oxford English Dictionary* offers a still largely untapped resource for examining in more detail, and more objectively, the impact of lexis on specific semantic domains and also at different levels within each domain (compare the work by Sylvester discussed above). Particularly where assessing impact on basic vocabulary is concerned, such work is made much more valuable if some perspective can be introduced on the relative frequencies of use of particular words within a thesaurus category: it is a quite different thing for a word to occur as a minor synonym in a particular meaning, and for it to become the usual, default realization of that meaning. (Compare Durkin (2014: 400–423), Durkin and Allan (2016) (on synonyms for 'sweet'), and the discussion of *carry* above.)

Diachronic frequency information is a major desideratum, but also likely to be some way off as a category of information readily derivable from historical corpora, especially as the most interesting and valuable information is likely to be at the level of specific meanings of words (compare discussion of *carry* and *bear* above), rather than of words or (most easily derived from a corpus) word forms not distinguished into separate homonyms. However, a rough sorting into more and less common synonyms in a particular meaning is often a more feasible task, as is an estimation of the period in which a particular lexical item crosses a certain threshold in frequency.

Close examination of the lexical make-up of substantial extracts from historical text samples from different genres (considering factors such as what proportion of borrowed lexemes each contains, what lexical fields they belong to, and when they first appeared in English) is likely to be the most revealing approach in tracing the development of the lexicon of Standard English in detail over time, but also hugely demanding in research hours, as well as raising difficult questions of classification of texts by genre (most acutely for the early periods which are of greatest interest).[15]

All such approaches are likely to necessitate engaging with the messiness and unpredictability of individual lexical histories, but pay rewards in giving clearer insights into the relationship of lexical borrowing in the Middle English period with the long-term development of the lexicon of Standard English.

---

15 Attractive areas for pilot studies would be those where specialized corpora already exist, such as the Helsinki *Corpus of Early English Medical Writing* or *Corpus of Early English Correspondence*, or other specialist corpora (compiled by various different institutions) listed at http://www.helsinki.fi/varieng/CoRD/index.html

Appendix 1 Loanwords from French and Latin among the 1000 most frequent words in the *British National Corpus*

I have followed the following conventions in this list:

- If an item is followed by brackets containing another item preceded by "hence", this means that there are two items both occurring in the high-frequency list, one of which is a borrowing and the other derived from it, e.g. "*base* (hence *basic*)" means that both *base* and its derivative *basic* occur in the high-frequency list; they are listed under 1300–1349 because this is the period when *base* was borrowed, although the derivative *basic* is first attested in the 1800s.
- If an item is followed by brackets containing "<" followed by another word, this means that the high-frequency word is not itself borrowed, but is formed from another borrowed word, by any of various word-formation processes (conversion, derivation, compounding), e.g. "*employment* (< *employ*)" means that *employment* (but not *employ*) occurs in the high-frequency list, and this occurs in the 1450–1499 part of the list of French borrowings because that is when *employ* was borrowed from French (although the derivative *employment* is first attested in the 1500s). Since in most cases the relation of the derived form to its parent is transparent and does not involve significant change of meaning, it is assumed here that the most important piece of information is the date of borrowing of the root word. In very many cases the derived form and the root word are close in date, often falling in the same one of the date bands employed here (e.g. *suddenly* has a first date of *c*1290, beside *sudden a*1300, thus both falling in the band 1250–1299).

1 Words borrowed from French

OE (in post-Conquest sources): *according to* (< *accord*), *service*, *war*
1150–1199: *court*, *standard*,
1200–1249: *air*, *authority*, *catch*, *change* (as noun and verb), *chapter*, *charge*, *city*, *degree*, *easy*, *fail*, *image*, *large*, *letter*, *matter* (noun), *measure* (noun), *oil*, *order* (hence *in order*), *park*, *pass* (verb), *pay* (verb), *piece*, *place* (noun, hence

place (verb), *replace*),[16] *point* (noun), *poor, price, prove, reason, rule* (noun), *save, simple* (hence *simply*), *story, term,*

1250–1299: *age, amount* (noun, < verb), *appeal, appear, arrive, available* (< *vail*, ultimately), *certain* (hence *certainly*), *chance, choice, clear* (hence *clearly*), *close* (verb), *company, contain, country, couple,*[17] *course, cover, demand, despite* (preposition < noun), *duty, enter, fine* (adjective), *foreign, garden, join, people, season, sir, size, sound, stage, suddenly* (< *sudden*), *treat* (hence *treatment*), *very* (earliest as adjective)

1300–1349: *account, achieve, allow, approach* (noun < verb), *argue, art, base* (hence *basic*), *car, claim* (as verb and noun), *contract* (noun), *cost, county, date, defence, difference, discover, disease, face* (noun and verb), *feature, force* (as noun and verb), *increase* (verb), *issue, language, level* (earliest as noun), *maintain, member, money, Mrs* (< *mistress*), *nice, number, office, paper, party, performance* (< *perform*), *power, proposal* (< *propose*), *purpose, push, quite, record* (noun), *return, river, round* (adverb and preposition, hence *around*, preposition and adverb), *space, sure, unit* (< *unity*), *university, value, view,*

1350–1399: *able, affair, apply, avoid, award* (noun), *benefit* (noun), *carry, close* (adjective), *community, customer, design* (verb), *determine, enjoy, ensure, environment* (< *environ*), *especially* (< *especial*), *establish, example* (hence *for example*), *express, financial* (< *finance*), *finish, hon (= honourable), increase* (noun), *just* (adverb, < *just*, adjective), *million, movement, officer, please* (earliest as verb), *point* (verb), *policy, property, publish, range, receive, remain, remember, remove, science, set* (noun), *sort, source, suppose, test* (noun), *total* (adjective), *village*

1400–1449: *agree, agreement, army, committee* (< *commit*), *control* (verb and noun), *employment* (< *employ*), *government, obtain, report* (noun), *rest* (noun), *royal, several, training* (< *train*),

1450–1499: *announce, bank,*[18] *department, effort, encourage, improve, page, police,*

1500–1549: *mention, post,*[19] *society,*

1550–1599: *design* (noun), *machine, model, national* (hence *international*), *procedure, research* (noun), *resource, responsibility* (< *responsible*)

---

16 There is also some evidence of borrowing of the Latin etymon of the French word in Old English, but it is extremely doubtful that there is any continuity with the later word.

17 Earlier (*a*1225) as verb.

18 The word denoting a financial institution is a loanword from French (and with probably also some direct input from Italian). The word denoting a bank of earth is probably of Scandinavian origin, but accounts for only a tiny proportion of the matches for the string *bank* in the *BNC*.

19 When showing either of the words meaning 'job' or 'mail' (probably also with some input directly from Italian); not when showing the word meaning 'piece of wood', which is a Latin/French borrowing attested earliest in Old English.

1600–1649: *attack* (noun), *detail, identify, list, plan* (noun, hence also verb), *risk, role*
1650–1699: *attitude, develop* (hence *development*), *group*,[20] *hotel*,

2 Words from Latin

OE: *box, church, cup, mile, offer, pound, school, spend, stop, street, turn*
1300–1349: *material*
1350–1399: *add, discuss, idea, private, secretary*
1400–1449: *admit, assume, create, explain, individual* (as adjective and hence also as noun), *picture, produce* (verb), *provide, result* (earliest as verb),
1450–1499: *act* (verb), *describe, fact, industrial, introduce, normal, occur, product, project* (noun),
1500–1549: *appropriate, exactly* (< *exact*), *expect, function, indicate* (earliest as participial adjective), *investment* (< *invest*), *political, population, success* (hence *successful*), *suggest*,
1550–1599: *analysis, area, basis, energy*,[21] *obviously* (< *obvious*), *sector, series, significant, various*,
1600–1649: *central, data/datum, fund* (noun), *previous, technology*,[22]

3 Words from Latin and/or French

(Following the analysis in *OED* for words already revised as part of its revision programme; in other instances, a provisional assessment has been made, on the basis especially of data in the entries in the *OED* and the *Middle English Dictionary*.)
OE (initially borrowed from Latin, but showing later French input): *April, cell, council, July, June, March, market, May, Mr* (< *master*), *note* (noun and verb), *October, oh, part, plant, study, table, title*
1150–1199: *serve*,
1200–1249: *case, cause* (hence *because*, also *'cos*), *circumstance, figure, form* (noun), *general* (hence *generally*), *person, question, special, state* (noun; hence

20 Showing some input also directly from Italian.
21 Probably also partly directly from Greek.
22 Probably also partly directly from Greek.

(via verb) *statement*), *suffer*, *use* (verb, hence also *used to*, *user*), *use* (noun), *visit* (verb)
1250–1299: *capital* (noun), *colour*, *during* (< *dure*), *election*, *element*, *evidence*, *form* (verb), *intend*, *move*, *natural*, *nature*, *second*, *style*, *tax* (earliest as verb),
1300–1349: *bill*, *character*, *condition*, *continue*, *current*, *doctor* (also as *Dr*), *final* (hence *finally*), *hospital*, *labour* (noun),[23] *minister*, *music*, *original*, *pattern*, *present* (verb and adjective), *profit*, *quality*, *region*, *require*, *response*, *single*, *station*, *subject*, *voice*
1350–1399: *accept*, *act* (noun), *action*, *actually* (< *actual*), *animal*, *application*, *argument*, *aspect*, *attention*, *centre*, *century*, *client*, *college*, *commission*, *common*, *consider*, *decide*, *different*, *difficulty* (hence *difficult*), *division*, *economic*, *effect*, *experience*, *family*, *future*, *history*, *information*, *institution*, *involve*, *major*, *minute*, *moment*, *necessary*, *operation*, *opportunity*, *particular* (hence *particularly*), *patient*, *per*, *personal*, *position*, *possible*, *president*, *pressure*, *principle*, *probably* (< *probable*), *problem*, *process* (noun), *provision*, *public*, *real* (hence *really*), *refer*, *relation* (hence *relationship*), *represent*, *sense*, *site*, *social*, *student*, *support* (verb and noun), *task*, *tend*, *usually* (< *usual*),
1400–1449: *activity*, *affect*, *compare*, *concern* (noun, < verb; hence also *concerned*), *decision*, *direction*, *discussion*, *economy*, *factor*, *important*, *include* (hence *including*), *legal*, *local*, *method*, *organisation*, *parent*, *period*, *practice* (< *practise*), *prepare*, *prime*, *rate*, *recent* (hence *recently*), *reduce*, *reflect*, *report* (verb), *security*, *serious*, *structure*, *union*,
1450–1499: *director*, *human*, *industry*, *interest* (noun), *military*, *modern*, *production*, *relate*, *situation*, *type*,
1500–1549: *association*, *attempt* (noun, < verb), *class*, *conference*, *education*, *event*, *perhaps*,[24]
1550–1599: *computer* (< *compute*), *exist*, *section*, *scheme*, *system*, *theory*,
1600–1649: *programme*, *similar*, *specific*,

References

Anderson, Robert T. 1963. 'Changing kinship in Europe'. *Kroeber Anthropological Society Papers* 28 1–48.

Crystal, David 2004. *The Stories of English*. London: Allen Lane.

23 Also counted separately in this frequency list when in attributive, i.e. adjectival, use, e.g. *labour regulations*, *Labour Party*.

24 A hybrid formation, from *hap*, an early Middle English borrowing from Scandinavian, with prefixation of French or Latin *per*, on the model of *perchance*, *peradventure*, and *percase*.

Durkin, Philip 2014. *Borrowed Words: A History of Loanwords in English*. Oxford: Oxford University Press.
Durkin, Philip 2018. 'Exploring the penetration of loanwords in the core vocabulary of Middle English: *Carry* as a test case', in *English Language and Linguistics* 22:2 265–82.
Durkin, Philip 2019. 'New light on early Middle English borrowing from Anglo-Norman: Investigating kinship terms in *grand-*', in *Anglia* 137:2 1–23.
Durkin, Philip and Allan, Kathryn 2016. 'Borrowing and copy: A philological approach to Early Modern English lexicology', in Anita Auer, Victorina González-Díaz, Jane Hodson and Violeta Sotirova (eds.) *Linguistics and Literary History: In honour of Sylvia Adamson*. Amsterdam: Benjamins. 71–86.
Finkenstaedt, Thomas and Wolff, Dieter with contributions by Neuhaus, H. Joachim and Herget, Winfried 1973. *Ordered Profusion: Studies in Dictionaries and the English Lexicon*. Heidelberg: Winter.
Fischer, Andreas 2002. 'Notes on kinship terminology in the history of English', in Katja Lenz and Ruth Möhlig (eds.) *Of dyuersitie & chaunge of langage: essays presented to Manfred Görlach on the occasion of his 65th Birthday*. Heidelberg: Winter. 115–128.
Goody, Jack 1983. *The Development of the Family and Marriage in Europe*. Cambridge: Cambridge University Press.
Haspelmath, Martin and Tadmor, Uri (eds.) 2009. *Loanwords in the World's Languages: A Comparative Handbook*. Berlin: De Gruyter Mouton.
Hughes, Geoffrey 2000. *A History of English Words*. Oxford: Blackwell.
Ingham, Richard 2009. 'Mixing languages on the manor', in *Medium Aevum* 78 80–97.
Ingham, Richard (ed.) 2010. *The Anglo-Norman Language and its Contexts*. York: York Medieval Press.
Ingham, Richard 2012. *The Transmission of Anglo-Norman: Language History and Language Acquisition*. Amsterdam: Benjamins.
Ingham, Richard 2018. 'The diffusion of higher-status lexis in medieval England: The role of the clergy', in *English Language and Linguistics* 22:2 207–24.
Leech, Geoffrey, Rayson, Paul, and Wilson, Andrew 2001. *Word Frequencies in Written and Spoken English: Based on the British National Corpus*. London: Longman.
Leisi, Ernst. 1955. *Das heutige Englisch: Wesenszüge und Probleme*. Heidelberg: Winter.
Miller, D. Gary. 2012. *External Influences on English: From its Beginnings to the Renaissance*. Oxford: Oxford University Press.
Rothwell, William 2010. 'Husbonderie and manaungerie in later medieval England: A tale of two Walters', in Ingham (2010) 44–51.
Scheler, Manfred 1977. *Der englische Wortschatz*. Grundlagen der Anglistik und Amerikanistik 9. Berlin: Erich Schmidt.
Schendl, Herbert and Wright, Laura (eds.) 2011. *Code-switching in Early English*. Berlin: Mouton de Gruyter.
Sylvester, Louise 2018. 'Contact effects on the technical lexis of Middle English: A semantic hierarchic approach', in *English Language and Linguistics* 22:2 249–64.
Trotter, David (ed.) 2000. *Multilingualism in Later Medieval Britain*. Cambridge: D. S. Brewer.
Trotter, David. 2010. 'Bridging the Gap: The (Socio-)linguistic Evidence of Some Medieval English Bridge Accounts', in Ingham (2010) 52–62.
Wright, Laura 1996. *Sources of London English: Medieval Thames Vocabulary*. Oxford: Oxford University Press.

Wright, Laura 2010. 'A Pilot Study on the Singular Definite Articles *le* and *la* in Fifteenth-Century London Mixed-Language Business Writing', in Ingham (2010) 130–142.
Historical Thesaurus of the Oxford English Dictionary, 2009. Christian Kay, Jane Roberts, Michael Samuels, and Irené Wotherspoon (eds.). Oxford: Oxford University Press.
Middle English Dictionary, 1952–2001. Eds. Hans Kurath, Sherman Kuhn, and Robert E. Lewis. Michigan: University of Michigan Press. http://quod.lib.umich.edu/m/med
The Oxford English Dictionary, first edition 1884–1928. (First issued as *A New English Dictionary on Historical Principles.*) Eds. Sir James A. H. Murray, Henry Bradley, Sir William A. Craigie and Charles T. Onions. *Supplement and Bibliography* (1933). *Supplement* (1972–1986); ed. Robert W. Burchfield. Second edition 1989, ed. John A. Simpson and Edmund S. C. Weiner. *Additions Series*, (1993–7), eds. John A. Simpson, Edmund S. C. Weiner, and Michael Proffitt. Third edition (in progress) as part of *OED Online* (March 2000-), eds. (2000–2013) John A. Simpson and (2013-) Michael Proffitt, http://www.oed.com

Louise Sylvester

12 The role of multilingualism in the emergence of a technical register in the Middle English period

Vocabulary does not feature much in discussions of the standardisation of English, and when it does, the tendency is to approach the issue from the viewpoint of the completed process. In considering standardisation as it relates to the lexicon, this paper looks to the emergence of English as a language of record following the centuries in which most documents were written in Medieval Latin, with some in Anglo-Norman French and many with multilingual elements or entirely in a syntactically regular mix of Medieval Latin, Anglo-Norman French and Middle English, depending on the text type (Wright 2011). This is the context from which distinctions such core versus non-core vocabulary can ultimately be made. What emerges from this study is that unlike what we see in regard to other levels of language, notably spelling and morphology, the establishment of anything like a standard in vocabulary seems to depend on increased variation. While the nature of the evidence means that we cannot assess frequency of usage for the vocabulary of the Middle English period, we can begin to make assessments about different registers, the co-existence of more general terms and lexical items which suggest the emergence of a technical register. It is evident that such distinctions require the availability of a set of variants for the expression of different levels of specificity within the same conceptual space.

In line with other considerations of the emergence of a standard language, we begin with Haugen's (1966) discussion of the processes necessary for the achievement of a standard. Haugen's notion of selection seems to offer a way in to thinking about standardisation in relation to vocabulary. Wright (2013) suggests that in the fifteenth century, during which monolingual English writing gradually replaced the mixed-language system in business writing, we witness the beginnings of a process not of selection, but of elimination, as part of the movement towards codification and the achievement of Haugen's element of *minimal variation of form* (1966: 931). With regard to lexis, the issue is complicated by the pressures on literary writing that arise from formal constraints since these tend to produce a need for a range of synonyms expressing the same idea. Lester (1996: 101–102) comments on the way in which the lexis of the alliterative poetry of the fourteenth and fifteenth centuries is noticeably different from that of the rhymed verse of the same period because the form required a range of alliterating terms for particular concepts; for example, 'man, warrior'

https://doi.org/10.1515/9783110687545-013

might be expressed by the general terms *knizt*, *lorde*, *mon* but also by the words *burne*, *freke*, *gome*, *hathel*, *lede*, *renk*, *schalk*, *segge*, *tulke*, or *wyze*. One of the outstanding questions in historical semantics concerns lexical obsolescence and replacement and semantic shift: we do not yet fully know why the vocabulary changes in these ways yet it seems clear that the answer must have a bearing on the standardisation of the vocabulary. In contrast to standardisation in the areas of phonology or spelling, this might not be produced by elimination. A set of near-synonyms can remain in the language, differentiated by semantics, pragmatics or register. In English these kinds of differentiations were made possible by multilingualism; that is, the presence of multiple terms expressing the same concept. This difference may have been one factor preventing full standardisation in the Old English period (Hogg 2002: 7), despite the elaboration evidenced by the use of Old English for what have been called 'the 'higher' functions associated with standard varieties (Beal 2016: 303).[1] The use of a variety of registers is important in this context, and I have argued that it is in the Middle English period that a technical register emerged (Sylvester 2016). Analysis of the patterns of lexical replacement and obsolescence and semantic shift in the technical register in Middle English may tell us something about process of lexical selection. In a project on technical terminology and semantic shift in Middle English, we have begun to trace the effects of the influx of French and other languages on the native vocabulary at different levels of the semantic hierarchy (Sylvester 2018b).[2]

Multilingualism thus appears to be key to the notion of standardisation of the lexicon, since it enabled the possibility of synonyms that have different sociolinguistic connotations (such as prestige) or functions (such as technicality). In relation to Middle English writing, Trotter (2006; 2012: 1790) raised the question of when Anglo-Norman words became English. While not all

1 Old English is, rather, marked by polysemy: a glance at the *Thesaurus of Old English* quickly reveals how hard the lexical items in OE have to work to encompass all the necessary meanings; an example is provided by *gesceaft*, a term which appears at 01|01 Earth, world :: As God's creation; 02 Creation; 02|02 Creation :: Created world; 02|03 Creation :: Created things, creatures; 02|03.03 Creation :: Created things, creatures :: Living being, creature; 02|03.03.04 Creation :: Living being, creature :: Created things, creatures :: Rational creature; 02.01.03.03 Fruitfulness, fertility :: Sex, generation; 03|03 Material, matter, substance :: An element, one of four elements; 03.05|03 Order, arrangement, disposition :: Ordered course (of events); 05.02|01 State, condition :: Natural state or condition; 05.02|02 State, condition :: External condition, state, position; 05.03.02.01.01|01 Event, issue, result :: An event, occurrence :: Ordered course of events; 05.04 Fate, lot, fortune, destiny; 05.04|01.01 Fate, lot, fortune, destiny :: Predestination :: An order of providence.

2 I am grateful to the Leverhulme Trust for funding the project *Technical language and semantic shift in Middle English* 2017–2020.

scholars accept Trotter's argument that it is anachronistic to speak of separate languages in the medieval period (2011: 157), many suggest that 'from the lexical point of view attempts at a clear distinction of language identity is futile, for such distinctions were certainly blurred in medieval England' (Hunt 2011: 64). Others point to the 'continuity of vocabulary between one language and another in medieval England' (Rothwell 2010: 20). This idea is further elaborated by the claim that '[e]ven for literate speakers of medieval England the various languages at their disposal were obviously less clearly distinct than often claimed by scholars' (Schendl 2002: 69). More recently this idea has been re-stated in Wright's observation that the 'boundaries between Middle English, Medieval Latin and Anglo-Norman were fuzzy by modern standards' (2013: 59).

Discussing the standardisation of English in the multilingual context of the medieval period, Schaefer (2006: 14; 2012: 529) sets out the process for a loanword as follows: 'it makes its first appearance in the target language as a markedly "foreign" element (diaglossic). If its first use is not a singular event, this element is socially (in the sense of "diastratically") marked and simultaneously or subsequently also stylistically marked. In the very end loans may also completely lose such marking when they have spread over all kinds of discourses and when their etymologically "foreign" provenance is no longer perceived'. This argument is based on a notion of borrowing that does not adequately account for the relationship between Anglo-Norman French and Middle English. Many scholars prefer to categorise the process in terms of a 'partial relexification of English from French and Latin sources' (Schendl 2000: 78) or a 'lexical transfer' (Trotter 2012: 1789). These conceptualisations draw attention to the extent to which the developments exceeded the bounds of what is generally understood as lexical borrowing. Equally, Schaefer's model depends on an understanding that the three languages in written use in medieval Britain were functionally separate, but does not account for the mixed-language writing that was general in business writing, and is found across a wide range of administrative documents – and, as Schendl (Chapter 11) shows, personal documents too.

1 An example from the *Lexis of Cloth and Clothing Project* database

The *LexP* database is a multilingual lexicographical resource that brings together the vocabulary items in use for cloth and clothing in use in medieval

Britain.[3] The data are drawn for the most part from the *Anglo-Norman Dictionary*, the *Dictionary of the Irish Language*, the *Dictionary of Medieval Latin from British Sources* (*DMLBS*), the *Dictionary of Old English*, the *Dictionary of the Older Scottish Tongue*, the *Geiriadur Prifysgol Cymru*, the *Middle English Dictionary* (*MED*), and the *Oxford English Dictionary* (*OED*).[4] The editors of the *LexP* database do not assume, however, that the attestation of a lexical item in a particular historical dictionary means that the term belongs only to that language. *LexP* database entries reflect this stance: terms may be listed as belonging to one or to several languages.

The phenomenon of terms whose senses are shared across a number of languages in use in medieval Britain occurs throughout the *LexP* database. An example is provided by the term *acton* (a quilted jacket, worn as padding underneath a breastplate, or worn alone, as a decorative garment worn on top of armour).[5] The *LexP* database shows that the term is attested in Anglo-French, Latin, Middle English, Old Scots, Welsh, and Irish. The earliest occurrence is proposed by the editors of the *MED* and the *OED* in *acton-maker* attested in the quotation 'Ric. le Aketonmaker', though the *MED* records this as sense 1(b) '~ maker'. The source cited by both dictionaries is Fransson's (1935) *Middle English Surnames*, suggesting that the term is a surname rather than a term for an occupation in 1328, at least as Fransson interprets the Assize Roll for Lincolnshire in which it occurs. Those familiar with the type of administrative document that contains information about names and occupations (not always distinguishable categories) will not be surprised to find that the term is preceded by the French determiner *le*. It is worth noting too that the term belongs on the edges of the semantic field of armour, though it is actually a garment. The term was sufficiently settled in Middle English to be used as a surname/occupation name from the mid-twelfth century: there are three quotations illustrating the term *aketouner* ('a maker of aketouns') in the *Middle English Dictionary*. The earliest citations for the garment sense of *aketoun*

---

3 I am grateful to the AHRC for funding the project *Lexis of Cloth and Clothing in Britain c. 700-c. 1450: Origins, Identification, Contexts and Change* 2006–2011.

4 These dictionaries were supplemented by *An Anglo-Saxon Dictionary based on the manuscript collections of Joseph Bosworth* and *Supplement*; *The illustrated Gaelic-English dictionary; Cregeen's Manx Dictionary*; *Fargher's English-Manx Dictionary*; the *Revised Medieval Latin Word-List*; *The non-Classical lexicon of Celtic Latinity*; *Dictionnaire de l'ancienne langue française et de tous ses dialectes du IXe au XVe siècle*; *Dictionnaire Étymologique de l'Ancien Français*; *Trésor de la langue française: dictionnaire de la langue du XIXe et du XXe siècle*; *Dictionnaire du Moyen Français*; *An Icelandic-English Dictionary*; *An Etymological Dictionary of the Norn Language in Shetland*. Full references may be found at http://lexisproject.arts.manchester.ac.uk/dictionaries/index.html accessed 17.04.2019

5 The definition is taken from the *LexP* database; note that the database uses *OED* headwords.

in *MED* is the Latin citation 'aketon pro defensione hominum ad arma' from the Accounts of the Exchequer in the Public Record Office of 1338. This citation floats above the definition and illustrative quotations in *OED*, presumably because of the language of the document from which it is drawn.[6] The quotations given for *acton* in the *LexP* database offer an insight into the ways in which vocabulary items from the ME period do not belong only to English. There are 22 citations drawn from five historical dictionaries and including a variety of genres including glosses, legal documents, accounts and literary works:

1. bombacinia: aketun (vars. haketouns, purpoyns, purpoyntis) ... rubea: wayd, en brasil ... galeros: chapel de quir, heumis ... ocreas: heses, hoseus, chausis de fer, esses ... toraces: wambesouns (vars. gambaysuns, gambisum vel uardecors, wadesuns) Gloss. [AND TLL (ii 136) ante 1300]
2. ionar ... 7 cotuin Historic. [eDIL Caithr. CC (11) circa 1100/1150]
3. qe chescun home defensable ... eit aketon, bacinet et launce Legal. [AND Parl Writs (ii 479)]
4. [186.46] ... La damoysele l'arma de estraunge armeyure: Pur aketoun ly bayle blaunche char e pure ... [186.74] ... La damoysele l'arma (=J.C.) de estraunge armeyure: Pur aketoun ly bayle blaunche char e pure, Pur cadaz e cotoun de saunk fu le encusture Poetic. [AND Lyric (187.46–74) circa 1200/1400]
5. quod durante guerra quilibet homo de terra laicus ... habeat pro corpore suo in defensione regni unam sufficientem aketonam [v.l. actonem], unum bacinetum [v.l. basinetum] et chirothecas de guerra ... et qui non habuerit aketonam ... habeat unum bonum hobirgellum vel unum bonum ferrum pro corpore suo Legal. (Sat. Rob. I c. 27) [DMLBS APScot (113) 1318]
6. quod tu uteris ij aketonibus, uno pro diebus ferialibus et alio pro festivis (Vis. S. Petr.) [DMLBS EHR (LVII 270) circa 1325]
7. Ric. le Aketonmaker.A maker of actons (as a surname), see AKETOUNER. [MED in Fransson Surn. (114) 1328]
8. Ac yna y hurdaud ermin ef yn varchaug ac y guisgaud arueu ymdanau nyt amgen actwn da dilis ysgafyn, a lluruc duy dyplic yr hon ny fuyssei dec arugein o funei y wlat. ac nyt oed araf a allei argyued y vn o hynny truy y

6 It seems worth noting that the editors of *MED* do not have access to the Accounts of the Exchequer in the Public Record Office; their citation comes from the *OED* slips. On the other hand, they include the quotation as the first for the sense 'A quilted or padded jacket worn under the armor for comfort and protection; also, a decorative garment worn over the armor'; indeed, the next quotation, drawn from a nineteenth-century article about the Wardrobe Accounts of Edward III also appears to be in Latin: 'Ad faciendum ix aketon coopertum cum fustien', though *fustian* is derived from French and occurs only in Medieval Latin as well as Middle English.

lluruc. ac ar vchaf hynny quire diogel, a chynsallt hossaneu lluryc a chrimogeu am y draet ay ysgeired ac ar warthaf hynny yspardunеu eureit. am y ben y dodet penguch burkwin a ffaylet. ac ar warthaf hynny helym eureit echdywynnedic. a guedy hynny y rodes y brenhin cledyf idaw ac y gwisgaud amdanaw. Romance. [GPC YBH (9. col. 17 535 -49a) circa 1250]

9. legavit . . . j aketonem cum platis et bacino, coleretto, cirotecis [DMLBS Reg. S. Aug. (302) circa 1350]
10. Ar marchawc a ymgyfodes arhynt ac yn llidiawc ac ae trewis ynteu ar y ysgwyd deheu yny dyrr y luric ae actwn. [LexP Hengwrt Selections (Williams) (330, 29–30) circa 1350]
11. [2050] . . . And next his sherte an aketoun, And ouer that an haubergeoun . . . And ouer that a fyn hauberk . . . Ful strong it was of plate, And ouer that his cote armour . . . [2065] . . . Hise iambeux were of quyrboily [vrr. quyrboilly, quirboile, quereboly, quyrbuly], His swerdes shethe of yuory . . . [2067] . . . His helm of latoun bright. Poetic, Romance. [MED Chaucer CT.Th. ((Manly-Rickert) B.2050–2067) circa 1390]
12. Mi plates shullen þi nailes be, myn acotoun þat spere tre þat stong þi swete syde. [MED Fadur & sone ((Bod 416) 18) circa 1400]
13. [3457] . . . The riche kynge . . . rawghte on his wedys, A reedde acton of rosse, the richeste of floures. . . . [3460] . . . One he henttis a hode of scharlette full riche, A pauys pillion hatt, þat pighte was full faire With perry of þe Oryent, and precyous stones . . . [3462] . . . Thane rysez the riche kynge . . . His gloues gayliche gilte and grauen by þe hemmys, With graynes of rubyes Arthurian, Heroic, Romance. (work ?a1400) [MED Morte Arth.(1) ((Thrn) 3457–3462) circa 1440]
14. [10025] . . . Hym self was armed fynly wel / Wyþ sabatons, & spores, & iaumbers of stel / Dublet & quysseux wiþ poleyns ful riche / Voydes, breche of maille, wyþ paunz non liche . . . [10029] . . . Hauberk wiþ plates yburnuscht ful wel / Vaumbras & rerbras, wyþ coters of stel / Þer-opon an aketon wiþ stof & al sylk, His cote of armes þer-on . . . [10040] . . . An helm he had on his hed / A riche corounal wiþ perre, al of brent golde / Þe nasel & bendeles of gold ful bryght, . . . Heroic, Historic. (work: a1338) [MED Mannyng Chron.Pt.1 ((Lamb 131) 10025–10043) ante 1450]
15. co nár bó dín lúirech leburlaidsech ná cotún comdlúta ná édedh arnaid allmurdo d'Fer tái Heroic, Poetic. [eDIL Fianaig. (98.2) ante 1419]
16. pro vij ulnis linee tele ad faciendum j alcotonem . . . et pro cotone ad illum alcotonem Accounts. [DMLBS Misae (124) circa 1209]
17. in cotone ad auketonum domini regis, sc. j li. et dim., xij d.; in eodem auketuno suendo, xij d. Accounts. [DMLBS Misae (269) 1213]
18. fieri facias duos . . . *acotimos [l. acotunos] Accounts. [DMLBS Cl (240b) 1215]

19. ad unum *acoconum [l. acotonem] cooperiendum Accounts. [DMLBS Cl (550b) 1223]
20. chalonem ... impignoravit pro quodam alketono Accounts. [DMLBS CurR (XII 2138) 1226]
21. ad ij alkethon' cend[allo] cooperiendas Accounts. [DMLBS Chanc. Misc. (3/3) 1235]
22. suscepit rex Ricardus ... a Saladino ... unum alcatonem satis levem, nulli spiculo penetrabile[m] Historic. [DMLBS M. PAR. (Min. II 18) circa 1190]

If we consider the dates of the citations, they suggest that the term is first recorded in a British manuscript in Irish at the start of the twelfth century (though we need to be aware of the accidents of historical evidence). Newton (1980: 28) notes that in the early 1340s, *aketons* 'appear frequently in English accounts and, though more rarely, on the Continent too'. The *LexP* database notes that the Irish form 'is used to refer to the cotton jacket and the material', suggesting a narrowing of the sense took place as the term's usage spread across the languages of medieval Britain. The Latin and Anglo-Norman occurrences precede those in Middle English but, as we might expect, the term continued in use in Medieval Latin into the mid-fourteenth century, which is in line with what we know about the language of local record-keeping in England (Stenroos 2017: 323). The *OED* editors note that the term is also used figuratively, though none of the usages illustrated with citations in that dictionary is labelled as such. The term is found in literary texts in Irish, Anglo-Norman and Middle English and these usages point to the ways in which literary writers in Middle English were able to draw on a range of registers to make use of general terms and vocabulary at the most precise levels of the semantic hierarchy drawn from a range of languages (Sylvester 2019: 98). We may note, too, Newton's observation that 'It is doubtful whether at any one time the exact differences between an aketon, a pourpoint, a doublet, a courtpiece and a jupon were absolutely defined. In France, the cote-hardie comes into this category, and in England, from the early 1360s, the paltok' (1980: 134). Of this list, the *LexP* database tells us that *pourpoint* is attested in A-F, L, ME, and OScots (and in MdE); *doublet* in AF, L, ME, Welsh, and OScots (and in ModE); *courtepy* in ME, AF, and L (and in MdE); *jupon* in AF, ME, L, and OScots, (and in MdE); and *paltock* in ME, AF, L, and OScots (and in MdE). All the terms signify a short, garment worn on the upper body usually by a man, sometimes under armour. There are some nuances of difference: a *courtepy* may be a short mantle made of rough-haired skins; a tabard or similar; while *paltocks* are often described as being made of rich fabric such as satin. There are some developments in sense over time: a *jupon* comes to signify short kirtle worn by women in the Early Modern period. Given that the terms all continue in use into the

Early Modern English, it does not seem reasonable to regard this lexical set as requiring reduction before standardisation could ensue; rather, the evidence suggests that standardisation depended on a range of near-synonyms.

2 An example from the *Bilingual Thesaurus of Everyday Life in Medieval England*

Further evidence of the shared vocabulary across the languages of medieval England comes from the *Bilingual Thesaurus of Everyday Life in Medieval England* (*BTh*).[7] This project collected vocabulary from *MED* and *AND* for seven occupational domains with the aim of providing insight into the interactions between the medieval French and English languages at a time of their overlapping use, and of discovering how far the knowledge and use of French extended down through the layers of later medieval English society. It seems worth consulting this resource because while I am suggesting that standardisation began in English not through the elimination of variation, but rather by an expansion of the vocabulary that allowed for a range of registers, I am concerned that this line of thinking does not slip into the (former) orthodoxies about French providing vocabulary relating solely to the interests of the ruling class. The methodology followed by the *BTh* team meant that only domain-specific terms were included and so it contains vocabulary at the lowest levels of the semantic hierarchy, denoting technical terminology in use in occupational domains such as Farming, Building, Manufacture, and Trade. There are, for example, no words at the level of Equipment related to sheep farming (a sub-category which sits below Instruments, which sits below Animal husbandry, which sits below Farming). There are, however, 11 terms for Shepherd, and four terms each in the two sub-groups *below* Equipment related to sheep farming, Shearing Equipment and Shepherd's Equipment:

SHEPHERD

ANGLO NORMAN:
Bercher (noun) 1200–1334
Languages of citation: French, Latin

7 I am grateful to the Leverhulme Trust for funding the Bilingual Thesaurus project from 2013–2016.

Pastur (noun) 1175–1245
Language of citation: French

Pasturel (noun) 1170–1325
Language of citation: French

MIDDLE ENGLISH:
Bercher (noun) 1166–1343
Languages of origin: Anglo-Norman, Medieval Latin
Languages of citation: French, English

Eue herde (noun) 1297–1424
Language of origin: Old English
Language of citation: ?English

Flokker (noun) 1302–1450
Language of origin: Old English
Languages of citation: Latin, English

Herde-man (noun) 1200–1450
Language of origin: Old English
Languages of citation: Latin, English

Hine (noun) 1275–1450
Language of origin: Old English
Languages of citation: Latin, English

Shep-herd(e) (noun) 1200–1450
Language of origin: Old English
Languages of citation: Latin, English

Shep-reve (noun) 1450–1250
Language of origin: Old English
Languages of citation: Latin, English

Trip(pe) herde (noun) 1305–1450
Language of origin: Anglo-Norman
Languages of citation: Latin, English

Of the 11 synonyms for 'shepherd', 5 derived from French and 6 derived from English, with 2 of the French terms attested in monolingual English texts (*bercher, trip(pe)herde*).

SHEARING EQUIPMENT

ANGLO NORMAN:
Cisaille (noun) 1216
Language of citation: French

Force (noun) 1200–1419
Language of citation: French

MIDDLE ENGLISH:
Cisours (noun) 1425–1450
Languages of origin: Old French, Middle English
Languages of citation: Latin, English

Shere (noun) 1300–1450
Language of origin: Old English
Languages of citation: Latin, English

SHEPHERD'S EQUIPMENT

ANGLO NORMAN:
Baston de berger (noun) 1200–1300
Languages of citation: French, Latin

Croce a pastur (noun) 1200
Languages of citation: French, Latin

MIDDLE ENGLISH:
Crok (noun) 1440
Languages of origin: Old English, Old Norse
Languages of citation: Latin, English

Staf (noun) 1121–1450
Languages of origin: Old English, Late Old English
Languages of citation: Latin, English

Of these 8 terms, 4 are of French etymology and 4 of English, with semantic overlapping of *force* and *shere*, and overlapping of *baston de berger*, *croce a pastur* and *staf*.

SHEEP SHEARER

ANGLO NORMAN:
Forcer (noun) 1292
Language of citation: French

Tondour (noun) 1275–1419
Language of citation: French

Tonsour (noun) 1300
Language of citation: French

Tunterier (noun) 1150
Language of citation: French

MIDDLE ENGLISH:
Shaver (noun) 1425–1450
Language of origin: Old English
Languages of citation: French, ?Latin, English

Sherer(e) (noun) 1425–1450
Language of origin: Old English
Languages of citation: Latin, English

Of the terms for sheep-shearer found in texts produced in England, 4 are French and 2 English. (Note that occupational surnames are not treated consistently in *MED*: 'Willielmus Bercharius', 'Alanus bercarius', 'Jehan le Bergier' are treated as attestations of the headword *bercher* and so appear in the *BTh.* 'Joh. Sherer', however, is labelled as a surname in *MED* and so does not appear in entries in the *BTh.* If it had been situated as part of *MED*'s evidence for usage, the *BTh.* would also have a Middle English term under Female Shearer, as attested by the *MED* citation 'Matilda le Scherher'.) Despite difficulties with the evidence that remains to us, however, it is clear that the two languages are intertwined at the higher and lower levels of the semantic hierarchy.

3 Conclusion

These findings support the idea that what emerged in the fourteenth and fifteenth centuries was not a resurgence of the Old English lexicon (as exemplified by literary and administrative texts), merely enriched by extra French additions. Rather, standardisation of vocabulary led to variation of expression within the same conceptual area, equating to having the lexical resources to describe things at the superordinate, basic and hyponymic levels. I have argued elsewhere (Sylvester 2018a) that the evidence of the database of the *Lexis of Cloth and Clothing Project* (*LexP*) suggests the development of a technolect in which nouns, in particular, were used widely – in Latin, French and English texts, with language-appropriate suffixes – and had acquired semantic precision. In this way the multilingualism of the later medieval period played a crucial role in three of the elements in Haugen's (1966) model of standardisation, i.e. selection of a norm, elaboration of function, and acceptance by the community. This process was made possible by the absence of the third element, codification: as noted above, the historical dictionaries have not, until recently, found ways to treat the attestations of medieval words in multilingual contexts. Examining the ways in which vocabulary is shared across languages, and the levels of the semantic hierarchy at which terms from different languages are found may offer a way out of the impasse produced by the widespread interpretation of the linguistic context of medieval Britain via the metaphor of competition. This turns up in, for example, Cottle's well-known *The Triumph of English* (1969), and is still being used in work as recent as Timofeeva's studies of the medieval religious lexis: "there is a lot of variation and competition between Middle English (ME) terms within the individual subdomains [. . .] and between English and French terms (*ire* and *erour*), which continues into the later periods" (Timofeeva 2018a: 58–59); "such core lexemes as *gospel* or *Easter* compete with *evangelium* and *pasque* and eventually survive, while dozens of other old religious terms are replaced with newer loans [. . .]. Just how this competition is resolved in early Middle English is the focus" (Timofeeva 2018b: 225). In his study of linguistic evolution, Samuels (1972: 67) posed a crucial question about change in the lexicon: "is it the availability (for mechanical, extralinguistic or extrasystemic reasons) of new forms that causes the shift, by differentiation from them, of older forms? Or is it the prior shift of the old form to a new meaning (by extension and limitation) which creates the need for a new form?" Returning to it may liberate us from a pervasive paradigm that appears to be limiting our thinking about the mechanisms and processes of lexical replacement and obsolescence and semantic shift.

In discussing the beginnings of the process of standardisation in the late medieval period, we are not yet talking about a fixed language variety that speakers were supposed to employ. Indeed, it is difficult to delineate the vocabulary of this variety since we are not able to make findings based on frequency of usage of lexical items. It would be helpful if we could be sure which terms were in general use by multiple speakers, that is, which words had been conventionalized, but, as Traugott (2012: 172) notes, it is difficult to know when this criterion is met in historical periods because a term may be attested only once because it was a nonce-term used by one speaker, or because evidence is lacking due to the contingencies of manuscript survival. The role of lexis in the standardisation of English comes much more sharply into focus in the sixteenth century, when we witness a heightened consciousness about the language and anxiety that its vocabulary was insufficient to express the philosophical and political ideas found in the Latin and Greek texts associated with the classical revival of the Early Modern period. The complaints are well rehearsed, and the fact of an established complaint tradition (Milroy and Milroy 1985; Crowley 2012; Beal 2016), albeit one that is said to begin with Higden and Caxton's translation of Trevisa (though the stigmatisation of northern forms does not seem to refer to lexical choices), suggests that by the sixteenth century we have moved to the notion of a standard as something to aim for. What we witness in the Middle English period is the evolution of a variety with a precise vocabulary, and with evidence of an emerging technical register which, as noted by Kloss (1967: 29), is one of the markers of a fully developed standard language.

References

Anglo-Norman Dictionary http://www.anglo-norman.net/gate/ accessed 01.05.2019.
Beal, Joan C. 2016. "Standardization". In Merja Kytö and Päivi Pahta (eds.). *The Cambridge Handbook of Historical Linguistics*. Cambridge: Cambridge University Press. 301–317.
Bilingual Thesaurus of Everyday Life in Medieval England https://thesaurus.ac.uk/bth/ accessed 02.05.2019.
Cottle, Basil. 1969. *The Triumph of English 1350–1400*. London: Blandford Press.
Crowley, Tony. 2012. "The Complaint Tradition". In Alexander Bergs and Laurel J. Brinton (eds.). *English Historical Linguistics* Volume 1. Handbooks of Linguistics and Communication Science 34/1. Berlin: De Gruyter Mouton. 980–994.
Fransson, Gustav. 1935. *Middle English Surnames of Occupation, 1100–1350. With an Excursus on Toponymical Surnames* (Lund Studies in English 3). Lund: C. W. K. Gleerup.
Haugen, Einar. 1966. "Dialect, Language, Nation". *American Anthropologist* 68: 922–935.
Hogg, Richard. 2002. *An Introduction to Old English*. Edinburgh: Edinburgh University Press.
Hunt, Tony. 2011. "The Languages of Medieval England". In Michael Baldzuhn and Christine Putzo (eds.). *Mehrsprachigkeit im Mittelalter*. Berlin: Walter de Gruyter. 59–68.
Kloss, H. 1967. "'Abstand Languages' and 'Ausbau Languages'". *Anthropological Linguistics* 9.7: 29–41.
Lester, G. A. 1996. *The Language of Old and Middle English Poetry*. Basingstoke: Macmillan.
Lexis of Cloth and Clothing Project database http://lexissearch.arts.manchester.ac.uk/ accessed 01.05.2019.
Middle English Dictionary https://quod.lib.umich.edu/m/med/ accessed 01.05.2019.
Milroy, James and Lesley Milroy. 1985. *Authority in Language: Investigating Language Prescription and Standardisation*. London: Routledge & Kegan Paul.
Oxford English Dictionary https://www.oed.com accessed 01.05.2019.
Rothwell, William. 2010. '"Strange", "Foreign", and "Alien": The Semantic History of Three Quasi-Synonyms in a Trilingual Medieval England'. *Modern Language Review* 105: 1–19.
Samuels, Michael. 1972. *Linguistic Evolution*. Cambridge: Cambridge University Press.

Schaefer, Ursula. 2006. "The Beginnings of Standardization: The Communicative Space in Fourteenth-Century England". In Ursula Schaefer (ed.). *The Beginnings of Standardization: Language and Culture in Fourteenth-Century England.* 73–90. Frankfurt: Peter Lang. 3–24.

Schaefer, Ursula. 2012. "Middle English: Standardization". In Alexander Bergs and Laurel J. Brinton (eds.). *English Historical Linguistics* Volume 1. Handbooks of Linguistics and Communication Science 34/1. Berlin: De Gruyter Mouton. 519–533.

Schendl, Herbert. 2000. "Linguistic Aspects of Code-Switching in Medieval English Texts. In David Trotter (ed.). *Multilingualism in Later Medieval Britain*. Cambridge: D S Brewer. 77–92.

Schendl, Herbert. 2002. "Mixed-Language Texts as Data and Evidence in English Historical Linguistics". In Donka Minkova and Robert Stockwell (eds.). *Studies in the History of the English Language: A Millennial Perspective.* Berlin and New York: Mouton de Gruyter, 51–78.

Stenroos, Merja. 2017. "Perspectives on Geographical Variation". In Laurel J. Brinton (ed.). *English Historical Linguistics: Approaches and Perspectives*. Cambridge: Cambridge University Press, 303–351.

Sylvester, Louise. 2016. "Technical Vocabulary and Medieval Text Types: A Semantic Field Approach". *Neuphilologische Mitteilungen* 117: 155–176.

Sylvester, Louise. 2018a. "A Semantic Field and Text-Type Approach to Late-Medieval Multilingualism". In Päivi Pahta, Janne Skaffari & Laura Wright (eds.). *Multilingual Practices in Language History: English and Beyond.* Language Contact and Bilingualism 15. Berlin: de Gruyter Mouton. 77–96.

Sylvester, Louise. 2018b. "'Contact effects on the Technical Lexis of Middle English: A Semantic Hierarchic Approach". *English Language and Linguistics* 22: 249–264.

Sylvester, Louise. 2019. 'The Role of Technical Vocabulary in the Construction of the Medieval Romance Text Type'. *Journal of English and Germanic Philology* 118: 73–99.

Timofeeva, Olga. 2018a. "Survival and loss of Old English religious vocabulary between 1150 and 1350". *English Language and Linguistics* 22: 225–247.

Timofeeva, Olga. 2018b. "*Mid ðare soðe luue ðe is icleped karite*: Pastoral care and lexical innovation in the thirteenth century". *Journal of the Spanish Society for Medieval English Language and Literature* (SELIM) 23: 55–85.

Traugott, Elizabeth Closs. 2012. "Semantics and Lexicon". In Alexander Bergs and Laurel J. Brinton (eds.). *English Historical Linguistics* Volume 1. Handbooks of Linguistics and Communication Science 34/1. Berlin: De Gruyter Mouton. 164–177.

Trotter, David. 2006. "Language Contact, Multilingualism, and the Evidence Problem. In Ursula Schaefer (ed.). *The Beginnings of Standardization: Language and Culture in Fourteenth-Century England*. Frankfurt: Peter Lang, 73–90.

Trotter, David. 2011. "Death, Taxes and Property: Some Code-Switching Evidence from Dover, Southampton, and York". In Herbert Schendl and Laura Wright (eds.). *Code-switching in Early English*. Berlin: Mouton de Gruyter. 155–189.

Trotter, David. 2012. "Middle English in Contact: Middle English Creolization". In Alexander Bergs and Laurel J. Brinton (eds.). *English Historical Linguistics* Volume 2. Handbooks of Linguistics and Communication Science 34/1. Berlin: De Gruyter Mouton, 1781–1793.

Wright, Laura. 2011. "On Variation in Medieval Mixed-Language Business Writing". In Herbert Schendl and Laura Wright (eds.). *Code-switching in Early English*. Berlin: Mouton de Gruyter. 191–218.

Wright, Laura. 2013. "The Contact Origins of Standard English". In Daniel Schreier and Marianne Hundt (eds.). *English as a Contact Language*. Studies in English Language. Cambridge: Cambridge University Press. 58–74.

Megan Tiddeman

13 More sugar and spice: Revisiting medieval Italian influence on the mercantile lexis of England

This article examines lexical evidence for direct borrowing from Italian in England's sugar and spice trade in the fourteenth and fifteenth centuries. This period of contact resulted in English vocabulary to describe various luxury commodities and how they were processed and measured.

Some of these lexemes can only be found in late medieval sources, others remain in use in modern English today – in either scenario, labelling them emphatically as 'Standard' or otherwise is problematic. As Sylvester states in Chapter 12, using lexical frequency as a measure of standardisation in the medieval period is evidently flawed given the haphazard survival rate of the textual corpus inherited. What scholars have demonstrated, however, is that mercantile language constituted an emerging technolect or set of universally understood terms which transcended linguistic boundaries (e.g. Sylvester 2016 / 2018, Trotter 2003 / 2011a, Wright 2002 / 2013). The semantic field of trade offers the ideal background to investigate the overlap and exchange of vocabulary from numerous languages in an 'everyday' context i.e. one not constrained to the experiences of a small, cultural elite. Sugar-related words such as *cot* and *caffatin* may have vanished from English records by 1500 but they still provide vital insight into the established lexicon of the professional communities involved and the way lexis was transferred between speakers and writers.

Conversely, frequency can be a helpful, if imperfect, measure in defining what constitutes Standard English today. Most of the Italian loanwords presented in this article (e.g. *candy, garble)* are found in the *Oxford Advanced Learner's Dictionary* (Hornby and Deuter: 2015), a resource which effectively codifies high-frequency vocabulary in the modern language for its readers (even if this is not its declared purpose). This does allow us to argue the case for such words (including ones limited to quite specific financial contexts such as *net* and *tare*) being considered Standard for the purposes of this analysis.

We take as our starting point an article from 1999, written by the late William Rothwell: former *Anglo-Norman Dictionary* editor and enthusiastic champion of the non-literary source. 'Sugar and Spice and All Things Nice: From Oriental Bazar to English Cloister in Anglo-French' analysed mercantile lexis against the backdrop of international commerce, highlighting trade routes that stretched from Italian

https://doi.org/10.1515/9783110687545-014

city states all the way to north-east England. This flow of goods (and words) connected English society not just to Europe but to the Middle East and beyond.

Northern Italians dominated the import of sugar and spices into late medieval England. Sugar was a sought-after luxury product[1] often for medicinal rather than culinary use. Maritime cities – Venice and Genoa in particular – made vast profits through their export to western Europe, exploiting their commercial dominance in the Middle East after the First Crusade in 1099 (Johnston 2011: 672). Sugar cane was grown locally in Sicily (where it had been introduced by the Arabs) but the very finest grades were sourced in the Venetian colonies on Cyprus (Adamson 2004: 28). *The Calendar State Papers of Venice* tell us that a single Venetian merchant sold 11,000 lbs (ie 11,000 lbs of sugar) of sugar in London in 1319 alone (Smith et al. 1830: 426).

Italy's position at the centre of the European sugar trade and its links around the Mediterranean are mirrored in the impressive variety of sugar types attested in the TLIO (*Tesoro della Lingua Italiana*). These are based on origin, characteristics or quality: e.g. *zucchero bambillonio* / *damaschino* / *tebaico* (from Babylon, Damascus and Thebes), *zucchero rosato / violato* (infused with rose or violet petals), *zucchero naibet / nebec* (infused with almond essence), *zucchero bianco / rosso* (refined and unrefined), *zucchero musciatto / muccara / caffettino* (compacted into cones or loaves), *zucchero tabarzet* (powdered sugar). In turn, cognates can be widely found in English records from the end of the thirteenth century, be they written in British Medieval Latin, Anglo-Norman or Middle English: e.g. *zucure rosate alexandrine* (AND2 **diacodion**), *zucre violette* (AND1 **violat**), *rede suger* (MED **sugre**), *zucar' caffatin'* (DMLBS **caffatinus**).

Ginger root or powder was also a popular (and expensive) import into medieval England and another market where Italian influence was particularly strong. The Florentine agent, Francesco Balducci Pegolotti, of the Bardi company, described three main grades for export in his well-known merchant handbook from c1335–43: high-quality *belledi* and *columbino*[2] gingers from India and the harder, smaller *micchino* from Mecca (cf. Evans 1935: 360, Bradley 1992: 112). This trio of gingers – *belendyn, columbyn et maykyn* – appears from

1 When the Bishop of Exeter died in 1310, he left 77lb of sugar in his will, worth £3 17s 2d (Trease 1959: 3).

2 Pegolotti's oft-cited description of the three grades of ginger referred to the *isola del Colombo d'India* and was originally taken to mean the city of Colombo on the island of Sri Lanka. The TLIO, DMF, MED and OED2 now all agree that it refers to Quilon (or Kollam) on the Malabar Coast of India, called *Columbum* in Latin.

3 For an extensive history of the Grocers company which traces its roots back to the Pepperers' Guild in the 1180s, see Nightingale (1995).

1414 in the accounts of the Worshipful Company of Grocers[3] and in several other English sources (see below). Pepper, nutmeg, cumin, cinnamon, cloves, aniseed, liquorice, treacle, dates, figs, raisins, fruits in syrup, candied peel, almonds, coconuts, pomegranates, oranges and quince jam are just some of the other treats available to English customers via the Italian trading empire (cf. Bradley 1992: 105–7, Ruddock 1951: 72–75).

In 'Sugar and Spice', Rothwell focused on two main sets of Anglo-Norman documentary sources. The first were from Southampton, a city with a deep-water harbour which welcomed large amounts of Genoese and Venetian traffic and which was at the heart of Anglo-Italian trade in the 1300s to mid-1400s. The *Local Port Book* and *Port Book of Southampton* record the arrival of expensive shipments including sugars, gingers, Egyptian silks and even elephant tusks. Some of these luxuries would also find their way into his second source – the contemporary monastic accounts of Durham Abbey, where the resident Benedictine order was not averse to indulging its sweet tooth.[4]

Rothwell had several key aims in writing his paper: to underline "the extent of overseas trade in the fourteenth and early fifteenth centuries revealed in just one set of documents" (1999: 656), to emphasize the crucial role of Anglo-Norman in recording such trade up to the mid-1400s and to highlight the value of the non-literary document. While he does not overtly identify borrowings from Italian, he does hint that Anglo-Norman represented a language of transmission, through which Italianisms could enter Middle English and British Medieval Latin: "French is the connection between Italian ships in Southampton and English monks in Durham" (1999: 652).[5] When we examine certain commodities which Rothwell picks out from these accounts, we do indeed find convincing lexical evidence of borrowing from Italian e.g. *gyngibre belendyn* or *sugre caffatin*.

The present paper considers the link between medieval Italian[6] and Anglo-Norman and, consequently, Middle English, in the semantic field of commerce. It

4 See also 'Glanures lexicologiques dans les documents des 14e et 15e siècles provenant de l'évêché de Durham' (Rothwell 2000).

5 In an earlier paper from 1993, Rothwell briefly comments on the importance of influential Italian banking companies like the Ricciardi and the Frescobaldi in England as part of the proliferation of the merchant class in general: this social change had wider, important linguistic consequences i.e. the widespread use of Anglo-Norman in business and administrative records (Rothwell 1993: 22–23).

6 The Italian merchant presence in late medieval England originated overwhelmingly from the north of the peninsula: Tuscan city states (Florence, Pisa, Lucca, and Siena) and the maritime powerhouses of Venice and Genoa. For the purposes of this article, I have used the basic label of 'Italian' in suggested etymologies. This is a useful but oversimplified catch-all for the

will focus on vocabulary related to the sugar and spice trades but which forms part of a wider pattern of borrowing in late medieval mercantile records in England. Furthermore, as the title of Rothwell's article suggests, we will see how non-literary Anglo-Norman and Middle English often came into contact with 'oriental' vocabulary (particularly of Arabic origin) via the medium of Italian dialects.

1 Anglo-Norman and Italian

No full-scale survey has ever been published on the Italian influence on insular French, in stark contrast to a number of studies which cover contact between Continental French and Italian, such as those by Vidos (1939, 1965), Hope (1971) and Fennis (1995). Together they analyse hundreds of borrowings in the fields of shipping and navigation, trade and finance, and warfare.[7]

Italian loanwords in insular French were first identified in 1913 in one of the sources Rothwell would later revisit: the accounts of Robert Florys, Water-Bailiff of Southampton in 1427–30. Their editor, Paul Studer, notes *fangot* ('bundle of cloth')[8] as being of Italian origin, enthusing that "the word must have been quite familiar to Southamptonians of A.D. 1428, seeing that it was commonly applied to bundles of exported cloth (!)" (Studer 1913: 50). In 1963, Brian Foster edited the later *Local Port Book of Southampton* (1435–36) and briefly mentions that close trading connections with Italy were visible in other examples of insular French vocabulary: AN *cotegnate* < It. *cotognato* ('quince jam'); AN *sarme* < It. *sarma* ('a measure of capacity'); AN *sport* < It. *sporta* ('a basket'); AN *comyt* < It. *comito* ('first officer on a galley') and AN *dosses* < It. *dossi* ('back skins') (Foster 1963: xiv).[9]

Tuscan, Venetian and Genoese regional languages with which the English merchant community came into contact. It is not within the scope of this article to provide phonological or morphological analyses of Italian dialectal variants or details of the transfer of lexis within these variants (e.g. from Sicilian into northern dialects). It is also worth noting that there are no references to the monumental *Lessico Etimologico Italiano* in this article because at the time of writing the relevant entries had not yet been published.

7 Precise totals from the medieval period can vary greatly depending on scholar and semantic field: see Schmitt 2003 and Schweickard 2008 for useful statistical breakdowns.

8 See also Tiddeman (2018: 125).

9 The borrowing of *dosses* from Italian *dossi* is unconvincing. It seems much more likely to be a spelling variation of AN *dos* ('back'), especially since the two forms appear within a month of each other in the Port Book: *Cl dosses de grey* / *Ml dos de grey* (see AND2 **dos**). Trotter agrees (2011a: 166).

David Trotter – who, like his mentor Rothwell, is another former AND editor – published two works in 2011 which consolidated both the concept of direct contact between Italian and Anglo-Norman and the need for wider study on the topic.[10] In ‘Death, taxes and property: Some code-switching evidence from Dover, Southampton and York’, he revisits the fifteenth-century Port Books as a prime example of a non-literary, multilingual source with, in this instance, the more unusual feature of Italianisms.[11] Trotter discusses the loanwords outlined by Studer and Foster (above) in more detail, and dwells on their implication for the wider field of medieval code-switching: it is highly unlikely that the Southampton scribe had much command of the Italian language but this peppering of the accounts with vocabulary not native to England (with no ‘switch-marking device’)[12] underlines the international dimension of maritime trade and how language contact was catalysed by real communicative situations (Trotter 2011a: 173–78). He also repeats his assertion that Italianisms could enter Anglo-Norman along a variety of transmission routes, including the royal dockyards at Rouen (the Clos de Gallées) where Genoese maritime terms (e.g. *calfater*, ‘to caulk’) used by skilled immigrant craftsman were absorbed into Norman lexis and then crossed the Channel (2011a: 170).[13] Trotter believed that while proof of lexical borrowing from Italian in English records such as these required further investigation, “the vehicle for linguistic commerce (i.e. the language in which the trade took place) was almost certainly French, whether insular or continental” (2011a: 182).

Finally, Schendl and Wright’s *Code-switching in Early English* highlights an important example of direct Anglo-Italian contact in the field of textiles:

> [...] the type of richly embroidered cloth known as *baudekin*, ultimately from an Arabic form *Baghdadi* ‘(cloth) of Baghdad’, passed into Italian *baldacco*, was then adopted into

10 The second article examined language contact in the opposite direction i.e. borrowings from Anglo-Norman, Middle English and (occasionally) British Medieval Latin found in a set of Sienese accounts written in London in 1305–08. See Trotter 2011b / Tiddeman 2012.

11 The other two sources examined are the Dover Castle inventories (1344–61) and various wills from York (1316–1491) which exhibit better known patterns of late English language mixing: in this case, a Latin-matrix with Anglo-Norman / Middle English lexemes or an insular French-matrix with Middle English lexemes.

12 This phenomenon entails the use of an Anglo-Norman definite article (usually *le* or *lé* / *lez*) to signal language switch mid-sentence and it most commonly precedes an Anglo-Norman / Middle English lexeme in a Latin-matrix administrative text. See also Trotter 2010, Wright 2010 and Ingham 2011 / 2013.

13 See also Trotter 2003 / 2006. Note that Trotter (2006c: 1779) also highlights the important role of Provençal in transmitting Italian shipping lexis into Continental French.

> Anglo-Norman where forms with and without /l/ vocalisation are found such as *baldekin*, *baudequin* [. . .] and then passed from Anglo-Norman into Middle English.
> (Schendl and Wright 2011:31)[14]

2 Middle English and Italian

It has been claimed that a surge in Italianisms in English did not begin until the mid-sixteenth century when Italian language learning became fashionable in noble circles during the Elizabethan period: the social and cultural achievements of the Renaissance were much admired and led to a rapid assimilation of borrowings in fields such as architecture (*cupola*, *duomo*, *piazza*), music and poetry (*duo*, *madrigal*, *violin*), science and mathematics (*algebra*, *romby*, *tariff*), and food and drink (*artichoke*, *mountflascon*, *pistachio*) (cf. Praz 1944: 27–37, Iamartino 2001: 22–28, Pinnavaia 2001: 155–64, Durkin 2014: 370–72). This coincided with the publication of William Thomas' first Italian grammar and glossary in England (1550), to be followed by John Florio's Italian-English dictionary *Worlde of Wordes* (1598).[15] A study by Durkin based on the OED3 corpus (A-ALZ and M-R-ZZ) shows a jump from twenty-two Italian loanwords attested in English in 1500–49 to 122 in 1550–99 which drops slightly to 98 in 1600–49 (Durkin 2014: 370–71). The same study shows that the two single biggest peaks in Italianisms as a proportion of all new words in English were in the second half of the sixteenth century and the first half of the eighteenth century.

Prior to 1500, the orthodox view has assumed that any Italian lexical influence on English soil was very small and restricted to a tiny cultural elite (cf. Dietz 2005). The only semantic field which has attracted widespread academic attention is that of literature. Borrowings in the works of Chaucer,[16] Gower, or Lydgate, multilingual authors with an interest in the famed *Tre Corone* (Dante, Petrarch and Boccaccio), have occupied scholars for centuries. It is widely accepted that all three authors were influenced by contemporary (or near contemporary) works

14 See also Tiddeman 2018 where I discuss this and other instances of borrowing of Italian fabric terminology into Anglo-Norman and Middle English.

15 For an overview of the contributions of Thomas and Florio to English lexicography, see O'Connor (1972) and for an intriguing examination of Italian language learning in early modern England, see Jason Lawrence's monograph *Who the Devil Taught Thee so much Italian?* (2005).

16 It should be remembered, of course, that Geoffrey Chaucer mingled just as much with merchants as he did with poets. He worked for over a decade as a bureaucrat, controlling customs on the Wool Wharf in London in close contact with visiting Italians and was sent to Genoa and Milan by Richard II on diplomatic trading missions (Lerer 2006).

in the Italian vernacular, especially Dante's *Divina Commedia* (c1308–20) and Boccaccio's *Decameron* (c1348–53).[17]

Such erudite usage is important, of course, and testimony to wider cultural links between England and Italy, even in the later Middle Ages. However, as we shall see in glossary below, literary borrowings from Italian in 'English' texts (be they Middle English, Anglo-Norman, British Medieval Latin or mixed-language of the sort used in accounts and inventories) are greatly outnumbered by more pragmatic borrowings to describe high-end commodities and commercial practices.

3 Untangling early Anglo-Italian contact

There is no doubt that Continental French played a key role in introducing some Italian loanwords into insular French pre-1450. We can confidently track the route of transmission of Genoese *poppa* ('stern of a ship') in the Rouen shipyards of the 1330s where northern Italian craftsmen were employed by the French king to build his fleet (Vidos 1965: 297–98, Trotter 2003: 23–24 / 2011a: 170); Continental French *poupe* was then later passed on into Anglo-Norman as *poupe* and eventually became English *poop*.

It can therefore be a complex issue deciding which Italianisms in Anglo-Norman are 'direct' and which are 'indirect' or 'Gallo-Italianisms' (i.e. passed on via Continental French). Loanwords such as *cotegnate* ('quince jam') attested in fifteenth-century Southampton but entirely absent from the Continental French corpus offer unproblematic evidence of direct contact. Yet all the Italian borrowings considered in detailed below (and numerous others in the wider field of merchant activity e.g. *carrack*, *carat*, *crimson, damask*) are also found in Continental French sources. This is hardly surprising given that Italian trade, banking and

17 See for example, Hines and Yeager (2010), Mortimer (2005) and Boitani (1983). Examples include *cerrial* (adj. 'of an oaktree' < It. *cerriale*), *cornuto* ('cuckold' < It. *cornuto*), *vecke* ('old woman' < It. *vecchia*). It is worth noting Rothwell's comments about Chaucer's borrowing of *cadence* ('rhythm in poetry / music' < It. *cadenza*) here. Earliest senses mean 'a fall' or 'falling off' but this was later adopted in Italian in a figurative sense to describe the voice or music rising and falling. It seems that Middle English (possibly via an unattested Anglo-Norman form) borrowed this secondary meaning significantly earlier (1380s) than Continental French (1520). Rothwell (1991: 180) comments: "Theoretically, the so-called learned borrowing 'cadence' ought to be introduced from the continent much later into a more highly educated society, but perversely appears in Chaucer's English in its musical sense some two centuries before being attested in the Renaissance French of the continent. Its appearance may well be a reminder of the well-documented presence of Italian bankers and merchants in fourteenth-century England."

shipping were also widespread in late medieval France (cf. Hope 1971: 55–56 / Trotter 2006). However, it would be wrong to assume that all Italianisms in the English mercantile record were first 'filtered through' Continental French. Whilst there was indeed a considerable influx of Italian military and maritime terms transmitted into early modern English via Continental French from the 1500s onwards,[18] we should not automatically superimpose this model of language contact onto the (trilingual) trading lexis of late medieval England.[19]

Overall, in numerous instances, we are surely dealing with a separate mercantile community with its own direct language contact with Italian dialects. Arguably, the name for a sought-after luxury like crystalized sugar, *(suchre) candi*, infiltrated the commercial vocabularies of England and France independently, given that its import was dominated by groups of Italian merchants in both countries. We have the earliest records of its purchase in the accounts of the English King's Spicer, c1242, whilst *candi* was first attested in France almost concurrently in 1256 in a medical treatise by the bilingual scholar, Aldobrandino da Siena. *Belendin* ginger from India – one of several types of the spice imported by Italian merchants – is listed by the Worshipful Company of Grocers. This was a royal London livery company whose founding members in 1348 included Vivian Roger of Lucca and which was also partly run from 1428 by Italians who trained their English apprentices (Bradley 2012: xxi / Nightingale 1995: 182, 185). Consequently, the attestations of this loanword are surely independent of parallel continental entries for *gig. baladit* found amongst the *Comptes de l'Argenterie des Rois de France* from 1359–60.

18 To take just two examples: OED2 **squadron** 'a small body of men / soldiers lined up in a square formation', att. 1562 (< CF *escadron*, att. c1375, < It. *squadrone*) / OED2 **gripe**[4] 'small, fast vessel used in the Levant', att. 1511 (< CF *grippe*, att. 1480, < It. *grippo*). See Vidos (1939: 448–51), Hope (1971: 41).

19 In his wide-ranging study on loanwords in the OED3, Durkin (2014: 262) confirms that words borrowed from French peak in Middle English in the late fourteenth century and that more "French and /or Latin" vocabulary was absorbed into English over the period 1350–1450 than at any other time. Crucially, this represents "the tail end of a period of trilingualism, in which an individual might be called on to express the same concepts in English, French or Latin, either in speech and writing. It is therefore unsurprising that when English comes to be used as a written medium in functions where one or both of the other languages had previously been used, we find that this is very often done using precisely those words that were equivalent and familiar in both of the other languages of this trilingual society". Such a model of commercial lexis transfer could equally well have applied to originally 'foreign' lexemes such as Italianisms than were absorbed during this period into Middle English from Anglo-Norman (or British Medieval Latin).

It seems clear that Anglo-Norman frequently played a role as a 'buffer' or language of transmission between Italian dialects (mainly Tuscan, Genoese or Venetian) and Middle English. Such a role has been thus far overlooked by the major dictionaries which often describe such loanwords in English simply as 'from French' e.g. OED2 **candy / tare.** While the label is technically correct, of course, this blanket term hides the reality of lexical transfer in merchant society and more subtle distinctions need to be drawn: what we are dealing with (in many cases) is an Italianism entering a language in England (Anglo-Norman), before being passed into another language in England (Middle English). If we are to accurately ascertain the extent of Italian language contact in late medieval England, we have to take this process into account.[20]

4 Glossary

The glossary below considers eight likely Italianisms in Anglo-Norman related to the sugar and spice trades, all of which were passed on into Middle English. As noted above, five of the lexemes remain in Standard English to this day (*candy, confection, garble, net, tare*) and three are not attested after the late medieval period (*belendin, caffatin, cot*). Five of the loanwords are also of Arabic origin: testament to Venice and Genoa's lucrative trading colonies in the Middle East and the Arab occupation of Sicily until the eleventh century.

Two key mercantile texts feature regularly, in addition to the Southampton and Durham material examined in Rothwell's 'Sugar and Spice'. These are the accounts of the Worshipful Company of Grocers from 1345–1463 (Anglo-Norman / Middle English-matrix) and the hosting accounts of Italian merchants in England from 1440–1444 (Anglo-Norman / Latin-matrix).[21] Two citations (for *net* and *tare*) are also included from the unpublished accounts of an English factor working in (Middle English / Latin / Tuscan-matrix).[22]

---

20 Another convincing argument for direct, early Anglo-Italian contact (although one which falls beyond the scope of this paper) is the presence of numerous insular Gallicisms and Middle Anglicisms in the Italian of Tuscan companies based in London in the 1300s and 1400s, such as the Gallerani, Salviati and Villani (see Tiddeman 2012, 2017 and 2018).

21 These Exchequer records (E101) are edited in English translation by Helen Bradley, *The Views of the Hosts of Alien Merchants, 1440–44* (2012). See also Tiddeman (2017: 222–28).

22 I am currently preparing an edition of these accounts for the British Academy, *The Cantelowe Accounts: Multilingual merchant records form Tuscany, 1450–51 (Archivio Salviati, Serie 1: 339).*

4.1 Belendin

AN *belendin* (adj.) 'referring to high-quality ginger, from the Indian west coast' < It. *belledi* < Ar. *beled* ('country')

Variants of *(gengiovo) belledi* appear alongside other imported Indian gingers in several Italian sources throughout the 1300s, such as Pegolotti's merchant handbook, the Statutes of Pisa and letters sent by the Datini company of Prato (TLIO **belledi** / AD **beledi, belladino** / OVI **belledi, Boliedi**). We also know it was still shipped out of Venice to western markets in the sixteenth century. In his edition of Venetian merchant letters from 1553–56, Ugo Tucci (1957: 350) glosses *beledi* as follows: "Gingembre des Indes d'excellente qualité [. . .] le *beledi* est le gingembre de plaine et fait dériver son nom du mot arable *beled* (pays) attribué au produit indigène par les Musulmans établis aux Indes, afin de le distinguer de ceux de provenance étrangère."

In England, the earliest citation is found in an Anglo-Norman medical receipt from the 1300s as ginger, like other spices, was widely used as a medicinal ingredient before it became a culinary one.

> *pernet une libre de gynger belentyn* ((Pop Med 34) (14th c.)[23] (AND2 **belendin**)

Gyngivre belendyn en racyns, purchased in London, is found in the Duchess of Norfolk's accounts (1394) and the spice appears with other ginger types (*mekyn, columbyn*) in the fifteenth-century Grocers accounts (1414), the Port Books of Southampton (1427–30) and a hosting account of Venetian merchants in the English capital (1443–43).

A citation not currently found in any dictionaries comes from a contemporary Latin-matrix View written on behalf of John Chichele, host to Geronimo Dandolo of Venice (cf. Bradley 2012: 281):

> *Item Jeronimus Dandillo mercator de Venise[. . .] zinziber belendyn ad valenciam iiijxxxviijli vjs* ((E010/128/31 ret. 33) (1440)

The term 'belendin ginger' transferred into late Middle English but we only have one extant example in an English-matrix text; *ginger valadyne* in the fifteenth-century *Book of Nurture* by John Russell, the product of an unexceptional bilabial to labio-dental shift:

23 While this source is named *Popular Medicine in Thirteenth Century England*, the citation containing *beletyn* is found in a fourteenth-century medical receipt written by John of Greenborough (Hunt 1990: 33–34).

Good gynger colombyne is best to drynke and ete; Gynger valadyne & maydelyn[24] *ar not so holsom in mete* (Russell Bk. Nurt 131–2) (a1475)[25] (MED **gingivere**)

Examples of this ginger type are not identified by the major Continental French dictionaries, although a record of *gig. baladit* occurs in the *Comptes de l'Argenterie des Rois de France* from 1359–60 (a text used in the DMF entry sub **columbin**[2]). These purchases of ginger are part of the expenses incurred by Jean II ('le Bon') of France whilst he was held for ransom in London by Edward III, after the Battle of Poitiers (cf. Yule 1875: 370).[26] We could speculate in this case, therefore, that the CF scribe's use of the form *baladit* was either influenced directly by Italian (but on English soil) or by insular French names for the ginger.

4.2 Caffatin

AN *caffatin* (adj.) 'referring to high-quality sugar loaves made in open, double-bottom moulds'

< It. *caffettino* < Ar. *quffa(t)* ('basket') / < It. *Caffa* ('Kaffa, a port on the Crimean peninsula)

Zucchero caffettino is first attested in the Sienese dialect of Cecco Angiolieri in a sonnet (c1275–1300) dedicated to Dante: the term is used as a metaphor for false promises ('it seems as sweet as caffetin sugar but it is salty'). More prosaically, the Bardi factor, Pegolotti,[27] refers to the quality and price of the sugar type nineteen times in his merchant handbook (c1335–43) and it also features in the Pisan Statues of 1322 (TLIO / OVI **caffettino**).

As Rothwell notes, this luxury import features in the Anglo-Norman accounts of Durham Abbey from c1348 onwards (see also AND2 **caffatin**):

24 *Maydelyn* ginger is not so easy to identify but it is presumably a variant of *maykyn* or Meccan ginger.

25 Note that the OED3 entry sub **ginger** dates this source as c.1460.

26 The king's lavish lifestyle as a 'prisoner' in London, whilst France struggled to scrape together an enormous ransom, is infamous and as Tuchman (1978: 169) noted: "Reading through Jean's accounts in the archives 500 years later, Jules Michelet, France's most vivid if not most objective historian, said they made him sick".

27 It is worth adding that the Florentine worked for the Bardi office in London for three years (1317–20) and was known to have dealt directly with the king, Edward II (Evans 1935: xvii-xx).

> 'zukr. de Skaffatyne' (c.1348; p.547), 'sucr. de Caffatyn' (1349–50; p.551) or 'zucre caffatyne' (1360; p.563) was most probably shipped from Caffa or Kaffa, a Black Sea port renowned for its trade in medieval times and held by the Genoese from the thirteenth to the fifteenth century. It is not mere chance that the Genoese galleys were the most numerous Italian vessels in the port of Southampton in the fourteenth and early fifteenth centuries.
> (Rothwell 1999: 655)

Caffatin sugar also appears in several other British Medieval Latin and Middle English sources from the 1300s and 1400s, including the King's Remembrancer, the Earl of Derby's accounts and medical treatises by Robert Thornton and (in translation) Guy de Chauliac:

> *zucar' caffatin'* (KR Ac 391/15 Arch.XXXI 101) (1349) (DMLBS **caffatinus**)
>
> *pro j pane suiguri caffretin* (Ac. H. Derby 11) (1390) (DMLBS **succarum**)
>
> *which Beneuenutus makeþ of zuccre candin or caffatyn [L caffatina], is preciouse in þis case.* (Chauliac 1 NY 12) (?a1425) (MED **caffatin**)
>
> *Sethe it efte with..a gude porcione of zucre caffatine* (Thrn.Med.Bk.(Thrn) 20/20) (c1440) (MED **caffatin**)

Whilst a link to Italian *caffettino* is clear in the case of these English attestations, the ultimate source of the borrowing is not. The AND takes Rothwell's view and defines *caffatin* as '(sugar) from Caffa, a Black Sea Port', with the term driving ultimately from the Genoese toponym for its thriving trading outpost, originally called Theodosia by the Greeks.The borrowing first appears in continental sources at the same time as insular ones (1328–42). The DMF entry sub **cafetin** gives the same gloss as the AND but then notes that there is an alternative etymon, *cafis* (also mentioned in the FEW: o.i. p.486a): 'Sucre jaune, couleur de résine, tel qu'on le portait de Chypre, d'Espagne ou de Sardaigne, dans des tonneaux appelés cafis.'

However, another convincing etymon to rival *Caffa* is the Arabic *quffa(t)* ('basket') as outlined in Rosella Mosti's TLIO article sub **caffettino** which describes loaves made from boiled sugar poured into moulds or baskets. Interestingly, it also refers the reader to the English term *basket-sugar* (cf. OED2 **basket**) which describes sugar made in the same way in the Straits Settlements, a nineteenth-century British colony in south-east Asia.

The potential role of an Italian intermediary in transmitting this Arabic term for loaf sugar into English commercial lexis is also suggested in the DMLBS entry sub **caffatinus**.

4.3 Confection

AN *confection* (n.) 'a preserve or sweetmeat such as candied fruit and nuts'

< It. *confezione* < Lat. *confectio* ('preparation')

As we have noted, the accounts of Durham Abbey and the Southampton Port Books detail numerous sweet treats imported into England from Italy in the 1300s and 1400s: such as *zucre caffatyne, suchre candi, cotegnate sport* ('basket') *de suchre pot* and *madrian.*[28] Both sources also record the purchase of 'confections', a more generic term covering preserves or sweetmeats made with sugar, spices, nuts, citrus fruits, rosewater and other expensive, exotic ingredients.

> *chardeqwns, confecions, dates, maces / In 3 lb. de confeccions* (Durham 594 / 605) (1384–85 / 1403–04)

> *xij pot de dates, vij cofyns de confections, valor xx s./ ij. casses de confections* (Port Bks 49 / 108) (1427–30) (AND2 **confection**)

Lydate and Gower[29] also both refer to such delicacies in Middle English:

> *Confection of cokes* (J. Gower Confessio Amantis III 23) (1393)

> *Of sondry metis and confecciouns, Off dyuers drynkes & manyfold vitaille.* (Lydgate, FP Bod 263, 7.902) (?a1439) (MED **confeccioun**)

An alternative and more widely attested name for these products was *confits*, from the past participle of the verb *confire* (AND2 **confire**^{2} / OED2 **comfit** / DMF **confit**) and ultimately, from the Latin *conficere* ('to prepare or produce').

The root of *confezione* is also the same Latin verb. The noun took on two distinct principal meanings: the action of making or achieving something and the end product, a mixture or preparation. This second semantic nuance split further into two sub-groups, the earlier medical confection and the later, culinary one. As both were based on the same ingredients – sugar and spices – and

28 *Madrian* appears to be a ginger conserve or sweetmeat which – as the OED3 entry sub **madrian** tentatively suggests – may be ultimately derived from the Italian *madria* ('Arabian ginger'). Italian attestations are admittedly thin on the ground, however, with the DEI entry sub **madria** offering only a single example from c1343. See also MED **madrian**, DMLBS **madria**, DEAF **madrïan,** DMF **madrian, FEW** XXI 139a o.i. / XXI 486b o.i.

29 It is also worth reiterating here that both these multilingual authors were inspired by great works of Italian literature and used unequivocal Italianisms in other parts of their work.

were made initially by the same practitioners, it was at times difficult to tell the difference. We cannot be sure if W. Burton, the King's 'spice confectioner' in 1403 would be considered today as a doctor or a cook (DMLBS **confectionarius**). But during the late Middle Ages, sugar work did eventually divide into two more distinct trades in England: the apothecary and the confectioner (cf. Richardson 2004, Trease 1964).

Interestingly, while confections as sweetmeats are found in Anglo-Norman, Middle English, British Medieval Latin and medieval Italian (TLIO / DEI **confezione**, OVI **confezioni, confectioni**)[30] from the thirteenth century onwards, I have found no trace of them in Continental French.[31] This may be a simple gap in the record or of no importance since all instances of *confection* could have been directly borrowed from Latin *confectio*. However, another theory is that this alternative name for *confits* is an Italianism in Anglo-Norman (in some source texts with Italian connections, at least), one that would be passed on into English and remain there.

4.4 Cot

AN *cot* (n.) 'a cooking: a term applied to sugar and the number of times it has been refined'

< It. *cotta / cotte* < Lat. *cocta* < Lat. *coquere* ('to cook')

In medieval Italian, the quality of sugar was defined by the number of times it had been 'cooked': i.e. boiled and left to recrystallize into a more refined white powder. Pegolotti describes, c1335, how the best sugar is the most cooked and by 1401, in the Datini Company correspondence, sugar is defined as *di uno / due / tre cotte* as a designator of its quality[32] (TLIO **cotta²** / OVI **cotto** / AD **cotta, cotte** / DEI **cotta**).

30 The culinary sense of *confezione* died out in the sixteenth century. Modern Italian retains only the meanings of 'making / production' or 'a package'.

31 *Confection* is attested in Continental French from the twelfth century onwards in the sense of 'action de confectionner, de réaliser qqc.', 'Action de confectionner par mélange, mélange', 'Remède composé, électuaire, préparation, mixture': see DMF / GDC / TLFi **confection**, FEW II-2, 1029b: **confection**, DEAF **confeccion**.

32 The meaning of *di tre cotte* in terms of 'the maximum extent' still lives on in modern Italian in the idiomatic expression *furbo di tre cotte* i.e. 'extremely cunning'.

By the last quarter of the sixteenth century, the whole process of triple refining sugar is clearly described in the first printed history of Sicily (where sugar was first introduced into Italy): *Le due deche dell'historia di Sicilia* (Fiorentino 1574: 29).[33] Melis (1976: 31) also notes the use of this quality grading system for sugar in his study of Italian merchants in Spain in the fourteenth to sixteenth centuries.

In the *Views of the Hosts*, we find convincing evidence that this labelling of sugar has been borrowed into Anglo-Norman as *cot(e)* with examples in two hosting accounts (one Latin-matrix) which both deal with Venetian merchants.

> *Item a Benet Augustyn sugre dune cot poisant ultra vijC xix libres a viij*^{d} *la libre summa xxiij*^{li} *xix*^{s} *iiij*^{d} (E101/128/30 ret.1) (1441–42)[34]

> *Item Jeronimus Dandillo mercator de Venise[...]sugre de j cote ad valenciam lxvj*^{li} *xiij*^{s} *iiij*^{d} (E010/128/31 ret. 33) (1440)

We find fourteen other examples in the Views of the more Anglicized variant *kute* used to describe high-quality sugar e.g.:

> *Item a Harry Purches iiijC libres lofe sugur de j kute pur xj*^{li}, *Item a Thomas Gybbus iiijC libres lofe sugur de iij kute pur xvj*^{li} *vj*^{s} *viij*^{d} (E101/128/30 ret. 4) (1441–42)

Eight references are to *iii kute* sugar and six to *i kute* and, unsurprisingly, the more refined product is the more expensive. In the examples cited above, 400lb of 'Grade 1' loaf sugar costs £11 whereas 400lb of 'Grade 3' costs £16 6s. 8d. Even if we decide that *kute* is simply a variant of Middle English *cute*, the case for a semantic loan, influenced by Italian, is a strong one.

Similarly, we have convincing late Middle English-matrix examples of the borrowing in the accounts of the London Grocers and Sir John Howard and in Russell's work on noble household management, the *Book of Nurture:*

> *Sugre of iij coet* (Grocer London 190/5) (1428)

> *He paid to Water of Colchestre for a li. sugre of ij kute [vr. kewte], xviij d* (Acc. Howard RC57, 305) (1465)

> *Sugre of iij cute white, hoot & moyst in his propurte.* (Russell Bk. Nurt (Hrl 4011) 138, 159) (a1475) (MED **cute**)

33 This text, by the Dominican friar Remigio Fiorentino, is a translation into Tuscan from a slightly earlier Latin work by Tomaso Fazello from 1558.

34 Note that the Italianism *talany* ('raw silk from Persia') also appears in this source (cf. Tiddeman 2017: 227 / 2018: 127).

With this in mind, it could be argued that the glosses in the relevant MED and OED entries are misleading. The first sense listed, *wyne cute*, clearly does refer to a boiled, sweetened wine that is served as a liquor and its name likely comes directly from the French past participle, *cuit*. However, attestations listed under the second sense relating to sugar ('of a liquor: reduced to one third / one half by boiling'), do seem to be influenced by the Italian grades of quality of *i, ii, iii cotte*. While these grades are, of course, obtained by boiling the sugar, some nuance of meaning has been lost in the MED entry. John Russell's instructions to take *Sugre of iij cute white, hoot & moyst in his propurte* do not mean that the sugar should be boiled until a third is left, rather that 'Grade 3' sugar should be used.

The reference to *gynger of iij cute* in another of Russell's recipes from the *Book of Nurture* (OED2 **cuit / cute**) is interesting. There is no equivalent use in the Italian corpora but the author must have meant 'high-quality / highly refined' ginger and borrowed Italian sugar terminology to apply to another spice supplied by these same merchants. It is noteworthy that all three suspected Italianisms in this source – ginger *valadyne / columbyne of iij cute* and *sugre iij cute* – all occur within a few lines of the same recipe.

4.5 Garbeler

AN *garbeler* (v.) 'to sift out the refuse from spices'

< It. *garbellare* < It. *garbello* < Ar. *gharbala / garbal* ('sieve')

Garbellare emerges in Romance in the Pisan Statutes of 1321 and also features in the merchant handbooks of Pegolotti (Florence) and Zibaldone (Venice). Attestations can be found in the Latin from 1269 (notably in Venice and Verona), according to the DEI sub **garbellare**. It is a commercial technical term, widely accepted to have come from the Arabic for 'sieve' or 'to sieve' (see, for example, Dietz 2005: 591). The inspection and *garbelling* of spices before sale to remove extraneous refuse (the *garble*) played an important part in their weight and price and was carried out by a designated official: the *garbler*.

In 1992, Rothwell discussed the verb *garbeller* in 'The French Vocabulary in the Archive of the London Grocers' Company' where it is attested several times, e.g:

> *le vendour purra acorder ové le chatour q'il puisse faire sanz garbeler [. . .] sy vous plese ordeygner qe lour Specerie soit garbelé* (Grocers 73) (1393)

toutz foitz apres q'il eyt garbellé ascun bale dez merchandisez (Grocers 75) (1394) (AND2 **garbeler**)

The same borrowing appears around twenty-five years later when the Worshipful Company of Grocers had shifted their accounting-keeping to a an English matrix:

No Maner Man..schall bye no Grene ȝinȝer..lesse þanne hit be Garbelyd by þe Garbelour (Grocer Lond. in Bk. Lond. E 202/239) (1419–20) (MED **garbelen**)

As we have seen, the Grocers was a London institution with especially close links to Italian trade and Italian traders (Bradley 2012: xxi). Whilst I would question Rothwell's dismissal of any potential direct Middle English-Italian contact at the time,[35] his article underlines the importance of specifically insular French *garbeler* as a vehicle for transferring this word family into the terminology of English trade:

This whole family of terms is unknown to G.[odefroy], T[obler] L[ommatzsch] and the AND. The FEW (2,ii. 1332a-1333a sub **cribellum**) has forms related to those found in the Grocers' Archive, but only at a much later date: "Mfr. nfr. *grabeler* 'passer (des épices) au crible' (16jh.-1653)"; "Nfr. *grabeaux 'morceaux rompus des drogues, poussière . . .* ' (seit 1640)"; "Nfr. *grabeleur* 'celui qui est chargé de grabeler une substance'; *grabelage* 'action de *grabeler*' (beide seit 1866)". (Rothwell 1992: 34)

Since the publication of his article, two Continental French citations of *garbeller* (or rather its past participle) have come to light in two spice-related contexts: one in 1305 in mercantile material in Bruges (DEAF ***grabellum**) and one in the legal journals of the French magistrate, Dauvet, in the 1450s (DMF **garbeller**). These two examples must surely also be linked to Italian *garbellare*, as are their Anglo-Norman cognates. As we see from Rothwell's comments above, the variant *grabeler* is not attested until the sixteenth century in France (where it also acquires a figurative meaning, 'to scrutinise closely', as used in Rabelais). It is worth pointing out though that the TLFi suggests that the verb evolved Middle Dutch *grabel* ('a sieve', att. 1439) which in turn is probably derived from Italian *garbello* and, ultimately, the same Arabic root. The FEW suggests an entirely different ultimate etymon (Latin *cribellum*) which appears a less convincing candidate given the frequent role of Arabic in spice-related etymologies.

What is very clear is that the *garbeller* word family appears more widely used in extant medieval merchant records in England than in France, with new

35 "This Anglo-French and Latin evidence from England not only makes necessary a drastic revision of the dates given in the FEW, but casts serious doubt on the validity of its Note 4 on p. 1333b: 'Auch e. *garble* aus dem it., vielleicht über das fr. entlehnt.'" (Rothwell 1992: 35).

insular derivations also emerging in several hosting accounts linked to Italian merchants in London e.g.:

> *a Thomas Nicholas iiij bales gynger & le garbeler* lj^{li} $iiij^{s}$ (E101/128/30 ret. 6) (1440)[36]

> *Item a dit Robert le mesme iour une petit bagge garbelage de peper longe* (E101/128/30 ret.1) (1441–42)

Thanks again to Rothwell's article, we see that *garbellore* appears as early as 1303 in British Medieval Latin: it is not given a separate headword in the DMLBS but features in the entry sub **granum**^{4} (the citation refers to sifting West African *grani paridisi*, also known as 'Guinea pepper'). This points to a much earlier use of these lexemes in the vernacular (Anglo-Norman, Middle English or both) than is implied by its first record in insular French-matrix and English-matrix texts from 1393 and c1419, respectively. Another key point is that *garbeller* was used in Anglo-Norman to refer to merchandise other than spices, suggesting that the concept was sufficiently embedded in the language of trade to take on new semantic roles.[37] See this condemnation of the 'seditious confederacy of Lombards' who were selling 'outrageously priced' bowstaffs that have not been properly 'garbelled' (i.e. sorted out into gradations of quality):

> *Ore est il ensi qe par la seducious confederacie de les Lombardes usantz as divers Portes de cest Roialme les Bowestaves ore sont a si outerageous price, c'est assavoir a viij li. le Cent, lou ils soloient estre venduz meis a xl s. et ensement ils suffrer ne voilent ascun garbelment d'iceux estre fait, meis vendont bons & mals a si excessif price ensemblement nient garbelez* (Stats ii 494, 1413–21) (AND2 **garbeler)**

In terms of morphological flexibility, this is an exceptionally prolific loanword. Home-grown derivations developed in Anglo-Norman, independent of the Italian equivalents: AND2 **garbelage / garbelment** (the process: cf. TLIO **garbellatura**); AND2 / MED **garbelure**, DMLBS **garbelura** (the remaining refuse: cf. TLIO **garbella**); AND2 / MED sub **garbelour** (the official carrying out the job: cf. TLIO **garbellatore**);[38] AND2 **garbelable / garbele** (adj. / p.p. to describe garbelled material, cf. TLIO **garbellato**). Note also the English noun *garble* ('the remaining refuse') which is only attested in English-matrix texts from c1503 and must surely derive either from unattested Anglo-Norman **garbel* or directly

36 Note the nominal use of *le garbeler* – a feature which is, so far, unique to this source.

37 There is also an example in the MED entry sub **garbelure** from 1428 referring to the the *garbalour of wax* (i.e. leftover or refuse wax).

38 Note, however, the attestation of *garbelatour* in the London Grocers documentation from 1419 (AND2 **garbelatour**) which is potentially an Italianism < *garbellatore*. See also DMLBS **garbelator** (att. 1442).

from Italian *garbella* (cf. OED2 **garble** (n.)). Further 'native' forms developed in Middle English *garbelarship* or 'office of the garbelour' (MED **garbelarship**); the gerund, *garbelinge* (MED **garbelinge**) and the past participle, *garbaled* (MED **garbelen**).

The verb *to garble* is also one of the most long-lived borrowings of medieval Italian origin in English. Its use to mean 'sifting or weeding out' endured until the nineteenth century and the later figurative sense of 'to change or distort meaning' (as in 'to garble one's words') is, of course, still found in Standard English today (OED2 **garble** (v.)).

4.6 Net

AN *net* (adj.) 'remaining weight of merchandise or price, after all deductions have been made'

< It. *netto* / *netta* < Lat. *nitidus* ('clean, bright, shiny')

Netto / *net* first emerged in Italian, French and English attached to a notion of cleanliness, be it physical or spiritual. The earliest meanings in Middle English of *net* (both attested c1330) are 'smart, trim and elegant' or 'desirable, good; decent, clean' and these come from Anglo-Norman *net*: 'clean, tidy, refined' / 'pure, chaste, pious' (AND2 net1).[39]

The shift to a commercial concept of a 'clean' weight or sum of money (i.e. that which remains when deductions have been taken from the gross) occurred in Italy (probably first in Tuscany) where it appears in accounts from 1300 (OVI / AD **netto, netta,** DEI **netto**). This specific usage – according to the FEW VII, 147a – was borrowed into Continental French in 1483 (but note the earlier presence of *restant de nect* in the accounts of Jacques Coeur in 1453, recorded by the DMF sub **net**).

The major dictionaries list only two citations of *net* being used in this way in Middle English, prior to 1500: one from the Worshipful Company of Grocers (a fruitful source of Italianisms, as we have seen) and one from the records of a wealthy English wool-trading family:

> *Þere was abayted For powdyr þe weyȝt Off iiijc lxviij lb. and pris þer uppon Nette at viij d. þe lb.* (R. W. Chambers & M. Daunt Bk. London Eng., 200) (1418)

39 This is at the root of modern English *neat* which emerged in the mid-fifteenth century (cf. OED3 **neat**, att. 1453) and, of course, French *nettoyer* (cf. AND2 **nettoier** att. c1275–1300).

> *Sum v sac d. viij cl[oves]. Ter xj cl[oves] Nett v sac xxiij cl[oves]*. (Cely Papers in Eng. Stud. 42 145) (1486) (OED3 **net adj. /n.4**)

Some important new citations of this semantic loan (not yet in any dictionary) can be found in two sources with strong Italian links. Firstly, the *Views of the Hosts* provides the first example of specific mercantile usage in an Anglo-Norman document, a decade earlier than the equivalent use in Central French. The account – written in Southampton – concerns the imports and exports of Paolo Morelli and his associates and records the net weight of some sacks of soap belonging to a Florentine merchant:

> *Peris de le Reype Florenteyne dischargy lij sackys de savone blanke que poysse net iijxxxixC & xxvij* libres (E101/128/31 r. 36) (1442–43)

In the multilingual *Cantelowe Accounts*, written in Pisa and Florence in 1450–51, the English author is clearly at ease with the concept of *net*. He uses the Italian shorthand n^{t} for *netto/a* several dozen times before a weight of wool or, occasionally, writes the word out in full. In the single English-matrix example, it is actually impossible to know whether Balmayn's abbreviation n^{t} stands for Italian *netto/a* or Middle English *net* but, in either case, the Tuscan influence on his English writing is undeniable:

> *Þe which summa ys xiij sackys et xxiij cloves. And so reste clere* n^{t}*: cc*^{o} *lj sackys cloves viij semis* (AS Serie 1: 339, 9c) (1450–51)

Overall, the evidence suggests (here, as in many other cases) that the financial term *net* entered England directly with Italian merchants: be it first into Anglo-Norman and then into Middle English, into Middle English directly or, very likely, both, depending on the source and the circumstances.

4.7 (Suchre) candy

AN *(suchre) candi* (n.) 'crystallized cane sugar, a luxury commodity first brought back from the Holy Land to Europe in the 1100s'

< It. *(zucchero) candi* < Ar. (*sukkar*) *qandī* ('crystalized sugar')
< Pers. *kand* ('sugar')

Along with rice and oranges, sugar was an 'exotic' foodstuff first introduced by Arabic speakers into Iberia and Sicily (Adamson 2004: 28). The first attestations of *çucheri candi* in Italian (as in English and French), referred to the crystallised sugar itself rather than to any sweetmeat or confectionary and were found in medical texts. The earliest is the Italian vernacular *Antidotarium Nicolai Parvum* (c1275), an anonymous collection of over 1200 pharmaceutical recipes, mostly from Greek sources, written in last quarter of the thirteenth century and a highly influential text at the Salerno School of Medicine (Prioreschi 2003: 472–74, TLIO / OVI **candi**). Another key source (itself originally based on several Latin texts) is *La sanità del corpo*, an Italian translation of the Continental French *Régime du corps* from 1256 by the bilingual author, Aldobrandino da Siena (cf. TL / TLFi **candi**).

Such texts were the result of the huge wave of influence of the more advanced traditions of Greco-Arabic medicine on Western Europe in the Middle Ages and it is certainly likely that in some English sources the Middle Eastern loanword *candi* was borrowed directly. One such source is the British Medieval Latin medical treatise *Rosa Anglica* (c1314), with its ten references to *saccharo/i candi*. Its author – Edward II's physician, John of Gaddesden – was the first of his profession to have been fully trained in England and not in the famous Montpellier school. Gaddesden cites numerous Greek, Latin and Arabic texts, such as the writings of the Khalif's physican, Abul-hassan Ali ben Ridhwan ben Ali ben Ja'far.[40]

As we have seen (cf. *confection*, above), there was little distinction between medicine and confectionary or between the trade of spicer and apothecary. Most 'treatments' – be they syrups or pastilles – were basically sweets made from sugar and spices. It was the English Pepperers who are first recorded as importing sugar into London in 1180 and by the early 1300s, "the versatile, honest and successful medieval spicer apothecary had to act as a shopkeeping spice specialist, pharmacist, international trader, artistic confectioner and alchemist" (Richardson 2004: 179). Indeed, our earliest attestation of *candi / candy* in an English record is from the BML accounts of the King's Spicer, Roger of Montpellier, a source edited by Trease in 1959:

> *pro candi et penid' 7d / pro candi 4d / pro zucar' et candi 3d /et pro penid' et candy 6d* (E101 /349/10 in Trease 1959: 39) (1242–43)

It seems very probable that such men who embraced a multitude of roles, both commercial and intellectual, encountered *candi* via the very merchants who

40 However, it is hard to know how much he read in the original or how much in translated extracts from other contemporary works, such as the *Practica seu Lilium medicinae*, from 1303, written by Bernard de Gordon in Montpellier (see Cholmeley 1912: 166–84, Prioreschi 2003: 369–70).

imported such products into their city as well as, or perhaps instead of, a scholarly term from Arabic.[41]

Vernacular *sugre candi* begins to appear within British Medieval Latin texts from the late 1300s onwards (DMLBS **succarum** / OED2 **sugar-candy**). Attestations in insular French-matrix texts are not numerous but once we consider sources like the Southampton Port Books and the *Views of the Hosts* in the 1400s, we can be fairly confident that *sucre candi*, 'the commodity', rather than 'the medical ingredient' was a lexeme reinforced over and over again in English lexis by its Italian sellers:

> *j. casset de suchre candy* (Port Bks 84) (1427–30) (AND1 **sucre**)

> *En primez ij barelles suger candy [. . .] En primez vendu a Nicholas Wifold ij barelles suger candy pur xxvijli xiijs vjd* (E010/128/31 ret 10) (1440–41)

Hope (1971: 32) lists *candi* as an Italian borrowing in Continental French but the loanword does not receive much attention in the major historical dictionaries. The FEW entry (XIX, 83b **qandi**) gives no other information beyond "sucre cristallisé en morceaux'. The TLFi's comment that "l'intermédiaire de l'ital. [. . .] est à écarter, *zucchero candito* n'étant à ce jour attesté qu'au xv^{e}s" is now out of date as we have evidence of *çucheri candi* from c1275 in Tuscan. The same is true of the comments in the OED2 entry sub **sugar-candy** which only mentions the later *zucchero candito* as a possible Italian source for the borrowing in England.

4.8 Tare

AN *tare* (n.) 'the weight of packaging which is deducted from the gross weight of merchandise'

< It. *tara* < Ar. *tarh* ('deduction') < Ar. *tarhah* ('to throw away')

The Arabic-derived *tara* was an everyday business term in medieval Italy with hundreds of extant citations in the OVI corpus. Pegolotti alone uses it 195 times in his merchant handbook (c1335–43). Generally, it referred to a deduction in the gross weight of merchandise so that wrapping or packaging was taken into

41 It should be pointed out that in Trease's edition, *candi/y* features alongside several medical preparations of Greco-Arabic origin such as *pennidi*, *diadragant* and *syrypis*.

account. It could also refer to deductions (often fixed by the civic authorities) in weight to compensate for imperfections or damage to the goods (OVI / AD / DEI **tara**).

Hope (1971: 51) and the TLFi recognise the likelihood that Italian *tara* acted as an intermediary for the transmission of this Arabism into Continental French in the fourteenth century. The FEW (XIX, 182b **tarh**), however, favours an earlier direct borrowing in the south of France via trade with North Africa. While attestations of the noun *tare* itself are not especially prolific in the Continental French dictionary corpora, we have several derivatives (e.g. the verb *tarer* and the past participle *tarrotté*) which suggest its use was well entrenched in commercial terminology.

In English records, the earliest examples of *tare* feature in both the Anglo-Norman and Middle English-Grocers accounts from c1379 onwards. In this source, as in the others below, there is a strong argument for direct Italian contact, as opposed to an indirect Italian borrowing, via Continental French.[42]

> *Poyvere et altres darrés achaté et vendu par lb pur chescun c sera abaté Gyngibre pur le tare [. . .]* (Grocers 56) (1379–80) (AND2 **garance**)

> *Ceaux sount les tares de dyverces darrés ordeynés et accedés par la compaynie* (Grocers 56) (1379–80) (AND1 **tare**)

> *and deliuered the powder ageyn to the Venicien, withe the Tares the some of vxxj lb. als right was, For lof sugre was worth at that day xv d. and powdre cassouns bot vij d.* (Grocer Lond. Kingdon 190) (1429) (MED **tare2**)

The *Cantelowe Accounts* also offer a valuable second source where *tare* is used in an late medieval English business text with very close Italian links in the first half of the fifteenth century. As with *net* (above), there is only one clear Middle English citation but the author uses the term (frequently abbreviated to *tar-* or just *t-*) over 200 times in the Tuscan-matrix section of his accounts.

> *The whych makyth in sackys CC° lxiiij° semis and v cloves semis, of the whych ys rebatyd for the tare of every poke j clove semis.* (AS Serie 1: 339, 7c) (1450–51)

In addition, the *Views of the Hosts* provide us with twenty-five new examples of *tare* in an Anglo-Norman text, all from the accounts of Thomas Walsingham, host to Venetians merchants in London e.g.:

42 The OED2 (sub **tare2**) simply derives the borrowing 'from French' and the earliest citation from England in the entry dates from 1486 (*Naval accounts and inventories of the reign of Henry VII*).

Item venduz a Marmeduke & Benedict Austyn iiij caas canelle qamont clere en argent <u>*tare*</u> *& tret rebatuz xxv^{li} xvij^{s}* (E101/128/31 ret. 10) (1442–43)

It is interesting that *tare* always appears in this text in a formulaic expression as shown below, with its fellow technical term *tret* and, sometimes, *gabelure* (cf. *garbeler*, above):

- *quamount clere en argent + tare & tret*
- *tare tret & garbelure*
- *tare tret & touz autres chargez + rebatuz +* [amount of money]

The citations of the commercial locution *Tare & Tret* in this mercantile source from the 1440s are certainly worthy of note as they are the only examples of the expression's use in an English medieval text pre-1500 (whether they are actually Anglo-Norman or Middle English lexemes, or both, is somewhat moot). Whilst *tare* was a standard deduction from gross weight for packaging, *tret* was a further but optional allowance of 1 lb in every 26 lbs for "such commodities as are liable to waste, moths, dust etc." (Fenning 1765: 203).[43] In English, *tret* appears in the *Chronicle* of the London trader, Richard Arnold, in 1502 but then not again until 1670. By the Victorian period, *Tare and Tret* had become a byword in English for basic arithmetic:

Your said suppliant shulde be rebated for the tare of euery of the said xij. bales [...] & for the <u>*tret*</u> *of ye same peper (R. Arnold Chron. f. xlvij/2)* (c1503)

We learnt <u>*Tare and Tret*</u> *together, at school* (Dickens Martin Chuzzlewit xix. 24) (1843) (OED2 **tret**)

The obvious etymon for *tret* in English is Anglo-Norman / Continental French *trait(e)*, perhaps an extension of the meaning of 'pull of the scale.'[44] However, it is tempting to ask if Italian, with its tradition of complex price deductions from

43 This is an eighteenth-century apprentice's guide: *The British youth's instructor or A new and easy guide to practical arithmetic.* It is written as a series of dialogues between Philo, the tutor, and Tyro, his pupil. See the chapter entitled *Tare & Tret* (pp. 202–09), for the explanation and practice calculations of the six weight allowances *Gross, Tare, Tret, Suttle, Closs and Neat* (cf. *net*, above).

44 See Weekley (1921: 1538): "AF, F. *trait* (pull) of the scale, from OF *traire*, to pull, L. *trahere*. The allowance compensated for the number of 'turns of the scale' which would result from weighing the goods in similar quantities. *Trait* is still so used in F. and *draft, draught* had a similar sense in ME: '*Un poids en équilibre ne treubuche point, si on n'y ajoute quelque chose pour le trait. Les petits poids ne reviennent pas aux grands à cause du trait*' (Furetière 1727)". Note that the current AND1 entry sub **trait** has no citations of the word being used in a commercial or indeed, weight-related, sense.

the value of bulk goods, was involved in some way in the development of the French technical term, just as it was for *tara*. *Tratta* (as a specific kind of tare or weight allowance) cannot be found as a headword in the major Italian historical dictionaries but Pegolotti does use it several times in this way, giving details of the rates for *tratta* for goods (grain, spices, wool etc.) in various countries. However, the lexeme is simply glossed as 'export duty' by the handbook's editor (Evans 1935: 443) and by Edler (1934: 305) in her *Glossary of Mediaeval Terms of Business.*

This Italian commercial terminology could have been behind the usage of Continental French *traitte / traicte* to mean 'droit perçu aux frontières sur la circulation des merchandise' from the mid-1300s (cf. TLFi **traite**[1] / DMF **traite**). It could also be the direct or indirect source of *tret* which appears in the Anglo-Norman London hosting accounts of the 1440s. Regardless, further investigation into the background of the locution *Tare and Tret* and its specific connotations in English business jargon in the sixteenth to nineteenth centuries seems long overdue.

5 Conclusion

The sugar and spice trade touched every corner of the known medieval world and its associated lexis was, at times, so widespread that it can be impossible to decipher what represents a 'simultaneous borrowing' with a clearly traceable etymon and what represents an 'international word', one that transcends geographical and linguistic borders (cf. Schendl and Wright 2011: 31). The situation is further complicated by the fact that insular French was, of course, a variant of a much larger dialectal group. It can be challenging to identify links between Anglo-Norman and Italian specifically because of the broader context of borrowing between medieval French and Italian. Some Italian borrowings in England were undoubtedly 'indirect', in that they entered Continental French first before appearing in Anglo-Norman.

However, this does not mean that the phenomenon of direct contact between Anglo-Norman and Italian should be dismissed. Indeed, in many cases, there is a strong argument for independent transmission of Italian lexis into English mercantile records, regardless of whether the borrowing is also attested in France. When we analyse lexemes such as the ones above, we find that there is convincing evidence for the existence of direct Italian transmission into insular French one path amongst several that formed a complex network of linguistic exchange.

Rothwell's *Sugar and Spice* hinted that Italian acted as bridge between East and West – the Oriental Bazaar and the English cloister – and this is further confirmed by the case studies analysed above. Italian dialects were instrumental as an intermediary, bringing Arabic lexis into England, either directly into Middle English or first into Anglo-Norman. Furthermore, as both Rothwell and Trotter have stressed on many occasions, non-literary texts and commercial records are of vital importance in understanding England's lexical past, the length and breadth of Anglo-Norman's legacy and its influence on Middle English. Such sources can also offer invaluable insight into the effects of a truly 'foreign' language, such as Italian, on the trilingual bureaucracy of English trade. As Iamartino highlights in his history of Anglo-Italian borrowing, it was the commercial semantic field which dominated prior to 1500, as opposed to that of literature. The later Middle Ages, he stresses, were characterised by a busy flow of trade and navigation which "non possono non favorire lo scambio e l'influsso interlinguistico" (2001: 19). The first cultural relations between Italy and England were forged at this stage and their remnants can still be found in English today. This phenomenon was by no means restricted to an individual commodity like sugar or ginger but encompassed trade it its widest sense.

Abbreviations

Languages

Ar.	Arabic
AN	Anglo-Norman
BML	British Medieval Latin
CF	Continental French
It.	Italian
Lat.	Latin
ME	Middle English
OE	Old English
Pers.	Persian

Bibliography

AD = Archivio Datini: Corpus Lemmatizzato del Carteggio Datini, http://aspweb.ovi.cnr.it.

Adamson, Melitta Weiss. 2004. *Food in Medieval Times* (Westport: Greenwood Press).

AND1 = William Rothwell et al. (eds.), *Anglo-Norman Dictionary*, 1st ed. (London: Modern Humanities Research Association, 1977–92).

AND2 = *Anglo-Norman Dictionary*, online (2nd) ed., http://www.anglo-norman.net.

Boitani, Piero. (ed.), 1983. *Chaucer and the Italian Trecento* (Cambridge: Cambridge University Press).
Bradley, Helen. 1992. *Italian Merchants in London c1350–c1450* (Royal Holloway and Bedford New College, University of London: PhD thesis).
Bradley, Helen. 2012. *The Views of the Hosts of Alien Merchants, 1440–1444* (London: The Boydell Press).
Cholmeley, H. P. 1912. *John of Gaddeston and the Rosa Medicinae* (Oxford: The Claredon Press).
DEAF = Kurt Baldinger et al. (eds.), *Dictionnaire Étymologique de l'Ancien Français* (Laval, Quebec: Presses de l'Université de Laval, 1971–), http://www.deaf-page.de.
DEI = Carlo Battisti and Giovanni Alessio, *Dizionario Etimologico Italiano* (Florence: Barbèra, 1950–57).
DMLBS = Ronald Edward Latham, David Howlett et al. (eds.), *Dictionary of Medieval Latin from British Sources* (Oxford: Oxford University Press, 1975–2013).
Dietz, Klaus. 2005. 'Die frühen italienischen Lehnwörter des Englischen', *Anglia*, 123: 573–631.
Durkin, Philip. 2014. *Borrowed Words: A History of Loanwords in English* (Oxford: Oxford University Press).
Edler, Florence. 1934. *Glossary of Mediaeval Terms of Business. Italian Series 1200–1600* (Cambridge: The Mediaeval Academy of America).
Evans, Allan. 1935. *La Practica della Mercatura* (Cambridge: Medieval Academy of America).
Fenning, Daniel. 1765. *The British youth's instructor or a new and easy guide to practical arithmetic*, 5th edn. (London: S. Crowder / M. Richardson / B. Collins).
Fennis, Jan. 1995. *Trésor du langage des galères: dictionnaire exhaustif, avec une introduction, des dessins originaux de René Burlet et des planches de Jean-Antoine de Barras de la Penne, un relevé onomasiologique et une bibliographie* (Tübingen: Niemeyer).
FEW = Walther von Wartburg et al. (eds.), *Französisches Etymologisches Wörterbuch: Eine Darstellung des Galloromanischen Sprachschatzes* (Basel: Zbinden, 1922–).
Fiorentino, Remigio. 1574. *Le due deche dell'historia di Sicila* http://www.liberliber.it/mediateca/libri/f/fazello/le_due_deche_dell_historia_di_sicilia/pdf/fazello_le_due_deche_dell_historia_di_sicilia.pdf (accessed 05/08/2018).
Foster, Brian. 1963. *The local port book of Southampton for 1435–36* (Southampton: The University Press).
GDC = *Godefroy Complément*, vols. 8–10 of Frédéric Godefroy (ed.), *Dictionnaire de l'Ancienne Langue Française et de Tous Ses Dialectes du IXe au XVe Siècle* (Paris: Vieweg, 1881–1902).
Hornby, Albert Sydney and Margaret Deuter. 2015. *Oxford Advanced Learner's Dictionary* (9th edition) (Oxford: Oxford University Press).
Ingham, Richard. 2011. 'Code-switching in the later medieval English lay subsidy rolls', in *Codeswitching in Early English*, ed. by Herbert Schendl and Laura Wright (Berlin: De Gruyter), pp. 95–114.
Ingham, Richard. 2013. 'Language-mixing in medieval Latin documents: vernacular articles and nouns' in *Multilingualism in Medieval Britain (c.1066–1520): Sources and Analysis*, ed. by Judith A. Jefferson and Ad Putter (Turnhout: Brepols), pp. 105–21.
Hines, John and Robert Yeager. 2010. *John Gower, Trilingual Poet: Language, Translation and Tradition* (Cambridge: Boydell and Brewer).
Hope, Thomas Edward. 1971. *Lexical borrowing in the Romance languages: a critical study of Italianisms in French and Gallicisms in Italian from 1100–1900* (Oxford: Blackwell).
Hunt, Tony. 1990. *Popular Medicine in Thirteenth-Century England* (Cambridge: D.S. Brewer).

Iamartino, Giovanni. 2001. 'La contrastività italiano-inglese in prospettiva storica', *Rassegna Italiana di Linguistica Applicata*, 33, 2–3: 7–130.
Johnston, Ruth A. 2011. *All Things Medieval: An Encyclopaedia of the Medieval World* (Santa Barbara: ABC-CLIO).
Lawrence, Jason. 2005. *Who the devil taught thee so much Italian? Italian language learning and literary imitation in early modern England* (Manchester: Manchester University Press).
Lerer, Seth. 2006. *The Yale Companion to Chaucer* (New Haven: Yale University Press).
MED = *Middle English Dictionary*, online ed. (Ann Arbor, MI: University of Michigan Press, 1952–2002), http://quod.lib.umich.edu/m/med.
Melis, Federigo. 1976. *Mercaderes italianos en Espana (Siglos xiv-xvi)* (Sevilla: Universidad de Sevilla).
Mortimer, Nigel. 2005. *John Lydgate's Fall of Princes: Narrative Tragedy in its Literary and Political Context* (Oxford: Oxford University Press).
Nightingale, Pamela. 1995. *A medieval mercantile community: the Grocers' Company & the politics & trade of London, 1000–1485* (New Haven: Yale University Press).
O'Connor, Desmond. 1972. 'John Florio's Contribution to Italian-English Lexicography', in *Italica*, 49: 49–67.
OED2 = *Oxford English Dictionary*, 2nd ed. (Oxford: Clarendon Press, 1989).
OED3 = *Oxford English Dictionary*, 3rd (online) ed. (New York: Oxford University Press, 2000) http://www.oed.com.
OVI = Opera del Vocabolario Italiano: Corpus OVI dell'Italiano Antico (Rome: Consiglio Nazionale delle Ricerche, 1998–), http://gattoweb.ovi.cnr.it.
Pinnavaia, Laura. 2001. *The Italian borrowings in the Oxford English Dictionary: a lexicographical, linguistic and cultural analysis* (Roma: Bulzoni).
Praz, Mario. 1944. *Richerche anglo-italiane* (Roma: Edizioni di Storia e Letteratura).
Prioreschi, Plinio. 2003. *A History of Medicine. Vol. 5: Medieval Medicine* (Omaha: Horatius Press).
Richardson, Tim. 2004. *Sweets: The History of Temptation* (London: Random House).
Rothwell, William. 1991. 'The missing link in English etymology: Anglo-French', *Medium Aevum*, 60: 173–96.
Rothwell, William. 1992. 'The French Vocabulary in the Archive of the London Grocers' Company', *Zeitschrift für französische Sprache und Literatur*, 102: 23–41.
Rothwell, William. 1993. 'The Legacy of Anglo-French: *faux amis* in French and English', *Zeitschrift für romanische Philologie*, 109: 16–46.
Rothwell, William. 1999. 'Sugar and Spice and All Things Nice: From Oriental Bazar to English Cloister in Anglo-French', *The Modern Language Review*, 94: 647–59.
Rothwell, William. 2000. 'Glanures lexicologiques dans les documents des 14e et 15e siècles provenant de l'évêché de Durham', *Zeitschrift für romanische Philologie*, 116: 213–36.
Ruddock, Alwyn. 1951. *Italian merchants and shipping in Southampton, 1270–1600* (Southampton: University College).
Schendl, Herbert and Laura Wright (eds.), 2011. *Code-Switching in Early English* (Berlin: De Gruyter).
Schmitt, Christian. 2003. 'Externe Sprachgeschichte des Französischen', in *Romanische Sprachgeschichte/ Histoire linguistique de la Romania: 1. Teilband / Tome 1*, ed. by Gerhard Ernst, Martin-Dietrich Gleßgen, Christian Schmitt and Wolfgang Schweickard (Berlin: De Gruyter) pp. 801–29.

Schweickard, Wolfgang. 2008. 'Storia interna dell'italino: lessico e formazione delle parole', in *Romanische Sprachgeschichte/ Histoire linguistique de la Romania: 3. Teilband / Tome 3*, ed. by Gerhard Ernst, Martin-Dietrich Gleβgen, Christian Schmitt and Wolfgang Schweickard (Berlin: De Gruyter) pp. 2847–72.
Smith, Sydney, Francis Jeffrey and Macavey Napier. 1830. 'Sugar Trade: Duties on Sugar', *The Edinburgh Review Or Critical Journal*, 50: 426–36.
Strohm, Paul. 2015. *The Poet's Tale: Chaucer and the year that made The Canterbury Tales* (London: Profile Books Ltd).
Studer, Paul. 1913. *The Port Books of Southampton or (Anglo-French) accounts of Robert Florys, Water-Bailiff and Receiver of Petty-Customs, A.D. 1427–1430* (Southampton: Southampton Record Society).
Sylvester, Louise. 2016. 'Technical Vocabulary and Medieval Text Types: A Semantic Field Approach', *Neuphilologische Mitteilungen*, 117: 155–76.
Sylvester, Louise. 2018. 'A Semantic Field and Text-Type Approach to Late-Medieval Multilingualism', in *Multilingual Practices in Language History: English and Beyond*, ed. by Päivi Pahta, Janne Skaffari & Laura Wright (Berlin: de Gruyter Mouton), pp. 77–96.
Tiddeman, Megan. 2012. 'Mercantile multilingualism: two examples of Anglo-Norman and Italian contact in the fourteenth century', in *Present and future research in Anglo-Norman: Aberystwyth Colloquium, July 2011*, ed. by David Trotter (The Anglo-Norman Online Hub), pp. 91–99.
Tiddeman, Megan. 2017. 'Early Anglo-Italian contact: new loanword evidence from two mercantile sources, 1440–1451' in *Merchants of Innovation: The Languages of Traders*, ed. by Esther-Miriam Wagner, Bettina Beinhoff and Ben Outhwaite (Berlin: De Gruyter Mouton), pp. 217–34.
Tiddeman, Megan. 2018. 'Lexical exchange with Italian in the textile and wool trades in the thirteenth to fifteenth centuries', *Medieval Clothing and Textiles*, 14: 113–40.
TLFi = Paul Imbs et al., eds., *Le Trésor de la Langue Française* (Paris: Éditions du Centre National de la Recherche Scientifique, 1971–89), http://atilf.atilf.fr/tlf.htm
Trease, George Edward. 1959. 'The Spicers and Apothecaries of the Royal Household in the Reigns of Henry III, Edward I and Edward II', *Nottingham Mediaeval Studies*, 3: 19–52.
Trease, George Edward. 1964. *Pharmacy in History* (London: Tindall and Cox).
Trotter, David. 2003. '*Oceano vox*: You never know where a ship comes from. On multilingualism and language-mixing in medieval Britain', in *Aspects of multilingualism in European language history*, ed. by Kurt Braunmüller and Gisella Ferraresi (Amsterdam: John Benjamins Publishing), pp. 15–33.
Trotter, David. 2006. 'Contacts linguistiques intraromans: roman et français / occitan', in *Histoire linguistique de la Romania. Manuel international d'histoire linguistique de la Romania*, Tome 2, ed. by Gerhard Ernst, Martin-Dietrich Gleßgen, Christian Schmitt and Wolfgang Schweickard (Berlin: De Gruyter), pp. 1776–85.
Trotter, David. 2010. 'Bridging the Gap: The (Socio)linguistic Evidence of Some Medieval English Bridge Accounts', in *The Anglo-Norman Language and its Contexts*, ed. by Richard Ingham (Woodbridge: York Medieval Press), pp. 52–62.
Trotter, David. 2011a. 'Death, taxes and property: some code-switching evidence from Dover, Southampton and York', in *Code-Switching in Early English*, ed. by Herbert Schendl and Laura Wright (Berlin: De Gruyter), pp. 155–89.
Trotter, David. 2011b. 'Italian merchants in London and Paris: evidence of language contact in the Gallerani accounts, 1305–08', in *Le changement linguistique en français: études en*

homage au professeur R. Anthony Lodge, ed. by Dominique Lagorgette and Tim Pooley (Chambéry: Presses de l'Université de Savoie), pp. 209–26.
Tucci, Ugo. 1957. *Lettres d'un marchand vénitien, Andrea Berengo (1553–1556)* (Paris: SEVPEN).
Tuchman, Barbara W. 1978. *A Distant Mirror: The Calamitous 14th Century* (New York: Ballantine Books).
Weekley, Ernest. 1921. *An Etymological Dictionary of Modern English* (New York: Dover Publications).
Wright, Laura. 2002. 'Code intermediate phenomena in medieval mixed-language texts', *Language Sciences*, 24: 471–89.
Wright, Laura. 2010. 'A pilot study on the singular definite articles *le* and *la* in fifteenth-century London mixed-language business writing', in *The Anglo-Norman Language and its Contexts*, ed. by Richard Ingham (Woodbridge: York Medieval Press), pp. 130–42.
Wright, Laura. 2013. 'The Contact Origins of Standard English', in *English as a Contact Language*. ed. by Daniel Schreier and Marianne Hundt (Cambridge: Cambridge University Press), pp. 58–74.
Vidos, Benedek Elemér. 1939. *Storia delle parole marinaresche italiane passate in francese: contributo storico-linguistico all'espansione della lingua nautica italiana* (Firenze: Leo S. Olschki).
Vidos, Benedek Elemér. 1965. *Prestito, espansione e migrazione dei termini tecnici nelle lingue romanze e non romanze: problemi, metodo e risultati* (Firenze: Leo S. Olschki).
Yule, Henry. 1875. *The Book of Ser Marco Polo, the Venetian: Concerning the Kingdoms and Marvels of the East*, Volume 2 (John Murray: London).

Richard Ashdowne

14 *-mannus* makyth *man(n)*? Latin as an indirect source for English lexical history

1 Introduction

No account of the emergence of a standard language can be complete without a discussion of vocabulary, and processes of lexical expansion (through derivation and borrowing) and selection (through promotion and stigmatisation, sometimes as a result of codification) are likely to feature in such a discussion. Establishing how Standard English developed its vocabulary is a daunting task, and one of many reasons for this is the difficult nature of the evidence: to assess the development of the lexicon, whether the development of new items and usages or the loss of old ones, it is necessary to be able to gauge what was a part of the lexicon at any given time. However, for much of the medieval period this task is complicated by a multilingual situation in which useful evidence for English appears not only in the monolingual English sources usually examined but also in sources in the other written languages of Britain (principally Latin, Anglo-Norman French, and the evolving mixed language derived from all three).

In recent years awareness has therefore grown that investigating the early lexical history of English must not be confined to consideration of the English sources alone. Of course the obvious fact that English borrowed vocabulary extensively from the languages that it came into contact with during the middle ages, most notably French and Latin, has for a long time led research to focus on this direction of transfer, not least in view of the prestige these languages are considered to have had.[1] Until recently, however, historians of English other than lexicographers have shown relatively little interest in transfers in the opposite direction, i.e. from English into the other languages of medieval Britain. Although such transfers are self-evidently of interest to the historians of those

1 See, for instance, Kastovsky (2006). More recently Lutz (2013) considers the role of prestige in contact between English and its donor languages, discussing the relationship with Latin at length, but not the possibility of two-way influence in respect of Latin and its consequent potential to shed light on the relative prestige of the languages in contact.

Richard Ashdowne, University College, Oxford

https://doi.org/10.1515/9783110687545-015

target languages, they should also not be neglected when investigating the lexical history of the source language English, because they may, indeed they often do, offer valuable indirect evidence of English to complement what can be found directly in English sources.

That additional attestations of lexical items or their meanings, and especially earlier ones, can be found as borrowings in other languages has been highlighted in, for instance, the work of Tony Hunt and David Trotter with reference to the multilingual context of medieval Britain and a focus on Anglo-Norman French in particular (e.g. Hunt 2003, Trotter 1996, 2017), following on from earlier work by William Rothwell (e.g. 1991, 1993, 1996, 2002).[2] For English it is noted by Durkin & Schad (2017: 334–5), who alongside their focus on borrowings into English from Latin discuss several examples of Latin words as evidence for earlier currency of English vocabulary. The theoretical basis for this is straightforward, that at the point of borrowing the target language receives a current usage (form and meaning) of the item in the source language, and so (subsequent) evidence in the target language implies earlier currency in the source language (albeit allowing for change within the target). The study presented here follows up their discussion and that of Wright (2013) by looking more closely at some possible Medieval Latin evidence for English, including some instances where Latin provides what appears to be, at present, the sole evidence for an English usage.

The material to be considered is the set of Medieval Latin lexical items that end in *-mannus* as documented in the *Dictionary of Medieval Latin from British Sources* (*DMLBS*).[3] These have been chosen as presenting in *-mannus* an unmistakeably English element (OE *mann*, ME *man*) which suggests that these items have their origins at least in part, if not wholly, in English, i.e. as borrowings. For instance, beside *DMLBS acremannus* there are *DOE æcermann*, *MED aker-man*, *OED acreman*. Although direct coinage within Latin and influence or interference from other local vernaculars (e.g. French or Welsh) cannot be discounted in principle for these terms, it is highly likely that in practice the majority of *-mannus*

2 See also Richter (2013), looking at a range of interacting languages that may lie behind behind Latin phrasing in a set of early 14th-cent. documents.

3 For the sake of clarity, lexical items are referred to throughout by the relevant dictionary citation forms unless otherwise indicated with quotation marks (e.g. because the form of a particular example is at issue), without prejudice to the fact that citations forms are editorially constructed labels of convenience and their spelling or form may not itself be attested. Stems in *DMLBS* citation forms are chosen to reflect supposed etymology, and in the case of material taken over from other languages this typically means relevant citation forms in the source language; the citation inflection of nouns is the nominative singular. The difficulties associated with language labels such as 'Latin' are discussed below.

items reflect straight (i.e. both form and meaning) borrowings into Latin of lexical usage in English as found by the Latin writers.[4]

Items of the *-mannus* type offer a further feature that may be helpful for the present study: the corresponding English items may be expected to be compounds or at least established collocations. In respect of form, the processes by which such items are formed in English are different from Latin in the period, making it less likely that the Latin *-mannus* items to be considered, which all seem to conform to English word-formation patterns, were formed solely within Latin from morphemes of English origin without any reference to fully formed English usages.[5] Moreover in respect of function, the observation that such items appear to be borrowed into Latin as recognisable semantic units suggests that these items correspond to English locutions that were themselves established and likely lexicalised, rather than simply compositional syntactic phrases containing *man(n)*.[6]

There are 64 relevant items ending in *-mannus* in *DMLBS*. For comparison, the English dictionaries together recognise at least 300 lexical items ending in *-man(n)* for the period before 1500, whether as compound or phrase: by no means all of these English items, therefore, have Latin correlates, but for this investigation it is valuable that many but not all of the *DMLBS* items appear,

4 Although many of the English bases from which *-man(n)* items with Latin *-mannus* parallels are formed also appear in Latin (e.g. *scira* 'shire' (*ASD scir*) alongside *scirmannus* (*ASD scirmann*)), *DMLBS* finds no evidence for a free form **mannus* or **manus* corresponding to *ASD mann* or *MED man*; in fact, the translation equivalence with Latin *homo* ('human being') was sufficiently strong for it to appear in the calque *landhomo* (alongside *landesmannus*) representing *land(es)mann*, albeit known from a single example and perhaps a nonce-formation. See also n. 6 below.

5 *DMLBS* gives brief etymological notes for most entries, which are primarily intended to clarify supposed word-structure and/or connections with other entries or vernacular forms in line with the chosen citation form; the presentation is problematic in the entries for many items for which the Latin evidence antedates the supposed English etymon. For *malamannus*, for instance, despite the etymology [cf. 2 *mala+mannus*, ME *molman*] seeming to suggest a process of compounding within Latin, the attested spellings in the quotations show that this is not really a Latin compound including *mala* but an English one consisting of two elements that, as it happens, correspond to attested Latin borrowings; using a comma in place of the '+' might have been clearer in conveying this. The present study is informed by the etymological material in the dictionaries consulted but not dependent on it.

6 In general these expectations are borne out uncontroversially for most items in the material considered but a small number do raise the question of whether *-mannus* was a productive suffix in Latin in medieval Britain and conceivably even a possible source for English borrowing rather than result of borrowing from English. In addition to discussion of individual items in section 3, this is discussed further in section 4.

like *acremannus*, to have attested English correlates because we thereby see the possibilities offered by this kind of evidence.[7]

From the number of terms it is clear that *-man(n)* was highly productive in English. The terms refer to people and they indicate distinctions and descriptions of sufficient relevance in society not only to be marked linguistically but also to reach the written record. Although the social significance of *-man(n)* and *-mannus* terms is not the focus of this study, the lexical field as a whole forms part of a developing terminology of social relations in English and holds much further interest once its make-up is established, for instance, by contributing to our understanding of the use of English within the multilingual medieval administrative system.

Excluded from consideration here are the 11 other *DMLBS* items ending in *-mannus* in which the second-element does not seem to represent English *-man*(*n*) in etymology: *Alamannus, Bragmannus* 1, *Bragmannus* 2, *Cenomannus, druchemannus, greetmannus, mannus* (inherited Latin = 'kind of horse'), *Musulmannus, Ostmannus* (but see 3.2 below), *ragemannus, Turcomannus.* Although some of these, or their English correlates, seem later to have been treated as containing English *-man* through folk etymology, they are excluded here because it would not be possible to draw reliable inferences about the direction of borrowing of these items into or from Latin, English, and their true etymological source. In addition to the *-mannus* items in *DMLBS* there is one relevant item in *-manus*, namely *yomanus* (cf. *MED yeman*), which is included for completeness.[8]

Following a discussion of the caution needed for the approach adopted here (2), the analysis (3) will proceed by taking the items in four descriptive groups, namely those where the Latin sources provide further exemplification and confirmation of dates and usages known from English sources (3.1 'Type A'), those where the Latin sources add to what is known from English sources of dates (3.2 'Type B') and usages (3.3 'Type C'), and those where Latin sources seem to provide the only evidence (3.4 'Type D'). Reasons of space preclude discussing every one of the 64 *-mannus* terms in detail, but selected examples illustrate the possibilities within each of the main groups. The final section (4) discusses the overall conclusions that can be drawn from the examination of the data.

---

7 *DMLBS* covers the use of Latin in British sources from the sixth century down to 1600, and although its coverage of the sixteenth century reflects the diminishing use of the language in that century, there is only one relevant item attested exclusively post-1500 (*yomanus*, 'yeoman').

8 The 16th-cent. date of its single Latin quotation puts it clearly in type A.

2 Methodological cautions

Working from indirect evidence inevitably leads to potential pitfalls, some of which go beyond those which should be familiar from considering direct evidence for lexical history. The issues do not fundamentally undermine the evidence presented here but they have a bearing on the kinds of method and conclusion available.

The foundation for this investigation is the assessment of the vocabulary of Latin and English presented respectively by the *DMLBS* on the one hand and a number of dictionaries of English on the other (*DOE*, *ASD*, *MED* and *OED*); *AND* has also been consulted where relevant. Dictionaries are much underestimated repositories of information and ideal for the purposes of this study: based on surveys of attested usage they all attempt to document the vocabulary of their language in their period, both lexical items and those items' range of meanings and use, including information about dates for each usage. However, the first caution is to note that, like all dictionaries, the ones used here all differ in their coverage and completeness, methodologies, and recentness. *DMLBS* is recently completed (2013; reissued with minor amendments 2018) but work began almost fifty years earlier (fascicule I between 1965 and 1975); *DOE* is in progress and available only for A to H; though complete in alphabetical coverage, much of *OED* remains as yet untouched by the on-going revision programme and so in a form published many decades ago, while the revised parts present a more current view. Because technology makes broader searching of large corpora of material now much more practical, more recent dictionaries are far more able to take account of published material than earlier ones, to say nothing of the increasing amount of material now available in published form that was largely inaccessible to earlier ones. For this reason, for instance, in the present work *DOE* is preferred to *ASD* where it is available.

Even if very current, however, no dictionary of a language before the present day should be thought of as a full record of the vocabulary of that language in the chosen period; at best it documents that language's usage as it survives in writing. Furthermore it is rare that a dictionary's underlying survey can be said to be fully comprehensive even of all the surviving written material. Further relevant evidence certainly exists outside that which is highlighted by the dictionaries used here.[9] For the present study this means that any findings

9 For instance, Wright (1996: 176–89) notes from Latin matrix contexts eight further items, of which *garthman*, *shoutman* and *tideman* have examples with explicit unambiguously Latin inflectional suffixes. The explicitly Latin forms do not antedate the English evidence for

must be tentative rather than categorical: absence of examples of a usage from a dictionary suggests it was not known to its compilers but not that it does not survive (or, indeed, never existed). Still, the thorough nature of the work of preparing these dictionaries makes it probable that vagaries of attestation have had a far greater effect on whether a usage is known of, and at what date, than whether dictionary surveys have overlooked a source that has survived and can provide an earlier or sole attestation of an item or usage.

To some degree all the dictionaries employed here acknowledge the 'parallel' evidence of the 'other' language(s), especially where it supplements or confirms direct evidence, to the point even of quoting Latin examples in the English dictionaries or English ones in the *DMLBS*. Accordingly, in many instances the exact same example appears in more than one dictionary, often marked as a parallel (e.g. *OED* often puts such quotations in square brackets or puts them within etymologies). To give one example, the same 1458 Latin quotation appears in both *DMLBS grithmannus* and *OED grith-man* (cpd. at *grith* n). Such overlaps doubtless reflect in part the compilers prudently consulting the other dictionaries and their surveys to supplement their own surveys and partly the difficulty, discussed below, of identifying what language ambiguous examples belong to. (Even their own surveys regularly offer examples apparently more suitable for inclusion as a direct evidence in a dictionary of the other language.) Moreover, senses or even whole entries that are supported overwhelmingly, sometimes exclusively, by parallel evidence are to be found in all of the dictionaries drawn on here.

It is also clear that the compilers take considerable account of the other dictionaries when identifying lexical items within their own material and suggesting senses for them: for instance, many *DMLBS* entries for items of English origin take account of the meaning(s) identified for the corresponding items in the relevant English dictionaries when attempting to identify sense(s) for the Latin quotations at hand. Since the present study is based on bringing together material for items across dictionaries, it is worth emphasising from the start that the aim is not to set the dictionaries in competition against each other so as to find and criticise their overlaps or gaps. It is, however, equally important to realise at the same time that any differences of sense and even of quotation between dictionaries can be expected to be limited as a result of their interdependence.

With all these cautions in mind it is clear that the results of examining the *-mannus* data will above all be qualitative, based on assessing each item, rather than quantitative statistical patterns which would at best be of dubious

---

garthman and *shoutman* (i.e. type A below), while for *tideman* the Latin provides an antedating (type B below).

significance, e.g. percentages of 'English' items first attested in vernacular or Latin in different periods or lexical fields, etc. The quotations chosen by editors for these dictionaries cannot be treated as amounting to coherent representative corpora (save of the policies and predilections of those editors) but they do provide qualitative evidence of usages that demonstrably existed at certain times, and they do so based on surveys and expertise which may be considered a reliable foundation. The method is, by means of comparison, to bring them together to see what fuller picture emerges and what further usages are implied to have existed.

There are four more general areas for caution to outline ahead of later fuller discussion in relation to the particular data. The first is that inevitably any philological study is hampered by the haphazard nature of the surviving evidence, however extensive it may be. Whether a lexical usage of the spoken language was ever also used in writing (or vice versa) and whether such a written use survives is to no small degree a matter of chance. The situation is complicated by the position of Latin in medieval Britain in general, when medium and function were major factors in the choice of language.[10] Moreover, it is very unlikely that the earliest attestations that do survive are the actual first occasions of those usages, or even the first in writing. This is a familiar problem, but attention is drawn to it because evidence of the kind discussed here can go some way to extending our knowledge, especially in view of the differential use of different languages for different functions and in different media, such as a Latin written record of business conducted orally in English.

The second point is that any way in which one language user can innovate is a way in which another could do likewise. Lexical items, especially borrowings, can have multiple histories, i.e. items can be independently coined or borrowed by different users on separate occasions (and similarly for the development of new senses). It is therefore not necessary to see all the examples (whether English, Latin or indeterminate) as deriving from one another chronologically back to a single first instance of innovation (i.e. borrowing): even examples of the 'same' usage may belong to separate histories, and it may not always be possible to join the dots of different data into a single picture with a single etymological line.[11]

The third is that, again especially for borrowed vocabulary, determining the linguistic affiliation of a lexical item, or even a whole text, is not straightforward and may sometimes not be possible. This difficulty is reflected in the way that our

---

10 On the position of Latin in medieval Britain and many of the other areas of caution discussed in this section see Ashdowne & White (2017b).

11 See, e.g., *anlepimannus* in 3.2 below and *foresposmannus* in 3.4 below.

dictionaries overlap in quotation, discussed above. Items may remain unintegrated within a Latin matrix (i.e. lack Latin inflections but be surrounded by unambiguously Latin words), be fully integrated (i.e. have explicit distinctively Latin inflections) or occupy some intermediate position (e.g. have abbreviation marks consistent with Latin inflection, leaving the spelled out form consistent with the source language); some items may seem not even to be borrowed but merely mentioned (e.g., '*ad omnes homines* <u>*vocatos grithmen*</u>', 'to all men <u>called grithmen</u>', quoted in both *OED* (*grith-man* cpd. at *grith* n.) and *MED* (*grith* 4b)). (This study is concerned only with so-called integral borrowing, i.e form and meaning borrowed together, and does not cover other interlingual phenomena such as calques, which would complicate the picture further.) Even if we leave aside the development in medieval Britain of a mixed business language with trilingual origins (English, French and Latin), borrowing can be considered a gradual process (or, in synchronic terms, a matter of degree) and there is ambiguity in certain inflections and abbreviations.[12] However, the aim of the present study allows us to treat the evidence all together, i.e. without need for the process of deciding a borderline between languages that dictionaries, in being of particular languages, must apply in deciding what to include.[13] This is of course not to say that assessing the extent to which a specific instance is Latin and/or English and/or Anglo-Norman French etc. is not worthwhile – far from it – but for present purposes it is not necessary, provided that in any given instance there are no grounds to suspect that the direction of transfer is other than English as source and Latin as target. (In presenting the evidence of this study, labels such as 'Latin', 'English', etc., though clearly a simplification, are nonetheless helpful at points in articulating the argument; their use takes account of matrix context and/or form as relevant, and they should typically be understood as indicating relative positions on a spectrum of linguistic affiliation rather than categorical judgements.)

Finally, after deciding what their overall evidence base is, dictionaries also have to decide how many and what lexical items to recognise from that evidence and to which lexical item to ascribe any individual example. Even if readings of

---

12 On mixed-language writing see, e.g., Wright (1996, 2017, both with references), arguing that the exploitation of such ambiguities lay at the heart of the development of the mixed language.

13 *DMLBS* errs on the side of inclusiveness, tending to recognise any instance where the word could be taken to have a Latin inflection (i.e. written in full or abbreviation), although its compilers were highly dependent on the faithfulness of printed editions to their sources, many of which did not make representing the exact original a priority, e.g. expanding abbreviations silently or supplying inflections to items which lacked any sign of abbreviation in manuscript. For similar reasons of clarity for users, even *DMLBS* itself adopts this kind of practice, as its introduction sets out. See also the discussion of *hidemannus* in 3.1 below, *anlepimannus* in 3.2 below, Durkin & Schad (2017: 335–9, esp. 336), Wright (2013), and Trotter (1996).

sources are certain, these decisions are also not straightforward in view of highly variable spelling; they are made harder still by difficulties in interpreting manuscript sources or doubtful transcripts in editions, and the like. For the most part it will be sensible, as here, to accept the judgements of the dictionaries on these matters, but especially where the available evidence is inconsistent, patchy or uncertain, an open mind should be kept to possible alternative interpretations: in the case, for instance, of *DMLBS hyredmannus* one article treats together the apparent correlates of two or perhaps three *DOE* items (cf. also *MED hired-man* and *hire-man*), and so too *lodmannus* and *lodesmannus* are treated together by *DMLBS* (cf. *MED lod-man* and *lodes-man*).[14] Dictionary compilers also generally need to choose appropriate citation forms, but for present purposes no significance is attached to them since they are typically normalised editorial labels and need not in fact be attested spellings (e.g. the stem *malamann-* does not appear in any quotation in *DMLBS malamannus*).

3 Analysis

For the sake of convenience in describing what can be observed, and especially what can be known from what sources, the *-mannus* items are divided into types based in part on whether the earliest evidence is 'Latin' or 'English', but overall these groups are not otherwise significant: so far as I can tell, it is a matter of chance attestation whether Latin borrowings of English *-man(n)* items survive, whether their English sources survive, and in what senses at what dates. For this material, at least, it is not possible to say why these and not the very many other known English *-man(n)* items show up in surviving Latin and do so when they do.

3.1 Type A: Latin provides confirmation but no earlier attestation or different meaning from the English

Thirty of the *DMLBS -mannus* items do not reveal anything substantially different in respect of date and meaning from what can be known of English from sources

14 Despite this *lodmannus* and *lodesmannus* are treated separately here in view of the evidence of separate English correlates and the clear alternative forms in Latin with and without the linking *-es-*. *hyredmannus* is not disentangled here because the *DMLBS* evidence is too scant to associate separately with the English correlates. Since all the English correlates can antedate the Latin for both sets, both are of the least revealing type A below.

in English. These items' first Latin attestations are spread across the centuries after the Conquest (grouped by century, alphabetically within each group):

11th cent.	*lagemannus, Northmannus, steormannus*
12th cent.	*burhmannus, castelmannus, ehtemannus, frithmannus, hyred-mannus, landesmannus, portmannus, sceidmannus, scirmannus, unfrithmannus*
13th cent.	*acremannus, bondemannus, landlesmannus, lodmannus, tething-mannus, toftmannus*
14th cent.	*bargemannus, bordmannus, gracemannus, hidemannus,* (*lodesman-nus*), *takmannus, werkmannus*
15th cent.	*belmannus, grithmannus, maltmannus, shermannus*
16th cent.	*yomanus*

A typical member of this group is ***acremannus*** ('class of smallholder') first cited in *DMLBS* from 1222 (Domesday of St Paul's) '*terre akermannorum*', but in both *DOE* ('peasant, ploughman') and *OED* ('cultivator of the ground, farmer; ploughman; manorial tenant') first cited from Ælfric's glossary, '*Agricola, æcermann*', more than 200 years earlier. (*OED* in fact also quotes as a parallel in its etymology an earlier Latin example from the mid-12th cent. overlooked by *DMLBS*.) Similarly *DMLBS* ***maltmannus*** ('maker or seller of malt') cited in two quotations from 1483 and 1484 postdates *MED malt-man* (at *malt* 2a) from 1294, '*Maultman*' (also quoted by *OED* directly from *MED*). The later Latin evidence here serves to confirm but not extend knowledge of these lexical items' early history and usage in English. Latin examples that postdate the earlier English instances may suggest continued currency of an English term in a particular meaning; however, they may also simply reflect continued currency of the term within Latin usage in the period after the borrowing and so provide at most a latest date for that borrowing.

For both *acremannus* and *maltmannus* there are significant differences in date between the earliest English and Latin evidence, but for some of this group the gaps are shorter, e.g. *DMLBS* ***belmannus*** (1405 'bell-ringer') alongside *MED bel(le-man* (1317 in personal name[15]; 1389 one 'who goes about ringing a bell and making announcements'), *DMLBS* ***bargemannus*** (1362) alongside *MED barge-man* (*c.*1332 perhaps in personal name), and *DMLBS* ***steormannus*** (*c.*1076 'one who steers a ship') alongside *ASD steormann* (*c.*1000; cf. also *steoresmann c.*1000).

15 On 'personal names', see the discussion of *hidemannus* below.

Although most of the 30 items listed above are straightforward, *DMLBS* ***bordmannus*** ('class of tenant' of the lowest rank, bordar) and *OED bordman* offer a case study in how the evidence may be distributed unexpectedly among the dictionaries, with the earliest Latin evidence apparently in the English dictionary and the only English evidence in the Latin one: (unrevised) *OED* has no English quotations but two Latin quotations from 17th-cent. glossaries apparently quoting Domesday, *MED* appears not to include an entry at all, and *DMLBS* has two quotations, one of uncertain date (effectively 1086×1331) and one of 1286 in which the item appears to be English within a Latin matrix. The *OED*'s two glossary/'Domesday' quotations are problematic in that Domesday in fact has only the abbreviation '*bor*'' and the expansions to '*bordmanni*' and '*bordimanni*' are editorial either in the later glossaries or some intermediate source; elsewhere the expansion of this abbreviation is taken to be *bordarius*, and these *OED* quotations therefore cannot be taken as antedating *DMLBS*'s Latin evidence of *bordmannus*. However, the *DMLBS* quotations are no less deserving of scrutiny. The 1286 quotation, from a Coram Rege roll (MS TNA PRO KB 27/98 r. 19), contains the word in the phrase '*qui appellantur bordmen*' ('who are called *bordmen*'). The manuscript is quite clear at this point in having '*bordmen*' in full with no mark of abbreviation, and the 'naming' formulation with *appellantur* is not uncommon in introducing a non-Latin term: it is therefore reasonable to take this as direct evidence of the term's existence in English, albeit quoted within a Latin matrix. Whether this 1286 English antedates or postdates the remaining possible Latin evidence, then, depends on the dating of the other quotation, from the Memoriale of Henry of Eastry (prior of Christ Church, Canterbury, ob. 1331). Here, as in the 17th-cent. glossaries, '*bordmannus*' and '*bormanni*' seem to be an expansion of Domesday '*bor*'' and the expansion must have occurred at some point between 1086 and the compilation of the Memoriale. Since Latin *bordarius*, *MED border(e)* and *AND bordier* were all in circulation during this period, *-mannus* forms would be an odd interpretation of the Domesday abbreviation unless *bordman* was in use in English at the time: this Latin seems to confirm the existence of the English item before 1330.

Steormannus offers further points of interest. First, none of the *DMLBS* quotations for *steormannus* shows any trace of the *-es-* of the English *steoresmann*, though both *steormann* and *steoresmann* seem to have been current in English: Latin evidence can potentially be taken into account for assessing their relationship to each other (cf. also *lodmannus*, *lodesmannus*).[16] Second, while Latin in

16 See also the etymological note on (-)*man* as an element in compounds at *OED man* n[1] 15, which in addition argues cogently against taking *-man* (or *-sman*) as a derivational suffix.

the medieval period had relatively invariable orthography for items of long standing in the language or their derivatives, borrowed vocabulary is attested in a much wider range of spellings for the same item, as in this case in *stermannus, stiremannum, stirmanni, estermannorum, sturemannis, esturmannis, sturmannis, steremanni*; the diversity may simply be free variation or the result of other factors, but in view of the continued close contact of Latin and English these forms can plausibly be considered alongside English, e.g. when looking at variation or change in spelling or its relation to pronunciation. Finally, two of these spellings show a prothetic *e-* which may well reveal a French influence at least, if not a mainly French etymology (cf. *AND esturman* as a French borrowing from a continental Germanic cognate of English *steormann*; note, however, the double *-nn-* of these Latin forms, which may contrast significantly with the AN *-n*, such that this would be at least in part a calque involving English morphology or influence). Even for *-mannus* items, then, which are clearly on the boundary of English and Latin, the broader multilingual context intrudes, with *estermannorum* in a document of 1173 and *esturmannis* in one of 1206 occurring in a period in which the writer would likely have had French as a native language.[17]

DMBLS ***gracemannus*** ('chief official of religious guild', 1363) presents three quotations from late 14th-cent. Lincolnshire guild documents. Several senses of *MED grace* could plausibly be present in this compound (e.g. relating it to divine favour or more wordly privilege). It belongs to type A because, though not noted in *MED grace*, *OED grace* or *AND grace*[1], a supplementary quotation in the *DMLBS* article notes the vernacular word in an earlier document of 1337: '*providetur quod .. le graceman offerat unum denarium pro missa*'. Despite its Anglo-Norman origin, this *le* does not imply the item marked with it is French: the formulation with *le* is a regular way in which vernacular vocabulary, whether English or French, is inserted unmodified into a Latin matrix and it marks the item as vernacular (rather than borrowed).[18]

In general this group does not add to the known semantics of an English item (for which see type C, 3.3 below), but *DMLBS* **hidemannus** ('tenant of hide-land'), which is attested from 1351, does show the item used in quotations other than as or passing into a personal name. This contrasts with *MED hide-man* (cpd. at *hide* n[2] 2a), which is directly attested only as or passing into a personal

17 *DMLBS* also covers some use of Latin outside the British Isles, including certain state records within continental territories held by the English crown, and so the *steormannus* entry also includes the form *esturmanniis* in a Gascon Roll of 1293.

18 Wright (2010; 2013: 20–3).

name in English. (*MED* also quotes the same 1351 Latin example as *DMLBS*.) In the lexical field denoted by *-mannus* words (people of a certain status, occupation, or the like) it is inevitable that many examples are of the word used alongside a given name (e.g. *Agnes Hydman*, 1334, at *MED hide* n^2 2a) or in other similar ways that can be considered as or approaching personal names. In these contexts an example is evidence of a form, but it is typically impossible to identify any semantics that can be reliably associated with it: even if the usage is not just part of a list or other irrelevant context, use as a name may reflect the semantics of the item from which the name emerged but need not do so explicitly or even at all.[19] For this reason, Latin evidence that does not antedate English may nonetheless supply additional context that can illuminate semantics. A second observation arises in connection with *hidemannus*: English *hideman* is also implied in the compound *hidemanlond*, for which *MED* (ibid.) has one quotation (1298, '*De v s. de Willelmo Margarete pro i hydemanland quondam Alexandri fratris sui*'), but in this quotation all the other words are clearly Latin (cf. *DMLBS*'s single quotation, ?1466, for *hidemanlandum*). Even if an edition's transcription in such circumstances is accurate and not overlooking a suspension mark at the end of *hydemanland*, it is clearly difficult to decide whether the linguistic affiliation of a word should be judged by its own form or the language of the surrounding text. Dictionaries tend to prefer formal criteria (such as alteration towards the target language's phonology, morphology and/or syntax) to distinguish when an item can be said to be used as part of the vocabulary of a language, but such adoption may be the end of a gradual process of integration which began without formal marking. Here, however, questions such as whether 1298 '*hydemanland*' is English or Latin can be set aside, since either way the existence of the item in English at or before that date is evident, and in this case that in turn implies the (earlier) existence of *hideman*.

DMLBS **lagemannus** ('magistrate or alderman in certain boroughs') raises similar matters to *hidemannus*: it is attested in the Exeter Domesday (1086) exactly contemporary with *OED lawman* (1b 'in the five Danish boroughs, one of a specified number of magistrates or aldermen') cited from Domesday (1086) in a likewise mainly Latin quotation '*In ipsa ciuitate erant xii Lageman, id est habentes sacam & socam*'; if this quotation were discounted (based on the Latin matrix), *DMLBS lagemannus* in this sense would belong to type B since *MED*

19 For instance, in 'John the butcher read a book' the context does not shed light on the semantics of 'butcher' even though John must be a butcher, while in 'John Butcher read a book' it would be coincidence if John were a butcher.

laue-man has English quotations only from 1208–13 onwards (all as or passing into personal name). That said, in at least one *DMLBS* quotation *lagemannus* may have the sense of *ASD lahmann* ('one whose duty it was to declare the law', = *OED lawman* 1a; both *ASD* and *OED* associate the relevant Latin quotation with that sense), and for this the English evidence (*c.*1000) already antedates the Latin in question (1130–5).

Both (unrevised) *OED toftman* (cpd. at *toft* n[1]) and *DMLBS* ***toftmannus*** essentially rely on the same pair of examples found in several interdependent 17th-cent. glossaries of legal terms: *OED* quotes *toftman* from one of 1672, although this can be antedated to Spelman's *Glossarium archaiologicum* of 1664, quoted by *DMLBS*. *OED* recognises *toftman* with the date of the glossary, although it seems likely that the form *toftman* can be taken as the reading of one of the glossary's two quotations from the same original source, *toftmanni* being the other; *DMLBS* by contrast gives *toftmanni* a presumed date (12..) for the glossary's original source. Since the source in question, identified as *Pri. Lew.* and apparently a Custumal of the Priory of Lewes (cf. Spelman, s.v. *lanceta*), remains unidentified, it is not yet possible to resolve the question of dating nor the accuracy of the 17th-cent. reports.

One more item in this group calls for comment in respect of meaning: *DMLBS* ***werkmannus*** ('labourer') is found referring to quarry workers (1376) and a kitchen worker (*c.*1438). While the meaning of the English correlate (*ASD weorcmann*, *MED werkman*) is clear, these Latin examples may offer an additional indication of what forms or fields of work could be referred to by the corresponding English term in their time.

The final item to mention under this heading is of both types A and B, namely *DMLBS* ***aldermannus***: this item has several senses, and as for *lagemannus* above, relative datings, here from comparing *aldermannus* with *DOE ealdormann* (*MED alder-man*, *OED ealdorman*, *alderman*), should be taken separately for the various senses. Straight lexical borrowing begins with a particular use on a particular occasion, which transmits the borrowed item with the part of its semantics appropriate to that situation; all its other possible uses may, but need not, follow. Moreover even with enduring contact, as between Latin and English, it is possible for the items in the two languages to develop semantically independent of each other as well as in parallel or through further borrowing. In the sense 'high-ranking Anglo-Saxon nobleman', the English evidence considerably antedates even the first reliably dated *DMLBS* attestation (12th century); in other senses, however, the Latin sources seem to provide evidence of earlier currency of meanings known later in sources in English.

3.2 Type B: Latin provides earlier evidence for English

Sixteen Latin *-mannus* items seem to provide some evidence of earlier currency than the parallel English in one or more senses.

Latin			English*
***DMLBS* lemma**	**date**	**sense(s)**	
socamannus	*c.*1075	sokeman, tenant who holds land in socage	*MED soke-man*, *c.*1130–5 (cf. also *AND sokeman*)
hundredmannus	1086	hundreder, bailiff or chief officer of a hundred	*MED hundred-man* ('chief officer of a hundred'), 1170, but only as or passing into personal name but cf. *DOE hundredmann* ('centurion, commander of a hundred men') and *hundredes mann* ('hundreder, presiding officer of a hundred') both antedating the Latin
cotmannus	1086	cot-man, cottar, tenant of cot or cottage	*MED cot-man*, 1207 as or passing into personal name, 1246 implied in *cotmanland* (cf. *hidemanland* in 3.1 above) (*OED* earlier quots. show the Latin word)
aldermannus	[*a*1114] 1111 *a*1118 1130	[ealdorman, nobleman] alderman, civic official bailiff of a hundred warden of a guild	[*DOE ealdormann*, ?10..] *MED alder-man* 3, *a*1130 *OED alderman* 1, *c.*1275 *OED alderman* 2, *c.*1316 (cf. also *AND alderman*)
smalmannus	1130	lesser tenant	*OED small man*, early 12th cent. as or passing into personal name, or in collocation *smallman's land* (cf. *hidemanland* in 3.1 above)
grasmannus	a1150	cottar	*MED gras-man* cpd. at *gras* 1b, 1327 (earlier quots. show the Latin word; but note 1300 '*gressemenlond*')
malamannus	1183	tenant for rent	*OED molman* 1277
gavelmannus	1224	gavel payer, tenant for rent	*MED gavel-man* cpd. at *gavel* n^{1} 1c, 1283 (earlier quots. show the Latin word)

(continued)

Latin			English*
***DMLBS* lemma**	**date**	**sense(s)**	
croftmannus	1238	tenant of croft	*MED croft-man* cpd. at *croft* 2a, 1327 as or passing into personal name only
ferthingmannus	*c.*1250	gild officer having authority over gildsmen in a quarter of town	*OED farthing-man* cpd. at *farthing* n, 16th cent.
anlepimannus	1270	?bondsman without tenement in manor	*MED onlepi-man* ('bachelor') cpd. at *on-lepi* adj d, 1277
bedemannus	1275 [1348]	crier [almsman]	*MED bede-man* 2, *c.*1378 [*MED bede-man* 3, ?*a*1200; cf. also *AND bedeman*]
undermannus	1276	subordinate, servant	*MED underman*, 1372
foremannus	1281 1284 1266 1304	man who goes before a plough guild officer (naut.) captain tenant of (part of) virgate	?*MED for(e-man* 2b ('one who goes in advance of another'), *a*1500 – ?*MED for(e-man* 2a ('leader of an army'), *a*1500 – (also *MED for(e-man* 1 ('chief servant, steward') from 1222; cf. also *AND forman*)
hengestmannus	1349	groom, henchman	*OED henchman* ('groom; squire or page of honour to prince'), 1377–80 (cf. also *AND henxman*)
carriagiamannus	1365	carriage-man, carrier	*MED cariage-man* ('carter') cpd. at *cariage* 1b, 1374

*The earliest relevant example quoted in any of *DOE*, *ASD*, *MED* and *OED*.

Like the items of type A in 3.1 above, some of these items have long gaps between the earliest dates of attestation of the parallel Latin and English items, others shorter gaps; however, in most cases the gap is less than a century. This variation is again most likely due to the effect of chance on whether attestation survives. Still, this is all an addition to what is known from purely English sources, and in some cases the Latin evidence appears to push the date back considerably at which English may be thought to have had the usage: to highlight one such example, *DMLBS* ***aldermannus*** in the sense of 'warden of a guild' antedates the earliest corresponding English evidence by nearly two centuries (*OED*; *MED* has the same earliest Latin quotation as *DMLBS* and its earliest English example is 1389).

By contrast, *DMLBS* ***anlepimannus*** (1270) is more or less contemporary with *MED onlepi-man* (1277) so as to make relatively little difference to our knowledge of when it was a lexical unit in English. Here, as for some of the items of type A, the interest instead lies in interpreting the sense of the item, which in Latin contexts (whether the word itself is inflected as Latin or English) seems to *DMLBS* to refer to a class of villein but in English contexts seems to refer to an unmarried man. If these were to be taken as different senses, this item would belong more properly to type C, but both *MED* and *OED* (at *onlepy* A2, a revised entry) take both types of context of usage together, suggesting the contexts in the Latin are indeed just contexts, a matter of what the word is used to refer to and not of what it means. They can do this because they evaluate a broader range of material than *DMLBS* including both context types, and some quotations suggest that even though the referents are on occasion mentioned in connection with payment of *chevagium* (perhaps even related to their unmarried condition), nevertheless it is the unmarried state – which is in line with the etymological make-up of the item – that defines the actual sense of the word. This shows the value of the approach adopted here of bringing together all the evidence for an item: *DMLBS* from Latin contexts (and typically forms clearly inflected as Latin) covers the apparent reference of this term; the wider view, as here in *MED*, allows the underlying sense to be seen, and it can be supplemented by dating evidence from the Latin. *OED* interestingly does not treat this item as a separate compound; however, the borrowing into Latin points to the adjective+noun sequence *onlepy+man* as being treated as at least a collocation and more probably as already a lexicalised compound in English.

In addition to the dating evidence presented in the table above, several items have points of interest raised by their quotations. The graduality of borrowing is starkly illustrated by the evidence for *malamannus/molman*. The ten quotations for *DMLBS* ***malamannus*** all show the item apparently integrated into the Latin context with explicit Latin nominal inflections. However, three of these, all plural, appear to have their nominal inflections added to a stem ending in *-menn-* (1300 '*lxvj molemenni*'; 1302: '*septem molmenni*'; 1403: '*molemennorum*'), i.e. showing both English and Latin plural marking. The distinctive English plural marking combined with explicit Latin plural morphology in two of these (1300 and 1302, both clearly unabbreviated in their manuscripts) or with ambiguous abbreviation in the third (1403: '*molemen*" is expanded editorially to '*molemennorum*') highlights the possibility of a word of English origin in a Latin text essentially still standing as the English word even if it has some slight formal disguise through the addition of explicit or abbreviated Latin inflection. We may think of this as showing minimal or very limited Latinisation. Three of *OED*'s four quotations at *molman* show the item in a Latin context and used in a 'naming' formula, e.g. the earliest 1277 quotation '*de consuetudinariis qui vocantur Molmen*' ('concerning customary tenants who are called *molmen*'), i.e. undisguised English without any Latinisation, albeit in a Latin context. As noted above, identifying linguistic affiliation of a particular example is not necessary for the purpose of establishing when a *-man(n)* item existed in English (unless we have reason to suspect that English acquired such a term from a Latin word in *-mannus* rather then the reverse). Nonetheless it is important to remember that Latin often, indeed perhaps typically, acquired its items from English sources through a process that could be gradual and/or iterative, including stages where the item in question was used in a Latin context though it remained wholly or largely English and could be marked as such in various ways. In particular, however, the plural *-menn-* forms with Latin inflections in a Latin context highlight the possibility that some singular forms in *-mann-* in a Latin context may similarly be relatively unintegrated despite explicit or abbreviated Latin inflection. (As it happens all ten *DMLBS* examples of *malamannus* are plural, but the principle is a general one.) The form of the word and the matrix context both require consideration for any assessment of the degree of integration, and even they may be insufficient to determine the extent to which an example is being treated as part of the source and/or target language.

There are ways other than date and sense in which Latin evidence may be considered useful alongside English. We have already seen examples of formal variation in morphology and spelling that may be useful as well as uses outside personal name contexts. *DMLBS* ***ferthingmannus***, however, illustrates the capacity for geographical distribution to be of interest. *OED farthing-man* (unrevised) is labelled as a Scottish usage and has a single quotation; *DMLBS* offers corroboration that this may be a regional usage in that its two quotations are from the Guild Statutes at Berwick. Similarly *DMLBS* ***carrigiamannus*** (one quotation) should be seen alongside the single English quotations in *MED cariage-man* (also from the Durham account rolls) and *OED carriage-man* (cpd. at *carriage*, from Barbour's *The Bruce*), with all three quotations from the late 14th century and the north of Great Britain.

In addition to the items listed in the table above, two further items require comment here. The first is ***tidemannus*** (Wright 1996: 187; 'construction worker whose work depends on the state of the tide'), which was overlooked in *DMLBS* but has unambiguously Latin forms (*c.*1384, '*vj Tydemannor[um] op[er]ant' cu'* *vno handram*') of which the earliest antedates *MED tide-man* (*c*.1410 in this sense; *AND tideman* = *MED* sense 2 is also antedated); (unrevised) OED *tidesman* offers no medieval quotations.

The second is *DMLBS* ***Ostmannus*** ('Ostman, invader or settler from Denmark or Norway (in Ireland)', *a*1188), corresponding to *MED ost-man*, *OED Ostman* (1264). Here the Latin evidence antedates the English, but although both show the distinctive *-man(n)* unit, the initial vowel *o-* shows that both must be at least in part borrowings from a third language, Old Icelandic (cf. English *east*). While it seems very likely Latin acquired the item from the English borrowing from that source, the involvement of a third language makes the relationships more uncertain.[20]

3.3 Type C: Latin provides additional senses for English

Some items have already been noted for which the Latin evidence may provide further clarification of the meaning of the English usage. However, a small number of items among the set go further by providing what could be taken to be a separate sense additional to those known for the English term.

DMLBS ***ridemannus*** ('riding bailiff', 1256) agrees in form with *OED rideman* (n[1], revised), which offers only one medieval quotation, from a late OE gloss ('*eques*, *rideman*'), together with some dated uses as or passing into a personal name (1256, 1259, 1290 etc.). Here, the specific use to refer to a class of bailiff found in the four *DMLBS* quotations, if correctly identified, is a sense not known in English in the period (it appears first as an anglicisation of the Latin in late-19th-cent. historical scholarship): the only sense that can be ascribed to the English of the OE gloss mentioned above would be some equivalence with *eques*, which does not seem to have this particular sense (*DMLBS eques* 'rider; mounted soldier; knight'). Of course, from so small a set of examples it is hard to be confident that there is a specific sense in the *DMLBS* evidence rather than merely the use of a broader 'rider' term in contextual reference to a 'riding bailiff'. However, taking the evidence together nonetheless helps to build a picture of the semantics of this term.

The remaining items are similarly open to discussion. The first of these is *DMLBS* ***foremannus*** (also listed under 3.2 above) at least in its senses 'guild officer' (1284, one quotation) and 'tenant of (part of) virgate' (1304, 1336, 13..).

20 Cf. also on *steormannus*, 3.1 above.

Across very many of the examples from *DMLBS* and *MED for(e-man* (unrevised *OED foreman* makes no significant contribution) the basic sense seems to be 'one who is ahead or in front of others (physically or figuratively with reference to status)'. That being so, it may be a matter of lexicographical division, i.e. reference rather than sense, that the 'leader' references to 'guild officer', 'captain (naut.)', 'chief servant' and 'leader of an army' have been separated out as senses and that there appear to be additional senses from the Latin evidence rather than a broader understanding of the classes of leader to whom the term could be applied; likewise, the role of the *foremannus* associated with ploughing cannot be wholly certain, whether he is so-called for his position relative to the plough or rather his status in connection with the operation. The connection with land tenure is in either case difficult. Here, as with *ridemannus*, we are left to conclude that the best picture of the English term *foreman* is likely to have to take account of the uses of *foremannus*, regardless of how the references in the examples are to be divided up among recognisable senses.

Next there is *DMLBS* ***bermannus***, which in addition to the meaning 'porter' (as *DOE bærmann*, *c*.1000; *MED ber(e)-man*, 1226) is identified as having the sense 'tenant charged with carrying service' (1285). In this case the additional sense can be taken as essentially lexicographical artefact: in the sole *DMLBS* quotation for the additional ('tenant') sense *bermannus* refers to someone with a duty to carry ('*debet cariare corredum domini archiepiscopi de mercato .. ad curiam*') but still therefore a person who carries. Without further evidence to demonstrate otherwise, at most this is not a distinctive additional sense but use in a particular context, albeit not one noted from the English examples.

The final item of this type is *DMLBS* ***sulungmannus*** ('one entitled to receive what is due from a suling', two quotations, from the Register of St Augustine's Canterbury). *MED suling-man* (cpd. at *suling*, *c*.1400) has only one quotation, in which the reference is to a service owed by the tenant of sulingland (i.e. ploughland of a certain area); this single quotation is from William Thorne's Chronicle of the abbots of St Augustine's Canterbury (in Latin), as printed in Twysden's 1652 *Historiae Anglicanae Scriptores Decem* (col. 2140, sub anno 1364), and reads '*Quae servicia & consuetudines ipsi tenentes annuatim faciunt & solummodo præter corporale servicium quod vocatur* Swollyngman' (Twysden prints 'Swollyngman' in a different fount, perhaps marking it as English, though it is not distinctively marked in the single manuscript for this passage). Clearly the Latin evidence quoted by *DMLBS* supplies a meaning that differs from the English, but more significantly the meaning is in line with what would be expected for a *-mannus*/*-man*(*n*) word; by contrast the English 'service' meaning is not expected, and it seems likely a word for 'service' needs to be understood from the earlier *servicium* ('except only the personal service that is called "swollyngman" [service]', i.e the personal service owed by a sulingman).[21]

3.4 Type D: Latin provides the sole evidence for English

Items of types A, B and C have revealed much in themselves, but they have also provided the necessary foundation for approaching the fifteen *DMLBS -mannus* items of this final type. Whereas for items of all three types A, B and C there has been a direct formal contact with English attestations to act as a control, for items of type D we must use the relationships observable when both Latin and English evidence are available as a basis for inference when only the Latin evidence is available. In that few of the items in this section have been discussed before as examples of *English* vocabulary, they are considered more thoroughly than those of the other types, and a reminder is appropriate at this point that no criticism is intended here of any absence from dictionaries of English. The items are discussed in chronological order of their earliest Latin attestation.

The single quotation for *ASD rædemann* ('horseman') antedates the earliest *DMLBS* quotations for ***radmannus*** (from Domesday), some of which include the form '*radman*', others '*radmanni*', all in the sense 'tenant who performs riding service'. If, however, *rædemann* does not represent a direct ancestor in view of its first vowel, Domesday provides the earliest evidence for our item. The Domesday quotations with '*radmanni*' show its currency in Latin and imply earlier currency in English. The question is what to make of the Domesday forms '*radman*' and, in the plural, '*radmans*'. *OED* (*radman*, revised) treats these forms as Anglo-Norman (French) borrowings from English and thus also only indirect evidence implying (earlier) currency in English; on that basis this item in English is known solely from non-English evidence.[22]

The two quotations for *DMLBS* ***sagemannus*** ('one who tells or provides information') are both from law texts of the first half of the 12th century, the Quadripartitus and the Laws of Henry the First. Quadripartitus has an English original of which it is essentially a Latin version: however, the English text at this point has '*bute swa min secga me sæde*' in parallel to '*nec verius inde scio quam mihi sagemannus meus dixit*'. The English form implied by the Latin can

21 Twysden appears to have used two manuscripts for his edition of Thorne: the entire section on the manors of Northborne and Ripple in which this text occurs in that edition seems to be absent from Corpus Christi College Cambridge MS 189 (where it would be expected on fos. 188r–v); his edition accurately transcribes the text of BL Add. MS 53710 (p. 335) for this sentence.

22 *radman* is not listed in *AND*.

be taken to derive from the same root as in the English parallel (*secgan* 'say'). However if the English text is not corrupted, there is an interesting difference here in the Latin not simply taking over the English form used at that point, and this may reflect the Anglo-Norman jurist's process of interpretation, choosing (or perhaps even coining) an English term to take over into Latin, one that is an unambiguous compound indicating a person and action. The Laws of Henry the First are thought to be the work of the same jurist.

DMLBS ***thingemannus*** ('?soldier, member of the Danish army', in a single quotation, also from the Laws of Henry the First) raises similar difficulties to those for *Ostmannus* (3.2 above); from *OED Thingman* (only from 1823, in historical reference) it seems to be an adaptation into English based on the Old Icelandic plural *þingmenn* (Cnut and his successors' housecarls or bodyguards). The *-mann-* in the root suggests the Latin item comes via English. However, in that at least 12 of the *DMLBS -mannus* items are attested in either the Quadripartitus or the Laws of Henry the First, the possibility of the writer using a familiar pattern and creating the Latin word as if based on an English word (or even taking the Old Icelandic plural as English and creating a backformation to add Latin plural inflection to) must be admitted.

The range of quotations for *DMLBS* ***avermannus*** ('tenant holding land by transport service', from *c.*1182) presents a strong case for inferring an English form such as *averman(n)*, the first element being *DOE eafor* ('?provision of conveyance'), *MED aver* n[1] ('draught horse'; cf. also unrevised *OED aver* n and *aver-*). Similarly *DMLBS* ***wicmannus*** ('tenant of or worker on a wick or (dairy-) farm', four quotations, from *c.*1230) implies a form such as *wicmann.*[23] In both these words, as in all of this type, the form that is implied requires consideration of both the Latin spellings (e.g. *wikemann-*, *wikmann-* and *wycmann-*) and the English evidence (cf. *ASD wic*, *MED wike* n[1], unrevised *OED wick* n[2] 3) for the base to which *-man(n)* is attached.

For *DMLBS* ***forewardmannus*** ('guild officer'), well attested in quotations ranging from from 1262 to 1479, while the meaning is unproblematic and the implied English *forewardman* seems plain enough, questions arise in supporting this with an etymology that connects the form and meaning. *DOE foreweard* adj notes the phrase *on forewearde* 'foremost, first in importance' (=*MED for(e-ward* adj & n 3), so *forewardman* is most likely to be a straightforward adj + noun compound, like *anlepiman* above. Still, it is one that should be seen alongside *DMLBS forewardinus* ('guild officer', from 1314, perhaps containing the regular

23 On the meaning of *wic* see Coates (1999).

Latin derivational suffix *-inus*, so 'someone who is *foreward*') and therefore, in turn, *MED wardein* (3a 'guild officer', from 1348; cf. *AND gardein*[1] 4, 13th cent.).[24]

DMLBS **smalmalamannus** ('unfree tenant who pays a small amount of rent'), in a single quotation from a 1272 Inquisition Post Mortem ('*de redditu annuo smalmolmennorum*', MS: '*smalmolmennor*"), is also recognised by *MED* (*mol* n^2 b and *smal* 5b) from the same sole source but as reported in the printed Calendar.[25] The distinctive Latin inflection, though partly abbreviated, suggests this can be taken as Latin evidence to some extent, though the *-menn-* plural may indicate minimal Latinisation (cf. *malamannus* in 3.2 above).

Also from 1272 in the same series of documents there is *DMLBS* ***forespos-mannus*** (unspecified 'class of tenant'), appearing twice in relation to two successive Sussex manors: from the context the reference to tenants is clear but both sense and etymology are less obvious. *MED* has *spouse man* ('male spouse, husband; bridegroom', at *spous(e* 2a) dated *a*1382 but apparently as a phrase ('*vois of þe spouse man & vois of þe spouse womman*'); *spouse* is also used of betrothed men. *Forespousman* would appear to mean a 'man before he is married': the connection of bachelorhood with tenancy is obscure, but we should note the contemporary parallel of *anlepimannus* discussed in 3.2 above.

DMLBS **drovemannus** ('drover', 1285) is known from only one quotation, apparently in the Latin form *drofmannus* ('*debet cum ij aliis drofmannis fugare omnes districciones factas*'), but this quotation also underlies the report by *MED drove-man* (cpd. at *drove* v 2b, not defined) from a secondary source. The etymology and meaning for this item ('person associate with droving (i.e. driving animals to market)') seem clear.

DMLBS **huttemannus** ('man in charge of a *hutta*', *c*.1295) must be seen alongside *DMLBS hutta* ('(?temporary) furnace for smelting lead (Devon)', *c*.1295). The meaning of *huttemannus* is in no doubt from the contexts and the identification of *hutta* as a smelting furnace similarly so, though the precise type of furnace is not certain nor how, if at all, it is distinguished from the *bola* (with which it appears in the phrase '*per bolas et huttas*'): the *bola* may perhaps have been a furnace with a natural draught (as suggested by *DMLBS bola*, cf. unrevised *OED bole* n^4) and the *hutta* equipped with some form of vent (cf. *DMLBS huttellum* 'smoke-vent, louver' of uncertain etymology, 1399); alternatively a less plausible connection could be made with *hutte* as a form of *OED hot* n^2 ('large basket for

24 *MED wardman* ('burgess representing a ward', from 1444) is unlikely to be relevant, being both late and more a fit in form than semantics, though its earlier existence cannot be ruled out since the relevant sense of *ward* can be traced back to at least the early thirteenth century.
25 On calendars as evidence in lexicography see Durkin & Schad (2017: 336).

carrying earth, sand, etc.' (?ore), or 'amount contained in a hot'; cf. *MED hotte* and *DMLBS hotta*)[26] or *OED hutte* ('variant of *hot* n², mass of foam on a boiling surface', ?*c*.1390).

Meaning and etymology are problematic for *DMLBS* ***contimannus*** too. The single quotation is dated 1299 (but the manuscript source itself is an 18th-cent. transcript of a now-lost original) and reads: '*contimanni: omnes contimanni petunt cum braciaverint x quarteria frumenti, dimidiam estricam*'. The context, which parallels *contimanni* with *falcatores* ('mowers') and *consuetudinarii* ('customary (unfree) tenant'), would suggest a class of tenant or worker, but *conti-* is obscure as an element of either Latin or English. If the reading is correct the form suggests connection with *MED counte* n³ (*OED county* n¹), but the lack of convincing semantic link between 'man associated with a county' and the context does not inspire confidence; this interpretation might imply a formation parallel to or in succession to *scirmannus* (equating Anglo-Norman-derived county and English shire) but such a connection is ruled out on grounds of the difference in meaning and separation in date.[27] More plausible is to see *contimannus* as representing *MED contre-man* ('one who lives in the open country, peasant', *c*.1300, also 1279 as or passing into personal name; *OED countryman*), which fits better semantically with the context. The difficulty here is the transcribed spelling but the fact of transcription could account for the letter *r* being overlooked, especially if it was in abbreviated form.

DMLBS ***cotsetlemannus*** ('tenant of cot-land', single quotation, 1323, also quoted as Latin in *MED cot-setle-man*, cpd. at *cot-setle* a; cf. *cotmannus* 3.3 above) is evidently *cotsetle* + *man*. In its basic sense *DOE cottsetla*, a compound of *cot* ('cottage') and *setla* ('occupant'), is a 'cottager', although from early on (and certainly in *MED* sense b) it is also used of the cottage or cot-land itself, either as a transferred use or through clipping from the compound or collocation *cotsetle-land*; *DMLBS cotsetla* shows both meanings. The form *cotsetleman* is therefore either a compound of *cotsetle* in its land sense, which seems more likely, or a recharacterisation of that noun in its person sense, perhaps prompted by the existence of the land sense making the term ambiguous (cf. *sagemannus* above).

A single quotation is the sole evidence for *DMLBS* ***sindermannus*** ('worker in potash', 1355) but both form (in quot. *syndermannis*) and meaning seem

26 *MED* treats *hutteman* (1267, attested only in surnames) as derived from *hotte*, but while in some or all the *MED* examples *hutteman* could well reflect the source for *DMLBS huttemannus* (so making it of types A or C), its own connection with *hotte* is not clearly established.

27 *DMLBS contus* ('pike, spear shaft; fish-spear; pot-stirrer') seems very unlikely to be relevant here in that it is an inherited Latin word which does not seem to have otherwise been borrowed into English and appears in glossaries, i.e. as a word requiring explanation.

unproblematic. By contrast *DMLBS* ***rewmannus*** ('one of a company of men, (in quots.) fellow suitor in a hundred court', 1414) has six quotations down to 1567; the forms too (*rewymanny*, *rewman'*, *rewmen'*, *rewmennorum*, *rewmannorum*, *reuuman'*), some showing *-menn-*, support the implied existence of an English *rewman*. The *rew-* element seems to be *MED rew* n^2 ('row of people or things'; 'company or group', *c.*1300; cf. *ASD rǽw*, *OED rew* n^1).

The last example of type D is *DMLBS* ***inmannus*** ('tenant who dwells within an estate'), from four quotations from the Register of St Augustine's, Canterbury. From the definition *DMLBS* implicitly takes the first element to be *MED in*, although the quotations do not suggest any particular class of tenant (e.g. '*in hoc manerio sunt quinque inmanni qui debent per ij dies levare fimum super carros et per ij dies in autumpno tassare in grangia domini*', 'in this manor there are five *inmanni* who are under duty to put dung on carts for two days and for two days in autumn to stack the harvest in the lord's barn'). An alternative might be to take the first element as *MED hine* (2b 'farm labourer'; cf. *DOE hiwan*, *OED hind* n^2 and cpd. *hind-man*, 1581), which would fit the context better, although the form, lacking *h-*, would be a less good match.[28]

4 Summary and conclusions

The examples in all four groups have shown what a wealth of material exists outside sources 'in English' that can nonetheless shed light on English lexical history. Most notable are the 15 lexical items implied for English that would not be known from sources in English alone, but new datings, meanings and contexts have been noted for many known items too. Plenty of these have been recognised previously, as the English dictionary references show, but in addition to the new specific observations here, there is much to be gained from seeing a linked set together. There are some broad patterns related to borrowing in this multilingual contact situation and connected with them some reflections to be made on methodological matters.

What emerges overall is that for a satisfactory identification of an English item it is important to have three things: the item should have (i) a recognisable form and (ii) a recognisable meaning, both of which come from the contexts of use, and (iii) a plausible etymology that connects the form and function. In our clearest examples, there has been no difficulty in recognising the meaning from

28 Medieval Latin spelling frequently drops or adds *h*, so this may be a minor concern.

the context or in identifying the constituent parts of the *-mannus* compound (or, rather, the base with which *-man(n)* has been combined): the latter is most straightforward when the base is one known to have existed as an independent word (e.g. *frith*) at the relevant time. Challenges arise when the form is unclear (e.g. *contimannus*) or the meaning is uncertain or hard to reconcile with the form (e.g. *anlepimannus, foresposmannus*). In the latter situation, which is surprisingly uncommon in this data-set given the scant and patchy evidence available, the Latin evidence may at least prompt and contribute to a wider discussion; any further material that emerges in time may help to resolve the question.

In an ideal situation when using borrowed vocabulary as indirect evidence, there would also be an account of the motivation for each term being borrowed. Motivations for borrowing have largely not been discussed here, for lack of useful evidence. Borrowing into the more or most prestigious language involved in a contact situation is less likely to be motivated by the prestige or cachet of the term or its reference, and other explanations must be sought, such as necessity (cf. Trotter 1996: 23). However, in the present data one example (*sagemannus*) was noted of a Latin *-mannus* word not corresponding to an English *-man(n)* word in a directly related English text, and the presence (?addition) of *-mannus* may suggest that straightforward 'necessity' is an insufficient explanation in at least this case and perhaps more generally.

To return to one other example discussed earlier, it is clear that there is a relationship between *bordmannus* and *bordarius*, the latter being the usual term in Latin and corresponding to AN *bordier*. In fact, several other *-mannus* items also have corresponding *-arius* forms built either to the same 'English' base (*cotarius, croftarius, gabularius, hidarius, hundredarius, sulungarius, toftarius, wicarius*) or to a Latin translation equivalent (e.g. *operarius, precarius*, cf. *werkmannus, bedemannus*). It is not clear whether these *-arius* terms should be seen as calques that are directly related to the corresponding English *-man(n)* items or related to them indirectly via the Latin *-mannus* ones, or whether they are simply independent formations internal to Latin (since in all these cases the English base has itself entered Latin too, e.g. *cota, crofta, sulunga*, etc., and is known from a date earlier than both *-arius* and *-mannus* items). The formal and functional oppositions between these *-mannus* and *-arius* forms have not, to my knowledge, previously been investigated and may shed light on the motivations for not only these borrowings and formations but also the other *-mannus* terms and perhaps even, more broadly, other medieval *-arius* coinages.The possibility that some *-mannus* usages, including perhaps *sagemannus*, represent coinages internal to Latin could then also be considered in this light (cf. also *thingemannus*). Indisputably productive English *-man(n)* must have been familiar to many users of Latin in medieval Britain and this might in itself have been sufficient as a source for borrowing *-man(n)* as a derivational suffix *-mannus*; however, if they were also familiar with some Latin items in *-mannus* in which at least the base to which *-mannus* was attached was somehow recognisable as English in origin (e.g. *hide*, *werk*, *toft*), it would be unsurprising for them to be able to coin new Latin terms in *-mannus* to other bases of English origin in accordance with this pattern, mirroring the way that English *-man(n)* could (but need not) have formed parallel items to the same bases. In such instances then the unit of borrowing would seem to be either the suffix alone or the pattern and thereby the suffix (and either way, separately, the bases) rather than each whole word. Such a borrowed or inferred Latin suffix *-mannus* might in fact be in alternation with *-arius* for some bases (rather than the whole *-mannus* and *-arius* words).[29]

However, notwithstanding *sagemannus* (and possibly *thingemannus*), which may in any case perhaps be due to the idiosyncrasy of a single individual writer, for the majority of the items considered here this possibility of internal Latin coinage seems far less probable than straightforward borrowing of whole forms already built within English. First, there are the numerous items of types A, B and C, for which both Latin and English are attested, albeit with differences of date and/or sense in some instances. A Latin-internal account is unnecessary for these items (unless one wants to claim independent formations or English borrowing from Latin, which seems similarly unnecessary). Moreover, the relevant bases in types A, B and C include those of all the *-arius* items listed above except *wicarius*. While the *-arius* alternation does make it more likely that *-mannus* could have been recognised as a suffix within its corresponding words, in fact here the alternation with this inherited productive Latin suffix suggests *-mannus* was not being recognised and liberated to form further Latin words to bases of English origin but rather itself being optionally replaced by a more Latin alternative.

Second, in the type D items, which are what are really at issue if *-mannus* were a productive Latin suffix, close attention is needed to the supposed base to which it is attached: in every instance a better case can be made for this base being of English origin than being well established within Latin, i.e. type D items would be, at most, English base morphemes previously absorbed within Latin that have been given an English suffix also absorbed within Latin, probably by a Latin user for whom, crucially, English *-man(n)* could behave in the same way. Such a restriction in base is surely significant. Even if it does not prove conclusively that all these *-mannus* items do represent borrowed English lexis, the ingredients and process are all of English origin. Moreover, if function is considered as well as form, the people referred to by these *-mannus* terms are ones to whom reference was

29 Or even *-homo* (n. 4 above).

surely made in English at least orally if not also in writing, i.e. they were recognised classes of individuals who required recording in various types of document. If the term used for them in English was not one that was borrowed as a *-mannus* term, some account will be needed of what that different term was in English, why it was not borrowed, and certainly why a Latin one was coined using some other combination of English ingredients to be used in its place.[30]

Even leaving aside such questions of competing formations, the evidence considered here has shown that not only the functions but also the forms of items of English vocabulary can be represented in a spectrum of ways outside of English matrix contexts, ranging from essentially quotation of English terms framed by naming formulations ('called X') through to full formal integration with, for instance, explicit and distinctive Latin inflections. These too would ideally be considered in connection with motivation, but there is a further diachronic aspect. The evidence has not been sufficient to associate this spectrum of forms with a process of gradual integration of terminology into Latin, nor was it the aim of the present study to do so; however, further work may show some useful connection between the degree of integration of forms and the confidence with which they can be ascribed to an English origin, although this will require larger surveys and exclusive concentration on original documents rather than editions.

Problems of dealing with sources have been a thread running through this study, whether difficulties of dating or of uncertain transmission or publication. Publications of sources focus on their content, making understandable editorial decisions that seek to make their texts accessible and useful for those working on topics related to the content. Content is the context for a lexical item and so it is no less essential to lexical study; indeed editorial decisions in published sources reflect interpretation from an expert on the particular source that is invaluable in practical terms to those interested in relatively small parts of that source. However, form is also critical in a way that may matter less to other users of editions,[31] and in particular, the representation of abbreviation has presented key questions. If one wanted to try to go beyond merely inferring the existence of English vocabulary items or usages at particular times and look at the processes of transfer as visible in the texts, clearly it would be essential to deal with the questions of different degrees of integration, including the significance of abbreviation, and it would require some investigation of the language users

30 Again, the problem of *sagemannus* cannot be wholly discounted, but the linguistic heritage of the writer in question (and his expectations of his readers) seems offer the most plausible avenue for explaining this.

31 A parallel might be made here with *mise-en-page*, which may matter only for certain kinds of study and may or may not be reproduced in editions.

involved in the process and their knowledge of the languages involved. While all Latin users in the period had Latin as a non-native language, they may have been native users of English or Anglo-Norman French (with whatever, if any, non-native knowledge of the other), or native users of both, to say nothing of the other contemporary languages present in Britain or the regional diversity of any of these languages.[32]

This leads to a final observation. It is striking that despite involving an English source and Latin target, all but one of the examples discussed here date from the post-Conquest era and many first appear in sources that can be supposed to be the work of native users of Anglo-Norman French.[33] This is particularly remarkable because 19 of the known English *-man(n)* items that correspond to Latin *-mannus* items are known to have been in English before the Conquest. The apparent near-total absence of borrowing into Latin of any of these items from English into Latin before the Conquest may well be merely the result of haphazard survival: Latin survives in greater quantities from the post-Conquest era, especially records, which are a text type in which meanings expressed by *-man(n)* words might be expected to have been more frequent. However, it is also the case that this greater survival reflects the massively increased use of Latin for record-keeping by the Anglo-Norman administrative apparatus.[34] While this distribution is chiefly a fact about Latin rather than English, accounts of English standardisation must consider the functions for

32 Welsh has not been discussed here but two items have raised the question of the relationship with Old Icelandic. Richter (2013) considers Welsh among other languages relevant to his material.

33 The single (pre-Conquest) exception is *Northmannus*. For this item the three pre-Conquest examples cited by *DMLBS* are all in the sense 'native of a northern country' in general (one quotation), or more specifically 'Dane' or 'Norwegian' (one quotation each). They may well reflect borrowings into Latin (by English users) of a proper term from the Germanic language(s) of the people referred to, even if English did already have its own cognate or similarly derived lexical item *Norþmann* (*ASD*).

34 This kind of distribution has been noted previously by Howlett (1997: 87–9): '[W]hen Anglo-Saxons wrote English, they wrote English, and when they wrote Latin, they wrote Latin. They did not contaminate their Latin with English. But from the very beginning of Norman traditions in England one encounters scores and hundreds of English words in Latin forms in hundreds of documents.' Howlett (2017: 68–9), restating this view, suggests that the distinction between vernacular and Latin was and had always been clear for speakers of English, but it was blurred for the Normans, whose spoken (Old) French and written Latin were much more closely related and alike. He implies that for the Normans it was easier and consequently became habitual to shift vernacular vocabulary from and into Latin, a habit which they carried over when encountering English vernacular terms needing to be rendered in Latin (or indeed French) and a practice which continued in the use of Latin in Britain thereafter.

which it was and was not used as the process went on, and the multilingual circumstances which brought the distribution about lie at the heart of the issues discussed in this study. Evidence for English lexical history is available in sources written in a variety of languages by users from a variety of linguistic heritages, and among these, Latin has been shown to be a much more important part of the picture than hitherto noticed. The material brought together here raises questions and provides some answers in respect of some straight borrowings from English into Latin, and it shows the potential for wider studies of other vocabulary, including calques, and fuller consideration of the other contemporary languages of Britain, especially Anglo-Norman French, to illuminate the lexical history of English and thereby the emergence of the vocabulary of the standard English language.

References

AND = *The Anglo-Norman Dictionary* http://www.anglo-norman.net

ASD = *An Anglo-Saxon Dictionary* ed. J. Bosworth & T. N. Toller (1898 & supplement 1921) http://bosworth.ff.cuni.cz/

DMLBS = *Dictionary of Medieval Latin from British Sources* ed. R.K. Ashdowne, D.R. Howlett, & R.E. Latham (British Academy, 2018)

DOE = *Dictionary of Old English*: A to I online, ed. A. Cameron, A. Crandell Amos, A. diPaolo Healey et al. (Toronto, Dictionary of Old English Project, 2018) https://doe.utoronto.ca

MED = *Middle English Dictionary*. ed. R. E. Lewis, et al. (Ann Arbor, University of Michigan Press, 1952–2001). Online edition in *Middle English Compendium*. ed. F. McSparran et al. (Ann Arbor, University of Michigan Library, 2000–2018) https://quod.lib.umich.edu/m/middle-english-dictionary/

OED = *The Oxford English Dictionary*, 3rd edn (in progress) OED Online, March 2000–, J. A. Simpson (ed. 2000–13), M. Proffitt (ed. 2013–), http://www.oed.com

Ashdowne, R., & C. White (eds), (2017a) *Latin in Medieval Britain* (London/Oxford, British Academy/Oxford University Press).

Ashdowne, R., & C. White (2017b) 'Introduction' in Ashdowne & White (eds), (2017a), 1–58.

Coates, R. (1999) 'New light from old wicks: the progeny of Latin *vicus*', *Nomina* 22: 75–114.

Durkin, P., & S. Schad (2017) 'The *DMLBS* and the *OED*: medieval Latin and the lexicography of English' in Ashdowne & White (eds), (2017a), 320–40.

Howlett, D. (1997) 'A Polyglot Glossary of the Twelfth Century' in S. Gregory & D. A. Trotter (eds), *De Mot en Mot: Aspects of Medieval Linguistics* (Cardiff, University of Wales Press), 81–91.

Howlett, D. (2017) 'The start of the Anglo-Latin tradition' in Ashdowne & White (eds), (2017a), 61–72.

Hunt, A. (2003) 'Anglo-Norman: Past and Future' in M. Goyens & W. Verbeke (eds), *The Dawn of the Written Vernacular in Western Europe* (Leuven, Leuven University Press), 379–89.

Kastovsky, D. (2006) 'Vocabulary' in R. M. Hogg & D. Denison (eds), *A History of the English Language* (Cambridge, Cambridge University Press), 199–270.
Lutz, A. (2013) 'Language contact and prestige', *Anglia* 131: 562–90.
Richter, M. (2013) 'Trace elements of obliterated vernacular languages in Latin texts' in M. Garrison, A. P. Orbán & M. Mostert (eds), *Spoken and Written Language: Relations Between Latin and the Vernacular Languages in the Earlier Middle Ages* (Turnhout, Brepols), 1–9.
Rothwell, W. (1991) 'The missing link in English etymology: Anglo-Norman', *Medium Ævum* 60: 173–96.
Rothwell, W. (1993) 'From Latin to Anglo-French and Middle English: the role of the multilingual gloss', *The Modern Language Review* 99: 581–99.
Rothwell, W. (1996) 'Playing "follow my leader" in Anglo-Norman Studies', *French Language Studies* 6: 177–210.
Rothwell, W. (2002) '*OED, MED, AND*: the making of a new dictionary of English', *Anglia* 119; 527–53.
Trotter, D. (1996) 'Language contact and lexicography: the case of Anglo-Norman' in H. F. Nielsen & L. Schøsler (eds), *The origins and development of emigrant languages: proceedings from the Second Rasmus Rask Colloquium, Odense University, November 1994* (Odense: Odense University Press), 21–39.
Trotter, D. (2017) 'Anglo-Norman, Medieval Latin, and words of Germanic origin' in Ashdowne & White (eds), (2017), 299–319.
Wright, L. (1996) *Sources of London English: Medieval Thames Vocabulary* (Oxford, Oxford University Press).
Wright, L. (2010) 'A pilot study on the singular definite articles *le* and *la* in fifteenth-century London mixed-language business writing' in R. Ingham (ed.), *The Anglo-Norman Languge and its Contexts* (York, York Medieval Press and The Boydell Press), 130–42.
Wright, L. (2013) 'On historical dictionaries and language boundaries: evidence from medieval mixed-language business writing' in L. Sikorska & M. Krygier (eds), *Evur happie & glorious, ffor I hafe at will grete riches* (Frankfurt am Main, Peter Lang), 11–26.
Wright, L. (2017) 'On non-integrated vocabulary in the mixed-language accounts of St Paul's Cathedral, 1315–1405' in Ashdowne & White (eds), (2017a), 272–98.

J. Camilo Conde-Silvestre

15 Communities of practice, proto-standardisation and spelling focusing in the Stonor letters

1 Standardisation, focusing and identity construction

In the opening section of her monograph on *Language Standardization and Language Change* (2004), Deumert summarises research on standardisation thus:

> Standardization is concerned with linguistic forms [. . .] as well as the social and communicative functions of language [. . .] In addition, standard languages are also discoursive projects and standardization processes are typically accompanied by the development of specific discourse practices. These discourses emphasize the desirability of uniformity and correctness in language use [. . .] [M]ost standard language histories have been shaped by dialect levelling and koineization [. . .] The majority of standard languages are thus composite varieties characterized by multiple selection, that is the complex recombination of features from various dialects and varieties. In other words, standard languages have 'multiple ancestors' and their history is shaped by various types of language contact. (Deumert 2004: 2)

Deumert highlights some key ideas: the composite quality of standard varieties, their multiple ancestry and the special role that language-contact and/or dialect-contact play in their inception. She also considers uniformity, and a discoursive dimension, as necessary accoutrements. This is also the commonly accepted background in English studies, at least since the collection of seminal essays in Wright (2000), and Benskin's (2004) problematisation of the "Chancery Standard" explanation as the most direct ancestor of the present-day standard. Since the single-ancestor theory has been discarded, the main directions of research have been, on the one hand, tracing the supralocalisation of features and varieties, mainly in domain-specific contexts (Nevalainen and Tieken-Boon van Ostade 2006; Nevalainen 2012; Beal 2016), and, on the other, viewing the processs from a multilingual perspective (Wright 2005; 2015; 2017).

The achievement of uniformity entails a systematic process of variant reduction which may be regulated by an external authority, leading to prescription

Note: Financial support for this research has been provided by the Fundacion Séneca (19331-PHCS-14), the Murcian Agency for Science and Technology (Programas de Apoyo a la Investigación).

https://doi.org/10.1515/9783110687545-016

and codification, or which may be based on "competition-selection process[es] [...] of cumulative micro-accommodation [...] and dialect convergence" that take place in the speech of individuals (Deumert 2004: 4). Le Page (1975) coined the term 'focusing' for this practice. In its initial formulation focusing was connected to 'projection': "the meaningful, identity negotiating acts of interpretation which motivate the linguistic choices of speakers" (Deumert 2004: 3). In this context of social-identity negotiation, focusing refers to the sociological observation that individuals change their verbal behaviour so as to accommodate to that of the group they wish to be identified with, creating uniform varieties in the process, which may then become norms. If individuals do not wish to identify with interlocutors, then the behaviour of the group will become diffused (Le Page 1988: 31; Deumert 2004: 3–4).

Focusing via inter-dialect contact and inter-speaker accommodation is fundamental in the initial historical stages of standardisation insofar as it favours the appearance of 'protostandards': "relatively uniform, collective norm[s] – models of 'good' or 'appropriate' usage – towards which speakers orient themselves in their linguistic performance, [...] they are not transmitted through institutionalized instruction and are not yet characterized by a prescriptive tradition [...] [but] are acquired primarily through exposure to and imitation of model texts and model speakers [...] in local and professional networks" (Deumert 2004: 5–6; see also Smith 1996: 65–66; Deumert and Vandenbussche 2003: 4–5; Nevalainen 2003). This is parallel to the label 'language standard' coined by Joseph (1987) in opposition to 'standardized languages'. An outstanding characteristic of 'protostandards', seen in the context of identity construction through social interaction, is that they "acquire a sense of 'oughtness', a moral imperative" which can come to be regarded as an important resource for the success of the users' social life (Deumert 2004: 5–6; see also Hechter and Opp 2001: xiii). Whether it is the incipient ideology of standardisation that leads to this sense of 'oughtness' or the other way round – awareness of focused varieties considered as moral imperatives that leads to the creation of the ideological environment – is an insoluble question.

Machan (2016) has questioned the possibility of identifying standards in the early history of English. There are two main reasons for this; on the one hand, due to the absence of "ordering principles for OE and ME dialects by which one variety could be selected or accepted among speakers in general" (2016: 65); on the other because historical linguists often adopt an aprioristic approach when dealing with the relevant material – inevitably 'bad data' – and because this often leads to "a selective reading of historical contexts" (2016: 64). Machan also questions that focusing is necessarily directed to the creation of language standards or protostandards, particularly in late Middle English, and considers it to be a general process of variant reduction and speech convergence "inevitable in language" for communication to suceed, and deriving from the mere need for solidarity between speakers (2016: 68):

> [S]peakers converged in their use of a variety because it was in their best communicative and social interest to do so, with the implication that many of the processes that produce a focused variety [. . .] are necessary for the production of any kind of language. And so to call only some usages focused [. . .] when all human language requires some degree of focusing implies that those usages have been formed in some non-normative way. (Machan 2016: 69)

Machan concludes that extending categories like standardisation or focusing to medieval English is an ideologically-laden historiographic exercise which is performed "to make linguistic history possible" (2016: 72) – the strategy of 'historical legitimization' (Milroy 2001: 548–549; Milroy and Milroy [1985] 2012: 169–172; Armstrong and Mackenzie 2013: 7). So, some varieties are labelled in this way to stamp them and the history they fashion with approval (as it were): "[t]he identification of medieval standards is a way to impose, retroactively, a teleology on the history of the language; it is a way to construct a narrative of inevitable progress to the present" (Machan 2016: 73). In my opinion, Machan's efforts to highlight this issue minimise the role that identity construction plays in focusing and, therefore, in triggering the initial stages of standardisation. As a result, an important facet of standardisation is left out of the discussion: its relationship to "the beliefs and attitudes, shared practices and discourses which shape and support the historical development" (Deumert and Vandenbussche 2003: 10). This derives from a human imperative that must necessarily have applied in the past, as it does in the present. It is my contention that the relationship of focusing to identity construction must have been instrumental, in certain contexts, in the formation of protostandards. With this purpose in mind, I make use of the concept of community of practice, based on the evidence afforded by the Stonor letters, a collection of mid-to-late fifteenth century correspondence. My analysis of the letters exchanged by members of this community of practice will concentrate on spelling and, in particular, attention will be paid to differences in spelling-focusing relating to choices of Germanic and Latin/Romance vocabulary.

2 Communities of practice and standardisation

The use of the community of practice (Lave and Wenger 1991; Wenger 1998) as an analytical construct in sociolinguistics has been foregrounded in the so called 'third wave' approach, as proposed by Eckert (2012). This complements the analysis of variation in terms of socio-demographic, static categories – like age, gender, socio-economic or professional background, etc. – to highlight local contexts where variation assumes its social meaning (Eckert 2000: 2–3; Meyerhoff 2002: 526–548). A community of practice, in connection with the study of language variation, is defined as follows:

> ... an aggregate of people who come together around some enterprise. United by this common enterprise, people come to develop and share ways of doing things, ways of talking, beliefs, values – in short, practices – as a function of their joint engagement in activity [...] A 'community of practice' is simultaneously defined by its membership and the shared practice in which that membership engages. (Eckert 2000: 35)

A community of practice involves three dimensions: (i) the mutual engagement of its members in common practices; (ii) the pursuit of a joint enterprise in which the members are involved and "defined by the participants in the very process of pursuing it" (Wenger 1998: 77–78); and (iii) a shared repertoire of resources, or ways of doing things, whether linguistic – language routines, styles – or not: gestures, tools, artifacts, dress, a common behaviour, etc. (72–73).[1]

The relevance of the third-wave approach and of communities of practice to the study of standardisation is, firstly, because seeing variation as practice means that "the meaning of individual variables is underspecified and takes in specificity in the context of discourse and in the construction of speech styles" (Eckert 2012: n.p.). This tenet helps avoid preconceptions and the apriorism which Machan has denounced. Secondly, because communities of practice can be instrumental in variable focusing, affording connections with identity and social meaning construction. It goes without saying that reconstructing groups, identities and social meanings from the past is difficult and often impossible; but this does not mean that language-users did not mutually engage in common enterprises, which required a shared repertoire of resources, including linguistic

---

1 Sociolinguists and discourse analysts distinguish the community of practice, which is often created with a specific goal and whose members tend to be aware of belonging to it, from other forms of interaction also pertinent to linguistic practices like 'discourse communities' and 'text communities'. Members of the former are usually engaged in a common enterprise and share interests, goals and beliefs which are revealed in their oral or written linguistic practices and often lead to some degree of conventionalisation in their discourse – as specific genres or rules of writing – whether the community is conscious of it or not (Watts 1999: 43; 2008: 41). The latter is a broader construct, involving any group of literate people sharing a particular range of written texts, their members not being "bound together by common practices and goals, but [...] by texts which refer to [them], address [them] and are used by [them]" (Jucker and Kopaczyk 2013: 5; Swales 1990: 21–32; Fitzmaurice 2010; Meurman-Solin 2012: 467). The main difference between these constructs and the community of practice lies in the awareness on the part of members of belonging to it, as well as on the nature and extend of the common enterprise; this may also mean that physical contact, at one or other stage, is established.

variables that were given social meanings. In fact, as Kopaczyk and Jucker (eds.) (2013) show, the construct has been successfuly applied to the interpretation of a number of linguistic features connected to specific groupings from the past such as (i) correspondents mutually engaged in some joint enterprise (Cruickshank 2013; Dossena 2013; Dylewski 2013; Włodarczyk 2013); (ii) scribes and printers engaged in producing manuscripts or books and exchanging or sharing resources with this aim (Rogos 2013; Rutkowska 2013; Sairio 2013; Tyrkkö 2013); (iii) other groups whose members were bound together by a common professional aim, such as monks at monastic houses in Anglo-Saxon England (Timofeeva 2013; 2016), members of the legal profession, like clerks and notaries in medieval and early modern Scotland (Kopaczyk 2013), communities of grammarians in eighteenth-century Britain participating in debates on the nature, sources and significance of their work (Buschmann-Göbels 2008; Watts 2008), and scientists exchanging ideas and aims within the Royal Society (Gotti 2013).

3 Oxfordshire *cofeoffees* and civil servants: A fifteenth-century community of practice in the Stonor letters

In Conde-Silvestre (2016; 2019) I reconstructed a late medieval community of practice. My evidence is drawn from the extant documents and letters addressed to different members of the Stonor family of Oxfordshire in the mid-to-late fifteenth century, gathered together in Carpenter (ed.) (1996). The documents in this collection range over ten generations from 1290 to 1483. From the evidence in the Stonor letters at least one community of practice can be reconstructed. This network belongs to the lifetime of Thomas Stonor II (22 March 1424–23 April 1474). The first son of Thomas Stonor I, Thomas Stonor II was seven when his father died and came under the guardianship of Thomas Chaucer (the poet's son) until 1434. From then until his majority in 1445 his estate was in the hands of John Warfield, Humphrey Forster and, later, Henry Doggett. After taking possession of his estate, he led the conventional life of the country gentleman, managing the family's lands and performing services to the community: as a Member of Parliament (1446–1447, 1449–1450), Knight Sheriff (1453–1454, 1465–1466), and as a participant in several commisions, of array and peace, in Oxfordshire and Berkshire (1468–1474) (Carpenter ed. 1996: 50–52). Over the course of his life, Thomas Stonor II had extensive contacts with a great variety of people, but he held a very specific relationship with some of his correspondents. This was based on *enfeoffment*. Originally, in the feudal system, enfeoffment applied to any grant of land by the lord in exchange for a pledge of service. By the mid-fifteenth century, however, it had developed into an specific legal action, often known as *enfeoffment to use*: "the act by landholders of entrusting their lands to a group of trustees for a period of time, who would reconvey them later to whoever was designated, the original holder or his heirs" (Noble 2009: 44; Rigby 1995: 265; Dyer 1997: 173). The aim of enfeoffment to use was to ensure that lndholders gained more freedom in the disposition of their lands by circumventing the traditional privileges of lords in a higher position, including the Crown. The alliance between *cofeoffees* was necessarily established on the basis of mutual service and trustworthiness, which can be qualified as one of the social meanings constructed in the letters: "acting together when necessary" and "shar[ing] an adherence to the value associated with the importance of land and the duties involved in being a feoffee or executor" (Noble 2009: 159). In this sense, certain relationships in the letters share a mutual concern, despite the involvement of people from different ranks and circles: "the Stonor correspondents reveal a shared value in their emphasis on trust in relationships. The processes between people that establish networks, norms and social trust and that help them cooperate for mutual benefit provide a social glue that has elsewhere been dubbed not cultural, but social capital" (Noble 2009: 191).[2] A group of people like this can be described as a community of practice, according to the three dimensions mentioned above: (i) the mutual engagement in the act of protecting and ensuring the adequate transmission of enfeoffed land, which was also (ii) the joint enterprise in which they all had mutual interest and were aware of, for which purpose they performed mutual services, and (iii) a repertoire of resources, including the letters that they exchanged.[3]

---

2 The didactic poem *Instructions to his Son* (c. 1474), by Peter Idley, is acknowledged as one of the intellectual sources behind the relevance of trustworthiness in mutual relationships. Idley compiled this pedagogical poem from different sources, including some sections of Robert Manning's *Handlyng Synne* (early fourteenth century) and John Lydgate's *Fall of Princes* (1431–1438) as well as homiletic precepts and pieces of moral advice; however, they were filtered "from within a mentality that reflects gentry culture as he knew it" (Noble 2009: 162). He was a neighbour and distant relative of the Stonors, which makes of this treatise an emblematic epitome of the identity of the family and their circle, and of the social meanings that they all represented.

3 Noble also highlights evidence in the Stonor letters of at least another network of gentlemen collaborating in a community of interests in the last third of the fourteenth century. This "horizontal grouping or network of local gentry" (Noble 2009: 127) operated spatially over the territory of the Thames valley (in Oxfordshire, Berkshire and Buckinghamshire), rather than in a single county, and it "seems to have provided the benefits of lordship in daily and non-

Some individuals mentioned in the Stonor collection – Richard Restwold (d. 1475), Thomas Hampden (c. 1424–1483) and Humphrey Forster (born c. 1415) – participated in this community from 1442–1443, when Thomas Stonor II was in his twenties, by acting together as feofees for the manor of Dodyngton in Buckinghamshire.[4] The relationship between these people lasted beyond these early years, either as neighbours or in the performance of services. The network also extended during Thomas's lifetime to other individuals who also participated in mutual acts of enfeoffment and worked together, sharing similar offices – Shire Knights, Sheriffs or Justices of the Peace – in the counties of Oxfordshire, Buckinghamshire or Berkshire: Thomas Ramsey I, Thomas Rokes (born c. 1424), Richard Quartermains, Sir Edward Langford, Richard Harcourt (1416–1486) and Thomas Mull.[5] My analysis is based on the fifteen letters that the members of this community of practice addressed to Sir Thomas Stonor II between 1463 and 1472. With the purpose of gathering more evidence, I have also analysed six letters that some of these correspondents addressed to Sir Thomas's son, William Stonor (1450–1491), in the 1470s, immediately after the former's death. The total number of words is 6410 (see Table 15.1).

In Conde-Silvestre (2016) I detailed choice of code as one of the shared resources used by the members of this community of practice: all the letters preserved were written in English. The use of English in personal letters at this date was already common, but French and Latin were still working languages in the country as other documents in the Stonor collection attest, including petitions, writs and legal proceedings in Latin and in mixed English and Latin. Some stylistic traits recurrent in the letters by members of this community of practice were also analysed. One remarkable stylistic characteristic of these letters in the multilingual context of late Middle English is the high rate of French lexical items, such as *conceyve* (< OF conceveir) and *disposicion* (< OF disposicion). In general, the Latin and French element is conspicuous in these letters and particularly affects legal terminology as some of the items in the following list show: *obligacion*

---

military life, in a neighbourly way, offering a reservoir of support for safeguarding the familiy's lands and status". The members of this group were united by "holding similar county offices, but also some affinity in their relationship to the honour of Wallingford and by their being linked by military service to the Black Prince" (157). Unfortunately, no individual letters by any member of this group have survived.

4 According to Noble: "[t]his enfeoffment encapsulates the network within which the young Thomas Stonor grew up, one of kinship combined with local gentry support" (2009: 171).

5 For the biographical profiles of these individuals see Noble (2009: 169–179, 186–187).

Table 15.1: Letters by members of the community of practice (CP) in the Stonor collection (1463–1477).

Author	No.	Date	Word count
Letters addressed to Thomas Stonor II			
Thomas Mull	69	1463	240
Thomas Hampden	75	c. 1465	196
Humphrey Forster	87	1466	369
Thomas Rokes	89	1467	319
Richard Quatermains	94	1467/68	270
Thomas Mull	100	1469	355
Richard Restwold	102	before 1470	99
Richard Harcourt	110	1470?	329
Thomas Mull	111	1470?	570
Humphrey Forster	115	1471	291
Richard Quatermains	116	1471	281
Sir Edward Langford	119	1472	247
Thomas Mull	121	1472	505
	123	1472	792
	124	1472	545
Letters addressed to William Stonor			
Thomas Ramsey I	144	1474	162
Richard Harcourt	145	1474	220
Thomas Ramsey I	177	1476	148
	179	1477	258
Thomas Hampden	187	c. 1477	91
Humphrey Forster	197	1477	123
Total			6410

(< OF obligacion), *puryficacion* (< OF purificacion), *accion* (< AN accioun), *instruccion* (< OF instruccion), *inquisicion* (< OF inquisicion), *possession* (< OF possession), *communicacion* (< OF communicacion), *direccion* (< Latin directionem), *commission* (< Latin commissionem), *innybucion* (< OF inibicion), *mension* (< OF mencion). The presence of Romance vocabulary points to the social status and education as members of the gentry of this community of practice.

4 Spelling focusing and proto-standardisation in the Stonor letters

4.1 Methodology

Here I look at spelling focusing as deployed in the letters exchanged by members of this community of practice. This is basically a comparative exercise, and I have also drawn evidence from a parallel corpus (a control group) of twenty-three letters preserved in the same collection. The letters were addressed to Thomas Stonor II by sixteen correspondents of variable rank and extraction in the period c. 1461–1474. The authors (see Table 15.2) include: (i) petitioners and receivers, John Goodman, Thomas Pratt, Oliver Wittonstall, William Swan, Thomas Taylour, William Harleston and Wadehill; (ii) the bailiffs at the manor of Ermington, John Frende, John Yeme and Thomas Matthew; (iii) the lawyer H. Unton and the under-sheriff R. Medford. Also included are (iv) other neighbours from the gentry ranks, Thomas Hampton and Thomas Gate, who did not share office with Thomas Stonor II or did not partake of the common enterprise of enfeoffment and, therefore, did not belong to the community of practice. Finally, (v) two letters by H.S., one of Sir Thomas's brothers in law, are included in this supplementary corpus. The total number of words is 6361, a similar figure to the total in the letters by members of the community of practice (6410). These figures are reduced to 6280 and 6040 respectively once some irrelevant data is left out, like numbers and dates. The material for analysis consists of the word lists drawn from both corpora, extracted by means of AntConc 3.4 (Anthony 2014) from the digital version available online from the *Middle English Compedium* at the University of Michigan repository (McSparran and Scaffner eds. 2001-). The word lists were then manually organised into types and the number of spelling variants for each type was calculated. Finally, the etymology of each type has been looked up in the *Oxford English Dictionary*.

Table 15.2: Letters by non-members of the CP in the Stonor collection (1461–1474).

Letters addressed to Thomas Stonor II			
Author	**No.**	**Date**	**Word count**
John Goodman	62	c. 1461	368
John Frende	63	1462	273
	64	c. 1462	321
Thomas Hampton	65	1462	595
	67	1462	442
H. Unton	68	1462	200
John Frende	71	1463?	110
Thomas Hampton	76	c. 1465	258
John Yeme	81	1466?	406
R. Medford	83	1466	310
John Croocker	92	1468	285
H.S.	98	c. 1469	191
	99	c. 1469	228
Thomas Pratt	103	c. 1470	137
	105	c. 1470	172
Oliver Wittonstall	107	c. 1470	158
	108	c. 1470	204
Wadehill	113	1471?	317
Thomas Matthew	126	1473?	404
Thomas Gate	130	1474?	446
William Swan	131	c. 1474	193
Thomas Taylour	132	c. 1474	151
William Harleston	135	1474	192
Total			6361

4.2 Results and interpretation

Despite the similar total number of words in both corpora the number of types in each of them is different: 771 in the collection of letters by members of the community of practice and 934 in the letters by non-members (see Table 15.3 and Figure 15.1).

Table 15.3: Types and tokens in letters by members of the CP and non-members, with indication of language of origin.

Members					Non-members				
Language	**Types**	**%**	**Tokens**	**%**	**Language**	**Types**	**%**	**Tokens**	**%**
OE	423	54.86	4860	80.46	OE	436	46.68	4943	78.71
ON	15	1.95	73	1.21	ON	14	1.50	73	1.16
Dutch	0	0	0	0	Dutch	6	0.64	6	0.10
French	243	31.52	745	12.34	French	277	29.66	760	12.11
Latin	20	2.59	65	1.08	Latin	31	3.32	80	1.27
Names	70	9.08	298	4.93	Names	170	18.20	418	6.66
Total	771		6040		Total	934		6280	

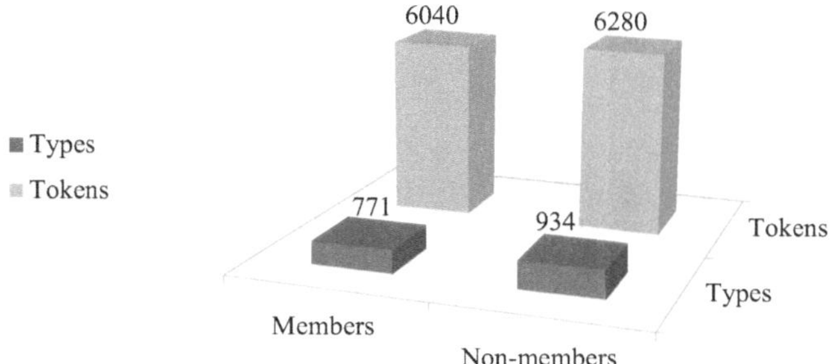

Figure 15.1: Types and tokens in letters by members of the CP and non-members.

Nevertheless, the distribution of vocabulary, as reflected also in Table 15.3, is similar in both corpora, with the highest percentage corresponding to Old English (OE) – 80.46% and 78.71% respectively for members and non-members – followed by French – 12.34% and 12.11% in each corpus. The percentage of Latin words is 1.08% in the letters by members and 1.27% in those by non-members. Finally, there is a small representation of Old Norse (ON) vocabulary – 1.21% and 1.16% – and a handful of Dutch words (6) in the letters by non-members (0.10%). A separate category for names has been considered, comprising both placenames, personal and family names. In this case the rates differ, with 4.93% in the letters by the community of practice and 6.66% in those by other correspondents to Sir Thomas. This may be due to the content of many of the letters in the latter group and the fact that, as documents issued by petitioners or receivers, detailed information on the people involved had to be supplied. It may also point to the closer and tighter links between members of the community of practice, which somehow is reflected in the lower reference to people outside the group.

When vocabulary is grouped according to its Germanic or Romance origin – the former comprising OE, ON and Dutch and the latter French and Latin – the distribution is also similar in both groups: 81.70% and 13.42% for Germanic and Romance vocabulary among members and 80.41% and 13.38% among non-members (see Figure 15.2). The distribution of types per group of languages shows, however, some differences, particularly as regards the Germanic ones, which reach 56.81% in the letters by members of the community of practice, but remains at 48.62% in letters by non-members. Similar rates are obtained for types of Romance origin: 34.11% and 32.98% respectively for members and non-members. As expected, the category of names shows the greatest differences with 18.20% of all types in the correspondence by non-members and 9.08% in letters by members (see Figure 15.3).

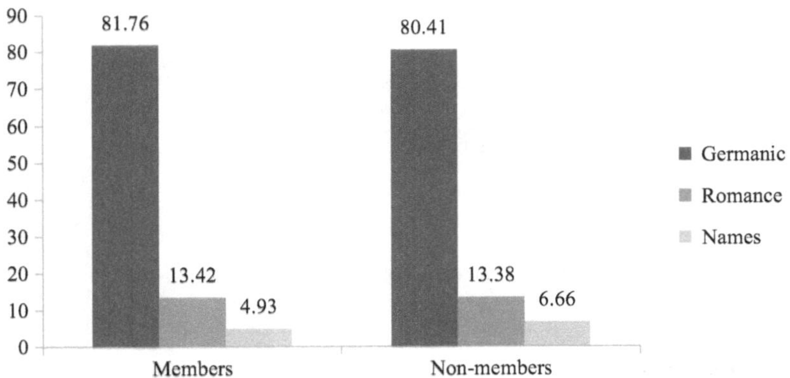

Figure 15.2: Tokens in letters by members of the CP and non-members, per group of languages (%).

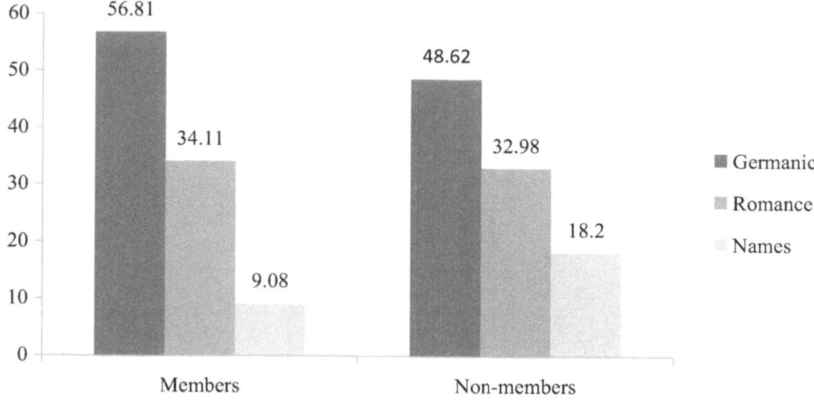

Figure 15.3: Types in letters by members of the CP and non-members, per group of languages (%).

Tracing the number of variants per type is an important indicator of spelling focusing. The information is displayed in Table 15.4. At first sight, the distribution of variants in each group is similar for one-variant types – 72.50% and 70.20% – and two-variant ones: 20.75% and 20.66% (see Table 15.4). Nevertheless, these figures should be viewed in connection with frequency of occurrence, since types with only one token in the corpus cannot be taken as evidence of spelling focusing or non-focusing. Accordingly 327 one-variant types from members (58.49%) and 446 from non-members (68.20%) should be left out of the analysis (see Table 15.5).

A comparison of the figures for one-variant types with the highest occurrence in both groups indicates focusing.[6] For members, 6.44% of one-variant types show a frequency of more than ten (up to 291, in the case of the conjunction *and*). This means that the same word was spelt the same on more than ten occasions by individuals belonging to the community of practice. The rate for one-variant types with a frequency of 5–9 words is 7.69% and rises to 37.83% for the lower frequency of 2–4 words. In contrast, rates for non-members are lower, with only 3.98% for the frequency between 10 and 277 (also the conjunction *and*), 4.28% for a frequency of 5–9 words and 23.55% for 2–4 words (see Table 15.5). These rates do not necessarily reflect coincidence with present-day English

6 No statistical analysis has been performed due to the conciseness of data limited to two groups of informants.

Table 15.4: Spelling variants per type in letters by members of the CP and non-members.

Members				Non-members			
Variants	**Types**	**%**	**Tokens**	**Variants**	**Types**	**%**	**Tokens**
1 variant	559	72.50	2474	1 variant	654	70.20	2186
2 variants	160	20.75	2351	2 variants	193	20.66	2470
3 variants	28	3.63	625	3 variants	46	4.93	682
4 variants	16	2.08	330	4 variants	22	2.36	442
5 variants	4	0.52	70	5 variants	7	0.75	96
6 variants	3	0.39	58	6 variants	6	0.64	250
7 variants >	1	0.13	33	7 variants >	6	0.64	154
Total	771		6040	Total	934		6280

Table 15.5: One-variant types and frequency of occurrence.

Members			Non-members		
Frequency	**Types**	**%**	**Frequency**	**Types**	**%**
1 word	327	58.49	1 word	446	68.20
2–4 words	153	37.83	2–4 words	154	23.55
5–9 words	43	7.69	5–9 words	28	4.28
> 10 (to 291) words	36	6.44	> 10 (to 277) words	26	3.98
Total	559		Total	654	

orthography, but spelling focusing as measured by internal consistency and reduced variation, irrespective of the particular spelling forms used.[7]

The same criterion has been followed with two-variant types (see Table 15.6). Types with a frequency of only two words have been discarded. These make up 23.75% (38 items) among members and 25.39% (49 items) among non-members. Two-variant types with a frequency of 3–4 words also indicate a low incidence of

7 See Conde-Silvestre (2019) for an analysis of spelling focusing as reflected in particular spelling combinations from the same corpus.

Table 15.6: Two-variant types and frequency of occurrence.

Members			Non-members		
Frequency	**Types**	**%**	**Frequency**	**Types**	**%**
2 words	38	23.75	2–4 word	49	25.39
3–4 words	41	25.63	3–4 words	63	32.64
5–10 words	41	25.63	5–10 words	39	20.21
11–20 words	18	11.25	11–20 words	18	9.33
> 21 (to 218) words	22	13.75	> 21 (to 197) words	24	12.44
Total	160		Total	193	

the type involved, although in this case the percentage is higher for non-members – 32.64% and 63 items – than for members: 25.63% and 41 items. It is possible to detect a higher degree of consistency among members of the community of practice when the frequency 5–10 words is considered, 25.63% vs. 20.21% among non-members. Differences are not so clear when two-variant types of higher frequency are taken into account, with only 1.92 in the frequency level of 11–20 words: 11.25% for members and 9.33% for non-members. The gap between both groups is reduced to 1.31 when two-variant types with the highest frequency (> 21 words, up to 218/197) are considered, with 13.75% and 12.44% respectively for members and non-members. These rates correspond to function words of the highest occurrence – I, OF, THE, FOR, BE, AS, THAT and IN – and the higher degree of focusing in both groups is the expected consequence of that frequency.

In the case of three- or more-variant types, a measurement of focusing is not yielded by high rates but, on the contrary, by lower figures. A high incidence of these types, particularly of those with four or more spelling variants, indicates a more diffused variety. The figures confirm greater internal consistency in the spellings used by the community of practice (see Table 15.4 and Figure 15.4), showing smaller percentages as the number of variants per type increases: 3.63% for three-variant types (28), 2.08% for four-variant ones (16) and 0.52%, 0.30% for five- and six-variant types respectively, with four and three items each. Only one type – the word WORSHIPFUL – has more than seven spelling variants, namely eleven, with a percentage of 0.13%. The rates for non-members are higher, with 4.93% for three-variant types (46), 2.36% for four-variant types (22), 0.75% for five-variant ones (7) and 0.64% for six-variant types (6). The number of words with more than seven variants is six, with a percentage of 0.64%, and includes IF, MASTERSHIP, RECOMMEND, RIGHT, THEM and WORSHIPFUL.

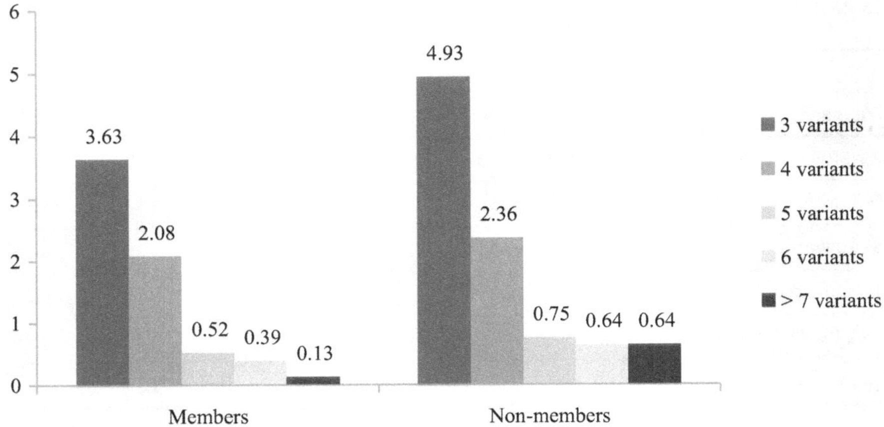

Figure 15.4: Types with three and more variants in letters by members of the CP and non-members.

I now look at the distribution of types and variants per group of languages: Germanic, Romance and names. The relevant data for members of the community of practice is given in Table 15.7, while figures for non-members appear in Table 15.8. For one-variant types only those with more that one occurrence have been considered, and for two-variant ones, only those with more than two occurrences.

Rates of Germanic one-variant types are 62.93% types for the community of practice and 54.32% for non-members: a sharp contrast of 8.61 points (see Table 15.7, Table 15.8 and Figure 15.5). Differences in rates for the Romance types are lower – 28.87% vs. 25.48% respectively, a contrast of 3.39 – but they soar when names are considered, with a difference of 12.01 points between the scores of non-members (20.19%) and members (8.18%). Rates for two-variant types for Germanic words and for names are more balanced, with 65.57% vs. 70.13% and 4.56 points for non-members, and 4.09% vs. 6.25%, with 2.16 points also for non-members. In the case of Romance vocabulary, members' rate of usage is higher, with 30.32% vs. 23.61% and a difference of 6.71. A high frequency of one- and two-variant types is regarded as spelling focusing, so the main differences between both groups lies in Romance vocabulary usage and names. Members of the community of practice used a more focused variety of Romance spellings than non-members, and non-members used a more focused spelling in the treatment of names.

A contrary situation affects names when the less-focused types are considered: three-, four- and five-or-more-variant types. As Figure 15.6 shows, there is

Table 15.7: Types and variants per language (members).

Lang.	1 variant > 2 f.		2 variants > 3 f.		3 variants		4 variants		5 variants		6 variants		7 > variants	
	Types	%	Types	%	Types	%	Types	%	Types	%	Types	%	Types	%
OE	142	61.20	77	63.11	18	64.29	14	87.50	1	25.00	2	66.6	1	100
ON	4	1.72	3	2.45	1	3.57	–	–	–	–	–	–	–	–
Dutch	–	–	–	–	–	–	–	–	–	–	–	–	–	–
French	62	26.71	33	27.04	7	25.00	2	12.50	2	50.00	–	–	–	–
Latin	5	2.15	4	3.27	0	0	0	0	–	–	1	33.3	–	–
Names	19	8.18	5	4.09	2	7.14	0	0	1	25.00	–	–	–	–
Total	232		122		28		16		4		3		1	

Table 15.8: Types and variants per language (non-members).

Lang.	1 variant > 2 f.		2 variants > 3 f.		3 variants		4 variants		5 variants		6 variants		7 > variants	
	Types	%	Types	%	Types	%	Types	%	Types	%	Types	%	Types	%
OE	108	51.92	101	70.13	30	65.22	13	59.09	6	85.71	5	83.33	3	60
ON	5	2.40	–	–	–	–	1	4.55	–	–	–	–	–	–
Dutch	–	–	–	–	–	–	–	–	–	–	–	–	–	–
French	47	22.58	33	22.91	11	23.92	8	36.37	1	14.29	–	–	1	20
Latin	6	2.88	1	0.69	–	–	–	–	–	–	–	–	1	20
Names	42	20.19	9	6.25	5	10.87	–	–	–	–	1	16.67	–	–
Total	208		144		46		22		7		6		5	

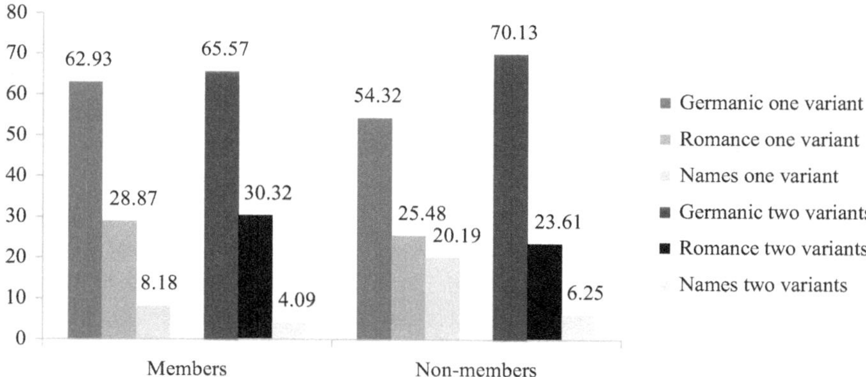

Figure 15.5: One- and two-variant types per group of languages (%).

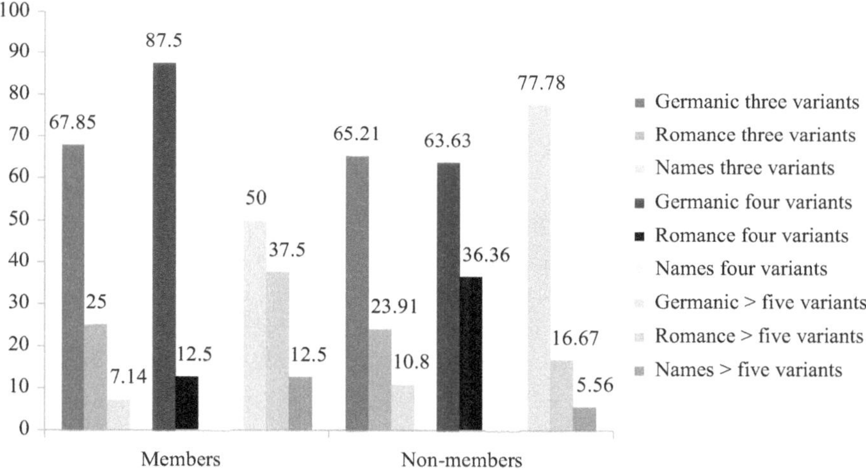

Figure 15.6: Three-, four- and five-or-more-variant types per group of languages (%).

a slight difference (3.66) in favour of members when names with three-variant types are considered: 7.14% vs. 10.8%. Notice that, in contrast to one- and two-variant types, the smaller figures here are a measurement of focusing, while higher rates point to more diffused spellings. Percentages are very similar in the case of types for names with five-or-more variants, with only one type in each group: WILLIAM.

Evidence is not conclusive when data for the other groups of languages is analysed. Very similar rates are obtained for Germanic items in the case of three-variant types: 67.85% for members and 65.21% for non-members. The tendency is confusing with four-variant types, with a very high rate for members (87.5%) and a much lower one for non-members (63.63%). This could point to a more focused variety among non-members of the community of practice, were it not for the contrary tendency in the case of five-or-more variants, with very high rates for non-members (77.78%) and lower ones for members (50%). If means are calculated, the behaviour of each group is very similar: 68.45 for members and 68.87 for non-members. The same is attested when Romance vocabulary is analysed, with similar rates for members and non-members in three-variant types – 25% vs. 23.91% – and contrary distributions in the case of four- and five-or-more-variant types: 12.5% and 37.5% for members vs. 36.36% and 16.67% for non members. There are similar means for each group – 25% vs. 26.51% – but with a slightly more focused variety among members as shown by the lower figure. However, the low number of items in each case makes these figures negligible in the general count.

5 Conclusion

The following data point to a higher degree of spelling focusing in the letters by members of the community of practice, also in relation to etymology:

- a higher rate of one- and two-variant types of mid frequency – 5–9 words and 5–10 words – with 7.69% (vs. 4.28%) and 25.63% (vs. 20.21%);
- lower rates for types with three- and four-variants, 3.63% (vs. 4.93%) and 2.08% (vs. 2.36%);
- the evidence of five-, six- and seven-or-more variant types, although small, also points in the same direction: 0.52% (vs. 0.75%), 0.39% (vs. 0.64%) and 0.13% (vs. 0.64%);
- the community of practice shows more focused practices with one-variant types of Germanic origin of mid-to-high occurrence – 62.93% (vs. 54.32%);
- in types of Romance origin, the community of practice shows more focused practices in two-variant types of mid-to-high frequency: 30.32% (vs. 23.61%),
- this is parallel to the use of lower rates when three-or-more-variant types of Romance origin are considered, and especially remarkable with four-variant ones: 12.5% (vs. 36.36%).

By contrast, non-members are only more consistent in the spelling of names: 20.19% (vs. 8.18%). The community of practice's more focused spellings in Romance word-types reflect the use of French and Latin as the languages of law and administration. This directly supports the thesis of this volume, which is that as English took over Anglo-Norman's pragmatic roles on the page, it took over its convention for spelling – that is, invariancy – too.

References

Anthony, Laurence. 2014. *AntConc* (Version 3.4.3) [Computer Software]. Tokyo, Japan: Waseda University. Available from http://www.laurenceanthony.net/

Armstrong, Nigel and Ian E. Mackenzie. 2013. *Standardization, Ideology and Linguistics.* Houndmills, Basingstoke: Palgrave MacMillan.

Beal, Joan C. 2016. Standardization. In Merja Kytö and Päivi Pahta (eds.). *The Cambridge Handbook of English Historical Linguistics*, 301–317. Cambridge: Cambridge University Press.

Benskin, Michael. 2004. Chancery Standard. In Christian Kay, Carole Hough and Irené Wotherspoon (eds.). *New Perspectives on English Historical Linguistics. Selected Papers from 12 ICEHL, Glasgow, August 21–26, 2002. Volume 2: Lexis and Transmission*, 1–40. Amsterdam and Philadelphia: John Benjamins.

Buschmann-Göbels, Astrid. 2008. *Bellum Grammaticale* (1712). A battle of books and a battle for the market. In Ingrid Tieken-Boon van Ostade (ed.). *Grammar, Grammarians and Grammar Writing in Eighteenth-Century Britain*, 81–100. Berlin: Mouton de Gruyter.

Carpenter, Christine (ed.). 1996. *Kingsford's Stonor Letters and Papers, 1290–1483.* Cambridge: Cambridge University Press.

Conde-Silvestre, J. Camilo. 2016. A 'third-wave' historical sociolinguistic approach to late Middle English correspondence: Evidence from the *Stonor Letters*". In Cinzia Russi (ed.). *Current Trends in Historical Sociolinguistics*, 46–66. Warsaw and Berlin: De Gruyter Open.

Conde-Silvestre, J. Camilo. 2019. Spelling focusing and proto-standardisation in a fifteenth-century community of practice. *Studia Neophilologica* 91 (1): 11–30.

Cruickshank, Janet. 2013. The role of communities of practice in the emergence of Standard Scottish English. In J. Kopaczyk and A. Jucker (eds.). 19–45.

Deumert, Ana. 2004. *Language Standardization and Language Change. The Dynamics of Cape Dutch.* Amsterdam and Philadelphia: John Benjamins.

Deumert, Ana and Wim Vandenbussche (eds.). 2003. *Germanic Standardizations. Past to Present.* Amsterdam and Philadelphia: John Benjamins.

Dossena, Marina. 2013. Mixing genres and reinforcing community ties in 19th century Scottish correspondence. In J. Kopaczyk and A. Jucker (eds.). 48–60.

Dyer, Christopher. 1997. The economy and society. In Nigel Saul (ed.). *The Oxford Illustrated History of Medieval England*, 137–173. Oxford: Oxford University Press.

Dylewski, Radosław. 2013. Communities of practice, idiolects and community grammar. Variation in the past of *to be* paradigms in the Civil War letters from Northwestern South Carolina. In J. Kopaczyk and A. Jucker (eds.). 61–82.

Eckert, Penelope. 2000. *Linguistic Variation as Social Practice*. Oxford: Blackwell.

Eckert, Penelope. 2012. Three waves of variation study: The emergence of meaning in the study of variation. *Annual Review of Anthropology* 41. 87–100. Also available online at https://web.stanford.edu/~eckert/PDF/ThreeWaves.pdf [Accessed 01/09/2016].

Fitzmaurice, Susan M. 2010. Mr Spectator, identity and social roles in an early eighteenth-century community of practice and the periodical discourse community. In Päivi Pahta, Minna Nevala, Arja Nurmi and Minna Palander-Collin (eds.). *Social roles and language practices in Late Modern English*, 29–54. Amsterdam and Philadelphia: John Benjamins.

Gotti, Maurizio. 2013. The formation of the Royal Society as a community of practice and discourse. In J. Kopaczyk and A. Jucker (eds.). 269–285.

Hechter, Michael and Karl-Dieter Opp, 2001. Introduction. In Michael Hechter and Karl-Dieter Opp (eds.). *Social Norms*, xi-xix. New York: Russell Sage Foundation.

Joseph, John Earl. 1987. *Eloquence and Power. The Rise of Language Standards and Standard Languages*. London: Frances Pinter.

Jucker, Andreas and Joanna Kopaczyk. 2013. Communities of practice as a locus of language change. In J. Kopaczyk and A. Jucker (eds.). 1–16.

Kopaczyk, Joanna. 2013. How a community of practice creates a text community. Middle Scots texts and administrative discourse. In J. Kopaczyk and A. Jucker (eds.). 225–250.

Kopaczyk, Joanna and Andreas Jucker (eds.). 2013. *Communities of practice in the history of English*. Amsterdam and Philadelphia: John Benjamins.

Lave, Jean and Étienne Wenger. 1991. *Situated Learning. Legitimate Peripheral Participation*. Cambridge: Cambridge University Press.

Le Page, Robert B. 1975. Projection, focussing, diffussion. *York Papers in Linguistics* 9: 123–142.

Le Page, Robert B. 1988. Some premises concerning the standardization of languages with special reference to Caribbean English. *International Journal of the Sociology of Language* 71: 25–36.

Machan, Tim William. 2016. Snakes, ladders, and standard language. In Tim William Machan (ed.). *Imagining Medieval English. Language Structures and Theories, 500–1500*, 54–77. Cambridge: Cambridge University Press.

McSparran, Frances and Paul Scaffner (eds.). 2001 *Middle English Compendium*. Ann Arbor: University of Michigan Digital Library Production Service. Available online at http://quod.lib.umich.edu/m/med [Accessed 01/09/2016]

Meurman-Solin, Anneli. 2012. Historical dialectology. Space as a variable in the reconstruction of regional dialects. In Juan M. Hernández-Campoy and J. Camilo Conde-Silvestre (eds.). *The Handbook of Historical Sociolinguistics*, 465–479. Oxford and Malden: Wiley-Blackwell.

Meyerhoff, Miriam. 2002. Communities of practice. In Jack K. Chambers, Peter Trudgill and Natalie Schilling-Estes (eds.). *The Handbook of Language Variation and Change*, 526–548. Oxford and Malden: Wiley-Blackwell.

Milroy, James. 2001. Language ideologies and the consequences of standardization. *Journal of Sociolinguistics* 5 (4): 530–555.

Milroy, James and Lesley Milroy. (1985) 2012. *Authority in Language. Investigating Standard English*. London: Routledge. (3rd edition)

Nevalainen, Terttu. 2003. English. In Ana Deumert and Wim Vandenbussche (eds.). *Germanic Standardizations. Past to Present*, 127–156. Amsterdam and Philadelphia: John Benjamins.

Nevalainen, Terttu. 2012. Variable focusing in English spelling between 1400 and 1600. In Susan Baddeley and Anja Voeste (eds.). *Orthographies in Early Modern Europe*, 127–165. Berlin: Mouton de Gruyter.

Nevalainen, Terttu and Ingrid Tieken-Boon van Ostade. 2006. Standardisation. In Richard Hogg and David Denison (eds.). *A History of the English Language*, 271–311. Cambridge: Cambridge University Press.

Noble, Elizabeth. 2009. *The World of the Stonors. A Gentry Society*. Woodbridge: The Boydell Press.

Rigby, S.H. 1995. *English Society in the Later Middle Ages. Class, Status and Gender*. London: MacMillan.

Rogos, Justyna. 2013. Crafting text languages. Spelling systems in manuscripts of the 'Man of Law's Tale' as a means of constructing a scribal community of practice. In J. Kopaczyk and A. Jucker (eds.). 105–121.

Rutkowska, Hanna. 2013. Typographical and graphomorphemic features of five editions of the *Kalender of Shepherdes* as elements of the early printers' community of practice. In J. Kopaczyk and A. Jucker (eds.). 123–149.

Sairio, Anni. 2013. Elizabeth Montagu's *Shakespeare Essay* (1769). The final draft and the first edition as evidence of two communities of practice. In J. Kopaczyk and A. Jucker (eds.). 177–197.

Swales, John M. 1990. *Genre Analysis: English in Academic and Research Settings*. Cambridge: Cambridge University Press.

Smith, Jeremy. 1996. *An Historical Study of English: Function, Form and Change*. London: Routledge.

The Oxford English Dictionary. 2000–2019. Third online edition, Oxford: Oxford University Press. http://www.oed.com/.

Timofeeva, Olga. 2013. *Of ledenum bocum to engliscum gereorde*. Bilingual communities of practice in Anglo-Saxon England. In J. Kopaczyk and A. Jucker (eds.). 201–223.

Timofeeva, Olga. 2016. The Viking outgroup in early medieval chronicles. *Journal of Historical Sociolinguistics* 2 (1), 83–121.

Tyrkkö, Jukka. 2013. Printing houses as communities of practice. Orthography in Early Modern medical books. In J. Kopaczyk and A. Jucker (eds.). 151–175.

Watts, Richard J. 1999. The social construction of standard English: Grammar writers as a 'discourse community'. In Tony Bex and Richard J. Watts (eds.). *Standard English: The Widening Debate*, 40–68. London: Routledge.

Watts, Richard J. 2008. Grammar writers in eighteenth-century Britain. A community of practice or a discourse community? In Ingrid Tieken-Boon van Ostade (ed.). *Grammar, Grammarians and Grammar Writing in Eighteenth-Century Britain*, 37–56. Berlin: Mouton de Gruyter.

Wenger, Étienne. 1998. *Communities of Practice. Learning, Meaning and Identity*. Cambridge: Cambridge University Press.

Włodarczyk, Matylda. 2013. Community or communities of practice? 1820 petitioners in the Cape Colony. In J. Kopaczyk and A. Jucker (eds.). 83–102.

Wright, Laura, (ed.). 2000. *The Development of Standard English, 1300–1800. Theories, Descriptions, Conflicts*. Cambridge: Cambridge University Press.

Wright, Laura. 2005. Medieval mixed-language business texts and the rise of standard English. In Janne Skaffari, Matti Peikola, Ruth Carroll, Risto Hiltunen and Brita Wårvik (eds.). *Opening Windows on Texts and Discourses of the Past*, 381–399. Amsterdam and Philadelphia: John Benjamins

Wright, Laura. 2015. The contact origins of standard English. In Daniel Schreier and Marianne Hundt (eds.). *English as a Contact Language*, 58–74. Cambridge: Cambridge University Press.

Wright, Laura. 2017. A multilingual approach to the history of standard English. In Päivi Pahta, Janne Skaffari and Laura Wright (eds.). *Multilingual Practices in Language History: New Perspectives*, 339–358. Berlin: Mouton de Gruyter.

Jesús Romero-Barranco

16 A comparison of some French and English nominal suffixes in early English correspondence (1420–1681)

1 Introduction

In this chapter, I compare the distribution of the English-etymology nominal suffixes -DOM, -HEDE, -NESS and -SHIP with the French-derived nominal suffixes -ATION, -AUNCE, -MENT, -AGE and -AL, as they occur in the *Parsed Corpus of Early English Correspondence* (*PCEEC*, a collection of 4,979 letters written between 1410 and 1681). I then relate their rates of usage to the age and social class of their authors. The survey finds that letter-writers used both English and French-derived suffixes at relatively similar rates until the decades following 1569, when use of English suffixes decreased. The social leaders in the diffusion of French-derived nominal suffixes were found to be the gentry and the professionals, that is, the middling social ranks, as opposed to the nobility and the non-gentry; and the leading age-group was 26–35 year olds. However, by the end of the period under study (1640–1681), the non-gentry had practically caught up, so that by the turn of the eighteenth century the picture is one of the nobility lagging behind. The use of French nominal suffixes on English bases (hybridisation of this sort showing that a suffix had become nativised) was also found to have been innovated by the middle social groups, the gentry and professionals. This finding supports the hypothesis that standardisation emanated from, and was spread by, the middle social ranks as they engaged in their daily businesses.

1.1 Noun suffixation

In English, speakers create new lexical units by means of three different mechanisms: (1) derivation or the addition of an affix to a base (i.e. *reload*, *readable*); (2) conversion, i.e. *the dead*; and (3) compounding, i.e. *get-together* (Marchand

---

Note: The present research has been funded by the Spanish Ministry of Science and Innovation (grant numbers FFI2014-57963-P and FFI2017-88060-P) and by the Autonomous Government of Andalusia (grant number P11-HUM7597). These grants are hereby gratefully acknowledged. I am also grateful to two anonymous reviewers.

https://doi.org/10.1515/9783110687545-017

1969: 2; Quirk et al. 1985: 1520; Huddleston and Pullum 2002: 1640–1719). I focus on the first mechanism, derivational suffixes. Derivational suffixes come into existence by way of two different processes: a former independent word such as -DOM or -HOOD, no longer used as such, and from suffixes that originated in another language, such as -AGE or -MENT from French (Marchand 1969: 211; Adams 2001: 154). According to Burnley (1992: 447), "of the forty or so [suffixes] which existed in Old English, about three-quarters persisted into Middle English, where they were joined by numerous additions from foreign sources".

Burnley identifies three stages in the process of vernacularization: (1) the foreign word containing an affix joins the lexicon; (2) the affix has a foreign status, being exclusively attached to foreign bases; and (3) the affix ceases to be considered as non-native, combining with bases of any origin (1992: 445–446; Durkin 2014: 327–328). In the last stage, morphological variation occurs, i.e. the same base is attested with different affixes, creating synonyms, one becoming part of the standard lexicon while the others remain nonstandard, e.g. *unagreeable, *displeasant, etc. (Kjellmer 2005: 156). Previous work on the topic includes Zbierska-Sawala (1989, 1993), who analyses the use of English and French nominal suffixation and verbal prefixation in early Middle English; Dalton-Puffer (1996), evaluating the French influence on Middle English morphology; Ciszek (2008), on the semantics, productivity and dialect distribution of English (-DOM, -SHIP, -HEDE and -NESS) and French (-AGE, -(E)RIE and -MENT) forming abstract nouns[1]; Lloyd (2011), on the semantic development of French (-ATION, -AUNCE, -MENT, -AGE and -AL); and Esteban-Segura, who shows that "alternation takes place with the suffixes -NESS and -SHIP on Germanic roots, but in a restricted number of words" (2011: 192).

In terms of route of entry as to how Latin and French suffixes came to be attached to English words, the pragmatic distribution is traditionally regarded as Latin for the most prestigious functions, used by the Church and universities; French for administration and ordinary everyday interaction among the French-speaking population; and English supposedly restricted to interaction in domestic

1 Ciszek (2002) focuses on Middle English -LY, Ciszek (2004) on French elements in early Middle English word derivation, Ciszek (2005) on the development of -SHIP in early Middle English, Ciszek (2006a) on late Middle English -SHIP, Ciszek (2006b) on -DOM in medieval English, Ciszek (2009) on late Middle English development of early Middle English coinages in -HEDE, and Ciszek (2012, 2013) on the decline in productivity of Middle English -ISH. Trips (2009) assesses the semantic development of -DOM, -HEDE and -SHIP from Old English to Modern English, concluding that they are the result of a process of lexicalisation rather than grammaticalisation. For the influence of French and Latin on the English lexicon see Dalton-Puffer (1996: 7), Ciszek (2008: 109), Trips (2014: 385).

domains (Pahta 2001: 213). However, there existed "extensive intermarriage, [as] the social elite had generally learned both languages [English and French], while descendants of the pre-1066 native population among the literate classes, especially tonsured clerks, administrators, and scribes, had acquired French via the educational system, which used French as a medium language" (Ingham 2011: 95). In terms of speech, it has been claimed that within Britain, "scarcely 1 per cent of ordinary people knew French" (Lloyd 2007: 13), and Durkin (2014: 224) observes that even though the Norman Conquest was the first step in the process, "it is also important to realize that [. . .] some of the word-forming elements that entered English from Latin and French did not become fully productive in English until the early Modern period". Therefore, speech seems to be less implicated in French nominal suffix adoption into English than the fifteenth-century practice of mixed-language writing, as demonstrated by Schendl (chapter 11).

2 Corpus and data retrieval

The timespan covered is 1420–1681 (Table 16.1); suffixes dated before 1420 have not been included due to their scarcity.

Table 16.1: The *Parsed Corpus of Early English Correspondence.*

PCEEC	
Historical period	**Tokens**
1420–1499 (M4)	364,317
1500–1569 (E1)	309,220
1570–1639 (E2)	910,675
1640–1681 (E3)	555,415
Total	2,139,627

Source: *Parsed Corpus of Early English Correspondence* (1410–1681), text version. 2006. Compiled by Terttu Nevalainen, Helena Raumolin-Brumberg, Jukka Keränen, Minna Nevala, Arja Nurmi and Minna Palander-Collin, with additional annotation by Ann Taylor. Helsinki: University of Helsinki and York. Distributed through the Oxford Text Archive.

The items under study were retrieved by means of *AntConc 3.2.4* (Anthony 2014) and manual disambiguation was carried out in order to exclude tokens not acting as nominal suffixes (such as *head* as a simplex noun rather than a suffix, or *torment* < Latin *tormentum*, where the derivational suffix was added in antiquity to the root of *torquēre* 'to twist', rather than to a root **tor-*). After the disambiguation process, the corpus amounted to 25,437 nominal suffix tokens. In order to calculate the morphological productivity of the suffixes, suffix spellings were normalized with *VARD*, i.e. *VARiant Detector* (Rayson et al. 2007), so that the number of hapax legomena of each item in each period could be counted.

3 Distribution

Table 16.2 below shows the total number of tokens for each set of suffixes after the process of manual disambiguation. English -NESS and -SHIP (5,439 and 5,382 tokens, respectively) and French -ATION (5,678 tokens) are the suffixes with the highest number of tokens in the corpus.

Table 16.2: Number of tokens of English and French nominal suffixes in the *PCEEC* 1420–1681.

	English suffixes				French suffixes				
	-DOM	-HEDE	-NESS	-SHIP	-AGE	-AL	-ATION	-AUNCE	-MENT
Tokens	525	225	5,439	5,382	1,464	497	5,678	2,878	3,349

Table 16.3 shows that over the time-period (1420–1681) -DOM, -NESS and -SHIP increased and -HEDE decreased. -DOM, -HEDE and -NESS reached their highest distributions 1500–1569 (*n.f.* 36.2, 12.3 and 423.3, respectively), -SHIP following later, 1570–1639 (*n.f.* 318.7).[2] After these distribution peaks the native suffixes underwent

Table 16.3: Diachronic distribution of English nominal suffixes 1420–1681 (*n.f.*).

	M4		E1		E2		E3	
	Raw	n.f.	Raw	n.f.	Raw	n.f.	Raw	n.f.
-DOM	35	9.6	112	36.2	207	22.7	171	30.8
-HEDE	83	22.8	38	12.3	80	8.8	24	4.3
-NESS	289	79.3	1,309	423.3	2,312	253.9	1,529	275.3
-SHIP	903	247.9	912	294.9	2,902	318.7	665	119.7

2 *n.f.* stands for normalized figures to one instance per 100,000 words.

a drop. By the end of the period -NESS and -SHIP were the most widely-used English-origin suffixes (*n.f.* 275.3 and 119.7, respectively).

Of the French-etymology suffixes, as Table 16.4 shows, the normalized frequencies reveal -MENT, -ATION and -AUNCE to have been the most widely-used suffixes (*n.f.* 124.9, 104 and 101 in the period 1420–1499, respectively). -MENT, -ATION, -AUNCE and -AGE remained the most frequent suffixes, although -MENT, -ATION and -AUNCE decreased towards the end of the period, with -AL spreading after 1639 but with a marginal distribution as compared to the other four French suffixes.

Table 16.4: Diachronic distribution of French nominal suffixes 1420–1681 (*n.f.*).

	M4		E1		E2		E3	
	Raw	**n.f.**	**Raw**	**n.f.**	**Raw**	**n.f.**	**Raw**	**n.f.**
-AGE	190	52.2	198	64	618	67.9	458	82.5
-AL	8	2.2	45	14.6	225	24.7	219	39.4
-ATION	379	104	1,071	346.4	2,512	275.8	1,716	309
-AUNCE	368	101	437	141.3	1,454	159.7	619	111.4
-MENT	455	124.9	572	185	1,512	166	810	145.8

Figure 16.1 shows the diachronic development of these groups as a whole. At the beginning of the period the French and English-derived nominal suffixes had a balanced distribution, the French-derived suffixes slightly predominating (*n.f.* 359.6 and 384.3, respectively), with both groups increasing until 1569 (the end of period E1), after which the English nominal suffixes minimally outnumbered the French ones (*n.f.* 766.8 over 751.2, respectively), but differences of usage remained

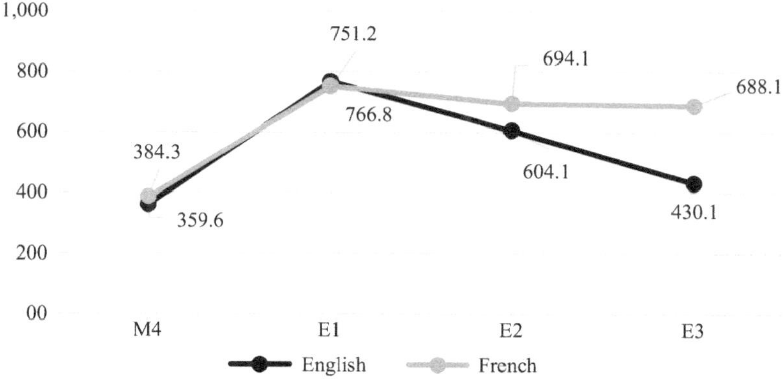

Figure 16.1: English vs. French nominal suffixes over the period 1420–1681 (*n.f.*).

minimal. However, from this point onwards, English and French-derived nominal suffixes followed distinct distribution paths: the use of French suffixes remained fairly stable until the end of the period (from *n.f.* 751.2 to 688.1 over the period 1500–1681), but the distribution of the English suffixes suffered a fairly sharp decrease (from *n.f.* 766.8 to 430.1 over the period 1500–1681).

4 Morphological productivity

Morphological productivity is defined by Plag (2003: 44) as the "property of an affix to be used to coin new complex words". Different approaches include type-token ratio (Kettunen 2014) and potential productivity (Baayen 1992, 1993). The type-token ratio (TTR) is the most common method of measuring lexical diversity, calculated as the division of the number of types by the number of tokens in a corpus (Kettunen 2014: 223). Here, TTR will be calculated by dividing the number of types of a particular nominal suffix (V_i) by the number of tokens corresponding to those types (N_i), as in (1):

(1) $TTR = V_i/N_i$

The potential productivity (P_P) of a morphological feature provides a trustworthy estimation of the "probability that new types will be encountered when the analysed corpus is increased" (Baayen 1992: 115–119). Thus, the (P_P) is the ratio between the number of hapax legomena with a given suffix (n_1) and the total number of tokens with that suffix in a corpus (N), as in (2):

(2) $P_P = n_1/N$

4.1 Morphological productivity 1420–1499

Tables 16.5 and 16.6 display the normalized frequency of hapax legomena ($HL_{n.f.}$),[3] the type/token ratio (TTR) and the potential productivity (P_P) of English and French suffixes, respectively. On quantitative grounds, these three are reliable

3 Hapax legomena are considered to have been neologisms, therefore, the number of hapax legomena (normalized to tokens per 100,000 words for the sake of comparison) in each period represents the number of neologisms in that particular period, that is, words that appear for the first time in our data.

Table 16.5: Morphological productivity of English suffixes in 1420–1499.

	M4		
	$HL_{n.f.}$	TTR	P_P
-DOM	1.4	0.14	0.14
-HEDE	1.4	0.1	0.06
-NESS	13.7	0.2	0.17
-SHIP	6.6	0.03	0.03

Table 16.6: Morphological productivity of French suffixes 1420–1499.

	M4		
	$HL_{n.f.}$	TTR	P_P
-AGE	5.8	0.16	0.11
-AL	1.1	0.63	0.5
-ATION	14.5	0.18	0.14
-AUNCE	12.9	0.14	0.13
-MENT	9.9	0.09	0.08

indicators of the morphological productivity of the suffixes and show the impact that the set of French suffixes had on their English counterparts. In the period 1420–1499, -NESS was the most productive, followed by -DOM and -HEDE.[4]

Table 16.6 shows that of the French-derived nominal suffixes, -AL was the most productive, followed by -ATION, -AUNCE, -AGE and -MENT.[5] -ATION and -AUNCE were the French-derived suffixes with the highest number of coinages in the period.

Focusing on individual suffixes irrespective of their etymology, -AL was the most productive suffix 1420–1499, followed by -NESS, -DOM, -ATION and -AUNCE. A

4 The number of hapax legomena is revealing inasmuch as it indicates the level of coinage of each suffix. If this indicator is observed in Table 16.5, it is found that -SHIP, the least productive English suffix 1420–1499 (P_P=0.03), is at the same time the second suffix with more hapax legomena in the period (*n.f.* 6.6).

5 P_P measures the ratio of hapax legomena with respect to the number of tokens of a particular suffix. This means that even though -AL is not the most occurrent nominal suffix in the period, it presents the highest score in the morphological productivity test.

comparison of productivity of both groups (Figure 16.2) shows that French suffixes were twice as productive as English suffixes 1420–1499. This chimes with Durkin's (2014: 224) observation cited above, that certain suffixes derived from "Latin and French did not become fully productive in English until the early Modern period" – or, here, the end of the Middle English period – that is, long after Anglo-Norman stopped being a spoken mother-tongue in England. The explanation for this seeming paradox is that these French suffixes resulted from the decades of mixed-language writing which preceded the spread of supralocal English varieties. Mixed-language consisted of a Latin matrix containing vocabulary from English and Anglo-Norman produced in Britain – that is, a variety of Anglo-Norman that was itself influenced by English. It was abandoned altogether in the later fifteenth century (see Wright (2011, 2017)). When written monolingual Anglo-Norman was abandoned in the first quarter of the fifteenth century, English filled its empty slot (see Stenroos, chapter 2). This English took over the characteristics of the Anglo-Norman it was replacing, including -AL, -ATION and -AUNCE.

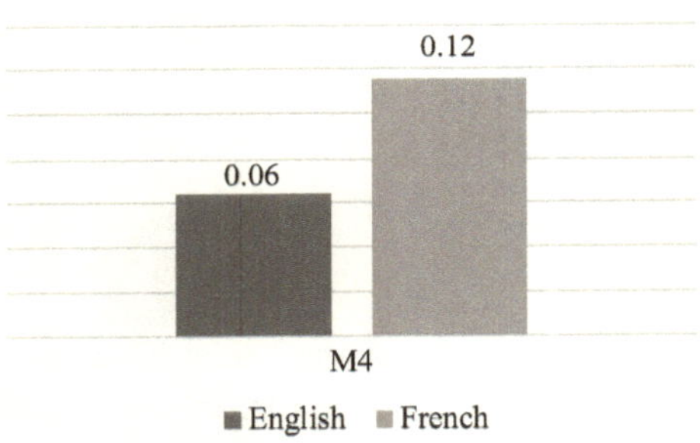

Figure 16.2: P_P of English and French nominal suffixes 1420–1499.

4.2 Morphological productivity 1500–1681

-HEDE was the most productive English-derived nominal suffix in 1500–1681, followed by -NESS, -SHIP and -DOM (Table 16.7). In spite of these figures, however, -NESS and -SHIP were the suffixes with the greatest contribution to the English lexicon, as their number of hapax legomena in each subperiod shows.

With regard to the French-derived set of nominal suffixes, -AL was the most productive until 1569, followed by -ATION and -MENT (Table 16.8). After that, -ATION was the most productive suffix, followed by -MENT, -AUNCE and -AGE. The suffixes with the highest scores in the potential productivity test are also the ones which contributed more to the English lexicon 1500–1681 (-ATION, -MENT and -AUNCE).

Table 16.7: Morphological productivity of English suffixes 1500–1681.

	E1			E2			E3		
	$HL_{n.f.}$	TTR	P_P	$HL_{n.f.}$	TTR	P_P	$HL_{n.f.}$	TTR	P_P
-DOM	1.9	0.06	0.05	0.7	0.03	0.03	0.9	0.04	0.03
-HEDE	1.3	0.13	0.11	0.9	0.11	0.10	1.1	0.25	0.25
-NESS	21	0.06	0.05	22.2	0.10	0.09	31.9	0.13	0.12
-SHIP	5.2	0.02	0.02	3.7	0.01	0.01	3.4	0.03	0.03

Table 16.8: Morphological productivity of French suffixes 1500–1681.

	E1			E2			E3		
	$HL_{n.f.}$	TTR	P_P	$HL_{n.f.}$	TTR	P_P	$HL_{n.f.}$	TTR	P_P
-AGE	5.5	0.15	0.09	3.8	0.09	0.06	5.8	0.11	0.07
-AL	2.6	0.22	0.18	1.3	0.07	0.05	2.5	0.09	0.06
-ATION	47.9	0.18	0.14	23.5	0.13	0.09	27.9	0.17	0.09
-AUNCE	16.5	0.13	0.12	8.6	0.06	0.05	8.3	0.13	0.07
-MENT	19.1	0.12	0.10	11.6	0.09	0.07	13.1	0.12	0.09

Figure 16.3 shows the potential productivity of English and French nominal suffixes 1500–1681. Three different stages can be distinguished: (1) French nominal suffixes are far more productive than their English counterparts 1500–1569;

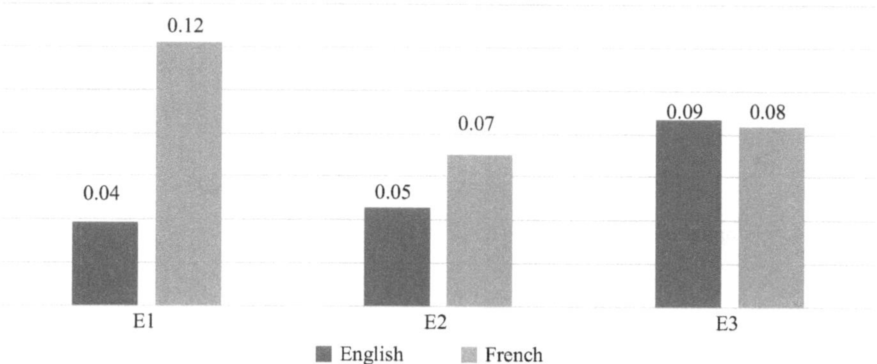

Figure 16.3: P_P of English and French nominal suffixes 1500–1681.

(2) both sets of nominal suffixes were more or less balanced in the period 1570–1639, albeit the French ones were still more productive; (3) both sets of nominal suffixes were even more balanced in the period 1640–1681.

5 Sociolinguistic analysis

Usage by different social groups in a given society contributes to the diffusion of linguistic innovations (Conde-Silvestre and Calle-Martín 2015: 67), so this section considers the informants of the corpus in order to ascertain whether social factors had any effect on choice of nominal suffix.

5.1 Age

The age of the informants reveals the group that used English suffixes most.[6] Figure 16.4 shows the percentages of English nominal suffix users grouped according to age, 1420–1681. There is no real discernible pattern, other than that English nominal suffixes were used least by the eldest and the youngest.

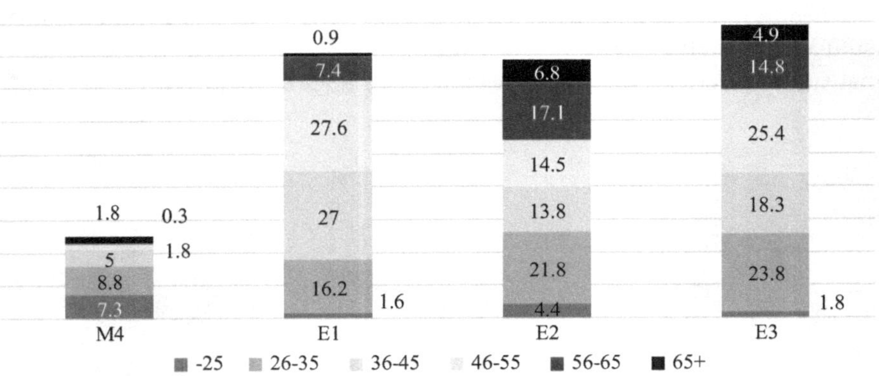

Figure 16.4: Informants' age and English nominal suffix usage (%).

6 Figures 16.4 and 16.5 do not include percentages corresponding to those informants with no biographical information.

The distribution of French-derived nominal suffixes across the age groups is found to be broadly similar (Figure 16.5), with people of middle years using them most.

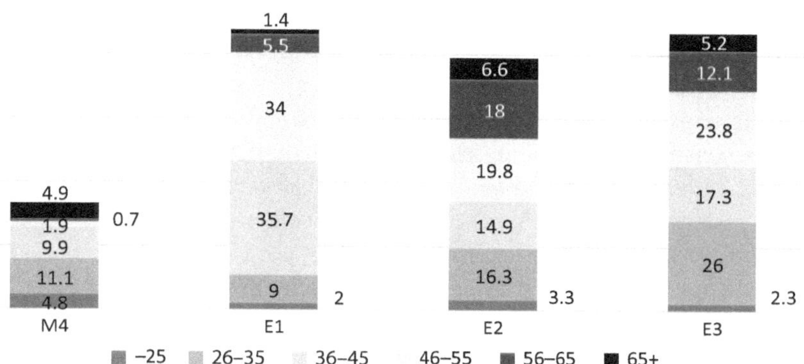

Figure 16.5: Informants' age and French nominal suffix usage (%).

5.2 Social class

The data has been divided into four different social groups (Table 16.9), based on the models proposed by Nevalainen and Raumolin-Brunberg (2003: 136–137: see also Nevalainen 1996: 58; Nevalainen and Raumolin-Brunberg 1996).

Table 16.9: Social stratification (adapted from Nevalainen 1996: 58).

Social group	Members belonging to the group
Nobility	Royalty, Duke, *Archbishop*, Marquess, Earl, Viscount
Gentry	Baron, Baronet, Knight, *Bishop*, Esquire, Gentleman, *Clergyman*
Professionals	Army Officer, Government Official, Lawyer, Medical Doctor, Teacher, etc.
Non-gentry	Merchant, Husbandman, Craftsman, Labourer, Cottager, etc.

When distinguishing social ranks in Early Modern English society, the gentry is usually subclassified into upper gentry (baronet, *bishop*, knight) and lower gentry (squire, gentleman, *clergyman*); however, no significant sociolectal difference was detected between these two subgroups in the use of nominal suffixes and therefore the gentry has been treated as a single group. Members of the clergy have been integrated (in italics) into the social groups to which they belong, rather than being treated seperately. Present-day studies suggest that linguistic innovators are usually found neither in the upper nor in the lower end of the social hierarchy but are located in the upper working class and the lower middle class, i.e. the groups that are more centrally located within the social hierarchy (Labov 1972: 294–295). This seems to have been the case historically also. For example, Nevalainen (2000) identified lawyers as the promoters of single as opposed to multiple negation, and Conde-Silvestre and Hernández-Campoy (2004) also demonstrated that the diffusion of incipient standard spellings in the fifteenth century were due to the role of lawyers. Lawyers are included in the group of Professionals in Nevalainen's social stratification chart given in Table 16.9, that is, neither the topmost group (the nobility) nor the lowest (the non-gentry). Figure 16.6 shows that English-derived nominal suffixes were used most by the middle-ranking groups, especially by the end of the period, but usage is fairly evenly distributed with the exception of the non-gentry, who used English-derived suffixes least.

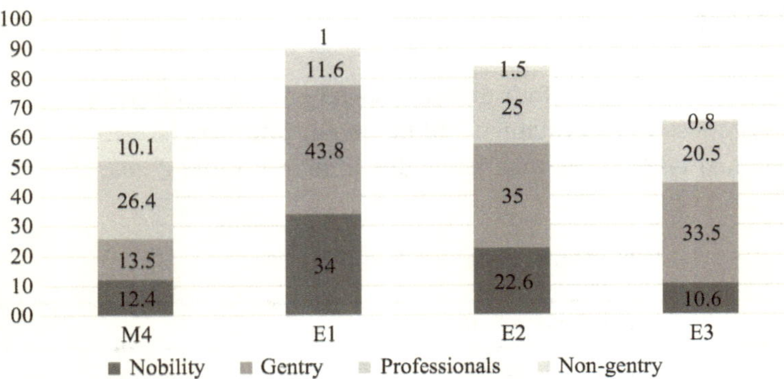

Figure 16.6: English nominal suffix usage according to social class 1420–1681 (%)[7].

By contrast, when it comes to writing French suffixes, a different panorama finally opens up. In Figure 16.7 the gentry is seen to have dominated, and the non-gentry are now visible as suffix-users too (merchants, producers of mixed-language writing, are included in this group), with considerable take-up over

7 Figure 16.6 and 16.7 do not include the percentages corresponding to those informants with no biographical information.

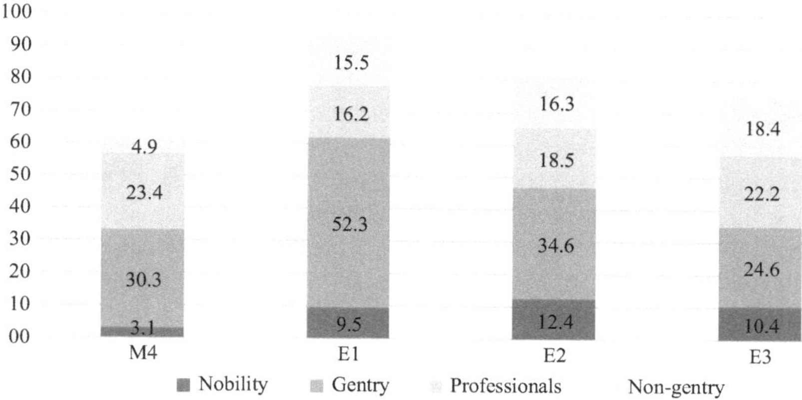

Figure 16.7: French nominal suffix usage according to social class 1420–1681 (%).

the fifteenth century. Commensurately, as lower social groups consolidated their usage of the set of French suffixes, the gentry's usage declined by half, from 52.3% in period E1 (1500–1569) to 24.6% in period E3 (1640–1681).

An interpretation of Figure 16.7 is that in 1420, French-derived nominal suffixes were mainly used in monolingual English by that sector of society which repeatedly wrote them in mixed-language contexts, the professionals and gentry. When Anglo-Norman was abandoned in the first half of the fifteenth century, monolingual English took over its empty slot and also many of its characteristics. When mixed-language dropped out of use in the later fifteenth century, written English absorbed its characterstics too – that is, French elements which had been integrated into mixed-language writing now became integrated into written monolingual English. Over the following two centuries, as English became the language of written record, French-derived suffixes were uptaken by the lower literate classes – who would largely have consisted of smaller traders and craftsmen, the lowest labouring classes remaining illiterate – so that French suffixes had become socially ubiquitous by 1570–1639 (E2). As the lower classes uptook them so the gentry abandoned them, allowing the hypothesis that these suffixes had become indexical of non-gentry writing and that the gentry were now distancing themselves. However, professionals continued to reach for Romance-derived suffixes when writing legal, medical, and bureaucratic text-types, and so the subset of French-derived nominal suffixes studied here went on to stabilise.

6 English v. non-English bases

The English set of suffixes was more prone to occur with English bases. Figure 16.8 provides the percentages of English suffixes occurring on non-English bases.[8] As shown, English suffixes -NESS, -SHIP and -DOM are found attached to non-English bases in proportions between 20% and 59% over the subperiods. -HEDE seems to have been more constrained, with proportions between 11.1% and 20%.[9] A comparison of the percentages from the beginning of the period to the end, 1420–1499 (M4) and 1640–1681 (E3), shows that English suffixes on non-English bases increased over the course of the Early Modern period.

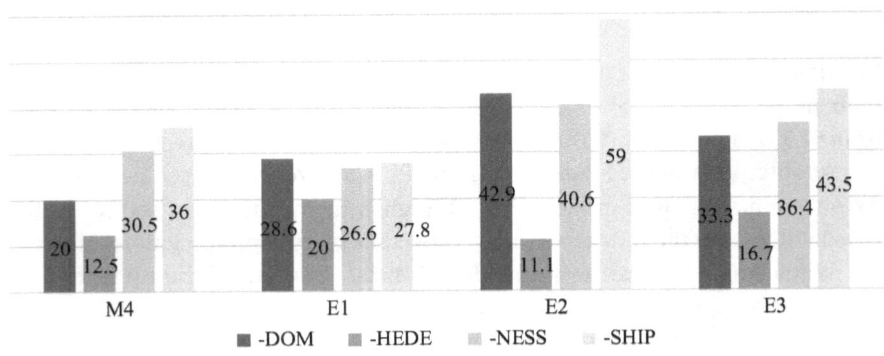

Figure 16.8: English suffixes attached to non-English bases 1420–1681 (%).

The proportions of English bases occurring with French suffixes are reproduced in Figure 16.9. These proportions represent the level of vernacularization of French suffixes as "(t)he application of a borrowed affix in native lexicogenesis is a mark of its assimilation by the native speakers of a language" (Miller 2012: 176). Figure 16.9 shows that -ATION was not yet vernacularized in our data, as there is no instance in which it is attached to an English base (-ATION was also found to occur with foreign bases only in Lloyd's study (2011: 195)). By 1500, -AGE and -AUNCE had become vernacularized, although data from PCEEC is scarce in this

8 The data in Figures 16.8 and 16.9 are based on the number of types of each of the suffixes.

9 In Ciszek (2008: 47–71), -HEDE is found to occur with 9 foreign bases and 5 bases that could not be classified, being ambiguous as to origin.

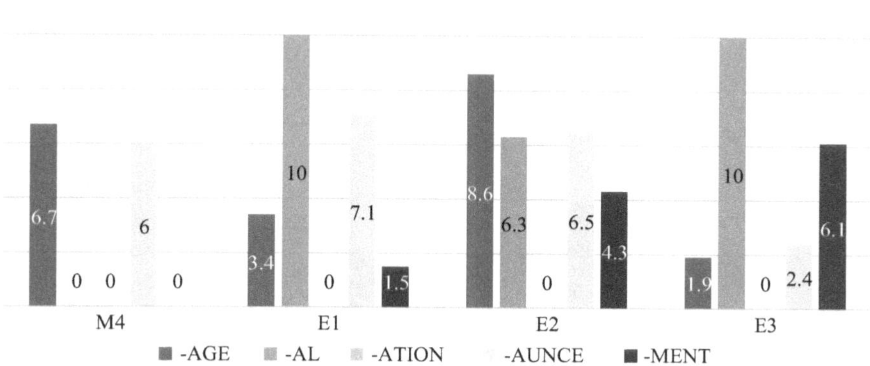

Figure 16.9: French suffixes attached to English bases (%).

period.[10] -MENT and -AL only occurred with English bases from 1500 onwards, being in this respect the last to vernacularise.[11] By the end of the period, 1681, -AL shows the highest percentages of occurrence with English bases.

The information in Figure 16.9 shows that the different French nominal suffixes were vernacularized at different points in time between 1420–1681. In order to get a more detailed account of these processes of vernacularization, the tokens of French suffixes occurring with English bases have been classified according to the social background of the informants, in order to identify the leading social group with regard to this practice. Figure 16.10 displays this classification.

Once again, the innovators were the middle social groups, the gentry and the professionals. Before 1499, the gentry and the non-gentry were the only groups to combine French suffixes with English bases. The phenomenon then spread among the others, although the professionals and the nobility followed different trends, with the proportions of usage by professionals rising towards the end of the period, but the rate of usage by the nobility decreasing over time. One explanation of these figures might be that the social classes who had used mixed-language writing in the fifteenth century remained linguistically adept, as it were, in the sixteenth and seventeenth centuries, uncoupling morphemes and reassigning them to new bases; whereas the more monolingual lower ranks, the non-gentry,

10 In the case of -AGE, the process of vernacularization had already started in early Middle English, as shown by Ciszek (2004, 2008).

11 Lloyd (2011: 195) accounts for instances where both -MENT and -AL are attached to 5 and 2 native bases in Middle English, respectively.

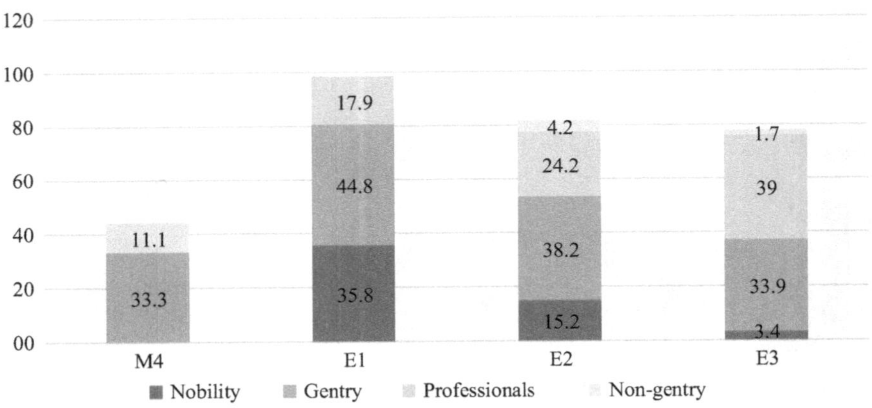

Figure 16.10: The use of French nominal suffixes on English bases classified according to social class (%).

although uptakers of French nominal suffixes as shown in Figure 16.7, may have taken over French-origin words fixed in their complete form.

7 Conclusions

This chapter surveys competition between English and French nominal suffixes (-DOM, -HEDE, -NESS and -SHIP vs. -AGE, -AL -ATION, -AUNCE and -MENT) in late Middle English and Early Modern English periods. The following conclusions have been reached:

In terms of distribution, the most frequent suffixes were -NESS and -SHIP and -ATION, respectively. The English-derived set of suffixes reached their highest distribution peaks between 1500–1569, with -NESS and -SHIP the most frequent English suffixes and -MENT, -ATION and -AUNCE the most frequent French suffixes. The distribution had levelled off by 1500, with English and French suffixes used equally until the late sixteenth century, after which use of English suffixes decreased.

The TTR and P_P were calculated in order to ascertain the level of morphological productivity of the items under study. In the fifteenth century, -NESS and -DOM were the most productive English nominal suffixes, and -AL, -ATION, -AUNCE -and -AGE were the most productive French nominal suffixes, with French suffixes as a group more productive in the fifteenth century. After 1500, -HEDE was the highest P_P scoring English suffix. With regard to French suffixes, two tendencies are detected: -AL was the most productive suffix until the end of E1 (1569), and -ATION took the lead from E2 onwards. If the P_P of both groups is compared, it can be seen that French nominal suffixes were more productive in the period 1500–1639, while English items obtained a higher score between 1640–1681.

The sociolinguistc analysis was divided into age and social class. With regard to age, it was found that the 26–35 age-group led the way with French-derived nominal suffixes, but that all age-groups apart from the youngest and eldest uptook them quickly, that is, between M4 (1420–1499) and E1 (1500–1569), which is to say, directly after the cessation of mixed-language writing. The comparison of suffix etymology and social class confirms that the gentry and the professionals were the social leaders in the diffusion of French-derived nominal suffixes, which points to business usage. The practice then spread to the neighbouring social groups, the nobility at the upper end and the non-gentry at the lower end, as part of the process of stabilisation and standardisation. The analysis of the etymology of the bases to which English and French suffixes were attached demonstrates that English suffixes were more versatile than their French counterparts, being combined with French bases prior to 1500. Here, the gentry and, to a lesser extent, the professionals were found to be responsible for their vernacularization.

In sum, with regard to the standardisation of English, this study of the spread of French-derived nominal suffixes -ATION, -AUNCE, -MENT, -AGE and -AL, as evidenced by the data in PCEEC, points to the demise of mixed-language writing in the later fifteenth century as a precursor to, and catalyst of, the diffusion of French-derived nominal suffixes into monolingual Standard English. This deduction is based on the picture provided by Figure 16.9, which shows that hybridisation of French suffixes onto English bases increased largely after 1500. Had the Norman Conquest alone been responsible for the incursion of French suffixes onto English bases, it would have been expected to have taken place within the French-speaking period, that is, influenced by the speech of those generations who still spoke French as a mother-tongue immediately following 1066. Rather, the dating here presented shows the influence of written mixed-language, where hybridisation of this sort was part of the mechanism of the text-type.

References

Adams, Valerie. 2001. *Complex Words in English*. London and New York: Routledge.
Anthony, Laurence. 2014. “AntConc 3.2.4: Computer Software.” Tokyo, Japan: Waseda University. http://www.laurenceanthony.net/.

Baayen, Harald. 1992. Quantitative Aspects of Morphological Productivity. In Geert Booij & Jaap van Marle, *Yearbook of Morphology 1991*, 109–49. Netherlands: Springer.
Baayen, Harald. 1993. On Frequency, Transparency and Productivity. In Geert Booij & Jaap van Marle, *Yearbook of Morphology 1992*, 181–208. Netherlands: Springer.
Burnley, David. 1992. Lexis and Semantics. In Norman Blake (ed.), *The Cambridge History of the English Language Vol. 2. 1066–1476*, 409–99. Cambridge: Cambridge University Press.
Ciszek, Ewa. 2002. ME -lich(e)/-ly. *Studia Anglica Posnaniensia* 38. 105–130.
Ciszek, Ewa. 2004. On Some French Elements in Early Middle English Word Derivation. *Studia Anglica Posnaniensia* 40. 111–19.
Ciszek, Ewa. 2005. The Development of-S(c)Hip(E) in Early Middle English. In Marcin Krygier and Liliana Sikorska (eds.), *Naked Wördes in English (Medieval English Mirror 2)*, 27–46. Frankfurt am Main: Peter Lang.
Ciszek, Ewa. 2006a. LME -ship(e). *Studia Anglica Posnaniensia* 42. 179–87.
Ciszek, Ewa. 2006b. -Dom in Medieval English. In Nikolaus Ritt, Herbert Schendl, Christiane Dalton-Puffer & Dieter Kastovsky (eds.), *Medieval English and its Heritage: Structure, Meaning and Mechanisms of Change*, 105–124. Frankfurt am Main: Peter Lang.
Ciszek, Ewa. 2008. *Word Derivation in Early Middle English*. Frankfurt am Main: Peter Lang.
Ciszek, Ewa. 2009. LME Development of EME Coinages in <hede>. *Kwartalnik Neofilologiczny* 56 (3). 321–327.
Ciszek, Ewa. 2012. The Middle English Suffix *-ish*: Reasons for Decline in Productivity. *Studia Anglica Posnaniensia* 47 (2–3). 27–39.
Ciszek, Ewa. 2013. The Suffix *-ish*: Its Semantic Development and Productivity in Middle English. In Laura Wright and Richard Dance (eds.), *The Use and Development of Middle English. Proceedings of the Sixth International Conference on Middle English, Cambridge 2008*, 129–143. Frankfurt am Main: Peter Lang.
Conde-Silvestre, Juan Camilo & Juan Manuel Hernández-Campoy. 2004. A Sociolinguistic Approach to the Diffusion of Chancery Written Practices in Late Fifteenth-century Private Correspondence. *Neuphilologische Mitteilungen* 105. 133–152.
Conde-Silvestre, Juan Camilo & Javier Calle-Martín. 2015. Zero *that*-clauses in the History of English. A Historical Sociolinguistic Approach (1424–1681). *Journal of Historical Sociolinguistics* 1 (1). 57–86.
Dalton-Puffer, Christiane. 1996. *The French Influence on Middle English Morphology: A Corpus-Based Study on Derivation*. Berlin, New York: Mouton de Gruyter.
Durkin, Philip. 2014. *Borrowed Words. A History of Loan Words in English*. Oxford: Oxford University Press.
Esteban-Segura, Laura. 2011. Suffixal Doublets in Late Middle English: '*-ness* vs *-ship*'. *Neuphilologische Mitteilungen* 112 (2). 183–94.
Huddleston, Rodney & Geoffrey K. Pullum. 2002. *The Cambridge Grammar of English*. Cambridge: Cambridge University Press.
Ingham, Richard. 2011. Code-switching in the Later Medieval English Law Subsidy Rolls. In Laura Wright and Herbert Schendl (eds.), *Code-switching in Early English*, 95–114. Berlin: Mouton de Gruyter.
Kettunen, Kimmo. 2014. Can Type-Token Ratio Be Used to Show Morphological Complexity of Languages? *Journal of Quantitative Linguistics* 21 (3). 223–45.

Kjellmer, Göran. 2005. Negated Adjectives in Modern English: A Corpus-based Study. *Studia Neophilologica* 77 (2). 156–70.
Labov, William. 1972. *Sociolinguistic Patterns*. Philadelphia: University of Pennsylvania Press.
Lloyd, Cynthia. 2007. From Denominal to Deverbal: The Suffix *-age* in Middle English. In Gabriella Mazzon (ed.), *Studies in Middle English Forms and Meanings (Studies in English Medieval Language and Literature 19)*, 145–64. Frankfurt & Main, Berlin, Bern, Brussels, New York, Oxford, Wien: Peter Lang.
Lloyd, Cynthia. 2011. *Semantics and Word-formation. The Semantic Development of Five French Suffixes in Middle English*. Frankfurt am Main, Berlin, Bern, Brussels, New York, Oxford, Wien: Peter Lang.
Marchand, Hans. 1969. *The Categories and Types of Present-Day English Word-Formation: A Synchronic-Diachronic Approach*. Munich: C. H. Beck'sche Verlagsbuchhandlung.
Miller, D. Gary. 2012. *External Influences on English from its Beginnings to the Renaissance*. Oxford: Oxford University Press.
Nevalainen, Terttu. 1996. Social Stratification. In Terttu Nevalainen & Helena Raumolin-Brunberg (eds.), *Sociolinguistics and Language History. Studies Based on the Corpus of Early English Correspondence*, 57–76. Amsterdam: Rodopi.
Nevalainen, Terttu. 2000. Processes of Supralocalisation and the Rise of Standard English in the Early Modern Period. In Ricardo Bermúdez-Otero, David Denison, Richard Hogg & Chris McCully (eds.), *Generative Theory and Corpus Studies: A Dialogue from 10 ICEHL*, 329–371. Berlin: Mouton de Gruyter.
Nevalainen, Terttu and Helena Raumolin-Brunberg. 1996. The Corpus of Early English Correspondence. In Terttu Nevalainen & Helena Raumolin-Brunberg (eds.), *Sociolinguistics and Language History. Studies Based on the Corpus of Early English Correspondence*, 39–54. Amsterdam: Rodopi.
Nevalainen, Terttu & Helena Raumolin-Brunberg. 2003. *Historical sociolinguistics. Language Change in Tudor and Stuart England*. London: Longman/Pearson Education.
Pahta, Päivi. 2001. Creating a New Genre: Contextual Dimensions in the Production and Transmission of Early Scientific Writing. *European Journal of English Studies* 5 (2). 205–220.
Plag, Ingo. 2003. *Word-Formation in English*. Cambridge: Cambridge University Press.
Quirk, Randolph, Sidney Greenbaum, Geoffrey Leech, Jan Svartvik & David Crystal. 1985. *A Comprehensive Grammar of the English Language*. London and New York: Longman.
Rayson, Paul, Dawn Archer, Alistair Baron, Jonathan Culpeper & Nicholas Smith. 2007. Tagging the Bard: Evaluating the Accuracy of a Modern POS Tagger on Early Modern English Corpora. In *Proceedings of Corpus Linguistics 2007, July 27–30, University of Birmingham, UK*. 1–14. http://ucrel.lancs.ac.uk/publications/CL2007/
Trips, Carola. 2009. *Lexical Semantics and Diachronic Morphology: The Development of -hood, -dom and -ship in the History of English*. Tübinger: Max Niemeyer Verlag.
Trips, Carola. 2014. Derivation and Historical Change. In Rochelle Lieber & Pavol Stekauer (eds.), *The Oxford Handbook of Derivational Morphology*, 384–406. Oxford: Oxford University Press.
Wright, Laura. 2011. On variation in medieval mixed-language business writing. In Herbert Schendl and Laura Wright (eds.), *Code-switching in Early English*, 191–218. De Gruyter Mouton: Berlin/ Boston.

Wright, Laura. 2017. On non-integrated vocabulary in the mixed-language accounts of St Paul's Cathedral, 1315–1405. In Richard Ashdowne and Carolinne White (eds.), *Latin in Medieval Britain. Proceedings of the British Academy* 206, 272–298. London: British Academy.

Zbierska-Sawala, Anna. 1989. On the Status of French Derivational Suffixes in Early Middle English. *Studia Anglica Posnaniensia* 22. 91–99.

Zbierska-Sawala, Anna. 1993. *Early Middle English Word-formation*. Frankfurt am Main, Berlin, Bern, New York, Paris, Wien: Peter Lang.

Joanna Kopaczyk

17 Textual standardisation of legal Scots *vis a vis* Latin

1 Latin and the standardising vernaculars

In this book on the development of Standard English in a multilingual context, a chapter on Scots – the other standardising Germanic language in the island of Great Britain in the medieval and early modern times[1] – provides a comparative background. The aim of this study is to shed light on the relationship between a standardising vernacular and the default omnipresent language of the public sphere – Latin. In medieval Scotland, as in England and elsewhere in Europe, Latin was the first language of legal record (Clanchy 1979; see also Melinkoff (1963) and Tiersma (1999: 19–27) for 'Law Latin' in England after the Norman Conquest). However, the Scots language took over the legal and administrative functions earlier than the vernacular down south. Scots had been present in Latin charters (Broun 2006, Broun and Tucker 2017) and emerged as a language of legal texts in the second half of the fourteenth century (MacQueen 2002). Unlike in England, Latin was the only language Scots had to compete with to take over the legal discourse wholesale.[2] As Barrow puts it, Scots was the sole vernacular in Scotland "which was sufficiently widespread, socially and geographically, to oust Latin save for solemn, ecclesiastical or academic purposes" (1997: 138). As an example, one may consider the process of vernacularisation in the unbroken record of civic

1 For selected general introductions to the history of Scots see McClure (1994), Macafee and Aitken (2002), and Millar (2012). The standardisation of Scots was not completed. The language came under pressure first from standardising English on the wave of socio-cultural developments which gained momentum in the late sixteenth century (the preponderance of English-language printed texts, the Reformation, the Union of the Crowns in 1604), and then from a largely standardised English prescriptive model after the Union of Parliaments in the early eighteenth century.

2 In England, the Statue of Pleading (1356) specified that legal proceedings should be carried out in English but recorded in Latin. The statute itself was written in French. See further in Melinkoff (1963) and Tiersma (1999: 28–34) on 'Law French' and legal trilingualism in England.

Note: I would like to extend my gratitude to Alpo Honkapohja for obtaining and sharing the images of the Cambridge MS Kk.1.5., and to the anonymous reviewers and the volume's editor for their constructive critique of the draft versions of this chapter. A version of this study was presented at the 11th International Conference on Middle English at the University of Florence (2019).

https://doi.org/10.1515/9783110687545-018

legal and administrative business conducted in the burgh of Aberdeen (Havinga 2020), although by no means was Latin completely gone from the record by the Early Modern period. Marshall McLuhan famously remarked that "print had the effect of purifying Latin out of existence" (1962: 228), but in the Scottish legal context Latin was used side-by-side with the vernacular even until the seventeenth century, as evidenced by the material consulted in this chapter.

This study traces the influence of Latin on Scots in medieval burgh laws. They constitute the earliest coherent body of legal regulations in Scotland, first compiled in Latin and copied for several centuries in this language, while simultaneously developing into a vernacular version. Since it would have been important to sustain the tenor of the law during its transmission through various manuscripts and through time, standardisation of the linguistic means by which the meaning was conveyed became desirable. Standardisation involves suppression of variation, and limits alternative readings, so it is justified to assume that legal discourse should favour this process in order to ensure stability and authority of the message. The question which immediately springs to mind in this context is what standardisation means across languages which are trying to capture the same legal meaning, and codify it for future dissemination. How did multilingual medieval scribes convey the same idea across time in the default language of the law, Latin? Did they draw on the Latin resources to construct the vernacular text of the laws? Did Latin contribute to the standardisation of the vernacular text?

To investigate these questions, this chapter compares selected Scottish burgh laws from six Latin manuscripts in order to extract the fragments of text that were already stable in Latin in terms of syntax and phraseology. Then the same laws from all eight extant Scots manuscripts are scrutinised to show exactly how the standardised Latin chunks were rendered across time in Scots. The vernacular manuscripts differ in this respect from each other; no two versions use exactly the same, standardised wording for the whole text of any given law. However, incipient textual standardisation can be discerned, which suggests a realisation on the part of the text compilers that an agreed version of the text would benefit the readers and users of the laws. After all, similar processes had already operated in the Latin versions.

The topic of the interaction between Scots and Latin in the development of early legal discourse in Scotland is complex. One should consider whether the scribes translated the same Latin version(s) of the laws, whether they copied previous Scots versions[3], whether each Scots version reflects a different engagement

3 Only one pair of the extant witnesses, Bute MS and Lumisden MS, has been recognised as an exemplar and a copy (see section 3. below).

(or the lack thereof) with the Latin text, and if it does, with which Latin text. Did the scribes have access to different Latin manuscripts which have not survived to our times? Did they know what had been standardised in Latin, and did it matter? These problems and questions are shared across vernacular legal cultures and are not easily answered – perhaps cannot be answered at all with certainty. This study uses a data-driven approach to trace the relationship between Latin and a medieval vernacular and provides a starting point for reconstructing the process of textual standardisation. The questions posed above can thus benefit from insights developed in an organic, text-centred way, while the findings can be used for informing comparisons across other European vernaculars, including English.

2 Textual standardisation in the language of legal texts

Typically conceived as a suppression of spelling variation and grammatical variation in historical texts (see e.g. Stein and Tieken-Boon van Ostade eds. 1993) and as a prescriptive codification of accent and grammar (Beal 2010; Tieken-Boon van Ostade 2008), linguistic standardisation[4] happens on all levels of language. It also happens on the level of *text*.

In structural terms, text is often seen as the highest level of linguistic complexity, situated above the level of the clause or sentence. However, it is a misconception to treat text simply as quantitatively larger than a sentence. Sentence fragments and even single words can be interpreted as text in appropriate circumstances, for example in public notices such as *No entry* or *Ladies* (Widdowson 2004: 6). When taken together to the level of text, the spelling units, morphemes, words, phrases and clauses build the overall potential meaning of the message in a cumulative manner. The final contextual interpretation of a message thus constructed is embedded in the surrounding discourse, which, in turn, makes text "a

4 In this chapter, I do not address the process whereby a version of a language becomes a 'standard language', or – in other words – is promoted to a non-regional prestigious position through a combination of various extralinguistic factors, e.g. cultural, economic, political or ideological (cf. Haugen 1966, Milroy and Milroy 1991 [1985]). This process may be referred to as *language standardisation*, and has been recently recast within Agha's (2003) enregisterment framework (Beal 2016). My interest lies in *linguistic standardisation* in the sense of suppression of variation on a specific level of the language system (for the conceptual division between the two types of standardisation, see Kopaczyk 2013: 42).

unit of language in use" (Halliday and Hasan 1976: 1). Elements of text may be similar or even identical in instances of text of the same kind. For example, it is conceivable to encounter the notices mentioned above in exactly the same linguistic format in many public spaces across the English-speaking world. It would make sense to see this as linguistic standardisation – after all, the intended meaning of barring entry or indicating that the bathroom facilities are dedicated to females could be expressed in a variety of ways. Still, this variation has been suppressed to a large extent and a standardised textual format has been arrived at.

It is also possible to see longer or shorter fragments of text recur in this way, while the rest of the text varies across its iterations. Consider the following linguistic choices recorded at the start of the entries concerning wrongful seizure of land, which may be found across medieval burgh court records in Scotland:

for ye wrangus haldyn fra him
for ye wrangus haldyn fra hir
for ye wrangus haldyn of ye land
for ye wrangus takyn of ye land
for ye wrangus takyn of ye landis
for ye wrangus takyn fra him
for ye wrangus takyn fra hir

In this illustration, the prepositional phrase fragment *for ye wrangus* 'for the wrongful' comes across as textually stable, while there is still some variation in the head of the noun phrase (*haldyn* 'holding' vs *takyn* 'taking') and the complementation patterns. It becomes clear that some fragments of text will be more prone to textual standardisation – defined above as suppression of variation – than others, and that these fragments do not have to be structurally complete, i.e. they do not have to be phrases. The question important for this chapter is whether textual standardisation of this kind in one language, be it of shorter or longer strings, can be prompted by the interaction with an earlier or co-existing version of the same text in a different language – in this case, in Scots and Latin, respectively.

Explicit interest in standardisation on the level of text is relatively recent in historical linguistics (Kopaczyk 2012, 2013) but the realisation that particular communicative events, which some scholars prefer to conceptualise as *genres*, are carried out within expected patterns goes back to Jauss's (1970) *Erwartungshorizon*, a 'horizon of expectations'. In literary criticism, that concept implies the existence of a set of rules, be it in relation to tropes, rhetorical tools, narrative structure, etc., which a writer has to follow in order to satisfy the definition of a given genre as understood by a particular interpretative community. People interacting by means of non-literary genres also have expectations as to the format and contents of the text. The departure from that expected format may invalidate the text and its purpose, especially in legal discourse where "highly codified, universally accepted interpretations" are preferred (Gotti 2012). Textual standardisation can thus be seen as a process which shapes genres into their expected form and ensures stability and authority. In a very mechanical way, the ultimate textual standardisation would result in all iterations of a particular type of text using exactly the same wording to achieve a given communicative aim. Unless copying directly from an earlier text, attaining this level of uniformity is practically impossible given the pressures put on the memory of the writer.[5] To aid the recall of expected formulaic structures, various guides to particular genres have been produced, from letter-writing manuals, to legal formularies. The inventory of Older Scots legal forms compiled by Gouldesbrough (1985) illustrates the range of document types which underwent textual standardisation (about one hundred genres, from *testament* to *extract decree of declarator of redemption*). These strictly regulated vernacular legal forms have a close relationship with their Latin counterparts and often co-existed with those.[6] The present study lays the ground for tracing this relationship by looking at texts at the core of early legal discourse – the laws themselves. Scottish burgh laws, dating back to the twelfth century, governed the life in early urban centres in Scotland and constitute the earliest collection of laws to be referred to in other records (Innes 1844: 32). The various administrative documents stem – directly or indirectly – from the application of those laws.

3 *Leges Burgorum* and *Lawis of burrowys*: Transmission of law across languages and time

The twelfth-century Scottish Lowlands were a scene of organised urbanisation, initiated by David I (1124–1153).[7] A feudal network of royal burghs with special trading privileges was set up as a source of revenue for the crown through burgage and other taxes (Duncan 1975: 470–477), with similar trends observable across

5 In speech, formulaicity is often aided by various mnemonic tools such as alliteration, rhyme, the use of binomials and other repetitive constructions. The links between orality and structural repetition in the language of the law form another fascinating research area, which falls outside the scope of the present chapter.

6 It is an unexplored area and a topic for further research on multilingual contexts for textual standardisation (also in a comparative perspective across different vernaculars and legal systems).

7 According to Fox, "there were 38 burghs in Scotland" at the end of the twelfth century (1983: 76). These were founded as royal burghs, then ecclesiastical and baronial burghs emerged. The numbers grew steadily to reach almost 200 by the end of the sixteenth century (Hall 2002: 7).

Europe – in Italy, Spain, the Netherlands, France and England (Innes 1868: xxi–xxxv). Customary oral legal codes most probably operated in the Scottish burghs before the emergence of a set of 120 laws,[8] put down in Latin as *Leges Quatuor Burgorum*, henceforth *Leges*, with the first extant manuscript dating back to c.1270 (see Table 17.2 below). Vernacular texts of the burgh laws co-existed alongside the Latin versions. The earliest extant manuscript containing the laws in Scots, is the Bute MS, dating back to the late fourteenth century (Taylor 2019: 49), henceforth *Lawis* (National Library of Scotland, henceforth NLS, MS 21246). In his comprehensive census of more manuscripts of legal literature in Scotland 1500–1700, Dolezalek (2010: 104) lists twelve more manuscripts containing the laws: eight have Latin and three have Scots versions, and one has both a Latin and a Scots version.[9] At the National Library of Scotland I tracked another three, which altogether gives eight extant manuscripts of this collection of laws, spread between the late fourteenth and early seventeenth centuries (see Table 17.1).[10]

Table 17.1: Catalogue details of all extant manuscript versions of *Lawis of ye burrowis*.

Reference label	Shelfmark	Date
ScA	NLS MS 21246**	la14c
ScB	NLS MS 25.4.15 (Adv. Lib. W.4.ult)	1455
ScC	NLS MS 25.5.7 (Adv. Lib. A.1.32)**	1470s
ScD	NLS MS 25.4.14 (Adv. Lib. W.4.28, Cokburn)**	la15c
ScE	NLS Acc 11218/5 (Adv. Lib. Fort Augustus A.1)	la15c
ScF	Cambridge MS Kk.1.5	la15c
ScG	NLS MS 7.1.9 (Adv. Lib. A.3.22, Malcolm)*	1560
ScH	NLS MS 7.1.10 (Adv. Lib. A.3.16, Lumisden)	1602

The earliest surviving witness of the *Lawis* (ScA) admittedly passed through the hands of John Skene, who consulted and heavily annotated it while working on the first printed version of the old laws, published in 1609 (Innes 1844: 181–182). As

8 The number and order of the chapters varies across manuscripts. Earlier oral vernacular legal practices shine through the Latin text which incorporates such specialised code-switched items as *twertnay* 'denial of culpability' (DSL *Thuertnay* n.) or *wrang et unlaw* 'a wrongdoing' (*Dictionary of the Scots Language*, henceforth DSL, *wrang* n., 3b; Kopaczyk 2011: 10–13).

9 Despite the title, some information in Dolezalek's census goes back to the fifteenth century. In his list of the burgh laws, the Cambridge UL Kk 1.5. (late fifteenth century) is split into two parts, both containing the Scots text.

10 In the discussion below, the reference labels from Tables 17.1 and 17.2 will be used. Manuscripts not listed as Scots in Dolezalek are marked with asterisks: double for a record missing altogether, and single for the MS listed as Latin only.

part of his preparations, a compilation of various legal texts, including the *Leges* (LatE) and the *Lawis* (ScH), was written in 1601–1602 by Skene's amanuensis who identified himself as Carolus Lumisden. He seems to have used ScA heavily in his rendition of the Lawis (Innes 1844: 208–209), which is confirmed by the results of this study (see especially section 5.6 and the Appendix).[11] At the start of the seventeenth century Latin still enjoyed authority in an increasingly vernacularised legal environment. Lumisden was clearly a bilingual writer in Latin and Scots, as was the scribe of NLS MS 25.4.14 (Cokburn, referred to in this study as ScD and LatB).

The two linguistic versions of the same collection of laws were compiled and accessed by bilingual professionals – scribes and early lawyers. It would then be justified to suggest that in the endeavour to establish the local language as an authoritative legal code *vis a vis* Latin, the practitioners drew on the Latin versions. It remains to be investigated how the laws were framed in the vernacular, to what extent the Scots *Lawis* were direct calques of the Latin *Leges*, how much cross-referencing was involved, what was left out, what was done in the vernacular differently and was missing from the Latin versions, and to what extent the emerging vernacular discourse norms relied on standardised Latin phrasing.

4 Interaction between Latin and Scots in the burgh laws

4.1 How do calques from Latin work?

For an earlier analysis of the relationship between the Latin and the Scots versions of the burgh laws, I created a database of the so-called points of contact between these two languages in the text of the laws. A point of contact is "any place in the text where the foreign-language version could have influenced a given linguistic choice in parallel fragments of the texts, containing the same meaning" (Kopaczyk 2011: 3).[12] The analysis of 120 chapters included in the parallel edition of the laws in Latin and Scots (Innes 1868), showed that calquing from Latin to Scots was the most prevalent strategy, accounting for 58% of the 607 types of language use influenced by the other language.[13] This number comprises: (1) direct calques (36%),

11 Interestingly, the versions of the *Lawis* in Lumisden's manuscript and Skene's print are not exact copies. In fact, the wording in the printed version does not seem to follow any previous manuscript (Kopaczyk 2020: 186–194).

12 Note that the influence went both ways.

13 Other types included borrowings and cognates.

where the meaning is rendered by direct lexical counterparts (adjusted the grammar of the language), e.g. L *bone fame* > Sc *gude fame*, L *ad curiam regis* > Sc *to the kingis court*; (2) incomplete calques (16%), where some Latin meaning is missing from the Scots counterpart, e.g. L *et nisi* 'and if' > Sc *bot gif*, L *leges et assisas burgorum* > Sc *law of burgh*; and (3) extended calques (6%), where the Scots version adds information to the Latin expression, e.g. L *duas uxores* > Sc *twa wyffis or ma*, L *ad puerum heredem* > Sc *till hyr chylder ayris*. In the discussion below, I will simply refer to all such constructions as calques. It should also be mentioned that Innes based his edition on a transcript prepared by Thomas Thomson for an antiquarian edition of the *Acts of the Parliaments of Scotland* (APS, Innes ed. 1844), and that the Latin version of the *Leges* in that edition was based to a large extent on the Berne MS (Innes 1844: 32, fn.2; see Table 17.2, LatA). Other scribes may have used different phrasing in places, a point which I take up in the next section.

Across the 120 chapters, the most frequent syntactic environment lending itself to a direct calque was a conditional clause. In Latin, the condition was introduced by means of several different strategies, which were, in turn, rendered in the vernacular in overlapping ways. Figure 17.1 presents the network of Scots and Latin translational equivalents.

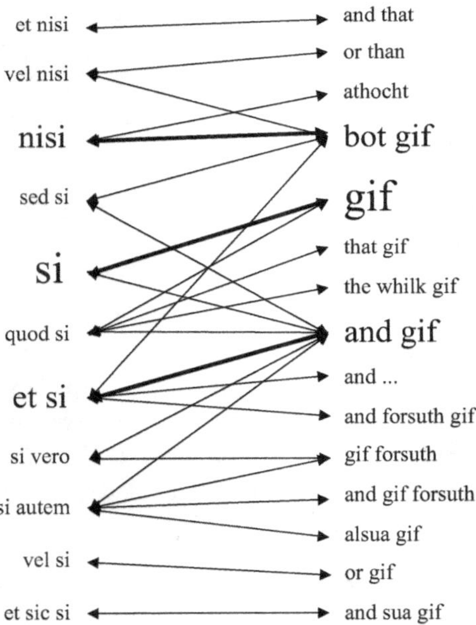

Figure 17.1: Latin conditional conjunctions in the *Leges Burgorum* and their Scots counterparts (based on Innes ed. 1844).

Across 120 chapters there were 134 conditional structures introduced in Latin by one of the expressions in the left column in Figure 17.1. The scribes utilised a range of stylistic variants, and only the infrequent ones had a single translational equivalent, e.g. L *vel si* > Sc *or gif*. The more popular ways of introducing a conditional clause could be rendered in Scots in multiple ways, e.g. L *si autem* prompts in the Scots version *and gif*, *gif forsuth*, *and gif forsuth* and *alsua gif*. One could interpret this stylistic variation as a lack of standardisation on the level of text; in other words, the scribes seem to be testing out various vernacular ways of rendering a Latin conditional clause. However, there are also traces of textual standardisation to be found in this material. By far the most frequent pairing was L *si* > Sc *gif* 'if' (63 tokens), followed by L *et si* > Sc *and gif* (20 tokens) and L *nisi* > Sc *bot gif* 'but if' (17 tokens). These are direct translational equivalents and seem to have been preferred by the compilers of the Scots versions of the laws over more impromptu translations.

4.2 Textual standardisation in Latin witnesses

Standardisation is a gradual process, presupposing more variation in patterns at the start and less variation towards the end of the investigated period. Ideally, one should be able to consult a range of contemporary versions of the same text at different points on the timeline, to compare the ratios of variation across time. Unfortunately, the material examined in this chapter is limited to a handful of manuscripts, both in Latin and in Scots, whose textual transmission and copying history is not straightforward. It is thus impossible to assess the degree of synchronic variation in the text. For this reason, the manuscripts will be treated collectively as equally important versions of the same text. Whenever the versions agree in the wording, an instance of textual standardisation can be postulated, assuming that the Latin versions show more similarities across the board than the Scots versions.

For a close-up on the textual stability in Latin I have selected four chapters of the *Leges* that have been previously been identified as containing calques from Latin in the Scots versions. These chapters concern various legal matters arising in medieval burghs:

a) Chapter 17: This law concerns the types of fines and taxes which could or could not be imposed by the burgh. The Latin versions vary quite substantially, mainly because the text incorporates Scots legal concepts:[14] *blodewit* 'a

14 These spellings are taken from the *APS* edition (Innes ed. 1844), as they vary across the manuscript witnesses, see the discussion of *stingisdint* below.

fine for bloodshed', *styngisdynt* 'a fine for assaulting someone with a wooden weapon', *merchet* 'a payment for marrying off the daughter of a tenant' and *herieth* 'the value of the best living animal', which appear in various orders, spellings, and may not all be present across the Latin manuscripts.

b) Chapter 23:[15] This law pertains to the inheritance of the house after the death of the tenant and resolves potential disputes between the heir and the widow.
c) Chapter 27: This law relates to the yearly payment of burgh rent, which every burgess was obliged to pay, in addition to building inhabitable property on his plot of land. However, there was an exemption in the first year, called *kirseth*, as stated by this law, which also specified further extenuating conditions for not building on the land.
d) Chapter 33: In case of overdue payment for debt, the burghs could seize goods or property, unless four mitigating circumstances were at work, as specified by this law.

The chapters were collated across six manuscripts representing a diachronic transmission of the laws in Latin. For comparison, I added the text prepared by Thomson for the *APS* (LatG, Innes ed. 1844). That edited version became the usual point of reference for anyone consulting the *Leges* (in both Latin and Scots), as the order of chapters varied among witnesses. Table 17.2 gives the details of the sources chronologically and assigns alphabetical labels which will be used in the remainder of the chapter for ease of reference.

Table 17.2: Latin versions of the *Leges Burgorum* consulted for this study.

Reference labels	Shelfmark	Date
LatA	NRS MS PA5/2 (Berne MS)	late 13c
LatB	NLS MS 25.4.14 (Adv. Lib. W.4.28, Cokburn)	late 15c
LatC	NLS MS 25.4.12	16c
LatD	NLS MS 25.5.9 (Adv. Lib. A.7.25, Bannatyne)	1520
LatE	NLS MS 7.1.10 (Adv. Lib. A.3.16, Lumisden)	1602
LatF	NLS MS 25.5.8 (Adv. Lib. A.2.20)	early 17c
LatG	APS (Innes ed.)	1844

In order to establish which parts of the Latin text were stable across witnesses and would offer a single wording to copy over to the Scots version, I used a free online collation tool Juxta Commons (Wheeles and Jensen 2013). The chapters were

15 This chapter is not present in one of the earliest versions of the *Lawis* (ScB).

diplomatically transcribed directly from manuscript and contained abbreviations, variant spellings and Scots words in the Latin text. These code-switched items showed substantial variation in form, e.g. the Scots term *stingisdint* 'an assault with a wooden weapon' becomes in the Latin versions: *stenges dint* (LatA), *steig(is) dynt* (LatB), *steingidint* (LatC), *styng(is) dynt* (LatD), *stangis dynne* (LatE), *stengis dint* (LatF), cf. *styngisdynt* in the Latin printed version (G). Since the interest of this study is not spelling variation in medieval Latin, I streamlined the text to achieve spelling consistency.[16] The transcripts were uploaded into Juxta Commons and a comparison set was prepared, see Figure 17.2.

The heat map in Figure 17.2 reflects the degree of difference between (LatA), the oldest surviving Latin version of the selected *Leges*, and the subsequent versions (for details, see Table 17.2). The darker the shading, the more the versions differ in wording at that location in the text. The differences may be of three types: additions, deletions, and alterations. Since our purpose is to establish the stable points of reference for the scribes who were creating the Scots versions of the text, the darkest strings can be disregarded as variable in Latin, and the focus should be placed on the white and lightest passages. The analysis below concentrates on whether these stable Latin chunks make their way into standardising legal discourse in Scots.

4.3 Comparing the *Leges* and the *Lawis*

The linguistically stable passages from the four selected chapters of the *Leges* – appearing as white and almost white in Figure 17.2 – have been juxtaposed with the text that carries the same information in the eight extant witnesses of the *Lawis* (see Table 17.1).The relevant chapters were transcribed diplomatically from manuscript *in situ* and from digital images[17] and the correspondences between the Scots and Latin versions were established. All stable Latin fragments and their Scots counterparts are listed in the Appendix chapter by chapter. If the Scots version was the same across several witnesses (disregarding spelling and minor grammatical differences), the text from these manuscripts is given in the

16 Specifically, I expanded abbreviations, replaced vocalic <v> with <u> as in *vxor* > *uxor*, consonantal <u> with <v> as in *uiuus* > *vivus*, and <æ> (only used in LatF) with <e> (in accordance with all the remaining witnesses) as in *hæres* > *heres*.

17 The *litterae notabiliores* and superscript characters were retained but abbreviations and macrons have been expanded in parentheses for the ease of reading. NLS MS 25.5.7 (ScC) has two types of a lower-case *d*, however this palaeographic distinction is not relevant to the aims of this chapter. Omissions of irrelevant material are indicated by an ellipsis.

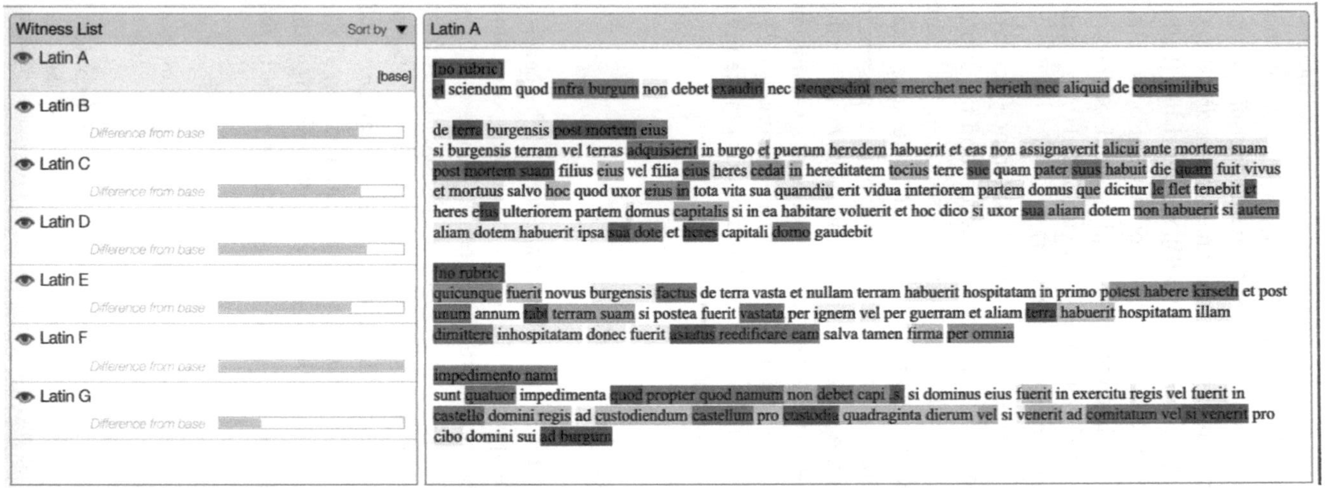

Witness List Sort by ▼

Latin A [base]

Latin B Difference from base

Latin C Difference from base

Latin D Difference from base

Latin E Difference from base

Latin F Difference from base

Latin G Difference from base

Latin A

[no rubric]
et sciendum quod infra burgum non debet exaudiri nec stengesdint nec merchet nec herieth nec aliquid de consimilibus

de terra burgensis post mortem eius
si burgensis terram vel terras adquisierit in burgo et puerum heredem habuerit et eas non assignaverit alicui ante mortem suam post mortem suam filius eius vel filia eius heres cedat in hereditatem tocius terre sue quam pater suus habuit die quam fuit vivus et mortuus salvo hoc quod uxor eius in tota vita sua quamdiu erit vidua interiorem partem domus que dicitur le flet tenebit et heres eius ulteriorem partem domus capitalis si in ea habitare voluerit et hoc dico si uxor sua aliam dotem non habuerit si autem aliam dotem habuerit ipsa sua dote et heres capitali domo gaudebit

[no rubric]
quicunque fuerit novus burgensis factus de terra vasta et nullam terram habuerit hospitatam in primo potest habere kirseth et post unum annum tali terram suam si postea fuerit vastata per ignem vel per guerram et aliam terra habuerit hospitatam illam dimittere inhospitatam donec fuerit asiatus reedificare eam salva tamen firma per omnia

impedimento nami
sunt quatuor impedimenta quod propter quod namum non debet capi .s. si dominus eius fuerit in exercitu regis vel fuerit in castello domini regis ad custodiendum castellum pro custodia quadraginta dierum vel si venerit ad comitatum vel si venerit pro cibo domini sui ad burgum

Figure 17.2: A Juxta Commons heat map of the degree of difference between the earliest extant Latin text of the *Leges Burgorum* (the Berne MS, here: Latin A) and subsequent versions.

Appendix in the same bullet point (with manuscript labels from Table 17.1). The consecutive bullet points are arranged to indicate similarities between the Scots versions, which means the order is not chronological (but it may well be). It is worth noting that some Scots manuscripts do not contain a passage directly corresponding to the Latin text, e.g. (1) has corresponding passages in all eight manuscripts, while (15) – in three. I come back to this point and offer a synthesis and discussion of emerging patterns below.

5 Discussion

If the Scots language of the laws were fully standardised at the time when the vernacular versions of the *Lawis* were being compiled, there would be little variation between the extant manuscripts. Just like a standardised opening of a letter or a benediction formula, the linguistic choices involved in transmitting the tenor of a particular law would have ideally been restricted to a single option. Clearly, this is not the case in the material consulted, see Appendix.

However, regardless of the variation, the impact of Latin on the word choices and syntactic structures is undeniable; the thirty seven fragments that were stable across the Latin witnesses are all attested in the Scots versions.[18] In other words, Scottish scribes did not invent the way of talking about a particular regulation from scratch but drew on the Latin text and strove to find the best way of capturing the same meaning, sometimes through a direct translation, and sometimes through adapting a given syntactic construction. There are also cases where more information is provided in the Scots version, as if the vernacular allowed for contextualising the law more than a generic Latin code. In the discussion below, I synthesize the specific strategies visible in the Scots material on the basis of the examples listed in the Appendix (example numbers in brackets). First, I present the instances of textual standardisation which were most likely prompted by the Latin text. Then I concentrate on the lexical choices and structural calques influenced by Latin in a substantial number of extant Scots manuscripts (four and above). The count of manuscripts sharing a pattern (regardless of spelling differences) is given, followed by the example number to be found in the Appendix. If the majority choice contrasts with only one manuscript which tackles the Latin chunk in its own way, that manuscript

18 In a few cases, although there were Scots versions of a given chunk in circulation, some individual manuscripts did not have a direct counterpart, see examples (15), (16), (17), (18), (21), (22), (26), (30) and (31). I discuss the omissions below.

is identified by its reference label from Table 17.1. Finally, I discuss the patterns shared across the Scots manuscripts which do not seem to have been prompted by the Latin counterparts. I interpret these chunks as instances of independent vernacular standardisation on the level of text.

5.1 Full textual standardisation due to Latin influence

Firstly, the selected laws contain passages where full textual standardisation seems to have taken place, as there is no variation across the Scots manuscripts from different places and periods. Out of thirty seven stable Latin fragments, five come up in the Scots material in exactly the same form: *sciendum quod* is rendered consistently as *(and) it is to wit* x8 (1), *et hoc dico* as *and . . . I say* x7 (19), *hospitatam . . . inhospitatam* as *biggit . . . unbiggit* x8 (DSL *big* v.1. to build) (29), *si dominus* as *gif . . . lord* x8 (33), and *si* as *gif* x8 (DSL *gif* conj. if, whether) (36). The latter two are a good illustration of the most common strategy in Scots for conveying condition, as suggested in the Latin text. It is noteworthy that performative constructions, even in the unusual first person in (19), were given a standardised rendition across the surviving witnesses.

5.2 Scots lexical choices influenced by Latin

Some stable Latin chunks promoted the same lexical choice across the a substantial number of Scots witnesses (at least four out of eight). There was one clear case of a stable equivalent passage containing a Latinate borrowing, close in form to the Latin prompt: *de* [+noun] *burgensis* rendered as *burgess* x6 vs *borow man* x1 (ScD) (3). In two other cases, the distribution of variants was more even across the Scots manuscripts: the Latin conjuction *salvo* rendered as *sauf* x4 vs *outtakand/outane yat* x3 (12), and the Latin *impedimenta* prompting *impedimentis* x4 vs *pointis* x3 vs *thyng(is)* x1 (ScD) (32). Thus, the direct lexical influence is rather limited and other cases of Latin influence are better described as structural calques.

5.3 Scots structural choices influenced by Latin

A few phraseological choices in the Scots material seem to be modelled on Latin. The binomial *vivus et mortuus* was given as *quyk and dede* x4 vs *leffand and ded* x1 (ScC) (11), so the structural frame was kept, and the lexical choices varied minimally.[19] The adverbial of time containing Latin *quam . . . die* was calqued directly as *that/the day* x5 vs *qwhill* x2 (10), the combination of a conjunction and a preposition forming the adverbial *et post* was rendered as *&/and eftyr* x5 vs *bot eftyr* x2 (26), the Latin *per ignem* was translated as *thru fyre* x5 vs *be fyre* 'by' x3 (28), while the Latin *vel* was typically rendered as *or* x4 vs *or eft(ir) yat* x1 (ScC) vs *or gyfe* 'if' x2 (35).

Several grammatical choices show prevalent tendencies across the Scots manuscripts in relation to their Latin counterparts. As for the verb phrase, the Latin present tense *adquisierit* prompted *gettis* x4 vs *has gottyn* x3 (4), and the Latin active voice *eas non assignaverit* was retained in *haf/has nocht assignit* x5 *vs he assigne to nane* x2 vs *lande be vnassignit* x1 (ScC) (7). Moving on to the noun phrase, the mass noun *terra* was treated as uncountable in the majority of cases: *of waste land* x5 vs *of a waste land* x3 (24). The Latin indicative pronoun *hoc* was most often retained as *yis* x6 vs *yat* x1 (ScB) (19), and the possessive *eius* was kept in the singular in the majority of Scots versions: *his* x6 vs *yar* x2 (33).

5.4 Textual standardisation regardless of Latin

The discussion so far has highlighted Latin influence in eighteen Scots contexts out of thirty seven corresponding stable Latin chunks, identified by the collation tool (cf. section 4.2., Fig. 17.2, and the list in the Appendix). The remaining nineteen contexts fall into two categories: either there was no prevalent variant prompted by Latin in the majority of Scots witnesses, or the prevalent variant was there, but it was not inspired by the Latin text. The latter option implies that textual standardisation was operating in Scots legal discourse regardless of the earlier, or indeed co-existing, Latin versions of the same laws.

The same lexical choices across four and more Scots manuscripts include *half of the hous* x4 vs *part* (as in Latin *partem domus*) x3 (14), *haue* x5 vs *joiß* x1 (ScG) (16), *morning gift* x4 vs *dowary* 'dowry' x3 (20), *maist(er)is / maister* (Gsg) x5 vs *lord(is)* x2 (37). Several scribes agree in their use of the preposition *within* x4 vs *in burgh* x3 where Latin has *in burgo* (5), and the preposition *till* x6 vs *to his ayre* 'to his heir' x1 (ScD) (6). The Latin conjuction *donec* 'till, as long as' was rendered as *quhil* x5 vs *quhil ye tym* x1 (ScB) vs *alß lang as* x1 (ScC) (30).

19 Two manuscripts (ScA and ScH) did not calque the binomial but used coordinated clauses. ScH is a copy of ScA, so their choices align in a vast majority of cases. Interestingly, in a non-binomial context, the preferred counterparts of the Latin *mortem* were *decess* x4 vs *dede* x3 (8).

In some cases, the Scots scribes chose the same grammatical construction where the Latin syntax lacked a direct counterpart. In terms of modals and auxiliaries, *sall* 'shall' x4 was chosen as frequently as *aucht* 'ought' x4 (2), and *he be* x6 was preferred over *he has* x1 (ScC) (30). In the noun phrase, where Latin had *puerum*, the indefinite article *a child* x6 was chosen over *ony child* x1 (ScD) (6), while for the Latin *uxor* in definite contexts the Scots scribes used *his wife* x4 vs *his spousyt wyfe* x3 vs (12), and *ye wif* x6 was preferred over *yat wif* x1 (ScC) (19). Complementation patterns around the verb *to buy* favoured *for (ye) bying of* [+NP] x5 vs *to by* [+NP] x1 (ScB) vs *for* [+NP] x2 (37), as in the Latin *pro cibo* 'for food'. In one case, four witnesses changed the temporal perspective carried by the Latin text: the original meaning in (8) foregrounded what the deceased had done with his possessions 'before' he died, and three manuscripts kept this reading, while four changed the focus to what should happen 'after' his death.

5.5 Shared additions, omissions, and alterations across Scots witnesses

There are also groups of manuscripts which alter the information available in the Latin text and do it by means of the same linguistic strategies on the level of syntax and in terms of lexical choices. In two cases more information was added in the majority of extant witnesses: in (1) four scribes added the conjunction *and* at the start of the chapter, while five scribes qualified the condition in (37) by mentioning that one had to dwell with the said lord (L *dominus*). Other lexical additions to the Latin text crop up in a few manuscripts but are not shared by the majority. These include: extending the noun phrase x1 (ScD) (5); adding a prepositional phrase *to nane* x4 vs *to na man* x2 (7); specifying whose property is talked about x2 (10); qualifying *domus* with adjectives: *head house* x3 vs *principal* x1 (ScC) (17); producing a binomial *wyn or duell* for Latin *habitare* x1 (ScD) (18); extending the conditional conjunction *si* to *and gif* x4 vs *bot and* x1 (ScE) (21); specifying *annum* as *yat ȝer* x4 vs *ye fyrst yhere* x3 (26); extending the meaning of Latin *in exercitu regis* 'in the king's army' to *in ye king(is) batall or in his ost* x1 (ScC) vs *in ye king(is) offys or(e) oste* x1 (ScD) (34). In a few cases, more information was added on the level of syntax in individual versions: the scribe of ScB added a short clause introducing the condition in (1), while ScD had the verb followed by a complement in *joys it aw* for *gaudebit* x1 (22).

Conversely, omissions of the content provided in the stable Latin fragments also happen across groups of Scots versions: reducing the Latin binomial to a single noun x6 (4); no mention of the hereditary context x4 vs *ayr(is)* as in Latin x2 (9); all manuscripts but two (ScA and ScC) rephrasing or omitting the relative pronoun Latin *quam* in (10); no mention of the condition that the widow shall remain a widow to exercise her right to the part of the house x4 vs as in Latin x3 (13); no mention of the Scots term for the inner part of the house (Sc *flet*) x4 vs x3 flagging the term as in Latin (15); finally, a counterpart of *et aliam* missing from all manuscripts (28). Some omissions were shared across fewer than four witnesses: no mention of land in the context of inheritance, simply calling it *heritage* x2 (10); no reference to the heir with regard to the other part of the house in three manuscripts (17) and their preference to live there (18); omission of the reference to enjoying the property x2 (22); no mention of the prerequisite of inhabiting the land, just possession x3 (25); Latin *postea* omitted from a conditional clause giving *and gif* x2 (27) – other manuscripts have some kind of adverbial of time, as mentioned above. Individual omissions are rare – only five such cases in the material: *oyir* 'other' on its own to render *aliam dotem* x1 (ScE) (21) while other manuscripts have two lexical options here; *burges* for *novus burgensis* in ScA and ScH (23)[20] while other manuscripts have a direct calque from Latin, the temporal adverbials in (26) and (30) missing from (ScF) and (ScE), respectively; and the conditional adverb in (31) missing from (ScB).

In a few cases individual scribes rephrased the Latin wording altogether: ScA and its copy ScH have a different wording and syntax in (3), ScG adapts the meaning of 'heir' as 'a child to all' (6), ScA and ScH rephrase the binomial as two clauses (11), ScG alters the meaning from the heir having the innermost part of the house to *ye heid hous* (17). These cases are rare, compared to the extent of shared practices elsewhere in the text.

5.6 Overall agreement between Scots versions

Even though the Scots manuscripts are not coeval – ScA has been dated to the second half of the fourteenth century, ScB, ScC, ScD, ScE and ScF come from the fifteenth century, ScG from 1560 and ScH from 1602 – they form tantalising clusters of similarity, see Figure 17.3.

Figure 17.3 captures the relationships between the Scots manuscripts of the *Lawis* as a Venn diagram (created with free online software Meta-Chart). The size of the circles represents the number of chunks directly corresponding to the stable Latin fragments identified above. The more a pair of manuscripts has in common, the closer they are arranged in the graph; with enough identical choices for

20 Note that ScH is a copy of ScA.

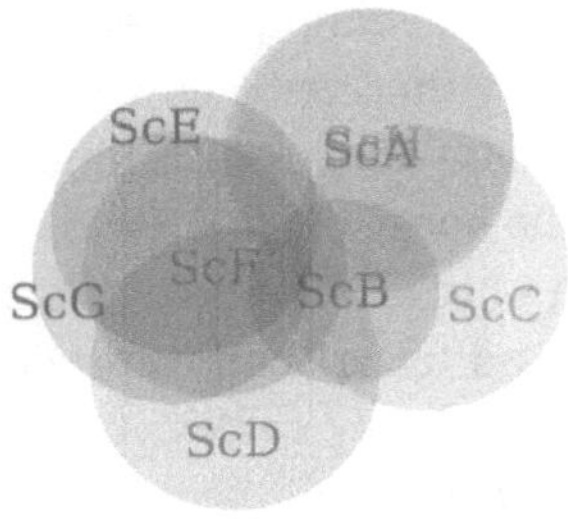

Figure 17.3: Similarities and overlaps between Scots manuscripts of the *Lawis* with regard to the corresponding stable fragments in Latin.

the Latin chunks, the circles start overlapping. It becomes clear that the surviving Scots manuscripts of the *Lawis* had various ways of carrying the same meaning and that full textual standardisation of that body of laws had not been achieved. In fact, no pair with the exception of ScA and its copy ScH, rendered the Latin material in exactly the same way; e.g. although very similar, ScE does not display exactly the same wordings, additions and omissions as ScF and ScG. It is unclear whether these manuscripts were copied directly from each other or from a missing exemplar. Even though we can observe budding textual stability across the witnesses, there are many differences between them also in the non-formulaic chunks, in the spelling, the ordering of the laws and their visual character (Kopaczyk 2020). It is possible that the scribes were working directly from the Latin text and transposing it into Scots on the go, perhaps with the help of an earlier Scots version, or inherited knowledge. As mentioned in section 3., the Latin and the Scots versions can be found within the same manuscript in two witnesses (LatB together with ScD, LatE together with ScH), which would support this theory.

6 Conclusions

The questions posed at the start are not straightforward to investigate. We know that multiple Latin versions of the laws existed alongside multiple Scots versions, we know that the scribes composing the texts were fluent in both languages, and we know that there are more differences in terms of phrasing the laws between the Scots manuscripts than there are between the Latin versions. In spite of these differences, the Scots texts do exhibit structural and lexical choices influenced by Latin. What we did not know, and this chapter is the first attempt to address this question, was whether these choices were similar across the vernacular versions, and whether the more stable Latin text of the *Leges* prompted textual standardisation in its vernacular counterparts. In other words, this study aimed to demonstrate how the local language of the laws – an innovative register at the time in any vernacular context – was being shaped through contact with the default pan-European language of the law – Latin.

The compilers of the Scots text of the burgh laws had to take decisions on how the transmission of binding legal provisions – from one language to another but also across time – was to be carried out. It is to be expected that care was taken to sustain the tenor of the laws, which, in principle, should remain stable during transmission. The detailed analysis of the mappings between the Latin text and the multiple vernacular versions confirms this assumption; only in rare cases was the Scots text incompatible with the Latin text in terms of the overall meaning.

Textual standardisation in the extant Scots witnesses is not complete. Figure 17.2 has shown overlaps between versions but no two versions were identical in their wording of the selected laws. However, stable Latin fragments have stable Scots counterparts (the same in 4–8 witnesses) in about 46% of cases (in this sample). The Scots versions show some degree of convergence, which can be interpreted as incipient textual standardisation, in several areas where the Latin witnesses all agree in wording. The performative chunks are stable across the witnesses and some syntactic and lexical choices inspired by Latin are preferred across multiple manuscripts. What is quite striking is that the same alterations, omissions and additions *vis a vis* Latin happen in the vernacular versions even though it is challenging to prove a direct copying link between the surviving material apart from ScA and ScH. The standardising passages in Scots which are not inspired by Latin could be the product of several factors working together, or separately: (1) the vernacular grammar – where Latin syntax is incompatible with Scots, (2) 'ways of saying things' inherited from earlier and/or co-existing oral legal practices, (3) stylistic preferences developed in Scots, and (4) copying traditions.

These findings point to the fact that Scots, as a vernacular undergoing functional elaboration in the medieval and early modern period, had its own means to produce seeds of textual standardisation. The people who produced the texts – scribes, clerks, notaries, and the communities of practice within which they operated – should be seen as the agents of linguistic standardisation on the level of text (as well as on other levels). The fact that they had Latin at their disposal alongside their vernacular(s), and that a pre-existing body of texts in Latin was available to them, created an environment where the resources and practices from one language could be replicated in the other. In this way, the Latin text provided a reference point but the local communities of practice developed further standardised 'ways of saying things' in the vernacular.

In other legal cultures and linguistic settings, e.g. in the south of England, these processes might have had their own peculiarities. Comparative research on textual standardisation is still pending. Essentially, however, the analysis of Scottish burgh laws in transmission provides an informative point of reference –

and a methodological case study – for similar research on the language of vernacular laws across Europe. The multilingual context and the impact of Latin on the genre will always have to be considered but it may well be that the textual stability is largely independent of Latin, as is the case in Scottish burgh laws.

Appendix

Chapter 17

(1) *sciendum quod*
– *It is to wyt* (ScA, ScB, ScH), *It is to vyt* (ScC)
– *And it is to wyt* (ScD), *And it is to wytte* (ScF), *And It is to wit* (ScE, ScG)

(2) *non debet*
– *acht no^{t} to be* (ScB), *aw noȝt to be* (ScC), *aucht nocht to be* (ScA, ScH)
– *sall nocht be* (ScD, ScF), *sall no^{t} be* (ScC, ScG)

Chapter 23

(3) *de* [+noun] *burgensis*
– *Off burgeß* [+noun] (ScC, ScG), *Off burges* [+noun] (ScE, ScF)
– *Off borow ma(n)nys* [+noun] (ScD)
– *Of* [+noun] *of a burges* (ScA, ScH)

(4) *si burgensis terram vel terras* [+verb]
– *Geyff aburgeß haß gottin land or land(is)* (ScC)
– *Gyfe aburges has gotyn ony land* (ScA), *Gyfe a burges has gotyn ony land* (ScH)
– *Gyff ye burges gettys ony lande* (ScD), *Gyff a burgeß gettis ony land* (ScE), *Giff a burgeß gettis ony land* (ScG)
– *Gyf a burges gett(is) ony land(is)* (ScF)

(5) *in burgo*
– *in burgh* (ScC), *in the burgh* (ScH), *in ye burgh* (ScA)
– *w^{t}in burgh* (ScE), *w^{t}in bur^{t}* (ScF), *wythin burche* (ScC)
– *within ye king(is) burgh* (ScD)

(6) *et puerum heredem habuerit*
– *and he hafe achylde tyl hys ayre* (ScA), *and he haue a chyld till h(is) ayre* (ScC), *and he haue a chylde till his aire* (ScE), *and he hafe a chylde tyl his ayre* (ScH)

– *and he haue a childe tyll ayre* (ScF)
– *ande he have ony chylde to ayre* (ScD)
– *and he hafe achild till aw* (ScG)

(7) *et eas non assignaverit*
– *and ye lande be vn assignit* (ScC)
– *and has no*ᵗ *assignit his land to nane* (ScE, ScG)
– *Ande hafe nocht assignyt his land(is) to na man* (ScD), *& haff nocht assegnit his landys to na ma(n)* (ScF)
– *and he assigne to nane* (ScA, ScH)

(8) *ante mortem suam*
– *befor h(is) destiß* (ScC)
– *before his dede* (ScA, ScH)
– *eftyr(e) his dede* (ScD)
– *eftyr his deceß* (ScE), *Eft(ir) his dysses* (ScF), *eftir his deceß* (ScG)

(9) *filius ... vel filia ... heres*
– *his son(n)e or doȝt(ir)* (ScC), *his sone or dochtyr* (ScE), his soin~ or docht(ir) (ScF), his son~ or docht(ir) (ScG)
– *his son~ or his docht(ir) ayr(is)* (ScD)
– *his ayre son or dochtyr* (ScA), *his ayre sone or dochtyr* (ScH)

(10) *hereditatem ... terre ... quam ... die ...*
– *all ye herytage ... ye quhilk ... yat day* (ScC), *ye h(er)etage ... y*ᵗ *day* (ScG)
– *ye heritage of all ye land(is) ... ye day* (ScD)
– *ye heretage of all of his fadir had y*ᵗ *day* (ScE), *ye herytage of all his fadre hayde yat day* (ScF)
– *ye eritage of al ye land ye quhilk ... qwhil* (ScA)
– *ye eritage of all ye land ... qwhil* (ScH)

(11) *fuit vivus et mortuus*
– *he vas leyffand and ded* (ScC)
– *he was quyk and dede* (ScD), *he wes quik and dede* (ScE), *he was qwheke and dede* (ScF), *he was quike and dede* (ScG)
– *he was in lyfe and qwhen he deid* (ScA, ScH)

(12) *salvo ... quod uxor*
– *outtakand yat h(is) spoussit vyff* (ScC), *Outetane yat hys spousyt wyfe* (ScA), *Outane yat his spousyt wyfe* (ScH)
– *sauff y*ᵗ *his wyfe* (ScD), *sauff y*ᵗ *his wyff* (ScE), *safe yat his wyfe* (ScF), *sauf y*ᵗ *his wife* (ScG)

(13) *tota vita sua quamdiu erit vidua*
- *all h(ir) lyff alß lang as scho Is vedow* (ScC), *al hyr lyfe als lang as scho is wydow* (ScA, ScH)
- *in all hir(e) lyfe* (ScD), *in all hyr liff* (ScE), *in all hire lyfe* (ScF), *In all hir life* (ScG)

(14) *interiorem partem domus*
- *ye Inn(er)mast part of ye howß* (ScC), *ye ennyr p(ar)t of ye hous* (ScA), *ye ennyr p(ar)t of ye house* (ScH)
- *ye e(n)n(ir)halfe of ye houß* (ScD), *the Inn(ir)half of the houß* (ScE), *the Innirhafe of the hous* (ScF), *ye Inn(ir) half of ye houß* (ScG)

(15) *que dicitur . . .*
- *yat is to say* (ScA)
- *ye quhilk is callyt* (ScC)
- *yat is callyt* (ScD)

(16) *tenebit*
- *sall haue* (ScC, ScE, ScF), *sal hafe* (ScA), *sall hafe* (ScD)
- *sall Joiß* (ScG)

(17) *heres . . . ulteriorem partem domus*
- *ye ayr ye Inn(ir) mast p(ar)t of ye p(ri)ncypall houß* (ScC)
- *his ayre ye vttyr p(ar)t of ye hede hows* (ScA)
- *ye ayre sall hafe ye toy(ir) halfe of ye hevyd houß* (ScD)
- *ye air ye heid houß* (ScG)

(18) *si in ea habitare voluerit*
- *gyfe he wyl dwel in it* (ScA), *geyff yat he vill duell in it* (ScC), *gyf he wyll dwell in it* (ScH)
- *gif hym lik(is) to wyn or duell yar(e) in* (ScD)

(19) *et hoc dico si uxor*
- *and yat I say geyff yat vyff* (ScC)
- *Ande yis I say gif ye wyfe* (ScD), *And yis I say gif the wyff* (ScE), *Ande y*[i]*s I say gyf ye wyfe* (ScF), *And yis I say gif ye wife* (ScG), *And yis I say gyfe the wyfe* (ScA, ScH)

(20) *dotem*
- *dowary* (ScB), *dowery* (ScA, ScH)
- *morwyngyft* (ScD), *mornyn gift* (ScE), *morowingeft* (ScF), *morowing gift* (ScG)

(21) *si aliam dotem habuerit ipsa . . .*
- *and geyff forsuth scho haue oy(ir) dowary* (ScC)
- *And gyfe scho has vthyr dowery* (ScA), *And gyfe scho has uthyr dowery* (ScH)

– *and gif scho has oyir(e) morwyngyft* (ScD)
– *bot and scho haue othis* (ScE)

(22) *et . . . gaudebit*
– *scho sal Ioys* (ScA), *scho sall Joyß* (ScC), *scho sall Joiß* (ScG), *scho sall joys* (ScH)
– *scho sall Joys it J aw* (ScD)

Chapter 27

(23) *novus burgensis*
– *new burges* (ScB, ScD), *nav burgeß* (ScC), *new burgeß* (ScG)
– *burgeß new* (ScE), *burges new* (ScF)
– *burges* (ScA, ScH)

(24) *de terra vasta*
– *of waist lande* (ScB), *off waste lande* (ScD), *of waist Land* (ScE), *of wast lande* (ScF), *of waste land* (ScG)
– *of awaste land* (ScA), *of a vast land* (ScC), *of a wast land* (ScH)

(25) *et nullam terram habuerit hospitatam*
– *and he haue na land* (ScE, ScG), *and he haff na lande* (ScF)
– *and he haf na land byggyt* (ScA), *& has na land biggit* (ScB), *& he haf na land byggyt* (ScH)
– *and he haue na land for-to duell in till* (ScC)
– *and he have na lande within ye burgh herberyt* (ScD)

(26) *et post . . . annum*
– *and eftyr yat yhere* (ScA), *& eft(ir) y*[t] *ȝer* (ScB), *and eft(ir) yat ȝher(e)* (ScC), *and aftyr yat yhere* (ScH)
– *And eft(ir) ye fyrst yher(e)* (ScD)
– *bot eftyr the first zere* (ScE), *bot eftir ye first zere* (ScG)

(27) *si postea*
– *& gif eft(ir) yat* (ScB)
– *and geyff eft(ir) uart(is)* (ScC)
– *Ande giff* (ScD), *And gif* (ScG)
– *And gif . . . syn(e)* (ScE), *gyf . . . syne* (ScF)
– *and eftyr yat gyfe* (ScA), *And eftir yat gyf* (ScH)

(28) *per ignem vel per guerram et aliam*
– *thru fyr or were* (ScB), *thrw fyre ot thrw were* (ScD), *throw fire or were* (ScF)
– *be fyr(e) or ver(e)* (ScC), *be fyre or were* (ScE), *be fire or were* (ScG)

– *be waste thrw fyre or were* (ScA), *be wast thrw fyre or were* (ScH)

(29) *hospitatam . . . inhospitatam*
– *biggyt . . . vnbiggyt* (ScA), *biggit . . . wnbiggit* (ScB), *byggyt . . . vnbyggyt* (ScC), *byggyd . . . vnbyggit* (ScD), *biggit . . . vnbiggit* (ScE), *bigit . . . wnbyggit* (ScF), *biggit . . . vn byggit* (ScG), *byggyt . . . unbiggyt* (ScH)

(30) *donec fuerit*
– *qwhil he be* (ScA), *quhill he be* (ScD), *qwhell he be* (ScF), *q(uh)ll he be* (ScG), *qwhyl he be* (ScH)
– *quhil ye tym he be* (ScB)
– *alß lang as he haß* (ScC)

(31) *salva tamen*
– *Neu(ir) ye les saufe* (ScA), *Neveryeles saufe* (ScH)
– *bot neu(ir) ye leß* (ScC), *Bot neu(ir) ye less* (ScF), *bot neu(ir)yeles* (ScG)
– *Bot non(e)theleß our all* (ScE)
– *saufande our(e) all* (ScD)

Chapter 33

(32) *impedimenta*
– *impedymentis* (ScA, ScH), *impedime(n)t(is)* (ScB), *impedyme(n)tt(is)* (ScC)
– *poyntis* (ScE), *poynttis* (ScF, ScG)
– *thyng(is)* (ScD)

(33) *si dominus eius*
– *gif his lorde* (ScB), *geyff h(is) lord* (ScC), *giff his lorde* (ScD), *gif his lord* (ScE), *gyfe his lorde* (ScF), *gyf his lord* (ScG)
– *gyfe yair lorde* (ScA), *gyfe yar lorde* (ScH)

(34) *in exercitu regis*
– *in ye kyngys oste* (ScA, ScH), *in y^t king(is) hoost* (ScB), *in the kingis oist* (ScE), *in the king(is) ost* (ScF), *in ye kingis oist* (ScG)
– *in ye king(is) batall or in his ost* (ScC)
– *in ye kyng(is) offys or(e) oste* (ScD)

(35) *vel fuerit in*
– *And ane oy(ir) is gif his lord war in* (ScB)
– *or eft(ir)yat he be in* (ScC)
– *or in* (ScD, ScE, ScF, ScG)
– *Or gyfe he be in* (ScA), *or gyfe he be in* (ScH)

(36) *si*
– *gif* (ScA, ScE, ScG), *geyff* (ScC), *giff* (ScD), *gef* (ScF), *gyfe* (ScH)

(37) *pro cibo domini sui*
– *for hys maystyr mete* (ScA), *for his masters mete* (ScH)
– *for bying off maist(ir) meit yat is his lorde with quham he Duellis.* (ScD)
– *for bying(e) of his mastr(is) mete w^t quham he dwellis* (ScE), *for bying(e) bying(e)* [sic] *off his mast(ir)ys mete wytht qwhame he dwellys* (ScF), *for bying of his maist(er)is mete w^t quham he duellis* (ScG)
– *fo ye bying of ye lord(is) mette vyth quham he duellis* (ScC)
– *to by his lord(is) met* (ScB)

Primary sources

Latin

Innes, Cosmo (ed.) 1844. *Acts of the Parliaments of Scotland*. Vol. 1. Edinburgh.
National Records of Scotland MS PA5/2 (Berne MS), http://stairsociety.org/resources/manuscript/the_berne_manuscript [Accessed August 2018]
National Library of Scotland MS 25.4.14 (Adv. Lib. W.4.28, Cokburn)
National Library of Scotland MS 25.4.12
National Library of Scotland MS 25.5.9 (Adv. Lib. A.7.25, Bannatyne)
National Library of Scotland MS 7.1.10 (Adv. Lib. A.3.16, Lumisden)
National Library of Scotland MS 25.5.8 (Adv. Lib. A.2.20)

Scots

Cambridge University Library MS Kk 1.5
National Library of Scotland MS 21246 (Bute)
National Library of Scotland MS 25.4.14 (Adv. Lib. W.4.28, Cokburn)
National Library of Scotland MS 25.4.15
National Library of Scotland MS 25.5.7
National Library of Scotland MS 7.1.9
National Library of Scotland MS 7.1.10 (Adv. Lib. A.3.16, Lumisden)
National Library of Scotland MS Acc 11218/5

References

Agha, Asif. 2003. The social life of a cultural value, *Language and Communication* 23: 231–273.
Barrow, Geoffrey. 1997. Non-literary manuscript production and survival in Scotland. In R. H. Britnell (ed.) *Pragmatic literacy, east and west, 1200–1330*. Woodbridge: Boydell. 131–146.

Beal, Joan C. 2010. Prescriptivism and the supression of variation. In Raymond Hickey (ed.) *Eighteenth-century English: Ideology and change*. Cambridge: Cambridge: University Press. 21–37.

Beal, Joan C. 2016. Standardization. In Merja Kytö & Päivi Pahta (eds.) *The Cambridge handbook of English historical linguistics*. Cambridge: Cambridge University Press. 301–317.

Broun, Dauvit. 2006. Scotland before 1100: Writing Scotland's origins. In B. Harris & A. R. MacDonald (eds.) *Scotland: Making and unmaking of the nation, c.1100–1700*. Dundee: Dundee University Press. 1–16.

Broun, Dauvit & Joanna Tucker. 2017. *Scribes and royal authority. Early charters from the National Records of Scotland*. Edinburgh: National Records of Scotland.

Clanchy, Michael T. 1979. *From memory to written record: England 1066–1307*. London: E. Arnold.

Dolezalek, Gero. 2010. *Scotland under Jus commune. Census of legal literature in Scotland, mainly between 1500 and 1660*. Vols. 1–3. Edinburgh: Stair Society.

DSL = *Dictionary of the Scots Language*, http://www.dsl.ac.uk [Accessed May 2019]

Duncan, A. A. M. 1975. *Scotland. The making of the kingdom*. Vol. 1. Edinburgh: Mercat Press.

Fox, R. 1983. Urban development, 1100–1700. In G. Whittington & Ian D. Whyte (eds.) *An historical geography of Scotland*. London: Academic Press. 73–92.

Gotti, Maurizio. 2012. Text and genre. In Lawrence Solan and Peter M. Tiersma (eds.) *The Oxford Handbook of Language and Law*. Oxford/New York: Oxford University Press.

Gouldesbrough, Peter. 1985. *Formulary of Old Scots legal documents*. Edinburgh: The Stair Society.

Innes, Cosmo (ed.) 1868. *Ancient laws and customs of the burghs of Scotland*. Vol.I. *A.D. 1124–1424*. Edinburgh: Scottish Burgh Records Society.

Hall, Derek. 2002. *Burgess, merchant and priest: Burgh life in the Scottish medieval town*. Edinburgh: Birlinn.

Haugen, Einar. 1966. Linguistics and language planning. In William Bright (ed.) *Sociolinguistics. Proceedings of the UCLA Sociolinguistics Conference 1964*. The Hague: Mouton. 50–71.

Havinga, Anna. 2020. The visibilisation of Scots in the Aberdeen Council Registers. In Jackson Armstrong & Edda Frankot (eds.) *Cultures of Law in Urban Northern Europe*. New York: Routledge.

Halliday, M.A.K. & Ruqaiya Hasan. 1976. *Cohesion in English*. London: Longman.

Jauss, Hans Robert. 1970. *Literaturgeschichte als Provokation der Literaturwissenschaft*. Frankfurt am Main: Suhrkamp.

Kopaczyk, Joanna. 2011. Latin and Scots versions of Scottish medieval burgh laws (*Leges Quatuor Burgorum*). *Scottish Language* 30. 1–17.

Kopaczyk, Joanna. 2012. Long lexical bundles and standardisation in historical legal texts. *Studia Anglica Posnaniensia* 47 (2–3). 3–26.

Kopaczyk, Joanna. 2013. *The legal language of Scottish burghs. Standardisation and lexical bundles 1380–1560*. Oxford: Oxford University Press.

Kopaczyk, Joanna. 2020. Unstable content, remediated layout: Urban laws in Scotland through manuscript and print. In Caroline Tagg and Mel Evans (eds.) *Historicising the Digital*. Mouton de Gruyter. 173–198.

Macafee, Caroline & †Aitken, A. J. 2002. A history of Scots to 1700. In *A Dictionary of the Older Scottish Tongue* Vol. XII, xxix-clvii. Online http://www.dsl.ac.uk/about-scots/history-of-scots/

MacQueen, Hector L. 2002. Laws and languages: Some historical notes from Scotland. *Electronic Journal of Comparative Law* 6 (2). Available at: http://www.ejcl.org/-&/art-&-&.html

McClure, J. Derrick. 1994. English in Scotland. In R. Burchfield (ed.) *The Cambridge history of the English language*. Vol. 5. *English in Britain and overseas*. Cambridge: Cambridge University Press. 23–93.

McLuhan, Marshall. 1962. *The Gutenberg galaxy. The making of typographic man*. London: Routledge & Kegan Paul.
Mellinkoff, David. 1963. *The language of the law*. Boston: Little Brown.
Millar, Robert McColl. 2012. Scots. In Alexander Bergs & Laurel J. Brinton (eds.) *English historical linguistics: An international handbook*. Vol. 2. Berlin: De Gruyter Mouton.
Milroy, James and Lesley Milroy. 1991 [1985] *Authority in language: Investigating language prescription and standardisation*. London: Routledge.
RPS = *Records of the Parliaments of Scotland to 1707*. University of St Andrews. https://www.rps.ac.uk/ (Accessed October 2018)
Stein, Dieter & Ingrid Tieken-Boon van Ostade (eds.) 1993. *Towards a Standard English 1600–1800*. Berlin / New York: Mouton De Grutyer.
Taylor, Alice. 2019. *The Laws of Medieval Scotland: Legal compilations from the thirteenth and fourteenth centuries*. Edinburgh: Stair Society.
Tieken-Boon van Ostade, Ingrid. 2008. *Grammars, grammarians, and grammar-writing in eighteenth-century England*. Berlin / New York: Mouton De Grutyer.
Wheeles D. & K. Jensen. 2013. Juxta Commons. In *Proceedings of the Digital Humanities 2013*. University of Nebraska-Lincoln, 17 July 2013. http://dh2013.unl.edu/abstracts/ab-142.html (accessed October 2018).
Widdowson, H.G. 2004. *Text, context, pretext. Critical issues in discourse analysis*. Oxford: Blackwell.

Laura Wright

18 Rising living standards, the demise of Anglo-Norman and mixed-language writing, and standard English

1 Introduction

> there is no doubt that the real wages of labourers rose very substantially between the crowded and crisis-torn early fourteenth century and the spacious later fifteenth century.
>
> Hatcher (2011: 5)

> commercialisation permeated the whole of medieval society. . . . The commercial life of the Middle Ages was based on the solid foundations of exchange of ordinary goods, which had a broad base throughout society. (Dyer 2011: 238)

In a series of papers (e.g. Wright 2001, 2013) I suggest that the standardisation of English is the long-term result of changes in living standards in the fourteenth century. A reduced population due to famine and Black Death in the first half of the fourteenth century resulted in a weakened demand on resources in the second. Living standards improved, expanding the market for manufactured and foreign goods as opposed to raw materials, and enabling growth of extensive food-supply networks. Historians view this as a process of standardisation, for example: "The history of the internal pottery industry confirms this interpretation of what was happening to internal market structures. Local pottery traditions were being superseded by a more standard range of pottery styles of superior manufacture. . . . A smaller number of potteries was supplying wares over distances characteristically wider than that of most earlier potteries" (Britnell 2000: 13). Over the fourteenth and fifteenth centuries weights, measures, and money all attracted standardisation legislation. Standardisation of commodities equates to variant reduction (a smaller number of potteries producing a reduced range of superior pots) and extended territorial reach (the superior pots became distributed over a wider distance). The parallel with the standardisation of English is direct: a reduced range of variants distributed over a wider territory.

Stenroos (Chapter 2) and Schipor (2018) show that the first writings in English were not the output of officialdom but initiated by less-wealthy, less-powerful classes. Stenroos reports "early texts in English are certainly found in much larger numbers in northern archives than in non-northern ones", that is, the people furthest from the seat of power. In a study of 7,070 Hampshire documents, Schipor (2018) locates the main usages of early passages in English in the

https://doi.org/10.1515/9783110687545-019

context of estate and money-management. In this chapter I consider the language of fourteenth and fifteenth-century financial texts, which were written in mixed-language (a syntactically regular mix of Medieval Latin, Anglo-Norman French and Middle English used for accounting) until the later fifteenth century and in supralocal Englishes thereafter. I take the beginnings of standardisation to equate to variant reduction – one instance of which is the reduction of languages from Latin, French, English and the business system of mixed-language, firstly to supralocal Englishes, and eventually to Standard English. As English-speakers became wealthier, identifiable by changing patterns of consumption and demand for more luxury goods, their voices began to be heard in English. English as a language of written record dates from the last quarter of the fourteenth century, which was a particularly turbulent time in terms of civic administration. Anglo-Norman stopped being a language learnt in childhood at this point, continuing on thereafter into the first quarter of the fifteenth century but showing the kinds of errors made by second-language-learners in adulthood. Mixed-language also shows systemic disruptions around the 1420s. I thus suggest that real-world social changes had an effect on language use: as living standards for the masses improved, so those masses began to protest and rebel, and to express what they had to say in writing. That voice was English rather than Anglo-Norman or Medieval Latin.

2 Historians' observations on the late fourteenth century rise in living standards

Historians have long identified a late-fourteenth and early-fifteenth century period of prosperity for the population at large, resulting from depopulation caused by famine (the Great Famine of 1315–17) and plague (the Black Death of 1348–9) exerting less pressure on food supply. Britnell (2000: 12–13) summarises Dyer (1989) on market changes, which derive from:

> the well-attested rising standard of living in rural society, as well as in towns, between 1349 and the mid fifteenth century, both amongst wage-earners and among tenant farmers. This had the effect of altering the composition of demand in rural society, and in particular it meant an increased demand for merchant wares at the expense of local manufactures. To some extent, no doubt, improvements in real wages were taken up in improved diet, but there can be little doubt that the elasticity of rural demand for manufactures was higher than that for grain or pastoral produce. Not all the growing manufacture of higher-quality cloth in Salisbury, Coventry, York, Norwich and Colchester during the later fourteenth century was destined for sale abroad. The expansion of these industries represented at least in part the substitution of town cloth for country cloth on the part of rural consumers.

In 1300 the poorest sector of society constituted over half the population. By 1524, that poorest sector had decreased to about a third. Over this period, consumers became better served by improved distribution networks, and had an increasing propensity to buy goods from abroad (Britnell 2000: 12, 13). So much so, that it has been dubbed an economical golden age, to the extent that Hatcher, taking a critical stance, debunks the more extreme claims, but even so affirms "there is no doubt that as the population plunged the average number of acres per head rose sharply, the proportions of the landless and near landless fell steeply, possibly from as much as two-thirds before 1349 to well under half in the later fifteenth century" (Hatcher 2011: 23–24).

Not only were poorer people becoming better off in the second half of the fourteenth century, food-supply networks had become more extensive. Dyer, summarising Galloway (2000) and Keene (2000), reports "a single grain market existed in southern England, in which prices of wheat moved in a synchronized fashion ... a reasonably efficient marketing network had been established ... The metropolitan role in distributing relatively expensive imported and manufactured goods seems to have been formed by the early fifteenth century" (Dyer 2000: 106). Keene, analysing debts owed to Londoners, says:

> In so far as the debts represent London's role as a force in the national economy, they seem to indicate a shift between 1424 and 1570 from close engagement with the counties of the South East, especially those lying towards the Low Countries, to a pattern of more extended linkages with interior counties to the north and west of London. This development, certainly a form of integration, is clearly indicated ... for middling- and larger-scale transactions the more distant counties were becoming more important for Londoners than the counties close to the city. ... We know from other evidence that London had enhanced its roles as an importer of manufactured goods from overseas and as a distributor of them to the internal market, and that presumably undermined manufactures in London's hinterland. (Keene 2000: 71–73)

From a linguistic point of view, merchants' trading chains distributing goods from source to customer across country and across Channel equate to weak-tie social networks, and we can map an expansion in trading networks between London and interior counties beyond the immediate hinterland onto an expanded weak-tie speaker-network. (For example, Keene (2000: 76) reports chapmen trading in 1570 between London and Shropshire, Cheshire, Yorkshire, Northumberland and Devon.) This trade expansion exerted a pressure towards uniform weights and measures, which hitherto had varied from place to place:

> the continual reiteration of the need for uniformity in weights and measures throughout the later medieval period demonstrates that the process of standardisation was gradual and difficult. Prevalent local customs, as well as matters of convenience for buyers and sellers, meant that local measures were still in use in several areas and trades. It was not until the

> late fourteenth century, when the focus began to switch from the units themselves to the practices employed, and when approved royal vessels were widely distributed, that substantial progress appears to have been made. . . . By 1429, all towns and boroughs were expected to have a common balance and weights . . . the distribution of weights and measures to an increasing number of towns by the fifteenth century suggests growing efforts and expenditure to uphold the process of standardisation. (Davis 2011a: 190–196)

To summarise: over the fourteenth and fifteenth centuries historians report processes of standardisation, both in goods, and in terms for weighing and measuring goods, and also in greatly extended networks for distributing goods. This considerable increase in organised commercial activity correlated with civic disturbances in London, and a period of change in the language of written record, from changes within the systems of Anglo-Norman and mixed-language, to subsequent abandonment of Anglo-Norman and mixed-language, to replacement of both by supralocal Englishes.

2.1 Social disruption in late fourteenth century London

Perhaps in part because of this rise in living standards for the population at large, late fourteenth-century London was a time of violent unrest from the point of view of City governance:

> The situation in the City of London in the last quarter of the fourteenth century was particularly turbulent and rent by factions. There were disputes between grocers and drapers struggling to dominate the export trade through Calais; and between different groups of drapers fighting over the distributive trade in cloth, between victuallers who wanted to maintain the food monopolies and the other crafts, known as the non-victuallers, who were anxious to open up a free market in food and so bring down costs, and between those characterised as radicals who wished to change the way in which the City was governed and those, conservatives, who resisted the constitutional changes or, at least, once they were in place and found to be unsatisfactory, struggled to restore the old order. There was no single 'big issue' that caused the turbulence of London in Richard II's reign. 'Parties' such as they were, were evanescent and temporary groupings. There were conflicting economic interests and, perhaps, class interests: masters fought to restrain the wages and opportunities of their workers, while merchants who traded goods abroad came into conflict with the artisans who made the goods. Barron in Barron & Wright (forthcoming)

In London, the City's 'Jubilee Book' (a book of civic job descriptions, procedural processes, and details of local government) was burnt in the Guildhall Yard in 1387. It is not known why it was burnt, but the text specifies: "And the Alderman ought to make his Clerk openly to Rede in Inglissh the poyntes that ensuen", and "also that al pleaters that pleaten withyn the Citee shuln pleate in Inglissh and in nonother man^{9} so that the lay people mown knowe the man^{9} of *þ*^{9} plees"

(Trinity College Cambridge, MS O.3.11, folios 145, 155, the manuscript dates from the 1480s but the text was written 1377–78 and updated until 1384). In London in the winter of 1388–9, guild certificates written in monolingual English emanated from the guilds of poorer parishioners (Barron & Wright: 1995):

> it is clear from the surviving London returns to the enquiry into guilds in 1388 that the crafts and parish fraternities were drawing up ordinances and oaths in English from a much earlier date. The Carpenters appear to have drawn up ordinances in English as early as 1333, the Pouchmakers in 1356, the Curriers in 1367–8, the Guild of the Virgin in St Stephen Coleman Street in 1369, the Guild of St Anne in St Lawrence Jewry in 1372 and the Joiners in St James Garlickhythe in 1375. There were probably many other craft and religious guilds in London using English for their ordinances and oaths whose returns to the 1388 enquiry have not survived. It seems likely that English was a much more utilitarian, governmental language in London in the mid-fourteenth century than the surviving records from the City's Guildhall archive would suggest.
>
> Barron in Barron & Wright (forthcoming)

Barron postulates that one reason for burning the Jubilee Book might have been the fact that it was written in English:

> If the governing of crafts could be conducted in English, why not that of the City? In this way City government would be made truly accessible and City officers could be brought to account more easily. It may have been this use of English which was the most destabilizing aspect of the Jubilee Book. The use of English enabled the entry of lay people into what Steven Justice has called 'clerkly space'. This caused monks and royal officials to throw up their hands in horror in 1381 and it seems to have provoked a similar reaction in London in 1384–87. When lay people entered clerkly space there were riots, unruly debates, shouting (rather than reason) and a plethora of opinions.
>
> Barron in Barron & Wright (forthcoming)

These unruly debates, shouting and plethora of opinions were expressed in English. Written English was not imposed by officialdom but emanated from the traders and craftspeople who came into conflict with the City's Mayor, Aldermen, Common Councilmen, Sheriffs, Constables, Sergeants and other law enforcement personnel, whose interests were bound up with maintaining the status quo. To borrow the metaphor of punctuated equilibrium from biology, long periods of equilibrium and stasis lead to language complexification (Trudgill 2011), whereas change and disruption, including the kind of social turmoil described by Barron, brings speakers from different backgrounds into contact, leading to language simplifications of various sorts. The abandonment of written Anglo-Norman and mixed-language can be characterised as one such simplification, leading to an outcome around 1500 of two written systems rather than four, namely Medieval Latin and supralocal Englishes.

3 Disruption and demise of Anglo-Norman and mixed-language

In the first quarter of the fifteenth century, scribes ceased writing in Anglo-Norman. A few decades later, they also stopped using the mixed-language system for financial accounts and inventories. Stenroos (Chapter 2), together with her colleagues working on a *Corpus of Middle English Local Documents 1399–1525*, found in a survey of 2,017 documents from around the country that up until the early fifteenth century, most documents were written in Medieval Latin, with a lesser amount in Anglo-Norman French. After the early fifteenth century, most documents were still written in Medieval Latin or Latin matrix, but the French component became replaced either by Medieval Latin or by Middle English; that is, after the first two decades of the fifteenth century, French became used less or abandoned altogether (according to text-type: lawyers retained French longest):

> In the fourteenth century, French appears in largely the same functions in which English appears in the fifteenth: correspondence, ordinances, oaths, conditions of obligation and occasional leases and sales. ... English virtually never occurs in bonds, final concords, inquests post mortem, letters of attorney, manorial court rolls, probates of wills and quitclaims. This means that Latin dominates the most common types of documents: in virtually any archive, the most common medieval documents are bonds, gifts, grants and quitclaims, as well as manorial court rolls, all documents that are for the most part written in Latin.
>
> ...
>
> In sum, when English appeared in local administrative writing, it appeared above all in the functional slots that had been occupied by French (Stenroos chapter 2)

Over the fifteenth century, use of French diminished but use of Latin did not, so that the fifteenth century can be characterised as the century when Anglo-Norman fell into disuse, rather than the century when English took over. During the fifteenth century English appears in local documents where intelligibility (from the point of view of the people involved) was paramount. Stenroos distinguishes between formulaic content for internal pragmatic use by other professionals which was usually written in Latin, and the more unpredictable components that needed to be understood by non-professionals which were written in Anglo-Norman until the early fifteenth century and in English thereafter. The switch from French to English in the more oral components was relatively swift; the Latin components in the less-oral components continued, not tailing off until the eighteenth century. With regard to Chancery documents, English is first found in incoming petitions written by the populace, rather than in outgoing official communications.

Schipor (2018) investigated 7,070 texts in the period 1399–1525 from three collections held at the Hampshire Record Office: the Winchester City Archives collection (municipal), the Winchester Diocese collection (episcopal) and the Jervoise family collection (manorial). She found that Anglo-Norman French texts ceased after 1425, and mixed-code ceased after 1455, with Latin remaining the main language of record throughout in the three collections. The majority of municipal and manorial texts were found to be multilingual in one way or another, with English appearing first together with multilingual 'events' (headings, marginalia, rubrics, commentary, switches of various sorts), before the appearance of passages of monolingual English. The shift to English was gradual and lengthy and not always linear (in manorial and municipal records that is; episcopal records remained predominantly Latin long after the fifteenth century), and manorial records contained more English than municipal records. English content was used in a variety of personal texts such as memoranda, correspondence, statements, personal conveyances, as well as documents recording monetary value and business transactions. From the early 1500s Schipor finds that English had become the means of expressing monetary and business transactions in the manorial collection; effectively, English emerged at the end of the fifteenth century as the language of financial dealing.

In a series of papers, Ingham has identified a period of disruption around the final decades of the fourteenth century in British Anglo-Norman French, which he attributes to the loss of the acquisition of the language in childhood. Ingham (2011) surveyed prepositional phrases in mixed-language contexts in the English Lay Subsidy Rolls of the fourteenth century. He found that the government constraint was operative (as it tends to be in present-day codeswitched varieties), so that unambiguously English prepositions (i.e. excluding *in* and *de*) were almost always followed by English determiners, and unambiguously French prepositions were almost always followed by French determiners. He infers that this regularity is indicative of speech: that the spoken reality behind the writing must have been bilingual English/French, lasting up until the final quarter of the fourteenth century. However, the Anglo-Norman system then became disrupted, and this can be seen with regard to the Anglo-Norman article *le*. *Le* is found borrowed into Latin-matrix texts from the early twelfth century in the context of personal names, placenames and topographical features in manorial accounts, and from the 1320s onwards modifying a range of nouns (Ingham 2009, 2012). Fourteenth-century *le* marked definiteness but not indefiniteness, following the same usage restriction as found in continental French writing. However in early fifteenth century Anglo-Norman and mixed-language writing, *le* (*la*, *les*, *del*, *des*, *al*, *as*) premodified indefinite nouns too, unlike continental French, marking English and French words rather than Latin ones – and in the case of mixed-language writing, blocking a case-ending on the noun. Thus *le* ceased to follow the usual French rules of distribution: traditionally syntactically appropriate until the last quarter of the fourteenth century, but appearing regardless of syntactic context in the early fifteenth.

3.1 Reduction of variants

My approach to investigating the origins of Standard English is to identify types of variant reduction, on the assumption that other qualities of standard languages such as codification and implementation could only come into force once the written variety had largely settled down in terms of spelling, morphology and word-choice. In this section I consider some types of variant reduction in Anglo-Norman, Medieval Latin and mixed-language writing, as I suggest in Section 4 that their influence can be discerned in supralocal Englishes (which preceded Standard English).

3.1.1 *le* + non-Latin noun

By the end of the fourteenth century, in mixed-language financial writing, all kinds of nouns were premodified by *le*, including those not derived from Latin or Anglo-Norman. In terms of weights and measures, the formula '*precium/pris/price le X*' was particularly productive. For example, the accounts of St Paul's Cathedral show:

> 1393 *ꝑcʾ le sakę* 'price the sack(load)', *ꝑcʾ le* C^{ne} (hundred), *ꝑcʾ le* M^{the} (thousand); 1394 *ꝑcʾ le bȝ* (bushel), *ꝑcʾ le nayl* (nail), *ꝑcʾ le lood* (load), 1397 *ꝑcʾ le taiß* (teise, a weight), *ꝑcʾ le ℔* (pound), 1398 *ꝑcʾ le borđ* (board), *ꝑcʾ le pecʾ* (piece), *ꝑcʾ le schide* (shide, a piece of wood), *ꝑcʾ le saplogʾ* (sap-log), *ꝑcʾ le staff*; 1400 *ꝑcʾ le rafter*; 1401 *ꝑcʾ le poste*; 1402 *ꝑcʾ le puncheon* (wooden beam), *ꝑcʾ le quartʾ* (quarter), 1402 *ꝑcʾ le sheƚƚ*, *ꝑcʾ le peire* (pair); 1403 *ꝑcʾ le pipe*; 1405 *ꝑcʾ le bote* (boatload)
>
> London Metropolitan Archive, CLC/313/L/D/001/MS25125/001, 003, 005, 007-8, 012, 014-5, 018-20, 022, 024-6, 028-36, 038-42, 044-6, Dean & Chapter of St Paul's Cathedral, London, Rental & Accounts

These nouns are all English, with the exception of the suspended 'libra', *℔*, which may have already anglicised in pronunciation to 'pound'. From the point of view of speech, Ingham suggests that an underlying oral codeswitching can be discerned in these [Latin (preposition) + French (article) + English (noun)] prepositional-phrase chunks. From the point of view of standardisation, a small piece of grammar can be seen coming into existence – the fact that it would not last would not have been apparent at the time.[1] This piece of grammar added to the invariant look of the page, because the earlier Latinate construction which it sat alongside had variable case-endings depending on preceding preposition, gender and number. (That is, [*le* + non-Latin noun, – case-ending] did not thoroughly oust the Latin prepositional phrase construction, rather, layering applied and both systems could be used together.) Examples are *apud wharfam* 'at the wharf' (where Latin preposition *apud* governs a Latin accusative singular case-ending -*am* on English *wharf*), and *in vaꝱ xxij Tidmannꝝ* 'in wages for 22 of the tidemen' (where Latin preposition *in* governs a Latin genitive plural case-ending -*orum*, expressed as abbreviation -ꝝ, on English compound *tide-man*). By contrast, [*le* + non-Latin noun] was almost invariant, only marking plurality. I demonstrate this claim with some prepositional phrases taken from the accounts of London Bridge for the year 1421–22, as written in column 1 according to the newer, anglifying pattern with *le* but without case-endings (other than marking plurality), and in column 2 as according to the older, Latin pattern minus *le* but with case-endings:

+ *le* – case-ending	– *le* + case-ending
ꝑ le Brighous 'for the Bridgehouse'	*ꝑ vnam tidam* 'for one tide'
ꝑ les Tides 'for the tides'	*ꝑ v tidas* 'for 5 tides'
ꝑ le ladyng 'for the loading'	*ꝑ ꝓbenꝱ equoꝝ* 'for the horses' provender'
ꝑ le lathe 'for the lathe'	*ꝑ ferris equoꝝ* 'for the horses' shoes'
ꝑ les Geauntes 'for the giants'	*ꝑ auditoribꝫ Compoti* 'for the auditors of the accounts'
ꝑ le Shoute 'for the shoutboat'	
ꝑ les weres 'for the weirs'	
ꝑ le dongeōn 'for the dungeon'	
de lestathelynges 'of the starlings (bridge-piers)'	*de teñ Pontꝭ* 'of the Bridge tenements'
de leskoggꝭ 'of the (mill)cogs'	*de arcubꝫ* 'of the arches'
de le briggehous 'of the Bridgehouse'	*de toto festo* 'of all the festival'
de lestokkꝭ 'from the stocks'	*de Mañio de Lambhithe* 'from the manor of Lambeth'
del Shoute 'of the shoutboat'	
del Trappe sup Pontem 'of the trapdoor over the Bridge'	
des vanes 'of the vanes'	

1 Although see Wright (2010) for the observation that the construction is still present in London church and place-names *St Mary le Bow, St Martin le Grand, St Mary le Strand, Marylebone, Horseleydown*, and now-obsolete names *St Christoper le Stocks, St Peter le Poor, St Michael le Quern*. Record of *le* + non-Latin word in these names postdates the abandonment of Anglo-Norman as a spoken language.

apud le Briggehous 'at the Bridgehouse'
apud le loke 'at the Lock'
apud le weyhous 'at the weighhouse'
vsqȝ le Tilhous 'to the Tilehouse'
vsqȝ le Lee 'towards the Lee'
cū le vernisshingꝰ 'with the varnishing'
cū le ffreyght 'with the freight'
in le Briggehous 'in the Bridgehouse'
in le Shoute 'in the shoutboat'
iuxta le Tilkylne 'next to the Tilekiln'
a les Shouteman 'to the shoutman'
circa les Geauntes 'around the giants'

vsqȝ aquam 'towards the water'
vsqȝ t̄râ 'towards the land'
cū vno ßuientꝰ 'with one servant'
cū indenturꝰ 'with the indenture'
in valta Capelle 'in the chapel vault'
in ꝑocħ 'in the parish'
iuxta leonem 'next to the lion'
ad ꝑuam Rammā 'at the small ram'

suꝑ Pontem 'above the Bridge'

London Metropolitan Archives, CLA/007/FN/03/002, MS Bridge House Weekly Payments, first series, volume 2, 1420x1421

In column 2, the Latin construction shows prepositions governing case-endings (and abbreviations representing case-endings) so that *pro*, for example, governs singular and plural noun suffixes spelt <*-am, -as, -is, -o, -ibus, -a, -es*>, plus abbreviated stems where case-endings are implied. By contrast, column 1 shows Latin prepositions followed by *le* (spelt <*le, les*>, and elided forms <*del, des*>), with just plurality marked on the following non-Latin, Anglo-Norman/English noun.[2] The newer system of [*le* + non-Latin noun] was one of morphological reduction, and had the effect of making mixed-language appear more and more English as English nouns preceded by *le* increased. In Wright (2013: 73) I relate this development of loss of synthetic morphology and loss of redundancy in mixed-language writing to Trudgill's (2010) observation that such changes are typical of systems learnt in adulthood.

3.1.2 Abbreviation and suspension symbols

Abbreviations were integral to the mixed-language system. They too made the text appear more English, as for example *ꝑ frengꝰ pellurꝰ coreis diu͛ß colorꝰ* 'for diverse coloured leather fringe trim' (pg 467), where the abbreviations permit

2 I say "non-Latin" because I know of no safe way of determining exactly when nouns of Anglo-Norman etymology became regarded as part of the English wordstock (*le* itself had ceased to be restricted to Anglo-Norman and become part of the Medieval Latin system). It seems counter-intuitive to insist that e.g. *varnishing*, n., is not attested in English until 1444–6 (c.f. *Middle English Dictionary*, vernishing ger.), when it is attested as shown above in the Bridge House Weekly Payments in 1421–22 in a mixed-language context, but the topic of mixed-language as evidence of the English lexicon is as yet under-theorised.

interpretations of both *diversis coloris* to match the Latin matrix and word-order but also *diverse colours* to match Anglo-Norman/English *freng̃*. Honkapoha & Liira (Chapter 9) consider rates of abbreviation loss in 14 different versions of Higden's *Polychronicon* written or printed in both Latin and English between the years 1342–1527. They find that the rate of abbreviation loss in Latin portions of text differed from the rate of loss in English portions. They also find that abbreviation variation decreased faster than spelling variation. Scribes copying both languages retained the abbreviation and suspension system in Latin texts considerably longer than they did in English ones, with more than half of the words in Latin texts carrying abbreviations in all but one manuscript copied before 1425. By contrast, the abbreviation density in English texts varied between the practices of individual scribes, dropping below 5% after 1450. This is a study of just one copied text so findings cannot be generalised; it remains to be seen whether a similar abbreviation-symbol reduction in later fifteenth-century English writing can be found in other texts and text-types. Certainly the view from mixed-language [*le* + non-Latin noun] chunks supports the finding, as Latin case-endings were frequently expressed via a suspension symbol, whereas Anglo-Norman/English nouns had a greater tendency to be written out in full as in the list above.

3.1.3 The payroll effect

As well as [*le* + non-Latin noun], another influence towards variant reduction seen in mixed-language financial writing is what I call the payroll effect. This is simply the matter of copying information (names, tasks, commodities, payments) literatim as the clerk copied over details of permanent staff from week to week (i.e. given information), and then added on the week's specific unpredictable particulars underneath (i.e. new information). Weekly given information tended to be invariant, either categorical or nearly so. Here are the spellings of surnames of 14 men who were paid weekly over the year 1420–21, extracted from the mixed-language Bridge House Weekly Payments:

Loy	54	100%	Neweman	24	96%
			Newemâ	1	4%
Clerk	58	100%			
			Silkestoñ	52	95%
Catelyñ	100	99%	Sylkestoñ	3	5%
Cately	1	1%			
			Houswif	47	94%
Sharp̂	55	98%	Houswyf	2	4%
Sharp	1	2%	Houswyff	1	2%

Warde	52	98%	Westoñ	27	93%
Warđ	1	2%	Weston	2	7%
Beek	62	97%	Stile	26	86%
Beeek	2	3%	Stille	2	2%
			Style	2	2%
Brys	51	96%	Sweteman	39	74%
Brŷs	1	2%	Swetman	13	24%
Bris	1	2%	Swetemâ	1	2%
			Bassett	33	62%
			Basset	19	36%
			Bassettℯ	1	2%

London Metropolitan Archives, MS Bridge House Weekly Payments, first series, volume 2, 1420x1421

No-one's name is spelt in more than three ways; no name displays a medieval Zipf's Law, 80/20 distribution with numerous minor variants. Walter Loy, the shouteman, looked after the shout, a type of barge. The word <shouteman> is also invariant, spelt exactly the same way 53 times as it was copied over each week. The payroll effect helped codify the appearance of accounts towards consistency, with its already highly codified layout on the page.

3.1.4 *les* + word-initial /s/

Another small piece of orthographical consistency is visible in the Bridge House Weekly Payments of 1420x21. This is deletion of word-final <s> and cliticisation when article *les* is followed by a noun beginning with /s/: *lestathelynges* (x2), *lestathelyngs* 'the staddelings or starlings', the protective outworks built around the bridge piers to protect them from the rush of water each tide; *lestokks* 'the Stocks', the name of a market; in contrast to *les Geauntes* (x4) 'the giants', *les Tides* 'the tides', *les Shouteman* 'the shoutman', *les weres* 'the weirs'. This system is governed phonetically rather than orthographically, triggered by word-initial /s/ but not word-initial /ʃ/.[3]

3 I am not sure whether there is a single exception: <leskoggs>. The full context is: *It̃p* emendacõe *de armatur de leskoggℯ Molenđ apđ leuesh^am ijs iiijđ*, 'Item for mending of equipment of the mill (s)cogs at Lewisham 2s 4d'. If the noun in question is 'cogs', as seems likely, then it is an exception – which is entirely expected at this date, as consistency had yet to develop. If it is 'scourges'

4 Supralocal London English

London is implicated in many textbook accounts of the spread of Standard English. The assumption has been that later fifteenth-century London monolingual English writing set the model for writing elsewhere; that London English equates to Standard English. Such an account ignores the fact that Standard English came to be written countrywide, and that Standard English does not show the kind of Southern morphology and orthography used in monolingual English supralocal London writing. For example, here are some linguistic features from a set of London English accounts for the year 1501–2:

- present plural *-n*: <ben, accompten>
- present singular *-th*: <apperitħ>
- zero-marked genitives: <at our lady ffayre>, <a tēnt that was late Thomas Pynder>
- elision of *at* + *the*: <atte>
- elision of definite article + following vowel, especially *a* and *o*: <thaccompte, tharreragis, thappurtenªncis, thabbot, tharchebisshop, thawbes, tharchaungeƚƚ, thawditours, thandę, tholde, thother, thuse>
- distinguishing of word-initial /ʃ/ from word-medial and word-final /ʃ/: *sh-* <shippes, shire, shamelx, sheañ, shaƚƚ, shewing, Sheffeld, sharpyng, shyvers, shovylles, shottyng, shougħtes> versus *-ssh* <fysshe, flesshe, Archebisshop, ꝑysshe, haƀdassher, asshelar, Maylasshe, Asshelarkę, bussheƚƚ, fornysshyng, Russhis, Rubysshe, wasshyng, Brusshis>. This was not categorical: <fishemongers, Bishopsgate, pyleshone, workemanship> also occur.
- distinguishing word-initial /ʤ/ from word-medial and word-final /ʤ/: <ghibet ghynne> ('gin' < *engine* was a high-frequency term in building accounts) versus <londonbridge, tharreragis, Charge, Chaunge, wharfage, Awgers, wagis, Seges, pagent, delygente, largely, Cariage, portage, straungears, Sergeaunte>. This was not categorical: <Georges, Gentilman, Geffrey> also occur.
- retention of Anglo-Norman <aun> trigraphs: <accomptauntę, Caunterbury, Chauntry, graunted, Allowaunce, cōmaundement, Marchaunte, Chaunge, tenauntę, plauncheborde, attendaunce, straungears, wexchaundeler, braunche, tharchaungeƚƚ, Sergeaunte>
- <y> where Standard English has <g>: <yeldhall>
- retention of Old English <d> where Standard English has <th>: <gadrid> 'gathered', <togyder> 'together'

(cf *Middle English Dictionary* attested form <skoges> under headword *scourge* n. 'whip') then it is not.

- unetymological <d> in <oder> 'other'
- Anglo-Norman plurals in <-lx>: <shamelx> 'shambles' (a market, from Old English *sc(e)amel* 'stall'), <juelx> 'jewels'

Examples taken from London Metropolitan Archives, CLA/007/FN/02/004, Bridgemasters' Annual Accounts and Rental, 1484–1509, volume 4, pages 221v–227v.

Standard English has none of these features, and neither does present-day London English: all were eventually to be abandoned. Yet they are part of the development towards Standard English, because when English became a language of written record, variants were reduced on the Anglo-Norman/Latin model, as both written languages were relatively invariant in spellings. Recall the smaller number of superior pots dispersed over a greater territory – none of these supralocal London features was limited to London and the South East, all were dispersed over a greater territory, and some lasted for centuries. The supralocal spread, ranging out over an increasing area, is itself a primary stage in the process of standardisation.

This supralocal London variety of 1500 shows traces of the Anglo-Norman component that preceded it. As the Anglo-Norman component dropped out of use in the first half of the fifteenth century in multilingual writing and English took its place, English also took over the relatively invariant, consistent spelling quality of Anglo-Norman and Medieval Latin, initiating the process of variant reduction. There are parallels between the Anglo-Norman cliticisation of preposition and definite article, as in *del* 'de + le' and *as* 'a + les', and English *atte* 'at + the'. There are parallels between the Anglo-Norman cliticisation of the definite article *l'* followed by a noun beginning with a vowel, as in *lestatut* 'le + estatut', and English *th'*, as in *thestate* 'the + estate', which still featured in written English in Shakespeare's time. The Anglo-Norman graphies of plural *-lx* and trigraph *-aun-* ranged over a widespread area (see for example Thengs (2013) for *-lx* plurals in local documents from Cheshire, Staffordshire and Shropshire, and Stenroos (Chapter 2) for *sealx* and *oder*). That these features did not last into Standard English is not material. Their significance to the process of standardisation lies in the 'fewer superior pots over a greater territory' analogue. The superiority in question can be related to what was deemed suitable for written Anglo-Norman (*-lx* plurals, cliticisation of the definite article, fewer variants per feature) was also felt to be suitable for newly-written English. The 'fewer' in question can also be related to the fact that two written systems, Anglo-Norman and mixed-language, were absorbed into one, English. That Anglo-Norman and mixed-language should exert pressure on written English is not surprising, both the realms of law and money-management where Anglo-Norman had predominated being conservative, conventionalised enterprises. Indeed it is likely that the more powerful the institution (I have adduced here the accounts of wealthy, perpetual institutions St Paul's Cathedral and London Bridge), the longer their archives are likely to contain Anglo-Norman and mixed-language writing, and the later they are likely to show the switch to monolingual English – which in the case of London Bridge, was 1479–80. Conversely the poorer parish guilds were already writing in monolingual English in the winter of 1388–9, with internal, non-extant, evidence that they had been doing so since the 1330s.

5 Discussion and summary

In this chapter I suggest that a rise in living standards in the second half of the fourteenth century and the first half of the fifteenth led to greater wealth and confidence in the poorer sectors of the population, expressed by unruly debates, a plethora of opinions and shouting, and visible in the abandonment of Anglo-Norman and commensurate increase in written English. Written English took over qualities from written Anglo-Norman, visible in supralocal Englishes of around 1500. The argument runs thus: habits acquired by scribes writing in the long traditions of Anglo-Norman and mixed-language worked their way into written English over the course of the fifteenth century. At first, in the earlier fourteenth century, scribes newly writing in English expressed themselves in an idiolectal, regional manner, with features following a 'linguistics of speech', Zipf's Law distribution of a few majority spellings with many minor variants (see Kretzschmar (2009) for 'linguistics of speech' ratios); but as use of written English increased, climbed the social scale and took on the pragmatic functions of Latin and French writing, it took on their more invariant characteristics too. This process was catalysed by the demise of childhood-acquired Anglo-Norman causing English to expand into new pragmatic functions, putatively propelled by social unrest. It progressed as no more than a series of tendencies, due to such forces as the relatively invariant spelling systems of Medieval Latin and Anglo-Norman, relatively invariant chunks of mixed-language such as [*le* + non-Latin noun], the payroll effect, and spelling preferences of individual scribes. Acting together with the highly codified appearance of financial accounts-keeping, the tendency towards a relatively invariant look became ported over to written English. ('Relatively' in all cases here means 'relative to writing in the fourteenth century', not 'relative to invariant present-day written Standard English'.) These forces acted together to exert pressure on the rest of the system – a slow accumulation of features from below, rather than a sudden official imposition from above.

However, by 1500 the resulting writing systems were still twofold, the continuation of Latin, and supralocal Englishes. Standard English had yet to develop and replace Latin. In London writing, third-person singular *-th* had yet to be replaced by *-s*, plural *-n* had yet to become abandoned, genitive groups had yet to assume the suffix *-'s*, definite article *the* had yet to become invariant, the digraph <sh> had yet to settle down to invariancy in all positions, words had yet to assume one unalterable shape on the page, and sentence structure had yet to conventionalise, among the many other features of Standard English. Selection in each case happened independently – better expressed as 'reduction to a single feature' rather than 'selection of a single feature', as 'selection' implies agency. As a system, standardisation would take another three hundred years before finally coming to look like its present-day instantiation.

The main contribution of this chapter has been to relate the change in writing systems to the populace and their real-world activities. It is a tenet of sociolinguistic studies that socially salient divisions become encoded in the voice, and I have sought to identify and foreground those socially salient people who spoke, and now wrote, in English. Barron identifies these speakers and writers primarily as members of trade and craft guilds:

> British Library, Ms Egerton 2885 ... was made by, or for, a London Fishmonger c. 1395, and contains many items out of the City's records, including an English translation of the charter granted to the City by Richard II in the first year of his reign. Such men had knowledge of Latin and French but they were also accustomed to using English in the books or ordinances or oaths associated with the crafts and fraternities to which they belonged. (Barron in Barron & Wright forthcoming)

Trade and craft guilds and parish fraternities were unions between brothers and sisters in a family kinship sense, in a work sense, and in a local neighbourhood sense. They can be characterised as dense, strong-tie social networks. I suggested in Section 2 that expanded merchants' networks extending into and out of London across the country and across the Channel equate to a community of practice with weak-tie networks. In terms of punctuated equilibrium, both weak-tie and strong-tie networks became disturbed over the fourteenth century, with the London population interrupted by means of civil unrest, and merchants from both home and elsewhere coming and going into new territories. This set in train processes of language simplification as a result of new speaker-contact in adulthood, eventually leading to Standard English, but this chapter stops at the end of the fifteenth century with supralocal Englishes and Medieval Latin (which was itself about to shift into Neo-Latin) continuing on as written norms into the next century.

References

Manuscripts

London Metropolitan Archives, CLA/007/FN/03/002, MS Bridge House Weekly Payments, first series, volume 2, 1420x1421.

London Metropolitan Archives, CLA/007/FN/02/004, Bridgemasters' Annual Accounts and Rental, volume 4, 1484x1509.

London Metropolitan Archive, CLC/313/L/D/001/MS25125/001, 003, 005, 007–8, 012, 014–5, 018–20, 022, 024–6, 028–36, 038–42, 044–6, Dean & Chapter of St Paul's Cathedral, London, MS Rental & Accounts, 1393x1405.

Printed matter

Barron, Caroline M. and Laura Wright. 1995. "The London Middle English Guild Certificates of 1388/89: i. Historical Introduction; ii. The Texts", *Nottingham Medieval Studies* 39. 108–145.

Barron, Caroline M. and Laura Wright (eds.). Forthcoming. *The Jubilee Book: Trinity College Cambridge, MS O.3.11*. London: London Record Society.

Bergstrøm, Geir. 2017. *Yeuen at Cavmbrigg' A Study of the Late Medieval English Documents of Cambridge*. University of Stavanger: PhD thesis.

Britnell, Richard. 2000. "Urban Demand in the English Economy, 1300–1600". In James A. Galloway (ed.). *Trade, Urban Hinterlands and Market Integration* c.*1300–1600*. Centre for Metropolitan History Working Papers Series, 3. London: Centre for Metropolitan History, Institute of Historical Research. 1–22.

Davis, James. 2011a. *Medieval Market Morality: Life, Law and Ethics in the English Marketplace, 1200–1500*. Cambridge: Cambridge University Press.

Davis, James. 2011b. "Market Regulation in Fifteenth-Century England." In Ben Dodds and Christian D. Liddy (eds.). 2011. *Commercial Activity, Markets and Entrepreneurs in the Middle Ages: Essays in Honour of Richard Britnell*. Woodbridge: Boydell. 81–106.

Dyer, Christopher. 1989. *Standards of Living in the Later Middle Ages: Social Change in England, c.1200–1520*. Cambridge: Cambridge University Press.

Dyer, Christopher. 2000. "Trade, Urban Hinterlands and Market Integration, 1300–1600: A Summing Up". In James A. Galloway (ed.). *Trade, Urban Hinterlands and Market Integration* c.*1300–1600*. Centre for Metropolitan History Working Papers Series, 3. London: Centre for Metropolitan History, Institute of Historical Research. 103–109.

Dyer, Christopher. 2011. "Luxury Goods in Medieval England". In Ben Dodds and Christian D. Liddy (eds.). 2011. *Commercial Activity, Markets and Entrepreneurs in the Middle Ages: Essays in Honour of Richard Britnell*. Woodbridge: Boydell. 217–238.

Galloway, James A. 2000. In "One Market or Many? London and the Grain Trade of England". In James A. Galloway (ed.). *Trade, Urban Hinterlands and Market Integration* c.*1300–1600*. Centre for Metropolitan History Working Papers Series, 3. London: Centre for Metropolitan History, Institute of Historical Research. 23–42.

Hatcher, John. 2011. "Unreal Wages: Long-Run Living Standards and the 'Golden Age' of the Fifteenth Century". In Ben Dodds and Christian D. Liddy (eds.). 2011. *Commercial Activity,*

Markets and Entrepreneurs in the Middle Ages: Essays in Honour of Richard Britnell. Woodbridge: Boydell. 1–24.

Ingham, Richard. 2009. "Mixing languages on the manor." *Medium Ævum* 78 (1). 80–97.

Ingham, Richard. 2011. "Code-switching in the later medieval English lay subsidy rolls." In Herbert Schendl and Laura Wright (eds.). *Code-Switching in Early English.* Berlin: Mouton de Gruyter. 95–114.

Ingham, Richard. 2012. "Language-mixing in Medieval Latin documents: Vernacular Articles and Nouns." In Ad Putter and Judith Jefferson (eds.). *Multilingualism in Medieval Britain (c. 1066–1520): Sources and Analysis.* Turnhout: Brepols. 105–121.

Keene, Derek. 2000. "Changes in London's Economic Hinterland as Indicated by Debt Cases in the Court of Common Pleas". In James A. Galloway (ed.). *Trade, Urban Hinterlands and Market Integration* c.*1300–1600.* Centre for Metropolitan History Working Papers Series, 3. London: Centre for Metropolitan History, Institute of Historical Research. 59–82.

Kretzschmar, William A., Jr. 2009. *The Linguistics of Speech.* Cambridge: Cambridge University Press.

Middle English Dictionary 1952–2001. https://quod.lib.umich.edu/m/middle-english-dictionary/dictionary.

Schipor, Delia. 2018. *A Study of Multilingualism in the Late Medieval Material of the Hampshire Record Office.* University of Stavanger: PhD thesis.

Thengs, Kjetil V. 2013. *English Medieval Documents of the Northwest Midlands A Study in the Language of a Real-Space Text Corpus.* University of Stavanger: PhD thesis.

Trudgill, Peter. 2010. "Contact and Sociolinguistic Typology". In Raymond Hickey (ed.). *The Handbook of Language Contact.* Oxford and Malden, MA: Wiley-Blackwell. 299–319.

Trudgill, Peter. 2011. *Sociolinguistic Typology: Social Determinants of Linguistic Complexity.* New York: Oxford University Press.

Wright, Laura. 1996. *Sources of London English: Medieval Thames Vocabulary.* Oxford University Press: Clarendon.

Wright, Laura. 2001. "The role of international and national trade in the standardisation of English". In Isabel Moskowich-Spiegel Fandiño, Begoña Crespo García, Emma Lezcano González and Begoña Simal González (eds.). *Re-interpretations of English. Essays on Language, Linguistics and Philology* (I). A Coruña: Universidade da Coruña. 189–207.

Wright, Laura. 2010. "A pilot study on the singular definite articles *le* and *la* in fifteenth-century London mixed-language business writing". In Richard Ingham (ed.). *The Anglo-Norman Languge and its Contexts.* York: York Medieval Press and The Boydell Press, 130–142.

Wright, Laura. 2013. "The Contact Origins of Standard English". In Daniel Schreier and Marianne Hundt (eds.). *English as a Contact Language.* Studies in English Language. Cambridge: Cambridge University Press. 58–74.

Index

abbreviations 10, 13, 59, 108, 201, 205, 206, 208, 209, 211, 269–274, 278, 280–299, 301–304, 307–311, 352, 418, 421, 427, 428, 438
accommodation 224, 226, 444
administrative texts 5, 23, 39–56, 67–8, 196–7, 320, 491
Audience Design theory 224

backformation 432
Black Death 513–516
borrowing 8–9, 343–362, 367, 381–405, 411–440
brevigraphs 291–293, 295, 296, 309

calques 329, 493–495, 499, 500
Central Midlands 3, 6, 12, 17–19, 24–26, 56, 106, 141, 181, 186
Chancery 4, 6, 14, 17–19, 24, 25, 32, 40, 41, 45, 46, 56, 58, 65, 68, 129, 160, 182, 183, 272, 273, 443
Chaucer 65, 124, 168, 176, 182, 183, 356, 386
cliticisation 526, 528
codeswitching 317, 319, 320, 492, 497, 520
community of practice 5, 11, 13, 186–187, 445–458, 462, 463
complexification 272, 273, 301, 310, 519

derivation 349, 398, 468
dialect swamping 26, 32
diffusion 217–219, 249, 257

East Midlands 3, 12, 17–23, 25, 29, 31, 33, 34, 89, 126, 194, 195

focusing 444–446, 451, 455–458, 461–463

government constraint 521
Gower 183, 186, 386, 393

Haugen 56, 181, 186, 216, 365, 376

identity 222, 227, 444–446
indexicality 223, 227, 231, 479
innovation 63–66, 68, 193, 211, 216, 217, 221–228, 255, 258, 356, 417, 478, 505

kinship 354
koineisation 31, 443

Jubilee Book 518, 519

layering 350, 351, 353, 357, 523
levelling 31, 193, 230, 443
lexical transfer 367, 389
loanwords 194, 344, 346, 348, 349, 351, 359, 367, 381, 384–389, 398, 401, 402
liturgy 239–243, 249, 260–262
London 3, 4, 6, 9, 11–13, 17–32, 43, 46–48, 56, 58–64, 71, 76, 78, 82, 88, 128, 129, 134, 165, 175, 178–187, 260
Lydgate 89, 126, 393, 448

morphological productivity 472–475, 482
multiplex networks 223, 225

orthography 102, 108, 149, 153, 160, 165–169, 171–173, 180–186, 191–193, 210, 218, 219, 223, 227, 230, 231, 273, 334, 526

palaeography 173, 184, 219, 289
Paston family 7, 14, 197, 198, 204, 207, 219–231, 255–256, 318
perplexity 166, 168–175, 182, 184–186
polysemy 356, 366

semantic hierarchy 366, 371, 372, 375, 376
simplification 272, 519, 528–530
Speaker Design Theory 227, 228
Stonor letters 11, 256, 447–461
strong-tie networks 13, 530
style-shifting 222, 225, 227
supralocalisation 4, 10, 11–13, 23, 68, 135, 193, 194, 196, 198, 210, 211, 223, 229, 231, 260, 516, 525, 527–530

https://doi.org/10.1515/9783110687545-020

synonymy 331–354, 358, 365, 366, 372, 373

technolect 14, 375, 381
Tyndale 242, 248
Types I-IV 3, 4, 6, 17, 19, 24–26, 40, 41, 65, 91, 128–30, 132–4, 141, 165, 180–184, 186, 272, 288, 289

variant pool 10, 13, 68, 142, 159, 273, 308, 309
variant reduction 3–6, 10, 13–14, 17, 23, 57, 67, 142, 159, 210, 270, 273, 301–2, 306–310, 517, 522, 528
visual diamorphs 310, 322, 325, 334, 336, 338, 339

weak-tie networks 13, 517, 530
Wycliffe 56, 141

Zipf 148, 216, 526, 529

www.ingramcontent.com/pod-product-compliance
Lightning Source LLC
Chambersburg PA
CBHW022102290426
44112CB00008B/516